Honda CB600F Hornet, CBF600 & CBR600F
Service and Repair Manual

by Matthew Coombs

(5572-328)

Models covered

CB600F Hornet 2007 to 2012
CB600FA Hornet 2007 to 2012
CBF600N 2008 to 2012
CBF600NA 2008 to 2012
CBF600S 2008 to 2012
CBF600SA 2008 to 2012
CBR600F 2011 and 2012
CBR600FA 2011 and 2012

© Haynes Publishing 2013

A book in the Haynes Service and Repair Manual Series

All rights reserved. No part of this book may be reproduced or transmitted in any form or by any means, electronic or mechanical, including photocopying, recording or by any information storage or retrieval system, without permission in writing from the copyright holder.

ISBN: 978 0 85733 572 2

ABCDE
FGHIJ
KLMNO
PQRST

Printed in the USA

Haynes Publishing
Sparkford, Yeovil, Somerset BA22 7JJ, England

Haynes North America, Inc
861 Lawrence Drive, Newbury Park, California 91320, USA

Haynes Publishing Nordiska AB
Box 1504, 751 45 Uppsala, Sweden

Contents

LIVING WITH YOUR HONDA

Introduction
The Birth of a Dream	Page	**0•4**
Acknowledgements	Page	**0•8**
About this manual	Page	**0•8**
Identification numbers	Page	**0•9**
Buying spare parts	Page	**0•9**
Safety first!	Page	**0•10**

Pre-ride checks
Engine oil level	Page	**0•11**
Brake fluid levels	Page	**0•12**
Suspension, steering and final drive	Page	**0•13**
Coolant level	Page	**0•14**
Tyres	Page	**0•15**
Legal and safety checks	Page	**0•15**

Bike spec	Page	**0•16**
Model development	Page	**0•18**

MAINTENANCE

Routine maintenance and servicing
Specifications	Page	**1•2**
Lubricants and fluids	Page	**1•2**
Maintenance schedule	Page	**1•3**
Component locations	Page	**1•4**
Maintenance procedures	Page	**1•7**

Contents

REPAIRS AND OVERHAUL

Engine, transmission and associated systems

Engine, clutch and transmission	Page	**2•1**
Cooling system	Page	**3•1**
Engine management system	Page	**4•1**

Chassis components

Frame and suspension	Page	**5•1**
Brakes, wheels and final drive	Page	**6•1**
Bodywork	Page	**7•1**

Electrical system

	Page	**8•1**

Wiring diagrams

	Page	**8•38**

REFERENCE

Tools and Workshop Tips	Page	**REF•2**
Security	Page	**REF•20**
Lubricants and fluids	Page	**REF•23**
Conversion factors	Page	**REF•26**
MOT Test Checks	Page	**REF•27**
Storage	Page	**REF•32**
Fault Finding	Page	**REF•35**
Technical Terms Explained	Page	**REF•46**

Index

	Page	**REF•50**

The Birth of a Dream

by Julian Ryder

There is no better example of the Japanese post-War industrial miracle than Honda. Like other companies which have become household names, it started with one man's vision. In this case the man was the 40-year old Soichiro Honda who had sold his piston-ring manufacturing business to Toyota in 1945 and was happily spending the proceeds on prolonged parties for his friends. However, the difficulties of getting around in the chaos of post-War Japan irked Honda, so when he came across a job lot of generator engines he realised that here was a way of getting people mobile again at low cost.

A 12 by 18-foot shack in Hamamatsu became his first bike factory, fitting the generator motors into pushbikes. Before long he'd used up all 500 generator motors and started manufacturing his own engine, known as the 'chimney', either because of the elongated cylinder head or the smoky exhaust or perhaps both. The chimney made all of half a horsepower from its 50 cc engine but it was a major success and became the Honda A-type.

Less than two years after he'd set up in Hamamatsu, Soichiro Honda founded the Honda Motor Company in September 1948. By then, the A-type had been developed into the 90 cc B-type engine, which Mr Honda decided deserved its own chassis not a bicycle frame. Honda was about to become Japan's first post-War manufacturer of complete motorcycles. In August 1949 the first prototype was ready. With an output of three horsepower, the 98 cc D-type was still a simple two-stroke but it had a two-speed transmission and most importantly a pressed steel frame with telescopic forks and hard tail rear end. The frame was almost triangular in profile with the top rail going in a straight line from the massively braced steering head to the rear axle. Legend has it that after the D-type's first tests the entire workforce went for a drink to celebrate and try and think of a name for the bike. One man broke one of those silences you get when people are thinking, exclaiming 'This is like a dream!' 'That's it!' shouted Honda, and so the Honda Dream was christened.

Honda C70 and C90 OHV-engined models

> 'This is like a dream!' 'That's it' shouted Honda

Mr Honda was a brilliant, intuitive engineer and designer but he did not bother himself with the marketing side of his business. With hindsight, it is possible to see that employing Takeo Fujisawa who would both sort out the home market and plan the eventual expansion into overseas markets was a masterstroke. He arrived in October 1949 and in 1950 was made Sales Director. Another vital new name was Kiyoshi Kawashima, who along with Honda himself, designed the company's first four-stroke after Kawashima had told them that the four-stroke opposition to Honda's two-strokes sounded nicer and therefore sold better. The result of that statement was the overhead-valve 148 cc E-type which first ran in July 1951 just two months after the first drawings were made. Kawashima was made a director of the Honda Company at 34 years old.

The E-type was a massive success, over 32,000 were made in 1953 alone, a feat of mass-production that was astounding by the

Introduction 0•5

standards of the day given the relative complexity of the machine. But Honda's lifelong pursuit of technical innovation sometimes distracted him from commercial reality. Fujisawa pointed out that they were in danger of ignoring their core business, the motorised bicycles that still formed Japan's main means of transport. In May 1952 the F-type Cub appeared, another two-stroke despite the top men's reservations. You could buy a complete machine or just the motor to attach to your own bicycle. The result was certainly distinctive, a white fuel tank with a circular profile went just below and behind the saddle on the left of the bike, and the motor with its horizontal cylinder and bright red cover just below the rear axle on the same side of the bike. This was the machine that turned Honda into the biggest bike maker in Japan with 70% of the market for bolt-on bicycle motors, the F-type was also the first Honda to be exported. Next came the machine that would turn Honda into the biggest motorcycle manufacturer in the world.

The C100 Super Cub was a typically audacious piece of Honda engineering and marketing. For the first time, but not the last, Honda invented a completely new type of motorcycle, although the term 'scooterette' was coined to describe the new bike which had many of the characteristics of a scooter but the large wheels, and therefore stability, of a motorcycle. The first one was sold in August 1958, fifteen years later over nine-million of them were on the roads of the world. If ever a machine can be said to have brought mobility to the masses it is the Super Cub. If you add in the electric starter that was added for the C102 model of 1961, the design of the Super Cub has remained substantially unchanged ever since, testament to how right Honda got it first time. The Super Cub made Honda the world's biggest manufacturer after just two years of production.

The CB250N Super Dream became a favorite with UK learner riders of the late seventies and early eighties

Honda's export drive started in earnest in 1957 when Britain and Holland got their first bikes, America got just two bikes the next year. By 1962 Honda had half the American market with 65,000 sales. But Soichiro Honda had already travelled abroad to Europe and the USA, making a special

The GL1000 introduced in 1975, was the first in Honda's line of Goldwings

Introduction

Carl Fogarty in action at the Suzuka 8 hour on the RC45

An early CB750 Four

point of going to the Isle of Man TT, then the most important race in the GP calendar. He realised that no matter how advanced his products were, only racing success would convince overseas markets for whom 'Made in Japan' still meant cheap and nasty. It took five years from Soichiro Honda's first visit to the Island before his bikes were ready for the TT. In 1959 the factory entered five riders in the 125. They did not have a massive impact on the event being benevolently regarded as a curiosity, but sixth, seventh and eighth were good enough for the team prize. The bikes were off the pace but they were well engineered and very reliable.

The TT was the only time the West saw the Hondas in '59, but they came back for more the following year with the first of a generation of bikes which shaped the future of motorcycling - the double-overhead-cam four-cylinder 250. It was fast and reliable - it revved to 14,000 rpm - but didn't handle anywhere near as well as the opposition. However, Honda had now signed up non-Japanese riders to lead their challenge. The first win didn't come until 1962 (Aussie Tom Phillis in the Spanish 125 GP) and was followed up with a world-shaking performance at the TT. Twenty-one year old Mike Hailwood won both 125 and 250 cc TTs and Hondas filled the top five positions in both races. Soichiro Honda's master plan was starting to come to fruition, Hailwood and Honda won the 1961 250 cc World Championship. Next year Honda won three titles. The other Japanese factories fought back and inspired Honda to produce some of the most fascinating racers ever seen: the awesome six-cylinder 250, the five-cylinder 125, and the 500 four with which the immortal Hailwood battled Agostini and the MV Agusta.

When Honda pulled out of racing in '67 they had won sixteen rider's titles, eighteen manufacturer's titles, and 137 GPs, including 18 TTs, and introduced the concept of the modern works team to motorcycle racing. Sales success followed racing victory as Soichiro Honda had predicted, but only because the products advanced as rapidly as the racing machinery. The Hondas that came to Britain in the early '60s were incredibly sophisticated. They had overhead cams where the British bikes had pushrods, they had electric starters when the Brits relied on the kickstart, they had 12V electrics when even the biggest British bike used a 6V system. There seemed no end to the technical wizardry. It wasn't that the technology itself was so amazing but just like that first E-Type, it was the fact that Honda could mass-produce it more reliably than the lower-tech competition that was so astonishing.

When in 1968 the first four-cylinder CB750 road bike arrived the world of motorcycling changed for ever, they even had to invent a new word for it, 'Superbike'. Honda raced again with the CB750 at Daytona and won the

Introduction 0•7

World Endurance title with a prototype DOHC version that became the CB900 roadster. There was the six-cylinder CBX, the CX500T – the world's first turbocharged production bike, they invented the full-dress tourer with the GoldWing, and came back to GPs with the revolutionary oval-pistoned NR500 four-stroke, a much-misunderstood bike that was more a rolling experimental laboratory than a racer. Just to show their versatility Honda also came up with the weird CX500 shaft-drive V-twin, a rugged workhorse that powered a new industry, the courier companies that oiled the wheels of commerce in London and other big cities.

It was true, though, that Mr Honda was not keen on two-strokes – early motocross engines had to be explained away to him as lawnmower motors! However, in 1982 Honda raced the NS500, an agile three-cylinder lightweight against the big four-cylinder opposition in 500 GPs. The bike won in its first year and in '83 took the world title for Freddie Spencer. In four-stroke racing the V4 layout took over from the straight four, dominating TT, F1 and Endurance championships with the RVF750, the nearest thing ever built to a Formula 1 car on wheels. And when Superbike arrived Honda were ready with the RC30. On the roads the VFR V4 became an instant classic while the CBR600 invented another new class of bike on its way to becoming a best-seller. The V4 road bikes had problems to start with but the VFR750 sold world-wide over its lifetime while the VFR400 became a massive commercial success and cult bike in Japan. The original RC30 won the first two World Superbike Championships is 1988 and '89, but Honda had to wait until 1997 to win it again with the RC45, the last of the V4 roadsters. In Grands Prix, the NSR500 V4 two-stroke superseded the NS triple and became the benchmark racing machine of the '90s. Mick Doohan secured his place in history by winning five World Championships in consecutive years on it.

In yet another example of Honda inventing a new class of motorcycle, they came up with the astounding CBR900RR FireBlade, a bike with the punch of a 1000 cc motor in a package the size and weight of a 750. It became a cult bike as well as a best seller, and with judicious redesigns continues to give much more recent designs a run for their money.

When it became apparent that the high-tech V4 motor of the RC45 was too expensive to produce, Honda looked to a V-twin engine to power its flagship for the first time. Typically, the VTR1000 FireStorm was a much more rideable machine than its opposition and once accepted by the market formed the basis of the next generation of Superbike racer, the VTR-SP-1.

One of Mr Honda's mottos was that technology would solve the customers' problems, and no company has embraced cutting-edge technology more firmly than Honda. In fact Honda often developed new technology, especially in the fields of materials science and metallurgy. The embodiment of that was the NR750, a bike that was misunderstood nearly as much as the original NR500 racer. This limited-edition technological tour-de-force embodied many of Soichiro Honda's ideals. It used the latest techniques and materials in every component, from the oval piston, 32-valve V4 motor to the titanium coating on the windscreen, it was – as Mr Honda would have wanted – the best it could possibly be. A fitting memorial to the man who has shaped the motorcycle industry and motorcycles as we know them today.

New Tricks

Usually, the tactic has been to copy what Suzuki did with the Bandit – although that was well before the financial slump arrived.

It is not being rude, far from it, to say that the first Bandits were parts-bin specials. Take one motor from a previous generation of sports bikes, wrap it in a steel frame, add basic suspension and brakes and you have cheap motorcycling. The success of the Bandit range

The CX500 – Honda's first V-Twin and a favorite choice of dispatch riders

The 2007 CB600F Hornet

Introduction

The 2008 CBF600N

The 2011 CBR600F

caught everyone by surprise, and it wasn't long before the other manufacturers followed suit. Here are the origins of the every more popular naked bike class. Do not confuse this with the retro class, which has never really caught on. The first true retros were Kawasaki's Zephyr range, all of which were extremely successful commercially. However, there wasn't a retro boom, there was a Zephyr boom.

Honda's shot in the naked war was the Hornet. It stuck to the original recipe apart from the not-insignificant matter of using a contemporary engine from the top of the middleweight range CBR600RR retuned for easier riding. That was in 1998. As befits a bike designed to be affordable, it hardly changed over its model life.

In 2007 Honda introduced a new-generation CBR600RR: new engine, new fuel injection system, new frame – a brand new motorcycle in fact. One might have expected it to be a year or two before the new motor found its way into the Hornet; but no, the F7 model got the new engine and a lot more. The Hornet went from being a rather dowdy-looking bike to getting the full streetfighter treatment in the manner pioneered by the Triumph Speed Triple. The British company's middleweight version, the Street Triple also appeared for the first time in 2007.

The F7-model Hornet got upside-down forks, sporty wheels and brakes, and sharp, angular styling complete with a little headlamp fairing that was supposed to remind you of Honda's wing logo. The 'double-R' super-sportster's motor cranks out 118hp at 13,500rpm and 66Nm of torque at 11,250rpm. Those are the numbers for an out-and-out sportster, which isn't just a road bike, it's the homologation model for Supersports 600 class racing at domestic and world championship level. By comparison, the new Hornet's motor made 100hp at 12,000rpm and 63.5Nm at 10,500rpm. In other words, the mid-range was fattened up nicely at the expense of a little bit off the top-end.

A year after the CBR600RR and CB600F Hornet appeared, Honda expanded the range with a very traditional naked bike, the CBF600N. The N was very much a throwback to the original nakeds, a basic bike with no bodywork, non-USD forks, and conventional styling – round headlamp, circular cross-section silencer. The engine is in a similarly mild state of tune – 76hp at 10,500rpm and 59Nm at 8,250rpm. There was also a half-faired version, the CBF600S, with equally restrained looks.

Perhaps the most daring move was to reintroduce the CBR600F model designation, the appellation given to the very first bike in the class back in 1987. The original bike was reinvented by putting a full fairing on the Hornet, changing almost nothing from the CB600F, including the engine tune. It's quite difficult to tell it from the double-R at distance, and it's interesting to note that Honda in all their official publications file the CBR600F under the heading of Sports Tourers alongside the VFRs.

The really clever part of this story is that Honda have produced three very distinct motorcycles using one engine tuned three different ways. Perhaps motorcyclists shouldn't be surprised, this sort of clever design has been commonplace in the car industry for many years. And Honda's full name is the Honda Motor Company.

Acknowledgements

Our thanks are due to Bransons Motorcycles of Yeovil who supplied the machines featured in the illustrations throughout this manual. We would also like to thank NGK Spark Plugs (UK) Ltd for supplying the colour spark plug condition photographs, the Avon Rubber Company for supplying information on tyre fitting and Draper Tools Ltd for some of the workshop tools shown.

Thanks are also due to Julian Ryder who wrote the introduction 'The Birth of a Dream' and to Honda (UK) Ltd. who supplied model photographs.

About this Manual

The aim of this manual is to help you get the best value from your motorcycle. It can do so in several ways. It can help you decide what work must be done, even if you choose to have it done by a dealer; it provides information and procedures for routine maintenance and servicing; and it offers diagnostic and repair procedures to follow when trouble occurs.

We hope you use the manual to tackle the work yourself. For many simpler jobs, doing it yourself may be quicker than arranging an appointment to get the motorcycle into a dealer and making the trips to leave it and pick it up. More importantly, a lot of money can be saved by avoiding the expense the shop must pass on to you to cover its labour and overhead costs. An added benefit is the sense of satisfaction and accomplishment that you feel after doing the job yourself.

References to the left or right side of the motorcycle assume you are sitting on the seat, facing forward.

We take great pride in the accuracy of information given in this manual, but motorcycle manufacturers make alterations and design changes during the production run of a particular motorcycle of which they do not inform us. No liability can be accepted by the authors or publishers for loss, damage or injury caused by any errors in, or omissions from, the information given.

Illegal copying

It is the policy of Haynes Publishing to actively protect its Copyrights and Trade Marks. Legal action will be taken against anyone who unlawfully copies the cover or contents of this Manual. This includes all forms of unauthorised copying including digital, mechanical, and electronic in any form. Authorisation from Haynes Publishing will only be provided expressly and in writing. Illegal copying will also be reported to the appropriate statutory authorities.

Identification numbers 0•9

Frame and engine numbers

The frame serial number is stamped into the right-hand side of the steering head. The engine number is stamped into the right-hand side of the upper crankcase. Both of these numbers should be recorded and kept in a safe place so they can be given to law enforcement officials in the event of a theft. The VIN plate is on the left-hand side of the frame, on the engine hanger. There is a colour code label on the sub-frame under the seat. The throttle bodies also have an ID number stamped into them.

The frame serial number, engine serial number, and colour code should also be kept in a handy place (such as with your driver's licence) so they are always available when purchasing or ordering parts for your machine.

Models are identified using the model name, i.e. CB600F, CBF600N, CBF600S, or CBR600F for standard models and CB600FA, CBF600NA, CBF600SA or CBR600FA for models with ABS. Where the information applies to both standard and ABS models it is expressed as CB600F/FA, CBF600N/NA, CBF600S/SA or CBR600F/FA. The production year is also given where necessary. The table below shows the extended model codes (as given on the VIN plate and colour code label) and the production year(s) they relate to.

CB600F/FA	Year
CB600F7/FA7	2007
CB600F8/FA8	2008
CB600F9/FA9	2009
CB600FA/FAA	2010
CB600FB/FAB	2011
CB600FC/FAC	2012

CBF600N/NA	Year
CBF600N8/NA8	2008
CBF600N9/NA9	2009
CBF600NA/NAA	2010-12

CBF600S/SA	Year
CBF600S8/SA8	2008
CBF600S9/SA9	2009
CBF600SA/SAA	2010-12

CBR600F/FA	Year
CBR600FB/FAB	2011
CBR600FC/FAC	2012

The frame number is stamped into the right-hand side of the steering head

The VIN plate (arrowed) is riveted to the left-hand side of the frame

The engine number is stamped into the right-hand side of the upper crankcase

The colour code label is on the rear sub-frame

Buying spare parts

Once you have found all the identification numbers, record them for reference when buying parts. Since the manufacturers change specifications, parts and vendors (companies that manufacture various components on the machine), providing the ID numbers is the only way to be reasonably sure that you are buying the correct parts for your model.

Whenever possible, take the worn part to the dealer so direct comparison with the new component can be made. Along the trail from the manufacturer to the parts shelf, there are numerous places that the part can end up with the wrong number or be listed incorrectly.

The two places to purchase new parts for your motorcycle – the franchised or main dealer and the parts/accessories store – differ in the type of parts they carry. While dealers can obtain every single genuine part for your motorcycle, the accessory store is usually limited to normal high wear items such as chains and sprockets, brake pads, spark plugs and cables, and to tune-up parts and various engine gaskets, etc. Rarely will an accessory outlet have major suspension components, camshafts, transmission gears, or engine cases.

Used parts can be obtained from breakers for roughly half the price of new ones, but you can't always be sure of what you're getting. Once again, take your worn part to the breaker for direct comparison, or when ordering by mail order make sure that you can return it if you are not happy.

Whether buying new, used or rebuilt parts, the best course is to deal directly with someone who specialises in your particular make.

Safety First!

Professional mechanics are trained in safe working procedures. However enthusiastic you may be about getting on with the job at hand, take the time to ensure that your safety is not put at risk. A moment's lack of attention can result in an accident, as can failure to observe simple precautions.

There will always be new ways of having accidents, and the following is not a comprehensive list of all dangers; it is intended rather to make you aware of the risks and to encourage a safe approach to all work you carry out on your bike.

Asbestos

● Certain friction, insulating, sealing and other products - such as brake pads, clutch linings, gaskets, etc. - contain asbestos. Extreme care must be taken to avoid inhalation of dust from such products since it is hazardous to health. If in doubt, assume that they do contain asbestos.

Fire

● Remember at all times that petrol is highly flammable. Never smoke or have any kind of naked flame around, when working on the vehicle. But the risk does not end there - a spark caused by an electrical short-circuit, by two metal surfaces contacting each other, by careless use of tools, or even by static electricity built up in your body under certain conditions, can ignite petrol vapour, which in a confined space is highly explosive. Never use petrol as a cleaning solvent. Use an approved safety solvent.

● Always disconnect the battery earth terminal before working on any part of the fuel or electrical system, and never risk spilling fuel on to a hot engine or exhaust.
● It is recommended that a fire extinguisher of a type suitable for fuel and electrical fires is kept handy in the garage or workplace at all times. Never try to extinguish a fuel or electrical fire with water.

Fumes

● Certain fumes are highly toxic and can quickly cause unconsciousness and even death if inhaled to any extent. Petrol vapour comes into this category, as do the vapours from certain solvents such as trichloro-ethylene. Any draining or pouring of such volatile fluids should be done in a well ventilated area.
● When using cleaning fluids and solvents, read the instructions carefully. Never use materials from unmarked containers - they may give off poisonous vapours.
● Never run the engine of a motor vehicle in an enclosed space such as a garage. Exhaust fumes contain carbon monoxide which is extremely poisonous; if you need to run the engine, always do so in the open air or at least have the rear of the vehicle outside the workplace.

The battery

● Never cause a spark, or allow a naked light near the vehicle's battery. It will normally be giving off a certain amount of hydrogen gas, which is highly explosive.

● Always disconnect the battery ground (earth) terminal before working on the fuel or electrical systems (except where noted).
● If possible, loosen the filler plugs or cover when charging the battery from an external source. Do not charge at an excessive rate or the battery may burst.
● Take care when topping up, cleaning or carrying the battery. The acid electrolyte, evenwhen diluted, is very corrosive and should not be allowed to contact the eyes or skin. Always wear rubber gloves and goggles or a face shield. If you ever need to prepare electrolyte yourself, always add the acid slowly to the water; never add the water to the acid.

Electricity

● When using an electric power tool, inspection light etc., always ensure that the appliance is correctly connected to its plug and that, where necessary, it is properly grounded (earthed). Do not use such appliances in damp conditions and, again, beware of creating a spark or applying excessive heat in the vicinity of fuel or fuel vapour. Also ensure that the appliances meet national safety standards.
● A severe electric shock can result from touching certain parts of the electrical system, such as the spark plug wires (HT leads), when the engine is running or being cranked, particularly if components are damp or the insulation is defective. Where an electronic ignition system is used, the secondary (HT) voltage is much higher and could prove fatal.

Remember...

✗ **Don't** start the engine without first ascertaining that the transmission is in neutral.
✗ **Don't** suddenly remove the pressure cap from a hot cooling system - cover it with a cloth and release the pressure gradually first, or you may get scalded by escaping coolant.
✗ **Don't** attempt to drain oil until you are sure it has cooled sufficiently to avoid scalding you.
✗ **Don't** grasp any part of the engine or exhaust system without first ascertaining that it is cool enough not to burn you.
✗ **Don't** allow brake fluid or antifreeze to contact the machine's paintwork or plastic components.
✗ **Don't** siphon toxic liquids such as fuel, hydraulic fluid or antifreeze by mouth, or allow them to remain on your skin.
✗ **Don't** inhale dust - it may be injurious to health (see Asbestos heading).
✗ **Don't** allow any spilled oil or grease to remain on the floor - wipe it up right away, before someone slips on it.
✗ **Don't** use ill-fitting spanners or other tools which may slip and cause injury.
✗ **Don't** lift a heavy component which may be beyond your capability - get assistance.

✗ **Don't** rush to finish a job or take unverified short cuts.
✗ **Don't** allow children or animals in or around an unattended vehicle.
✗ **Don't** inflate a tyre above the recommended pressure. Apart from overstressing the carcass, in extreme cases the tyre may blow off forcibly.
✔ **Do** ensure that the machine is supported securely at all times. This is especially important when the machine is blocked up to aid wheel or fork removal.
✔ **Do** take care when attempting to loosen a stubborn nut or bolt. It is generally better to pull on a spanner, rather than push, so that if you slip, you fall away from the machine rather than onto it.
✔ **Do** wear eye protection when using power tools such as drill, sander, bench grinder etc.
✔ **Do** use a barrier cream on your hands prior to undertaking dirty jobs - it will protect your skin from infection as well as making the dirt easier to remove afterwards; but make sure your hands aren't left slippery. Note that long-term contact with used engine oil can be a health hazard.
✔ **Do** keep loose clothing (cuffs, ties etc. and long hair) well out of the way of moving mechanical parts.

✔ **Do** remove rings, wristwatch etc., before working on the vehicle - especially the electrical system.
✔ **Do** keep your work area tidy - it is only too easy to fall over articles left lying around.
✔ **Do** exercise caution when compressing springs for removal or installation. Ensure that the tension is applied and released in a controlled manner, using suitable tools which preclude the possibility of the spring escaping violently.
✔ **Do** ensure that any lifting tackle used has a safe working load rating adequate for the job.
✔ **Do** get someone to check periodically that all is well, when working alone on the vehicle.
✔ **Do** carry out work in a logical sequence and check that everything is correctly assembled and tightened afterwards.
✔ **Do** remember that your vehicle's safety affects that of yourself and others. If in doubt on any point, get professional advice.
● If in spite of following these precautions, you are unfortunate enough to injure yourself, seek medical attention as soon as possible.

Pre-ride checks

Note: *The Pre-ride checks outlined in the owner's manual covers those items which should be inspected on a daily basis.*

Engine oil level

Before you start:
✔ Make sure the motorcycle is on level ground.
✔ Start the engine and let it idle for 3 to 5 minutes.
Caution: Do not run the engine in an enclosed space such as a garage or workshop.
✔ Stop the engine and allow the oil level to stabilise for 2 to 3 minutes. Support the motorcycle upright by having an assistant hold it.

Bike care:
● If you have to add oil frequently, check whether you have any oil leaks from the engine joints, oil seals and gaskets. If not, the engine could be burning oil, in which case there will be white smoke coming out of the exhaust (see *Fault Finding*).

The correct oil:
● Modern, high-revving engines place great demands on their oil. It is very important that the correct oil for your bike is used.
● Always top up with a good quality motorcycle oil of the specified type and viscosity and do not overfill the engine. Do not use oils designed for use in car engines.
Caution: Do not use chemical additives or oils labelled "ENERGY CONSERVING". Such additives or oils could cause clutch slip.

Oil type	API grade: SG or higher JASO T 903 grade: MA
Oil viscosity	SAE 10W30

1 The oil level inspection window is located on the right-hand side of the engine. If necessary wipe the window so that it is clean.

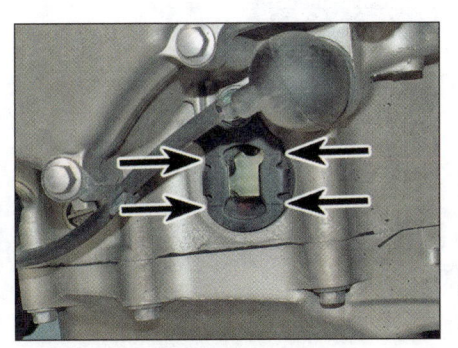

2 With the motorcycle held upright, the oil level should lie between the upper and lower level lines (arrowed).

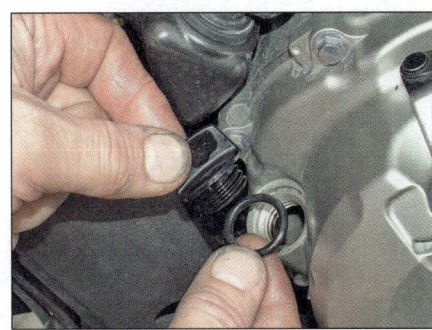

3 If the level is near, on or below the lower line, unscrew the oil filler cap from the clutch cover, noting the O-ring.

4 Top up the engine with the recommended grade and type of oil to bring the level almost up to the upper line on the inspection window. Do not overfill.

5 Make sure the filler cap O-ring is in good condition and correctly seated in the cap.

0•12 Pre-ride checks

Brake fluid levels

> **Warning:** Brake hydraulic fluid can harm your eyes and damage painted surfaces, so use extreme caution when handling and pouring it and cover surrounding surfaces with rag. Do not use fluid that has been standing open for some time, as it is hygroscopic (absorbs moisture from the air) which can cause a dangerous loss of braking effectiveness.

Before you start:

✔ The front brake fluid reservoir is on the right-hand handlebar. The rear brake fluid reservoir is located under the side cover on the right-hand side.
✔ Make sure you have the correct hydraulic fluid – DOT 4.
✔ Wrap a rag around the reservoir being worked on to ensure that any spillage does not come into contact with painted surfaces.
✔ When checking the fluid in the front reservoir turn the handlebars so the reservoir is level.
✔ When checking the fluid in the rear reservoir support the motorcycle upright. On CB600F/FA and CBR600F/FA models remove the right-hand side cover (see Chapter 7).

Bike care:

● The fluid in the front and rear brake master cylinder reservoirs will drop as the brake pads wear down. If the fluid level is low check the brake pads for wear (see Chapter 1), and replace them with new ones if necessary (see Chapter 6).
● If either fluid reservoir requires repeated topping-up there is a leak somewhere in the system. Check for signs of fluid leakage from the hydraulic hoses and/or brake system components – if found, rectify immediately (see Chapter 6).
● Check the operation of both brakes before taking the machine on the road; if there is evidence of air in the system (spongy feel to lever or pedal), it must be bled (see Chapter 6).

FRONT

1 The front brake fluid level is visible through the window in the reservoir body – it must be above the LOWER level line (arrowed).

2 If the level is on or below the LOWER line, undo the reservoir cover screws and remove the cover, diaphragm plate and diaphragm.

3 Top up with new clean DOT 4 hydraulic fluid, until the level is up to the upper level line (arrowed) cast inside the reservoir. Do not overfill and take care to avoid spills (see **Warning** above).

4 Wipe any moisture off the diaphragm with a tissue.

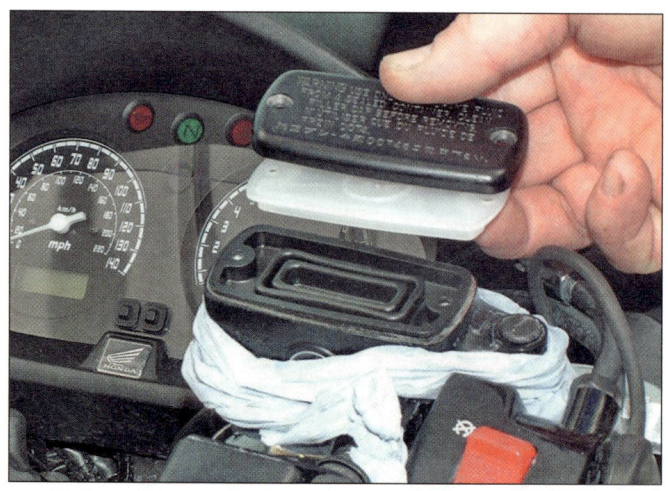

5 Make sure that the diaphragm is correctly seated before fitting the plate and cover. Secure the reservoir cover with its screws.

Pre-ride checks

REAR

1 The rear brake fluid level is visible through the reservoir body – it must be between the UPPER and LOWER level lines (arrowed).

2 If the level is on or below the LOWER line, unscrew the reservoir bolt and displace the reservoir so the cap is clear.

3 Unscrew the reservoir cap, then remove the diaphragm plate and diaphragm. Relocate the reservoir and loosely fit the bolt to support it.

4 Top up with new clean DOT 4 hydraulic fluid, until the level is up to the UPPER line. Do not overfill and take care to avoid spills (see **Warning** opposite).

5 Wipe any moisture off the diaphragm with a tissue. Make sure that the diaphragm is correctly seated before fitting the plate and cap, then fit the reservoir and tighten the bolt.

Suspension, steering and final drive

Suspension and Steering:
- Check that the front and rear suspension operates smoothly without binding (see Chapter 1).
- Check that the suspension is adjusted as required (see Chapter 5).
- Check that the steering moves smoothly from lock-to-lock.

Drive chain:
- Check that the chain isn't too loose or too tight, and adjust it if necessary (see Chapter 1).
- If the chain looks dry, lubricate it (see Chapter 1).

Coolant level

> **Warning:** *DO NOT remove the pressure cap from the filler neck to add coolant. Topping up is done via the coolant reservoir tank filler. DO NOT leave open containers of coolant about, as it is poisonous.*

Before you start:

✔ Check the coolant level when the engine is at normal working temperature. Take the motorcycle on a short run to allow it to reach normal temperature.

✔ Stop the engine. Support the motorcycle on the centrestand (where fitted) or otherwise using an auxiliary stand, making sure it is upright and on level ground.
✔ On CB600F/FA and CBR600F/FA models the coolant reservoir is located behind the seat cowl on the left-hand side and is visible by removing the seat.
✔ On CBF600N/NA and S/SA models the coolant reservoir is located behind the footrest bracket on the left-hand side.

Caution: Do not run the engine in an enclosed space such as a garage or workshop.

Bike care:

● Use only the specified coolant mixture of 50% distilled water and 50% corrosion inhibited ethylene glycol anti-freeze – ready-mixed coolant is available in one litre containers. It is important that the correct proportion of anti-freeze is used in the system all year round, and not just in the winter. Do not top the system up using only water, as the system will become too diluted.
● Do not overfill the reservoir tank. If the coolant is significantly above the UPPER level line at any time, the surplus should be siphoned or drained off to prevent the possibility of it being expelled out of the overflow hose.
● If the coolant level falls steadily check the system for leaks (see Chapter 1). If no leaks are found and the level continues to fall, it is recommended that the machine is taken to a Honda dealer for a pressure test.

CB600F/FA and CBR600F/FA

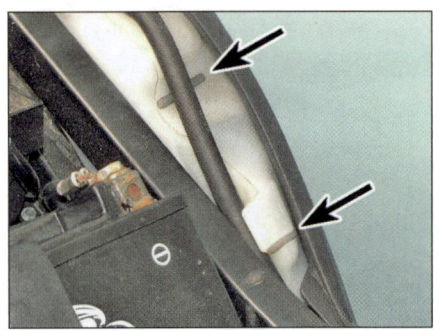

1 Remove the seat (see Chapter 7). The coolant level should lie between the upper and lower level lines (arrowed) that are marked on the reservoir.

2 If the coolant level is on or below the LOWER line, remove the reservoir filler cap.

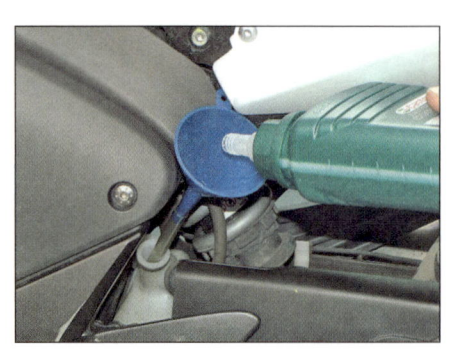

3 Top up the reservoir with the recommended coolant mixture to the UPPER level line, using a suitable funnel if required. Fit the cap. Install the seat (see Chapter 7).

CBF600N/NA/S/SA

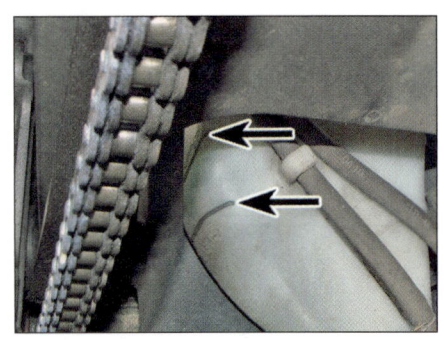

1 The coolant level should lie between the upper and lower level lines (arrowed) that are marked on the reservoir.

2 If the coolant level is on or below the LOWER line, remove the reservoir filler cap.

3 Top up the reservoir with the recommended coolant mixture to the UPPER level line, using a suitable funnel if required. Fit the cap.

Pre-ride checks

Tyres

The correct pressures:
- The tyres must be checked when **cold**, not immediately after riding. The pressure inside the tyre will increase when the tyre is hot. Note that tyre pressure will also change from one day to the next as air temperature changes.
- Correct tyre pressure will increase tyre life and provide maximum stability and ride comfort. Incorrect pressure will cause abnormal tread wear and unsafe handling. Low tyre pressures may cause the tyre to slip on the rim or come off.
- Use an accurate pressure gauge. Many forecourt gauges are wildly inaccurate. If you buy your own, spend as much as you can justify on a quality gauge.
- The pressures given apply to all models and all loads, including a passenger.

Front	Rear
36 psi (2.5 Bar)	42 psi (2.9 Bar)

Tyre care:
- Check the tyres carefully for cuts, tears, embedded nails or other sharp objects and excessive wear. Operation of the motorcycle with excessively worn tyres is extremely hazardous, as traction and handling are directly affected.
- Pick out any stones or nails that may have become embedded in the tyre tread. If left, they will eventually penetrate through the casing and cause a puncture.
- Make sure a dust cap is fitted. If air escapes when the cap is removed the valve core could be loose – a simple tool that is cheaply available and sometimes incorporated in the cap is needed to tighten the valve. Check the condition of the valve.
- If tyre damage is apparent, or unexplained loss of pressure is experienced, seek the advice of a tyre fitting specialist without delay.

Tyre tread depth:
- At the time of writing UK law requires that tread depth must be at least 1 mm over 3/4 of the tread breadth all the way around the tyre, with no bald patches. Many riders, however, consider 2 mm tread depth minimum to be a safer limit. Honda recommends a minimum of 1.5 mm on the front and 2 mm on the rear, but note that German law requires a minimum of 1.6 mm for each tyre.
- Most tyres incorporate wear indicators in the tread. Identify the location marking on the tyre sidewall to locate the indicator bar and replace the tyre if the tread has worn down to the bar.

1 Remove the dust cap from the valve. Do not forget to fit the cap after checking the pressure.

2 Check the tyre pressures when **cold**.

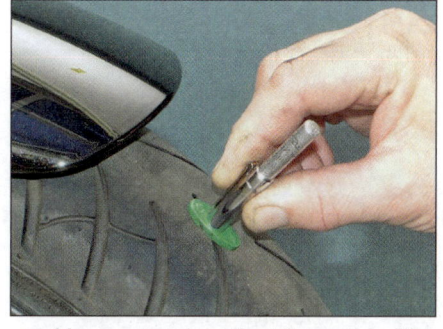

3 Measure tread depth at the centre of the tyre using a depth gauge.

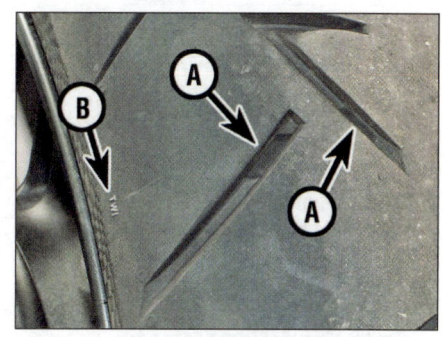

4 Tyre tread wear indicators (A) and its location marking (B) on the edge or sidewall (according to manufacturer).

Legal and safety checks

Lighting and signalling:
- Take a minute to check that the headlights, tail and brake lights, licence plate light, instrument lights and turn signals all work correctly.
- Check that the horn sounds when the button is pressed.
- A working speedometer, graduated in mph, is a statutory requirement in the UK.

Safety:
- Check that the throttle grip rotates smoothly when opened and snaps shut when released, in all steering positions. Also check for the correct amount of freeplay (see Chapter 1).
- Check that the brake lever and pedal, clutch lever and gearchange lever operate smoothly. Lubricate them at the specified intervals or when necessary (see Chapter 1).
- Check that the engine shuts off when the kill switch is operated. Check the starter interlock circuit (see Chapter 1).
- Check that stand return springs hold the stand(s) up securely when retracted.

Fuel:
- This may seem obvious, but check that you have enough fuel to complete your journey. If you smell petrol (gasoline) or notice signs of fuel leakage, rectify the cause immediately.
- Ensure you use the correct grade fuel – see Chapter 4 Specifications.

Bike spec

Dimensions and weights

CB600F/FA
2007 to 2010 models
- Overall length .... 2085 mm
- Overall width .... 760 mm
- Overall height .... 1090 mm
- Wheelbase .... 1435 mm
- Seat height .... 800 mm
- Ground clearance .... 135 mm
- Kerb weight
  - F models .... 198 kg
  - FA models .... 205 kg
- Maximum weight capacity .... 188 kg

2011-on models
- Overall length .... 2150 mm
- Overall width .... 750 mm
- Overall height .... 1070 mm
- Wheelbase .... 1435 mm
- Seat height .... 800 mm
- Ground clearance .... 135 mm
- Kerb weight
  - F models .... 202 kg
  - FA models .... 207 kg
- Maximum weight capacity .... 188 kg

CBF600N/NA
- Overall length .... 2160 mm
- Overall width .... 765 mm
- Overall height .... 1110 mm
- Wheelbase .... 1490 mm
- Seat height .... 785 ± 15 mm
- Ground clearance .... 136 mm
- Kerb weight
  - N models .... 213 kg
  - NA models .... 218 kg
- Maximum weight capacity .... 195 kg

CBF600S/SA
- Overall length .... 2160 mm
- Overall width .... 765 mm
- Overall height .... 1240 to 1285 mm
- Wheelbase .... 1490 mm
- Seat height .... 785 ± 15 mm
- Ground clearance .... 136 mm
- Kerb weight
  - S models .... 217 kg
  - SA models .... 222 kg
- Maximum weight capacity .... 195 kg

CBR600F/FA
- Overall length .... 2150 mm
- Overall width .... 740 mm
- Overall height .... 1150 mm
- Wheelbase .... 1435 mm
- Seat height .... 800 mm
- Ground clearance .... 135 mm
- Kerb weight
  - F models .... 206 kg
  - FA models .... 211 kg
- Maximum weight capacity .... 188 kg

Bike spec

Engine – all models
Type	Four-stroke in-line four
Capacity	599 cc
Bore	67.0 mm
Stroke	42.5 mm
Compression ratio	
CB600F/FA and CBR600F/FA models	12.0 to 1
CBF600N/NA/S/SA models	11.6 to 1
Cooling system	Liquid cooled
Clutch	Wet multi-plate
Transmission	Six-speed constant mesh
Final drive	Chain and sprockets
Camshafts	DOHC, chain-driven
Fuel system	PGM-FI fuel injection
Ignition system	Computer-controlled digital transistorised with electronic advance

Chassis

CB600F/FA and CBR600F/FA
Frame type	Mono backbone
Rake and trail	25°, 99 mm
Fuel tank	
Capacity (including reserve)	
CB600F/FA 2007 to 2010 models	19.0 litres
CB600F/FA 2011-on models	18.7 litres
CBR600F/FA models	18.4 litres
Reserve volume	approx. 3.5 litres
Front suspension	
Type	41 mm USD oil-damped cartridge-type telescopic forks
Travel	109 mm
Adjustment	
CB600F/FA 2007 and 2008 models	none
CB600F/FA 2009-on models	Spring pre-load and rebound damping
CBR600F/FA models	Spring pre-load and rebound damping
Rear suspension	
Type	Single shock absorber, aluminium swingarm
Travel (at axle)	128 mm
Adjustment	
CB600F/FA 2007 and 2008 models	Spring pre-load
CB600F/FA 2009-on models	Spring pre-load and rebound damping
CBR600F/FA models	Spring pre-load and rebound damping
Wheels	17 inch 5-spoke alloy
Tyres	
Front	120/70-ZR17M/C (58W)
Rear	180/55-ZR17M/C (73W)
Front brake	
F models	Twin 296 mm floating discs with twin piston sliding calipers
FA models	Twin 296 mm floating discs with triple piston sliding calipers
Rear brake	Single 240 mm disc with single piston sliding caliper

CBF600N/NA/S/SA
Frame type	Mono backbone
Rake and trail	26°, 110 mm
Fuel tank	
Capacity (including reserve)	20.0 litres
Reserve volume	approx. 4.0 litres
Front suspension	
Type	41 mm oil-damped telescopic forks
Travel	108 mm
Adjustment	Spring pre-load
Rear suspension	
Type	Single shock absorber, single-sided aluminium swingarm
Travel (at axle)	120 mm
Adjustment	Spring pre-load
Wheels	17 inch 6-spoke alloy
Tyres	
Front	120/70-ZR17M/C (58W)
Rear	160/60-ZR17M/C (69W)
Front brake	
N and S models	Twin 296 mm floating discs with twin piston sliding calipers
NA and SA models	Twin 296 mm floating discs with triple piston sliding calipers
Rear brake	Single 240 mm disc with single piston sliding caliper

CB600F/FA (Hornet)

The CB600F/FA was launched in 2007.

The engine is based on, and was developed alongside, the in-line four cylinder liquid-cooled engine used in the 2007-on CBR600RR, but with minor differences and re-tuned to provide greater torque output and therefore more flexible drive in the low and mid-ranges. Drive to the double overhead camshafts that actuate the four valves per cylinder is by chain from the right-hand end of the crankshaft. The clutch is a conventional wet multi-plate unit actuated by cable, and the gearbox is 6-speed. Drive to the rear wheel is by chain and sprockets.

Honda's PGM-FI fuel injection system supplies fuel and air to the engine via 36 mm throttle bodies and two intake valves per cylinder, with exhaust gases exiting via another two valves per cylinder into a four-into-one under-slung exhaust system with closed-loop catalytic converter. An electronic engine management system controls both the injection system and the ignition system. All Europe models feature Honda's immobiliser system (HISS).

The engine sits in an aluminium mono-backbone frame with hangers holding the engine at the front, and using the engine as a stressed member.

Front suspension is by upside-down oil-damped 41 mm forks with cartridge dampers; from 2009-on the forks have adjustable spring pre-load and rebound damping. Rear suspension is by an aluminium box-section swingarm and a single shock absorber with adjustable spring pre-load, and adjustable rebound damping from 2009-on.

The hydraulic braking system on the standard model has two twin piston sliding calipers acting on 296 mm discs at the front, and a single piston sliding caliper acting on a 240 mm disc at the rear. The A model has a combined anti-lock (C-ABS) braking system, with two triple piston sliding calipers acting on 296 mm discs at the front, and a single piston sliding caliper acting on a 240 mm disc at the rear. When the rear brake is applied the system actuates the centre piston in the right-hand caliper via a delay valve and a proportional control valve.

In 2011 a new integrated headlight and instrument assembly was fitted, along with a new seat cowl, tail light and tail unit. The Hornet name was dropped in 2012, though the bike itself remained the same.

Available in black, yellow, blue and red in 2007, white, silver, black, yellow and blue in 2008, white, silver, black, yellow and red in 2009 and 2010, yellow, white and black in 2011, and grey, blue and white in 2012.

CBF600N/NA and CBF600S/SA

The CBF models were launched in 2008, with N models being of naked design and S models having a half-fairing with adjustable windshield.

The engine is the same as the in-line four cylinder liquid-cooled engine used in the CB600F/FA Hornet. Drive to the double overhead camshafts that actuate the four valves per cylinder is by chain from the right-hand end of the crankshaft. The clutch is a conventional wet multi-plate unit actuated by cable, and the gearbox is 6-speed. Drive to the rear wheel is by chain and sprockets.

Honda's PGM-FI fuel injection system supplies fuel and air to the engine via 32 mm throttle bodies and two intake valves per cylinder, with exhaust gases exiting via another two valves per cylinder into a four-into-one exhaust system with closed-loop catalytic converter. An electronic engine management system controls both the injection system and the ignition system. All Europe models feature Honda's immobiliser system (HISS).

The engine sits in an aluminium mono-backbone frame with hangers holding the engine at the front, and using the engine as a stressed member. All models have an adjustable seat.

Front suspension is by oil-damped 41 mm forks with adjustable spring pre-load. Rear suspension is by an aluminium box-section swingarm and a single shock absorber with adjustable spring pre-load.

The hydraulic braking system on the standard model has two twin piston sliding calipers acting on 296 mm discs at the front, and one single piston sliding caliper acting on a 240 mm disc at the rear. The A models have a combined anti-lock (C-ABS) braking system, with two triple piston sliding calipers acting on 296 mm discs at the front, and a single piston sliding caliper acting on a 240 mm disc at the rear. When the rear brake is applied the system actuates the centre piston in the right-hand caliper via a delay valve and a proportional control valve.

Available in blue, silver, black, and red in 2008 to 2010. In 2011 and 2012 N models came in white, green and black, and S models came in white/black, red/black, green/black and black.

CBR600F/FA

The CBR600F/FA was launched in 2011. It is basically a sports version of the Hornet, having lower handlebars and a fairing, without being nearly as sport-focused as the CBR600RR.

The engine is the same as the in-line four cylinder liquid-cooled engine used in the Hornet and CBF models. Drive to the double overhead camshafts that actuate the four valves per cylinder is by chain from the right-hand end of the crankshaft. The clutch is a conventional wet multi-plate unit actuated by cable, and the gearbox is 6-speed. Drive to the rear wheel is by chain and sprockets.

Honda's PGM-FI fuel injection system supplies fuel and air to the engine via 36 mm throttle bodies and two intake valves per cylinder, with exhaust gases exiting via another two valves per cylinder into a four-into-one under-slung exhaust system with closed-loop catalytic converter. An electronic engine management system controls both the injection system and the ignition system. All Europe models feature Honda's immobiliser system (HISS).

The engine sits in an aluminium mono-backbone frame with hangers holding the engine at the front, and using the engine as a stressed member.

Front suspension is by upside-down oil-damped 41 mm forks with cartridge dampers, and adjustable spring pre-load and rebound damping. Rear suspension is by an aluminium box-section swingarm and a single shock absorber with adjustable spring pre-load and rebound damping.

The hydraulic braking system on the standard model has two twin piston sliding calipers acting on 296 mm discs at the front, and one single piston sliding caliper acting on a 240 mm disc at the rear. The A model has a combined anti-lock (C-ABS) braking system, with two triple piston sliding calipers acting on 296 mm discs at the front, and a single piston sliding caliper acting on a 240 mm disc at the rear. When the rear brake is applied the system actuates the centre piston in the right-hand caliper via a delay valve and a proportional control valve.

Available in white/black, white/red and black/grey.

Chapter 1
Routine maintenance and servicing

Contents

	Section number
Air filter	18
Battery	20
Brake fluid level check	see *Pre-ride checks*
Brake system	3
Clutch	4
Coolant level check	see *Pre-ride checks*
Cooling system	9
Crankcase breather	2
Drive chain and sprockets	1
Engine oil and filter	8
Engine oil level check	see *Pre-ride checks*
Engine wear assessment	see Chapter 2
Fuel system	5
Headlight aim	11
Idle speed control system	see Chapter 4
Nuts and bolts	17
PAIR (pulse secondary air) system	10
Stand, pivot points and throttle cable lubrication	16
Spark plugs	7
Sidestand, centrestand and starter interlock circuit	12
Steering head bearings	14
Suspension	13
Throttle cables	6
Tyre pressure check	see *Pre-ride checks*
Valve clearances	19
Wheels, tyres and wheel bearings	15

Degrees of difficulty

| **Easy,** suitable for novice with little experience | **Fairly easy,** suitable for beginner with some experience | **Fairly difficult,** suitable for competent DIY mechanic | **Difficult,** suitable for experienced DIY mechanic | **Very difficult,** suitable for expert DIY or professional |

Specifications

Engine
Cylinder numbering	1 to 4 from left to right
Spark plug type	
NGK	CR8EH-9
Denso	U24FER9
Spark plug electrode gap	0.8 to 0.9 mm
Engine idle speed	
CB600F/FA and CBR600F/FA	1350 ± 100 rpm
CBF600N/NA/S/SA	1300 ± 100 rpm
Valve clearances (COLD engine)	
Intake valves	0.20 ± 0.03 mm
Exhaust valves	0.28 ± 0.03 mm

Cycle parts
Drive chain slack	
CB600F/FA and CBR600F/FA	30 to 40 mm
CBF600N/NA/S/SA	20 to 30 mm
Clutch cable freeplay	10 to 20 mm at lever end
Throttle cable freeplay	2 to 6 mm
Tyre pressures (cold)	see *Pre-ride checks*
Steering head bearing pre-load (see text)	8.8 to 13.7 N (0.9 to 1.4 kgf; 2.0 to 3.1 lbf)

Lubricants and fluids
Engine oil type	SAE 10W30, API grade SG or higher, JASO T 903 MA, motorcycle oil
Engine oil capacity	
Oil change	2.7 litres
Oil and filter change	2.8 litres
Coolant type	50% distilled water, 50% corrosion inhibited ethylene glycol anti-freeze
Coolant capacity	
CB600F/FA and CBR600F/FA	
Radiator and engine	2.9 litres
Reservoir	0.38 litres
CBF600N/NA/S/SA	
Radiator and engine	2.42 litres
Reservoir	0.35 litres
Brake/clutch fluid	DOT 4
Drive chain	SAE 80 or 90 gear oil or aerosol chain lubricant suitable for O-ring chains
Steering head bearings	Urea based multi-purpose grease with EP2 rating
Steering head bearing adjuster nut threads	Engine oil
Stand pivots	Multi-purpose grease
Wheel bearing seal lips	Multi-purpose grease
Clutch lever pivot	Multi-purpose grease
Gearchange lever/rear brake pedal/footrest pivots	Multi-purpose grease
Gearchange linkage rod ball joints	Multi-purpose grease
Swingarm pivot bearings and seals	
CB600F/FA to 2010 and CBF600N/NA/S/SA	Lithium based multi-purpose grease with EP2 rating grease
CB600F/FA 2011-on and CBR600F/FA	Molybdenum disulphide grease
Shock absorber pivot bearings and seals	
CB600F/FA to 2010 and CBF600N/NA/S/SA	Lithium based multi-purpose grease with EP2 rating grease
CB600F/FA 2011-on and CBR600F/FA	Molybdenum disulphide grease
Shock absorber pre-load adjuster ring	Molybdenum paste
Throttle and clutch cables	Aerosol cable lubricant
Throttle and clutch cable ends	Multi-purpose grease
Front brake lever pivot and master cylinder pushrod end	Silicone grease
Brake caliper slider pins and boots	Silicone grease
Rear master cylinder pushrod and boot	Silicone grease

Torque settings
Engine oil drain plug	30 Nm
Engine oil filter	26 Nm
Fork clamp bolts (top yoke)	22 Nm
Rear axle nut	98 Nm
Spark plugs	16 Nm
Steering head bearing adjuster nut	
CB600F/FA and CBR600F/FA	26 Nm
CBF600N/NA/S/SA	25 Nm
Steering stem nut	103 Nm
Timing inspection cap	18 Nm

Maintenance schedule

Note: The Pre-ride checks outlined in the owner's manual cover those items which should be inspected before every ride. Also perform the pre-ride inspection at every maintenance interval (in addition to the procedures listed). The intervals listed below are the intervals recommended by the manufacturer for the models covered in this manual.

Pre-ride
- ☐ See 'Pre-ride checks' at the beginning of this manual

After the initial 600 miles (1000 km)
Note: This check is performed by a Honda dealer after the first 600 miles (1000 km) from new. Thereafter, maintenance is carried out according to the following intervals of the schedule.

Every 600 miles (1000 km)
- ☐ Check, adjust, clean and lubricate the drive chain (Section 1)

Every 4000 miles (6000 km) or 6 months
- ☐ Clean the crankcase breather (Section 2)
- ☐ Check the brake pads for wear (Section 3)
- ☐ Check the spark plugs (Canada models only) (Section 7)

Every 8000 miles (12,000 km) or 12 months
Carry out the items under the 4000 mile (6000 km) check, plus the following:
- ☐ Check the brake system and brake light switch operation (Section 3)
- ☐ Check the clutch (Section 4)
- ☐ Check the fuel system and hoses (Section 5)
- ☐ Check the throttle cables and adjust if necessary (Section 6)
- ☐ Check the spark plugs (Europe models) (Section 7)
- ☐ Fit new spark plugs (Canada models only) (Section 7)
- ☐ Change the engine oil and fit a new filter (Section 8)
- ☐ Check the cooling system (Section 9)
- ☐ Check the PAIR (pulse secondary air) system (Section 10)
- ☐ Check the headlight beam aim (Section 11)
- ☐ Check the stand(s) and starter interlock circuit (Section 12)
- ☐ Check the front and rear suspension (Section 13)

Every 8000 miles (12,000 km) or 12 months (continued)
- ☐ Check the steering head bearings and adjust if necessary (Section 14)
- ☐ Check the condition of the wheels, wheel bearings and tyres (Section 15)
- ☐ Lubricate the clutch, gearchange and brake levers, brake pedal, stand pivots, and the throttle cables (Section 16)
- ☐ Check the tightness of all nuts, bolts and fasteners (Section 17)

Every 12,000 miles (18,000 km) or 18 months
Carry out all the items under the 4000 mile (6000 km) check, plus the following:
- ☐ Clean and check the air filter element (Section 18)

Every 12,000 miles (18,000 km) or two years
Carry out all the items under the 4000 mile (6000 km) check, plus the following:
- ☐ Change the brake fluid (Section 3)

Every 16,000 miles (24,000 km) or two years
Carry out all the items under the 8000 mile (12,000 km) check, plus the following:
- ☐ Fit new spark plugs (Europe models) (Section 7)
- ☐ Check the valve clearances and adjust if necessary (Section 19)

Every 24,000 miles (36,000 km) or two years
Carry out all the items under the 12,000 mile (18,000 km) and 8000 mile (12,000 km) checks, plus the following:
- ☐ Change the coolant (Section 9)

Non-scheduled maintenance
- ☐ Check the battery (Section 20)
- ☐ Change the front fork oil (Section 13)
- ☐ Re-grease the swingarm and shock absorber bearings (Section 13)
- ☐ Re-grease the steering head bearings (Section 14)

1•4 Component locations

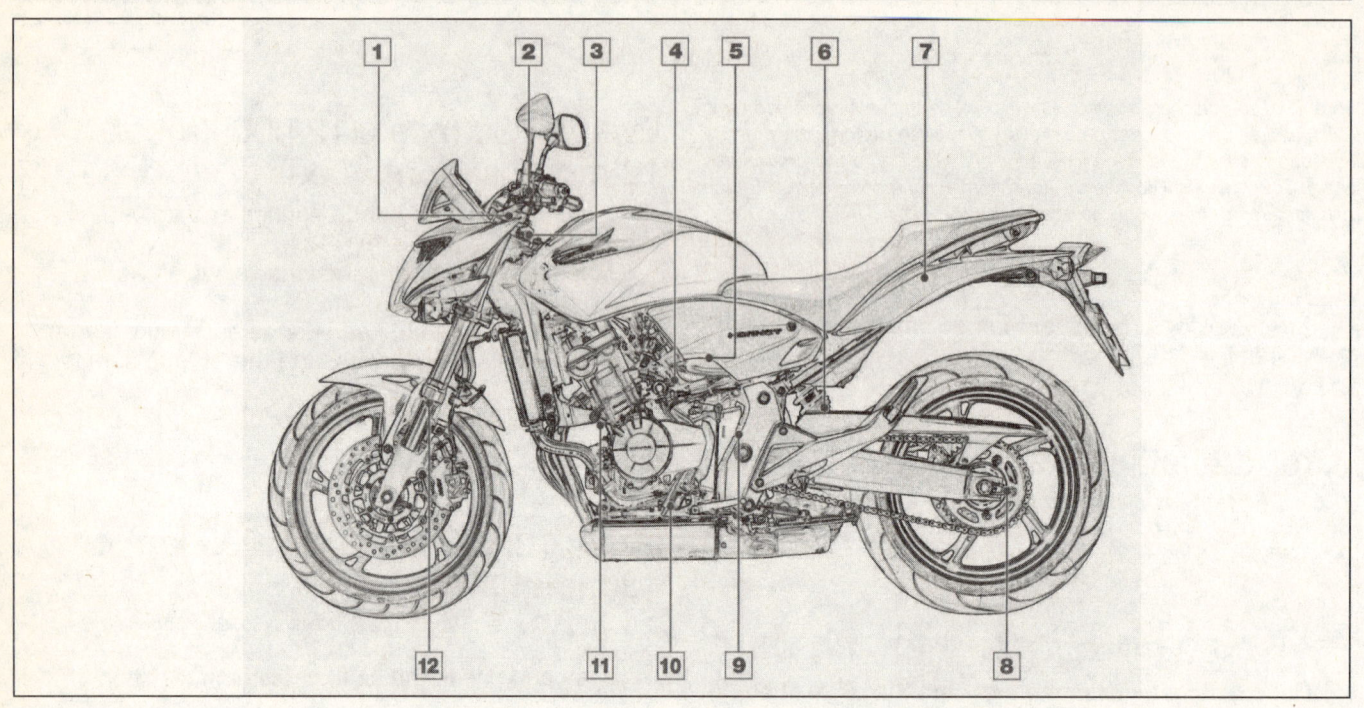

Component locations on the left side – CB600F/FA

1. Front fork pre-load and damping adjuster (2009-on)
2. Clutch cable adjuster and upper end
3. Steering head bearing adjuster
4. Crankcase breather collector
5. Air filter
6. Rear shock pre-load adjuster
7. Coolant reservoir tank
8. Drive chain adjuster
9. Drive chain slider
10. Coolant drain bolt on water pump
11. Coolant drain bolt in cylinder jacket
12. Front fork seal

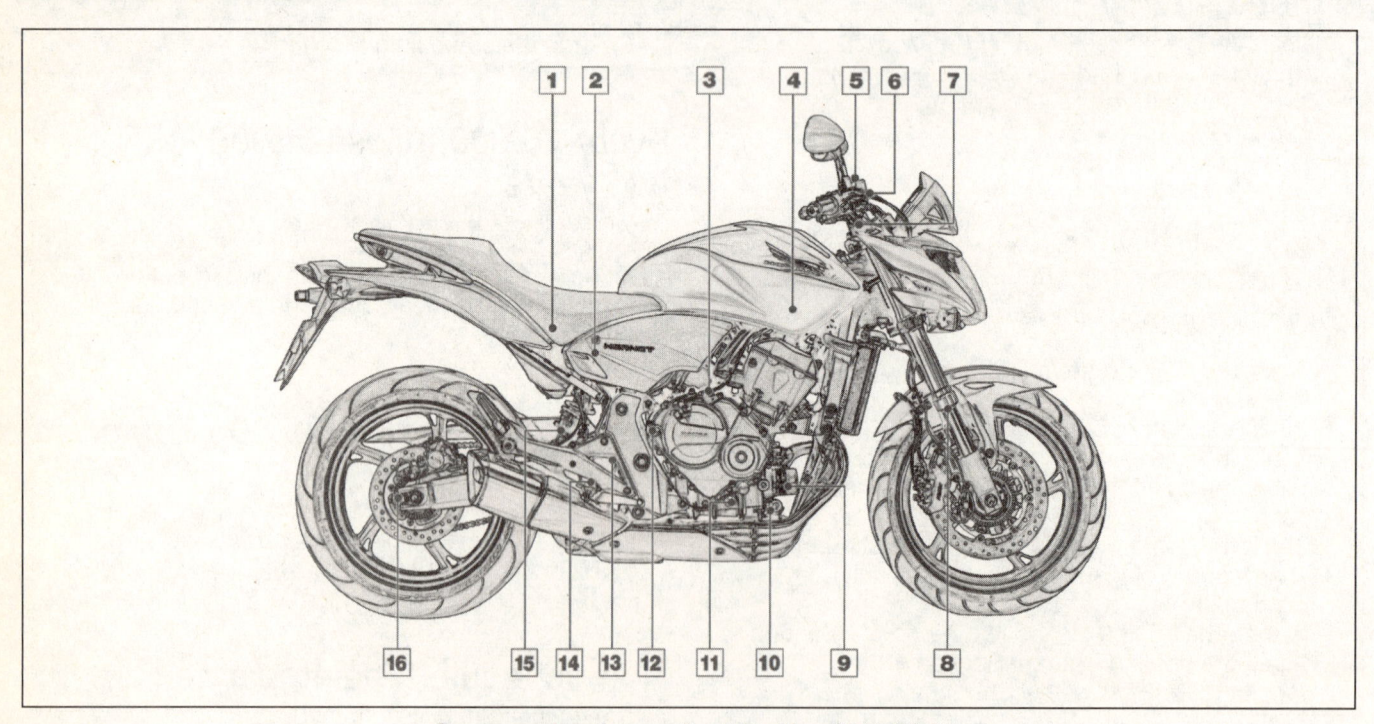

Component locations on the right side – CB600F/FA

1. Battery
2. Rear brake fluid reservoir
3. Clutch cable adjuster at lower end
4. Cooling system pressure cap
5. Front brake fluid reservoir
6. Throttle cable upper adjuster
7. Front fork pre-load and damping adjuser (2009-on)
8. Front fork seal
9. Engine oil filter
10. Engine oil drain plug
11. Engine oil level inspection window
12. Engine oil filler cap
13. Rear brake light switch
14. Rear brake pedal height adjuster
15. Rear shock damping adjuster (2009-on)
16. Drive chain adjuster

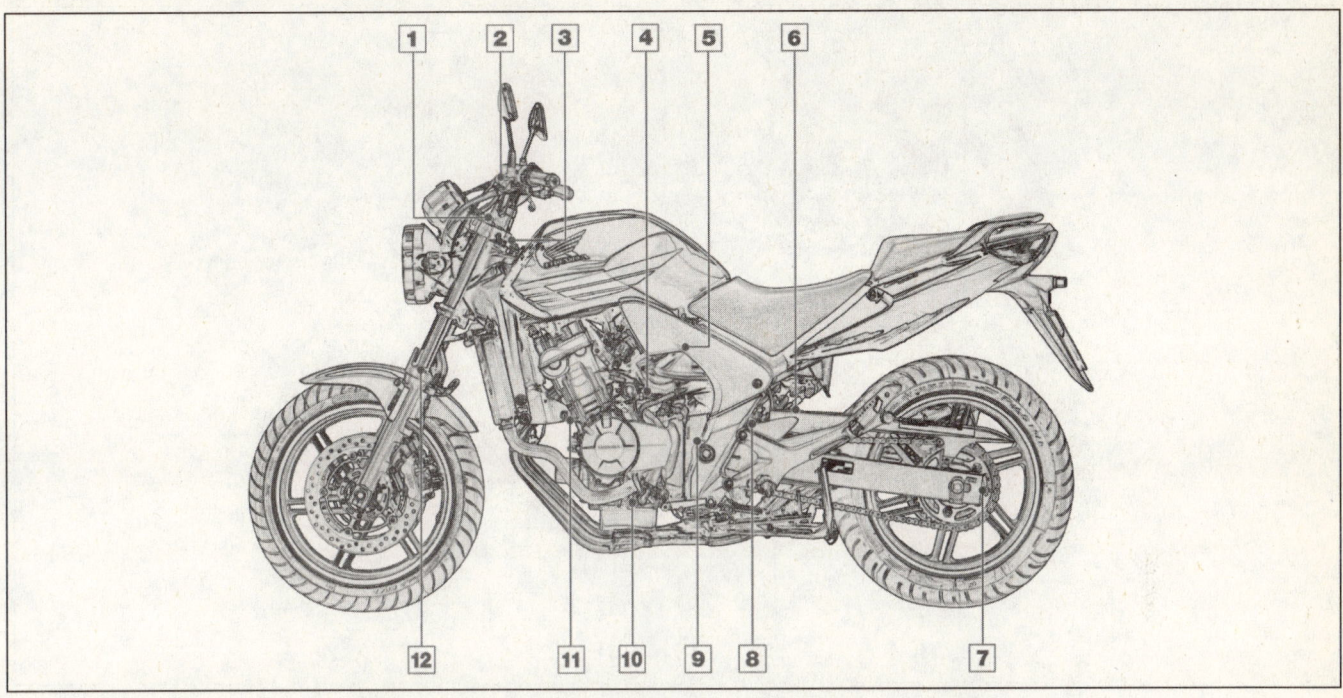

Component locations 1•5

Component locations on the left side – CBF600N/NA (and S/SA)

1. Front fork pre-load adjuster
2. Clutch cable adjuster and upper end
3. Steering head bearing adjuster
4. Crankcase breather collector
5. Air filter
6. Rear shock pre-load adjuster
7. Drive chain adjuster
8. Coolant reservoir tank
9. Drive chain slider
10. Coolant drain bolt on water pump
11. Coolant drain bolt in cylinder jacket
12. Front fork seal

Component locations on the right side – CBF600N/NA (and S/SA)

1. Battery
2. Rear brake fluid reservoir
3. Clutch cable adjuster at lower end
4. Cooling system pressure cap
5. Front brake fluid reservoir
6. Throttle cable upper adjuster
7. Front fork pre-load adjuser
8. Front fork seal
9. Engine oil filter
10. Engine oil drain plug
11. Engine oil level inspection window
12. Engine oil filler cap
13. Rear brake light switch
14. Rear brake pedal height adjuster
15. Drive chain adjuster

1•6 Component locations

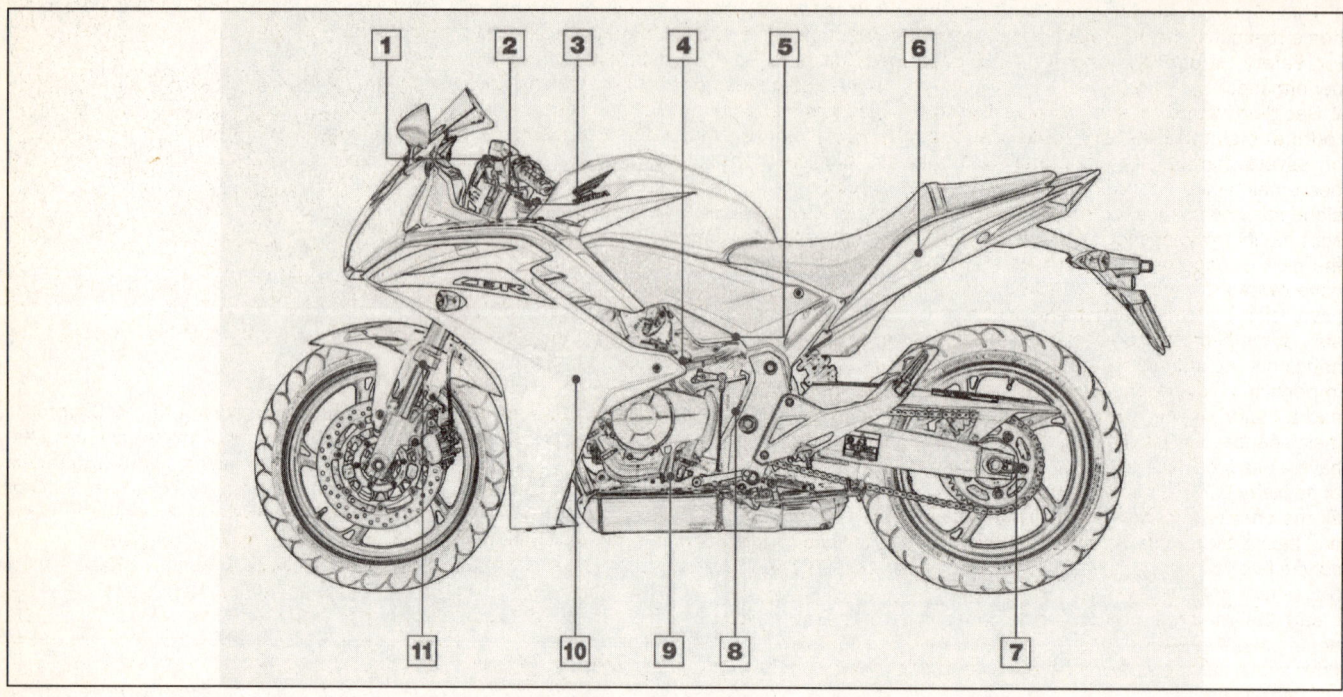

Component locations on the left side – CBR600F/FA

1. Clutch cable adjuster and upper end
2. Front fork pre-load and damping adjuster
3. Steering head bearing adjuster
4. Crankcase breather collector
5. Air filter
6. Coolant reservoir tank
7. Drive chain adjuster
8. Drive chain slider
9. Coolant drain bolt on water pump
10. Coolant drain bolt in cylinder jacket
11. Front fork seal

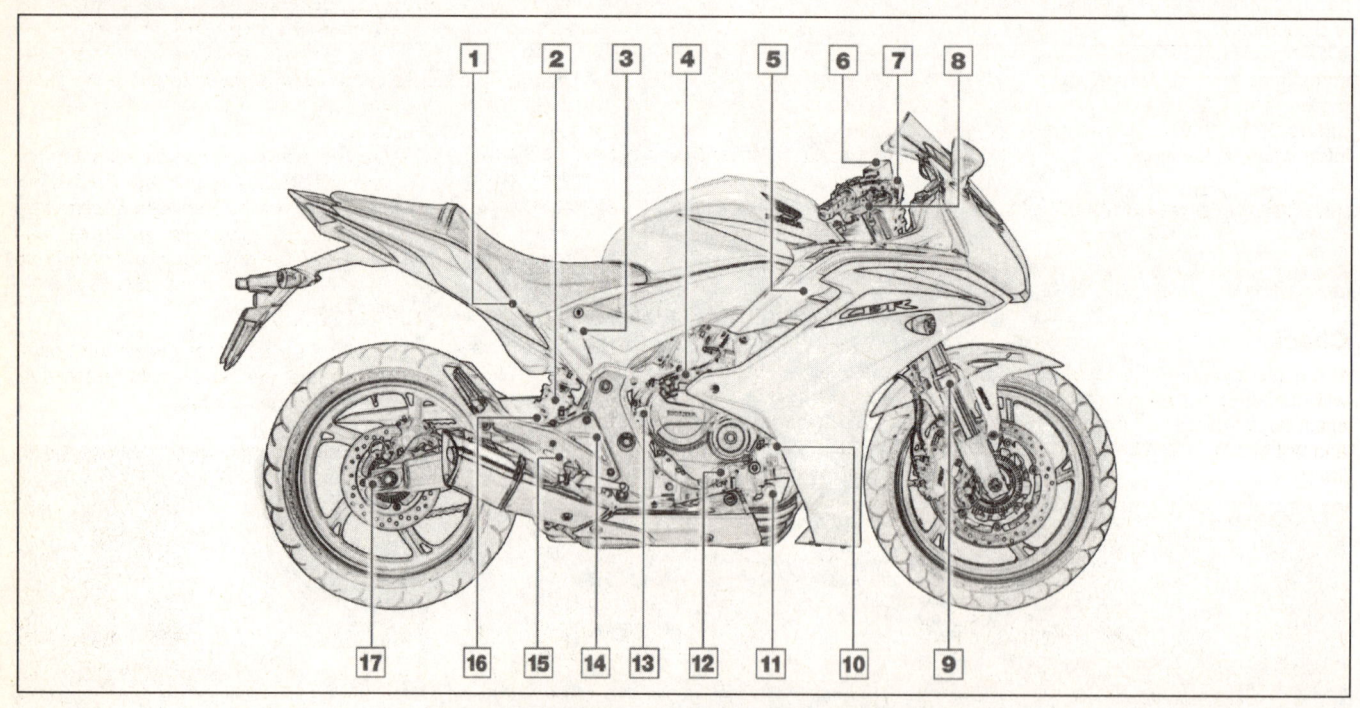

Component locations on the right side – CBR600F/FA

1. Battery
2. Rear shock pre-load adjuster
3. Rear brake fluid reservoir
4. Clutch cable adjuster at lower end
5. Cooling system pressure cap
6. Front brake fluid reservoir
7. Throttle cable upper adjuster
8. Front fork pre-load and damping adjuser
9. Front fork seal
10. Engine oil filter
11. Engine oil drain plug
12. Engine oil level inspection window
13. Engine oil filler cap
14. Rear brake light switch
15. Rear brake pedal height adjuster
16. Rear shock damping adjuster
17. Drive chain adjuster

Routine maintenance and servicing 1•7

1 This Chapter is designed to help the home mechanic maintain his/her motorcycle for safety, economy, long life and peak performance.

2 Deciding where to start or plug into the routine maintenance schedule depends on several factors. If your motorcycle has been maintained according to the warranty standards and has just come out of warranty, start routine maintenance as it coincides with the next mileage or calendar interval. If you have owned the machine for some time but have never performed any maintenance on it, start at the nearest interval and include some additional procedures to ensure that nothing important is overlooked. If you have just had a major engine overhaul, then start the maintenance routine from the beginning. If you have a used machine and have no knowledge of its history or maintenance record, combine all the checks into one large service initially and then settle into the specified maintenance schedule.

3 Before beginning any maintenance or repair, clean the machine thoroughly, especially around the oil filter, oil drain plug, body panels, drive chain, suspension, wheels, etc. Cleaning will help ensure that dirt does not contaminate the engine and will allow you to detect wear and damage that could otherwise easily go unnoticed. If you use a pressure washer make sure you do not direct the jet at wheel bearing and suspension seals and at the steering head, or at any electrical/ignition components and connectors.

4 Certain maintenance information is sometimes printed on labels attached to the motorcycle. If the information on the labels differs from that included here, use the information on the label.

1 Drive chain and sprockets

Check

1 A neglected drive chain won't last long and will quickly damage the sprockets. Routine chain adjustment and lubrication isn't difficult and will ensure maximum chain and sprocket life.

2 To check the chain, place the bike on its sidestand and shift the transmission into neutral. Make sure the ignition switch is OFF.

3 Push up on the bottom run of the chain and measure the slack midway between the two sprockets, then compare your measurement to that listed for your model in this Chapter's Specifications **(see illustration)**. As the chain stretches with wear, adjustment will periodically be necessary (see below). Since the chain will rarely wear evenly, roll the bike forward so that another section of chain can be checked (having an assistant to do this makes the task a lot easier); do this several times to check the entire length of chain, and mark the tightest spot.

Caution: Riding the bike with a chain that is too tight or too loose could lead to damage.

4 In some cases where lubrication has been neglected, corrosion and dirt may cause the links to bind and kink, which effectively shortens the chain's length and makes it tight. Thoroughly clean and work free any such links, then highlight them with a marker pen or paint. Take the bike for a ride.

5 After the bike has been ridden, repeat the measurement for slack in the highlighted area. If the chain has kinked again and is still tight, replace it with a new one (see Chapter 6). A rusty, kinked or worn chain will damage the sprockets and a tight chain can damage transmission bearings. If in any doubt as to the condition of a chain, it is far better to install a new one than risk damage to other components and possibly yourself.

6 Check the entire length of the chain for damaged rollers, loose links and pins, and missing O-rings and replace it with a new one if necessary. **Note:** *Never install a new chain on old sprockets, and never use the old chain if you install new sprockets – replace the chain and sprockets as a set.*

Adjustment

CB600F/FA and CBR600F/FA

7 Move the bike so that the tightest point of the chain is at the centre of its bottom run, then put it on the sidestand.

8 Slacken the rear axle nut **(see illustration)**.

9 Turn each adjuster bolt evenly **(see illustration)** until the amount of freeplay specified at the beginning of the Chapter is obtained at the centre of the bottom run of the chain – if the chain was slack turn the bolts clockwise; if the chain was tight turn them anti-clockwise, then move the wheel forwards in the swingarm to take up the gap.

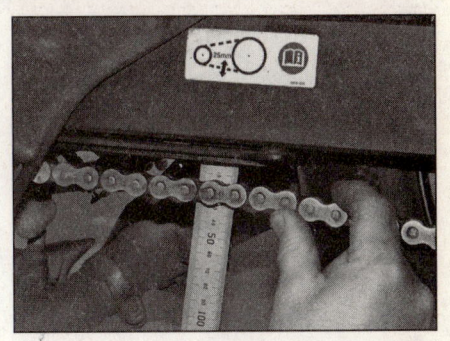

10 Following adjustment, check that the index notches on each adjustment marker are in the same position in relation to the lines on the swingarm **(see illustration)**. It is important the position is the same on each side otherwise the rear wheel will be out of alignment with the front. If there is a difference in the positions, adjust one side so that its position is exactly the same as the other. Check the chain freeplay again and readjust if necessary.

11 Also check the alignment of the wear decal on the left-hand side with the top index line on the swingarm **(see illustration 1.10)**. When the red REPLACE CHAIN zone meets the line, the drive chain has stretched excessively and must be replaced with a new one (see Chapter 6).

12 When adjustment is complete tighten the axle nut to the torque setting specified at the beginning of the Chapter **(see illustration 1.8)**. Recheck the adjustment as above, then place the machine on an auxiliary stand and spin the wheel to make sure it runs freely.

CBF600N/NA/S/SA

13 Move the bike so that the tightest point of the chain is at the centre of its bottom run, then put it on the sidestand.

1.3 Push up on the chain and measure the slack

1.8 Slacken the axle nut (arrowed)

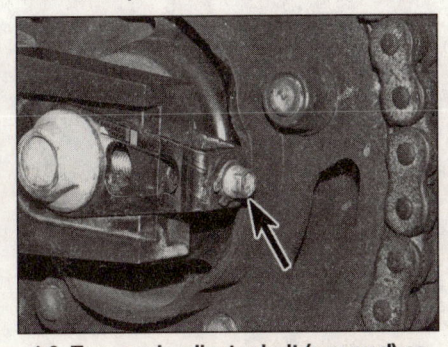

1.9 Turn each adjuster bolt (arrowed) as required

1.10 Make sure the notches are in the same position each side relative to the lines on the swingarm. When the red zone aligns with the lines, fit a new chain

Routine maintenance and servicing

1.14 Slacken the axle nut (arrowed)

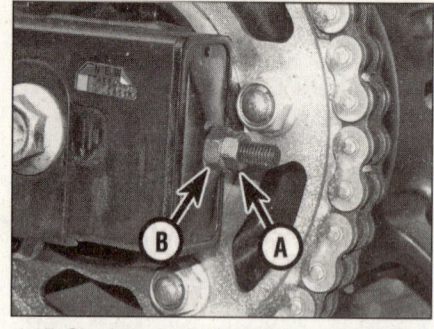

1.15 Slacken the locknut (A) on each side, then turn each adjuster nut (B) as required

1.16 Make sure the index lines are in the same position each side relative to the slot in the swingarm.

14 Slacken the rear axle nut **(see illustration)**.
15 Slacken the locknut on the adjuster on each side of the swingarm **(see illustration)**. Turn each adjuster nut evenly until the amount of freeplay specified at the beginning of the Chapter is obtained at the centre of the bottom run of the chain – if the chain was slack turn the nuts clockwise; if the chain was tight turn them anti-clockwise, then move the wheel forwards in the swingarm to take up the gap.
16 Following adjustment, check that the index lines on each adjustment marker are in the same position in relation to the rear edge of the slot in the swingarm **(see illustration)**. It is important the position is the same on each side otherwise the rear wheel will be out of alignment with the front. Always make sure that each adjuster is butted against the end of the swingarm. If there is a difference in the positions, adjust one side so that its position is exactly the same as the other. Check the chain freeplay again and readjust if necessary.
17 Also check the alignment of the index arrow on the marker with the wear decal on the left-hand side **(see illustration)**. When the arrow meets the red REPLACE CHAIN zone, the drive chain has stretched excessively and must be replaced with a new one (see Chapter 6).
18 When adjustment is complete, counter-hold the adjuster nuts and tighten the locknuts **(see illustration 1.15)**. Now tighten the axle nut to the torque setting specified at the beginning of the Chapter **(see illustration 1.14)**. Recheck the adjustment as above, then place the machine on its centrestand and spin the wheel to make sure it runs freely.

Cleaning and lubrication

19 If required, wash the chain using a dedicated aerosol cleaner, or in paraffin (kerosene) or a suitable non-flammable or high flash-point solvent that will not damage the O-rings, using a soft brush to work any dirt out if necessary **(see illustration)**. Wipe the cleaner off the chain and allow it to dry. If the chain is excessively dirty remove it from the machine and allow it to soak in the paraffin or solvent (see Chapter 6).
Caution: Don't use petrol (gasoline), an unsuitable solvent or other cleaning fluids which might damage the internal sealing properties of the chain. Don't use high-pressure water to clean the chain. The entire process shouldn't take longer than ten minutes, otherwise the O-rings could be damaged.
20 The best time to lubricate the chain is after the motorcycle has been ridden. When the chain is warm, the lubricant will penetrate the joints between the side plates better than when cold. **Note:** *Honda specifies SAE 80 to SAE 90 gear oil or an aerosol chain lube that it is suitable for O-ring chains; do not use any other chain lubricants – the solvents could damage the O-rings.* Apply the lubricant to the area where the sideplates overlap – not the middle of the rollers **(see illustration)**.

1.17 When the arrow aligns with the red zone, fit a new chain

> **HAYNES HiNT** *Apply the lubricant to the top of the lower chain run, so centrifugal force will work the oil into the chain when the bike is moving. After applying the lubricant, let it soak in a few minutes before wiping off any excess.*

> ⚠ **Warning: Take care not to get any lubricant on the tyres or brake system components.** If any of the lubricant inadvertently contacts them, clean it off thoroughly using a suitable solvent or dedicated brake cleaner before riding the machine.

1.19 Using a chain cleaning brush

1.20 Apply the lubricant to the overlapping sections of the sideplates

Routine maintenance and servicing 1•9

1.21a Check the sprocket teeth . . .

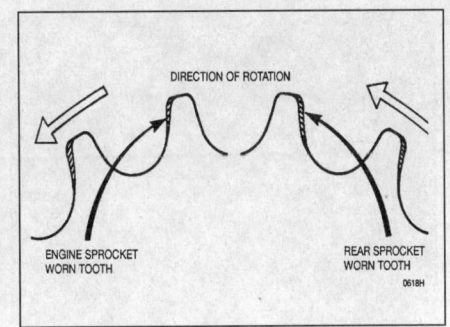

1.21b . . . in the areas indicated

1.22 Check the amount of wear on the slider – wear limit markers (arrowed) are provided top and bottom

Sprocket check

21 Remove the front sprocket cover (see Chapter 6). Check the teeth on the front and rear sprockets for wear **(see illustrations)**. If the teeth are worn excessively, replace the chain and both sprockets with a new set.

22 With the sprocket cover removed check the amount of wear on the chain slider around the front of the swingarm **(see illustration)**. If the rubbing surfaces of the slider have worn to the markers remove the swingarm and replace the slider with a new one (see Chapter 5). Note that you'll need to clean all old chain grease and road dirt off the slider in order to see the markers clearly.

2 Crankcase breather

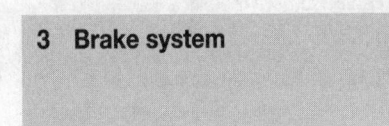

Note: *The crankcase breather should be checked more frequently if the bike is constantly ridden in wet conditions or at full throttle, or if it has fallen over, or whenever deposits are seen in the drain collector.*

1 On CBR600F/FA models remove the left-hand fairing side panel (see Chapter 7).
2 Check for any deposits in the air filter housing drain collector **(see illustration)**. If the collector is nearly full disconnect the ECT sensor wiring connector. Lift the hose and wiring out of its guide on the air filter housing.
3 Release the clamp, remove the collector and allow any deposits to drain into a rag.
4 Clean the collector and check its condition – replace it with a new one if there are any cracks or splits. Fit the collector and secure it with the clamp.
5 Fit the wiring and hose into its guide and connect the ECT sensor wiring connector **(see illustration 2.2)**.
6 On CBR600F/FA models install the left-hand fairing side panel (see Chapter 7).
7 Check the condition of the crankcase breather hose that runs between the middle of the valve cover and the right-hand side of the air filter housing **(see illustration)**. Check for cracks and splits and replace it with a new one if any are evident – raise the fuel tank for access (see Chapter 4). Make sure the hose is not kinked or trapped, and is securely connected at each end.

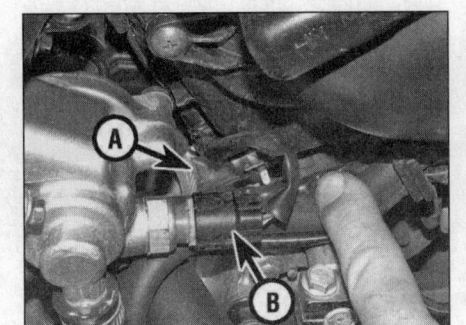

2.2 Check the collector (A) – to drain it disconnect the wiring connector (B) and lift the hose and wiring out of the guide

3 Brake system

Brake pad wear check

1 Each brake pad has wear indicators in the form of cut-outs in the side of the material **(see illustration)**. The wear indicators should be plainly visible by looking from the top of each front caliper, and from behind the rear caliper, but note that an accumulation of road dirt and brake dust could make them difficult to see **(see illustration)**.
2 If the pads are worn to the beginning of the cut-outs, they must be replaced with new ones.
Note: *Some after-market pads may use different indicators to those on the original equipment.*

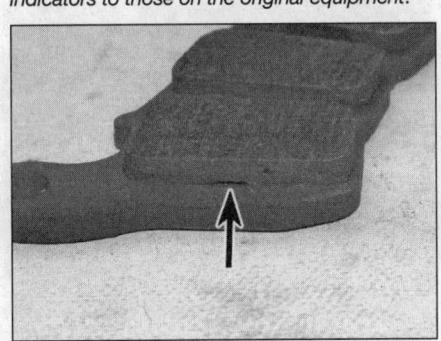

2.7 Crankcase breather hose (arrowed)

3 If the indicators are difficult to see, the amount of friction material remaining is easily visible, and it will be obvious when the pads need replacing. Honda do not specify a minimum thickness for the friction material, but anything less than 1 mm should be considered excessively worn.
4 Also check for different amounts of wear in the pads in each caliper, and uneven wear across each brake pad in each front caliper, which is indicative of a sticking or seized piston. If found, the caliper(s) must be overhauled (see Chapter 6).
5 If the pads are dirty or if you are in doubt as to the amount of friction material remaining, remove them for inspection (see Chapter 6). If the pads are excessively worn, also check the brake discs (see Chapter 6).
6 Refer to Chapter 6 for details of pad removal and installation.

3.1a Brake pad wear indicator cut-out (arrowed) . . .

3.1b . . . and where to look for it

Routine maintenance and servicing

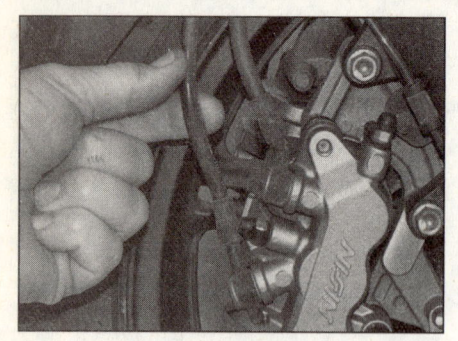

3.10 Check all hoses, pipes and unions for cracks and leaks

3.12 Rear brake light switch adjuster ring (arrowed)

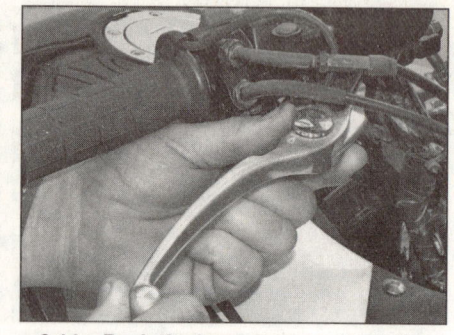

3.14a Push the lever away and turn the adjuster as required . . .

Brake system check

7 A routine general check of the brake system will ensure that any problems are discovered and remedied before the rider's safety is jeopardised.
8 Check the brake pads for wear (see above) and make sure the fluid level in each reservoir is correct (see *Pre-ride checks*).
9 Check the brake lever and pedal pivots for sloppy or rough action, excessive play, bends, and other damage. Replace any damaged parts with new ones (see Chapter 5). Clean and lubricate the lever and pedal pivots if their action is stiff or rough (see Section 16). If the lever or pedal is spongy, bleed the brakes (see Chapter 6).
10 Look for leaks at the hose and pipe connections and check for cracks in the hoses, pipes and unions **(see illustration)**. If leakage or cracked or damaged hoses are found, renew the hoses as described in Chapter 6. Make sure all brake hose and pipe fasteners are tight. Similarly check for any signs of fluid leakage from the caliper and master cylinder – overhaul and seal renewal will be necessary if found (see Chapter 6).
11 Make sure the brake light operates when the front brake lever is pulled in. The front brake light switch, mounted on the underside of the master cylinder, is not adjustable. If it fails to operate properly, check it (see Chapter 8).
12 Make sure the brake light is activated just before the rear brake takes effect. The rear brake light switch is mounted behind the right-hand footrest bracket. If adjustment is necessary, hold the switch body and turn the adjuster ring until the brake light is activated when required – do not turn the switch itself **(see illustration)**. If the brake light comes on too late or not at all, turn the ring clockwise so the switch is drawn up out of its bracket. If the brake light comes on too soon or is permanently on, turn the ring anti-clockwise so the switch is drawn down into the bracket. If the switch doesn't operate the brake light, check it (see Chapter 8).
13 On CB600FA, CBR600FA and CBF600NA/SA models (ABS-equipped) raise the front wheel off the ground; do this on CBF600NA/SA models by placing the bike on its centrestand and having an assistant press down on the rear, and on all other models by using a front paddock stand. Press the rear brake pedal down and check that the front wheel is locked by the brake. If the wheel can be turned, there is a fault in the linked braking system (see Chapter 6).
14 The front brake lever has a span adjuster that alters the distance of the lever from the handlebar. On early models each setting is identified by a notch in the adjuster ring aligning with the arrow on the lever – push the lever away from the handlebar and turn the adjuster ring to alter the span, making sure that the notch specific to the desired setting is aligned with the arrow on the lever **(see illustration)**. On late models each setting is identified by a number on the adjuster aligning with the triangular index mark on the lever – push the lever away from the handlebar and turn the adjuster ring until the setting which best suits the rider is obtained, then release the lever **(see illustration)**. Do not set the adjuster between the defined settings.
15 The height of the rear brake pedal can be adjusted to suit the rider's preference if required. Slacken the locknut securing the clevis on the master cylinder pushrod, then turn the pushrod using a spanner on the hex at the top of the rod until the pedal is at the desired height **(see illustration)**. On completion tighten the locknut. Note that at a low setting the bottom of the pushrod must clear the clevis by 1 mm and at a high setting must still be visible under the top of the clevis. Adjust the rear brake light switch after adjusting the pedal height (see Step 12).

Brake fluid change

16 The brake fluid should be changed at the prescribed interval. Refer to Chapter 6 for details. Ensure that all the old fluid is pumped from the hydraulic system and that the level in the fluid reservoir is checked and the brakes tested before riding the motorcycle.

4 Clutch

1 Check that the clutch lever operates smoothly and easily.
2 If the clutch lever operation is heavy or stiff, remove the cable (see Chapter 2) and lubricate it (see Section 16). If the cable is still stiff, replace it with a new one. Install the lubricated or new cable (see Chapter 2).
3 With the cable operating smoothly, check that it is correctly adjusted. Periodic adjustment is necessary to compensate for wear in the

3.14b . . . on late models aligning the required setting with the index mark (arrowed) . . .

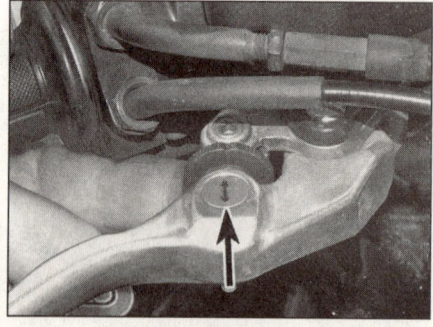

3.14c . . . and on early models aligning the notch with the index mark (arrowed)

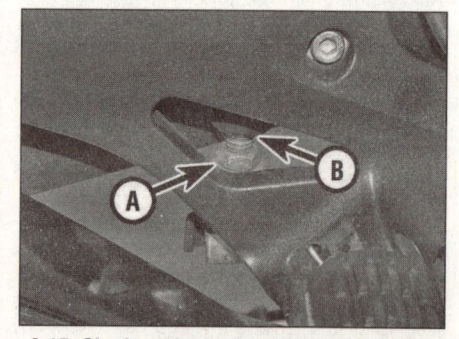

3.15 Slacken the locknut (A) and turn the pushrod using the hex (B) to adjust pedal height

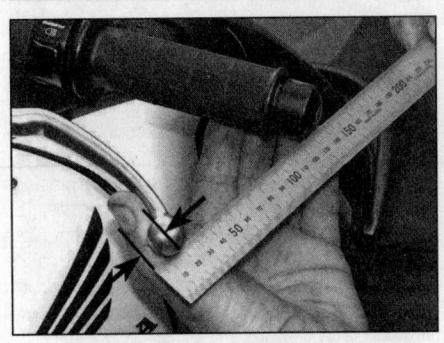

Routine maintenance and servicing 1•11

4.3 Freeplay measured from the centre of the ball end of the lever when at rest to the point freeplay is taken up

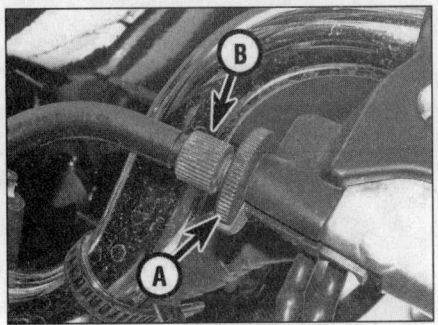

4.4 Slacken the lockring (A) and turn the adjuster (B) as required

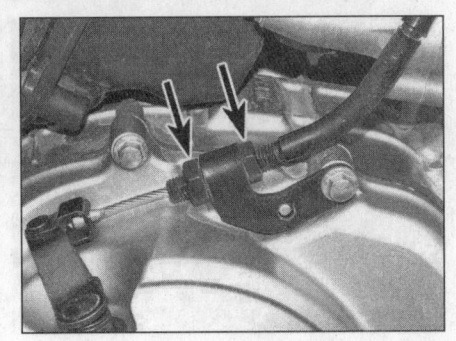

4.8 Slacken and adjust the nuts (arrowed) as described

clutch plates and stretch of the cable. Check that the amount of freeplay at the clutch lever end is within the specifications listed at the beginning of the Chapter **(see illustration)**.

4 If adjustment is required, this can be done first at the lever end of the cable. Loosen the adjuster lockring, then turn the adjuster in or out until the required amount of freeplay is obtained **(see illustration)**. To increase freeplay, thread the adjuster into the lever bracket. To reduce freeplay, thread the adjuster out of the bracket.

5 Make sure that the slot in the adjuster and the lockring, are not aligned with the slot in the lever bracket – these slots are to allow removal of the cable, and if they are all aligned while the bike is in use the cable could jump out. Also make sure the adjuster is not threaded too far out of the bracket so that it is only held by a few threads – this will leave it unstable and the threads could be damaged. Tighten the lockring on completion.

6 If all the adjustment has been taken up at the lever, thread the adjuster all the way into the bracket to give the maximum amount of freeplay, then back it out one turn – this resets the adjuster to its start point.

7 Now set the correct amount of freeplay using the adjuster on the clutch end of cable. The adjuster is set in a bracket on the clutch cover on the right-hand side of the engine.

8 Use the nuts on each end of the threaded section of the cable to adjust freeplay **(see illustration)**. To increase freeplay, slacken the front nut and tighten the rear nut until the freeplay is as specified, then tighten the front nut. To reduce freeplay, slacken the rear nut and tighten the front nut until the freeplay is as specified, then tighten the rear nut. Subsequent adjustments can now be made using the lever adjuster only.

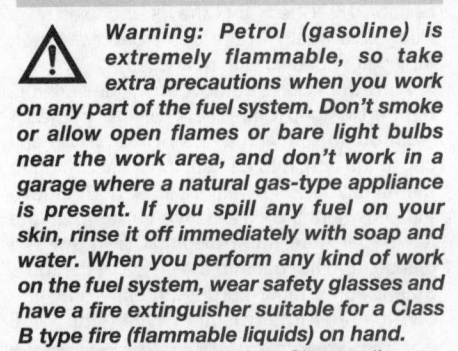

5 Fuel system

⚠ **Warning: Petrol (gasoline) is extremely flammable, so take extra precautions when you work on any part of the fuel system. Don't smoke or allow open flames or bare light bulbs near the work area, and don't work in a garage where a natural gas-type appliance is present. If you spill any fuel on your skin, rinse it off immediately with soap and water. When you perform any kind of work on the fuel system, wear safety glasses and have a fire extinguisher suitable for a Class B type fire (flammable liquids) on hand.**

1 Remove the fuel tank (see Chapter 4).
2 Check the fuel tank, the fuel supply hose, the tank drain and breather hoses, the throttle body vacuum hoses and idle system hoses for signs of leaks, cracks, deterioration or damage. In particular check that there are no leaks from the fuel hose or hose unions. Replace hoses with new ones as required, referring to the relevant section in Chapter 4. Note the routing of each hose and how it is secured – it is advisable to make a sketch of the hoses before removing them to ensure they are correctly installed. Make sure each new hose is fully pushed onto its union. Use new clamps if necessary where fitted.

3 Check the joint between the fuel pump mounting plate and the tank, and between the fuel level sensor and the tank. If there is evidence of fuel leakage, check the mounting nuts are tight (see Chapter 4 Specifications for the pump plate nut torque setting). If the leak persists, remove the pump or level sensor as required and fit a new seal (see Chapter 4).

4 Inspect the joints between the fuel rails, the injectors and the throttle bodies. If there are any leaks, remove the fuel rails and fit new seals and O-rings to the injectors and/or rails as required (see Chapter 4).

5 Fuel filter renewal is not a service item. The filter and strainer are integral with the fuel pump, and are not available as a separate component. If fuel starvation is experienced, and all other possibilities have been checked, a blocked filter or strainer could be the cause; in this event a new pump assembly must be installed (see Chapter 4).

6 Throttle cables

1 Make sure the throttle grip rotates smoothly and freely from fully closed to fully open with the front wheel turned at various angles. The grip should return automatically from fully open to fully closed when released. If the throttle sticks, check and lubricate the cable and twistgrip as described below.

Cable freeplay check and adjustment

2 Check for a small amount of freeplay in the cables, measured in terms of the amount of twistgrip rotation before the throttle opens, and compare the amount to that listed in this Chapter's Specifications **(see illustration)**. If it's incorrect, adjust the cables to correct it as follows.

3 Initially adjust freeplay using the adjuster in the throttle opening cable where it leaves the throttle pulley housing on the handlebar. Loosen the locknut and turn the adjuster in or out as required until the specified amount of freeplay is obtained (see this Chapter's Specifications), then retighten the locknut **(see illustration)**.

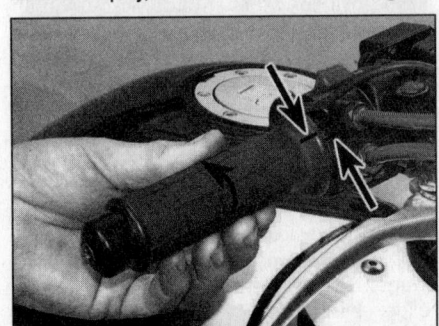

6.2 Throttle cable freeplay is measured in terms of twistgrip rotation

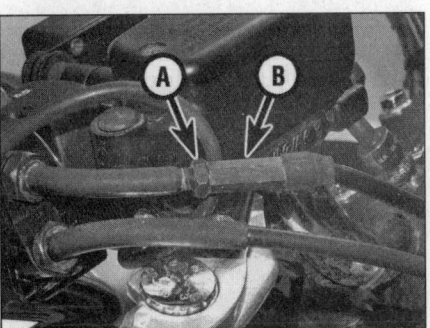

6.3 Slacken the adjuster locknut (A) and turn the adjuster (B) as required

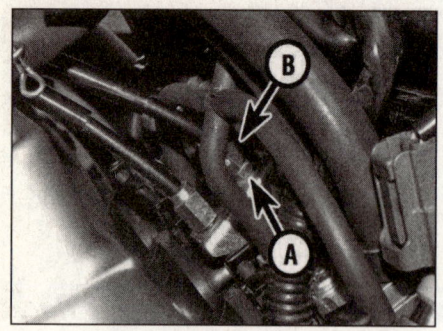

1•12 Routine maintenance and servicing

6.5 Throttle cable adjuster locknut (A) and adjuster (B)

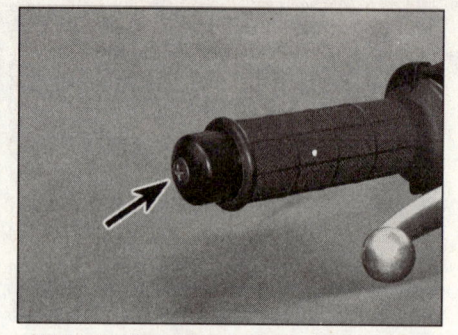

6.7 Undo the screw (arrowed) to free the end-weight and twistgrip

4 If the adjuster has reached its limit of adjustment, reset it to its start point by turning it fully in, so that freeplay is at a maximum, then raise the fuel tank (see Chapter 4) to access the adjuster at the throttle body end.
5 The adjuster is on the rear cable in the bracket. Slacken the adjuster locknut, then screw the adjuster in or out as required, making sure the captive nut remains held in the bracket, thereby threading itself along the adjuster as you turn it, until the specified amount of freeplay is obtained, then tighten the locknut **(see illustration)**. Subsequent adjustments can be made at the throttle twistgrip end when required. If the cable cannot be adjusted as specified, replace it with a new one (see Chapter 4). Check that the throttle twistgrip operates smoothly and snaps shut quickly when released.

⚠ **Warning: Turn the handlebars all the way through their travel with the engine idling. Idle speed should not change. If it does, the cables may be routed incorrectly. Correct this condition before riding the bike.**

Cable and twistgrip lubrication

6 If the throttle sticks, this is probably due to a cable fault. Detach the cables from the throttle pulley (see Chapter 4) and lubricate them (see Section 16). Check that the inner cables slide freely and easily in the outer cables. If not, replace the cables with new ones.
7 With the cables removed, make sure the throttle twistgrip rotates freely on the handlebar – dirt combined with a lack of lubrication can cause the action to be stiff. If necessary, undo the handlebar end-weight screw and remove the end-weight, then slide the twistgrip off the handlebar **(see illustration)**. Clean any old grease from the bar and the inside of the tube. Smear some multi-purpose grease onto the bar, then refit the twistgrip. When fitting the end-weight, align the boss with the cut-out on the inner weight inside the handlebar. Clean the threads of the screw, then apply a suitable non-permanent thread locking compound, hold the weight and tighten the screw.
8 Install the cables, making sure they are correctly routed (see Chapter 4). If this fails to improve the operation of the throttle, the cables must be replaced with new ones. Note that in very rare cases the fault could lie in the throttle bodies. Remove the air filter housing and check the action of the throttle pulley and linkage (see Chapter 4).

7 Spark plugs

Check

Special tool: *A wire gauge or feeler gauge set is necessary for measuring the spark plug gap (see illustrations 7.9a and b).*

1 Make sure your spark plug socket is the correct size (16 mm hex) before attempting to remove the plugs – a suitable one is supplied in the motorcycle's tool kit which is stored under the passenger seat.
2 Raise or remove the fuel tank (see Chapter 4). Remove the PAIR system control valve along with its hoses (see Chapter 4). Remove the ignition coils (see Chapter 4).
3 Clean the area around each spark plug cap to prevent any dirt falling into the spark plug channels.
4 Using either the plug removing tool supplied in the bike's toolkit or a deep spark plug socket and extension, unscrew and remove the plugs **(see illustrations)** – lay the plugs out in order so you know which cylinder each comes from.
5 Before cleaning the plug refer to the colour spark plug chart at the end of this manual and compare the firing end of each plug to those shown, identifying any abnormal condition and assessing its cause if necessary.
6 Clean the electrodes using a wire brush – if any deposits do not come off replace the plugs with new ones. Cleaning spark plugs by sandblasting is fine as long as you blow them with compressed air and clean them with a high flash-point solvent afterwards. Also clean any deposits off the white ceramic body of the plug.
7 Check the condition of the cleaned electrodes. Both the centre and side electrodes should have square edges and the side electrodes should be of uniform thickness. Check for evidence of a cracked or chipped insulator around the centre electrode. Check the plug threads, the washer and the ceramic insulator body for cracks and other damage.
8 If in doubt concerning the condition of the plugs, replace them with new ones, as the expense is minimal.
9 If the plugs can be re-used check the gap between the electrodes with a feeler gauge or wire type gauge **(see illustrations)**. The gap

7.4a Unscrew the plug . . .

7.4b . . . and lift it out with the tool – the rubber insert should grip around the plug top

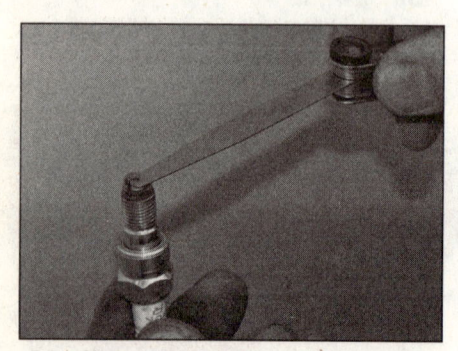

7.9a Using a feeler blade to measure the spark plug electrode gap

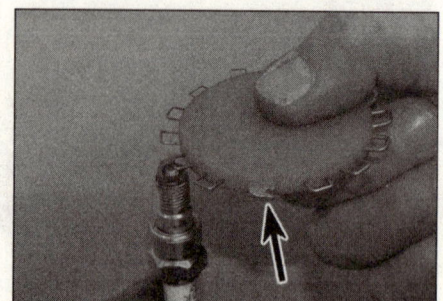

7.9b Using a wire gauge to measure the spark plug electrode gap – note the adjuster (arrowed)

Routine maintenance and servicing 1•13

TOOL TIP

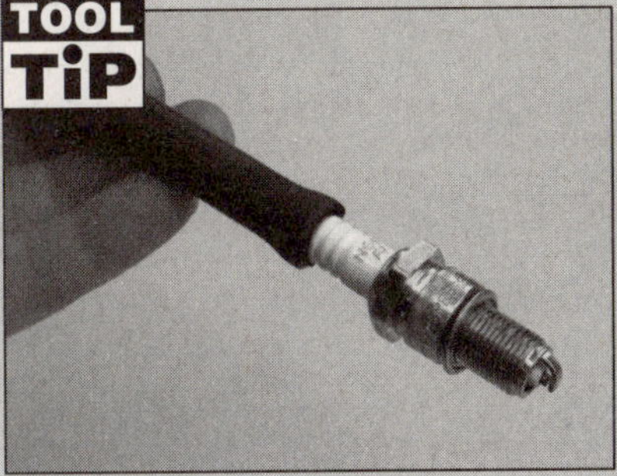

As the plugs are quite recessed, slip a short length of hose over the end of the plug to use as a tool to thread it into place. The hose will grip the plug well enough to turn it, but will start to slip if the plug begins to cross-thread in the hole – this will prevent damaged threads.

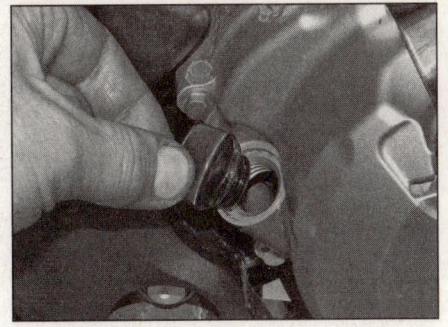

8.3 Unscrew the oil filler cap to act as a vent

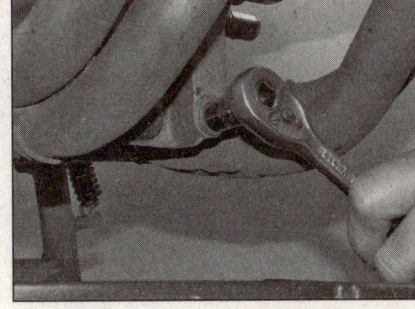

8.4a Unscrew the oil drain plug . . .

should be as given in the Specifications at the beginning of this chapter. If the electrodes have worn and the gap is wider than it should be, or for some reason the gap is narrower than it should be (if the plug has been dropped for instance) carefully bend the outer electrode as required to restore the correct gap – wire gauges have a special adjuster incorporated.

10 Fit the plug into the end of the tool, then use the tool to insert the plug **(see illustration 7.4b)**. Alternatively there are dedicated plug insertion tools, or you can use some hose (see *Tool Tip*). Thread the plugs as far as possible into the head turning the tool or hose by hand, making sure they do not cross-thread. Once the plugs are finger-tight, tighten them using a spanner on the tool supplied or a socket drive **(see illustration 7.4a)**. If a torque wrench can be applied, tighten the spark plugs to the torque setting specified at the beginning of the Chapter. Otherwise, if new plugs are being used tighten them by 1/2 a turn after the washer has seated, and if the old plugs are being reused tighten them by 1/8 to 1/4 turn after they have seated, according to feel. Do not over-tighten them.

11 Install the ignition coils, PAIR system control valve and fuel tank (see Chapter 4).

HAYNES HINT: *Stripped plug threads in the cylinder head can be repaired with a thread insert – see 'Tools and Workshop Tips' in the Reference section.*

Renewal

12 At the prescribed interval, whatever the condition of the existing spark plugs, remove the plugs as described above and install new ones.

8 Engine oil and filter

Special tool: *A filter removing tool is necessary for this job. You can purchase one as a Honda spare part (as a kit along with the oil filter or separately) or alternatively there are several after-market options (see Step 5).*

⚠️ **Warning:** *Be careful when draining the oil, as the exhaust, the engine, and the oil itself can cause severe burns.*

1 Consistent routine oil and filter changes are the single most important maintenance procedure you can perform. The oil not only lubricates the internal parts of the engine, transmission and clutch, but it also acts as a coolant, a cleaner, a sealant, and a protector. Because of these demands, the oil takes a terrific amount of abuse and should be replaced often with new oil of the recommended grade and type. The oil filter should be changed with every oil change.

HAYNES HINT: *Saving a little money on the difference in cost between a good oil and a cheap oil won't pay off if the engine is damaged.*

2 Before changing the oil, warm up the engine so the oil will drain easily. The oil drain plug is in the front of the sump on the left-hand side, and the filter is on the front of the crankcase. On CBR600F/FA models remove the fairing side panels (see Chapter 7).

3 Position a large clean drain tray below the engine, so it is under the drain plug and the filter. Unscrew the oil filler cap from the clutch cover to vent the crankcase and to act as a reminder that there is no oil in the engine **(see illustration)**.

4 Unscrew the oil drain plug and allow the oil to flow into the tray **(see illustrations)**. Remove the sealing washer from the drain plug – you may have to cut it off. A new washer must be used.

5 Unscrew the filter using a filter socket (one can be obtained with the new filter from Honda dealers under part No. 07HAA-PJ70101, or otherwise there are commercially available equivalents available), filter pliers, or a filter removing strap or a chain-wrench, and tip any residual oil into the drain tray **(see illustrations)**. The filter socket is preferable

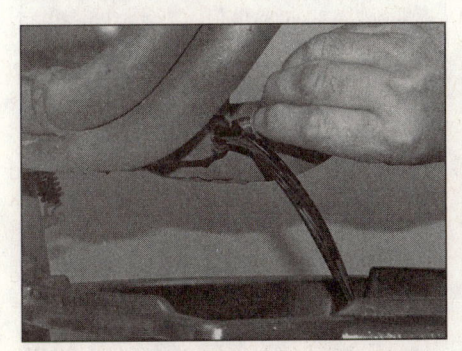

8.4b . . . and allow the oil to completely drain

8.5a Unscrew the filter using a filter removing socket or strap . . .

8.5b . . . and allow the oil to drain

1•14 Routine maintenance and servicing

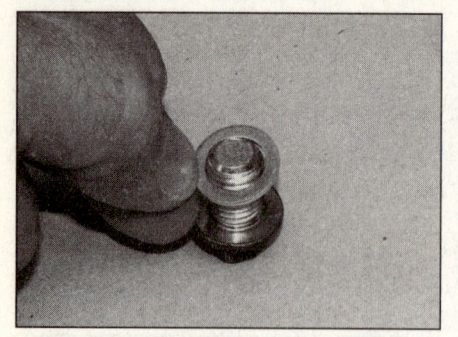

8.6a Fit a new sealing washer onto the drain plug...

8.6b ...and tighten the plug to the specified torque

8.7 Measure the length of exposed thread

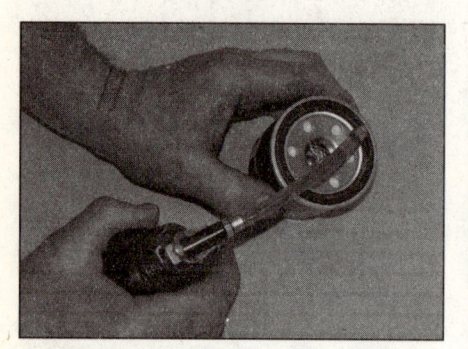

8.8a Smear clean oil onto the seal...

8.8b ...then fit the filter and tighten it as described

8.9a Add the specified type and amount of oil...

because it provides a means of tightening the new filter to the correct torque.

6 When the oil has completely drained, fit the new sealing washer onto the plug, then fit the plug into the sump and tighten it to the torque setting specified at the beginning of the Chapter **(see illustrations)**. Do not overtighten it as the threads in the sump are easily damaged.

7 Before fitting the filter measure the length of exposed thread on the oil filter boss to check that it didn't unscrew when removing the filter – there should be 16 to 17 mm of thread exposed **(see illustration)**.

8 Smear clean engine oil onto the threads and rubber seal on the new filter, then thread the filter onto the engine **(see illustrations)**. Tighten it to the specified torque setting using the filter socket if available, or tighten the filter as tight as possible by hand, or by the number of turns specified on the filter itself or its packaging. **Note:** *Do not use a strap or chain-type filter removing tool to tighten the filter as you will damage it.*

9 Refill the engine using the recommended type and amount of oil (see Specifications) **(see illustration)**. With the motorcycle vertical, the oil level should lie just below the upper level line on the inspection window, but do not go above it **(see illustration)**. Check the condition of the O-ring on the filler cap and replace it with a new one if it is damaged or worn **(see illustration)**. Fit the filler cap.

10 Start the engine and let it run for two or three minutes (make sure that the oil pressure light extinguishes after a few seconds). Shut it off, wait a few minutes, then check the oil level again. If necessary, add more oil to bring the level between the upper and lower level lines.

11 Check around the drain plug and the filter for leaks. If leaks are evident, and the plug and filter are correctly tightened using a new washer and a lubricated seal, there is another cause (such as dirt or corrosion) that must be investigated before riding the bike.

12 The old oil drained from the engine cannot be re-used and should be disposed of properly. Check with your local refuse disposal company, disposal facility or environmental agency to see whether they will accept the used oil for recycling. Don't pour used oil into drains or onto the ground.

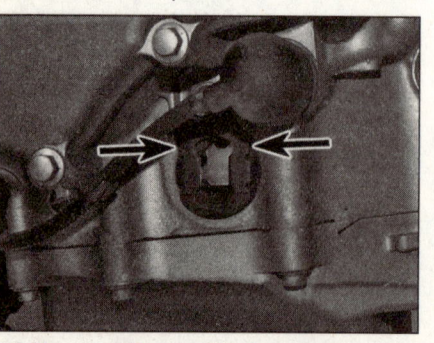

8.9b ...so the level is almost up to the upper level lines (arrowed)

8.9c Make sure the O-ring is in good condition and correctly seated

HAYNES HINT *Check the old oil carefully – if it is very metallic coloured, then the engine is experiencing wear from break-in (new engine) or from insufficient lubrication. If there are flakes or chips of metal in the oil, then something is drastically wrong internally and the engine will have to be disassembled for inspection and repair. If there are pieces of fibre-like material in the oil, the clutch is experiencing excessive wear and should be checked.*

Note: It is illegal and anti-social to dump oil down the drain. To find the location of your local oil recycling bank in the UK, call 08708 506 506 or visit www.oilbankline.org.uk

OIL CARE — FOLLOW THE CODE

Routine maintenance and servicing 1•15

9.2 Where fitted detach and remove the grille

9.3 Check all the coolant hoses as described

9 Cooling system

Check

⚠ **Warning: The engine must be cool before beginning this procedure.**

1 Check the coolant level in the reservoir (see *Pre-ride checks*).

2 On CBR600F/FA models remove the fairing side and upper panels (see Chapter 7). On CB600F/FA and CBF600N/NA models remove the radiator grille **(see illustration)**. On all models raise the fuel tank (see Chapter 4).

3 Examine each rubber coolant hose along its entire length. Look for cracks, abrasions and other damage. Squeeze each hose at various points to see whether they are dried out or hard **(see illustration)**. They should feel firm, yet pliable, and return to their original shape when released. If necessary, replace them with new ones (see Chapter 3).

4 Check for evidence of leaks at each cooling system hose connection, and around the pump on the left-hand side of the engine, at the inlet union on the back of the cylinder block and the outlet union and thermostat housing on the back of the cylinder head, and on CB600F/FA and CBR600F/FA models around the oil cooler on the front of the engine. Tighten the hose clips carefully to prevent future leaks. If the pump is leaking around the cover, check that the bolts are tight. If they are, remove the cover and replace the cover and cover plate O-rings with new ones (see Chapter 3).

5 To prevent leakage of coolant from the cooling system to the lubrication system and vice versa, two seals are fitted on the pump shaft. The coolant seal on the water pump side is of the mechanical type and bears on the rear face of the impeller. The oil seal, which is mounted behind the mechanical seal, is of the normal feathered lip type. On the underside of the pump housing there is a drain hole **(see illustration)**. If either seal fails, the drain allows the coolant or oil to escape. If on inspection the drain shows signs of continuous leakage, particularly with the engine running, remove the pump and replace it with a new one (see Chapter 3) – it comes as an assembly and the seals are not available separately. Honda states that a small amount of coolant weeping is normal, so you may have to decide for yourself the difference between that and continuous leakage – if in doubt seek the advice of your dealer.

6 Check the radiator on the front of the engine for leaks and other damage. Leaks in the radiator leave tell-tale scale deposits or coolant stains on the outside of the core below the leak. If leaks are noted, remove the radiator (see Chapter 3) and have it repaired or replace it with a new one – do not use a liquid leak-stop compound to try to repair leaks.

7 Check the radiator fins for mud, dirt and insects, which may impede the flow of air through it. If the fins are dirty, remove the radiator (see Chapter 3) and clean it using water or low pressure compressed air directed through the fins from the inner side of the radiator. If the fins are bent or distorted, straighten them carefully with a screwdriver. If the airflow is restricted by bent or damaged fins over more than 20% of the radiator's surface area, replace the radiator with a new one.

⚠ **Warning: Do not remove the pressure cap when the engine is hot. It is good practice to cover the cap with a heavy cloth and turn the cap slowly anti-clockwise. If you hear a hissing sound (indicating that there is still pressure in the system), wait until it stops, then continue turning the cap until it can be removed.**

8 Remove the pressure cap from the filler neck, noting the *Warning* **(see illustration)**.

9 Check the condition of the coolant in the system. If it is rust-coloured or if accumulations of scale are visible, drain, flush and refill the system with new coolant (see below). Check the antifreeze content of the coolant with an antifreeze hydrometer – a 50% content should give a reading of 1.084 at 5°C to 1.074 at 25°C, varying accordingly in between. The system must have the correct coolant mixture (see Specifications) – if the coolant is weak (too little anti-freeze) there will not be adequate protection against freezing and corrosion, and if it is too strong the ability to cool the engine is reduced. If the hydrometer indicates an incorrect mixture, drain, flush and refill the system (see below).

10 The function of the pressure cap is crucial to the correct running of the cooling system. Check the cap seal for cracks and other damage. If the coolant level consistently drops and/or the

9.5 Check the pump drain hole (arrowed) for signs of leakage

9.8 Remove the pressure cap as described

1•16 Routine maintenance and servicing

9.12a Oil cooler (arrowed) and its hoses – CB600F/FA and CBR600F/FA

9.12b Oil cooler (arrowed) – CBF600N/NA/S/SA

bike overheats, and no evidence of leaks can be found, have the cap pressure checked by a Honda dealer, or just fit a new one. If a new cap does not cure the problem have the entire system pressure checked by a dealer.

11 Fit the cap by turning it clockwise until it reaches the first stop then push down on it and continue turning until it can turn no further. Start the engine and let it reach normal operating temperature, then check for leaks again. As the coolant temperature increases, the electric fan (mounted on the back of the radiator) should come on automatically and the temperature should begin to drop. If not, refer to Chapter 3 and check the fan and fan circuit.

12 Check the oil cooler on the front of the engine for any signs of oil leakage between it and the engine **(see illustrations)**. If there is leakage check the cooler bolt(s) is/are tight. If the leakage persists you will have to fit a new O-ring between the cooler and the engine (see Chapter 2). On CB600F/FA and CBR600F/FA models check that the coolant hoses are secure on the cooler unions, and that there is no evidence of leakage from the body of the cooler. If there is, the cooler is damaged and must be replaced with a new one.

13 Install the fuel tank, radiator grille, and fairing panels as required according to model.

Coolant change

⚠ **Warning: Allow the engine to cool completely before performing this maintenance operation. Also, don't allow anti-freeze to come into contact with your skin or the painted surfaces of the motorcycle. Rinse off spills immediately with plenty of water. Anti-freeze is highly toxic if ingested. Never leave anti-freeze lying around in an open container or in puddles on the floor; children and pets are attracted by its sweet smell and may drink it. Check with local authorities (councils)** about disposing anti-freeze – many have collection centres that dispose it safely. Anti-freeze is also combustible, so don't store it near open flames.

Draining

14 Raise the fuel tank (see Chapter 4). On CB600F/FA and CBR600F/FA models remove the seat cowl, and on CBR600F/FA models also remove the fairing side and upper panels (see Chapter 7).

15 Remove the pressure cap from the filler neck on the thermostat cover by turning it anti-clockwise until it reaches a stop **(see illustration 9.8)**. If you hear a hissing sound (indicating there is still pressure in the system), wait until it stops. Now press down on the cap and continue turning the cap until it can be removed. Also remove the coolant reservoir cap.

16 Position a suitable container beneath the water pump on the left-hand side of the engine. Unscrew the drain bolt and allow the coolant to completely drain **(see illustrations)**. A new sealing washer is needed, but keep the old one for use during flushing if required.

17 Now position the container beneath the front of the engine. Unscrew the cylinder drain bolt and allow the coolant to completely drain from the cylinder jacket **(see illustration)**. Retain the old sealing washer for use during flushing.

18 Disconnect the radiator overflow hose from the bottom of the reservoir and allow the reservoir to drain into the container **(see illustrations)**. Mop up any spilt coolant.

Flushing

19 Flush the system with clean tap water by inserting a hose in the filler neck. Allow the water to run through the system until it is clear and flows out cleanly. If the radiator is extremely corroded, remove it (see Chapter 3) and have it cleaned by a specialist. Also flush the reservoir, then reconnect the hose.

20 Clean the drain holes then fit the drain bolts using the old sealing washers.

21 Fill the cooling system via the filler neck with clean water mixed with a flushing compound **(see illustration 9.27)**. Make sure the flushing compound is compatible with aluminium components, and follow the manufacturer's instructions carefully. Fit the pressure cap.

22 Start the engine and allow it to reach

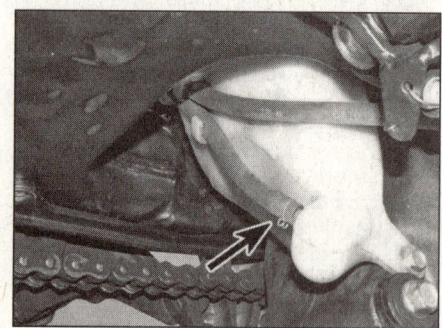

9.16a Unscrew the bolt (arrowed) . . .

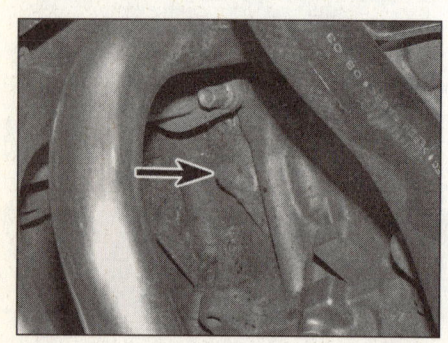

9.16b . . . and allow the coolant to drain

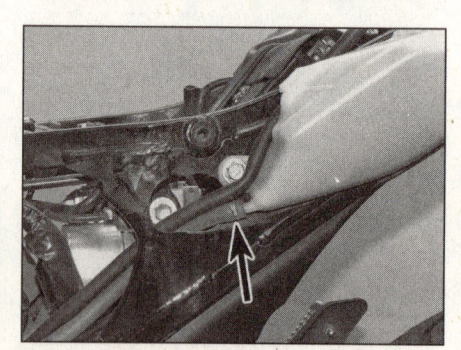

9.17 Cylinder jacket drain bolt (arrowed)

9.18a Radiator overflow hose (arrowed) – CB600F/FA and CBR600F/FA

9.18b Radiator overflow hose (arrowed) – CBF600N/NA/S/SA

Routine maintenance and servicing 1•17

9.26 Fit a new sealing washer onto each drain bolt

9.27 Fill the system as described

normal operating temperature. Let it run for about ten minutes.
23 Stop the engine. Let it cool for a while, then cover the pressure cap with a heavy rag and turn it anti-clockwise to the first stop, releasing any pressure that may be present in the system. Once the hissing stops, push down on the cap and remove it completely.
24 Drain the system once again.
25 Fill the system with clean water and repeat Steps 22 to 24.

Refilling
26 Fit the drain bolts using new sealing washers and tighten them **(see illustration)**. Reconnect the reservoir hose **(see illustration 9.18a or b)**.
27 Support the bike upright on level ground. Fill the system to the base of the radiator filler neck with the proper coolant mixture (see this Chapter's Specifications) **(see illustration)**.
Note: *Pour the coolant in slowly to minimise the amount of air entering the system, and when full carefully waggle the bike from side to side to dislodge any trapped air.* Fill the reservoir to the UPPER level line (see *Pre-ride checks*).
28 Start the engine and allow it to idle for 2 to 3 minutes. Flick the throttle twistgrip part open 3 or 4 times, so that the engine speed rises to approximately 4000 to 5000 rpm, then stop the engine. Any air trapped in the system should bleed back to the radiator filler neck.
29 If necessary, top up the coolant level to the base of the radiator filler neck, then fit the pressure cap, and top up the reservoir to the UPPER level line, then fit the cap.

30 Start the engine and allow it to reach normal operating temperature, then shut it off. Let the engine cool then remove the pressure cap as described in Step 23. Check that the coolant level is still up to the base of the radiator filler neck. If it's low, add the specified mixture until it reaches the base of the filler neck. Refit the cap.
31 Check the coolant level in the reservoir and top up if necessary. Check the system for leaks.
32 Install the fuel tank, seat cowl and fairing panels as required according to model.
33 Do not dispose of the old coolant by pouring it down the drain. Instead pour it into a heavy plastic container, cap it tightly and take it into an authorised disposal site or service station – see **Warning** at the beginning of this Section.

10 PAIR (pulse secondary air supply) system

1 To reduce the amount of unburned hydrocarbons released in the exhaust gases, a pulse secondary air supply (PAIR) system is fitted. The system consists of the control valve (mounted above the valve cover on the top of the engine), the reed valves (fitted in the valve cover) and the hoses between the air filter housing, the control valve and the reed valves **(see illustration 10.3)**. The control valve is actuated electronically by the ECM.
2 Under normal operating conditions, the valve allows filtered air to be drawn through the reed valves and cylinder head passages and into the exhaust ports. The air mixes with the exhaust gases, causing any unburned particles of the fuel in the mixture to be burnt in the exhaust port/pipes. This process changes a considerable amount of hydrocarbons and carbon monoxide into relatively harmless carbon dioxide and water. The reed valves in the valve cover are fitted to prevent the flow of exhaust gases back up the cylinder head passages and into the air filter housing.
3 The system is not adjustable and requires little maintenance. Raise the fuel tank (see Chapter 4). Check that the hoses are not kinked or pinched, are in good condition and are securely connected at each end **(see illustration)**. Replace any hoses that are cracked, split or generally deteriorated with new ones.
4 Refer to Chapter 4 for further information on the system and for checks if it is believed to be faulty.

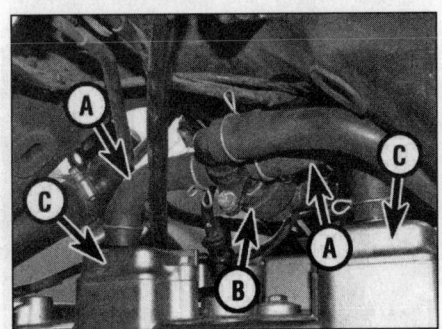

11 Headlight aim

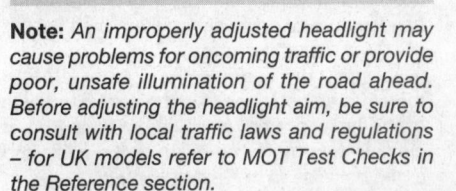

Note: *An improperly adjusted headlight may cause problems for oncoming traffic or provide poor, unsafe illumination of the road ahead. Before adjusting the headlight aim, be sure to consult with local traffic laws and regulations – for UK models refer to MOT Test Checks in the Reference section.*

1 The headlight beam can adjusted horizontally and vertically. Before making any adjustment, check that the tyre pressures are correct and the suspension is adjusted as required. Make any adjustments to the headlight aim with the machine off its stand and on level ground, with the fuel tank half full and with an assistant sitting on the seat. If the bike is usually ridden with a passenger on the back, have a second assistant to do this.

CB600F/FA and CBR600F/FA
2 To move the beam up or down turn the upper-right adjuster knob **(see illustrations)**. Turn it clockwise to move the beam up, and anti-clockwise to move it down.

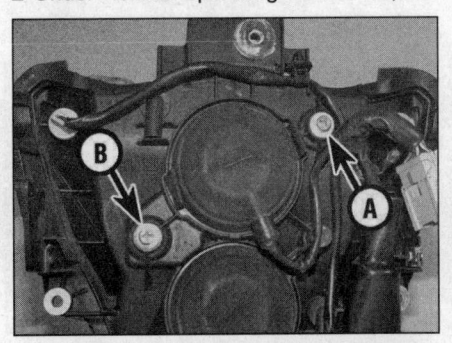

10.3 Check the PAIR system hoses (A) as described. PAIR control valve (B) and reed valve housings (C)

11.2a Vertical adjuster (A), horizontal adjuster (B) – 2007 to 2010 CB600F/FA

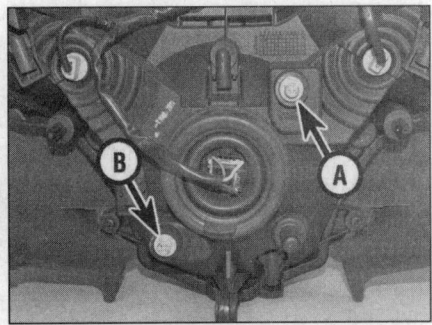

11.2b Vertical adjuster (A), horizontal adjuster (B) – 2011-on CB600F/FA and CBR600F/FA

1•18 Routine maintenance and servicing

11.4 Slacken the bolt (arrowed) on each side – CBF600N/NA

11.5 Horizontal adjustment screw (arrowed) – CBF600N/NA

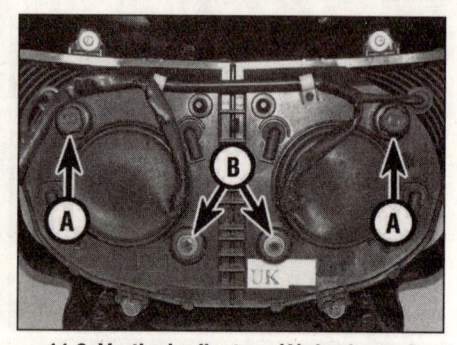

11.6 Vertical adjusters (A), horizontal adjusters (B) – CBF600S/SA

3 To move the beam to the right or left turn the lower-left adjuster knob **(see illustration 11.2a or b)**. On 2007 to 2010 CB600F/FA models turn it clockwise to move the beam to the right, and anti-clockwise to move it to the left. On 2011-on CB600F/FA models and all CBR600F/FA models turn it clockwise to move the beam to the left, and anti-clockwise to move it to the right.

CBF600N/NA

4 To move the beam up or down slacken the headlight mounting bolts slightly and pivot the headlight up or down as required, then tighten the bolts **(see illustration)**.
5 To move the beam to the right or left turn the small adjuster screw in the right-hand side of the headlight rim **(see illustration)**. Turn it clockwise to move the beam to the right, and anti-clockwise to move it to the left.

CBF600S/SA

6 To move the beam up or down turn the adjuster knob on the top outer corner of the relevant beam **(see illustration)**. Turn it clockwise to move the beam up, and anti-clockwise to move it down.
7 To move the beam to the right or left turn the adjuster knob on the bottom inner corner of the relevant beam **(see illustration 11.6)**. When adjusting the left-hand beam turn the adjuster clockwise to move the beam to the right, and anti-clockwise to move it to the left. When adjusting the right-hand beam turn the adjuster clockwise to move the beam to the left, and anti-clockwise to move it to the right.

12 Sidestand, centrestand and starter interlock circuit

1 Check the stand springs for damage and distortion **(see illustration)**. The springs must be capable of retracting the stand fully and holding it retracted when the motorcycle is in use. If a spring is sagged or broken it must be replaced with a new one.
2 Lubricate the stand pivots regularly (see Section 16).
3 Check the stand and its mount(s) for bends and cracks. Stands can often be repaired by welding.
4 Check the operation of the starter interlock circuit as follows:
- Make sure the transmission is in neutral, then retract the stand and start the engine. Pull in the clutch lever and select a gear. Keeping the clutch lever pulled in, extend the sidestand. The engine should stop as the sidestand is extended.
- Make sure the engine is in neutral and the sidestand is down, then start the engine. Pull the clutch lever in and select a gear. The engine should cut out.
- Check that when the sidestand is down the engine can only be started if the transmission is in neutral, and when the sidestand is up and the transmission is in gear the engine can only be started if the clutch lever is pulled in.

5 If the circuit does not operate as described, check the sidestand switch, neutral switch, clutch switch and diodes, and the circuit between them (see Chapter 8).

13 Suspension

1 The suspension components must be maintained in top operating condition to ensure rider safety. Loose, worn or damaged suspension parts decrease the motorcycle's stability and control.

Front suspension check

2 While standing alongside the motorcycle, apply the front brake and push on the handlebars to compress the forks several times. See if they move up-and-down smoothly without binding **(see illustration)**. If binding is felt, the forks should be disassembled and inspected (see Chapter 5).
3 Inspect each fork inner tube for scratches, corrosion and pitting in the area of travel through the seals, which will cause seal failure, and for oil leakage, which means the seal has failed **(see illustration)**. If the corrosion damage is excessive, new inner tubes should be fitted (see Chapter 5), or the fitted ones must be re-chromed using hard chrome. If leakage is evident, the seals must be replaced with new ones (see Chapter 5).
4 Carefully lever the dust seal out using a flat-bladed screwdriver and inspect the area

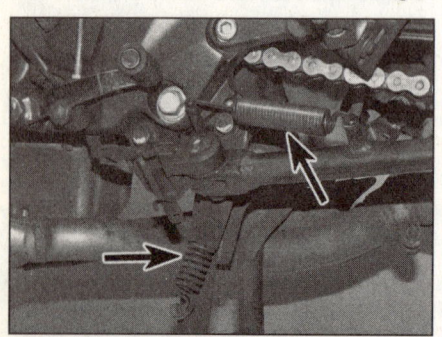

12.1 Check the sidestand springs and on CBF600 models the centrestand springs (arrowed)

13.2 Compress the forks to check their action

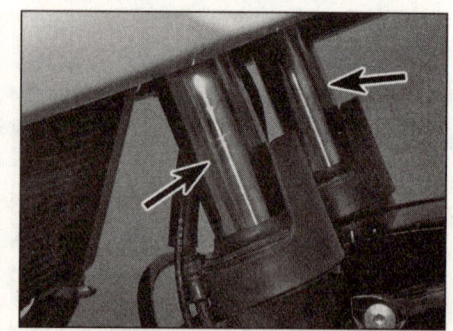

13.3 Check the inner tubes (arrowed) for pitting and signs of oil leakage

Routine maintenance and servicing 1•19

around the oil seal **(see illustration)**. If there is evidence of corrosion on the oil seal and/or its retaining ring, spray the area with a penetrative lubricant. If the seal is corroding (from water getting under the rubber) it must be replaced with a new one (see Chapter 5). Press the dust seal back into the outer tube on completion.

5 Check the tightness of all suspension nuts and bolts to be sure none have worked loose, referring to the torque settings specified at the beginning of Chapter 5.

Rear suspension check

6 Inspect the rear shock absorber for fluid leakage. If leakage is found, the shock must be replaced with a new one (see Chapter 5).

7 With the aid of an assistant to support the bike, compress the rear suspension several times **(see illustration)**. It should move up-and-down freely without binding. If any binding is felt, the worn or faulty component must be identified and checked. The problem could be due to either the shock absorber or its bush or bearing, or the swingarm bearings.

8 On CBF600N/NA/S/SA models place the motorcycle on its centrestand so that the rear wheel is off the ground. On all other models support the bike using an auxiliary stand that does not take the weight of the bike through any part of the rear suspension. Grab the swingarm and rock it from side-to-side **(see illustration)** – there should be no discernible movement at the rear.

9 Next, grasp the top of the rear wheel and pull it upwards **(see illustration)** – there should be no discernible freeplay before the shock absorber begins to compress.

10 If there's a little movement or a slight clicking can be heard, check the swingarm pivot bolt nut is tight, referring to the torque setting in Chapter 5, and re-check for movement. Also check the shock absorber mounting bolts/nuts. If there is still some noise or freeplay after everything has been correctly tightened then there is either a worn bush or bearing in the shock absorber mountings, or worn swingarm bearings. The worn components must be identified and replaced with new ones (see Chapter 5).

11 You can make a more accurate assessment by isolating the swingarm from the shock absorber – remove the rear wheel (see Chapter 6) and the bolt securing the shock absorber to the swingarm (see Chapter 5).

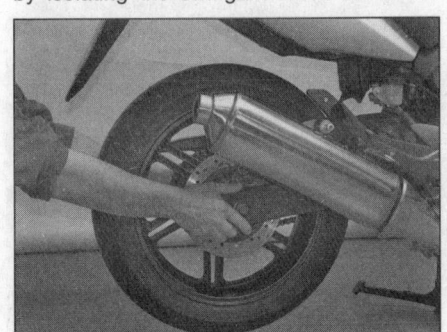

12 Grasp the rear of the swingarm with one hand and place your other hand at the junction of the swingarm and the frame. Try to move the rear of the swingarm from side-to-side. Any wear (play) in the bearings should be felt as movement between the swingarm and the frame at the front. If there is any play, the swingarm will be felt to move forward and backward at the front (not from side-to-side). Next, move the swingarm up and down through its full travel. It should move freely, without any binding or rough spots. If there is any play in the swingarm or if it does not move freely, remove the bearings for inspection (see Chapter 5).

13 With the shock absorber detached check the sleeve and bearing in the lower mount for corrosion and wear and failure of the seals, referring to Chapter 5 for details, and clean and re-grease or replace components as required.

Front fork oil change

14 Although there is no set interval for changing the fork oil, the oil will degrade over a period of time and lose its damping qualities. Refer to Chapter 5 for details of front fork removal, oil draining and refilling. The forks do not need to be completely disassembled to change the oil.

Rear suspension bearing lubrication

15 Although there is no set interval for re-greasing the suspension bearings, over a considerable mileage, and if the bike is often ridden in wet conditions (or through incorrect use of jet washers) the seals may fail and allow dirt and water to get in, in which case the grease in the bearings will be washed out or will harden.

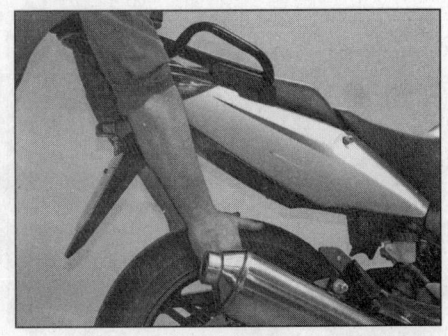

16 The shock absorber and swingarm should be removed periodically and the bearings cleaned and re-greased as necessary (see Chapter 5).

14 Steering head bearings

Freeplay check and adjustment

1 Steering head bearings can become dented, rough or loose during normal use of the machine. In extreme cases, worn or loose steering head bearings can cause steering wobble – a condition that is potentially dangerous.

Check

2 On CBF600N/NA/S/SA models place the motorcycle on its centrestand on level ground, and raise the front wheel off the ground, either by having an assistant press down on the rear, or by placing a jack under the engine (use a piece of wood between the jack head and the engine to spread the weight). On all other models raise the front wheel off the ground using an auxiliary stand or stands that do not interfere with movement of the steering. Always make sure that the bike is properly supported and secure.

3 Point the front wheel straight-ahead and slowly move the handlebars from lock to lock. Any dents, tightness or roughness in the bearing races will be felt – if the bearings are too tight the bars will not move smoothly and freely. Again point the wheel straight-ahead, and tap the front of the wheel to one side. The wheel should 'fall' under its own weight to the limit of its lock, indicating that the bearings are not too tight (take into account the restriction that cables, hoses and wiring may have). Check for similar movement to the other side.

4 If a spring balance (graduated zero to 30N) is available, attach one end around the fork tube and hold it out at right angles to the yoke **(see**

13.4 Carefully prise the seal out and check for corrosion

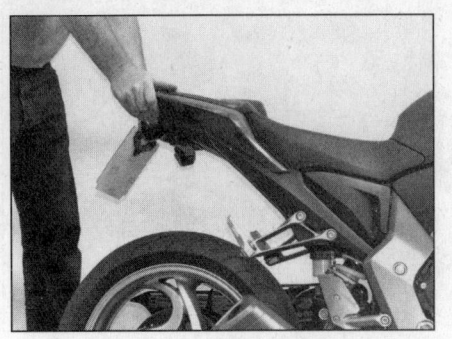

13.7 Compress the rear suspension to check its action

13.8 Checking for play in the swingarm bearings

13.9 Checking for play in the rear shock mountings

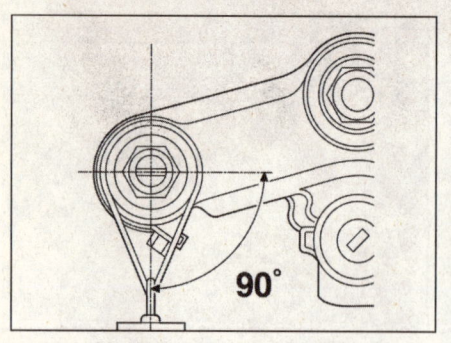

1•20 Routine maintenance and servicing

14.4 Checking steering head bearing pre-load using a spring balance

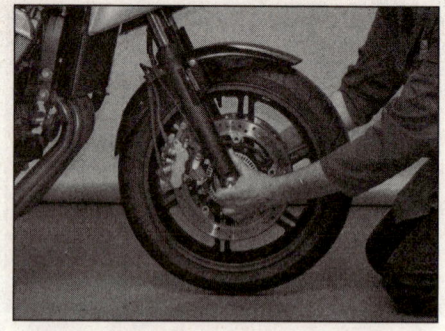

14.5 Feeling for play in the steering head bearings

14.6 Instrument/headlight bracket bolts (arrowed) – early Hornet shown

illustration). With the steering straight-ahead, pull on the balance and check the reading at which the handlebars start to turn. If the reading is below the minimum value specified in the pre-load range given in the Specifications at the beginning of the Chapter, the steering head is too loose, if the reading is above the maximum value specified the steering head is too tight. If the steering doesn't perform as described, and it's not due to the resistance of cables or hoses, then the bearings should be adjusted as described below.

5 Next, grasp the bottom of the forks and gently pull and push them forward and backward (see illustration). Any looseness or freeplay in the steering head bearings will be felt as front-to-rear movement of the forks. If play is felt, adjust the bearings as described below.

Adjustment

Special tool: Either the Honda special tool (part No. 07916-3710101), equivalent peg spanner, or a suitably sized C-spanner is necessary for this procedure – see Step 11.

6 As a precaution against accidental damage, remove the fuel tank and any fairing panels as required according to model (see Chapters 4 and 7). On CB600F/FA models remove the instrument cluster and headlight assembly (see Chapter 8), then unscrew the bracket bolts on the underside of the top yoke (see illustration).

> **HAYNES HINT:** Make sure you are not mistaking any movement between the bike and stand, or between the stand and the ground, for freeplay in the bearings. Do not pull and push the forks too hard – a gentle movement is all that is needed. Freeplay between the fork tubes due to worn bushes can also be misinterpreted as steering head bearing play – do not confuse the two.

7 On CBF600N/NA models refer to Chapter 8 and remove the instrument cluster – this procedure includes displacing the handlebars and the top yoke.

8 On all other models displace the handlebars and rest them on some rag, tying or supporting them so they are secure (see Chapter 5). Unscrew the steering stem nut (see illustration). Slacken the fork clamp bolts in the top yoke (see illustration).

9 Gently ease the top yoke up off the forks and support it clear, using rag to protect other components (see illustration).

10 On all models bend the lockwasher tabs out of the notches in the locknut (see illustration). Unscrew the locknut using your fingers (see illustration) – it shouldn't be tight. If it is tight use a C-spanner located in one of the notches (see illustration 14.11). Remove the lockwasher (see illustration). Inspect the tabs for cracks or signs of fatigue. If there is

14.8a Unscrew the steering stem nut . . .

14.8b . . . and slacken the fork clamp bolt (arrowed) on each side . . .

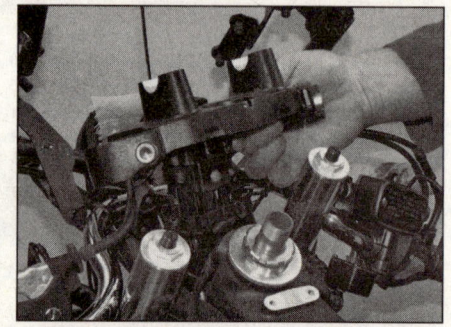

14.9 . . . then gently ease the yoke up off the forks and support it securely

14.10a Bend down the tabs securing the locknut . . .

14.10b . . . then unscrew the locknut . . .

14.10c . . . and remove the lockwasher

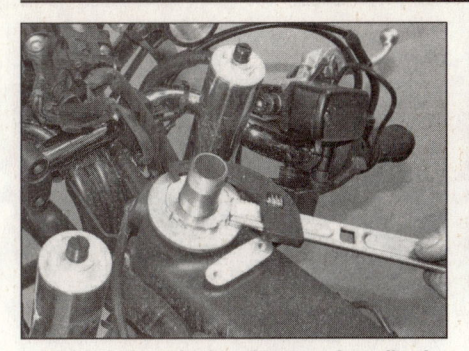

Routine maintenance and servicing 1•21

14.11 Adjust the bearings as described using a C-spanner

14.13 Fit the tabs into the notches in the adjuster nut

14.14 Bend the tabs up into the notches in the locknut

any sign of damage, discard the lockwasher and use a new one; otherwise the old one can be re-used, but note that Honda recommend using a new one as a matter of course.

11 To turn the adjuster nut you need either a C-spanner or the Honda service tool (part No. 07916-3710101) or a suitable peg spanner, which can be made by cutting castellations into an old socket **(see illustration)**. Slacken the adjuster nut slightly until pressure is just released. If the Honda tool or a peg spanner is available, tighten the adjuster nut to the torque setting specified at the beginning of the Chapter, then turn the steering from lock-to-lock five times, then reapply the specified torque setting to the nut. If the tool is not available, tighten the adjuster nut using a C-spanner until all freeplay is taken up, yet the steering is able to move freely. The object is to set the adjuster nut so that the bearings are under a very light loading, just enough to remove any freeplay, but not so much that the steering is prevented from moving freely from side-to-side. If the torque setting is applied check the physical feel as described as well. If you have the spring balance (see Step 4), set the adjuster nut so that the steering starts to move at around the mid-point of the pre-load range given in the Specifications at the beginning of the Chapter. **Caution: Take great care not to apply excessive pressure because this will cause premature failure of the bearings.**

12 If the bearings cannot be correctly adjusted, disassemble the steering head and check the bearings and races (see Chapter 5).

13 With the bearings correctly adjusted, fit the lockwasher, using a new one if the tabs are weakened or cracked, onto the adjuster nut and fit the two short tabs into the notches in the adjuster nut **(see illustration)**.

14 Fit the locknut and tighten it finger-tight **(see illustration 14.10b)**. Tighten the locknut further (but no more than 90°) until its notches align with the remaining lockwasher tabs, making sure the adjuster nut does not turn as well (though that is unlikely). Secure the locknut in position by bending up the long lockwasher tabs into its notches **(see illustration)**.

15 On CBF600N/NA models refer to Chapter 8 and install the instrument cluster.

16 On all other models fit the top yoke onto the steering stem and forks **(see illustration 14.9)**. Fit the steering stem nut and tighten it to the torque setting specified at the beginning of the Chapter **(see illustration 14.8a)**. Tighten the fork clamp bolts to the specified torque **(see illustration 14.8b)**.

17 Install the handlebars (see Chapter 5).

18 Check the bearing adjustment as described above and re-adjust if necessary.

19 Install the instrument/headlight components or bolts (Chapter 8), fuel tank (Chapter 4) and fairing panels (Chapter 7) as required according to model.

Lubrication

20 Over a considerable time the grease in the bearings will be dispersed or will harden allowing the ingress of dirt and water.

21 The steering head should be disassembled periodically and the bearings cleaned and re-greased (see Chapter 5, Sections 9 and 10).

15.2 Check each valve as described and make sure a cap is fitted

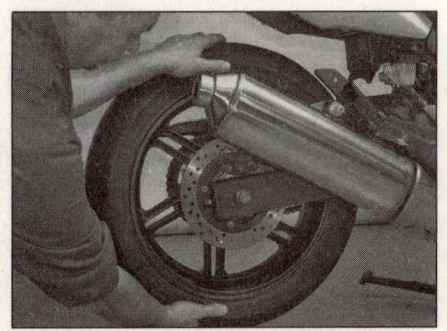

15.5 Checking for play in the wheel bearings

15 Wheels, tyres and wheel bearings

Wheels

1 Cast wheels are virtually maintenance free, but they should be kept clean and checked periodically for cracks and other damage. Never attempt to repair cast wheels – if damaged they must be replaced with new ones. Also check wheel run-out and alignment (see Chapter 6). Check that the wheel balance weights are fixed firmly to the wheel rim. If you suspect that a weight has fallen off, have the wheel rebalanced by a motorcycle tyre specialist.

Tyres

2 Check the tyre pressures, condition and tread depth thoroughly – see *Pre-ride checks*. Check the valve rubber for signs of damage or deterioration and have it replaced with a new one if necessary by a tyre-fitting specialist. Also, make sure the valve stem cap is in place and tight **(see illustration)**.

Wheel bearings

3 Wheel bearings will wear over a considerable mileage and should be checked periodically to avoid handling problems.

4 On CBF600N/NA/S/SA models place the motorcycle on its centrestand. When checking the front wheel raise the wheel off the ground, either by having an assistant press down on the rear, or by placing a jack under the engine (use a piece of wood between the jack head and the engine to spread the weight). On all other models support the motorcycle upright using an auxiliary stand so that the wheel being examined is off the ground.

5 Check for any play in the bearings by pushing and pulling the wheel against the hub **(see illustration)**. When checking the front wheel turn the handlebars to full lock on one side and hold the wheel against the lock. Also rotate the wheel and check that it turns smoothly and without any grating noises (bearing in mind that the brakes and final drive chain make some noise – do not confuse them).

6 If any play is detected in the hub, or if the wheel does not rotate smoothly (and this is not due to brake or transmission drag), the wheel

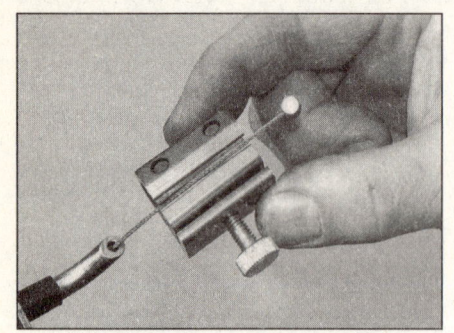

Routine maintenance and servicing

16.3a Fit the cable into the adapter . . .

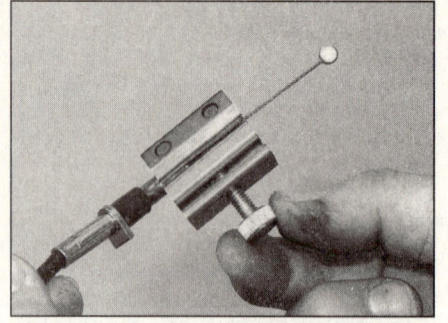

16.3b . . . and tighten the screw to seal it in . . .

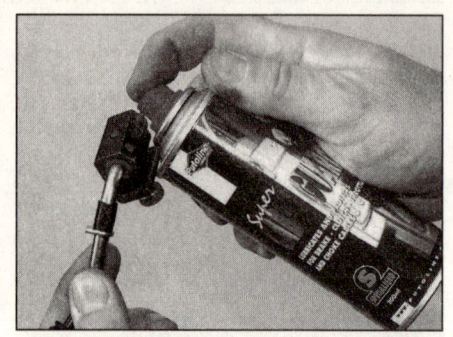

16.3c . . . then apply the lubricant using the nozzle provided inserted in the hole in the adapter

should be removed and the bearings inspected for wear or damage (see Chapter 6).

16 Stand, lever pivots and throttle cable lubrication

Pivot points

1 Since the controls, cables and various other components of a motorcycle are exposed to the elements, they should be checked and lubricated periodically to ensure safe and trouble-free operation.

2 The footrest pivots, clutch and brake lever pivots, brake pedal and gearchange lever pivots and linkage, and stand pivots should be lubricated frequently. In order for the lubricant to be applied where it will do the most good, the component should be disassembled and cleaned (see Chapter 5). The lubricant recommended by Honda for each application is listed at the beginning of the Chapter. If an aerosol lubricant is being used, it can be applied to the pivot joint gaps and will usually work its way into the areas where friction occurs, so less disassembly of the component is needed (however it is always better to do so and clean off all corrosion, dirt and old lubricant first). If motor oil or light grease is being used, apply it sparingly as it may attract dirt (which could cause the controls to bind or wear at an accelerated rate). **Note:** *An alternative lubricant for the control lever pivots is a dry-film lubricant (available from many sources by different names).*

Cables

Special tool: *A cable lubricating adapter is necessary for this procedure* **(see illustration 16.3c).**

3 To lubricate the cables, disconnect the relevant cable at its upper end, then lubricate it with a pressure adapter and aerosol cable lubricant **(see illustrations)**. See Chapter 4 for throttle cable disconnection, and Chapter 2 for the clutch cable.

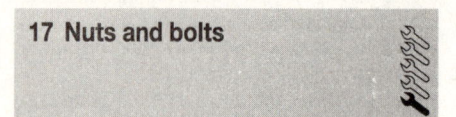

17 Nuts and bolts

1 Since vibration of the machine tends to loosen fasteners, all nuts, bolts, screws, etc. should be periodically checked for proper tightness.
2 Pay particular attention to the following, referring to the relevant Chapter:
 Spark plugs
 Engine oil drain plug
 Lever and pedal bolts
 Footrest and stand bolts
 Engine mounting bolts/nuts
 Shock absorber and swingarm pivot bolts/ nuts
 Handlebar bolts
 Front fork clamp bolts (top and bottom yoke) and fork top bolts
 Steering stem nut
 Front wheel axle bolt and axle clamp bolts
 Rear wheel axle nut
 Front sprocket bolt and rear sprocket nuts
 Brake caliper and master cylinder mounting bolts
 Brake hose banjo bolts and caliper bleed valves
 Brake disc bolts
 Exhaust system bolts/nuts

3 If a torque wrench is available, use it along with the torque settings given at the beginning of this and other Chapters.

18 Air filter

Caution: *If the machine is continually ridden in wet or dusty conditions, the filter should be replaced more frequently.*

1 Remove the left-hand side cover (see Chapter 7).
2 Undo the air intake duct screws and displace the duct **(see illustration)** – there is no need to disconnect the vacuum hose from the diaphragm valve (you can just rest the duct on the footrest) unless you prefer to do so, or if you are removing the air filter housing/ throttle body assembly **(see illustration)**.
3 Withdraw the filter element from the housing **(see illustration)**.
4 Clean the filter by tapping it on a hard surface to dislodge any dirt, then use compressed air to blow through it, directing the air in the opposite way to normal flow, i.e. from the outside **(see illustration)**. Do not use any solvents or cleaning agents on the element. If the element is excessively dirty or

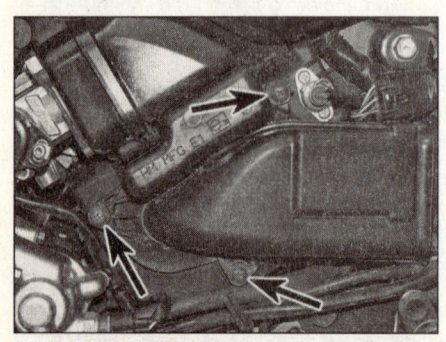

18.2a Undo the screws (arrowed) and displace the duct . . .

18.2b . . . and if required disconnect the vacuum hose

18.3 Withdraw the filter element

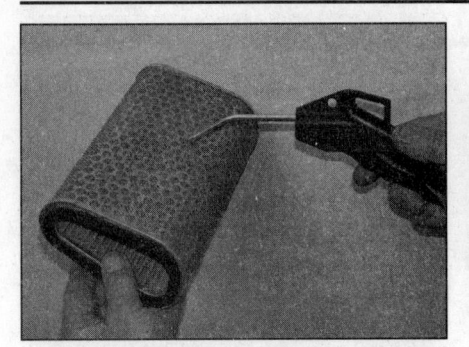

Routine maintenance and servicing

18.4 Direct the air in the opposite direction of normal flow

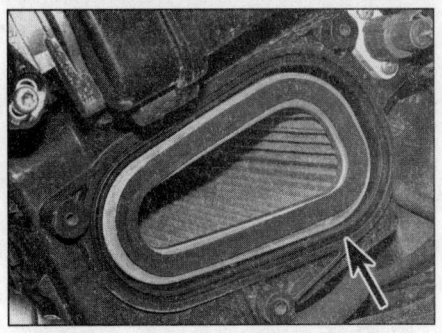

18.6 Check the air duct seal (arrowed)

is damaged replace it with a new one.
5 Fit the filter element into the housing, making sure it seats properly **(see illustration 18.3)**.
6 Make sure the air duct seal is in good condition and seated in its groove – fit a new one if necessary **(see illustration)**. If disconnected, connect the vacuum hose to the diaphragm valve **(see illustration 18.2b)**. Fit the air duct and tighten the screws **(see illustration 18.2a)**.
7 Install the side cover (see Chapter 7).

19 Valve clearances

Special tool: *A set of feeler gauges is necessary for this job* **(see illustration 19.7)**.
1 The engine must be completely cool for this maintenance procedure, so let the bike stand overnight before beginning.
2 Remove the spark plugs (see Section 7). Remove the valve cover (see Chapter 2). Either retract and lock the cam chain tensioner plunger if the tool described is available, or remove the tensioner if not (see Chapter 2).
3 Make a chart or sketch of all valve positions so that a note of each clearance can be made against the relevant valve. The cylinders are numbered 1 to 4 from left to right. The intake valves are on the back of the cylinder head and the exhaust valves are on the front.
4 Unscrew the timing inspection cap from the clutch cover **(see illustration)**. Check the condition of its O-ring and obtain a new one if necessary.
5 To check the valve clearances the engine must be turned so that the valve being checked is closed. The engine can be turned using a socket on the timing rotor bolt and turning it in a clockwise direction only **(see illustration 19.6a)**.
6 Turn the engine clockwise until the line next to the T mark on the timing rotor aligns with the static timing mark, which is a notch or pointer in the inspection hole rim, and the IN and EX marks on the intake and exhaust camshaft sprockets respectively are facing away from each other and are flush with the cylinder head top surface **(see illustrations)**. If the sprocket marks are facing towards each other, rotate the engine clockwise one full turn (360°) until the line next to the T mark again aligns with the static timing mark. The sprocket marks will now be facing away.
7 With the engine in this position, check the clearances on the Nos. 1 and 3 cylinder intake valves, remembering there are two valves per cylinder. Insert a feeler gauge of the same thickness as the correct valve clearance (see Specifications) between the camshaft lobe and the follower of each valve and check that it is a firm sliding fit – you should feel a slight drag when the you pull the gauge out **(see illustration)**. If not, use the feeler gauges to obtain the exact clearance. Record the measured clearance on the chart.
8 Now rotate the engine 180° clockwise until the line next to the T mark on the timing rotor is diametrically opposite the static timing mark – the scribed line on the rotor will now be in the 12 o'clock position **(see illustration)**. With the engine in this position, check the clearances on the Nos. 2 and 4 cylinder exhaust valves using the method described in Step 7.
9 Now rotate the engine 180° clockwise until the line next to the T mark aligns with the static timing mark again **(see illustration 19.6b)**. With the engine in this position, check the clearances on the Nos. 2 and 4 cylinder

19.4 Unscrew the timing inspection cap (arrowed)

19.6a Turn the engine clockwise using the bolt . . .

19.6b . . . until the line next to the T mark aligns with the notch (arrowed) . . .

19.6c . . . and the camshaft sprocket marks are as shown

19.7 Insert the feeler gauge between the base of the cam lobe and the top of the follower as shown

19.8 Turn the engine 180° so the marks are aligned as shown

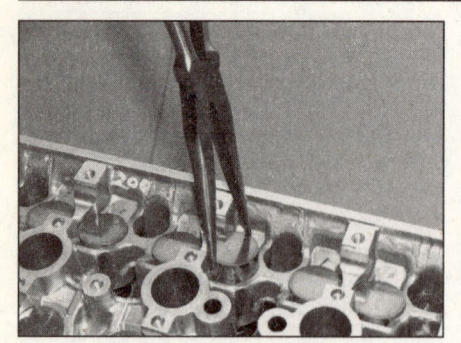

Routine maintenance and servicing

19.13a Carefully lift out the follower . . .

19.13b . . . and retrieve the shim (arrowed) from inside it . . .

19.13c . . . or from the top of the valve

intake valves using the method described in Step 7.

10 Now rotate the engine 180° clockwise until the line next to the T mark on the timing rotor is once again diametrically opposite the static timing mark and the scribed line is at the 12 o'clock position **(see illustration 19.8)**. With the engine in this position, check the clearances on the Nos. 1 and 3 cylinder exhaust valves using the method described in Step 7.

11 When all clearances have been measured and charted, identify whether the clearance on any valve falls outside the specified range. If any do, the shim must be replaced with one of a thickness that will restore the correct clearance.

12 Shim replacement requires removal of the camshafts (see Chapter 2). Place rags over the spark plug holes and the cam chain tunnel to prevent a shim from dropping into the engine on removal. Work on one valve at a time to prevent the possibility of mixing up the followers, which must be returned to their original location. If you want to remove more than one shim and follower at a time, store them in a marked container or bag, denoting which cylinder and which valve the shim and follower are from, so that they do not get mixed up.

13 With the camshaft removed, remove the cam follower of the valve in question using a magnet or the suction created by a valve lapping tool, or long nosed pliers can be used with care **(see illustration)**. Retrieve the shim either from the inside of the follower or pick it out of the top of the valve spring retainer using either a magnet, a screwdriver with a dab of grease on it (the shim will stick to the grease), or a very small screwdriver and a pair of pliers

(see illustrations). Do not allow the shim to fall into the engine.

14 Measure and record the thickness of the shim using a micrometer **(see illustration)**.

15 Calculate the required replacement shim by using the formula $a = (b - c) + d$, where a is the required replacement shim size, b is the measured valve clearance, c is the specified valve clearance, and d is the existing shim thickness. For example:

The measured clearance of an exhaust valve is 0.35 mm, so b = 0.35

The specified clearance range for an exhaust valve is 0.25 to 0.31 mm, the mid-point being 0.28 mm, so c = 0.28

The thickness of the existing shim is 2.00 mm, so d = 2.0

Therefore, the required replacement shim $a = 0.35 - 0.28 + 2.0$ (a = 2.07 mm). The nearest available size to this is 2.075 mm (Step 16).

Note: *If the required replacement shim is greater than 2.900 mm (the largest available), the valve is probably not seating correctly due to a build-up of carbon deposits and should be checked and cleaned or resurfaced as required (see Chapter 2).*

16 Shims are available in 0.025 mm increments from 1.200 mm to 2.900 mm. A size mark should be stamped on one face of the shim – a shim marked 175 is 1.75 mm thick. Obtain the replacement shim, then lubricate it with molybdenum disulphide oil (a 50/50 mixture of molybdenum disulphide grease and engine oil) and fit it into the recess in the top of the valve spring retainer with the size mark facing up **(see illustration 19.13c)**.

17 Check that the shim is correctly seated, then lubricate the follower with molybdenum disulphide oil and fit it onto the valve, making sure it fits squarely in its bore **(see illustration)**. Repeat the process for any other valves until the clearances are correct, then install the camshafts (see Chapter 2).

18 Rotate the crankshaft clockwise several turns to seat the new shim(s), then check the clearances again.

19 Release the cam chain tensioner plunger, or refit the tensioner if it was removed, then install the valve cover (see Chapter 2). Install the spark plugs (see Section 7).

20 Fit the timing inspection cap using a new O-ring if required, and smear the O-ring with oil and the cap threads with grease **(see illustration)**. Tighten the cap to the torque setting specified at the beginning of the Chapter.

20 Battery

1 All models covered in this manual are fitted with a sealed MF (maintenance free) battery. **Note:** *Do not attempt to remove the battery caps to check the electrolyte level or battery specific gravity.* Removal will damage the caps, resulting in electrolyte leakage and battery damage. All that should be done is to check that the terminals are clean and tight and that the casing is not damaged or leaking. See Chapter 8 for further details.

2 If the machine is not in regular use, disconnect the battery and give it a refresher charge every month to six weeks (see Chapter 8).

19.14 Check the thickness of the shim using a micrometer

19.17 Fit the follower onto the valve

19.20 Use a new O-ring if necessary

Chapter 2
Engine, clutch and transmission

Contents

	Section number
Alternator	see Chapter 8
Cam chain tensioner	8
Cam chain, tensioner blades and front guide	10
Camshafts and followers	9
Clutch	14
Clutch cable	15
Clutch check	see Chapter 1
Component access	2
Connecting rod and main bearing information	21
Connecting rods and bearings	23
Crankcases and cylinder bores	20
Crankcase separation and reassembly	19
Crankshaft and main bearings	22
Crankshaft position sensor	see Chapter 4
Cylinder head and valve overhaul	12
Cylinder head removal and installation	11
Engine disassembly and reassembly general information	5
Engine removal and installation	4
Engine wear assessment	3
Gearchange mechanism	16

	Section number
General information	1
Neutral switch	see Chapter 8
Oil and filter change	see Chapter 1
Oil cooler	6
Oil level check	see Pre-ride checks
Oil pressure switch	see Chapter 8
Oil pump	18
Oil sump, strainer and pressure relief valve	17
Piston rings	25
Pistons	24
Running-in procedure	29
Selector drum and forks	28
Spark plugs	see Chapter 1
Starter clutch and gears	13
Starter motor	see Chapter 8
Transmission shafts overhaul	27
Transmission shafts removal and installation	26
Valve clearance check and adjustment	see Chapter 1
Valve cover	7
Water pump	see Chapter 3

Degrees of difficulty

| Easy, suitable for novice with little experience | Fairly easy, suitable for beginner with some experience | Fairly difficult, suitable for competent DIY mechanic | Difficult, suitable for experienced DIY mechanic | Very difficult, suitable for expert DIY or professional |

Specifications

General
Type	Four-stroke in-line four
Capacity	599 cc
Bore	67.0 mm
Stroke	42.5 mm
Compression ratio	
CB600F/FA and CBR600F/FA	12.0 to 1
CBF600N/NA/S/SA	11.6 to 1
Cylinder numbering	1 to 4 from left to right
Firing order	1-2-4-3
Cooling system	Liquid cooled
Lubrication	Wet sump, trochoid pump
Clutch	Wet multi-plate
Transmission	Six-speed constant mesh
Final drive	Chain

Camshafts and followers

Intake cam lobe height
  CB600F/FA and CBR600F/FA
    Standard .... 36.24 to 36.32 mm
    Service limit (min) .... 36.22 mm
  CBF600N/NA/S/SA
    Standard .... 34.38 to 34.62 mm
    Service limit (min) .... 34.36 mm
Exhaust cam lobe height
  CB600F/FA and CBR600F/FA
    Standard .... 35.42 to 35.50 mm
    Service limit (min) .... 35.40 mm
  CBF600N/NA/S/SA
    Standard .... 33.86 to 34.10 mm
    Service limit (min) .... 33.84 mm
Oil clearance
  Standard .... 0.020 to 0.062 mm
  Service limit (max) .... 0.10 mm
Runout (max) .... 0.05 mm
Cam follower diameter
  Standard .... 25.978 to 25.993 mm
  Service limit (min) .... 25.97 mm
Cam follower bore diameter
  Standard .... 26.010 to 26.026 mm
  Service limit (max) .... 26.04 mm

Cylinder head

Warpage (max) .... 0.10 mm

Valves, guides and springs

Valve clearances... see Chapter 1
Stem diameter
  Intake valve
    Standard .... 3.975 to 3.990 mm
    Service limit (min) .... 3.965 mm
  Exhaust valve
    Standard .... 3.965 to 3.980 mm
    Service limit (min) .... 3.955 mm
Guide bore diameter – intake and exhaust valves
  Standard .... 4.000 to 4.012 mm
  Service limit (max) .... 4.040 mm
Stem-to-guide clearance
  Intake valve
    Standard .... 0.010 to 0.037 mm
    Service limit (max)................................... 0.075 mm
  Exhaust valve
    Standard .... 0.020 to 0.047 mm
    Service limit (max)................................... 0.085 mm
Seat width – intake and exhaust valves
  Standard .... 0.90 to 1.10 mm
  Service limit (max) .... 1.50 mm
Valve guide height above cylinder head
  Intake valve... 17.1 to 17.4 mm
  Exhaust valve .... 13.3 to 13.6 mm
Valve spring free length
  Intake
    Standard .... 40.19 mm
    Service limit (min) .... 39.4 mm
  Exhaust
    Standard .... 39.76 mm
    Service limit (min) .... 39.0 mm

Engine, clutch and transmission

Starter clutch
Starter driven gear hub OD
    Standard .... 45.657 to 45.673 mm
    Service limit (min) .... 45.642 mm
Starter idle gear ID
    Standard .... 10.013 to 10.035 mm
    Service limit (max) .... 10.05 mm
Starter idle gear shaft OD
    Standard .... 9.991 to 10.000 mm
    Service limit (min) .... 9.98 mm

Clutch
Friction plates 8
Plain plates 7
Friction plate thickness
    Standard .... 2.92 to 3.08 mm
    Service limit (min) .... 2.6 mm
Plain plate warpage (max) .... 0.3 mm
Spring free length
    Standard .... 48.2 mm
    Service limit (min) .... 47.2 mm
Clutch guide OD
    Standard .... 34.996 to 35.004 mm
    Service limit (min) .... 34.986 mm
Clutch guide ID
    Standard .... 24.993 to 25.003 mm
    Service limit (max) .... 25.013 mm
Primary driven gear ID
    Standard .... 41.000 to 41.016 mm
    Service limit (max) .... 41.026 mm
Input shaft OD at clutch guide
    Standard .... 24.980 to 24.990 mm
    Service limit (min) .... 24.960 mm

Oil pump
Oil pressure (at oil pressure switch, with engine warm) .... 72 psi (5.1 Bar) @ 6000 rpm, oil @ 80°C
Inner rotor tip-to-outer rotor clearance
    Standard .... 0.15 mm
    Service limit (max) .... 0.20 mm
Outer rotor-to-body clearance
    Standard .... 0.15 to 0.21 mm
    Service limit (max) .... 0.35 mm
Rotor end-float
    Standard .... 0.04 to 0.09 mm
    Service limit (max) .... 0.17 mm
Oil pump drive sprocket ID
    Standard .... 35.025 to 35.145 mm
    Service limit (max) .... 35.155 mm
Oil pump drive sprocket guide ID
    Standard .... 25.000 to 25.021 mm
    Service limit (max) .... 25.031 mm
Oil pump drive sprocket guide OD
    Standard .... 34.950 to 34.975 mm
    Service limit (min) .... 34.940 mm
Input shaft OD at sprocket guide
    Standard .... 24.980 to 24.990 mm
    Service limit (min) .... 24.960 mm

Selector drum and forks
Selector fork end thickness
    Standard .... 5.93 to 6.00 mm
    Service limit (min) .... 5.90 mm
Selector fork bore ID
    Standard .... 12.000 to 12.018 mm
    Service limit (max) .... 12.03 mm
Selector fork shaft OD
    Standard .... 11.957 to 11.968 mm
    Service limit (min) .... 11.95 mm

Cylinder bores
Bore
   Standard... 67.000 to 67.015 mm
   Service limit (max) .... 67.100 mm
Warpage (max) .... 0.10 mm
Ovality (out-of-round) (max) .... 0.10 mm
Taper (max).. 0.10 mm
Cylinder compression.. 189 psi (13.3 Bar) @ 350 rpm

Crankshaft and bearings
Main bearing oil clearance
   Standard... 0.020 to 0.038 mm
   Service limit (max) .... 0.05 mm
Runout (max) .... 0.05 mm

Connecting rods
Small-end internal diameter
   Standard... 16.030 to 16.044 mm
   Service limit (max) .... 16.050 mm
Small-end-to-piston pin clearance
   Standard... 0.03 to 0.05 mm
   Service limit (max) .... 0.07 mm
Big-end side clearance
   Standard... 0.15 to 0.30 mm
   Service limit (max) .... 0.35 mm
Big-end oil clearance
   Standard... 0.028 to 0.052 mm
   Service limit (max) .... 0.06 mm

Pistons
Piston diameter (measured 6 mm up from skirt, at 90° to piston pin axis)
   Standard... 66.965 to 66.985 mm
   Service limit (min) .... 66.90 mm
Piston-to-bore clearance
   Standard... 0.015 to 0.050 mm
   Service limit (max) .... 0.10 mm*
Piston pin diameter
   Standard... 15.994 to 16.000 mm
   Service limit (min) .... 15.98 mm
Piston pin bore diameter in piston
   Standard... 16.002 to 16.008 mm
   Service limit (max) .... 16.02 mm
Piston pin-to-piston pin bore clearance
   Standard... 0.002 to 0.014 mm
   Service limit (max) .... 0.04 mm

*If the piston-to-bore clearance exceeds the service limit, the cylinders can be rebored – Honda supply +0.25 oversize pistons and rings. Following rebore, the piston-to-bore clearance must be as standard for normal pistons

Piston rings
Ring end gap (installed)
  Top ring
   Standard... 0.10 to 0.20 mm
   Service limit (max).. 0.40 mm
  Second ring
   Standard... 0.21 to 0.31 mm
   Service limit (max).. 0.50 mm
  Oil ring side-rail
   Standard... 0.20 to 0.70 mm
   Service limit (max).. 1.0 mm
Ring-to-groove clearance
  Top ring
   Standard... 0.03 to 0.06 mm
   Service limit (max).. 0.10 mm
  Second ring
   Standard... 0.015 to 0.050 mm
   Service limit (max).. 0.08 mm

Engine, clutch and transmission 2•5

Transmission
Gear ratios (no. of teeth)
  CB600F/FA and CBR600F/FA
    Primary reduction .... 2.111 to 1 (76/36)
    Final reduction .... 2.688 to 1 (43/16)
    1st gear... 2.750 to 1 (33/12)
    2nd gear.. 1.938 to 1 (31/16)
    3rd gear... 1.556 to 1 (28/18)
    4th gear... 1.348 to 1 (31/23)
    5th gear... 1.208 to 1 (29/24)
    6th gear... 1.095 to 1 (23/21)
  CBF600N/NA/S/SA
    Primary reduction .... 2.111 to 1 (76/36)
    Final reduction .... 2.625 to 1 (42/16)
    1st gear... 2.750 to 1 (33/12)
    2nd gear.. 1.938 to 1 (31/16)
    3rd gear... 1.556 to 1 (28/18)
    4th gear... 1.304 to 1 (30/23)
    5th gear... 1.150 to 1 (23/20)
    6th gear... 1.041 to 1 (25/24)
Input shaft 5th and 6th gears ID
  Standard... 28.000 to 28.021 mm
  Service limit (max) .... 28.04 mm
Input shaft 5th and 6th gears bush OD
  Standard... 27.959 to 27.980 mm
  Service limit (min) .... 27.94 mm
Input shaft 5th and 6th gears gear-to-bush clearance
  Standard... 0.020 to 0.062 mm
  Service limit (max) .... 0.10 mm
Input shaft 5th gear bush ID
  Standard... 24.985 to 25.006 mm
  Service limit (max) .... 25.016 mm
Input shaft OD at 5th gear bush point
  Standard... 24.967 to 24.980 mm
  Service limit (min) .... 24.96 mm
Input shaft-to-bush clearance at 5th gear bush point
  Standard... 0.005 to 0.039 mm
  Service limit (max) .... 0.06 mm
Output shaft 1st gear ID
  Standard... 24.000 to 24.021 mm
  Service limit (max) .... 24.04 mm
Output shaft 2nd, 3rd and 4th gears ID
  Standard... 31.000 to 31.025 mm
  Service limit (max) .... 31.04 mm
Output shaft 2nd gear bush OD
  Standard... 30.955 to 30.980 mm
  Service limit (min) .... 30.94 mm
Output shaft 3rd and 4th gears bush OD
  Standard... 30.950 to 30.975 mm
  Service limit (min) .... 30.93 mm
Output shaft 2nd gear gear-to-bush clearance
  Standard... 0.020 to 0.070 mm
  Service limit (max) .... 0.10 mm
Output shaft 3rd and 4th gears gear-to-bush clearance
  Standard... 0.025 to 0.075 mm
  Service limit (max) .... 0.11 mm
Output shaft 2nd gear bush ID
  Standard... 27.985 to 28.006 mm
  Service limit (max) .... 28.021 mm
Output shaft OD at 2nd gear bush point
  Standard... 27.967 to 27.980 mm
  Service limit (min) .... 27.96 mm
Output shaft-to-bushing clearance at 2nd gear bush point
  Standard... 0.005 to 0.039 mm
  Service limit (max) .... 0.06 mm

2•6 Engine, clutch and transmission

Torque settings

Cam chain tensioner blades and guide	
Lower tensioner blade pivot bolt	12 Nm
Upper tensioner blade pivot bolt	20 Nm
Front guide blade pivot bolt	12 Nm
Camshaft holder bolts	12 Nm
Camshaft sprocket bolts	20 Nm
Clutch nut	128 Nm
Clutch spring bolts	12 Nm
Connecting rod nuts	26 Nm
Crankcase bolts	
Lower crankcase 8 mm crankshaft journal bolts	
Torque setting	15 Nm
Angle setting	+ 120°
Lower crankcase 10 mm bolt	39 Nm
Lower crankcase 6 mm bolts	12 Nm
Upper crankcase 8 mm bolt	24 Nm
Upper crankcase 6 mm bolts	12 Nm
Cylinder head 9 mm bolts	47 Nm
Engine mountings	
CB600F/FA and CBR600F/FA	
Front mounting bracket-to-frame bolt nuts	49 Nm
Front mounting bolts	59 Nm
Upper and lower rear mounting bolt nuts	59 Nm
CBF600N/NA/S/SA	
Front mounting bracket-to-frame bolt nuts	49 Nm
Front mounting bolts	59 Nm
Upper and lower rear mounting bolt nuts	59 Nm
Swingarm pivot bolt nut	98 Nm
Swingarm pivot bracket bolt nuts	69 Nm
Oil cooler bolt (CB600F/FA and CBR600F/FA)	59 Nm
Oil pipe bolts	12 Nm
Oil pump body bolts	12 Nm
Oil pump driven sprocket bolt	15 Nm
Selector drum bearing/fork shaft retainer bolts	12 Nm
Selector drum cam bolt	23 Nm
Starter clutch bolt	83 Nm
Stopper arm bolt	12 Nm
Timing inspection cap	18 Nm
Transmission input shaft bearing retainer plate bolts	12 Nm
Valve cover bolts	10 Nm

1 General information

The engine/transmission unit is a liquid-cooled in-line four cylinder. The sixteen valves are operated by double overhead camshafts that are chain driven off the right-hand end of the crankshaft. The engine/transmission is a unit assembly constructed from aluminium alloy. The crankcase divides horizontally.

The crankcase incorporates a wet sump, pressure-fed lubrication system which uses a trochoidal oil pump that is chain-driven off the back of the clutch. The system has an oil strainer in the pick-up, a pressure relief valve in the feed from the pump to the filter, an oil filter, an oil cooler, and an oil pressure switch in the main gallery.

The alternator is on the left-hand end of the crankshaft. The water pump is on the left-hand side of the engine, and its drive shaft is keyed to the oil pump drive shaft. The ignition timing triggers are on the outside of the starter clutch body on the right-hand end of the crankshaft. The crankshaft position sensor is mounted in the clutch cover.

Power from the crankshaft is routed to the transmission via the clutch. The clutch is of the wet, multi-plate type and is gear-driven off the crankshaft. The clutch is operated by cable. The transmission is a six-speed constant-mesh unit. Final drive to the rear wheel is by chain and sprockets.

2 Component access

Operations possible with the engine in the frame

The components and assemblies listed below can be removed without having to remove the engine/transmission assembly from the frame. If however, a number of areas require attention at the same time, removal of the engine is recommended.

- Valve cover
- Cam chain tensioner and blades
- Camshafts and cam chain
- Cylinder head
- Clutch
- Gearchange mechanism
- Alternator
- Oil filter and oil cooler
- Oil sump, oil pump, oil strainer and oil pressure relief valve
- Starter motor
- Starter clutch/timing rotor
- Water pump

Operations requiring engine removal

It is necessary to remove the engine/transmission assembly from the frame to gain access to the following components.

- Crankshaft and bearings
- Connecting rods and bearings
- Pistons, piston rings and cylinder bores
- Transmission shafts
- Selector drum and forks

Engine, clutch and transmission 2•7

3 Engine wear assessment

Cylinder compression check

Special tool: *A compression gauge is needed. You are best off using the type with a threaded hose and adaptor to fit the spark plug holes (use either the Honda gauge and adapter (part No. 07RMJ-MY50100) or an aftermarket version) – there are cheaper ones that have a coned rubber tip that is pressed onto the spark plug hole, but they are not as good, especially when access is restricted. Depending on the outcome of the initial test, a squirt-type oil can may also be needed.*

1 Poor engine performance can be caused by leaking valves, incorrect valve clearances, a leaking head gasket, or worn pistons, piston rings or cylinder walls. A cylinder compression check will highlight these conditions and can also indicate the presence of excessive carbon deposits in the cylinder head, and a leakdown test (for which special equipment is needed – consult a Honda dealer) will pinpoint the actual cause(s) of the problem.

2 Start by making sure the valve clearances are correctly set (see Chapter 1). Also make sure the battery is fully charged.

3 Run the engine until it is at normal operating temperature.

4 Remove the spark plugs (see Chapter 1).

5 Raise the fuel tank and disconnect the fuel pump wiring connector (see Chapter 4) – note that depending on the type of gauge being used you may prefer to remove the fuel tank to improve access (see Chapter 4).

6 Make sure the gauge hose/adapter threads are the same as the spark plug **(see illustration)**. Fit the gauge into the No. 1 cylinder spark plug hole.

7 With the ignition switch ON, the kill switch set to RUN, and the throttle held fully open, turn the engine over on the starter motor until the gauge reading has built up and stabilised **(see illustration)**.

8 Compare the reading on the gauge to the cylinder compression figure specified at the beginning of the Chapter. Repeat for the remaining cylinders.

9 If a reading is low, it could be due to a worn cylinder bore, piston or rings, failure of the head gasket, or worn valve seats. To determine which is the cause, pour a small quantity of engine oil into the spark plug hole to seal the rings, then repeat the compression test. If the figures are noticeably higher the cause is a worn cylinder, piston or rings. If there is no change the cause is a leaking head gasket or worn valve seats.

10 If the reading is high there could be a build-up of carbon deposits in the combustion chamber. Remove the cylinder head and scrape all deposits off the piston and cylinder head.

3.6 Select the correct adapter and fit it onto the gauge hose

3.7 Checking cylinder compression

Leak-down (cylinder leakage) test

11 A leak down or 'cylinder leakage' test is similar to a compression test in that it tells you how well a cylinder is sealing, but it does so by testing how much pressure is lost through leakage, as opposed to how much pressure is created through compression. Many professionals prefer a leak test to a compression test as it more accurately pin-points the cause of the problem before any disassembly is done. However the required equipment is more expensive than for a compression test and a source of compressed air is essential. If you think a test is needed take the bike to a suitably equipped dealer or workshop. If you decide to purchase your own equipment follow the manufacturer's instructions.

12 A leakage test can also be used in conjunction with a compression test to diagnose other kinds of problems, such as a faulty valve train component, incorrect valve timing, faulty ignition or fuel delivery problems.

Engine oil pressure check

Special tool: *An oil pressure gauge is required to perform this test.*

13 An oil pressure check can provide useful information about the condition of the engine's lubrication system, and can also be used as an indicator of excessive wear in the engine if no specific faults with the lubrication or pressure warning system are found.

14 The oil pressure warning light should come on when the ignition switch is turned ON and extinguish a few seconds after the engine is started. If the light stays on, or comes on whilst the engine is running, low oil pressure is indicated – stop the engine immediately and carry out an oil level check *(see Pre-ride checks)*. If the oil level is correct, remove the sump and check the oil pick-up strainer for a blockage (Section 17). Also check the drained oil for sludge that reduces its ability to flow. Note that it is possible that the cause of the light staying on or coming on while the engine is running is an electrical fault, so make sure the oil pressure switch, warning light and circuit are all functioning correctly (see Chapter 8). If all appears good an oil pressure check must be carried out.

15 To check the oil pressure, a suitable gauge and adapter (which screws into the main oil gallery in place of the oil pressure switch) will be needed. Honda can provide a gauge and adapter (part Nos. 07506-3000001 and 07510-4220100) for this purpose, or one can be obtained commercially. You will also need some rags to catch and mop up any residual oil that gets lost in between removing the oil pressure switch and installing the gauge – place the bike on its sidestand so that the oil gathers at the other end of the gallery to reduce spillage.

16 Check the oil level (see *Pre-ride checks*).

17 Remove the oil pressure switch (see Chapter 8). Screw the gauge adapter in its place. Connect the oil pressure gauge to the adapter.

18 Warm the engine up to normal operating temperature, then briefly increase the engine speed to 6000 rpm whilst watching the gauge reading. The oil pressure should be similar to that given in the Specifications at the start of this Chapter.

19 If the pressure is significantly lower than the standard, and the pick-up strainer is clean, either the pressure relief valve is stuck open, the oil pump or its drive mechanism is faulty, the oil strainer or filter is blocked, or there is other engine damage. Also make sure the correct grade oil is being used. Begin diagnosis by checking the oil filter, strainer and relief valve (see Section 17), then check the oil pump (Section 18). If those items check out okay, chances are the bearing oil clearances are excessive and the engine needs to be overhauled.

20 If the pressure is too high, either an oil passage is clogged, the relief valve is stuck closed or the wrong grade of oil is being used.

21 If the pressure is as it should be, and if not already done, then check the oil pressure switch, warning light and circuit (see Chapter 8).

22 Stop the engine and let it cool, then remove the gauge and adapter and install the oil pressure switch (see Chapter 8).

⚠ **Warning: Be careful when removing the pressure gauge adapter as the exhaust pipes, the engine and the oil itself can cause severe burns.**

23 Check the oil level (see *Pre-ride checks*).

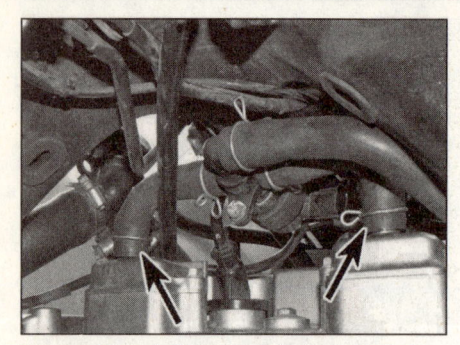

2•8 Engine, clutch and transmission

4.8 Detach the hoses (arrowed) and remove the PAIR valve

4.9 Remove the crankcase breather hose (arrowed)

4 Engine removal and installation

Caution: *The engine is very heavy. Engine removal and installation should be carried out with the aid of at least one assistant; personal injury or damage could occur if the engine falls or is dropped.*

Note: *As each mounting bolt is removed store it along with any related washer, nut and spacer to avoid parts getting mixed up, making installation easier.*

Removal

1 Support the bike upright using the centrestand where fitted, or an auxiliary stand or stands that will not interfere with engine removal – a rear paddock stand is ideal. Make sure the bike is on level ground, and tie the front brake on. Work can be made easier by raising the machine to a suitable working height on an hydraulic ramp or a suitable platform. Make sure the motorcycle is secure and will not topple over (also see *Tools and Workshop Tips* in the Reference section).

2 On all models remove the seat(s) and side covers (see Chapter 7). On CBR600F/FA and CBF600S/SA models remove the fairing side panels (see Chapter 7). On CBF600N/NA/S/SA models remove the left-hand seat cowl (see Chapter 7).

3 If the engine is dirty, particularly around its mountings, wash it thoroughly. This will make work much easier and rule out the possibility of caked on lumps of dirt falling into some vital component.

4 Drain the engine oil and the coolant (see Chapter 1). If required remove the oil filter (see Chapter 1).

5 Disconnect the negative (–ve) lead from the battery (see Chapter 8).

6 Remove the fuel tank and the air filter housing and throttle body assembly (see Chapter 4). Plug the engine intake manifolds with clean rag.

7 Remove the radiator along with its hoses, noting their routing (see Chapter 3). Detach and remove any remaining coolant hoses, noting their positions and routing.

8 Detach the PAIR system hoses from the valve cover and remove the PAIR control valve along with the hoses **(see illustration)**.

9 Detach the crankcase breather hose and remove it **(see illustration)**.

10 Pull the caps off the spark plugs.

11 Remove the exhaust system (see Chapter 4).

12 Remove the front sprocket (see Chapter 6). Slip the drive chain off the end of the output shaft and let it rest against the front of the swingarm.

13 Disconnect the alternator wiring connector (black 3-pin, 3 yellow wires) from the regulator/rectifier **(see illustrations)**. Release the wiring from its clamps and feed it down to the alternator, noting its routing.

14 Unscrew the sidestand switch bolt and displace the switch **(see illustration)**. Release the switch wiring from its guides and clamps and position it clear, noting its routing.

15 If required, remove the thermostat housing and coolant inlet union (see Chapter 3).

16 If required, remove the starter motor (see Chapter 8). If not, pull back the rubber cover on its terminal, then unscrew the nut and disconnect the lead **(see illustration)**. Also unscrew the mounting bolt securing the earth lead and detach the lead.

17 Remove the horn (see Chapter 8). Release the wiring from the bracket.

18 Release the oil pressure switch wiring from the swingarm pivot bracket **(see illustration)**.

19 Unscrew the bolt securing the clutch cable bracket to the clutch cover **(see illustration)**. Displace the bracket, noting how it locates, and free the cable end from the release arm

4.13a Alternator wiring connector (arrowed) – CB and CBR models

4.13b Alternator wiring connector (arrowed) – CB and CBF models

4.14 Side stand switch bolt (arrowed)

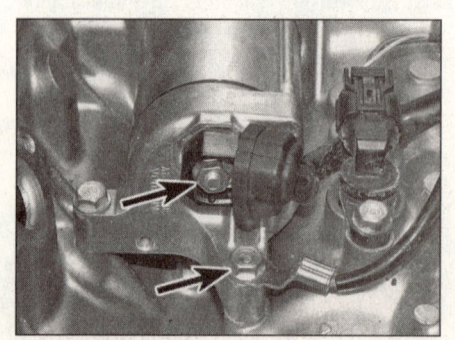

4.16 Unscrew the nut and bolt (arrowed) and detach the leads

4.18 Release the wire clamp and guide (arrowed)

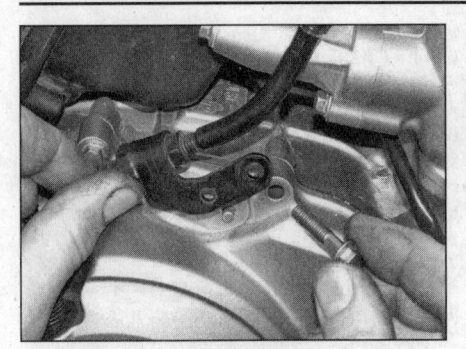

Engine, clutch and transmission 2•9

4.19a Unscrew the bolt and detach the bracket . . .

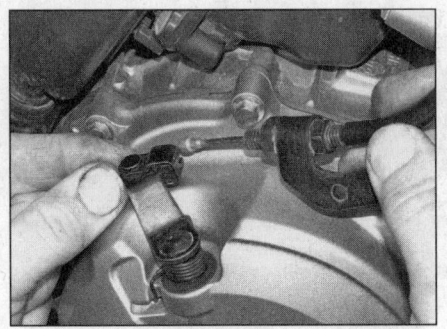

4.19b . . . then detach the cable end

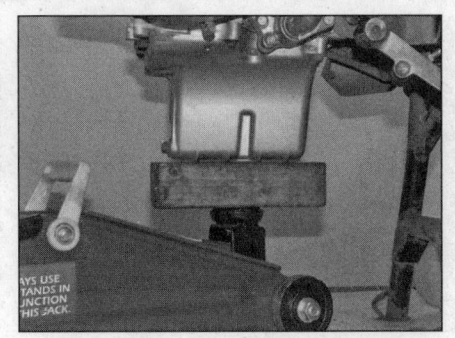

4.20 Support the engine with a jack

4.21a Unscrew the front bolt (arrowed) on each side . . .

4.21b . . . and remove the spacers

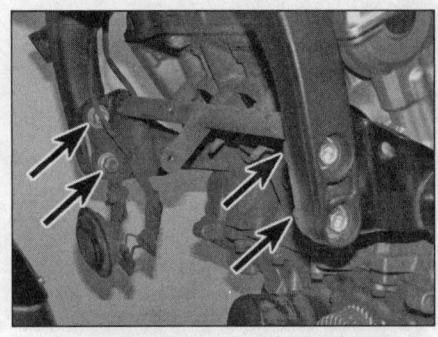

4.22 Front bracket nuts (arrowed)

(see illustration). Position the cable clear of the engine.

20 At this point, position an hydraulic or mechanical jack under the engine with a block of wood between the jack head and sump (see illustration). Make sure the jack is centrally positioned so the engine will not topple in any direction when the last mounting bolt is removed. Raise the jack to take the weight of the engine, but make sure it is not lifting the bike and taking the weight of that as well. The idea is to support the engine so that there is no pressure on any of the mounting bolts once they have been slackened, so they can be easily withdrawn.

21 Unscrew the front mounting bolts and remove the spacers, noting which fits where (see illustrations).

22 Unscrew the front mounting bracket nuts and remove the washers/horn bracket/fairing brackets as required according to side and model (see illustration). Withdraw the bolts and remove the bracket.

23 On CBF600N/NA/S/SA models slacken the swingarm pivot bolt nut and the nuts on the right-hand ends of the swingarm pivot bracket bolts, counter-holding the bolt heads if necessary (see illustration). Withdraw the bracket bolts from the left, then draw the left-hand pivot bracket out just enough until it can be turned slightly anti-clockwise, pivoting on the swingarm bolt (see illustration).

24 Unscrew the nut from the lower rear mounting bolt (see illustration). Check that the engine is properly supported by the jack, then withdraw the bolt. Remove the spacer from between the engine and frame on the right-hand side.

25 Unscrew the nut from the upper rear mounting bolt (see illustration). Support the engine and withdraw the bolt. Remove the spacer from the right-hand side.

26 The engine can now be removed from the frame (see Caution above). Check that

4.23a Unscrew the nuts (arrowed) . . .

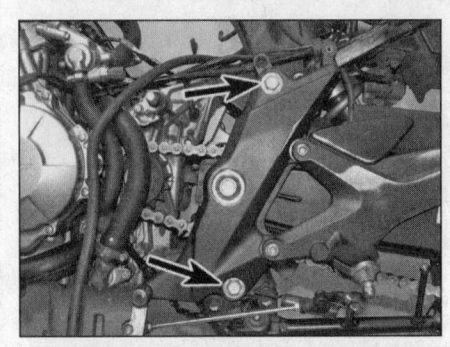

4.23b . . . then withdraw the bolts (arrowed) and pivot the bracket round

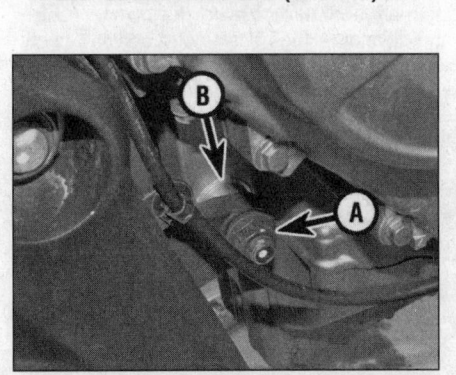

4.24 Unscrew the nut (A), withdraw the bolt and remove the spacer (B) – lower mounting

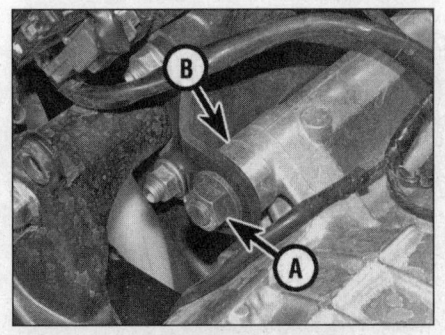

4.25 Unscrew the nut (A), withdraw the bolt and remove the spacer (B) – upper mounting

2•10 Engine, clutch and transmission

4.30 On CBR models make sure the fairing brackets (arrowed) are correctly fitted

all wiring, cables and hoses are free and clear, then carefully lower the jack a bit and manoeuvre the engine as required to clear the frame. Fully lower the jack, then with the aid of an assistant remove the jack from under the engine and remove the engine.

Installation

Note: To prevent corrosion which could lead to bolts being seized, smear copper grease onto the bolt shafts, not the threads, to prevent the possibility of them seizing in the collars or the engine or frame.

27 Manoeuvre the engine into position under the frame and lift it onto the jack. Raise the engine to align all the mounting bolt holes, making sure that all cables and wiring are correctly routed and do not get trapped. Note that it may be necessary to adjust the jack as some of the bolts are installed and tightened to realign the other bolt holes.
28 Install the upper and lower rear mounting bolts (on CBF600N/NA/S/SA models the upper bolt is shorter than the lower) from the left-hand side, fitting the spacers between the engine and frame on the right-hand side **(see illustrations 4.25 and 4.24)**. Fit and finger-tighten the nuts.
29 On CBF600N/NA/S/SA models realign and position the left-hand swingarm pivot bracket, then insert the bracket bolts from the left **(see illustration 4.23b)**. Fit the bracket bolt nuts and tighten them and then the swingarm pivot bolt nut to the torque settings specified at the beginning of the Chapter **(see illustration 4.23a)**.
30 Locate the front mounting bracket and insert the bolts **(see illustration 4.22)**. Fit the horn bracket/ fairing brackets/washers according to side and model **(see illustration)**. Tighten the nuts finger-tight.
31 Install the front mounting bolt on each side with its spacer **(see illustration 4.21a)** – the longer spacer goes with the longer bolt in the left-hand side **(see illustration 4.21b)**. Tighten the bolts finger-tight.
32 Tighten the front mounting bracket nuts to the torque setting specified at the beginning of the Chapter **(see illustration 4.22)**.
33 Tighten the nut on the lower rear bolt to the specified torque, then tighten the nut on the upper bolt to the specified torque **(see illustrations 4.24 and 4.25)** – counter-hold the bolt heads if required.
34 Tighten the front bolts to the specified torque **(see illustration 4.21a)**.
35 The remainder of the installation procedure is the reverse of removal, noting the following points:
- Use new gaskets on the exhaust pipe connections.
- Make sure all wires, cables and hoses are correctly routed and connected, and secured by any clips or ties.
- Refill the engine with the correct type and quantity of oil and coolant (see Chapter 1).
- Adjust the throttle and clutch cable freeplay.
- Adjust the drive chain (see Chapter 1).
- Start the engine and check that there are no oil or coolant leaks. Adjust the idle speed (see Chapter 1).

5 Engine disassembly and reassembly general information

1 Before beginning the engine overhaul, read through the related procedures to familiarise yourself with the scope and requirements of the job. Overhauling an engine is not all that difficult, but it is time consuming. Check on the availability of parts and make sure that any necessary special tools are obtained in advance.
2 Most work can be done with a decent set of typical workshop hand tools, although a number of precision measuring tools are required for inspecting parts to determine if they are worn.
3 To ensure maximum life and minimum trouble from a rebuilt engine, everything must be assembled with care in a spotlessly clean environment.

Disassembly

4 Before disassembling the engine, thoroughly clean and degrease its external surfaces. This will prevent contamination of the engine internals, and will also make the job a lot easier and cleaner. A high flash-point solvent, such as paraffin (kerosene) can be used, or better still, a proprietary engine degreaser such as Gunk. Use old paintbrushes and toothbrushes to work the solvent into the various recesses of the casings. Take care to exclude solvent or water from the electrical components and intake and exhaust ports.

⚠ *Warning: The use of petrol (gasoline) as a cleaning agent should be avoided because of the risk of fire.*

5 When clean and dry, position the engine on the workbench, leaving suitable clear area for working. Gather a selection of small containers, plastic bags and some labels so that parts can be grouped together in an easily identifiable manner. Also get some paper and a pen so that notes can be taken. You will also need a supply of clean rag, which should be as absorbent as possible.
6 Before commencing work, read through the appropriate section so that some idea of the necessary procedure can be gained. When removing components note that great force is seldom required, unless specified (checking the specified torque setting of the particular bolt being removed will indicate how tight it is, and therefore how much force should be needed). In many cases, a component's reluctance to be removed is indicative of an incorrect approach or removal method – if in any doubt, re-check with the text.
7 When disassembling the engine, keep 'mated' parts that have been in contact with each other during engine operation together (i.e. pistons with their piston rings and connecting rods, valves with their followers, shims and other components, etc). These 'mated' parts must be reinstalled together and in their original location.
8 A complete engine/transmission disassembly should be done in the following general order with reference to the appropriate Sections.
   Remove the valve cover
   Remove the camshafts
   Remove the cylinder head
   Remove the starter motor (see Chapter 8)
   Remove the starter clutch
   Remove the cam chain and blades
   Remove the clutch
   Remove the gearchange mechanism
   Remove the alternator (see Chapter 8)
   Remove the oil sump
   Remove the oil pump
   Separate the crankcase halves
   Remove the crankshaft
   Remove the transmission shafts and the selector drum and forks
   Remove the connecting rods and pistons

Reassembly

9 Reassembly is accomplished by reversing the general disassembly sequence.

6 Oil cooler

Note: The oil cooler can be removed with the engine in the frame. If the engine has been removed, ignore the steps that do not apply.

CB600F/FA and CBR600F/FA
Removal
1 The cooler is located on the front of the engine next to the oil filter.
2 Drain the engine oil (see Chapter 1). Drain the coolant (see Chapter 1).
3 Slacken the clamp securing each hose

Engine, clutch and transmission 2•11

6.3 Slacken the clamps (arrowed) and detach the hoses

6.4 Unscrew the bolt and remove the cooler

6.6 Fit a new O-ring into the groove

to the cooler and detach the hoses **(see illustration)**.
4 Unscrew the bolt with its sealing washer and remove the cooler **(see illustration)**. Remove the O-ring – a new one must be used.
5 Check the cooler body for cracks and dents and any evidence of coolant leakage and replace it with a new one if necessary. Also check the hoses for splits, cracks, hardening and deterioration and fit new ones if required.

Installation

6 Installation is the reverse of removal, noting the following:
- Ensure the mating surfaces of the crankcase and the cooler are clean and dry.
- Use a new O-ring on the cooler body and smear it with clean engine oil. Make sure it seats in its groove **(see illustration)**.
- Seat the tabs on the bottom of the cooler body on each side of the lug on the crankcase. Use a new sealing washer and smear it and the bolt threads with oil, and tighten the bolt to the torque setting specified at the beginning of the Chapter.
- Make sure the coolant hoses are pressed fully onto their unions and are secured by the clamps **(see illustration 6.3)**.
- Fill the engine with the correct type and quantity of oil (see Chapter 1).
- Refill the cooling system (see Chapter 1).

CBF600N/NA/S/SA
Removal

7 The cooler is located on the front of the engine next to the oil filter.

8 Drain the engine oil (see Chapter 1).
9 Unscrew the bolts and remove the cooler **(see illustration)**. Remove the O-ring – a new one must be used.
10 Check the cooler body for cracks and any evidence of oil leakage and replace it with a new one if necessary.

Installation

11 Installation is the reverse of removal, noting the following:
- Ensure the mating surfaces of the crankcase and the cooler are clean and dry.
- Use a new O-ring on the cooler body and smear it with clean engine oil. Make sure it seats in its groove.
- Fill the engine with the correct type and quantity of oil (see Chapter 1).

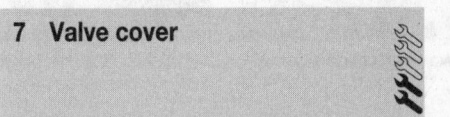

7 Valve cover

Note: *The valve cover can be removed with the engine in the frame. If the engine has been removed, ignore the steps that do not apply.*

Removal

1 Remove the fuel tank (see Chapter 4).
2 Detach the crankcase breather hose **(see illustration 4.9)**. Detach the PAIR system hoses from the valve cover and air filter housing **(see illustration 4.8)**. Disconnect the PAIR control valve wiring connector and remove the valve along with the hoses.
3 Remove the ignition coils (see Chapter 4).
4 Unscrew the four valve cover bolts and lift the cover off the cylinder head **(see illustrations)**. If it is stuck, do not try to lever it off with a screwdriver. Tap it gently around the sides with a rubber hammer or block of wood to dislodge it. Take care not to damage the radiator fins. Note the rubber washers for the bolts and remove them if they are loose **(see illustration 7.11a)**.
5 The rubber gasket is normally glued into the groove in the cover, and is best left there if it is reusable. If the gasket is in any way damaged, deformed or deteriorated, remove it **(see illustration 7.10a)**.
6 Note the four dowels that link the PAIR system air passages between the valve cover and cylinder head and remove them for safekeeping if they are loose (which is unlikely), taking care not to drop them if they are not in the valve cover **(see illustration 7.10a)**.
7 If required, remove the PAIR system reed valves (see Chapter 4).

Installation

8 If removed, install the PAIR system reed valves (see Chapter 4).
9 If removed, fit the PAIR system dowels into the valve cover **(see illustration 7.10a)**.
10 Examine the valve cover gasket for signs of damage or deterioration and fit a new one if necessary. If a new one is used, clean

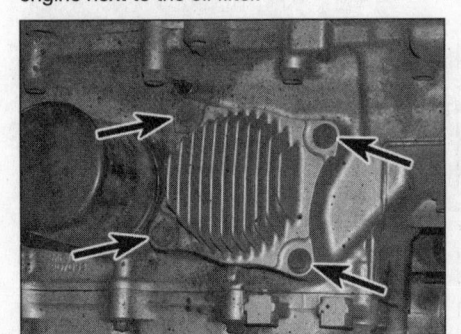

6.9 Oil cooler bolts (arrowed)

7.4a Unscrew the bolts (arrowed) . . .

7.4b . . . and remove the valve cover

2•12 Engine, clutch and transmission

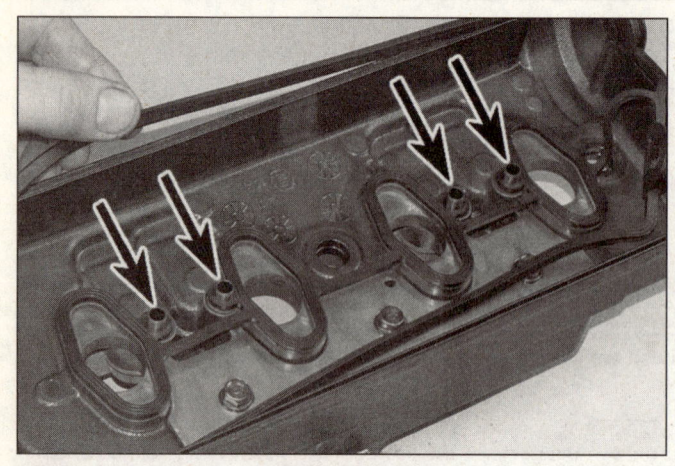

7.10a Make sure the gasket locates in the groove and over the dowels (arrowed)

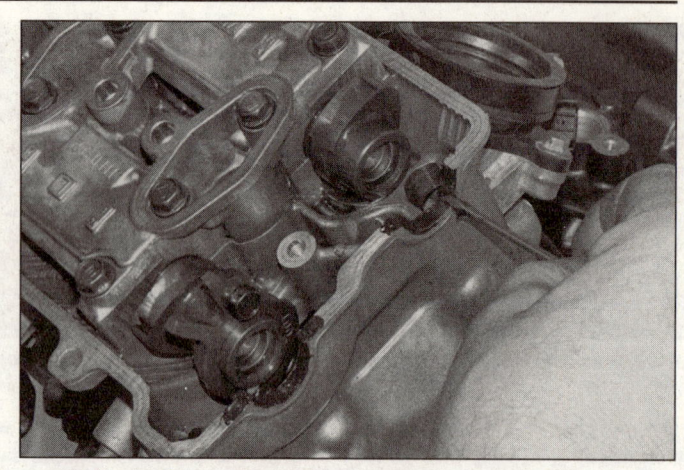

7.10b Apply a sealant to the cut-outs in the cylinder head

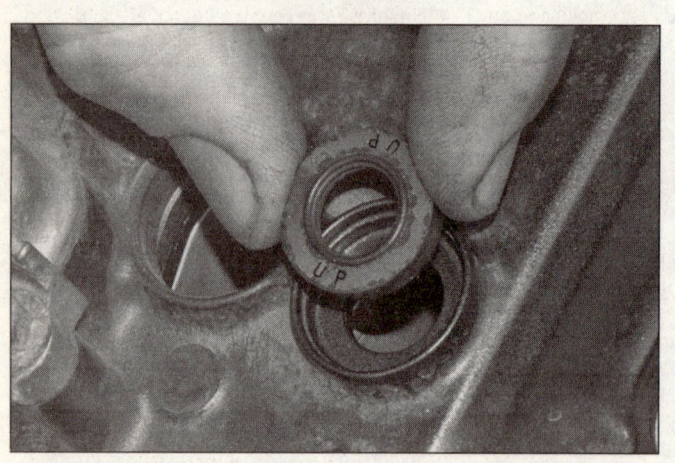

7.11a Make sure the UP marks on the washers face up

7.11b Fit the bolts and tighten them to the specified torque

all traces of the old glue from the groove in the cover and clean it and the cylinder head mating surface with solvent. Fit the new gasket into the perimeter groove and around the plug bores and over the dowels, using a suitable glue, sealant or grease to hold it in place, and making sure it (see illustration). Also apply a suitable sealant to the cut-outs in the cylinder head (see illustration).

11 If removed, fit the rubber washers into the cover, using new ones if required, and making sure the UP marks face up (see illustration). Position the valve cover on the cylinder head, making sure the gasket stays in place (see illustration 7.4b). Fit the cover bolts and tighten them to the torque setting specified at the beginning of the Chapter (see illustration).

12 Install the remaining components in the reverse order of removal.

8 Cam chain tensioner

Note: *The cam chain tensioner can be removed with the engine in the frame. If the engine has been removed, ignore the steps that do not apply. Before removing the tensioner it is good practice to set the No. 1 cylinder at TDC on its compression stroke so that you can check the timing marks in case the chain jumps around the sprocket when the tensioner is removed – refer to Section 9, Steps 1 to 3, and on completion to Steps 31 to 33.*

Removal

1 For best access and to prevent the possibility of damage remove the right-hand

8.2 Unscrew the cap bolt and remove the washer

side cover, and on CBR600F/FA models the fairing side panel and upper panel (see Chapter 7).

2 Unscrew the tensioner cap bolt and remove the sealing washer (see illustration).

3 If the Honda tensioner holding tool (part No. 070MG-0010100) is available, fit it onto the end of the tensioner and turn it clockwise until the plunger is fully retracted and held (see illustration). Unscrew the tensioner mounting bolts and withdraw the tensioner from the engine (see illustration 8.4a).

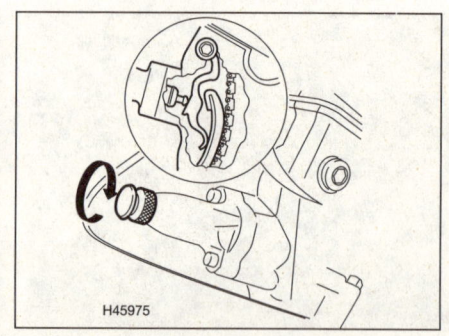

8.3 Using the Honda tool to retract the tensioner plunger

Engine, clutch and transmission 2•13

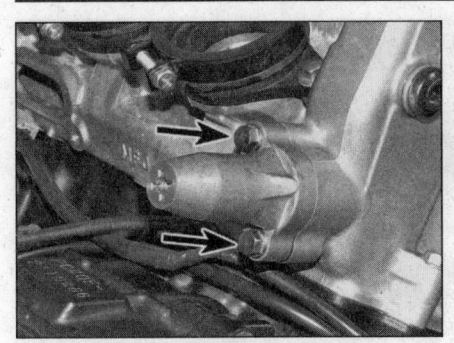

8.4a Slacken the mounting bolts (arrowed) slightly . . .

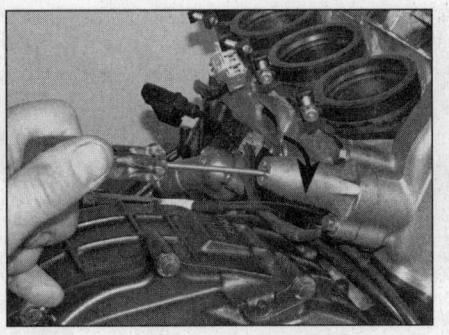

8.4b . . . then insert the screwdriver and retract the plunger . . .

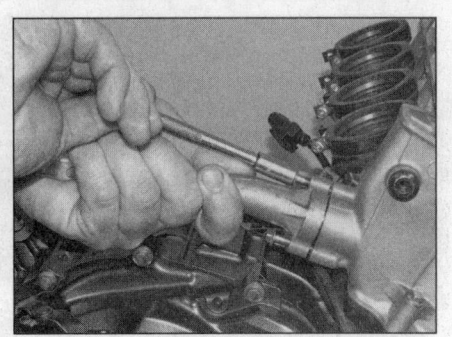

8.4c . . . and unscrew the mounting bolts

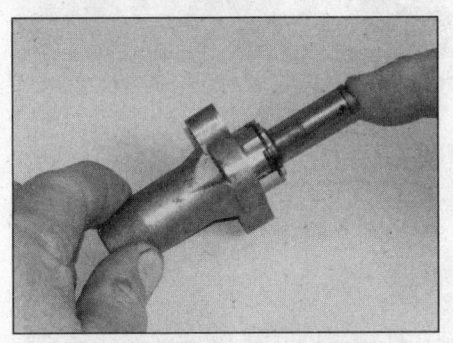

8.6 The plunger must not move in when pushed

8.8a Insert the screwdriver and retract the plunger . . .

4 If the holding tool is not available, first slacken the tensioner mounting bolts slightly **(see illustration)**. Insert a small flat-bladed screwdriver in the end of the tensioner so that it engages the slotted plunger **(see illustration)**. Turn the screwdriver clockwise until the plunger is fully retracted and hold it in this position while unscrewing the tensioner mounting bolts **(see illustration)**. Remove the bolts, then withdraw the tensioner from the engine and release the screwdriver **(see illustration 8.4c)** – the plunger will spring back out once the screwdriver is removed, but can be easily reset on installation.
5 Remove the gasket and sealing washer – new ones must be used on installation. Do not attempt to dismantle the tensioner.

Installation

6 Check that the plunger cannot be pushed into the body **(see illustration)** – if it can, fit a new tensioner. Check that the plunger moves smoothly when wound into the tensioner and springs back out freely when released **(see illustration 8.8a)**. Make sure the tensioner and cylinder block surfaces are clean and dry.
7 If the Honda holding tool is being used and has been removed, fit it onto the end of the tensioner as before and turn it clockwise until the plunger is fully retracted and held. Fit a new gasket onto the tensioner body, then fit the tensioner with its mounting bolts and tighten them **(see illustrations 8.8b and c)**. Remove the tool, then fit the tensioner cap bolt with a new sealing washer and tighten it **(see illustration 8.2)**.
8 If the tool is not available, insert a small flat-bladed screwdriver in the end of the tensioner so that it engages the slotted plunger **(see illustration)**. Turn the screwdriver clockwise until the plunger is fully retracted and hold it in this position whilst the tensioner is installed. Fit a new gasket onto the tensioner body, then fit the tensioner with its mounting bolts and tighten them **(see illustrations)**. Release and remove the screwdriver, then fit the tensioner cap bolt with a new sealing washer and tighten it **(see illustration 8.2)**.
9 Fit the side cover/panels according to model (see Chapter 7).

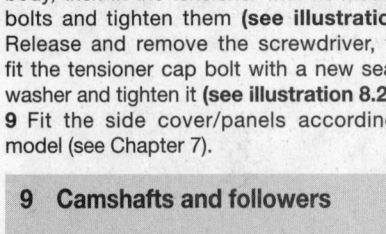

9 Camshafts and followers

Note: *The camshafts can be removed with the engine in the frame. Place clean rags over the spark plug holes and the cam chain tunnel to prevent any component from dropping into the engine.*

Removal

1 Remove the spark plugs (see Chapter 1). Remove the valve cover (see Section 7).
2 Unscrew the timing inspection cap from the clutch cover **(see illustration)**. Check the condition of its O-ring and obtain a new one if necessary.
3 The engine must be turned so that the No. 1 piston is at TDC (top dead centre) on its compression stroke. Turn the engine using a suitable spanner or socket on the timing rotor bolt and turning it in a clockwise direction only until the line next to the T mark on the timing rotor aligns with the static timing mark, which is a notch in the inspection hole rim, and the IN and EX marks on the intake and exhaust camshaft sprockets respectively are facing away from each other and are flush with the

8.8b . . . then fit a new gasket onto the tensioner . . .

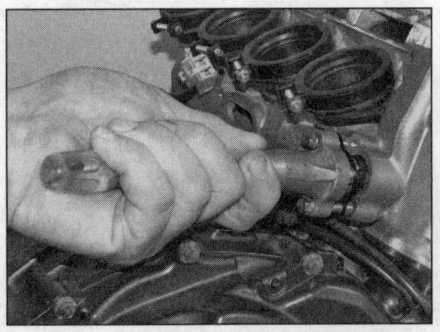

8.8c . . . and install the tensioner

9.2 Remove the timing inspection cap

2•14 Engine, clutch and transmission

9.3a Turn the engine clockwise using the bolt . . .

9.3b . . . until the line next to the T mark aligns with the notch (arrowed) . . .

9.3c . . . and the camshaft sprocket marks are as shown

9.4 Unscrew the bolts and remove the guide

cylinder head top surface **(see illustrations)**. If the marks are facing towards each other, rotate the engine clockwise one full turn (360°) until the line next to the T mark again aligns with the static timing mark. The sprocket marks will now be facing away.

4 Either remove the cam chain tensioner (see Section 8), or if you prefer, using the tensioner holding tool as described in Section 8, Step 3, retract and lock the tensioner plunger. Unscrew the bolts securing the top cam chain guide and remove it **(see illustration)**.

5 There are three camshaft holders, each bridging both camshafts **(see illustration)**. Of the two larger holders, the one on the right-hand end is marked R and the one on the left-hand end L, and these letters are at the front **(see illustration)**. Mark an arrow on

9.5a Camshaft holders (arrowed)

9.5b Note the ID letter and the bolt numbers on each holder

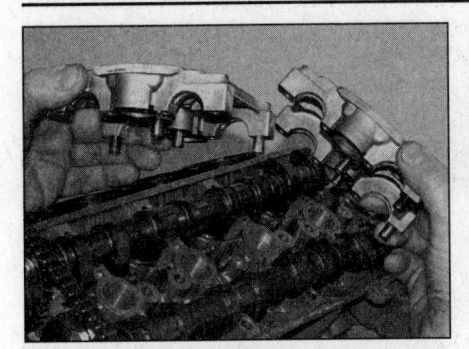

Engine, clutch and transmission 2•15

9.6a Unscrew the bolts as described and remove the holders

9.6b Remove the sealing rings and discard them

9.7 Note the identity mark on each camshaft

the small holder adjacent to the cam chain to denote which side points to the front of the engine. Note the numbers marked on the holders, adjacent to each bolt – these numbers denote the **tightening** sequence for the holder bolts.

6 Unscrew the camshaft holder bolts, slackening them evenly and a very little at a time in a **reverse** of the tightening sequence marked on the holders. Remove the bolts, noting which fits where as there are different lengths, and lift off the holders, noting how they fit **(see illustration)**. Note the sealing washers fitted with the eight bolts around the spark plug bores **(see illustration 9.28c)**. Remove the sealing rings from their grooves around the spark plug holes on the underside of the holders, noting how they also locate around the PAIR system air passage dowels **(see illustration)**. Discard them as new ones must be used. Do not remove the dowels unless they are loose and liable to drop out.

Caution: Make sure the holders lift up squarely and evenly and do not stick on a dowel or distort from some of the bolts being slackened more than the others as they or a camshaft could easily break.

7 If both camshafts are being removed, remove the intake camshaft first. Carefully lift each camshaft off the head and disengage the sprocket from the chain **(see illustrations 9.27a and 9.26a)**. The camshafts are marked for identification – the intake camshaft is marked FG and the exhaust camshaft is marked FG/EX **(see illustration)**. If the marks aren't clear make your own as the camshafts must be installed in their original location.

8 While the camshafts are out do not rotate the crankshaft – the chain may drop down and bind between the crankshaft and case, which could damage these components. Wire the chain to another component or secure it using a rod of some sort to prevent it from dropping. Place rags over the spark plug holes and the cam chain tunnel to prevent anything from dropping into the engine on removal.

9 If the followers and shims are being removed from the cylinder head, obtain a container which is divided into sixteen compartments, and label each compartment with the location of a valve, i.e. intake or exhaust camshaft, left or right valve. If a container is not available, use labelled plastic bags (egg cartons also do very well!). Remove the cam follower of the valve in question using a magnet or the suction created by a valve lapping tool, or long nosed pliers can be used with care **(see illustration)**. Retrieve the shim from the inside of the follower or pick it out of the top of the valve spring retainer using either a magnet, a screwdriver with a dab of grease on it (the shim will stick to the grease), or a very small screwdriver and a pair of pliers **(see illustrations)**. Do not allow the shim to fall into the engine.

10 The camshaft sprockets are identical and are therefore interchangeable, but if you need to remove them mark them according to the camshaft they fit on. Also make alignment marks between the sprocket and the camshaft so that the sprocket can be installed the correct way round to avoid confusion when setting up the timing. Unscrew the sprocket bolts and take the sprockets off the camshafts **(see illustration)**.

Inspection

11 Inspect the bearing surfaces of the camshaft holders and cylinder head and the corresponding journals on the camshafts **(see illustration)**. Look for score marks, deep

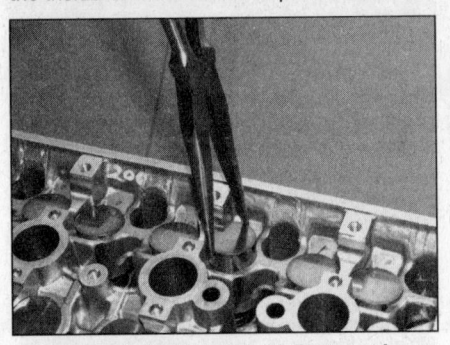

9.9a Carefully lift out the follower using a lapping tool, grips or a magnet . . .

9.9b . . . and retrieve the shim from inside it . . .

9.9c . . . or from the top of the valve

9.10 Camshaft sprocket bolts

9.11 Check all related bearing surfaces

2•16 Engine, clutch and transmission

9.12 Measure the height of the camshaft lobes with a micrometer

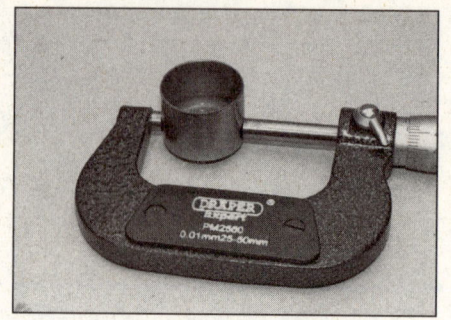

9.21a Measure the external diameter of each follower . . .

9.21b . . . and the internal diameter of each bore

scratches and evidence of spalling (a pitted appearance). Check the oil passages for clogging.

12 Check the camshaft lobes for heat discoloration (blue appearance), score marks, chipped areas, flat spots and spalling. Measure the height of each lobe with a micrometer **(see illustration)** and compare the results to the minimum height listed in this Chapter's Specifications. If damage is noted or wear is excessive, the camshaft must be replaced with a new one.

13 Check the amount of camshaft runout by supporting each end on V-blocks, and measuring any runout using a dial gauge. If the runout exceeds the specified limit the camshaft must be replaced with a new one.

> **HAYNES HiNT** *Refer to Tools and Workshop Tips in the Reference section for details of how to read a micrometer and dial gauge.*

14 Next, check the camshaft journal oil clearances. In order to negate the probability of the camshafts rotating (due to the fact that some of the lobes will be depressing their valves) as the holder bolts are tightened down, which will disturb the Plastigauge and lead to a false measurement, the cylinder head should be removed and the valves removed from it (see Sections 11 and 12). Clean the camshafts and the bearing surfaces in the cylinder head and camshaft holder with a clean lint-free cloth, then lay each camshaft in its correct location in the cylinder head (see Step 7).

15 Cut some strips of Plastigauge and lay one piece on each journal, parallel with the camshaft centreline. Make sure the camshaft holder dowels are installed **(see illustration 9.28a)**. If the valves are installed, fit the holders and tighten the bolts as described in Step 28. If the valves have been removed, fit the holders as described in Step 28, noting that you can do each holder separately rather than all three at the same time, and tighten the bolts evenly and a little at a time in a criss-cross sequence to the torque setting specified at the beginning of the Chapter, making sure the holders are pulled down squarely onto the dowels. While doing this, don't let the camshafts rotate, or the Plastigauge will be disturbed and you will have to start again.

16 Now unscrew the camshaft holder bolts as described in Step 6 (valves installed) or evenly and a little at a time in a criss-cross sequence (valves removed), and lift off the holder.

17 To determine the oil clearance, compare the crushed Plastigauge (at its widest point) on each journal to the scale printed on the Plastigauge container. Compare the results to this Chapter's Specifications. If the oil clearance is greater than specified, replace the camshaft with a new one and recheck the clearance. If the clearance is still too great, also replace the cylinder head and holder with new ones.

> **HAYNES HiNT** *Before replacing the camshafts, cylinder head or holders because of damage, check with motorcycle cylinder head specialists to see whether worn components can be renewed. Due to the cost of new components it is recommended that all options be explored before condemning them as trash!*

18 Except in cases of oil starvation, the cam chain should wear very little. If the chain has stretched excessively, which makes it difficult to maintain proper tension, or if it is stiff or the links are binding or kinking, replace it with a new one. Refer to Section 10 for replacement.

19 Check the sprockets for wear, cracks and other damage, and replace them with new ones if necessary (see Steps 10 and 22). If the sprockets are worn, the cam chain is also worn, and so probably is the sprocket on the crankshaft. If severe wear is apparent, the entire engine should be disassembled for inspection.

20 Inspect the cam chain guides and tensioner blade (see Section 10).

21 Inspect the outer surface of each cam follower for evidence of scoring or other damage. If a follower is in poor condition, it is probable that the bore in the cylinder head in which it works is also damaged. Check for clearance between each follower and its bore. Measure the outer diameter of each follower and the inner diameter of its bore and compare the results to the Specifications **(see illustrations)**. If any follower is worn beyond its service limit replace it with a new one. If any bore is worn beyond its limit, is seriously out-of-round or tapered, replace the cylinder head with a new one.

Installation

22 If separated, fit the sprockets onto the camshafts. Make sure they are installed the correct way round and in their original location as identified by the marks made on removal (Step 10) **(see illustration 9.10)**. Clean the threads of the bolts and apply a suitable non-permanent thread locking compound to the sprocket bolts and tighten them to the torque setting specified at the beginning of the Chapter.

23 If removed, lubricate each shim and its follower with molybdenum disulphide oil (a 50/50 mixture of molybdenum disulphide grease and engine oil). Fit each shim into its recess in the top of the valve spring retainer with the size mark facing up, making sure it is correctly seated **(see illustration)**. **Note:** *It is most important that the shims and followers are returned to their original valves otherwise the valve clearances will be inaccurate.* Fit each follower, making sure it fits squarely in its bore **(see illustration)**.

9.23a Fit each shim into its recess . . .

9.23b . . . then fit the follower onto the valve

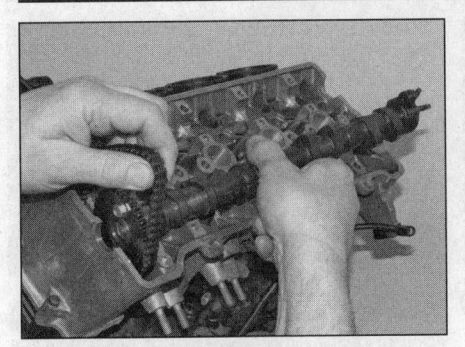

Engine, clutch and transmission 2•17

9.26a Fit the chain round the exhaust cam sprocket . . .

9.26b . . . and align the EX mark as shown

9.27a Fit the chain round the intake cam sprocket . . .

9.27b . . . and align the IN mark as shown

9.28a Fit the holders . . .

9.28b . . . fitting the longer bolts fit where the dowels are positioned

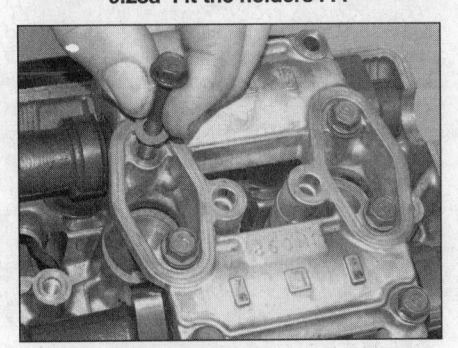

9.28c Fit new sealing washers with the spark plug bore bolts

24 Make sure the bearing surfaces on the camshafts and in the cylinder head are clean, then apply molybdenum disulphide oil (a 50/50 mixture of molybdenum disulphide grease and engine oil) to each of them. Also apply it to the camshaft journals and lobes. Make sure that none gets on the mating surfaces between the holder and the head, or in the bolt holes.

25 Check that the line next to the T mark on the timing rotor aligns with the notch in the inspection hole rim (see illustration 9.3b). If both camshafts have been removed, install the exhaust camshaft first, then the intake.

26 Lay the exhaust camshaft (marked FG/EX) onto the head with the EX mark on the sprocket facing forward and level with the cylinder head top mating surface, and fitting the cam chain around the sprocket, pulling up on the chain to remove all slack in the front run between the crankshaft and the camshaft (see illustrations).

27 Lay the intake camshaft (marked FG) onto the head with the IN mark on the sprocket facing back and level with the cylinder head top mating surface, and fitting the cam chain around the sprocket, pulling on it to remove all slack from between the two camshaft sprockets (see illustrations). Any slack in the chain must lie in the rear run between the intake camshaft and the crankshaft, to be taken up later by the tensioner.

28 Make sure the bearing surfaces in the camshaft holders are clean, then apply molybdenum disulphide oil (a 50/50 mixture of molybdenum disulphide grease and engine oil) to each of them. Make sure the camshaft holder bolt dowels and PAIR system air passage dowels are installed. Fit new sealing rings into the grooves around the spark plug holes on the underside of the main holders, making sure they also locate around the PAIR system air passage dowels (see illustration 9.6b). Lay the holders in the head making sure they are correctly positioned (see Step 6) (see illustration). Apply clean engine oil to the threads and under the heads of all the camshaft holder bolts. Fit the bolts, fitting the six longer ones where the dowels are fitted, and not forgetting new sealing washers with the eight bolts around the spark plug bores, and tighten them finger-tight (see illustrations). First gradually and evenly tighten the bolts until the holders contact the head, making sure they are drawn down squarely and the dowels all locate. Now tighten all the bolts evenly and a little at a time in the correct sequence (i.e. 1 to 20), and to the torque setting specified at the beginning of the Chapter.

Caution: Whilst tightening the bolts, make sure the holders are being pulled evenly and squarely down and are not binding on the dowels or tilting to one side – if they do, adjust the relevant bolts until the holders are again square to the head. A holder or camshaft is likely to break if they are not tightened down evenly and squarely.

29 If the tensioner tool was used to retract and hold the tensioner plunger, remove it to release the plunger. If the tensioner was removed, use a piece of wooden dowel to press on the back of the cam chain tensioner blade via the tensioner bore in the cylinder block to ensure that any slack in the cam chain is taken up and transferred to the rear run of the chain (where it will later be taken up by the tensioner). At this point check that all the timing marks are still in **exact** alignment as described in Step 3

(see illustration and 9.3b and c). Note that it is easy to be slightly out (one tooth on the sprocket) without the marks appearing

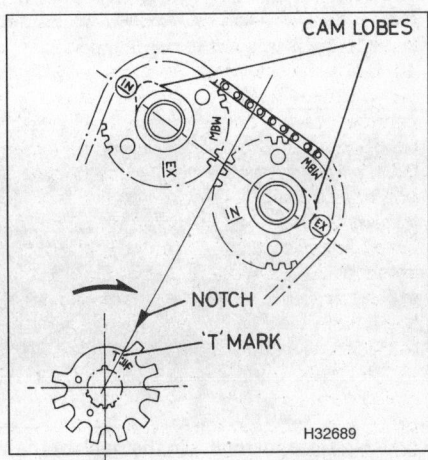

9.29 Timing mark alignment

2•18 Engine, clutch and transmission

9.32 Fit the cap O-ring and smear it and the threads with grease

drastically out of alignment. If the marks are out, verify which sprocket is misaligned, then either reinstall the tensioner locking tool and retract the plunger, or remove the wooden dowel. Unscrew the sprocket's bolts and slide it off the camshaft, then disengage it from the chain. Move the camshaft round as required, then fit the sprocket back into the chain and onto the camshaft, and check the marks again. With everything correctly aligned, apply a suitable non-permanent thread locking compound to the sprocket bolts and tighten them to the torque setting specified at the beginning of the Chapter.

Caution: *If the marks are not aligned exactly as described, the valve timing will be incorrect and the valves may strike the pistons, causing extensive damage to the engine.*

30 Fit the cam chain top guide and tighten its bolts **(see illustration 9.4)**. Either install the cam chain tensioner (see Section 8), or remove the tensioner holding tool, according to the method you used earlier.

31 Turn the engine clockwise through two full turns and check again that all the timing marks still align (see Step 3) **(see illustrations 9.3a, b and c and 9.29)**. Check the valve clearances and adjust them if necessary (see Chapter 1).

32 Fit the timing inspection cap using a new O-ring if required, and smear the O-ring with oil and the cap threads with grease **(see illustration)**. Tighten the cap to the torque setting specified at the beginning of the Chapter.

33 Install the valve cover (see Section 8). Install the spark plugs (see Chapter 1).

10 Cam chain, tensioner blades and front guide

Note: *The cam chain and its blades can be removed with the engine in the frame. If the engine has been removed, ignore the steps which do not apply.*

Removal

1 Remove the camshafts – this procedure involves removing the top guide blade (see Section 9).
2 Remove the starter clutch (see Section 13).
3 Draw the cam chain off the crankshaft sprocket and out of the engine **(see illustration)**. If required, slide the sprocket off the end of the crankshaft, noting the offset wide splines that mean it can only be installed in one position **(see illustration)**.
4 Unscrew the lower tensioner blade pivot bolt and draw the blade out of the engine **(see illustration)**. Remove the collar from the inner side of the blade pivot **(see illustration)**.
5 Unscrew the front guide blade pivot bolt and draw the blade out of the top of the engine **(see illustration)**.
6 Unscrew the upper tensioner blade pivot bolt and draw the blade out of the top of the engine **(see illustration)**. Remove the sealing washer and fit a new one on installation.

Inspection

Cam chain

7 Check the chain for binding, kinks and any obvious damage and replace it with a new one if necessary. Check the camshaft and crankshaft sprocket teeth for wear and replace the cam chain, camshaft sprockets and crankshaft with a new set if necessary.

Tensioner and guide blades

8 Check the sliding surface and edges of the blades for excessive wear, deep grooves, cracking and other obvious damage, and replace them with new ones if necessary.

Installation

9 Installation of the sprocket, chain and blades is the reverse of removal. Make sure the top of the lower tensioner blade sits to

10.3a Remove the cam chain . . .

10.3b . . . then slide the sprocket off the shaft

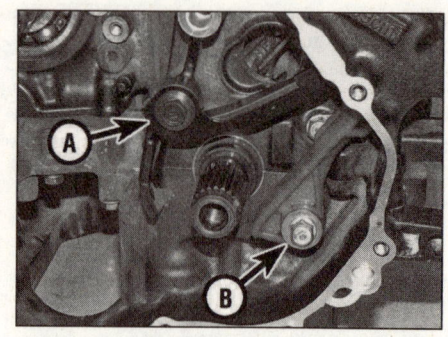

10.4a Lower tensioner blade pivot bolt (A), front guide blade pivot bolt (B)

10.4b Note the collar in the back of the pivot

10.5 Unscrew the pivot bolt and draw the blade out of the engine

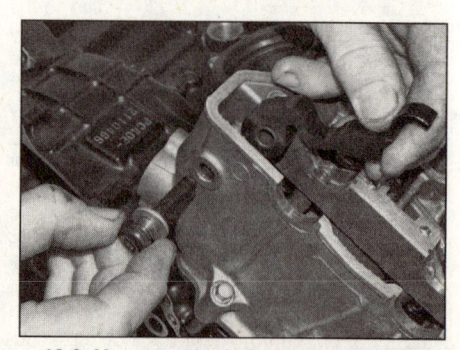

10.6 Unscrew the bolt and remove the upper tensioner blade

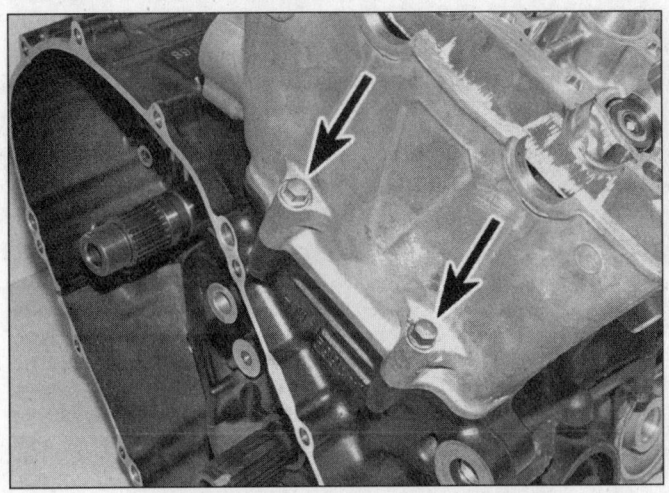

Engine, clutch and transmission 2•19

11.5a Cylinder head 6 mm bolts (arrowed)

11.5b Cylinder head 9 mm bolts (arrowed)

the front of the upper tensioner blade **(see illustration 8.3)**. Use a new sealing washer on the upper tensioner blade bolt **(see illustration 10.6)**. Do not omit the collar that fits in the lower tensioner blade pivot **(see illustration 10.4b)**. Clean the threads of all the bolts and apply a suitable non-permanent thread locking compound, and tighten them to the torque settings specified at the beginning of the Chapter.

11 Cylinder head

Note: *The cylinder head can be removed with the engine in the frame. If the engine has been removed, ignore the steps that do not apply.*

Removal

1 Remove the exhaust system (see Chapter 4).
2 Remove the air filter housing and throttle body assembly (see Chapter 4).
3 Remove the thermostat housing (see Chapter 3).
4 Remove the camshafts, followers and shims (see Section 9). If not already done (i.e. if the holding tool was used when removing the camshafts) remove the cam chain tensioner (see Section 8).
5 The cylinder head is secured by two 6 mm bolts and ten 9 mm bolts with fitted washers (i.e. they can't be separated from the bolts) **(see illustrations)**. First unscrew and remove the 6 mm bolts. Now unscrew and remove the 9 mm bolts, slackening them evenly and a little at a time in a criss-cross pattern working from the outside to the middle until they are all loose.
6 Hold the cam chain up and pull the cylinder head up off the block, then pass the cam chain down through the tunnel **(see illustration)**. Do not let the chain fall into the crankcase – secure it with a piece of wire or metal bar to prevent it from doing so. If the head is stuck, tap around the joint faces with a soft-faced mallet. Do not attempt to free the head by inserting a screwdriver between the head and block mating surfaces – you'll damage them.
7 Remove the cylinder head gasket and discard it – a new one must be used. If they are loose, remove the dowels from the crankcase or the underside of the cylinder head **(see illustration 11.11)**.
8 Check the cylinder head gasket and the mating surfaces on the cylinder head and crankcase for signs of leakage, which could indicate warpage. Refer to Section 12 and check the cylinder head gasket surface for warpage.
9 Clean all traces of old gasket material from the cylinder head and crankcase. If a scraper is used, take care not to scratch or gouge the soft aluminium. Be careful not to let any of the gasket material fall into the crankcase, the cylinder bore or the oil and coolant passages.

Installation

10 Ensure both cylinder head and crankcase mating surfaces are clean. If removed, fit the dowels **(see illustration 11.11)**.
11 Lay the new head gasket over the cam chain and blades and onto the crankcase, locating it over the dowels and making sure all the holes are correctly aligned **(see illustration)**. Never reuse the old gasket.

11.6 Carefully lift the head up off the block

11.11 Fit the dowels (arrowed) then lay the new gasket on the block

2•20 Engine, clutch and transmission

12 Carefully fit the cylinder head onto the block, making sure it locates correctly onto the dowels and that if not removed the upper tensioner blade sits to the rear of the lower blade **(see illustration 11.6)**. Feed the cam chain up through the tunnel as you install the head, then secure it in place with a piece of wire to prevent it from falling back down.

13 Apply some molybdenum disulphide oil (a 50/50 mixture of molybdenum disulphide grease and engine oil) to the threads and the underside of the heads and washers of the 9 mm bolts **(see illustration)**. Note that if new bolts are fitted, first remove any anti-rust coating by cleaning them with solvent. Fit the bolts and tighten them all finger-tight. Now tighten them evenly and a little at a time in a criss-cross pattern working from the middle to the outside to the torque setting specified at the beginning of the Chapter.

14 Fit the 6 mm bolts and tighten them **(see illustration 11.13)**.

15 Install the remaining components in a reverse of their removal sequence, referring to the relevant Sections or Chapters (see Steps 4 to 1).

12 Cylinder head and valve overhaul

1 Because of the complex nature of this job and the special tools and equipment required, most owners leave servicing of the valves, valve seats and valve guides to a professional. However, you can make an initial assessment of whether the valves are seating correctly,

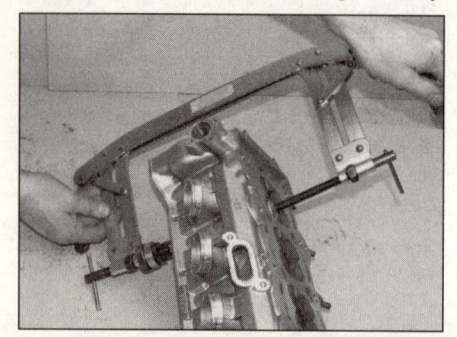

12.6a Compressing the valve springs using a valve spring compressor

12.6b Make sure the compressor locates correctly both on the top of the spring retainer . . .

11.13 Lubricate the bolts and tighten them as described to specified torque setting

and therefore sealing, by pouring a small amount of solvent into each of the valve ports. If the solvent leaks past any valve into the combustion chamber area the valve is not seating correctly and sealing.

2 With the correct tools (a valve spring compressor is essential – make sure it is suitable for motorcycle work), you can also remove the valves and associated components from the cylinder head, clean them and check them for wear to assess the extent of the work needed, and, unless seat cutting or guide replacement is required, grind in the valves and reassemble them in the head.

3 A dealer service department or specialist can replace the guides and re-cut the valve seats.

4 After the valve service has been performed, be sure to clean it very thoroughly before installation on the engine to remove any metal particles or abrasive grit that may still be present from the valve service operations. Use compressed air, if available, to blow out all the holes and passages.

Disassembly

5 Before proceeding, arrange to label and store the valves along with their related components in such a way that they can be returned to their original locations without getting mixed up **(see illustration)**. Either use the same container as the cam followers and shims are stored in (see Section 9), or obtain a separate container and label each compartment accordingly. Alternatively, labelled plastic bags will do just as well.

12.6c . . . and on the bottom of the valve

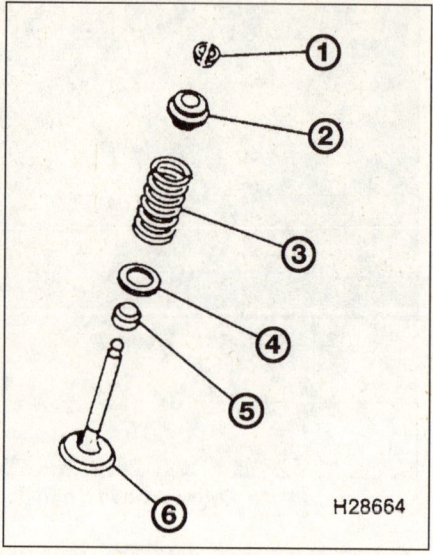

12.5 Valve components

1 Collets
2 Spring retainer
3 Spring
4 Spring seat
5 Valve stem oil seal
6 Valve

6 Compress the valve spring on the first valve with a spring compressor, making sure it is correctly located onto each end of the valve assembly **(see illustration)**. On the top of the valve the adaptor needs to be about the same size as the spring retainer – if it is too big it will contact the follower bore and mark it, and if it is too small it will be difficult to remove and install the collets **(see illustration)**. On the underside of the head make sure the plate on the compressor only contacts the valve and not the soft aluminium of the head **(see illustration)** – if the plate is too big for the valve, use a spacer between them. Do not compress the spring any more than is absolutely necessary.

Caution: Take great care not to mark the cam follower bore with the spring compressor.

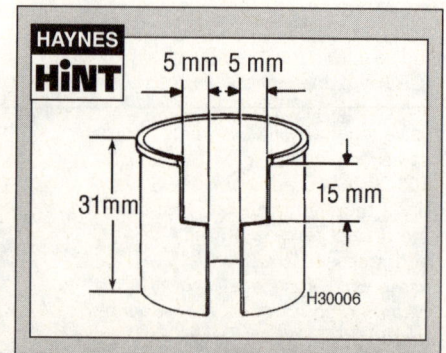

HAYNES HiNT

Protect the follower bore in the cylinder head from scratches by the valve spring compressor using either the Honda tool (Part No. 07HMG-MR70002) or by fabricating a shield from a 35 mm film canister. Cut the canister to the dimensions shown.

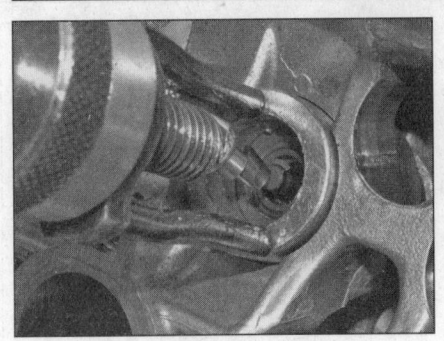

12.7a Remove the collets . . .

12.7b . . . the spring retainer and spring . . .

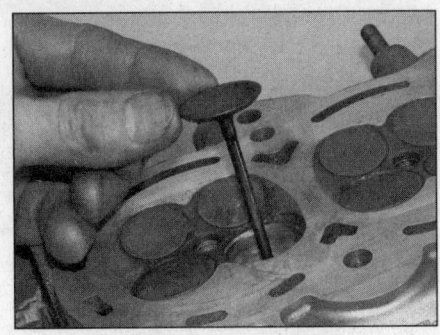

12.7c . . . and the valve

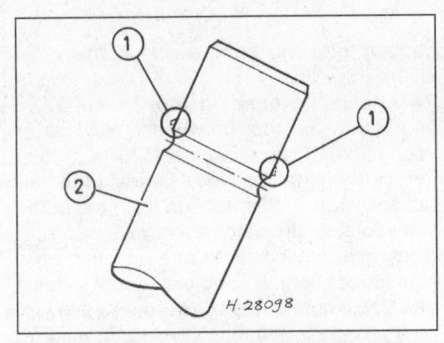

12.7d If the valve stem (2) won't pull through the guide, deburr the area above the collet groove (1)

12.8a Pull the seal off the valve stem . . .

12.8b . . . then remove the spring seat

7 Remove the collets, using a magnet or a screwdriver with a dab of grease on it **(see illustration)**. Carefully release the valve spring compressor and remove the spring retainer, noting which way up it fits, the spring and the valve **(see illustrations)**. If the valve binds in the guide and won't pull through, push it back into the head and deburr the area around the collet groove with a very fine file or whetstone **(see illustration)**.

8 Pull the valve stem seal off the top of the valve guide with pliers and discard it (the old seals should never be reused), then remove the spring seat noting which way up, it fits – using a magnet is the easiest way to remove the seat from the head **(see illustrations)**.

9 Repeat the procedure for the remaining valves. Remember to keep the parts for each valve together so they can be reinstalled in the same location.

10 Clean the cylinder head with solvent and dry it thoroughly. Compressed air will speed the drying process and ensure that all holes and recessed areas are clean. **Note:** *Do not use a wire brush mounted in a drill motor to clean the combustion chambers as the head material is soft and may be scratched or eroded away by the wire brush.*

11 Clean all of the valve springs, collets, retainers and spring seats with solvent and dry them thoroughly. Do the parts from one valve at a time so that no mixing of parts between valves occurs.

12 Scrape off any deposits that may have formed on the valve, then use a motorised wire brush to remove deposits from the valve heads and stems. Again, make sure the valves do not get mixed up.

Inspection

13 Inspect the head very carefully for cracks and other damage. If cracks are found, a new head is required. Check the camshaft bearing surfaces for wear and evidence of seizure. Check the camshafts and holders for wear as well (see Section 9).

14 Using a precision straight-edge and a feeler gauge set to the warpage limit listed in the specifications at the beginning of the Chapter, check the head gasket mating surface for warpage. Refer to *Tools and Workshop Tips* in the Reference section for details of how to use the straight-edge. If the head is warped beyond the limit specified at the beginning of this Chapter, consult a Honda dealer or take it to a specialist repair shop for an opinion, though be prepared to have to buy a new one.

15 Examine the valve seats in the combustion chamber. If they are pitted, cracked or burned, the head will require work beyond the scope of the home mechanic. Measure the valve seat width and compare it to this Chapter's Specifications **(see illustration)**. If it exceeds the service limit, or if it varies around its circumference, overhaul is required.

16 Working on one valve and guide at a time, measure the valve stem diameter **(see illustration)**. Clean the valve's guide using a guide reamer to remove any carbon build-up – insert the reamer from the underside of the head and turn it clockwise only. Now measure the inside diameter of the guide (at

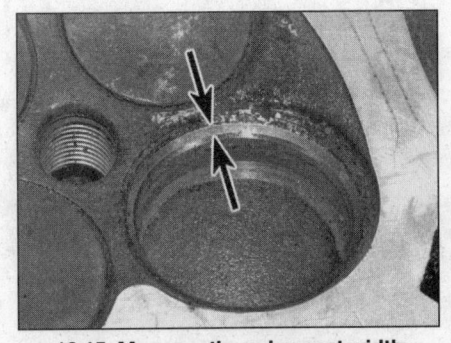

12.15 Measure the valve seat width

12.16a Measure the valve stem diameter with a micrometer

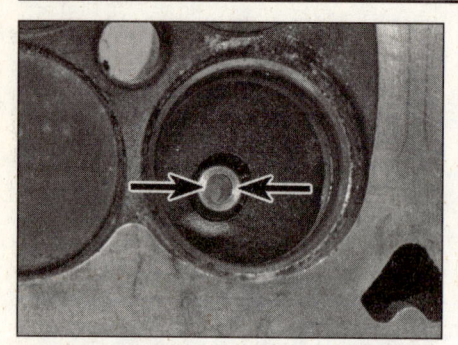

12.16b Measure the valve guide with a small bore gauge, then measure the bore gauge with a micrometer

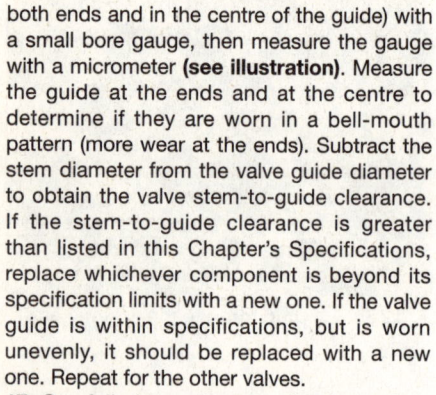

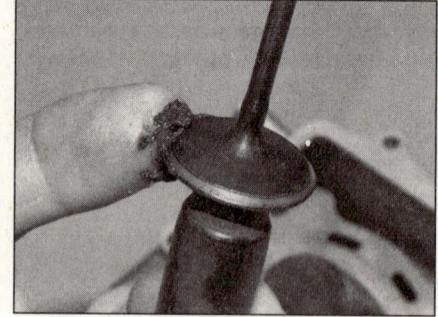

12.23 Apply dabs of paste round the valve face

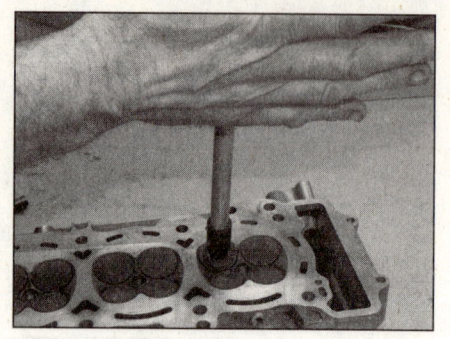

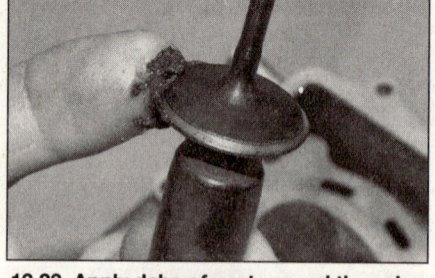

12.24 Rotate the valve grinding tool back and forth between the palms of your hands

both ends and in the centre of the guide) with a small bore gauge, then measure the gauge with a micrometer **(see illustration)**. Measure the guide at the ends and at the centre to determine if they are worn in a bell-mouth pattern (more wear at the ends). Subtract the stem diameter from the valve guide diameter to obtain the valve stem-to-guide clearance. If the stem-to-guide clearance is greater than listed in this Chapter's Specifications, replace whichever component is beyond its specification limits with a new one. If the valve guide is within specifications, but is worn unevenly, it should be replaced with a new one. Repeat for the other valves.

17 Carefully inspect each valve face, stem and collet groove area for cracks, pits and burned spots.

18 Rotate the valve and check for any obvious indication that it is bent, in which case it must be replaced with a new one. Check the end of the stem for pitting and excessive wear. The presence of any of the above conditions indicates the need for valve servicing.

19 Check the end of each valve spring for wear and pitting. Measure the spring free lengths and compare them to the specifications **(see illustration 14.13)**. If any spring is shorter than specified it has sagged and must be replaced with a new one. Also place the spring upright on a flat surface and check it for bend by placing a ruler against it, or alternatively lay it against a set-square. If the bend in any spring is excessive, it must be replaced with a new one.

20 Check the spring seats, retainers and collets for obvious wear and cracks. Any questionable parts should not be reused, as extensive damage will occur in the event of failure during engine operation.

21 If the inspection indicates that no overhaul work is required, the valve components can be reinstalled in the head.

Reassembly

22 Unless a valve service has been performed, before installing the valves they should be ground in (lapped) to ensure a positive seal between the valves and seats. This procedure requires coarse and fine valve grinding compound and a valve grinding tool (either hand-held or drill driven – note that some drill-driven tools specify using only a fine grinding compound). If a grinding tool is not available, a piece of rubber or plastic hose can be slipped over the valve stem (after the valve has been installed in the guide) and used to turn the valve.

23 Apply a small amount of coarse grinding compound to the valve face **(see illustration)**. Smear some molybdenum disulphide oil (a 50/50 mixture of molybdenum disulphide grease and engine oil) to the valve stem, then slip the valve into the guide **(see illustration 12.29)**. **Note:** *Make sure each valve is installed in its correct guide and be careful not to get any grinding compound on the valve stem.*

24 Attach the grinding tool to the valve and rotate the tool between the palms of your hands. Use a back-and-forth motion (as though rubbing your hands together) rather than a circular motion (i.e. so that the valve rotates alternately clockwise and anti-clockwise rather than in one direction only) **(see illustration)**. If a motorised tool is being used, take note of the correct drive speed for it – if your drill runs too fast and is not variable, use a hand tool instead. Lift the valve off the seat and turn it at regular intervals to distribute the grinding compound properly. Continue the grinding procedure until the valve face and seat contact area is of uniform width, and unbroken around the entire circumference.

25 Carefully remove the valve and wipe off all traces of grinding compound, making sure none gets in the guide. Use solvent to clean the valve and wipe the seat area thoroughly with a solvent soaked cloth.

26 Repeat the procedure with fine valve grinding compound, then use solvent to clean the valve and flush the guide, and wipe the seat area thoroughly with a solvent soaked cloth. Repeat the entire procedure for the remaining valves. On completion thoroughly clean the entire head again, then blow through all passages with compressed air. Make sure all traces of the grinding compound have been removed before assembling the head.

27 Working on one valve at a time, lay the spring seat in place in the cylinder head with its shouldered side facing up **(see illustration)**. As it is easy to cock the seat on the top of the valve guide, and then tricky to get it to sit properly, fit it using a rod (such as a screwdriver) as a guide for it to slide down.

28 Fit a new valve stem seal onto the guide, using finger pressure, a stem seal fitting tool or an appropriate size deep socket, to push the seal squarely onto the end of the valve guide until it is felt to clip into place **(see illustration)**. Make sure the seal does not get cocked sideways as it could be damaged – using a rod as a guide as for the seat helps.

29 Coat the valve stem with molybdenum disulphide oil (a 50/50 mixture of molybdenum disulphide grease and engine oil), then slide

12.27 Fit the spring seat using a rod to guide it if necessary

12.28 Fit a new valve stem seal and press it squarely into place

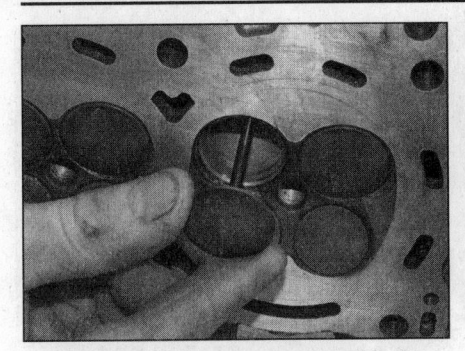

Engine, clutch and transmission 2•23

12.29 Lubricate the stem and slide the valve into its correct location

12.30a Fit the spring ...

12.30b ... then fit the spring retainer

it into its guide, rotating it slowly to avoid damaging the seal **(see illustration)**. Check that the valve moves up-and-down freely in the guide.

30 Next, fit the spring, with the closer-wound coils facing down into the cylinder head **(see illustration)**. Fit the spring retainer, with its shouldered side facing down so that it fits into the top of the spring **(see illustration)**.

31 Apply a small amount of grease to the collets to help hold them in place. Compress the valve spring with a spring compressor, making sure it is correctly located onto each end of the valve assembly (see Step 6) **(see illustrations 12.6a, b and c)**. Do not compress the spring any more than is necessary to slip the collets into place. Locate each collet in turn into the groove in the valve stem using a screwdriver with a dab of grease on it **(see illustration)**. Carefully release the compressor, making sure the collets seat and lock in the retaining groove.

32 Repeat the procedure for the remaining valves. Remember to keep the parts for each valve together and separate from the other valves so they can be reinstalled in the same location.

33 Support the cylinder head on blocks so the valves can't contact the work surface, then tap the end of each valve stem lightly to seat the collets in their grooves **(see illustration)**.

> **HAYNES HINT**: *Check for proper sealing of the valves by pouring a small amount of solvent into each of the valve ports. If the solvent leaks past any valve into the combustion chamber the valve grinding operation on that valve should be repeated.*

34 After the cylinder head and camshafts have been installed, check the valve clearances and adjust as required (see Chapter 1).

13 Starter clutch and gears

Note: *The starter clutch can be removed with the engine in the frame. If the engine has been removed, ignore the steps that do not apply.*

Check

1 The operation of the starter clutch can be checked while it is in situ. Remove the

12.31 Locate each collet in its groove in the top of the valve stem

starter motor (see Chapter 8). Check that the reduction gear is able to rotate freely clockwise as you look at it via the starter motor aperture, but locks when rotated anticlockwise **(see illustration)**. If not, the starter clutch is faulty and should be removed for inspection.

Removal

2 Remove the clutch cover (see Section 14, Steps 1 to 4).

3 To prevent the crankshaft from turning while unscrewing the starter clutch bolt, wedge a thick piece of rag material or a piece of

12.33 Seat the collets as described

13.1 Check the gear turns as described

2•24 Engine, clutch and transmission

13.3a Using a piece of aluminium to jam the gears . . .

13.3b . . . while unscrewing the bolt

13.3c Remove the idle gear and shaft

aluminium (DO NOT use steel) between the starter idle and driven gears at the top as shown **(see illustration)**. Unscrew the bolt and remove the washer **(see illustration)**. Remove the idle gear shaft and gear as an assembly, along with the washers if not already removed **(see illustration)**.

4 Slide the starter clutch off the shaft, noting the offset wide splines that mean it can only be installed in one position **(see illustration)**. Remove the thrust washer **(see illustration)**.

5 If you need to remove the reduction gear first remove the clutch (see Section 14). Remove the reduction gear **(see illustration)**.

Inspection

6 With the starter clutch face down on a workbench, check that the starter driven gear rotates freely clockwise and locks against the rotor anti-clockwise **(see illustration)**. If it doesn't, the starter clutch should be dismantled for further investigation.

7 Withdraw the starter driven gear from the starter clutch **(see illustration)**. If the gear appears stuck, rotate it clockwise as you withdraw it to free it from the starter clutch. Remove the needle bearing **(see illustration)**.

8 Check the condition of the sprags inside the

13.4a Slide the starter clutch off . . .

13.4b . . . and remove the thrust washer

13.5 Remove the reduction gear

13.6 Check the operation of the clutch as described

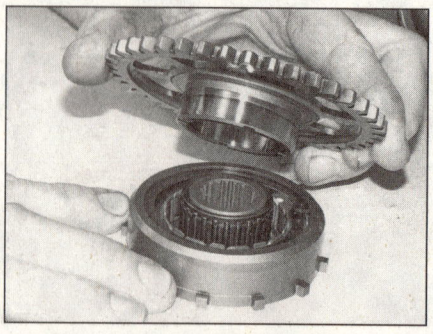

13.7a Withdraw the driven gear . . .

13.7b . . . and remove the bearing

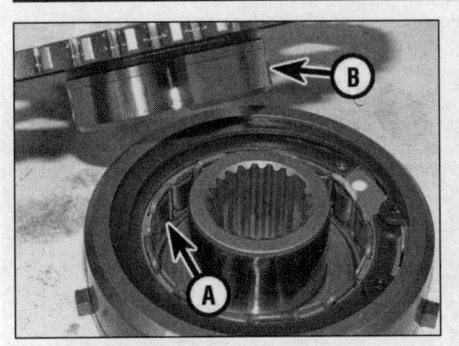

Engine, clutch and transmission 2•25

13.8a Check the sprags (A) and the surface of the hub (B)

13.8b Remove the circlip . . .

13.8c . . . and push the sprag assembly out

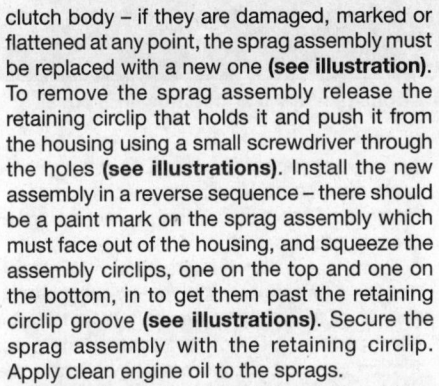

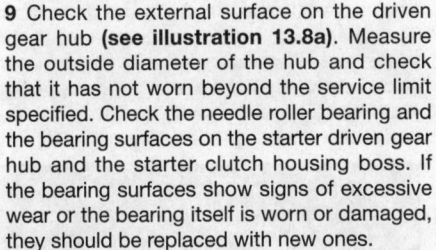

clutch body – if they are damaged, marked or flattened at any point, the sprag assembly must be replaced with a new one **(see illustration)**. To remove the sprag assembly release the retaining circlip that holds it and push it from the housing using a small screwdriver through the holes **(see illustrations)**. Install the new assembly in a reverse sequence – there should be a paint mark on the sprag assembly which must face out of the housing, and squeeze the assembly circlips, one on the top and one on the bottom, in to get them past the retaining circlip groove **(see illustrations)**. Secure the sprag assembly with the retaining circlip. Apply clean engine oil to the sprags.

9 Check the external surface on the driven gear hub **(see illustration 13.8a)**. Measure the outside diameter of the hub and check that it has not worn beyond the service limit specified. Check the needle roller bearing and the bearing surfaces on the starter driven gear hub and the starter clutch housing boss. If the bearing surfaces show signs of excessive wear or the bearing itself is worn or damaged, they should be replaced with new ones.

10 Check the teeth of the reduction and idle gears and the corresponding teeth of the starter driven gear and starter motor drive shaft. Replace the gears and/or starter motor if worn or chipped teeth are discovered on related gears. Also check the idle gear shaft for damage, and check that the gear is not a

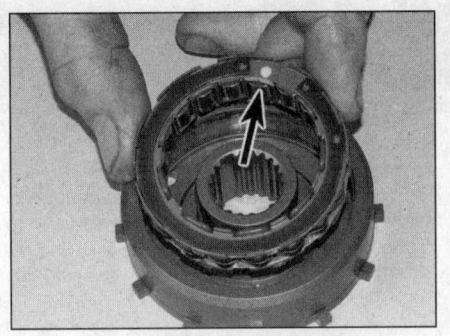

13.8d Fit the assembly with the paint mark (arrowed) facing out . . .

loose fit on it. Check the reduction gear shaft ends and the bores they run in for wear.

Installation

11 Lubricate the needle roller bearing with clean engine oil and fit it over the starter clutch boss **(see illustration 13.7b)**. Lubricate the outside of the starter driven gear hub with clean engine oil, then fit the gear into the clutch, rotating it clockwise as you do so to spread the sprags and allow the hub to enter **(see illustration 13.7a)**.

12 If removed, lubricate the reduction gear shaft ends with clean engine oil then locate the inner end of the shaft in its bore in the crankcase, engaging it with the starter motor

13.8e . . . and squeeze the assembly circlips in to get them past the groove

shaft teeth if installed **(see illustration 13.5)**. Install the clutch (see Section 14).

13 Slide the thrust washer onto the crankshaft and against the cam chain sprocket **(see illustration 13.4b)**. Align the wide splines on the starter clutch with those on the crankshaft and slide the starter clutch on with the driven gear on the inside **(see illustration 13.4a)**.

14 Apply clean oil to the threads and under the head of the starter clutch bolt. Fit the bolt with its washer and tighten it to the torque setting specified at the beginning of the Chapter, noting that the rag or piece of aluminium to prevent crankshaft rotation must now be wedged between the primary drive and driven gears at the bottom as shown **(see illustrations)**.

13.14a Fit the lubricated bolt with its washer

13.14b Fit the wedge between the gears at the bottom (arrow) while tightening the bolt

2•26 Engine, clutch and transmission

14.3 CKP sensor wiring connector (arrowed)

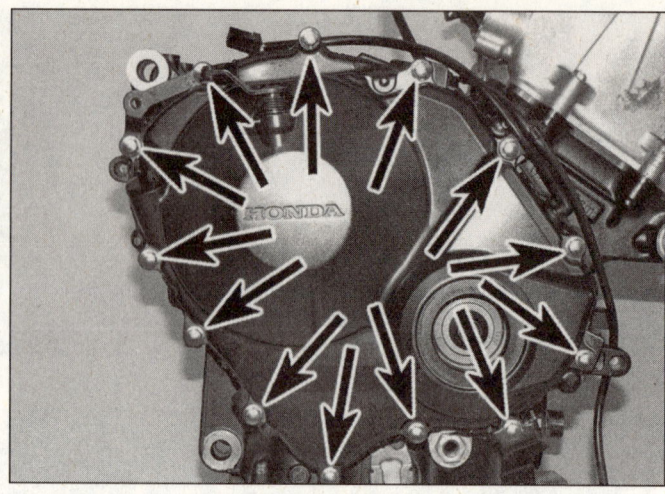

14.4a Unscrew the bolts (arrowed) and remove the cover

15 Lubricate the idle gear shaft with clean engine oil and fit it into the gear. Locate the idle gear, shouldered side inwards, between the reduction gear and the driven gear and slide the shaft into its bore in the crankcase **(see illustration 13.3c)**.
16 Install the clutch cover (see Section 14, Steps 29 to 32).

14 Clutch

Note 1: *The clutch can be removed with the engine in the frame. If the engine has been removed, ignore the steps that don't apply.*
Note 2: *The clutch nut must be discarded and a new one used on installation – it is best to obtain the new nut in advance.*

Removal

1 On CBR600F/FA models remove the right-hand fairing side panel (see Chapter 7). On all models drain the engine oil (see Chapter 1).
2 Unscrew the bolt securing the clutch cable bracket **(see illustration 4.19a)**. Displace the bracket, noting how it locates, and free the cable end from the release arm **(see illustration 4.19b)**.
3 Raise the fuel tank (see Chapter 4). Trace the crankshaft position (CKP) sensor wiring from the top of the clutch cover and disconnect it at the red 2-pin wiring connector **(see illustration)**. Feed the wiring down to the cover, noting the routing.
4 Working evenly in a criss-cross pattern, unscrew the clutch cover bolts, noting the wiring clamp, and on CBR600F/FA models the fairing bracket **(see illustration)**. Remove the cover, turning the release lever arm back (anti-clockwise) as you do to disengage the shaft from the pull-rod. Note that there is a thrust washer and a wave washer on the end of the idle gear shaft which may come away with the cover and could therefore drop from it – if they stay on the end of the shaft remove them for safekeeping if required **(see illustration)**. Be prepared to catch any residual oil. Remove the four dowels from either the cover or the crankcase if they are loose. Do not turn the engine with the clutch cover removed or the reduction gear could be damaged.
5 Working in a criss-cross pattern, gradually slacken the clutch spring bolts until pressure is released **(see illustration)**. To prevent the assembly from turning, cover it with a rag and hold it securely – the bolts are not very tight. If available, have an assistant to hold the clutch while you unscrew the bolts. Remove the bolts and springs, then remove the pressure plate **(see illustration)**. Remove the pull-rod from either the back of the pressure plate or the end of the shaft.
6 Remove the clutch friction and plain plates, hooking them out as necessary, noting how they fit and keeping them in order **(see illustration)**. Note how the tabs on the outer friction plate locate in the shallow slots in the housing, while the rest sit in the deep slots. The outer and inner friction plates are different to the rest – the outer plate has larger friction sections than the others, and the inner friction plate has a larger internal diameter so that it fits over the anti-judder spring and spring

14.4b Remove the thrust washer and wave washer (arrowed) if required

14.5a Unscrew the bolts (arrowed) and remove the springs . . .

14.5b . . . then remove the pressure plate and pull-rod (arrowed)

14.6 Remove the clutch plate assembly

Engine, clutch and transmission 2•27

14.7a Unstake the nut . . .

14.7b . . . then unscrew it as described and remove the washers

seat. All other plates have one coloured tab end. To prevent confusion, make sure you keep the plates in the correct order. Remove the anti-judder spring and spring seat, noting which way round they fit **(see illustrations 14.26b and a)**.

7 The clutch nut is staked against the input shaft. Unstake the nut using a hammer and punch – take care not to damage the threads on the end of the shaft **(see illustration)**. To remove the clutch nut, the input shaft must be locked. This can be done in several ways. If the engine is in the frame, engage 6th gear and have an assistant hold the rear brake on hard with the rear tyre in firm contact with the ground. Alternatively, the Honda service tool (part No. 07724-0050002), or a similar commercially available tool can be used to stop the clutch centre from turning whilst the nut is slackened **(see illustration)**. Unscrew the nut and remove the spring washer and the thrust washer **(see illustrations 14.25b and a)**. Discard the nut – a new one must be used on installation.

8 Remove the clutch centre and the thrust washer from the shaft **(see illustrations 14.24b and a)**.

9 Ease out the clutch guide and needle bearing from between the clutch housing and the input shaft – this can be done using pliers on the raised tab and by sliding the housing on the shaft to help push them along if necessary **(see illustration)**. Remove the clutch housing. Note how the holes in the back of the housing engage with the pins on the oil pump drive sprocket.

10 If required, lock the oil pump driven sprocket to prevent it from turning and unscrew the bolt **(see illustration 18.2)** – block the opening to the sump with rag in case you drop the bolt. Remove the driven sprocket, the chain and the drive sprocket together **(see illustration)**. Remove the drive sprocket guide **(see illustration)**. If required unscrew the chain guide bolts and remove the guides, noting how they locate over the pins – note the collar fitted into the inner side of the front guide **(see illustration)**.

Inspection

11 After an extended period of service the clutch friction plates will wear and promote clutch slip. Measure the thickness of each friction plate using a Vernier caliper **(see illustration)**. If any plate has worn to or beyond the service limits given in the Specifications at the beginning of the Chapter, or if any of the plates smell burnt or are glazed, replace all the friction plates with a new set.

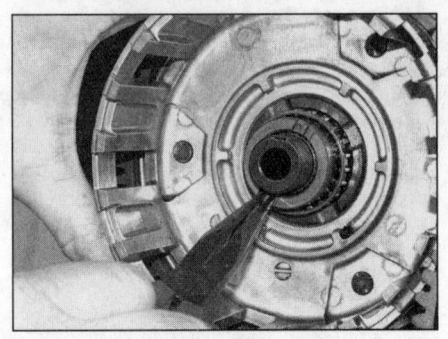

14.9 Ease the bearing and guide out from the middle of the housing then remove the housing

14.10a Remove the sprockets and chain . . .

14.10b . . . and the guide

14.10c Chain guide bolts (arrowed)

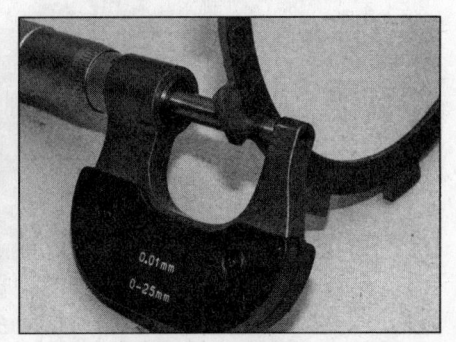

14.11 Measuring clutch friction plate thickness

2•28 Engine, clutch and transmission

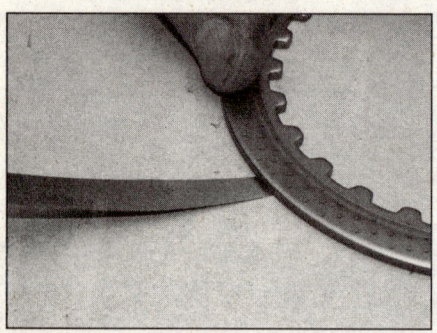

14.12 Check the plain plates for warpage

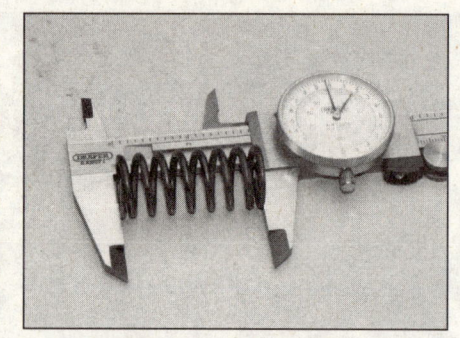

14.13 Measure the free length of the clutch springs and check them for bend

14.14a Check the friction plate tabs and housing slots . . .

14.14b . . . and the plain plate teeth and centre slots as described

14.15 Check the bearing and the bearing surfaces in the housing and on the guide

12 The plain plates should not show any signs of excess heating (bluing). Check for warpage using a flat surface and feeler gauges **(see illustration)**. If any plate exceeds the maximum permissible amount of warpage, or shows signs of bluing, replace all the plain plates with a new set.

13 Measure the free length of each clutch spring using a Vernier caliper **(see illustration)**. Place each spring upright on a flat surface and check it for bend by placing a ruler against it, or alternatively lay it against a set square. If any spring is below the minimum free length specified or if the bend in any spring is excessive, replace all the springs with a new set. Also check the anti-judder spring and spring seat for damage or distortion and replace them with new ones if necessary.

14 Inspect the friction plates and the clutch housing for burrs and indentations on the edges of the protruding tabs on the plates and/or the slots in the housing **(see illustration)**. Similarly check for wear between the inner teeth of the plain plates and the slots in the clutch centre **(see illustration)**. Wear of this nature will cause clutch drag and slow disengagement during gear changes as the plates will snag when the pressure plate is lifted. With care a small amount of wear can be corrected by dressing with a fine file, but if this is excessive the worn components should be replaced with new ones.

15 Inspect the needle roller bearing and the bearing surfaces in the clutch housing and on the clutch guide **(see illustration)**. If there are any signs of wear, pitting or other damage the affected parts must be replaced with new ones.

16 Using a Vernier caliper, measure the internal and external diameter of the clutch guide, the internal diameter of the clutch housing and the external diameter of the input shaft where the guide sits **(see illustration 14.15)**. Compare the measurements to the specifications at the beginning of the Chapter and replace any part that is worn beyond its service limit with a new one. Similarly measure the internal and external diameter of the oil pump drive sprocket guide, the internal diameter of the sprocket and the external diameter of the input shaft where the guide sits **(see illustration)**.

17 Check the pressure plate and its bearing and the pull-rod for signs of wear or damage and roughness **(see illustration)**. Check that the bearing outer race is a good fit in the centre of the pressure plate, and that the inner race rotates freely without any rough spots.

14.16 Check the related surfaces as described

14.17 Check the pressure plate and its bearing

Engine, clutch and transmission 2•29

14.18a Withdraw the shaft

14.18b Removing the seal

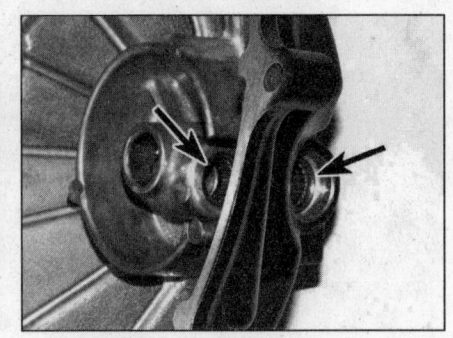

14.18c Check the bearings (arrowed)

Check the pull-rod end and the corresponding cut-out in the release lever shaft for signs of wear or damage. Replace any parts necessary with new ones.

18 Check the release mechanism in the clutch cover for a smooth action. If the action is stiff or rough, withdraw the shaft, noting how the return spring ends locate, and remove the washer **(see illustration)**. Check the oil seal in the top of the cover – it can be removed by levering it out with a seal hook or screwdriver **(see illustration)**. Clean and check the two needle bearings in the cover **(see illustration)**. Press the new seal in **(see illustration)**. Lubricate the bearings with oil and the seal lips with grease before installing the shaft. Make sure the return spring ends locate correctly **(see illustration)**.

19 Check the teeth of the primary driven gear on the back of the clutch housing and the corresponding teeth of the primary drive gear on the crankshaft. Replace the clutch housing and/or crankshaft with a new one if worn or chipped teeth are discovered.

Installation

20 Remove all traces of old sealant from the crankcase and clutch cover surfaces. Note that if removed the starter reduction gear must be installed now as it cannot be fitted once the clutch is in place – see Section 13, Step 12.

21 If removed, clean the threads of the oil pump drive chain guide bolts and apply a suitable non-permanent thread locking compound. Make sure the collar is fitted into

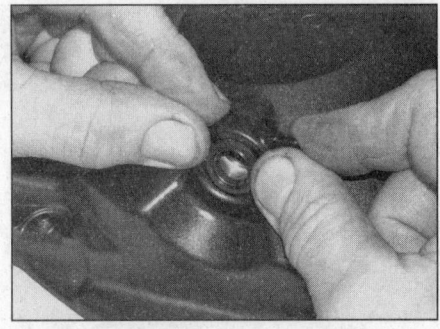

14.18d Press the new seal in

the front guide, then fit the guides, locating their holes over the pins, and tighten the bolts **(see illustration 14.10c)**. Smear the inside and outside of the oil pump drive sprocket guide and the inside of the sprocket with molybdenum disulphide oil (a 50/50 mixture of molybdenum disulphide grease and engine oil). Slide the guide onto the input shaft with the flanged end inwards **(see illustration 14.10b)**.

22 Slide the oil pump drive sprocket onto the guide, making sure the pins face out **(see illustration 14.10a)**. Slip the chain around the sprocket. Engage the driven sprocket with the chain, making sure the OUT mark faces out, then locate the sprocket on the oil pump **(see illustration 18.18)**. Clean the threads of the sprocket bolt and apply a suitable non-permanent thread locking compound, and tighten it to the torque setting specified

14.18e Make sure the spring ends (arrowed) locate correctly

at the beginning of the chapter, locking it as before **(see illustration 18.2)**. Oil the chain.

23 Smear the inside and outside of the clutch guide, the inside of the clutch housing and the needle bearing with molybdenum disulphide oil (a 50/50 mixture of molybdenum disulphide grease and engine oil) **(see illustration 14.15)**. Position the clutch housing and hold it then slide the clutch guide and needle bearing onto the shaft and into the centre of the housing **(see illustrations)**. Make sure that the primary drive and driven gear teeth engage and the pins on the oil pump drive sprocket locate in the holes in the rear of the housing – turn the driven sprocket with your finger while pressing on the housing until the pins are felt to locate and the housing moves in a bit further, then double-check by making sure the sprocket can't turn independently of the housing **(see illustration)**.

14.23a Position the housing over the shaft and engage the primary gears . . .

14.23b . . . then slide the guide and bearing in . . .

14.23c . . . and check everything has engaged correctly

2•30 Engine, clutch and transmission

14.24a Fit the thrust washer . . .

14.24b . . . and the clutch centre

14.25a Fit the thrust washer and the spring washer, with the OUT mark facing out

14.25b Fit a new clutch nut . . .

14.25c . . . and tighten it to the specified torque

14.25d Stake the nut against the detent in the shaft end . . .

14.25e . . . as shown

24 Slide the thrust washer onto the shaft (see illustration). Slide the clutch centre onto the shaft splines (see illustration).
25 Fit the thrust washer and the spring washer with its OUT mark facing out (see illustration). Smear the new clutch nut threads and seat with oil, then thread it onto the input shaft and, using the method employed on removal to lock the shaft (see Step 7), tighten the nut to the torque setting specified at the beginning of the Chapter (see illustrations). Stake the collar of the nut into the indent on the end of the shaft (see illustrations).

26 Fit the anti-judder spring seat into the clutch centre, then fit the spring so that its outer edge is raised off the seat and facing outwards (see illustrations).
27 Coat each clutch plate with engine oil prior to installation, then build up the plates as follows: fit the friction plate with the larger internal diameter over the spring and spring seat (see illustration), then fit a plain plate, then alternate standard friction plates (with one coloured tab end) and plain plates until all except the outer plate (with the larger friction sections) are installed, then fit that with its tabs fitting

14.26a Fit the anti-judder spring seat and spring . . .

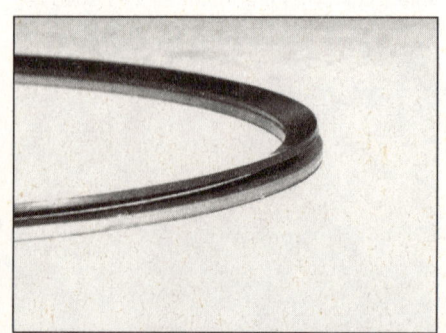

14.26b . . . with the spring's outer edge raised off the seat

14.27a Fit the friction plate with the larger internal diameter first, locating it around the anti-judder assembly . . .

Engine, clutch and transmission 2•31

14.27b ... then fit a plain plate ...

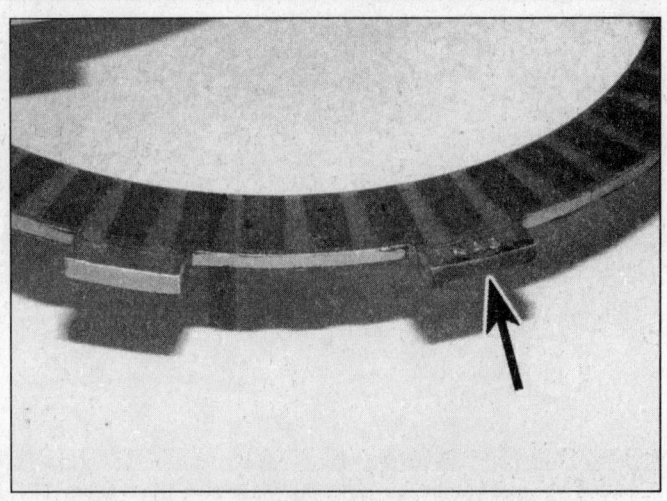

14.27c The standard plates have one coloured tab end (arrowed) ...

14.27d ... and the outer plate has larger friction sections (arrowed)

14.27e Locate the tabs on the outer friction plate into the shallow slots in the housing

into the shallow slots in the housing **(see illustrations)**.

28 Lubricate the bearing in the pressure plate. Fit the pull-rod into the shaft **(see illustration)**. Fit the pressure plate onto the clutch, engaging the protrusions on its inner rim in the slots in the clutch centre **(see illustration 14.5b)**. Fit the springs and the bolts and tighten them evenly in a criss-cross sequence to the specified torque setting **(see illustration)**. Counter-hold the clutch housing to prevent it turning when tightening the spring bolts.

29 If removed fit the wave washer and the thrust washer onto the end of the starter idle gear shaft **(see illustration 14.4b)**. Lubricate the reduction and idle gear shaft outer ends with oil.

30 Apply a smear of a suitable sealant (such as Three Bond 1207B or equivalent RTV sealant – ask your dealer) to the entire mating surface on the clutch cover **(see illustration)**. Also apply the sealant 10 to 15 mm either side of the crankcase joints on the mating surface

14.28a Fit the pull-rod into the shaft

14.28b Fit the springs and bolts and tighten them as described

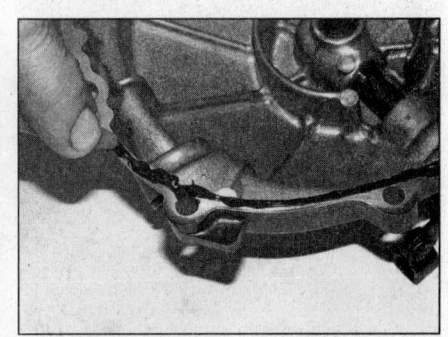

14.30a Apply sealant to the cover ...

2•32 Engine, clutch and transmission

14.30b ... and crankcase joints (A). Make sure the dowels (B) are fitted

14.30c Fit the cover making sure the release mechanism engages

with the clutch cover. Fit the four dowels into the crankcase if removed **(see illustration)**. Fit the cover, pulling the release lever arm back (anti-clockwise) as you do then moving it forward so that it engages behind the pull-rod end as you push the cover home on the dowels and shaft ends **(see illustration)**. Fit the bolts (except the clutch cable bracket bolt) finger tight, not forgetting the wiring clamp and on CBR600F/FA models the fairing bracket, then tighten them evenly and a little at a time in a criss-cross pattern **(see illustration 14.4a)**.

31 Reconnect the crankshaft position (CKP) sensor wiring connector **(see illustration 14.3)**. Engage the clutch cable end in the release lever arm, then locate the bracket on the cover and tighten the bolt **(see illustrations 4.19b and a)**.

32 Fill the engine with the correct type and quantity of oil (see Chapter 1). Lower the fuel tank (see Chapter 4). On CBR600F/FA models install the fairing panel (See Chapter 7).

15 Clutch cable

1 Fully slacken the lockring on the adjuster at the handlebar end of the cable, then thread the adjuster fully in **(see illustration)**. This provides freeplay in the cable and resets the adjuster to the beginning of its span.

2 Raise the fuel tank (see Chapter 4).

3 Slacken the nuts on the threaded section of the cable in the bracket on the clutch cover, then thread the front nut as far up as it will go and thread the rear nut off **(see illustration)**. Slide the cable into the bracket to get some freeplay and free the cable end from the release lever, noting how it fits **(see illustration)**. Draw the cable out of the bracket **(see illustration)**.

4 Align the slots in the adjuster and lockring at the handlebar end of the cable with that in the lever bracket, then pull the outer cable end from the socket in the adjuster and release the inner cable from the lever **(see illustrations)**.

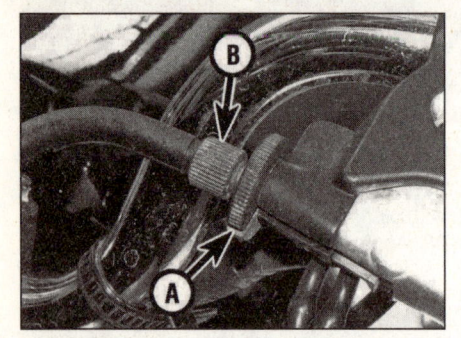

15.1 Slacken the lockring (A) and turn the adjuster (B) in

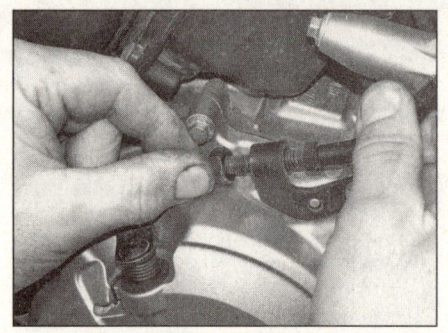

15.3a Thread the front nut up and the rear nut off . . . . .

15.3b ... then free the end from the release lever ...

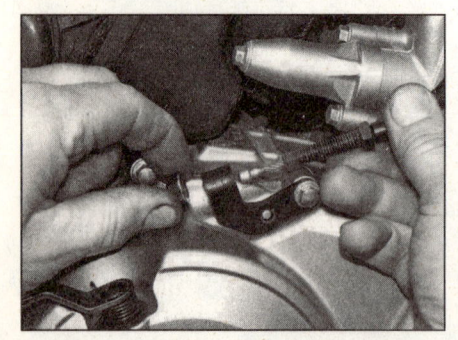

15.3c ... and draw the cable out of the bracket

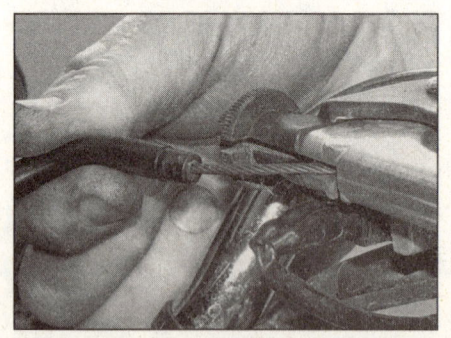

15.4a Align the slot(s) and free the cable from the adjuster ...

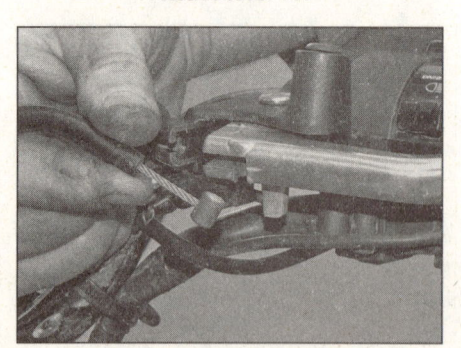

15.4b ... and from the lever

Engine, clutch and transmission 2•33

16.2 Note the alignment of the clamp on the shaft

16.4a Unscrew the bolt (arrowed) and remove the plate

16.4b Withdraw the shaft/arm assembly, noting how it fits

Remove the cable from the machine, noting its routing.

> **HAYNES HiNT**
> Before removing the cable from the bike, tape the lower end of the new cable to the upper end of the old cable. Slowly pull the lower end of the old cable out, guiding the new cable down into position. Using this method will ensure the cable is routed correctly.

5 Installation is the reverse of removal. Apply grease to the cable ends. Make sure the cable is correctly routed. Adjust the amount of clutch lever freeplay (see Chapter 1).

16 Gearchange mechanism

Note: *The gearchange mechanism can be removed with the engine in the frame. If the engine has been removed, ignore the steps that don't apply.*

Removal

1 Make sure the transmission is in neutral. Remove the clutch (see Section 14) – there is no need to remove the oil pump drive and driven sprockets and chain. Block the holes into the sump with clean rag to prevent anything falling in.

2 Unscrew the gearchange linkage arm pinch bolt and slide the arm off the shaft, noting how the slit in the arm aligns with the punch mark on the shaft **(see illustration)**.
3 Wrap a single layer of thin insulating tape around the gearchange shaft splines to protect the oil seal lips as the shaft is removed.
4 Unscrew the gearchange mechanism retainer plate bolt and remove the plate **(see illustration)**. Note how the gearchange shaft centralising spring ends fit on each side of the locating pin in the casing, and how the pawls on the selector arm locate onto the pins on the end of the selector drum cam. Grasp the end of the shaft and withdraw the shaft/arm assembly **(see illustration)**. Retrieve the washer from the crankcase if it didn't come with the shaft.
5 If required, note how the stopper arm spring ends locate and how the roller on the arm locates in the neutral detent on the selector drum cam, then unscrew the stopper arm bolt and remove the arm, the washer and the spring, noting how they fit **(see illustration)**.

Inspection

6 Check the selector arm for cracks, distortion and wear of its pawls, and check for any corresponding wear on the pins on the selector drum cam **(see illustration)**. Check the arm moves up smoothly and freely and returns under pressure of its spring **(see illustration)**. Also check the stopper arm roller

16.5 Note how the spring ends locate, and how the roller sits in the neutral detent, then unscrew the bolt (arrowed) and remove the arm

and the detents in the selector drum cam for any wear or damage, and make sure the roller turns freely **(see illustration)**. Replace any components that are worn or damaged with new ones. If required, refer to the illustrations in Section 28 and remove the selector drum cam by unscrewing the bolt in its centre. Note the locating pin in the end of the drum and remove it for safekeeping if required. On installation, locate the pin in the wider cut-out in the back of the cam. Clean the threads of the cam bolt and apply a suitable non-permanent thread locking compound, and tighten it to the torque setting specified at the beginning of the Chapter.
7 Inspect the shaft centralising spring and the stopper arm return spring for fatigue, wear or

16.6a Check the selector arm pawls and the pins . . .

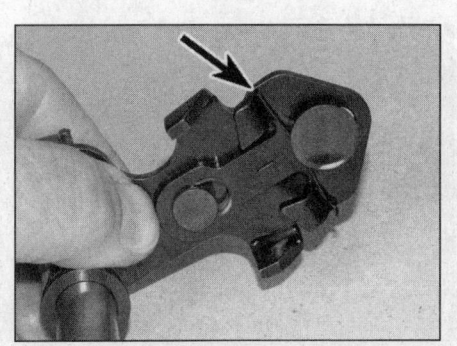

16.6b . . . and check the action of the arm and its spring (arrowed)

16.6c Check the stopper arm roller and cam as described

16.7 Check the springs (arrowed)

16.8a Unscrew the bolt (arrowed) and remove the plate . . .

16.8b . . . then lever out the seal

16.8c Check the bearing (arrowed)

16.8d Press the new seal into its housing

damage **(see illustration)**. If any is found, the components must be replaced with new ones. To replace the shaft spring, slide the inner washer off the shaft, then remove the circlip and slide the outer washer and the spring off the shaft, noting how its ends locate. Fit the new spring, locating the ends on each side of the tab, and the outer washer and secure them with the circlip, making sure it locates in its groove. Slide the inner washer against the circlip. Also check that the centralising spring locating pin in the crankcase is securely tightened. If it is loose, remove it, clean the threads and apply a non-permanent thread locking compound, then tighten it.

8 Check the gearchange shaft is straight and look for damage to the splines. If the shaft is bent you can attempt to straighten it, but if the splines are damaged the shaft must be replaced with a new one. Also check the condition of the shaft oil seal in the left-hand side of the crankcase. If it is damaged, deteriorated or shows signs of leakage it must be replaced with a new one – unscrew the seal retainer plate bolt and remove the plate **(see illustration)**. Lever out the old seal with a seal hook or screwdriver **(see illustration)**. With the seal removed, check the condition of the needle bearing, and replace that as well if necessary – refer to *Tools and Workshop Tips* in the Reference Section **(see illustration)**. Fit the new bearing and press or drive the new seal squarely into place using your fingers, a seal driver or suitable socket **(see illustration)**. Fit the retainer plate and tighten its bolt.

Installation

9 If removed, clean the threads of the stopper arm bolt and apply a suitable non-permanent thread locking compound. Fit the bolt through the stopper arm, then fit the washer and the stopper arm return spring onto the bolt **(see illustration)**. Fit the arm, locating the roller onto the neutral detent on the selector drum and making sure the spring ends are positioned correctly **(see illustration)**. Tighten the bolt to the torque setting specified at the beginning of the Chapter. Check that the arm and spring ends are correctly positioned **(see illustration 16.5)**.

10 Check that the shaft centralising spring is properly positioned and slide the washer onto the shaft if removed **(see illustration 16.7)**. Apply some grease to the lips of the gearchange shaft oil seal in the left-hand side of the crankcase. Slide the shaft into place and push it all the way through the case until the splined end comes out the other side **(see illustration 16.4b)**. Locate the selector arm pawls onto the pins on the selector drum and the centralising spring ends onto each side of the locating pin in the crankcase **(see illustration)**. Clean the threads of the retainer plate bolt and apply a suitable non-permanent thread locking compound, then fit the plate and tighten the bolt **(see illustration 16.4a)**.

11 Remove the rag that was blocking the sump, then install the clutch (see Section 14).

12 Remove the insulating tape from around the gearchange shaft splines. Slide the gearchange linkage arm onto the shaft, aligning its slit with the punch mark on the shaft **(see illustration 16.2)**. Fit the pinch bolt and tighten it.

16.9a Assemble the stopper arm components as shown . . .

16.9b . . . then fit the arm and tighten the bolt

16.10 Make sure everything is correctly positioned then fit the retainer plate

Engine, clutch and transmission 2•35

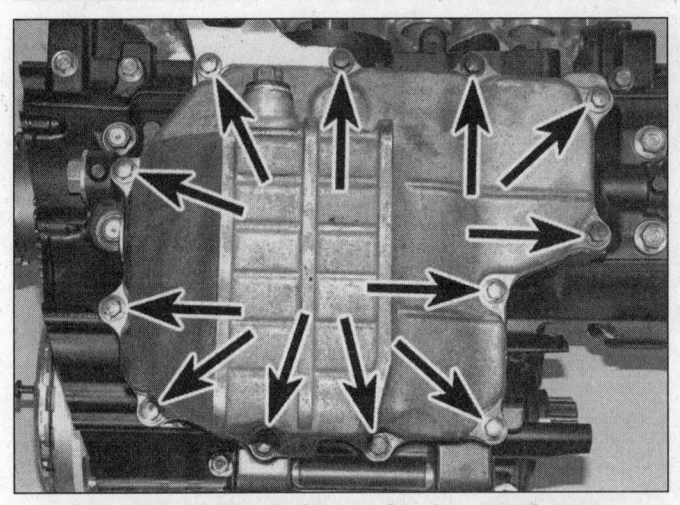

17.3 Unscrew the bolts (arrowed) and remove the sump

17.4 Remove the strainer, noting how the tab locates in the groove

17 Oil sump, oil strainer and pressure relief valve

Note: *The oil sump, strainer and pressure relief valve can be removed with the engine in the frame. If the engine has been removed, ignore the steps that don't apply.*

Removal

1 Remove the exhaust system (see Chapter 4).
2 Drain the engine oil (see Chapter 1).
3 Slacken the sump bolts evenly in a criss-cross sequence to prevent distortion, then remove the bolts and remove the sump **(see illustration)**.
4 Pull the strainer out, noting how it locates **(see illustration)**. Remove the rubber seal – a new one must be used.
5 Pull the pressure relief valve out of its socket **(see illustration)**. Remove the O-ring – a new one must be used.

Inspection

6 Remove all traces of sealant from the sump and crankcase mating surfaces, and clean the inside of the sump with solvent. Blow the sump dry with compressed air if available.
7 Clean the oil strainer in solvent and

17.5 Pull the relief valve out of its socket

remove any debris caught in the mesh **(see illustration)**. If the strainer gauze is damaged, replace the strainer with a new one.
8 Push the relief valve plunger into the valve body and check that it moves smoothly and freely against spring pressure **(see illustration)**. If not, remove the circlip, noting that it is under spring pressure, then remove the washer, spring and plunger. Clean all components in solvent, then check the plunger and the valve body for evidence of scoring, wear and any other damage. If any is found, replace the relief valve with a new one – individual components are not available. Otherwise, coat the plunger

17.7 Clean the mesh (arrowed)

with oil and fit it closed end first back into the valve and recheck the movement. If it is good, install the spring and washer and secure them with the circlip.

Installation

9 Fit a new O-ring onto the relief valve and smear it with clean oil **(see illustration)**. Push the valve into its socket in the sump **(see illustration and 17.5)**.
10 Fit a new rubber seal smeared with clean oil into the strainer orifice in the crankcase **(see illustration)**. Do not fit it onto the strainer as it will distort when the strainer is fitted onto the

17.8 Push the plunger into the body and check that it moves smoothly

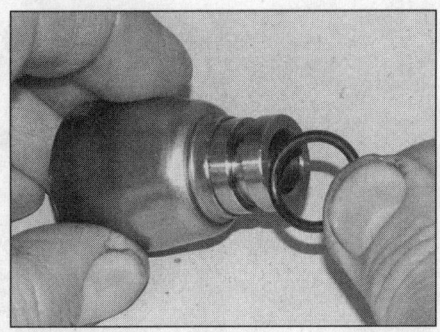

17.9 Fit a new O-ring onto the relief valve body

17.10a Lubricate the rubber seal and fit it into the crankcase

2•36 Engine, clutch and transmission

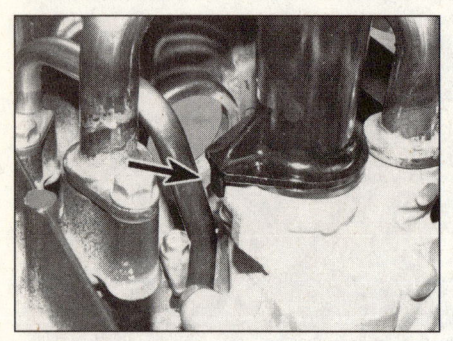

17.10b Locate the tab (arrowed) in the slot

17.11a Apply the sealant . . .

17.11b . . . then install the sump

pump. Fit the strainer, locating the tab in the cut-out in the crankcase **(see illustration)**.
11 Clean the mating surfaces of the sump and crankcase with solvent. Apply a suitable sealant (such as Three Bond 1207B or equivalent RTV sealant – ask your dealer) to the sump mating surface **(see illustration)**. Position the sump onto the crankcase and fit the bolts finger-tight **(see illustration)**. Tighten the bolts evenly and a little at a time in a criss-cross pattern **(see illustration 17.3)**.
12 Install the exhaust system.
13 Fill the engine with the correct type and quantity of oil as described in Chapter 1. Start the engine and check that there are no leaks around the sump.

18 Oil pump

Note: *The oil pump can be removed with the engine in the frame. If the engine has been removed, ignore the steps which don't apply.*

Removal

1 Remove the clutch cover (Section 14, Steps 1 to 4), and the sump and oil strainer (Section 17).
2 Lock the oil pump driven sprocket to prevent it from turning and unscrew the bolt (see illustration). Remove the driven sprocket **(see illustration 18.18)**.
3 Unscrew the large oil pipe bolts and remove the pipe **(see illustration)**. Remove the sealing rings – new ones must be used. Note that removal of the small oil pipe is not necessary for oil pump removal, but if required it can be unbolted from the crankcase, although the water pump must first be removed (see Chapter 3) **(see illustration)**. Remove the O-rings – new ones must be used.
4 Unscrew the pump mounting bolts and remove the pump, noting how it fits **(see illustration)**. Remove the dowels from either the crankcase or the pump if they are loose **(see illustration)**.

18.2 Lock the sprocket and unscrew its bolt

18.3a Large oil pipe bolts (arrowed)

18.3b Small oil pipe bolts (arrowed)

18.4a Unscrew the bolts (arrowed) and remove the pump

18.4b Remove the dowels (arrowed)

Engine, clutch and transmission 2•37

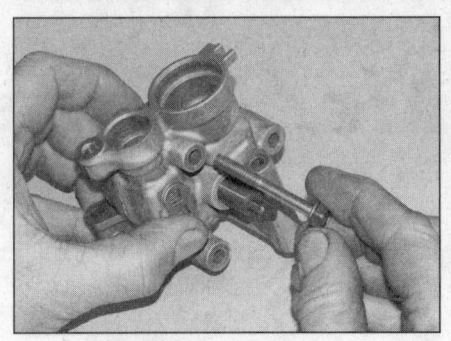

18.5a Unscrew the bolts . . .

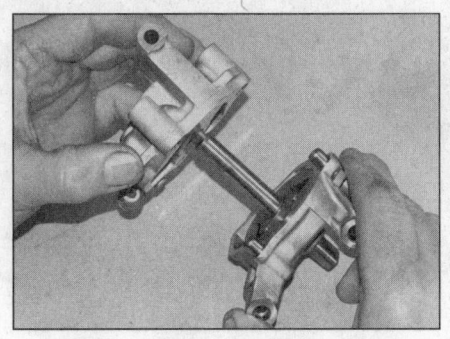

18.5b . . . and remove the cover . . .

18.5c . . . and the dowels

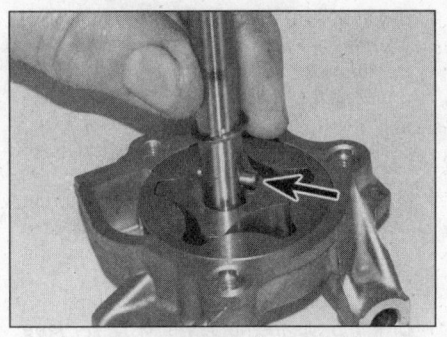

18.5d Remove the washer and drive pin (arrowed) . . .

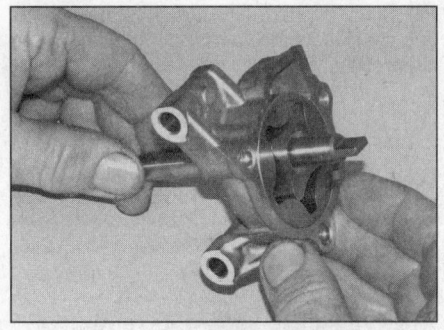

18.5e . . . and withdraw the shaft

18.5f Remove the rotors

Inspection

5 Unscrew the pump body bolts and draw the cover off the shaft **(see illustrations)**. Remove the dowels from the cover or body if loose **(see illustration)**. Remove the thrust washer and drive pin, noting how it fits, then withdraw the shaft from the pump **(see illustration)**. Remove the inner and outer rotors, marking which way round the outer rotor fits **(see illustration)**.

6 Clean all the components in solvent. Also clean the oil pipes, and blow through them with compressed air.

7 Inspect the pump body and rotors for scoring and wear. If any damage, scoring or uneven or excessive wear is evident, replace the pump with a new one (individual components are not available).

8 Fit the inner and outer rotors into the pump body, then insert the shaft. Measure the clearance between the inner rotor tip and the outer rotor with a feeler gauge and compare it to the service limit listed in the specifications at the beginning of the Chapter **(see illustration)**. If the clearance measured is greater than the maximum listed, replace the pump with a new one.

9 Measure the clearance between the outer rotor and the pump body with a feeler gauge and compare it to the maximum clearance listed in the specifications at the beginning of the Chapter **(see illustration)**. If the clearance measured is greater than the maximum listed, replace the pump with a new one.

10 Lay a straight-edge across the rotors and the pump body and, using a feeler gauge, measure the rotor end-float (the gap between the rotors and the straight-edge **(see illustration)**. If the clearance measured is greater than the maximum listed, replace the pump with a new one.

11 Check the pump drive chain and drive and driven sprockets for wear or damage, and replace them with a new set if necessary.

12 If the pump is good, make sure all the components are clean, then lubricate them with new engine oil.

13 Fit the outer rotor into the pump body the same way as noted on removal **(see illustration 18.5f)**. Fit the inner rotor into the outer rotor with the cut-outs in the inner rotor facing out **(see illustration 18.5f)**. Slide the drive shaft through the inner rotor and pump body, making sure the end with the driven sprocket bolt hole is on the outer side and the tabbed end is on the inner side **(see illustration 18.5e)**. Slide the drive pin into its hole in the driveshaft and locate it into the cut-outs in the inner rotor, then slide the thrust washer onto the shaft so it covers the drive pin **(see illustration 18.5d)**. Fit the dowels if

18.8 Measure the inner rotor tip-to-outer rotor clearance

18.9 Measure the outer rotor-to-body clearance

18.10 Measure rotor end-float

2•38 Engine, clutch and transmission

18.16a Locate the pump and align the driveshaft if necessary . . .

18.16b . . . and fit the longest bolt as shown

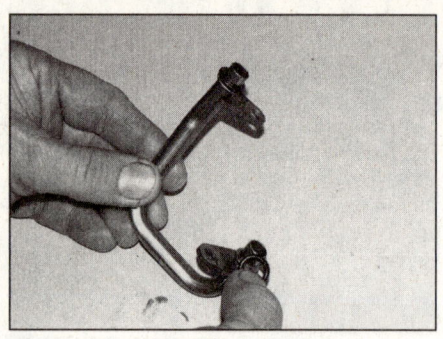

18.17a Fit new O-rings onto the small pipe

removed (see illustration 18.5c). Slide the cover onto the pump (see illustration 18.5b). Fit the bolts, longest one in the position shown, and tighten them to the torque setting specified at the beginning of the Chapter (see illustration 18.5a).
14 Rotate the pump shaft by hand and check it turns the rotors smoothly and freely.

Installation

15 Pour some clean engine oil into the pump and rotate the shaft to prime the pump. Fit the pump locating dowels if removed (see illustration 18.4b).
16 Manoeuvre the pump into position and onto the dowels – if the water pump has not been removed rotate the oil pump drive shaft to align the tab on its end with the slot in the water pump shaft (see illustration). Fit the mounting bolts, longest bolt in the position shown, and tighten them (see illustration).
17 Clean the threads of the oil pipe bolts. If the small pipe was removed fit a new O-ring smeared with oil onto each end (see illustration). Locate the pipe in the crankcase, then apply a suitable non-permanent thread locking compound to the bolts and tighten them (see illustration 18.3b). Fit a new sealing ring smeared with oil onto each end of the large pipe (see illustration). Locate the pipe in the pump and crankcase, then apply a suitable non-permanent thread locking compound to the bolts and tighten them to the torque setting specified at the beginning of the Chapter, tightening the rear bolt first (see illustration 18.3a).
18 Engage the pump driven sprocket with the chain, making sure the OUT mark faces out, then locate the sprocket on the shaft (see illustration). Clean the threads of the sprocket bolt and apply a suitable non-permanent thread locking compound, and tighten it to the torque setting specified at the beginning of the chapter (see illustration 18.2).
19 Install the oil strainer and sump (Section 17) and the clutch cover (Section 14, Steps 29 to 32), and if removed the water pump (see Chapter 3).

19 Crankcase separation and reassembly

Note 1: *To separate the crankcase halves, the engine must be removed from the frame.*
Note 2: *The 8 mm crankshaft journal bolts in the lower crankcase are of the stretch type, which can only be used in a running engine once, though they can be used when performing the oil clearance check detailed in Section 22 to prevent having to buy two sets of new bolts. The new bolts come pre-coated with an oil additive that must not be cleaned off.*

Separation

1 To access the pistons, connecting rods, crankshaft, bearings, transmission shafts and selector drum and forks, the crankcase must be split into its two halves.
2 Before the crankcases can be separated the following components must be removed:
Valve cover (Section 7)
Camshafts (Section 9) – see Note*
Cylinder head (Section 11) – see Note*
Alternator (Chapter 8)
Starter clutch (Section 13)
Cam chain and blades (Section 10) – see Note*
Clutch, oil pump drive chain and sprockets (Section 14)
Water pump (Chapter 3)
Gearchange mechanism (Section 16) – see Note*
Oil cooler (Section 6)
Starter motor (Chapter 8)
Oil sump, strainer and pressure relief valve (Section 17)
Oil pump (Section 18)
Speed sensor (Chapter 8)
Note*: *If the crankcases are being separated to inspect the crankshaft without removing it, the camshafts and cylinder head can remain in situ. To remove the crankshaft without removing the connecting rods and pistons, the camshafts must be removed but the head can stay. However, if removal of the connecting rod assemblies is intended, full disassembly of the top-end is necessary. To inspect or remove the transmission shafts and selector drum and forks, the camshafts and cylinder head can remain in situ. The gearchange mechanism can remain in situ unless the transmission and selector drum and forks are being removed.*
3 Unscrew the three 6 mm upper crankcase bolts and the 8 mm bolt evenly, a little at a time and in a criss-cross sequence until they are finger-tight, then remove them, noting the bolts fitted with sealing washers (see illustration).

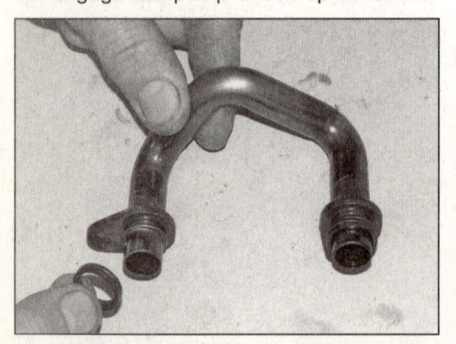

18.17b Fit new sealing rings onto the large pipe

18.18 Fit the sprocket into the chain with the OUT mark out

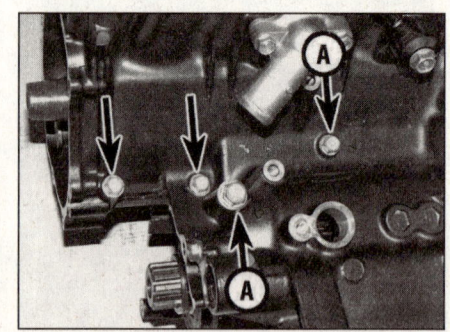

19.3 Upper crankcase bolts (arrowed) – the bolts marked A have sealing washers

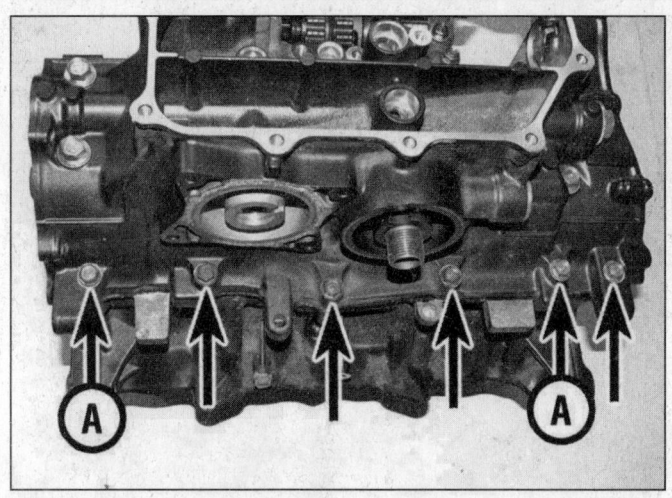

Engine, clutch and transmission 2•39

19.5a Lower crankcase 6 mm bolts (arrowed) – the bolts marked A have sealing washers. . .

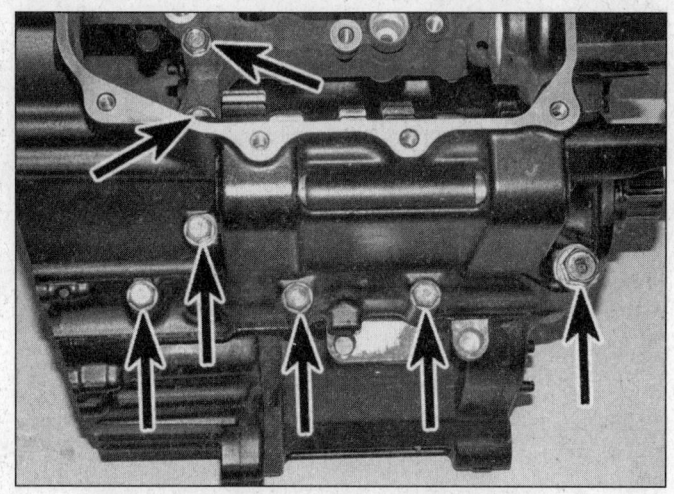

19.5b Lower crankcase 6 mm bolts and 10 mm bolt

Note: *As each bolt is removed, store it in its relative position in a cardboard template of the crankcase halves* **(see illustration 19.5c)**. *This will ensure all bolts and washers are installed in the correct location on reassembly. Note that new sealing washers should be used on assembly where fitted, though it is wise to keep the old ones with the bolts for the time being as a pattern for the new ones.*

4 Turn the engine upside down and support it as required using wooden blocks.

5 Unscrew the one 10 mm and the twelve 6 mm lower crankcase bolts evenly, a little at a time and in a criss-cross sequence until they are finger-tight, then remove them, noting the 6 mm bolts along the front are fitted with sealing washers **(see illustrations)**. **Note:** *As each bolt is removed, store it in its relative position in a cardboard template of the crankcase halves* **(see illustration)**. *This will ensure all bolts are installed in the correct location on reassembly.*

6 Now unscrew the ten 8 mm crankshaft journal bolts evenly, a little at a time and in a reverse of the tightening sequence, i.e. starting from the outside and working to the centre, until they are finger-tight, then remove them **(see illustration)**.

7 Carefully lift the lower crankcase half off the upper half, using a soft-faced hammer to tap around the joint to initially separate the halves if necessary **(see illustration)**. **Note:** *If the halves do not separate easily, make sure all fasteners have been removed. Do not try and separate the halves by levering against the crankcase mating surfaces as they are easily scored and will leak oil in the future if damaged.* The lower crankcase half will come away leaving the crankshaft, transmission shafts and selector drum and forks in the upper crankcase half.

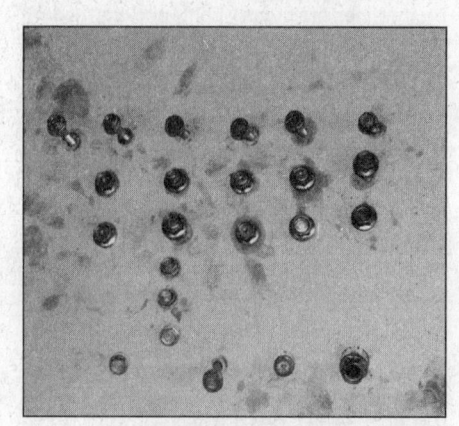

19.5c Cardboard template for storing the lower crankcase bolts

8 Remove the three locating dowels from the crankcase if they are loose (they could

19.6 Crankshaft journal bolts (arrowed) – the bolts marked (A) are longer

19.7 Carefully separate the crankcase halves

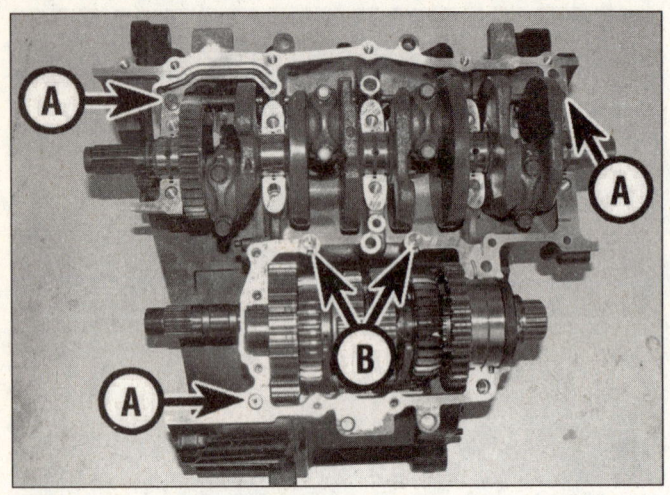

2•40 Engine, clutch and transmission

19.8 Remove the dowels (A) if they are loose, and the oil jets (B)

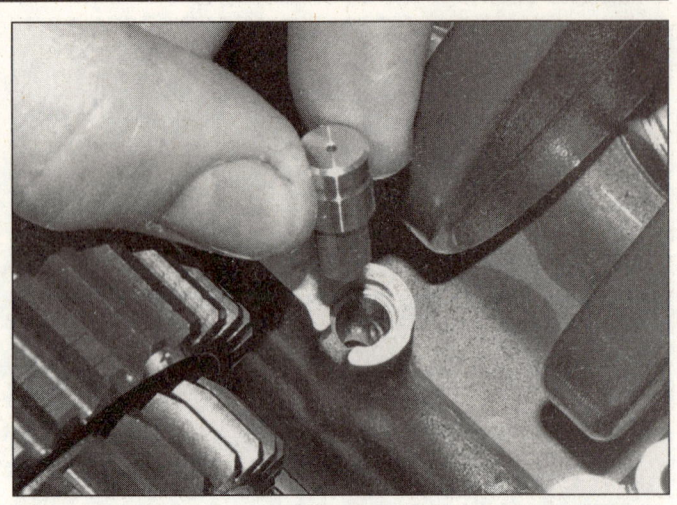

19.13 Fit the oil jets with the flats against the corresponding flats in the bores

be in either crankcase half), and the two oil jets, noting how they fit **(see illustration and 19.13a and b)**.

9 Refer to Sections 20 to 28 for the removal and installation of the components housed within the crankcases.

Reassembly

10 Remove all traces of sealant from the crankcase mating surfaces.

11 Ensure that all components and their bearings are in place in the upper and lower crankcase halves. If the transmission shafts have not been removed, check the condition of the oil seal on the left-hand end of the output shaft and replace it with a new one if it is damaged or deteriorated – it is advisable to fit a new one as a matter of course **(see illustration 26.11)**.

12 Generously lubricate the crankshaft and transmission shafts, particularly around the bearings, with clean engine oil, then use a rag soaked in high flash-point solvent to wipe over the mating surfaces of both crankcase halves to remove all traces of oil.

13 If removed, fit the three locating dowels and the two oil jets in the upper crankcase half **(see illustration 19.8)** – align the flat sides of the jets with the flats in the crankcase **(see illustration)**.

14 Apply a small amount of suitable sealant (Three-Bond 1207B or equivalent RTV sealant – ask your dealer) to the outer mating surface of the lower crankcase half as shown **(see illustrations)**.

Caution: Apply the sealant only to the shaded areas. Do not apply an excessive amount as it will ooze out when the case halves are assembled and may obstruct oil passages. Do not apply the sealant close to any of the bearing shells or surfaces, or oil passages.

15 Check again that all components are in position, particularly that the bearing shells are still correctly located in the lower crankcase half. Carefully fit the lower crankcase half down onto the upper crankcase half, making sure the dowels locate correctly **(see illustration 19.7)**.

16 Check that the lower crankcase half is correctly seated.

Caution: The crankcase halves should fit together without being forced. If the casings are not correctly seated, remove the lower crankcase half and investigate the problem. Do not attempt to pull them together using the crankcase bolts as the casing will crack and be ruined.

17 Fit the ten NEW 8 mm crankshaft journal bolts – there are two different lengths, with four longer ones, so make sure all are correctly positioned as shown **(see illustration 19.6)**. Secure all bolts finger-tight at first, then tighten them evenly, in three stages and in

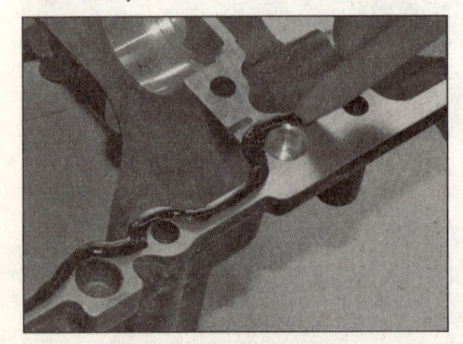

19.14a Apply the sealant . . .

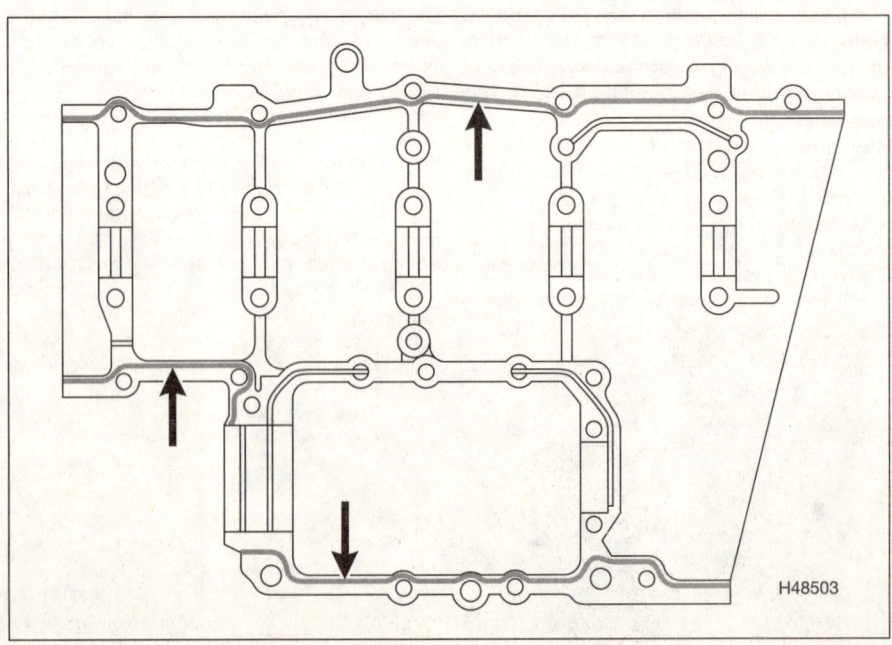

19.14b . . . to the shaded area shown

Engine, clutch and transmission 2•41

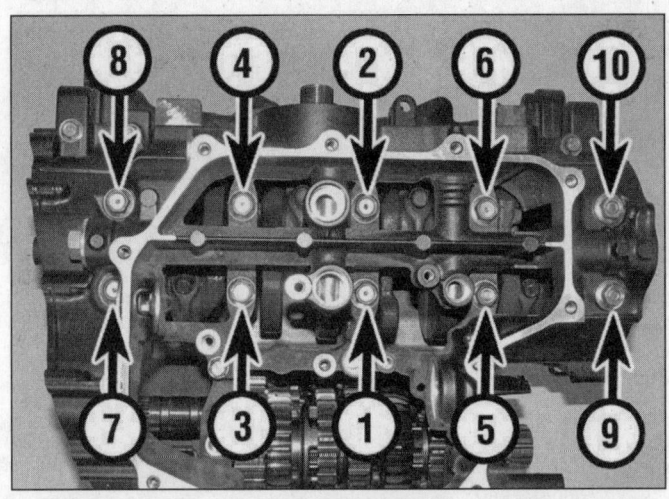

19.17a Tighten the bolts in sequence to the specified torque setting . . .

19.17b . . . and through the specified angle

the numerical sequence shown to the torque setting specified at the beginning of the Chapter **(see illustration)** – tighten them in increments of 5 Nm to ensure three equal stages up to the specified torque. Now, using a degree disc, tighten each bolt in turn and in one go by a further 120°, again following the numerical sequence **(see illustration)**.
18 Clean the threads of the twelve 6 mm and one 10 mm lower crankcase bolts and insert them in their original locations **(see illustrations 19.5a and b)** – do, not forget to fit new sealing washers with the two 6 mm bolts shown at the front **(see illustration)**. Secure all bolts finger-tight at first, then tighten the 10 mm bolt to its specified torque. Now tighten the 6 mm bolts evenly and a little at a time in a criss-cross sequence starting in the middle and working outwards to the specified torque setting.
19 Turn the engine over. Clean the threads of the three 6 mm and one 8 mm upper crankcase bolts and insert them in their original locations **(see illustration 19.3)** – do not forget to fit new sealing washers with the innermost 6 mm bolt and the 8 mm bolt. Secure the bolts finger-tight at first, then tighten them to the specified torque settings.
20 With all crankcase fasteners tightened, check that the crankshaft and transmission

19.18 Use new sealing washers where directed

shafts rotate smoothly and easily. Check that the transmission shafts rotate freely and independently in neutral, then rotate the selector drum by hand and select each gear in turn whilst rotating the input shaft. Check that all gears can be selected and that the shafts rotate freely in every gear. If there are any signs of undue stiffness, tight or rough spots, or of any other problem, the fault must be rectified before proceeding further.
21 Install all other removed assemblies in a reverse of the sequence given in Step 2.

20 Crankcases and cylinder bores

Crankcases

1 After the crankcases have been separated, remove the crankshaft, connecting rods and pistons, transmission shafts and selector drum and forks, speed sensor, neutral switch and oil pressure switch, referring to the relevant Sections of this Chapter and Chapter 8 for the speed sensor and oil pressure and neutral switches. If there are any other components or assemblies that have not been removed as part of your stripdown procedure, for example the starter motor or the coolant inlet union, remove these as well, referring to the relevant Chapter. Also remove the transmission input shaft bearing in the crankcase if required, but note that if you do a new one must be fitted – see Section 27.
2 Clean the crankcases and all oil passages, including the oil jets and oil jet pipes, with new solvent and dry them with compressed air, blowing it through the passages, jets and pipes.
3 Remove all traces of old gasket sealant from the mating surfaces. Clean up minor damage to the surfaces with a fine sharpening stone or grindstone.
Caution: *Be very careful not to nick or gouge the crankcase mating surfaces or oil leaks will result. Check both crankcase halves very carefully for cracks and other damage.*
4 Small cracks or holes in aluminium castings can be repaired with an epoxy resin adhesive as a temporary measure. Permanent repairs can only be done by argon-arc welding, and only a specialist in this process is in a position to advise on the economy or practical aspect of such a repair. If any damage is found that can't be repaired, replace the crankcase halves as a set.
5 Damaged threads can be economically reclaimed using a diamond section wire insert, for example of the Heli-Coil type (though there are other makes), which are easily fitted after drilling and re-tapping the affected thread.
6 Sheared studs or screws can usually be removed with extractors, which consist of a tapered, left-hand thread screw of very hard steel. These are inserted into a pre-drilled hole in the stud, and usually succeed in dislodging the most stubborn stud or screw. If a stud has sheared above its bore line, it can be removed using a conventional stud extractor which avoids the need for drilling.

> **HAYNES HiNT** *Refer to Tools and Workshop Tips for details of installing a thread insert and using screw extractors.*

7 Install all other components and assemblies, referring to the relevant Sections of this and the other Chapters, before reassembling the crankcase halves.

Cylinder bores

Note: *The liners are made of aluminium and so great care must be taken not to scratch or gouge them. Do not attempt to separate the cylinder liners from the cylinder block.*
8 Check the cylinder walls carefully for scratches and score marks.

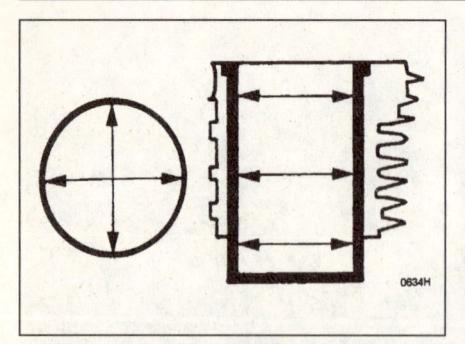

2•42 Engine, clutch and transmission

20.10a Measure the cylinder bore in the directions shown . . .

20.10b . . . using a telescoping gauge, then measure the gauge with a micrometer

9 Using a precision straight-edge and a feeler gauge set to the warpage limit listed in the specifications at the beginning of the Chapter, check the block gasket mating surface for warpage. Refer to *Tools and Workshop Tips* in the Reference section for details of how to use the straight-edge. If warpage is excessive the crankcases must be replaced with new ones.

10 Using telescoping gauges and a micrometer (see *Tools and Workshop Tips*), check the dimensions of each cylinder to assess the amount of wear, taper and ovality. Measure near the top (but below the level of the top piston ring at TDC), centre and bottom (but above the level of the oil ring at BDC) of the bore, both parallel to and across the crankshaft axis **(see illustrations)**. Compare the results to the specifications at the beginning of the Chapter. If the cylinders are worn, oval or tapered beyond the service limit they can be re-bored – an oversize (+ 0.25) set of pistons and rings are available. Note that the person carrying out the re-bore must be aware of the piston-to-bore clearance for the oversize pistons and rings (see Specifications).

11 If the precision measuring tools are not available, take the upper crankcase to a Honda dealer or specialist motorcycle repair shop for assessment and advice.

21 Connecting rod and main bearing information

1 Even though new main and connecting rod bearings are generally fitted during engine overhaul, the old bearings should be retained for close examination as they may reveal valuable information about the condition of the engine.

2 Bearing failure occurs mainly because of lack of lubrication, the presence of dirt or other foreign particles, overloading the engine and/or corrosion. Regardless of the cause of bearing failure, it must be corrected before the engine is reassembled to prevent it from happening again.

3 When examining the bearings, lay them out on a clean surface in the same general position as their location on the crankshaft journals. This will enable you to match any noted bearing problems with the corresponding crankshaft journal.

4 Dirt and other foreign particles get into the engine in a variety of ways. They may be left in the engine during assembly or they may pass through filters or breathers, then get into the oil and from there into the bearings. Metal chips from machining operations and normal engine wear are often present. Abrasives are sometimes left in engine components after reconditioning operations, especially when parts are not thoroughly cleaned using the proper cleaning methods. Whatever the source, foreign objects often end up imbedded in the soft bearing material and are easily recognised. Large particles will not imbed in the bearing and will score or gouge the bearing and journal. The best prevention for this cause of bearing failure is to clean all parts thoroughly and keep everything spotlessly clean during engine reassembly. Regular oil and filter changes are also recommended.

5 Lack of lubrication or lubrication breakdown has a number of interrelated causes. Excessive heat (which thins the oil), overloading (which squeezes the oil from the bearing face) and oil leakage or throw off (from excessive bearing clearances, worn oil pump or high engine speeds) all contribute to lubrication breakdown. Blocked oil passages will starve a bearing of lubrication and destroy it. When lack of lubrication is the cause of bearing failure, the bearing material is wiped or extruded from the steel backing of the bearing. Temperatures may increase to the point where the steel backing and the journal turn blue from overheating.

6 Riding habits can have a definite effect on bearing life. Full throttle low, speed operation, or labouring the engine, puts very high loads on bearings, which tend to squeeze out the oil film. These loads cause the bearings to flex, which produces fine cracks in the bearing face (fatigue failure). Eventually the bearing material will loosen in pieces and tear away from the steel backing. Short trip riding leads to corrosion of bearings, as insufficient engine heat is produced to drive off the condensed water and corrosive gases produced. These products collect in the engine oil, forming acid and sludge. As the oil is carried to the engine bearings, the acid attacks and corrodes the bearing material.

7 Incorrect bearing installation during engine assembly will lead to bearing failure as well. Tight fitting bearings which leave insufficient bearing oil clearances result in oil starvation. Dirt or foreign particles trapped behind a bearing shell result in high spots on the bearing which lead to failure.

8 To avoid bearing problems, clean all parts thoroughly before reassembly, double check all bearing clearance measurements and lubricate the new bearings with clean engine oil during installation.

> **HAYNES HiNT** *Refer to Tools and Workshop Tips for bearing fault finding.*

22 Crankshaft and main bearings

Note: *To remove the crankshaft the engine must be removed from the frame and the crankcase halves separated.*

Removal

1 Remove the engine from the frame (see Section 4) and separate the crankcase halves (see Section 19).

2 Using paint or a felt marker pen, mark the relevant cylinder identity on the front face of each connecting rod and cap to ensure that they are fitted the correct way around and onto the correct rod on reassembly **(see illustration)**. Note that the number already across the rod and cap indicates rod size grade **(see illustration 23.21b)**.

3 Unscrew the connecting rod cap nuts **(see illustration)**. Separate the caps from the

22.2 Mark the relevant cylinder number on each connecting rod and cap

22.3 Unscrew the nuts and remove the connecting rod caps

Engine, clutch and transmission 2•43

22.4 Lift the crankshaft out of the crankcase

22.5 Remove the shells from their housings

22.6 Primary drive gear (arrowed)

crankpin **(see illustration 22.26b)**. Push the rods and pistons up to the tops of the bores so that the bottom ends are clear of the crankshaft, taking care to keep the rods clear of the cylinder liners – it is best to protect the liners with some rag **(see illustration 22.26a)**.
Note: *If no work is to be carried out on the piston/connecting rod assemblies there is no need to remove them from the bores. If you do remove them, refer to Section 23.*
4 Lift the crankshaft out of the upper crankcase half, bringing the cam chain with it if it hasn't been removed, and taking care not to dislodge the main bearing shells **(see illustration)**. Wrap some rag around each connecting rod to protect the cylinder walls.
5 Remove the main bearing shells from the crankcase halves **(see illustration)**. Keep the shells in order. If required remove the oil jet pipes (see Section 20, Step 2).

Inspection

6 Clean the crankshaft with solvent, squirting it under pressure through all the oil passages. Also clean through the oil jet pipes. If available, blow the crank dry with compressed air, and also blow through the oil passages. Check the primary drive gear for wear or damage **(see illustration)**. If any of the main gear teeth are excessively worn, chipped or broken, the crankshaft must be replaced with a new one. If wear or damage is found, also inspect the primary driven gear on the back of the clutch housing (see Section 14).
7 Refer to Section 21 and examine the main bearing shells. If they are scored, badly scuffed or appear to have been seized, new bearings must be installed. Always replace the main bearings as a set. If they are badly damaged, check the corresponding crankshaft journals. Evidence of extreme heat, such as discoloration, indicates that lubrication failure has occurred. Be sure to thoroughly check the oil pump and pressure relief valve as well as all oil holes and passages before reassembling the engine.
8 Give the crankshaft journals a close visual examination, paying particular attention where damaged bearings have been discovered. If the journals are scored or pitted in any way a new crankshaft will be required. Note that undersizes are not available, precluding the option of regrinding the crankshaft.

9 Place the crankshaft on V-blocks and check the runout at the centre main bearing journal using a dial gauge. Compare the reading to the maximum specified at the beginning of the Chapter. If the runout exceeds the limit, the crankshaft must be replaced with a new one.

Oil clearance check

10 Whether new bearing shells are being fitted or the original ones are being reused, the main bearing oil clearance should be checked before the engine is reassembled. Main bearing oil clearance is measured with a product known as Plastigauge.
11 Clean both sides of the bearing shells and the bearing housings in both crankcase halves.
12 Press the bearing shells into their cut-outs, ensuring that the tab on each shell engages in the notch in the crankcase **(see illustration 22.5)**. Make sure the bearings are fitted in the correct locations and take care not to touch any shell's bearing surface with your fingers.
13 Ensure the shells and crankshaft are clean and dry. Lay the crankshaft in position in the upper crankcase **(see illustration 22.4)**. Fit the three crankcase dowels if removed **(see illustration 19.8)**.
14 Cut five lengths of the appropriate size Plastigauge (they should be slightly shorter than the width of the crankshaft journals). Place a strand of Plastigauge on each (cleaned) journal, avoiding the oil hole **(see illustration)**. Make sure the crankshaft is not rotated.
15 Fit the crankcase locating dowels if removed. Carefully fit the lower crankcase half onto the upper half **(see illustration 19.7)**. Check that the lower half is correctly seated.
Note: *Do not tighten the crankcase bolts if the casing is not correctly seated.* Fit the ten 8 mm crankshaft journal bolts – there are two different lengths, with four longer ones, so make sure all are correctly positioned as shown **(see illustration 19.6)**. Secure all bolts finger-tight at first, then tighten them evenly, in three stages and in the numerical sequence shown to the torque setting specified at the beginning of the Chapter **(see illustration 19.17a)** – tighten them in increments of 5 Nm to ensure three equal stages up to the specified torque. Now, using a degree disc, tighten each bolt in turn by a further 120°, again following the numerical sequence **(see illustration 19.17b)**.
16 Slacken each bolt evenly and a little at a time in a reverse of the tightening sequence, i.e. starting from the outside and working to the centre, until they are all finger-tight, then remove the bolts. Carefully lift off the lower crankcase half, making sure the Plastigauge is not disturbed.
17 Compare the width of the crushed Plastigauge on each crankshaft journal to the scale printed on the Plastigauge envelope to obtain the main bearing oil clearance **(see illustration)**. Compare the reading to the specifications at the beginning of the Chapter.
18 On completion carefully scrape away all traces of the Plastigauge material from the crankshaft journal and bearing shells; use a fingernail or other object which is unlikely to score them.

22.14 Place a strip of Plastigauge carefully on the journal

22.17 Measure the crushed Plastigauge to establish the oil clearance

2•44 Engine, clutch and transmission

22.21a Main bearing journal size numbers

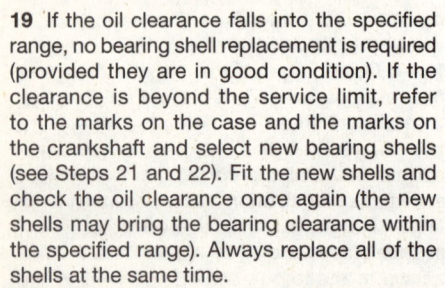

22.21b Main bearing housing size letters

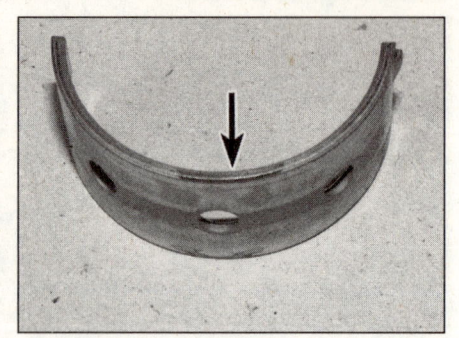

22.22 Bearing shell colour code (arrowed)

19 If the oil clearance falls into the specified range, no bearing shell replacement is required (provided they are in good condition). If the clearance is beyond the service limit, refer to the marks on the case and the marks on the crankshaft and select new bearing shells (see Steps 21 and 22). Fit the new shells and check the oil clearance once again (the new shells may bring the bearing clearance within the specified range). Always replace all of the shells at the same time.

20 If the clearance is still greater than the service limit listed in this Chapter's Specifications (even with replacement shells), the crankshaft journals are worn and the crankshaft should be replaced with a new one.

Main bearing shell selection

21 Replacement bearing shells for the main bearings are supplied on a selected fit basis. Code letters and numbers stamped on the crankshaft and crankcase are used to identify the correct replacement bearings. The crankshaft main bearing journal size numbers are stamped on the outside of the left-hand crankshaft web and will be either 1, 2 or 3 **(see illustration)**. The first letter, after the L, is for the left-hand journal, and the numbers correspond consecutively for each journal. The corresponding main bearing housing size letters are stamped into the left-hand side of the upper crankcase half and will be either A, B or C **(see illustration)**. The left-hand letter corresponds to the left-hand journal, and the letters correspond consecutively from left to right.

22 A range of bearing shells is available.

To select the correct bearing for a particular journal, use the table below and cross-refer the main bearing journal size number (stamped on the crank web) with the main bearing housing size letter (stamped on the crankcase) to determine the colour code of the bearing required. For example, if the journal code is 3, and the housing code is A, then the bearing required is green. The colour is marked on the side of the shell **(see illustration)**.

Main bearing journal code	Main bearing housing code		
	A	B	C
1	Pink	Yellow	Green
2	Yellow	Green	Brown
3	Green	Brown	Black

Installation

23 Clean both sides of the bearing shells and the bearing cut-outs in both crankcase halves. If new shells are being fitted, ensure that all traces of the protective grease are cleaned off using paraffin (kerosene). Wipe the shells and crankcase halves dry with a lint-free cloth. Make sure all the oil passages and holes are clear, and blow them through with compressed air if available and not already done. If removed install the oil jet pipes (Section 19, Step 13).

24 Press the bearing shells into their locations. Make sure the tab on each shell engages in the notch in the casing **(see illustration 22.5)**. Make sure the bearings are fitted in the correct locations and take care not to touch any shell's bearing surface with your fingers. Lubricate the bearing surface of each

22.26a Pull the connecting rod onto the crankpin . . .

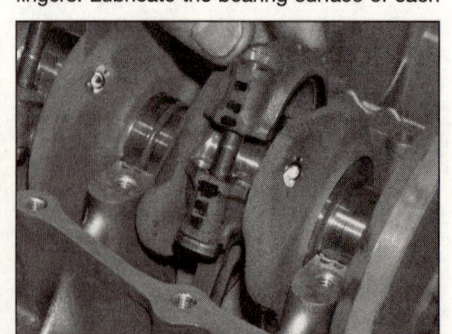

22.26b . . . and fit the cap

shell with molybdenum disulphide oil (a 50/50 mixture of molybdenum disulphide grease and clean engine oil).

25 Remove the rag from around the connecting rods. Lower the crankshaft into position in the upper crankcase, making sure all bearings remain in place **(see illustration 22.4)**.

26 Lubricate the crankpins with molybdenum disulphide oil (a 50/50 mixture of molybdenum disulphide grease and clean engine oil). Carefully pull the connecting rods onto the crankpins, taking care not to mark the cylinders **(see illustration)**. Fit the caps onto the rods **(see illustration)**. Make sure each cap is fitted the correct way around so the previously made markings align, and that the rod is facing the right way (see Step 2 and Section 23).

27 Apply some clean oil to the threads and under the heads of the connecting rod nuts, then fit them and tighten them finger-tight **(see illustration 22.3)**. Now tighten them evenly and alternately to the torque setting specified at the beginning of the Chapter – tighten them in two increments of 9 Nm and one of 8 Nm to ensure even tightening up to the specified torque. It is highly advisable to have an assistant to hold the crankshaft down in the crankcase while tightening the nuts as it could jump out.

28 Carefully turn the crankshaft – if there are any signs of roughness or tightness, try tapping the bottom of the connecting rod caps as this may relieve tightness, but if in doubt remove the caps and check the bearing clearance (Section 23).

29 Check again to make sure that all components have been returned to their original locations using the marks made on disassembly.

30 Reassemble the crankcase halves (see Section 19).

23 Connecting rods and bearings

Note 1: *To remove the connecting rods the engine must be removed from the frame and the crankcases separated.*
Note 2: *The connecting rod bolts can only be used in a running engine once, though they*

Engine, clutch and transmission 2•45

23.5 Push the piston and connecting rod assembly up and withdraw it from the top of the cylinder

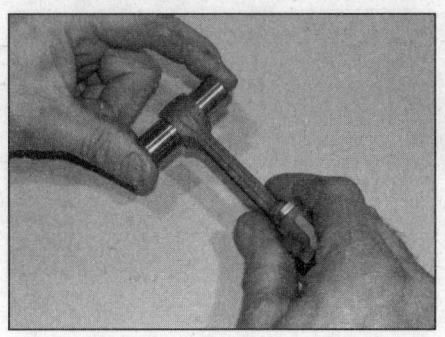

23.9a Check for freeplay between the rod and pin

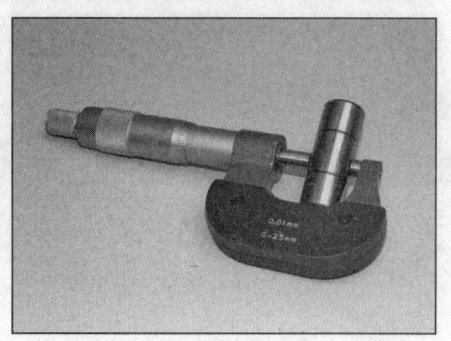

23.9b Measure the external diameter of the pin and the internal diameter of the connecting rod small-end

can be used to do the oil clearance check to prevent having to buy two sets of new bolts.

Removal

1 Remove the engine from the frame (see Section 4) and separate the crankcase halves (see Section 19).
2 Before removing the rods from the crankshaft, measure the side clearance (the gap between the connecting rod big-end and the crankshaft web) with a feeler gauge. If the clearance is greater than the service limit listed in this Chapter's Specifications, replace the rods with new ones. If the clearance is still excessive, replace the crankshaft with a new one.
3 Using paint or a felt marker pen, mark the relevant cylinder identity on the front face of each connecting rod and cap to ensure that they are fitted the correct way around and onto the correct rod on reassembly **(see illustration 22.2)**. The piston crown is marked IN, and this mark faces the intake side of the cylinder, and the bearing shell notch in the big-end of the connecting rod should face the same way, to the back of the engine (intake side) **(see illustration 24.2)**.
4 Remove the crankshaft (see Section 22, Steps 3 and 4). Wrap some rag around each connecting rod to protect the cylinder walls.
5 Raise the crankcase onto wooden blocks to provide room for the connecting rod/piston assemblies to be removed from the tops of the bores. Alternatively turn the crankcase on its side, but remove the transmission output shaft first otherwise it will fall out (see Section 26). Push each piston/connecting rod assembly up its bore and remove it from the top making sure the connecting rod does not mark the cylinder walls **(see illustration)**.

> **HAYNES HiNT** To ease removal of the pistons, carefully remove any ridge of carbon built up on the top of each cylinder bore using a scraper, Stanley blade or scouring cloth. If there is a pronounced wear ridge, remove it using a ridge reamer.

Caution: Do not try to remove the piston/connecting rod from the bottom of the cylinder bore. The piston will not pass the crankcase main bearing webs. If the piston is pulled right to the bottom of the bore the oil control ring will expand and lock the piston in position. If this happens it is likely the ring will break.

6 Keep the rod, cap, nuts, and the bearing shells (if they are to be reused) together in their correct positions to ensure correct installation – fit the caps back onto the rods and finger-tighten the nuts to make sure.
7 Remove the pistons from the connecting rods if required (see Section 24), but note that if you are doing a big-end oil clearance check they must be on the rods to prevent them rotating on the crankpin and upsetting the Plastigauge.

Inspection

8 Check the connecting rods for cracks and other obvious damage.
9 Apply clean engine oil to the piston pin, slide it into the connecting rod small-end and check for any freeplay between the two **(see illustration)**. Measure the pin external diameter in its centre and the small-end bore diameter, then calculate the difference to obtain the small-end-to-piston pin clearance **(see illustration)**. Compare the result to the specifications at the beginning of the Chapter. If the clearance is greater than specified, replace the components that are worn beyond their specified limits with new ones.
10 Refer to Section 21 and examine the connecting rod bearing shells. If they are scored, badly scuffed, corroded, or appear to have seized, new shells must be installed. Remove them by pushing their centres out to the side then lifting them out **(see illustration)**. Always replace the shells in the connecting rods as a set. If they are badly damaged, check the corresponding crankpin. Evidence of extreme heat, such as discoloration, indicates that lubrication failure has occurred. Be sure to thoroughly check the oil pump and pressure relief valve as well as all oil holes and passages before reassembling the engine.
11 Have the rods checked for twist and bend by a Honda dealer if you are in doubt about their straightness.

Oil clearance check

12 Whether new bearing shells are being fitted or the original ones are being reused, the connecting rod bearing oil clearance should be checked prior to reassembly. Check the clearance on one rod at a time.
13 Clean both sides of the bearing shells and the bearing housings in both the connecting rod and cap.
14 Press the bearing shells into their housings, making sure the tab on each shell engages the notch in the connecting rod/cap **(see illustration 23.10)**. Make sure the bearings are fitted in the correct location and take care not to touch any shell's bearing surface with your fingers. Refer to Step 25 and fit the rod and piston into its correct cylinder, making sure it is the correct way round. Lay the crankshaft in the upper crankcase half, then pull the connecting rod onto the crankpin **(see illustrations 22.4 and 22.26a)**.
15 Cut a length of the appropriate size Plastigauge (it should be slightly shorter than the width of the crankpin). Place a strand of Plastigauge on the crankpin journal, making sure it is not over the oil hole **(see illustration 22.14)**. Fit the cap onto the rod **(see illustrations 22.26b)**. Make sure the cap is fitted the correct way around so the previously made markings align. Apply some clean oil to the threads and under the heads of the connecting rod nuts. Secure the nuts finger-tight at first, then tighten them evenly and alternately in two stages to the torque setting specified at the beginning of the Chapter

23.10 Remove the shells

23.21a Crankpin journal size letters

23.21b Connecting rod size number

for a particular big-end, use the table below and cross-refer the crankpin journal size letter (stamped on the web) with the connecting rod size number (stamped on the rod). For example, if the crankpin size is B, and the connecting rod size is 1, then the bearing required is green. The colour is marked on the side of the shell **(see illustration 22.22)**.

Crankpin journal code	Connecting rod code	
	1	2
A	Yellow	Green
B	Green	Brown

Installation

23 If removed fit the pistons onto the connecting rods (see Section 24).
24 Clean both sides of the bearing shells and the bearing housings in both cap and rod. If new shells are being fitted, ensure that all traces of any protective grease are cleaned off using paraffin (kerosene). Wipe the shells, cap and rod dry with a clean lint free cloth. Fit the bearing shells in the connecting rods and caps, making sure the tab on each shell engages the notch **(see illustration 23.10)**. Lubricate the shells with molybdenum disulphide oil (a 50/50 mixture of molybdenum disulphide grease and clean engine oil). Make sure the bolt heads are all correctly seated.
25 Lubricate the piston and rings and the cylinder bore with clean engine oil. Wrap some rag round the bottom of the connecting rod. Insert the piston/connecting rod assembly into the top of its bore, taking care not to allow the connecting rod to mark the bore **(see illustration 23.5)**. Make sure the IN mark on the piston crown and the connecting rod bearing shell notch are on the intake side of the bore. Carefully compress and feed each piston ring into the bore until the piston crown is flush with the top of the bore **(see illustration)**. If available, a piston ring compressor makes installation a lot easier – fit the compressor around the piston and over the rings and tighten it to compress the rings, then locate the assembly on the top of the bore and tap the top of the piston using a wooden or plastic tool (such as the handle end of a hammer) until the piston is completely in the bore **(see illustrations)**.

– tighten them in two increments of 9 Nm and one of 8 Nm to ensure even tightening up to the specified torque, all the time ensuring that the crankshaft does not rotate. It is highly advisable to have an assistant to hold the crankshaft down in the crankcase while tightening the nuts as it could lift.
16 Slacken the nuts and remove the connecting rod cap. Compare the width of the crushed Plastigauge on the crankpin to the scale printed on the Plastigauge envelope to obtain the connecting rod bearing oil clearance **(see illustration 22.17)**. Compare the reading to the specifications at the beginning of the Chapter.
17 On completion carefully scrape away all traces of the Plastigauge material from the crankpin and bearing shells using a fingernail or other soft object that is unlikely to score the shells.

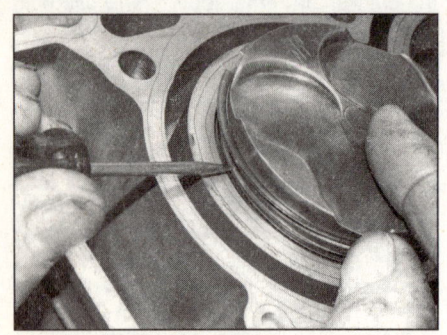

18 If the clearance is within the range listed in this Chapter's Specifications and the bearings are in perfect condition, they can be reused. If the clearance is beyond the service limit, replace the bearing shells with new ones (see Steps 21 and 22). Check the oil clearance once again (the new shells may be thick enough to bring bearing clearance within the specified range). Always replace all of the shells at the same time.
19 If the clearance is still greater than the service limit listed in this Chapter's Specifications, the crankpin is worn and the crankshaft should be replaced with a new one.
20 Repeat the oil clearance check for the other connecting rods.

Bearing shell selection

21 Replacement bearing shells for the big-end bearings are supplied on a selected fit basis. Code letters and numbers stamped on the crankshaft and connecting rod are used to identify the correct replacement bearings. The crankpin journal size letters are stamped on the outside of the left-hand crankshaft web, and will be either an A or B **(see illustration)**. The first letter after the L is for the No. 1 cylinder connecting rod (left-hand journal), and the letters correspond consecutively for each cylinder. The connecting rod size code number is marked across the flat face of the connecting rod and cap and will be either a 1 or 2 **(see illustration)**.
22 A range of bearing shells is available. To select the correct bearing shell colour code

23.25a Carefully compress and feed each ring in

23.25b Fit the compressor over the piston and rings . . .

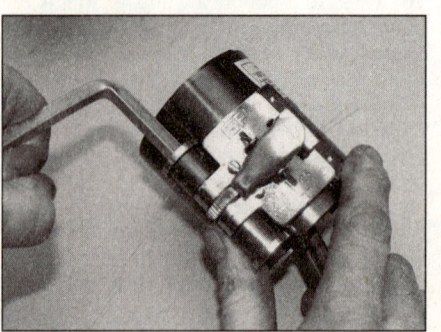

23.25c . . . then compress the rings by tightening the bands on the compressor using an Allen key

23.25d Fit the rod into the bore and rest the compressor on the crankcase . . .

Engine, clutch and transmission 2•47

23.25e ... then tap the top of the piston with a soft tool so that it enters

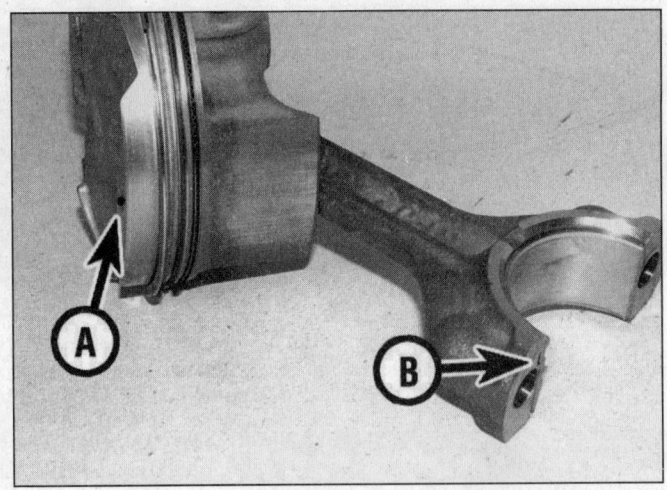

24.2 The piston IN mark (A) is on the same side as the bearing shell notch (B)

26 Install the crankshaft (see Section 22).
27 Reassemble the crankcase halves (see Section 19).

24 Pistons

Note: *To remove the pistons the engine must be removed from the frame and the crankcase halves separated.*

Removal

1 Remove the connecting rods (see Section 23).
2 Before removing the piston from the connecting rod, use a sharp scriber or felt marker pen to write the cylinder identity on the crown of each piston (or on the inside of the skirt if the piston is dirty and going to be cleaned). Each piston crown should already be marked IN, though the mark is likely to be invisible until the piston is cleaned, and this mark faces the intake side of the cylinder, the same way as the bearing shell notch in the big-end of the connecting rod **(see illustration)**.
3 Carefully prise out the circlip on one side of the piston using needle-nose pliers or a small flat-bladed screwdriver inserted into the notch **(see illustration)**. Push the piston pin out from the other side to free the piston from the connecting rod **(see illustration)**. If required remove the other circlip. New circlips must be used. When the piston has been removed, slide its pin back into its bore so that related parts do not get mixed up.

HAYNES HINT *If a piston pin is a tight fit in the piston bosses, use a heat gun to heat the area around the piston pin – this will expand the alloy piston sufficiently to release its grip on the pin. If the piston pin is particularly stubborn, extract it using a drawbolt tool, but be careful to protect the piston's working surfaces.*

4 Using your thumbs or a piston ring removal and installation tool, carefully remove the rings from the pistons **(see illustrations 25.10, 25.9b, 25.7c, b and a)**. Do not nick or gouge the pistons in the process. Carefully note which way up each ring fits and in which groove as they must be installed in their original positions if being reused. The upper surface of the top ring should be marked RE at one end, and the second (middle) ring marked RNE. The top and middle rings can also be identified by the fact that the top ring is not as wide as the second (middle) ring, and their cross-section profiles are different.
5 Scrape all traces of carbon from the tops of the pistons. A hand-held wire brush or a piece of fine emery cloth can be used once most of the deposits have been scraped away. Do not use a wire brush mounted in a drill motor to remove deposits from the pistons – the piston material is soft and will be eroded away by the wire brush.
6 Use a piston ring groove cleaning tool to remove any carbon deposits from the ring grooves. If a tool is not available, a piece broken off an old ring will do the job. Be very careful to remove only the carbon deposits. Do not remove any metal and do not nick or gouge the sides of the ring grooves.
7 Once the deposits have been removed, clean the pistons with solvent and dry them thoroughly. If the identification mark previously made on the piston is cleaned off, be sure to re-mark it with the correct identity. Make sure the oil return holes below the oil ring groove are clear.

Inspection

8 Carefully inspect each piston for cracks around the skirt, at the pin bosses and at the ring lands. Normal piston wear appears as even, vertical wear on the thrust surfaces of the piston. If the skirt is scored or scuffed, the engine may have been suffering from overheating and/or abnormal combustion, which caused excessively high operating temperatures. Also check that the circlip grooves are not damaged.
9 A hole in the top of the piston, in one extreme, or burned areas around the edge of the piston crown, indicate that pre-ignition or knocking under load have occurred. If you find evidence of any problems the cause must be corrected or the damage will occur again (see *Fault Finding* in the *Reference* section).

24.3a Prise out the circlip using a suitable tool in the notch ...

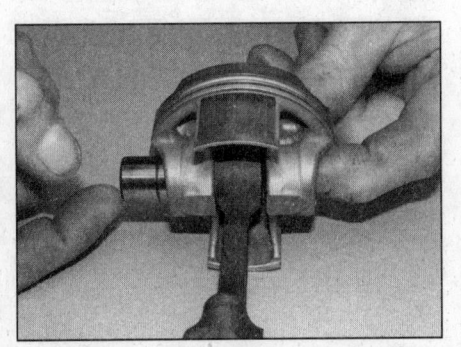

24.3b ... then push out the pin and separate the piston from the rod

2•48 Engine, clutch and transmission

24.10 Measure the piston ring-to-groove clearance with a feeler gauge

24.11 Measure the piston diameter with a micrometer at the specified distance from the bottom of the skirt

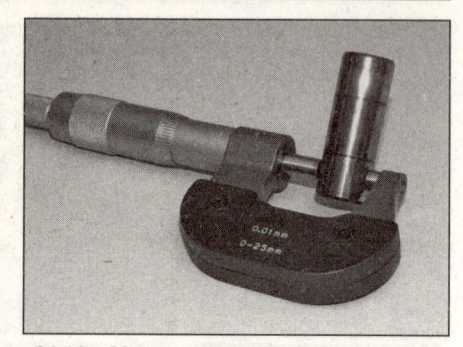

24.12a Measure the external diameter of the pin . . .

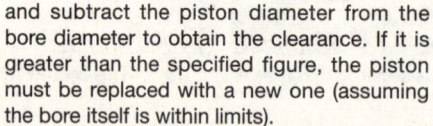

24.12b . . . and the internal diameter of the bore in the piston

10 Measure the piston ring-to-groove clearance by laying each piston ring in its groove and slipping a feeler gauge in beside it **(see illustration)**. Make sure you have the correct ring for the groove (see Step 4). Check the clearance at three or four locations around the groove. If the clearance is greater than specified, replace both the piston and rings as a set. If new rings are being used, measure the clearance using the new rings. If the clearance is greater than that specified, the piston is worn and must be replaced with a new one.

11 Check the piston-to-bore clearance by measuring the bore (see Section 20), then measure the piston 6 mm up from the bottom of the skirt and at 90° to the piston pin axis **(see illustration)**. Make sure each piston is matched to its correct cylinder. Refer to the Specifications at the beginning of the Chapter and subtract the piston diameter from the bore diameter to obtain the clearance. If it is greater than the specified figure, the piston must be replaced with a new one (assuming the bore itself is within limits).

12 Apply clean engine oil to the piston pin, insert it into the piston and check for any freeplay between the two. Measure the pin external diameter near each end **(see illustration)**, and the pin bore in each side of the piston **(see illustration)**. Calculate the difference to obtain the piston pin-to-piston pin bore clearance. Compare the result to the specifications at the beginning of the Chapter. If the clearance is greater than specified, replace the components that are worn beyond their specified limits. If not already done (see Section 23), repeat the measurements between the pin and the connecting rod small-end.

Installation

13 Inspect and install the piston rings (see Section 25).
14 Lubricate the piston pin, the piston pin bore and the connecting rod small-end bore with molybdenum disulphide oil (a 50/50 mixture of molybdenum disulphide grease and clean engine oil).
15 When fitting the pistons onto the connecting rods make sure the IN mark on the piston crown faces the same way as the bearing shell notch in the big-end **(see illustration 24.2)**.
16 If both circlips were removed fit one *new* circlip into one side of the piston (do not reuse old circlips). Line up the piston on its correct connecting rod, and insert the piston pin from the other side **(see illustration)**. Secure the pin with another *new* circlip **(see illustration)**. When fitting the circlips, compress them only just enough to fit them in the piston, and make sure they are properly seated in their grooves with the open end away from the removal notch.
17 Install the connecting rods (see Section 23) and reassemble the crankcase halves (see Section 19).

25 Piston rings

Note: *It is good practice to replace the piston rings with new ones when an engine is being overhauled.*

Removal

1 See Section 24, Steps 1 to 4.

Inspection

2 Whether re-using the old rings or fitting new ones, check the installed end gaps with the rings installed in the bore, as follows. Lay out each piston with its ring set and keep them together so the rings will be matched with the same piston and bore during the measurement procedure and engine assembly.
3 Insert the top ring into the top of the bore and square it up with the bore walls by pushing it in with the top of the piston **(see illustration)**. The ring should be at least 20 mm

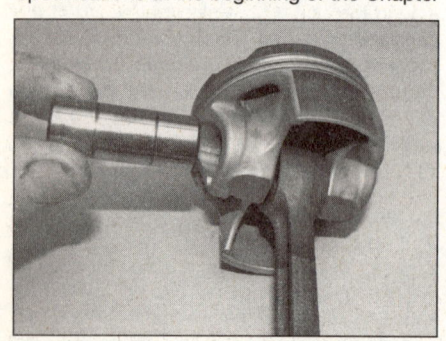

24.16a Slide the pin through the piston and rod . . .

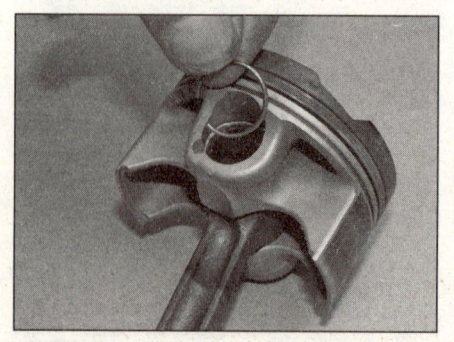

24.16b . . . and secure it with new circlips

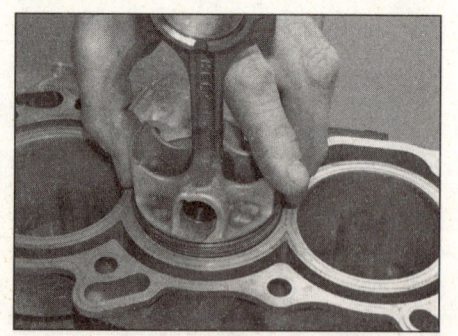

25.3a Set the ring square in its bore using the piston . . .

25.3b ... and measure the end gap using a feeler gauge

25.7a Fit the oil ring expander in its groove ...

25.7b ... then fit the lower side rail ...

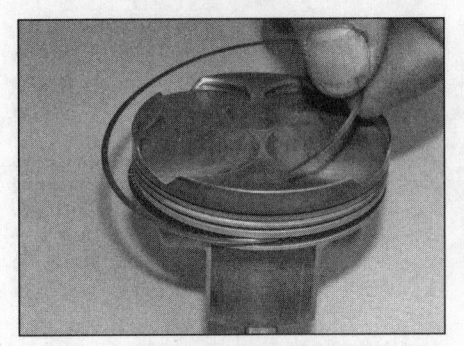

25.7c ... and the upper side rail on each side of it

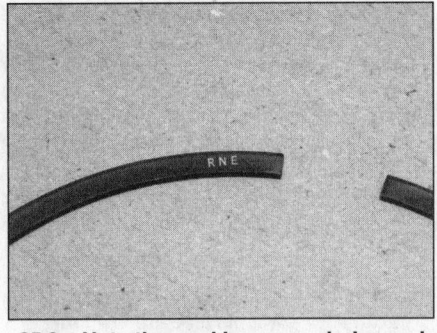

25.9a Note the marking on each ring and make sure it faces up

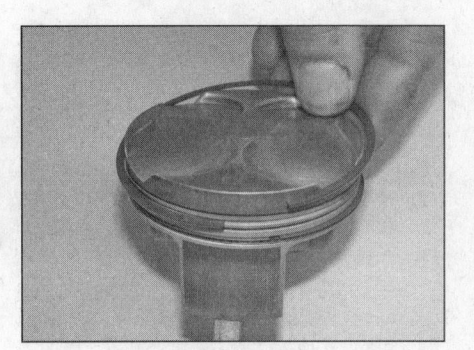

25.9b Fit the second (middle ring) ...

below the top edge of the bore, so it is within its area of travel in the bore. Slip a feeler gauge between the ends of the ring and compare the measurement to the specifications at the beginning of the Chapter **(see illustration)**.

4 If the gap is larger or smaller than specified, double check to make sure that you have the correct rings before proceeding; excess end gap is not critical unless it exceeds the service limit.

5 If the service limit is exceeded with new rings, check the bore for wear (see Section 20). If the gap is too small, the ring ends may come in contact with each other during engine operation, which can cause serious damage.

6 Repeat the procedure for the middle ring and the oil control ring side-rails, but not the expander ring. Remember to keep the rings, pistons and bores matched up.

25.10 ... and the top ring as described

Installation

7 Fit the oil control ring (lowest on the piston) first. It is composed of three separate components, namely the expander and the upper and lower side-rails. Slip the expander

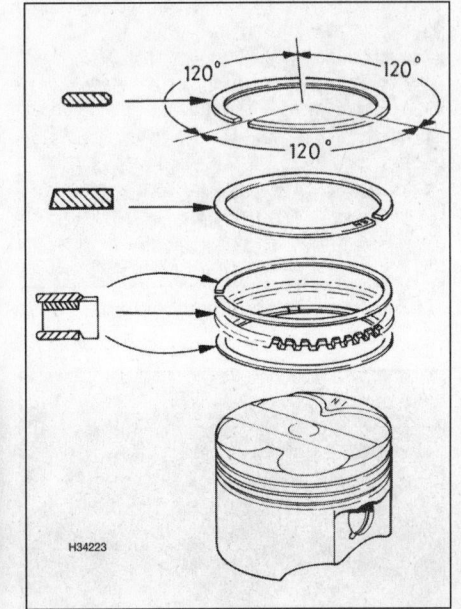

25.11 Piston ring profiles and ring end gap positions

Stagger the end gaps as shown. Note that the oil ring rail end gaps must be 20 mm or more from each other

into the groove, making sure the ends don't overlap **(see illustration)**. Next fit the lower side-rail **(see illustration)**. Do not use a piston ring installation tool on the side-rails as they may be damaged. Instead, place one end of the side-rail into the groove between the expander and the ring land. Hold it firmly in place and slide a finger around the piston while pushing the rail into the groove. Next, fit the upper side-rail in the same manner **(see illustration)**. Check that the ends of the expander have not overlapped.

8 After the three oil ring components have been installed, check to make sure that both the upper and lower side-rails can be turned smoothly in the ring groove.

9 Fit the second (middle) ring next – it should be marked RNE at one end, and it can also be identified by its cross-section profile **(see illustration 25.11)**. Make sure that the ring is installed with the identification letters facing up. Fit the ring into the middle groove in the piston **(see illustration)**. Do not expand the ring any more than is necessary to slide it into place. To avoid breaking the ring, use a piston ring installation tool.

10 Finally, fit the top ring, marked RE, in the same manner into the top groove in the piston **(see illustration)**. Make sure the identification letter near the end gap is facing up.

11 Once the rings are correctly installed, check they move freely without snagging and stagger their end gaps as shown **(see illustration)**.

2•50 Engine, clutch and transmission

26.2a Remove the output shaft

26.2b Remove the bearing dowel from its hole . . .

26.2c . . . and the retainer from its groove

26 Transmission shafts removal and installation

Note: To remove the transmission shafts the engine must be removed from the frame and the crankcases separated.

Removal

1 Remove the engine from the frame (see Section 4) and separate the crankcase halves (see Section 19).
2 Lift the output shaft out of the casing, noting how it engages with the input shaft and its selector forks, and how the hole in the needle bearing housing locates onto the dowel **(see illustrations)**. If the shaft is stuck, use a soft-faced hammer and gently tap on the ends. Remove the bearing dowel – if it is not in its hole in the crankcase, remove it from the bearing on the shaft **(see illustration)**. Also remove the ball bearing half-ring retainer from either the crankcase or the bearing **(see illustration)**. Remove the oil seal and discard it as a new one must be used **(see illustration 26.11)**.
3 Remove the selector forks (see Section 28) – the drum can stay in place, but remove it as well if required.
4 Unscrew the transmission input shaft bearing retainer plate bolts and remove the plate, noting how it fits **(see illustration)**.
5 Draw the input shaft a little way out of the crankcase until the right-hand bearing is clear (the left-hand bearing should stay in the crankcase, then slide the right-hand bearing off the end of the shaft and lift the shaft out of the crankcase **(see illustrations)**. Note the thrust washer on the left-hand end of the shaft – if it is not there it may be stuck to the bearing.
6 If necessary, the transmission shafts can be disassembled and inspected for wear or damage (see Section 27).
7 Referring to *Tools and Workshop Tips* (Section 5) in the Reference Section, check the bearings on the shafts and in the crankcase. Replace the bearings with new ones if necessary, noting that the left-hand bearing on the output shaft is not available separately from the shaft.

Installation

8 Make sure the thrust washer is on the left-hand end of the input shaft **(see illustration 27.20b)**. Position the shaft in the crankcase then fit the right-hand bearing onto the outer end of the shaft with its marked side facing out **(see illustration 26.5b)**. Slide the shaft in locating the inner end in the left-hand bearing and pressing the right-hand bearing into the crankcase **(see illustration)**.
9 Clean the threads of the bearing retainer plate bolts and apply a suitable thread locking compound. Fit the plate with the OUTSIDE mark facing out, and tighten the bolts to the torque setting specified at the beginning of the Chapter **(see illustration 26.4)**.
10 Install the selector drum (if removed) and the selector forks (see Section 28).
11 Lubricate the left-hand end of the output shaft with clean oil and slide the new oil seal on **(see illustration)**. Smear the seal outer lips with oil.
12 Fit the output shaft needle bearing dowel

26.4 Unscrew the bolts (arrowed) and remove the plate

26.5a Draw the shaft and bearing out . . .

26.5b . . . then slide the bearing off and remove the shaft

26.8 Push the bearing into its housing until it seats

26.11 Lubricate the end of the shaft and fit the oil seal

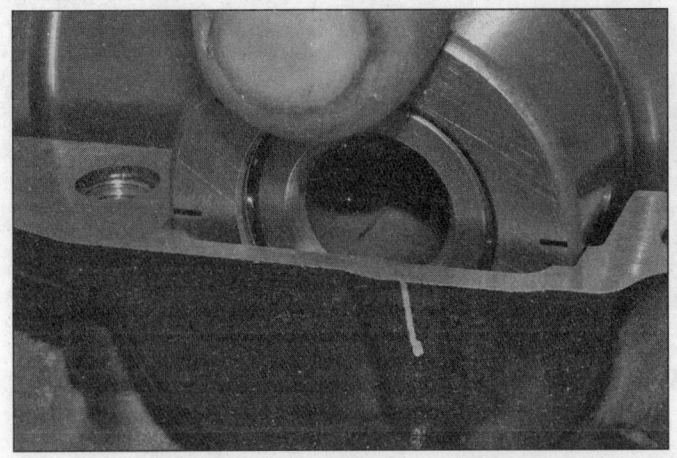

Engine, clutch and transmission 2•51

26.13a Align the marks with the mating surface

26.13b Make sure the locating pin (A) and oil seal rim (B) locate correctly

into its hole in the crankcase, and the half-ring retainer into its slot **(see illustrations 26.2b and c)**.

13 Lower the output shaft into position in the upper crankcase **(see illustration 26.2a)**, making sure the selector forks locate in their pinion grooves, the hole in the needle bearing engages correctly with the dowel (align the marks on the outer face of the bearing with the crankcase mating surfaces for alignment), the groove in the ball bearing engages correctly with the retainer in the bearing housing, the locating pin sits in the cut-out in the crankcase, and the oil seal lip locates in the crankcase groove **(see illustrations)**.
Caution: If the ring retainer or dowel do not locate correctly, the crankcase halves will not seat properly.
14 Position the gears in the neutral position and check the shafts are free to rotate easily and independently (i.e. the input shaft can turn whilst the output shaft is held stationary) before proceeding further. Also check that each gear can be selected by turning the input shaft with one hand and the selector drum with the other.
15 Reassemble the crankcase halves (see Section 19).

27 Transmission shafts overhaul

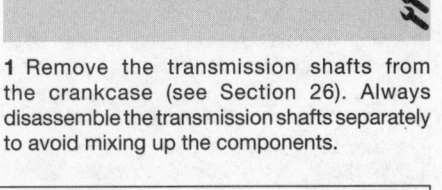

1 Remove the transmission shafts from the crankcase (see Section 26). Always disassemble the transmission shafts separately to avoid mixing up the components.

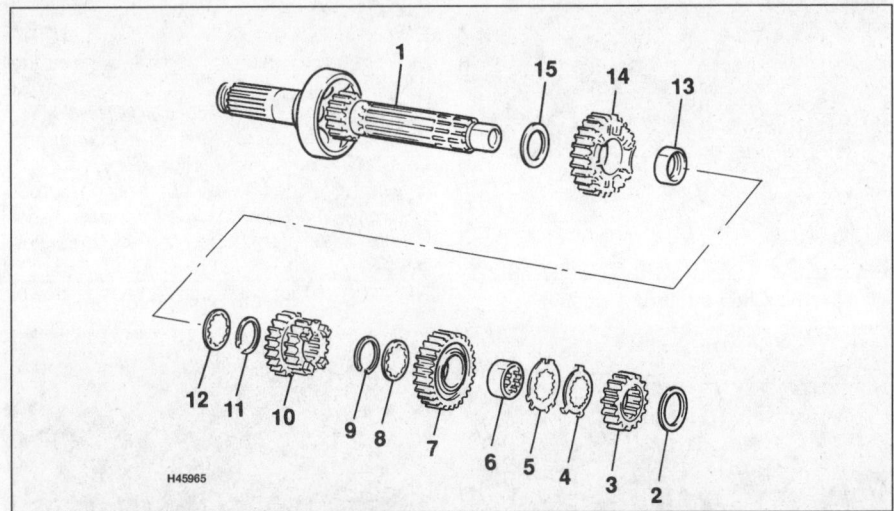

HAYNES HINT *When disassembling the transmission shafts, place the parts on a long rod or thread a wire through them to keep them in order and facing the proper direction.*

Input shaft

Disassembly

2 Mark the outer face of the 2nd gear pinion on the left-hand end of the shaft so it can re-fitted the same way round. Slide the thrust washer and the pinion off the shaft **(see illustration and 27.20b and a)**.
3 Slide the tabbed lockwasher off the shaft, then turn the slotted splined washer to offset the splines and slide it off the shaft **(see illustrations 27.19c and a)**. Slide the 6th gear pinion and its splined bush off the shaft, followed by the splined washer **(see illustrations 27.18c, b and a)**.
4 Remove the circlip, then slide the combined 3rd/4th gear pinion off the shaft **(see illustrations 27.17b and a)**.
5 Remove the circlip, then slide the splined washer, the 5th gear pinion and its bush, and the thrust washer off the shaft **(see illustrations 27.16e, d, c, b and a)**. The 1st gear pinion is integral with the shaft **(see illustration)**.

27.2 Transmission input shaft components

1 Input shaft and bearing
2 Thrust washer
3 2nd gear pinion
4 Tabbed lockwasher
5 Slotted splined washer
6 6th gear pinion splined bush
7 6th gear pinion
8 Splined washer
9 Circlip
10 Combined 3rd/4th gear pinion
11 Circlip
12 Splined washer
13 5th gear pinion bush
14 5th gear pinion
15 Thrust washer

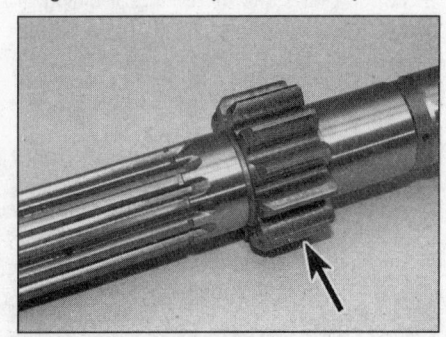

27.5 1st gear pinion (arrowed) is part of the shaft

27.6a Locate the knife-end behind the inner race and expand it . . .

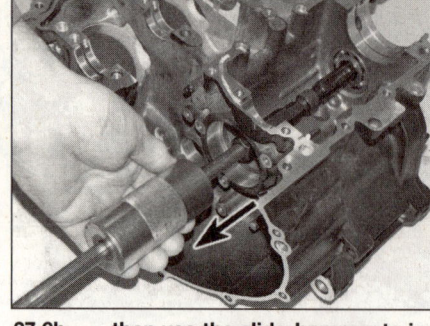

27.6b . . . then use the slide-hammer to jar the bearing out

27.11 Measure the dimensions of the related components as listed in the Specifications

27.15 Fit the bearing into the crankcase

6 If required, remove the left-hand bearing from the crankcase – you will need an expanding puller to lock behind the bearing inner race and a slide-hammer attachment to jar the bearing out **(see illustrations)**. Heat around the bearing housing first using a hot air gun to make removal easier

Inspection

7 Wash all of the components in clean solvent and dry them off.
8 Check the gear teeth for cracking, chipping, pitting and other obvious wear or damage. Any pinion that is damaged as such must be replaced with a new one.
9 Inspect the dogs and the dog holes in the gears for cracks, chips, and excessive wear especially in the form of rounded edges. Make sure mating gears engage properly. Replace the paired gears as a set if necessary.
10 Check for signs of scoring or bluing on the pinions, bushes and shaft. This could be caused by overheating due to inadequate lubrication. Check that all the oil holes and passages are clear. Replace any damaged pinions or bushes.
11 Check that each pinion moves freely on the shaft or its bush but without undue freeplay. Check that each bush moves freely on the shaft but without undue freeplay. If the necessary equipment is available the individual components for which dimensions are given in the Specifications at the beginning of this Chapter can be measured to assess the extent of wear **(see illustration)**.
12 The shaft is unlikely to sustain damage unless the engine has seized, placing an unusually high loading on the transmission, or the machine has covered a very high mileage. Check the surface of the shaft, especially where a pinion turns on it, and replace the shaft if it has scored or picked up, or if there are any cracks. Damage of any kind can only be cured by replacement.
13 Check the washers and circlips and replace any that are bent or appear weakened or worn. Use new ones if in any doubt. Note that it is good practice to renew all circlips when overhauling gearshafts.

Reassembly

14 During reassembly, apply molybdenum disulphide oil (a 50/50 mixture of molybdenum disulphide grease and clean engine oil) to the mating surfaces of the shaft, pinions and bushes. When installing the circlips, do not expand their ends any further than is necessary. Install the stamped circlips and washers so that their chamfered side faces away from the thrust side (see *Tools and Workshop Tips* in the Reference section).
15 If removed, fit the ball bearing into the crankcase with its marked side facing out of the housing, referring to *Tools and Workshop Tips* in the Reference Section **(see illustration)**. Put the new bearing in the freezer for a while, and when it is cold heat the bearing housing with a hot air gun. Fit the bearing and tap it squarely in using a socket or bearing driver that bears on the outer race until it seats.
16 Slide the thrust washer onto the left-hand end of the shaft, followed by the 5th gear pinion bush **(see illustrations)**. Fit the 5th gear pinion onto the bush with its dogs facing away from the integral 1st gear **(see illustration)**. Slide the splined washer onto the shaft, then fit the circlip, making sure that

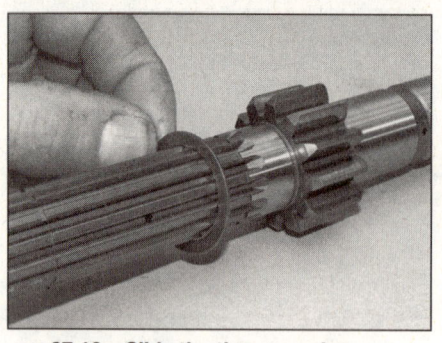

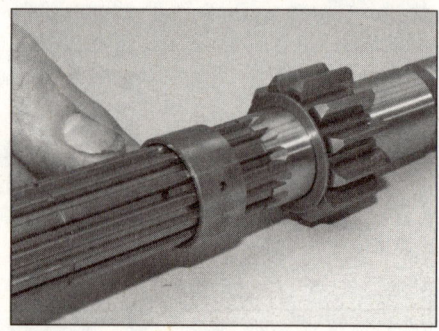

27.16a Slide the thrust washer . . .

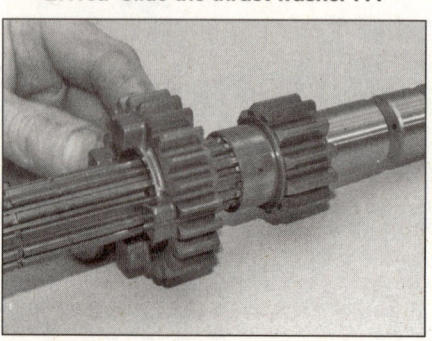

27.16b . . . the 5th gear pinion bush . . .

27.16c . . . the 5th gear pinion . . .

27.16d . . . and the splined washer onto the shaft . . .

Engine, clutch and transmission 2•53

27.16e ... and secure them with the circlip ...

27.16f ... making sure it locates properly in its groove

27.17a Slide the combined 3rd/4th gear pinion onto the shaft ...

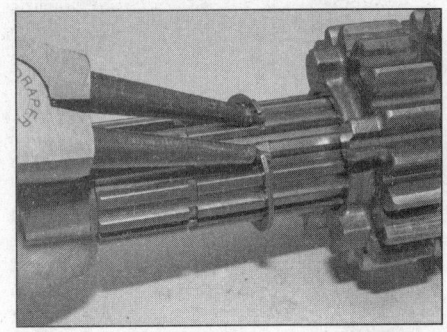

27.17b ... and secure it with the circlip ...

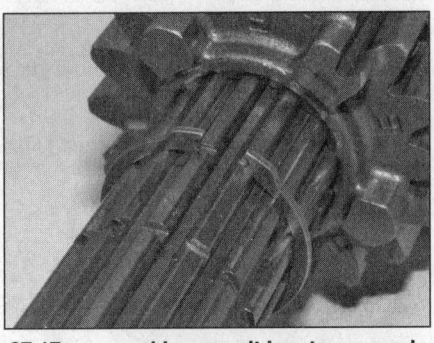

27.17c ... making sure it locates properly in its groove

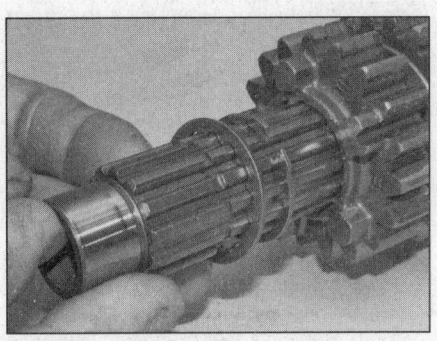

27.18a Slide the splined washer ...

27.18b ... the 6th gear pinion splined bush ...

27.18c ... and the 6th gear pinion onto the shaft

27.19a Slide on the slotted splined washer ...

27.19b ... and locate it as shown ...

27.19c ... then slide on the tabbed lockwasher and locate its tabs in the slots

it locates correctly in the groove in the shaft (see illustrations).

17 Slide the combined 3rd/4th gear pinion onto the shaft with the larger 4th gear pinion facing the 5th gear pinion (see illustration). Fit the circlip, making sure it is locates correctly in its groove in the shaft (see illustrations).

18 Slide the splined washer onto the shaft, followed by the 6th gear pinion splined bush, aligning the oil hole in the bush with the hole in the shaft (see illustrations). Slide the 6th gear pinion onto the bush, with its dogs facing the 3rd/4th gear pinion (see illustration).

19 Slide the slotted splined washer onto the shaft and locate it in its groove, then turn it in the groove so that the splines on the washer align with the splines on the shaft and secure the washer in the groove (see illustrations). Slide the tabbed lockwasher onto the shaft, locating the tabs in the slots in the outer rim of the splined washer (see illustration).

20 Slide the 2nd gear pinion onto the end of the shaft with the mark made on removal

27.20a Slide the 2nd gear pinion . . .

27.20b . . . and the thrust washer onto the shaft

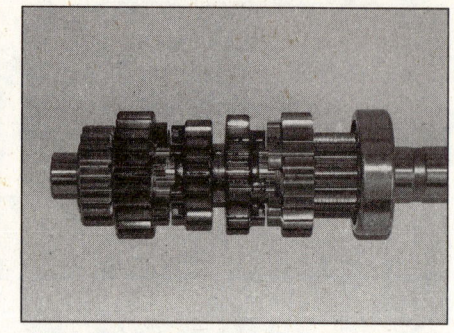

27.21 The complete input shaft should be as shown

facing out **(see illustration)**. Fit the thrust washer **(see illustration)**.

21 Check that all components have been correctly installed **(see illustration)**.

Output shaft

Disassembly

22 Slide the outer race and the needle bearing off the right-hand end of the shaft **(see illustration and illustrations 27.37e and d)**.
23 Slide the thrust washer off the shaft, followed by the 1st gear pinion and its needle roller bearing, the thrust washer and the 5th gear pinion **(see illustrations 27.37c, b and a, and 27.36b and a)**.
24 Remove the circlip, then slide the splined washer, the 4th gear pinion and its splined bush off the shaft **(see illustrations 27.35d, c, b and a)**.
25 Slide the tabbed lockwasher off the shaft, then turn the slotted splined washer to offset the splines and slide it off the shaft **(see illustrations 27.34c and a)**.
26 Slide the 3rd gear pinion and its splined bush, followed by the splined washer, off the shaft **(see illustrations 27.33c, b and a)**.
27 Remove the circlip, then slide the 6th gear pinion off the shaft **(see illustrations 27.32b and a)**.
28 Remove the circlip, then slide the splined washer, the 2nd gear pinion and its bush off the shaft **(see illustrations 27.31d, c, b and a)**.

Inspection

29 Refer to Steps 7 to 13 above.

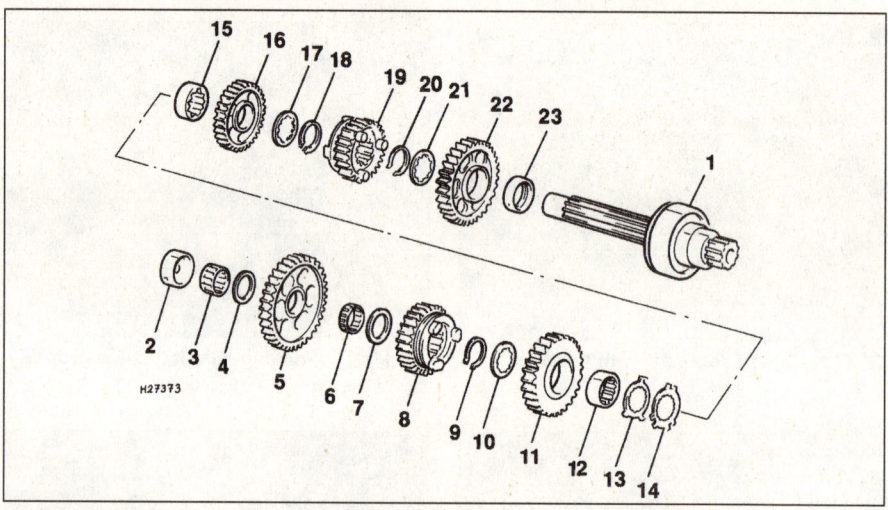

27.22 Transmission output shaft components

1 Output shaft and bearing
2 Needle roller bearing outer race
3 Needle roller bearing
4 Thrust washer
5 1st gear pinion
6 Needle roller bearing
7 Thrust washer
8 5th gear pinion
9 Circlip
10 Splined washer
11 4th gear pinion
12 4th gear pinion splined bush
13 Tabbed lockwasher
14 Slotted splined washer
15 3rd gear pinion splined bush
16 3rd gear pinion
17 Splined washer
18 Circlip
19 6th gear pinion
20 Circlip
21 Splined washer
22 2nd gear pinion
23 2nd gear pinion bush

Reassembly

30 During reassembly, apply engine oil to the mating surfaces of the shaft, pinions and bushes. When installing the circlips, do not expand the ends any further than is necessary. Install the stamped circlips and washers so that their chamfered side faces away from the thrust side (see *Tools and Workshop Tips* in the Reference section).
31 Slide the 2nd gear pinion bush onto the shaft, then slide the 2nd gear pinion onto the bush with its dog holes facing away from the bearing, followed by the splined washer **(see illustrations)**. Fit the circlip, making sure it

27.31a Slide the 2nd gear pinion bush . . .

27.31b . . . the 2nd gear pinion . . .

27.31c . . . and the splined washer onto the shaft . . .

Engine, clutch and transmission 2•55

27.31d . . . and secure them with the circlip . . .

27.31e . . . making sure it locates in the groove

27.32a Slide the 6th gear pinion onto the shaft . . .

27.32b . . . and secure it with the circlip . . .

27.32c . . . making sure it locates in the groove

27.33a Slide the splined washer . . .

locates correctly in its groove in the shaft (**see illustrations**).

32 Slide the 6th gear pinion on with its selector fork groove facing away from the 2nd gear pinion, then fit the circlip, making sure it is locates correctly in its groove in the shaft (**see illustrations**).

33 Slide the splined washer and the 3rd gear pinion splined bush onto the shaft, making sure the oil hole in the bush aligns with the hole in the shaft, then slide the 3rd gear pinion onto its bush with its dog holes facing the 6th gear pinion (**see illustrations**).

34 Slide the slotted splined washer onto the shaft and locate it in its groove, then turn it in the groove so that the splines on the washer align with the splines on the shaft and secure the washer in the groove (**see illustrations**).

27.33b . . . the 3rd gear pinion splined bush . . .

Slide the lockwasher onto the shaft, locating the tabs on the lockwasher in the slots in the outer rim of the splined washer (**see illustration**).

27.33c . . . and the 3rd gear pinion onto the shaft

35 Slide the 4th gear pinion splined bush onto the shaft, making sure the oil hole in the bush aligns with the hole in the shaft (see

27.34a Slide the slotted splined washer onto the shaft . . .

27.34b . . . and locate it as shown

27.34c Slide the lockwasher onto the shaft and engage it with the slotted washer

2•56 Engine, clutch and transmission

27.35a Slide the 4th gear pinion splined bush . . .

27.35b . . . the 4th gear pinion . . .

27.35c . . . and the splined washer onto the shaft . . .

27.35d . . . and secure them with the circlip . . .

27.35e . . . making sure it locates in the groove

27.36a Slide the 5th gear pinion . . .

27.36b . . . and the thrust washer onto the shaft

27.37a Slide the needle bearing . . .

27.37b . . . the 1st gear pinion . . .

illustration). Slide the 4th gear pinion onto its bush with its dog holes facing away from the 3rd gear pinion **(see illustration)**. Slide the splined washer on, then fit the circlip, making sure it is locates correctly in its groove in the shaft **(see illustrations)**.

36 Slide the 5th gear pinion onto the shaft with its selector fork groove facing the 4th gear pinion, followed by the thrust washer **(see illustrations)**.

37 Slide the 1st gear pinion needle roller bearing onto the shaft, then slide the 1st gear pinion onto the bearing with its dog holes facing the 5th gear pinion. Fit the thrust washer, then fit the needle roller bearing and its outer race over the end of the shaft **(see illustrations)**.

27.37c . . . and the thrust washer onto the shaft . . .

27.37d . . . then fit the bearing onto the end of the shaft . . .

27.37e . . . and the outer race over the bearing

Engine, clutch and transmission 2•57

27.38 The assembled output shaft should be as shown

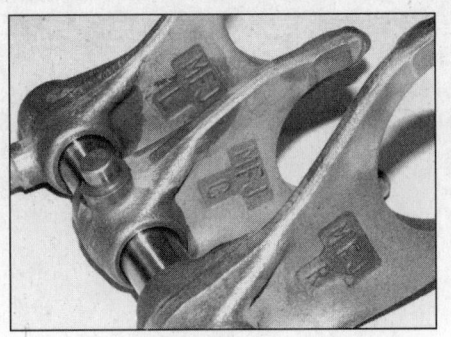

28.3 Note the identification markings on the forks

28.4 Unscrew the bolts (arrowed)

38 Check that all components have been correctly installed **(see illustration)**.

28 Selector drum and forks

Note: *To remove the selector drum and forks the engine must be removed from the frame and the crankcases separated.*

Removal

1 The selector drum and forks are located in the upper crankcase half. Remove the engine (see Section 4) and separate the crankcase halves (see Section 19).
2 Remove the transmission output shaft (see Section 26). If not already done, remove the gearchange mechanism (see Section 16).
3 Before removing the selector forks, note that each fork carries an identification letter **(see illustration)**. The right-hand fork has R, the centre fork C, and the left-hand fork L. These letters all face the right-hand (clutch) side of the engine. If no letters are visible, mark them yourself using a felt pen. The R and L forks fit into the output shaft and the C fork fits into the input shaft.
4 Unscrew and remove the selector drum bearing/fork shaft retainer bolts **(see illustration)**.
5 Support the selector forks and withdraw the shaft from the casing, then remove the forks **(see illustrations 28.14d, c, b and a)**. Withdraw the selector drum from the right-hand side of the engine **(see illustration)**.
6 Once removed from the case, slide the forks back onto the shaft to keep them in the correct order.

Inspection

7 Inspect the selector forks for any signs of wear or damage, especially around the fork ends where they engage with the groove in the pinion. Check that each fork fits correctly in its pinion groove. Check closely to see if the forks are bent. If the forks are in any way damaged they must be replaced with new ones.
8 Measure the thickness of the fork ends and compare the readings to the specifications **(see illustration)**. Replace the forks with new ones if they are worn beyond their specifications.
9 Check that the forks fit correctly on their shaft **(see illustration)**. They should move freely with a light fit but no appreciable freeplay. Measure the internal diameter of the fork bores and the corresponding diameter of the fork shaft **(see illustrations)**. Replace the forks and/or shaft with new ones if they are worn beyond their specifications. Check that the fork shaft holes in the casing are neither worn nor damaged.
10 Check the selector fork shaft is straight by rolling it along a flat surface. A bent rod will cause difficulty in selecting gears and make the gearchange action heavy. Replace the shaft with a new one if it is bent.
11 Inspect the selector drum grooves and selector fork guide pins for signs of wear or damage **(see illustration)**. If either component

28.5 Withdraw the selector drum

28.8 Measure the fork end thickness

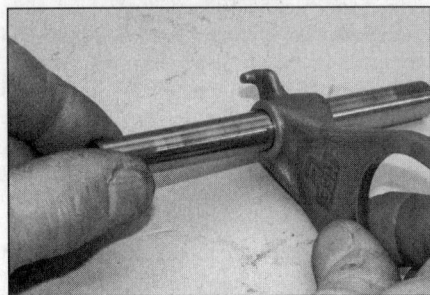

28.9a Check the fit of each fork on the shaft . . .

28.9b . . . then measure the fork shaft OD . . .

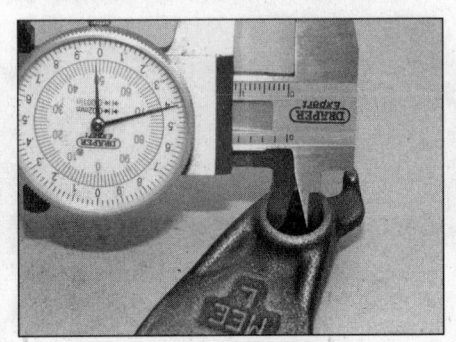

28.9c . . . and the fork bore ID

28.11 Check the guide pins and their grooves in the drum

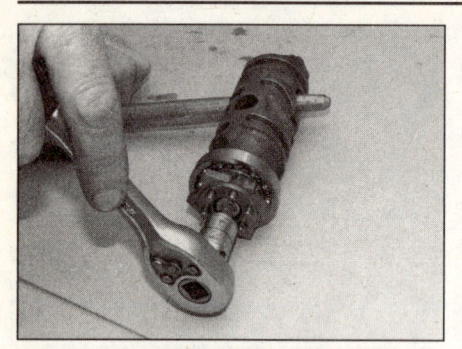

2•58 Engine, clutch and transmission

28.12a Counter-hold the drum as shown and unscrew the bolt

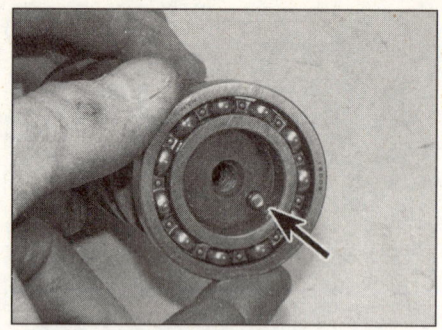

28.12b Remove the old bearing and fit a new one. Note the locating pin (arrowed)

28.12c Locate the cut-out (arrowed) over the pin

28.12d Apply a threadlock to the bolt

shows signs of wear or damage the fork(s) and drum must be replaced with new ones.

12 Check that the selector drum bearing rotates freely and has no sign of freeplay between it and the casing. To fit a new bearing, remove the selector drum cam by unscrewing the bolt in its centre – pass a rod through the drum to counter-hold it **(see illustration)**. Note the locating pin in the end of the drum and remove it for safekeeping if required. Remove the old bearing and fit a new one (see *Tools and Workshop Tips* in the Reference Section if necessary) **(see illustration)**. Fit the selector drum cam, locating the pin in the wider cut-out in the back of the cam **(see illustration)**. Clean the threads of the cam bolt and apply a suitable non-permanent thread locking compound, and tighten it to the torque setting specified at the beginning of the Chapter **(see illustration)**.

Installation

13 Slide the selector drum into position in the crankcase **(see illustration 28.5)**. Make sure the drum end locates into its bore in the casing, and position it so that the neutral contact is against the neutral switch.
14 Lubricate the selector fork shaft with clean engine oil and slide it into the crankcase, locating each fork in the correct order and way round (see Step 3), fitting each fork's guide pin in its groove in the selector drum, and fitting the centre fork ends in its pinion groove in the input shaft **(see illustrations)**.
15 Clean the threads of the selector drum retainer bolts, then apply a suitable non-permanent thread locking compound. Fit the bolts and tighten them to the torque setting specified at the beginning of the Chapter **(see illustration 28.4)**.
16 Install the transmission output shaft, then reassemble the crankcase halves and the rest of the engine.

29 Running-in procedure

1 Make sure the engine oil and coolant levels are correct (see *Pre-ride checks*). Make sure there is fuel in the tank.
2 Turn the engine kill switch to the ON position and shift the gearbox into neutral. Turn the ignition ON.
3 Start the engine and allow it to run with no throttle applied until it reaches operating temperature.

⚠ *Warning: If the oil pressure warning light doesn't go off, or it comes on while the engine is running, stop the engine immediately.*

4 If the oil pressure warning light does not go out, stop the engine immediately and try to find the cause – refer to Section 3. If an engine is run without oil pressure, even for a short period of time, severe damage will occur.
5 Check carefully for oil and coolant leaks and make sure the transmission and controls, especially the brakes, function properly before road testing the machine.
6 Treat the machine gently for the first few miles to make sure oil has circulated throughout the engine and any new parts installed have started to seat.
7 Even greater care is necessary if new pistons/rings or a new crankcase/bores have been fitted, and the bike will have to be run in as when new. This means greater use of the transmission and a restraining hand on the throttle until at least 300 miles (500 km) have been covered. There's no point in keeping to any set speed limit – the main idea is to keep from labouring the engine and to gradually increase performance up to the 300 miles (500 km) mark. Experience is the best guide, since it's easy to tell when an engine is running freely.
8 Upon completion of the road test, and after the engine has cooled down completely, recheck the valve clearances (see Chapter 1) and check the engine oil and coolant levels (see *Pre-ride checks*).

28.14a Slide the shaft in and through the R fork . . .

28.14b . . . the C fork . . .

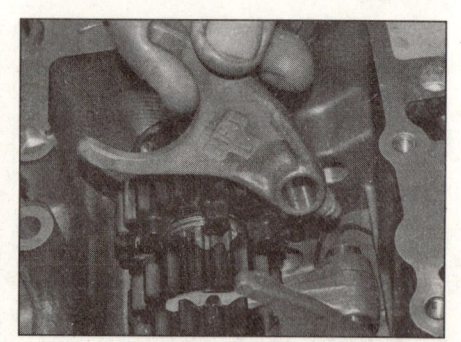

28.14c . . . and the L fork and into its bore in the crankcase

Chapter 3
Cooling system

Contents

	Section number		Section number
Coolant change	see Chapter 1	General information	1
Coolant hoses, pipes and unions	8	Oil cooler	see Chapter 2
Coolant level check	see Pre-ride checks	Radiator	5
Coolant reservoir	7	Temperature display and ECT sensor	3
Cooling fan and fan relay	2	Thermostat and housing	4
Cooling system checks	see Chapter 1	Water pump	6

Degrees of difficulty

Easy, suitable for novice with little experience	**Fairly easy,** suitable for beginner with some experience	**Fairly difficult,** suitable for competent DIY mechanic	**Difficult,** suitable for experienced DIY mechanic	**Very difficult,** suitable for expert DIY or professional

Specifications

Coolant
Mixture type and capacity .... see Chapter 1

ECT sensor
Resistance @ 80°C .... 2.1 to 2.6 K-ohms
Resistance @ 120°C .... 650 to 730 ohms

Thermostat
Opening temperature .... 80 to 84°C
Fully open .... 95°C
Valve lift .... 8 mm (min)

Radiator
Cap valve opening pressure .... 16 to 20 psi (1.1 to 1.4 Bar)

Torque settings
Cooling fan assembly – CB600F/FA and CBF600N/NA/S/SA
   Fan blade nut .... 2.7 Nm
   Fan shroud bolts .... 8.5 Nm
   Fan motor bolts .... 5 Nm
Cooling fan assembly – CBR600F/FA
   Fan blade nut .... 2.7 Nm
   Fan bracket bolts .... 8.5 Nm
   Fan motor nuts .... 5 Nm
ECT sensor .... 23 Nm
Thermostat housing cover bolts .... 12 Nm
Water pump bolts .... 12 Nm

3•2 Cooling system

1 General information

The cooling system uses a water/anti-freeze coolant to carry away excess heat from the engine and maintain as constant a temperature as possible. The cylinders are surrounded by a water jacket from which the heated coolant is circulated by thermo-syphonic action in conjunction with a water pump, which is driven by the oil pump. The hot coolant passes upwards to the thermostat and through to the radiator. The coolant then flows across the core of the radiator, then to the water pump and back to the engine. On CB600F/FA and CBR600F/FA models the coolant is also circulated around the oil cooler.

A thermostat is fitted in the system to prevent the coolant flowing through the radiator when the engine is cold, therefore accelerating the speed at which the engine reaches normal operating temperature. An engine coolant temperature (ECT) sensor mounted in the thermostat housing provides information to the engine management system ECM (engine control module), and to the temperature gauge and/or warning light on the instrument panel, according to model. A cooling fan fitted to the back of the radiator aids cooling in extreme conditions by drawing extra air through. The fan motor is controlled by a relay which receives a signal from the ECM which in turn receives information from the ECT sensor.

The complete cooling system is partially sealed and pressurised, the pressure being controlled by a valve contained in the spring-loaded radiator cap. By pressurising the coolant the boiling point is raised, preventing premature boiling in adverse conditions. The overflow pipe from the system is connected to a reservoir into which excess coolant is expelled under pressure. The discharged coolant automatically returns to the radiator by the vacuum created when the engine cools.

Warning: Do not remove the pressure cap from the radiator when the engine is hot. Scalding hot coolant and steam may be blown out under pressure, which could cause serious injury. When the engine has cooled, place a thick rag, like a towel, over the pressure cap; slowly rotate the cap anti-clockwise to the first stop. This procedure allows any residual pressure to escape. When the steam has stopped escaping, press down on the cap while turning it anti-clockwise and remove it.

Caution: Do not allow anti-freeze to come in contact with your skin or painted surfaces of the motorcycle. Rinse off any spills immediately with plenty of water. Anti-freeze is highly toxic if ingested. Never leave anti-freeze lying around in an open container or in puddles on the floor; children and pets are attracted by its sweet smell and may drink it. Check with the local authorities about disposing of used anti-freeze. Many communities will have collection centres which will see that anti-freeze is disposed of safely.

Caution: The cooling system must be filled with either a pre-mix coolant, or anti-freeze and distilled water mixed in the correct proportion. The anti-freeze contains corrosion inhibitors which are essential to avoid damage to the cooling system. A lack of these inhibitors could lead to a build-up of corrosion which would block the coolant passages, resulting in overheating and severe engine damage. Distilled water must be used as opposed to tap water to avoid a build-up of scale which would also block the passages.

2 Cooling fan and fan relay

Cooling fan

Check

1 The cooling fan is on the back of the radiator. If the engine is overheating and the cooling fan does not come on, check the cooling fan fuse (see Chapter 8). If the fuse is good, check the relay (see below).

2 To test the cooling fan motor, raise the fuel tank (see Chapter 4). Release the fan wiring connector from the retainer and disconnect it **(see illustrations)**. Using a 12 volt battery and two jumper wires with suitable connectors, connect the battery positive (+) lead to the black/blue wire terminal on the fan side of the wiring connector, and the battery negative (–) lead to the black wire terminal on the connector. Once connected the fan should operate. If it does not, and the connector and wiring between it and the motor is good, then the fan motor is faulty.

Removal and installation – CB600F/FA and CBF600N/NA/S/SA

3 Remove the radiator (see Section 5).
4 Unscrew the fan shroud bolts, noting the washers, and remove the fan assembly **(see illustration)**.
5 If required unscrew the fan blade nut and remove the blade **(see illustration)**. Free the wiring from the guide. Undo the three bolts

2.2a Release the catch using a small screwdriver . . .

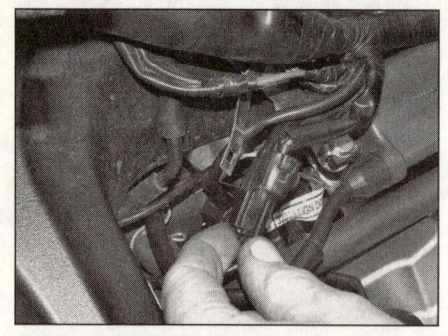

2.2b . . . and slide the connector off . . .

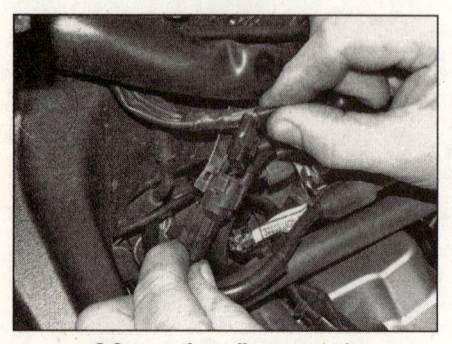

2.2c . . . then disconnect it

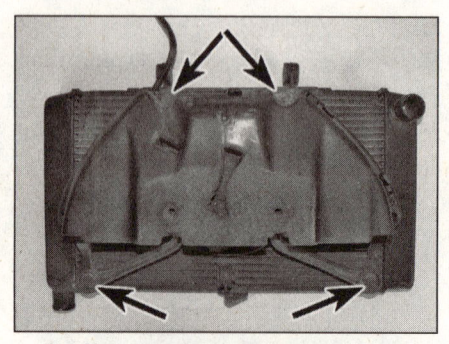

2.4 Unscrew the bolts (arrowed) and remove the shroud

2.5a Fan blade nut (arrowed)

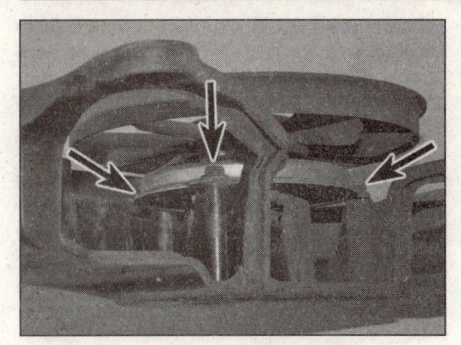

2.5b Fan motor bolts arrowed)

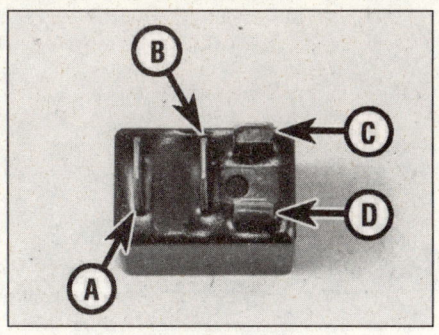

2.15 Fan relay terminal identification

on the front of the fan motor and separate the motor from the shroud **(see illustration)**.
6 Installation is the reverse of removal. Tighten the fan motor bolts to the torque setting specified at the beginning of the Chapter. Clean the threads of the motor shaft. Align the flats on the shaft with those in the bore in the fan blade. Apply a suitable non-permanent thread locking compound to the fan blade nut and tighten it to the specified torque. Tighten the shroud bolts to the specified torque.
7 Install the radiator (see Section 5).

Removal and installation – CBR600F/FA

⚠️ **Warning: The engine must be completely cool before carrying out this procedure.**

8 Remove the radiator (see Section 5).
9 Unscrew the bolts and remove the fan assembly.
10 If required unscrew the fan blade nut and remove the blade. Undo the three nuts on the front of the fan motor and separate the motor from the bracket.
11 Installation is the reverse of removal. Tighten the fan motor nuts to the torque setting specified at the beginning of the Chapter. Clean the threads of the motor shaft. Align the flats on the motor shaft with those in the bore in the fan blade. Apply a suitable non-permanent thread locking compound to the fan blade nut and tighten it to the specified torque. Tighten the bracket bolts to the specified torque.
12 Install the radiator (see Section 5).

Cooling fan relay

Check

13 If the engine is overheating and the cooling fan does not come on, first check the cooling fan fuse (see Chapter 8).
14 If the fuse is good, remove the relay (see Steps 19 and 20).
15 Set a multimeter to the ohms x 1 scale and connect it across the relay's A and B terminals **(see illustration)**. There should be no continuity (infinite resistance). Using a fully-charged 12 volt battery and two insulated jumper wires, connect the positive (+) terminal of the battery to the C terminal on the relay, and the negative (–) terminal to the D terminal on the relay. At this point the relay should be heard to click and the multimeter read 0 ohms (continuity). If this is the case the relay is proved good. If the relay does not click when battery voltage is applied and still indicates no continuity (infinite resistance) across its terminals, it is faulty and must be replaced with a new one.
16 If the relay is good, check for battery voltage at the red/green wire in the wiring connector with the ignition switch ON. If there is no voltage, check the wiring between the relay and the fusebox for continuity, referring to the relevant wiring diagram at the end of Chapter 8. Next check for voltage in the black/white wire, and if there is none check the wire to the engine stop relay for continuity, then check the engine stop relay (see Chapter 4, Section 7). If voltage is present, check that there is continuity to earth in the black/blue wire with the ignition switch OFF. If there is no continuity, check the wiring between the relay, the fan wiring connector, the fan, then back to the connector and then in the green wire to earth. If all is good check the green/blue wire for continuity to the ECM (engine control module).
17 If the fan is on the whole time, refer to Steps 19 and 20 and remove the relay – the fan should stop. If it does, the relay is defective and must be replaced with a new one.
18 If the fan works but is suspected of cutting in at the wrong temperature, check the ECT sensor (see Section 3).

Removal and installation

19 On CB600F/FA and CBR600F/FA models, remove the seat cowl (see Chapter 7). On CBF600N/NA/S/SA models, remove the left-hand seat cowl (see Chapter 7).
20 Move the rubber retainer aside then pull the relay off the connector **(see illustrations)**.
21 Installation is the reverse of removal.

3 Temperature display and ECT sensor

Temperature display

1 On CBF600N/NA/S/SA models the circuit consists of the ECT sensor mounted in the thermostat housing and the warning light in the instrument cluster.
2 On CB600F/FA and CBR600F/FA models the circuit consists of the ECT sensor mounted in the thermostat housing and the digital display, temperature indicator symbol and warning light in the instrument cluster. When the ignition is first switched on all the segments in the LCD display should come on temporarily – this serves as an indication that the display is functioning correctly (if not, refer to Chapter 8). Under normal operating conditions, when the coolant temperature is below 34°C the display will show '- -'. When the temperature is between 35°C and 132°C the display will show the actual temperature. Once the temperature reaches 122°C the display will start to flash, and the temperature indicator symbol and the warning light will come on. If this occurs

2.20a Cooling fan relay – 2007 to 2010 CB models

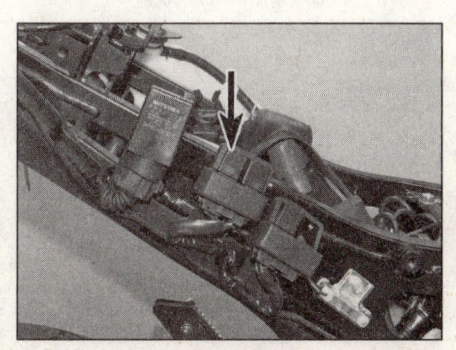

2.20b Cooling fan relay – 2011-on CB and CBR models

2.20c Cooling fan relay – CBF models

3•4 Cooling system

3.3 ECT sensor wiring connector (arrowed)

4.3 Pull the cap (A) off, unscrew the bolt (B) then slacken the clamp (C) and detach the hose

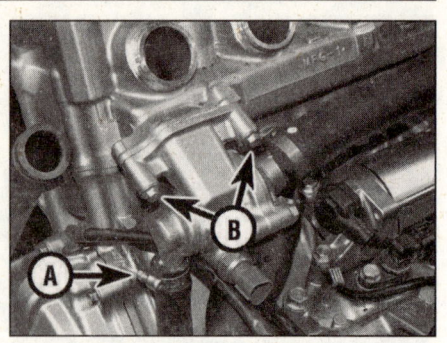

4.5 Slacken the clamp (A) and detach the hose. Thermostat housing bolts (B)

stop the engine and check the coolant level in the reservoir (see *Pre-ride checks*). If the temperature goes above 132°C the display will continue to show 132°C.

3 If the temperature warning light does not come on, disconnect the ECT sensor wiring connector **(see illustration)**. Using a jump wire, connect the green/blue (2007 to 2010 CB600F/FA and all CBF600N/NA/S/SA models) or grey/red (2011-on CB600F/FA and CBR600F/FA models) wire terminal in the connector to earth. Turn the ignition ON – the indicator symbol and/or warning light (according to model) should come on. If so, replace the sensor with a new one. If not, refer to Chapter 8 and disconnect the instrument wiring connector. Check the green/blue or grey/red wire for continuity between the ECT sensor and instrument cluster wiring connectors. If there is no continuity repair the wiring. If there is continuity the instrument board could be faulty – refer to Chapter 8.

4 If the light is on the whole time, disconnect the ECT sensor wiring connector **(see illustration 3.3)**. Turn the ignition ON – if the light is off the sensor is faulty. If the light is still on, refer to Chapter 8 and disconnect the instrument wiring connector. Check the green/blue (2007 to 2010 CB600F/FA and all CBF600N/NA/S/SA models) or grey/red (2011-on CB600F/FA and CBR600F/FA models) wire for continuity to earth – if there is continuity, locate the fault and repair it. If not the instrument board could be faulty (see Chapter 8).

ECT sensor

Check

5 The resistance of the sensor changes with changes in temperature – see the Specifications at the beginning of the chapter. While in theory it is possible to bench-test the sensor at those temperatures, in practice the test is difficult to set up and perform.

6 However you can test the resistance of the sensor in the bike with the engine cold, warm and hot. Disconnect the ECT sensor wiring connector **(see illustration 3.3)**. Connect the positive probe of a multimeter set to read resistance to the green/blue (2007 to 2010 CB600F/FA and all CBF600N/NA/S/SA models) or grey/red (2011-on CB600F/FA and CBR600F/FA models) wire terminal on the switch and the negative probe to the body of the switch and take several readings as the engine warms up. Resistance should decrease as temperature increases – if the sensor fails it is most likely to give a zero, constant, or infinite resistance reading at all temperatures.

Removal and installation

⚠️ **Warning: The engine must be completely cool before carrying out this procedure.**

7 The sensor is mounted in the thermostat housing **(see illustration 3.3)**. Drain the cooling system (see Chapter 1).

8 Disconnect the ECT sensor wiring connector.

9 Unscrew and remove the sensor, and discard the sealing washer.

10 Fit a new sealing washer onto the sensor. Fit the sensor and tighten it to the torque setting specified at the beginning of the Chapter. Connect the wiring.

11 Refill the cooling system (see Chapter 1).

4 Thermostat and housing

1 The thermostat is automatic in operation and should give many years service without requiring attention. In the event of a failure, the valve will probably jam open, in which case the engine will take much longer than normal to warm up. Conversely, if the valve jams shut, the coolant will be unable to circulate and the engine will overheat. Neither condition is acceptable – the fault must be investigated promptly.

Housing removal

⚠️ **Warning: The engine must be completely cool before carrying out this procedure.**

2 Drain the cooling system (see Chapter 1).

3 Pull the cap off the No. 4 cylinder spark plug. Unscrew the filler neck bolt. Draw the neck out, slacken the clamp securing the large hose to the back of the neck and detach the hose **(see illustration)**.

4 Disconnect the ECT sensor wiring connector **(see illustration 3.3)**.

5 Slacken the clamp securing the by-pass hose to the thermostat housing and detach the hose **(see illustration)**.

6 Unscrew the housing bolts and remove the housing, bringing the large bore hose with it and noting its routing **(see illustration 4.5)**. Remove the O-ring – a new one must be used. Detach the hose if required.

Thermostat removal

7 Remove the housing (Steps 2 to 6).

8 Unscrew the cover bolts and detach it from the housing **(see illustration)**. Withdraw the thermostat, noting how it fits **(see illustration)**.

Thermostat check

9 Examine the thermostat visually before

4.8a Unscrew the bolts (arrowed) and detach the cover...

4.8b ...then withdraw the thermostat from the housing

Cooling system 3•5

carrying out the test. If it remains in the open position at room temperature, it should be replaced with a new one. Also check the condition of the seal.

10 Suspend the thermostat by a piece of wire in a container of cold water. Place a thermometer capable of reading temperatures up to 110°C in the water so that the bulb is close to the thermostat **(see illustration)**. Heat the water, noting the temperature when the thermostat opens, and compare the result with the specifications given at the beginning of the Chapter. Also check the amount the valve opens after it has been heated for a few minutes and compare the measurement to the specifications. If the readings obtained differ from those given, the thermostat is faulty and must be replaced with a new one.

11 In the event of thermostat failure, if the thermostat is permanently closed, as an emergency measure only it can be removed and the machine used without it (this is better than leaving it in as the engine will overheat). If it is permanently open you are better to leave it in. In both cases take care when starting the engine from cold as it will take much longer than usual to warm up. Ensure that a new unit is installed as soon as possible.

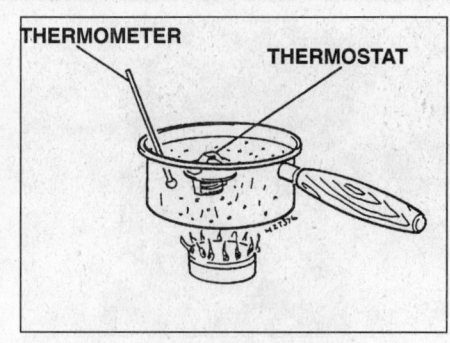

Installation

12 Check the thermostat seal for signs of damage or deterioration and fit a new one if necessary **(see illustration)**. Fit the thermostat into the housing with the stamp mark at the top, and aligning the rib with the groove **(see illustration 4.8b)**.
13 Fit the cover and tighten the bolts to the torque setting specified at the beginning of the Chapter **(see illustration)**.
14 Reconnect the hose if detached. Fit a new O-ring into the groove in the housing **(see illustration)**.
15 Feed the hose up to the filler neck then fit the housing and tighten the bolts **(see illustrations 4.5)**.
16 Connect the by-pass hose and tighten the clamp. Connect the ECT sensor wiring **(see illustration 3.3)**.

4.10 Thermostat testing set-up

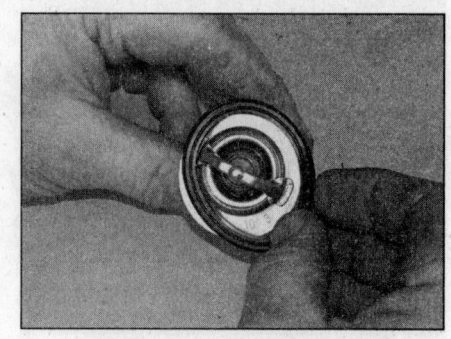

4.13 Fit the cover onto the housing as shown

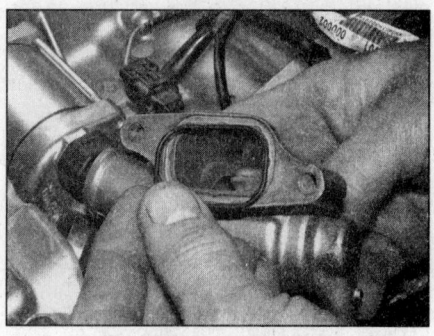

17 Connect the hose to the filler neck and tighten the clamp **(see illustration 4.3)**. Fit the neck and tighten the bolt. Fit the cap onto the spark plug.
18 Fill the cooling system (see Chapter 1).

5 Radiator

Note: *If the radiator is being removed as part of the engine removal procedure, detach the hoses from their unions on the engine rather than on the radiator and remove the radiator complete with its hoses. Note the routing of the hoses.*

4.12 Fit a new seal if necessary

4.14 Use a new O-ring

Removal

⚠ **Warning: The engine must be completely cool before carrying out this procedure.**

1 Drain the cooling system (see Chapter 1).
2 Release the fan wiring connector from the retainer and disconnect it **(see illustrations 2.2a, b and c)**.
3 Slacken the clamps securing the hoses to the radiator and detach them **(see illustrations)**.
4 On all except CBR600F/FA models release the horn wiring from the right-hand side of the fan shroud.
5 Unscrew the lower mounting bolt, noting the washer **(see illustration)**. Unscrew the radiator upper mounting bolts, noting the

5.3a Detach the hose (arrowed) from the right-hand side of the radiator . . .

5.3b . . . and from the left-hand side

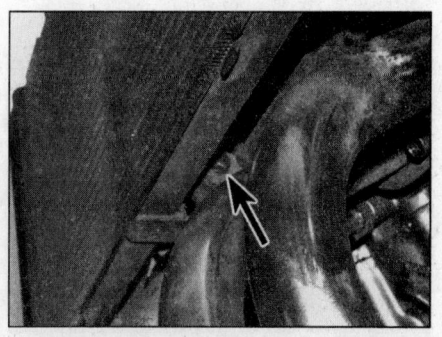

5.5a Unscrew the lower mounting bolt (arrowed) . . .

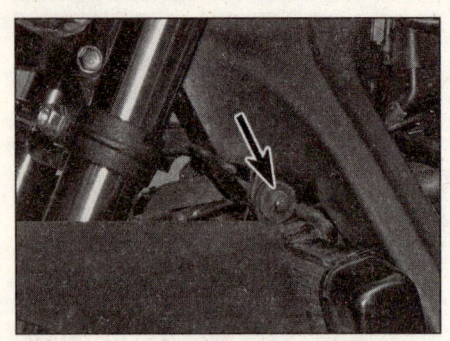

3•6 Cooling system

5.5b . . . then the upper bolt (arrowed) on each side

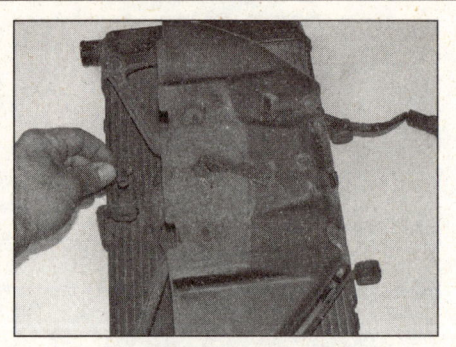

5.7 Note the collars and check the condition of the grommets

washers, and remove the radiator, taking care not to catch the fins on anything **(see illustration)**.

6 On CB600F/FA and CBF600N/NA models remove the radiator grille if required.

7 Note the arrangement of the collars and rubber grommets in the radiator mounts **(see illustration)**. Replace the grommets with new ones if they are damaged, deformed or deteriorated.

8 Check the radiator for signs of damage and clear any dirt or debris that might obstruct air flow and inhibit cooling. If the radiator fins are badly damaged or broken the radiator must be replaced with a new one. To enable full examination and cleaning, remove the cooling fan (see Section 2).

Installation

9 Installation is the reverse of removal, noting the following.

- Ensure the coolant hoses are in good condition (see Chapter 1), and are securely retained by their clamps, using new ones if necessary.
- Make sure the rubber grommets are in place.
- Make sure the collars are correctly fitted in the grommets *(see illustration 5.7)*.
- Make sure that the fan wiring is correctly connected.
- On completion refill the cooling system as described in Chapter 1.

Pressure cap check

10 If problems such as overheating or loss of coolant occur, check the entire system as described in Chapter 1. If there are no obvious problems and leaks the pressure cap opening pressure should be checked by a Honda dealer with the special tester required to do the job. If the cap is defective, replace it with a new one.

6 Water pump

Check

1 Refer to Chapter 1, Section 9.

Removal

2 Drain the coolant (see Chapter 1).

3 Remove the front sprocket cover (see Chapter 6). Displace the sidestand switch and free its wiring from the clamps and position it clear (see Chapter 8).

4 Slacken the clamps securing the coolant hoses to the pump and detach the hoses, noting which fits where **(see illustration)**. Unscrew the pipe union bolt and remove the pipe **(see illustration)**. Remove the seal – a new one must be used.

5 Unscrew the two pump mounting bolts, then draw the pump from the crankcase, noting how it fits **(see illustrations)**. It may be necessary to lever it out to overcome the O-ring on the pump body. Remove the O-ring from the rear of the body – a new one must be used **(see illustration 6.9a)**.

6 To remove the cover, unscrew the remaining bolts **(see illustrations)**. Remove the O-ring – a new one must be used **(see illustration 6.8)**. Do not attempt to remove the impeller and seals – the pump comes as an assembly and no internal components are available.

7 Wiggle the water pump impeller back-and-

6.4a Slacken the clamps (arrowed) and detach the hoses

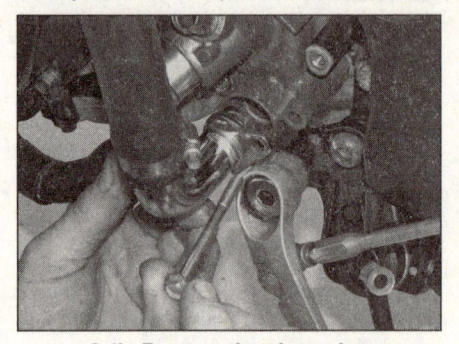

6.4b Remove the pipe union

6.5a Unscrew the bolts (arrowed) . . .

6.5b . . . and withdraw the pump

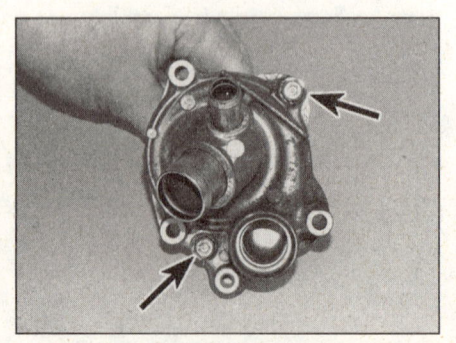

6.6a Unscrew the bolts (arrowed) . . .

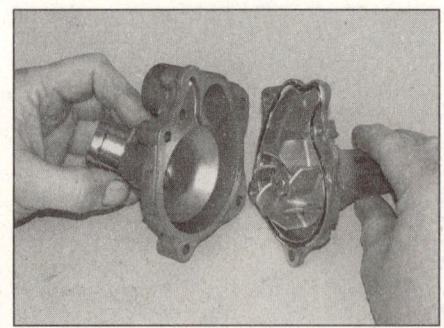

6.6b . . . and remove the cover

Cooling system 3•7

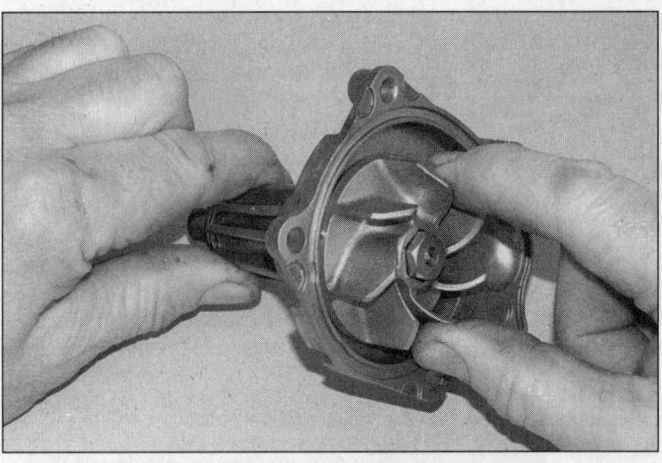

6.7 Check the pump impeller as described

6.8 Fit the new O-ring into its groove

6.9a Fit a new O-ring onto the body

6.9b Align the slot with the tab (arrowed)

forth and in-and-out **(see illustration)**. If there is excessive movement, replace the pump with a new one. Also check for corrosion or a build-up of scale in the pump body and clean or replace the pump as necessary.

Installation

8 If the cover was removed smear the new O-ring with grease and fit it into its groove **(see illustration)**. Fit the cover onto the pump **(see illustration 6.6b)**. Fit the two bolts and tighten them to the torque setting specified at the beginning of the Chapter **(see illustration 6.6a)**.

9 Apply a smear of engine oil to the new pump body O-ring and fit it into the groove in the body **(see illustration)**. Slide the pump into the crankcase, aligning the slot in the shaft end with the tab on the oil pump shaft **(see illustration)**. Make sure the bolt holes are aligned. Fit the two bolts and tighten them to the torque setting specified at the beginning of the Chapter **(see illustration 6.5a)**.

10 Fit a new seal onto the pipe union **(see illustration)**. Fit the union onto the pump and tighten the bolt **(see illustration 6.4b)**. Fit the coolant hoses onto the pump and secure them with their clamps **(see illustration 6.4a)**.

11 Refill the cooling system (see Chapter 1). Fit the sidestand switch (see Chapter 8). Install the front sprocket cover (see Chapter 6).

7 Coolant reservoir

Removal

CB600F/FA and CBR600F/FA

1 The coolant reservoir is located behind the seat cowl on the left-hand side. Remove the cowl (see Chapter 7). Get a suitable container to drain the coolant into.

2 Detach the breather hose from the top of the reservoir **(see illustration)**.

6.10 Fit a new seal

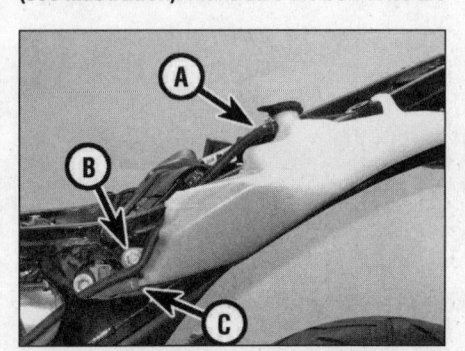

7.2 Breather hose (A), mounting bolt (B), overflow hose (C) – early CB shown

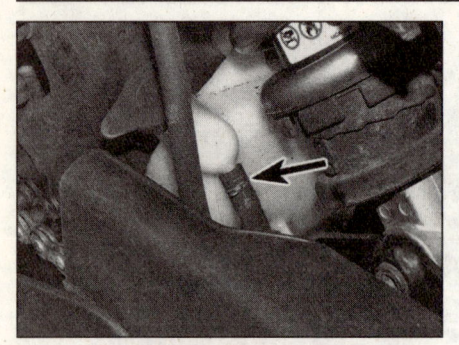

3•8 Cooling system

7.5a Detach the breather hose (arrowed)...

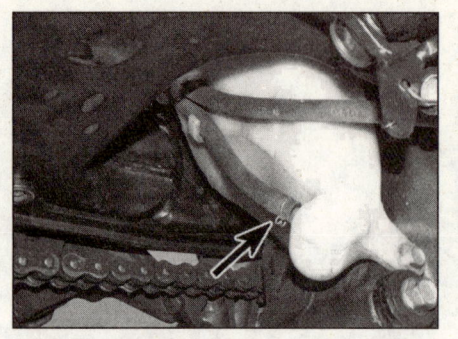

7.5b ...then detach the overflow hose and drain the reservoir

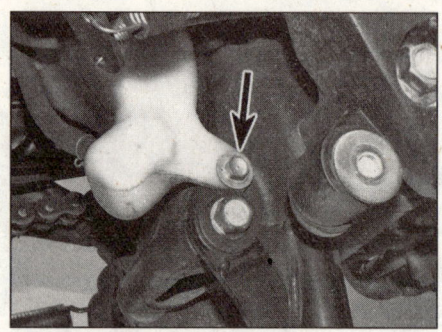

7.6 Reservoir bolt (arrowed)

3 Unscrew the bolt or undo the screws (according to model) and displace the reservoir, then remove the cap and tip the coolant into the container. Detach the radiator overflow hose from the bottom of the reservoir.

CBF600N/NA/S/SA

4 The coolant reservoir is located behind the footrest bracket on the left-hand side. Get a suitable container to drain the coolant into.
5 Detach the breather hose from the top of the reservoir **(see illustration)**. Detach the radiator overflow hose from the bottom of the reservoir and drain the coolant into the container **(see illustration)**.
6 Unscrew the bolt then unhook and remove the reservoir **(see illustration)**.

Installation

7 Installation is the reverse of removal. Refill the reservoir to the UPPER level line with the specified coolant mixture (see *Pre-ride checks*).

8 Coolant hoses, pipes and unions

Removal

1 Before removing a hose, drain the coolant (see Chapter 1).
2 Use a screwdriver to slacken the larger-bore hose clamps, then slide them back along the hose and clear of the union spigot. The smaller-bore hoses are secured by spring clamps which can be expanded by squeezing their ears together with pliers.

Caution: *The radiator unions are fragile. Do not use excessive force when attempting to remove the hoses.*

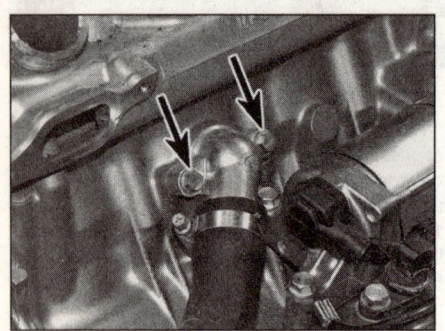

8.4 Inlet union bolts (arrowed)

8.7 Use a new O-ring

3 If a hose proves stubborn, release it by rotating it on its union before working it off. If all else fails, cut the hose with a sharp knife. Whilst this means replacing the hose with a new one – it is preferable to buying a new radiator.
4 The inlet union to the cylinder block can be removed by unscrewing its bolts **(see illustration)**. If the union is removed, the O-ring must be replaced with a new one. The outlet from the cylinder head goes into the thermostat housing, which is covered in Section 4.

Installation

5 Slide the clamps onto the hose and then work the hose on to its union as far as the spigot where present.

> **HAYNES HiNT** *If the hose is difficult to push on its union, soften it by soaking it in very hot water, or alternatively a little soapy water on the union can be used as a lubricant.*

6 Rotate the hose on its unions to settle it in position before sliding the clamps into place and tightening them securely.
7 If the inlet union to the cylinder block has been removed, fit a new O-ring into the groove, using a dab of grease to hold it in place if necessary **(see illustration)**. Install the union and tighten the mounting bolts.
8 Refill the cooling system (see Chapter 1).

Chapter 4
Engine management system

Contents

Section number

Air filter	see Chapter 1
Air filter housing and throttle bodies	3
Air intake system	10
Catalytic converter	18
Clutch switch	see Chapter 8
Engine control module (ECM)	8
Exhaust system	16
Fuel gauge and level sensor	14
Fuel injection system description	5
Fuel injection system fault diagnosis	6
Fuel injection system relays	9
Fuel injection system sensors	7
Fuel pressure check	12
Fuel pump	13
Fuel rails and injectors	4

Section number

Fuel system check	see Chapter 1
Fuel tank	2
General information and precautions	1
Idle speed control system	11
Ignition coils	20
Ignition switch	see Chapter 8
Ignition system check	19
Ignition timing	21
Immobiliser system	22
Neutral switch	see Chapter 8
Pulse secondary air (PAIR) system	17
Sidestand switch	see Chapter 8
Spark plugs	see Chapter 1
Throttle cable check and adjustment	see Chapter 1
Throttle cables	15

Degrees of difficulty

| **Easy,** suitable for novice with little experience | **Fairly easy,** suitable for beginner with some experience | **Fairly difficult,** suitable for competent DIY mechanic | **Difficult,** suitable for experienced DIY mechanic | **Very difficult,** suitable for expert DIY or professional |

Specifications

General information
Cylinder numbering	1 to 4 from left to right
Firing order	1-2-4-3
Spark plugs	see Chapter 1

Fuel
Grade	Unleaded. Minimum 91 RON (Research Octane Number) for Europe

Fuel tank

Capacity (including reserve of 3.5 litres) – CB and CBR models
CB600F/FA 2007 to 2010 models	19.0 litres
CB600F/FA 2011-on models	18.7 litres
CBR600F/FA models	18.4 litres
Capacity (including reserve of 4 litres) – CBF models	20.0 litres

Fuel injection system

Idle speed
CB600F/FA and CBR600F/FA models	1350 ± 100 rpm
CBF600N/NA/S/SA models	1300 ± 100 rpm
Fuel pressure at specified idle speed	50 psi (3.5 Bar)
Minimum fuel flow rate	189 cc every 10 seconds

Fuel injection system test data

Crankshaft position (CKP) sensor
Resistance	approx. 450 ohms at 20°C (68°F)
Minimum peak voltage output	0.7 volt
Engine coolant temperature (ECT) sensor resistance	2.3 to 2.6 K-ohms at 20°C (68°F)
Fuel injector resistance	11 to 13 ohms at 20°C (68°F)
Intake air temperature (IAT) sensor resistance	1 to 4 K-ohms between 20 to 30°C (68 to 86°F)
Oxygen sensor heater resistance	10 to 40 ohms at 20°C (68°F)

4•2 Engine management system

Air intake system
Air intake control valve resistance .... 28 to 32 ohms @ 20°C

Fuel level sensor
Resistance
  CB600F/FA and CBR600F/FA
    Full position .... 8 to 12 ohms
    Empty position .... 234 to 240 ohms
  CBF600N/NA/S/SA
    Full position .... 6 to 10 ohms
    Empty position .... 86 to 90 ohms

PAIR system
PAIR system control valve solenoid resistance .... 23 to 27 ohms @ 20°C

Ignition coils
Note: *All values given are only accurate at 20°C (68°F)*
Primary winding resistance .... approximately 3.5 ohms
Secondary winding resistance
  With plug caps .... approximately 31 K-ohms
  Without plug caps .... approximately 21 K-ohms
Plug cap resistance .... approximately 5 K-ohms
Initial voltage (see text)................................ Battery voltage (approximately 12 volts)
Minimum peak voltage (see text) .... 100 volts
Ignition timing (F mark)
  CB600F/FA and CBR600F/FA .... 5° BTDC at idle
  CBF600N/NA/S/SA .... 4° BTDC at idle

Torque settings
Exhaust system
  All mounting bolts/nuts................................. 22 Nm
  Downpipe flange nuts................................. 12 Nm
  Shield screws .... 12 Nm
  Silencer clamp bolt................................... 22 Nm
Footrest bracket bolts .... 37 Nm
Fuel pump assembly mounting plate nuts .... 12 Nm
Fuel rail bolts .... 5 Nm
Fuel tank pivot bolt nut
  CB600F/FA and CBR600F/FA .... 12 Nm
  CBF600N/NA/S/SA .... 16 Nm
PAIR system reed valve cover bolts...................... 12 Nm
Timing inspection cap .... 18 Nm

1 General information and precautions

General information

Fuel system

The fuel supply system consists of the fuel tank with internal fuel pump assembly (incorporating the pressure regulator, filter and strainer) and fuel level sensor, the fuel hose, the fuel rails, the fuel injectors, the throttle body assembly, and the throttle cables. The fuel pump is switched on and off via a relay. The engine management system, known as PGM-FI, supplies fuel and air to the engine via 36 mm throttle bodies on CB600F/FA and CBR600F/FA models, and 32 mm throttle bodies on CBF600N/NA/S/SA models. The injectors are operated by the Engine Control Module (ECM) using the information obtained from the various sensors it monitors (refer to Section 5 for more information on the operation of the fuel injection system).

All models have a fuel gauge incorporated in the instrument cluster, actuated by the level sensor inside the fuel tank.

Ignition system

The transistorised electronic ignition system is combined with the fuel injection system, both being controlled by the ECM. The ignition system comprises a timing rotor, crankshaft position sensor (CKP sensor), the ECM, the ignition coils and the spark plugs. There are two conventional coils, one firing cylinders 1 and 4, the other firing cylinders 2 and 3, operating on the 'wasted spark' principal.

The triggers on the timing rotor, which are incorporated in the starter clutch housing on the right-hand end of the crankshaft, generate a signal in the CKP sensor as the crankshaft rotates. The CKP sensor sends that signal to the ECM which, in conjunction with information received from the throttle position sensor and engine coolant temperature sensor, calculates the ignition timing and supplies the ignition coils with the power necessary to produce a spark at the plugs. There is no provision for adjusting the ignition timing.

The system incorporates a safety interlock circuit which will cut the ignition if the sidestand is extended whilst the engine is running and in gear, or if a gear is selected whilst the engine is running and the sidestand is down. It also prevents the engine from being started if the sidestand is down and the engine is in gear. The engine can be started with the sidestand up when it is in gear as long as the clutch lever is pulled in.

All UK models are fitted with an immobiliser system (HISS – Honda Ignition Security System) as standard. The system will not allow the engine to be started unless the correct key is used. The immobiliser system has its own fault diagnosis function.

Note: *Individual engine management system components can be checked but not repaired. If system troubles occur, and the faulty component can be isolated, the*

Engine management system 4•3

only cure for the problem in most cases is to replace the part with a new one. Keep in mind that most electronic parts, once purchased, cannot be returned. To avoid unnecessary expense, make very sure the faulty component has been positively identified before buying a new part.

Precautions

⚠️ *Warning: Petrol (gasoline) is extremely flammable, so take extra precautions when you work on any part of the fuel system. Always remove the battery (see Chapter 8). Don't smoke or allow open flames or bare light bulbs near the work area, and don't work in a garage where a natural gas-type appliance is present. If you spill any fuel on your skin, rinse it off immediately with soap and water. When you perform any kind of work on the fuel system, wear safety glasses and have a fire extinguisher suitable for a class B type fire (flammable liquids) on hand.*

With the fuel injection system, some residual pressure will remain in the fuel feed hoses and fuel rail assemblies after the motorcycle has been used. Before disconnecting any fuel hose, release fuel system pressure as described in Section 2. It is vital that no dirt or debris is allowed to enter the fuel tank or the fuel rail assembly whilst the fuel hoses are disconnected. Any foreign matter in the fuel system components could result in injector damage or malfunction. Ensure the ignition is switched OFF before disconnecting or reconnecting any fuel injection system wiring connector. If a connector is disconnected or reconnected with the ignition switched ON, the ECM may be damaged.

Always perform service procedures in a well-ventilated area to prevent a build-up of fumes.

Never work in a building containing a gas appliance with a pilot light, or any other form of naked flame. Ensure that there are no naked light bulbs or any sources of flame or sparks nearby.

Do not smoke (or allow anyone else to smoke) while in the vicinity of petrol (gasoline) or of components containing it. Remember the possible presence of vapour from these sources and move well clear before smoking.

Check all electrical equipment belonging to the house, garage or workshop where work is being undertaken (see the Safety first! section of this manual). Remember that certain electrical appliances such as drills, cutters etc, create sparks in the normal course of operation and must not be used near petrol (gasoline) or any component containing it. Again, remember the possible presence of fumes before using electrical equipment.

Always mop up any spilt fuel and safely dispose of the rag used.

Any stored fuel that is drained off during servicing work must be kept in sealed containers that are suitable for holding petrol (gasoline), and clearly marked as such; the containers themselves should be kept in a safe place. Note that this last point applies equally to the fuel tank if it is removed from the machine; also remember to keep its filler cap closed at all times.

Read the *Safety first!* section of this manual carefully before starting work.

2 Fuel tank

⚠️ *Warning: Refer to the precautions given in Section 1 before starting work.*

Raise

1 Make sure the fuel cap is secure.

2 Remove the seat(s) and the side covers (see Chapter 7).

3 On CBR600F/FA models remove the fairing side panels and upper panels, and on CBF600S/SA models remove the fairing side panels (see Chapter 7).

4 On CB600F/FA and CBR600F/FA models unscrew the regulator/rectifier bracket bolts and move the assembly back so it is clear of the tank (see illustration).

5 Prepare a suitable piece of wood to fit between the front tank bracket and the frame (see illustration). Unscrew the front mounting bolts, noting the washers (see illustration). Raise the front of the tank, then unscrew the retaining strap nut and detach the strap (see illustration). Raise the tank further and locate the support – make sure it is secure.

Removal

Note: *Removing the tank involves a certain amount of unavoidable fuel spillage, which is obviously dangerous. Refer to the precautions given in Section 1 before starting work, and have plenty of rag to hand. Once the tank has been removed, rest it on some soft rag to prevent damaging the paintwork or hose unions. Try to time the removal procedure with a near empty tank, which makes it much easier to lift.*

6 Raise the tank as described above.

7 Disconnect the fuel pump and level sensor wiring connectors (see illustration).

8 To eliminate any residual pressure in the fuel system start the engine and let it idle until it stops, then turn the ignition off.

2.4 Unscrew the bolts (arrowed) and move the assembly back

2.5a We used a piece of 4 x 2 wood, about 18 inches long, to support the tank

2.5b Unscrew the tank front mounting bolts (arrowed) . . .

2.5c . . . and the retaining strap nut (arrowed)

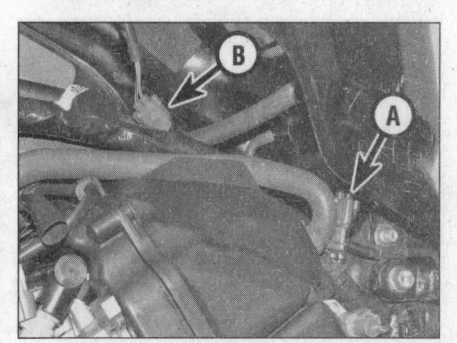

2.7 Fuel pump wiring connector (A), fuel level sensor wiring connector (B)

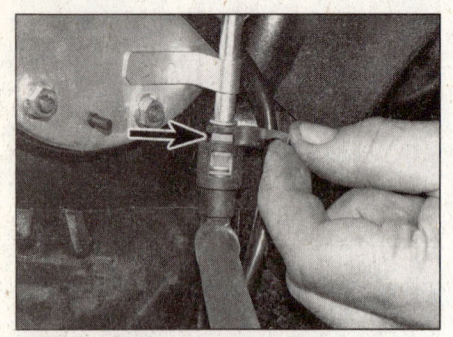

4•4 Engine management system

2.10a Pull the rubber restrictor out of the retainer then press the retainer tabs (arrowed) in and pull the connector off

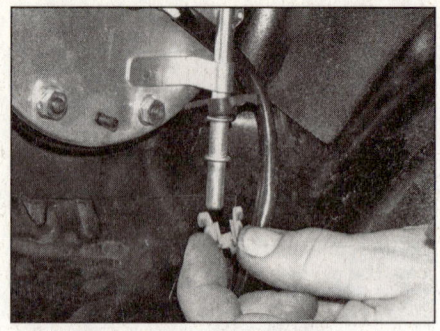

2.10b Remove the retainer from the pipe union

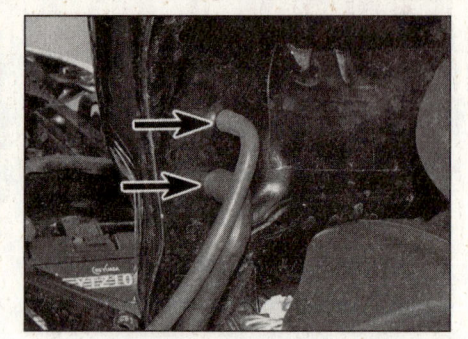

2.11 Detach the hoses (arrowed)

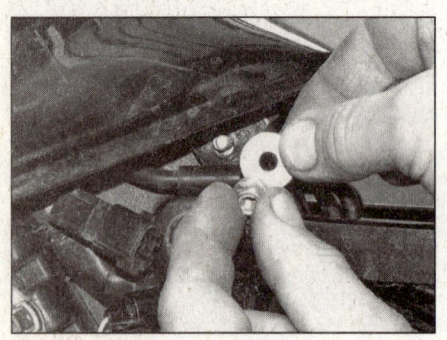

2.13a Unscrew the nut . . .

2.13b . . . withdraw the bolt . . .

2.13c . . . and remove the tank

9 Disconnect the battery negative (–) lead (see Chapter 8).

10 Clean any dirt from the quick-release connector on the fuel hose. Place a wad of rag for catching any residual fuel in the hose under the connector. Pull the rubber restrictor out of the connector retainer, noting how it seats **(see illustration)**. Press the retainer tabs in and pull the connector off the pipe union. Remove the retainer **(see illustration)** – note that Honda specify to replace it with a new one whenever the fuel hose is disconnected. Also check the condition of the restrictor and replace it with a new one if necessary. Seal the union and the connector with a piece from a plastic bag or the finger from a latex glove, secured with an elastic band, to prevent dirt getting in.

11 Disconnect the fuel tank drain and breather hoses **(see illustration)**.

12 Remove the support from the front of the tank and lower the tank.

13 Unscrew the nut on the tank pivot bolt, then withdraw the bolt, noting the washers on CBF600N/NA/S/SA models **(see illustrations)**. Carefully lift the tank off the frame and remove it **(see illustration)**. Remove the collars from the mounting grommets if required **(see illustrations 2.15a and b)**.

14 Check all the tank rubbers and hoses for signs of damage or deterioration and replace them with new ones if necessary.

Installation

15 Fit the mounting rubbers and collars into their mounts if removed – the collars for the front mounts fit from the underside **(see illustrations)**.

16 Depending on how the tank has been stood and how full it is there is the possibility of fuel having made its way into the breather pipe which could spurt out of the hose on the base when it is moved – be prepared with some rag for this. Once the tank is upright the pipe will fill itself with air.

17 Position the tank on the frame and insert the pivot bolt, with its washer on CBF600N/NA/S/SA models **(see illustration 2.13b)**. Fit the nut, again with its washer on CBF models, and tighten it to the torque setting specified at the beginning of the Chapter for your model. Raise and support the tank as before.

18 Connect the fuel tank drain and breather hoses **(see illustration 2.11)**.

19 If removed fit the rubber restrictor onto the pipe union above the second rib. Fit a new retainer into the connector, aligning the tabs with the holes **(see illustration)**. Fit the

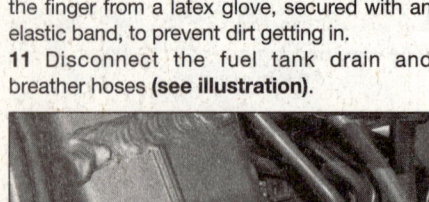

2.15a Check all tank mounting rubbers . . .

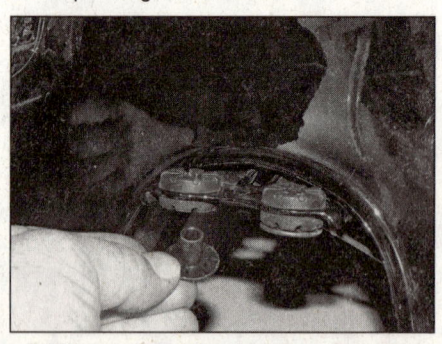

2.15b . . . and make sure the collars are fitted as described

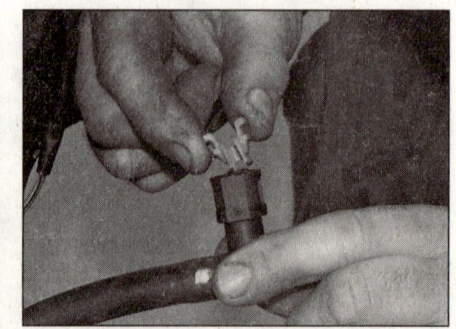

2.19a Fit a new retainer into the connector . . .

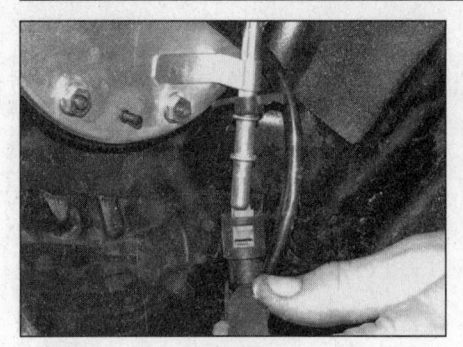

Engine management system 4•5

2.19b ... then push the connector onto the union

3.4 Release the clamp (arrowed) and unscrew the bracket bolt

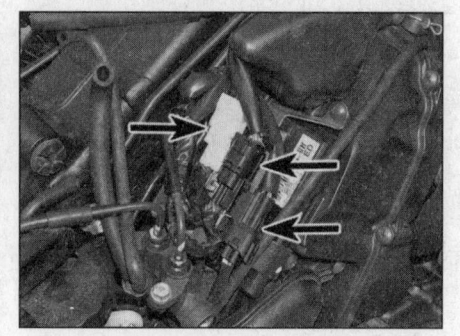

3.5 Disconnect and release the wiring connectors (arrowed – CB shown)

connector onto the pipe and push it until both retainer tabs click into place, then try to pull the connector off to make sure it has locked **(see illustration)**. Fit the rubber restrictor into the retainer, so the tabs cannot be pushed in **(see illustration 2.10a)**.

20 Connect the fuel pump and level sensor wiring connectors **(see illustration 2.7)**. Make sure all the hoses and wiring are securely connected.

21 Connect the battery (see Chapter 8). Make sure the kill switch is set to RUN, then turn the ignition ON to allow the fuel pump to pressurise the system, then turn it off. Repeat a couple of times and each time check for leaks at the hose connector.

22 Remove the prop and pivot the tank down, making sure the hoses do not get squashed or kinked. Fit the tank strap onto the frame and tighten the nut, then lower the tank **(see illustration 2.5b)**. Fit and tighten the front mounting bolts with their washers **(see illustration 2.5a)**.

Repair

23 Repairs to the fuel tank should be carried out by a professional who has experience in this critical and potentially dangerous work. Even after cleaning and flushing of the fuel system, explosive fumes can remain and ignite during repair of the tank.

24 If the fuel tank is removed from the bike, it should not be placed in an area where sparks or open flames could ignite the fumes coming out of the tank. Be especially careful inside garages where a natural gas-type appliance

3.7 Disconnect the CKP sensor wiring connector

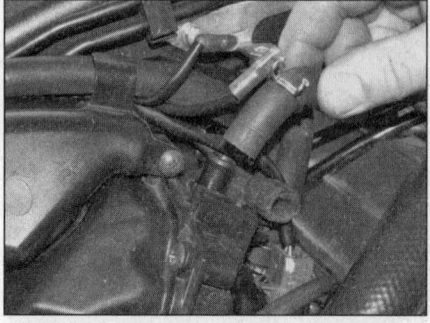

3.8 Disconnect the crankcase breather hose

is located, because the pilot light could cause an explosion.

3 Air filter housing and throttle bodies

Warning: Refer to the precautions given in Section 1 before starting work.

1 The air filter housing and throttle bodies are removed as an assembly, and can be separated after removal if required.

Removal

2 Remove the fuel tank (see Section 2).
3 Remove the air filter (see Chapter 1).
4 Detach the throttle cables from the twistgrip on the handlebar (see Section 15). Release the cable clamp (CBF600S/SA models only) and

unscrew the guide bracket bolt, then draw the cables out from under the top yoke and out of the guide, noting their routing **(see illustration)**.
5 Disconnect the throttle body sub-loom wiring connectors and the oxygen sensor wiring connector **(see illustration)**. Release the connectors from the ECM retainer.
6 Remove the ECM (Section 8) – if there is a security bracket the ECM must be removed together with the air filter housing.
7 Disconnect the CKP sensor wiring connector **(see illustration)**.
8 Disconnect the crankcase breather hose **(see illustration)**.
9 Remove the upper resonator chamber from the right-hand side of the housing **(see illustration)**.
10 Remove the air intake duct and lower resonator chamber from the right-hand side of the housing **(see illustrations)**.

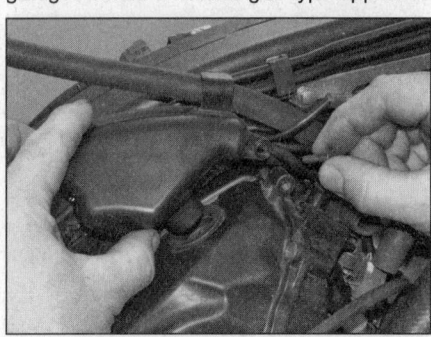

3.9 Undo the screw and lift the chamber off the housing

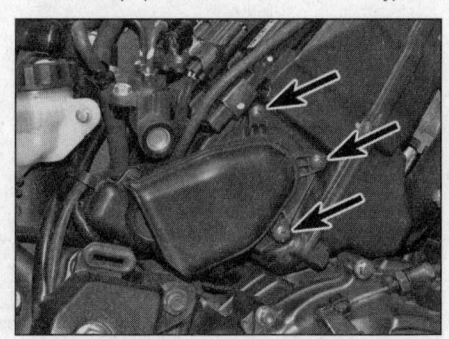

3.10a Air intake duct screws (arrowed) – CB and CBR models

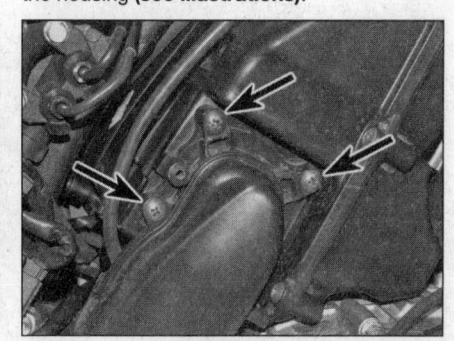

3.10b Air intake duct screws (arrowed) – CBF models

3.11 Disconnect the wiring connectors (arrowed) from each coil

3.12 Disconnect the ECT sensor wiring connector

3.13 Disconnect the sub-loom wiring connector

3.14a Disconnect the hose . . .

3.14b . . . and the wiring connector (arrowed)

3.15a Release the hose and wiring from the guide (arrowed)

11 Disconnect the wiring connectors from the ignition coils **(see illustration)**.
12 Disconnect the ECT sensor wiring connector **(see illustration)**.
13 Disconnect the wiring sub-loom wiring connector **(see illustration)**.
14 Disconnect the PAIR system supply hose from the air filter housing and the wiring connector from the control valve **(see illustrations)**.
15 Release the hoses and wiring from the guides on the left-hand side of the housing **(see illustration)**. Disconnect the overflow hose from the cooling system filler neck and draw it clear **(see illustration)**.
16 Release the wiring loom from its peg on the underside of the sub-frame **(see illustrations)**. Unscrew the air filter housing mounting bolt **(see illustration)**.
17 Fully slacken the clamps on the cylinder

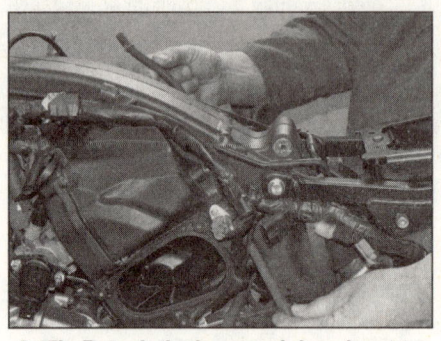

3.15b Detach the hose and draw it out to the left

head side of the intake rubbers for cylinders 1 to 3, and on the throttle body side for No. 4 **(see illustrations)**. Draw the housing/throttle

3.16a Release the catch using a small screwdriver . . .

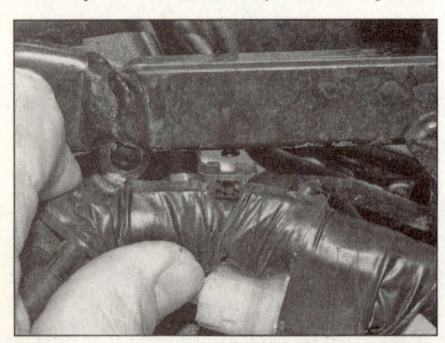

body assembly back and manoeuvre it out to the left, keeping the mounting bolt lug clear of the frame and the starter motor lead and any

3.16b . . . and draw the loom holder off the peg

3.16c Unscrew the bolt (arrowed)

3.17a Slacken the clamps (arrowed) . . .

Engine management system 4•7

3.17b ... and the clamp (arrowed)

3.17c Keep the lug clear of the frame ...

3.17d ... the wiring and hoses clear of the reservoir (arrowed) ...

3.17e ... and draw the assembly out to the left

other wiring and hoses clear of the vacuum reservoir on the underside of the housing, and bringing the throttle cables with it, noting their routing **(see illustrations)**. Cover or plug the intake ducts and rubber on the cylinder head.
Caution: Tape over or stuff clean rag into each cylinder head intake after removing the throttle body assembly to prevent anything getting in.
Caution: Do not snap the throttle cam/valves from fully open to fully closed once the cables have been disconnected because this can lead to engine idle speed problems.

Installation

18 Installation is the reverse of removal, noting the following:
- Do not forget to remove the covers or plugs from the intake ducts and rubber on the cylinder head.
- Check the condition of the intake rubbers and replace them with new ones if necessary (see Step 33).
- Check the condition of all hoses and replace them with new ones if they are in any way damaged or deteriorated.
- Make sure the intake rubber clamps are correctly orientated with the hole in each clamp over the peg on the rubber.
- Lubricate the inside of the rubbers with a light smear of engine oil to aid installation. Tighten the intake rubber clamps so that the gap between the ends is 6 to 8 mm.
- The air filter housing bolt threads into a rubber wellnut fitted in a hole in the frame, rather than threading directly into the frame itself. The wellnut is held in its hole only by a rubber rim, and when fitting the bolt it is possible to push on the nut, at which point the rim gives way and the nut disappears inside the frame. To prevent this happening make sure the mount in the housing is perfectly aligned with the nut before inserting the bolt, and push the mount against the rubber rim to help keep it in place; insert the bolt carefully, making sure the threads have engaged before using a tool.
- Make sure all wiring connectors are securely connected.
- Make sure all cables, hoses and wiring are correctly routed.
- Make sure the right-hand air duct O-ring is in good condition and seated in its groove – fit a new O-ring if necessary.
- Check throttle cable freeplay at the twistgrip and adjust if necessary (see Chapter 1).

Disassembly (throttle body removal)

19 Disconnect the IAT sensor wiring connector **(see illustration)**.

3.19 IAT sensor wiring connector (A), air intake control valve wiring connector (B)

3.21 TP sensor wiring connector (arrowed)

3.22 MAP sensor wiring connector (arrowed)

3.23 Fuel injector wiring connectors (arrowed)

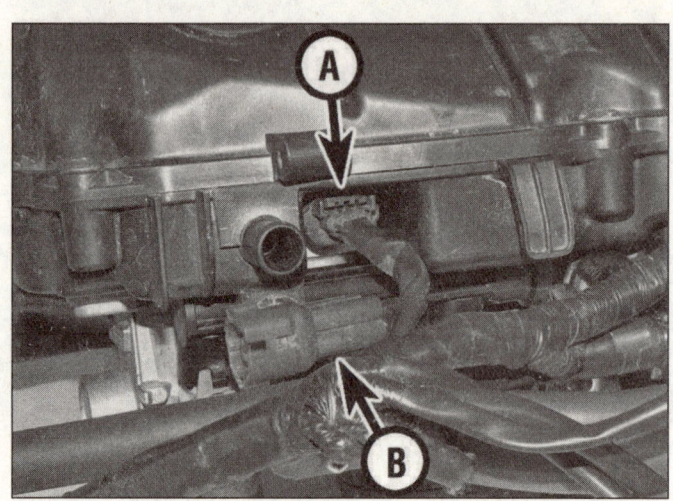

3.24 Idle speed control valve wiring connector (A), CKP sensor connector (B)

20 Disconnect the air intake control valve wiring connector **(see illustration 3.19)**.
21 Disconnect the throttle position sensor wiring connector **(see illustration)**.
22 Disconnect the MAP sensor wiring connector **(see illustration)**.
23 Make a note of which connector fits onto which injector. Disconnect the wiring connectors from the injectors **(see illustration)**.
24 Disconnect the wiring connector from the idle speed control valve **(see illustration)**.
25 Release the CKP sensor connector from its holder **(see illustration 3.24)**. Release the wiring sub-loom from the guides, noting its routing, and remove it **(see illustration)**.
26 Remove the air duct seal from the left-hand side of the housing, and from the right-hand side if required **(see illustration)**. Detach the vacuum hose from the No. 4 throttle body **(see illustration)**. Undo the screws

3.25 Note the routing of the wiring in the guides (arrowed) and remove the sub-loom

3.26a Remove the left-hand air duct seal

3.26b Pull the vacuum hose off

Engine management system 4•9

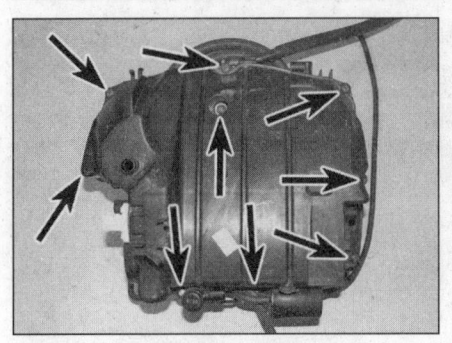

3.26c Upper section screws (arrowed)

3.26d Remove the mesh . . .

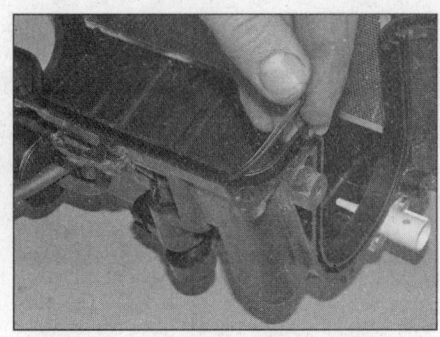

3.26e . . . and the seals if required

securing the upper section of the housing and remove it **(see illustration)**. Remove the mesh screen and the housing seals (the large perimeter one and the small centre one for the recessed screw bore) if required **(see illustrations)**.

27 Disconnect the vacuum hose from the MAP sensor **(see illustration)**. Undo the air funnel/throttle body mounting screws, then remove the funnels and detach the throttle body assembly from the lower section of the housing **(see illustrations)**. Remove the throttle body seals **(see illustration)** – new ones must be used.

28 If you want to detach the fuel hose clean any dirt from the quick-release connector. Place a wad of rag for catching any residual fuel in the hose under the connector. Pull the rubber

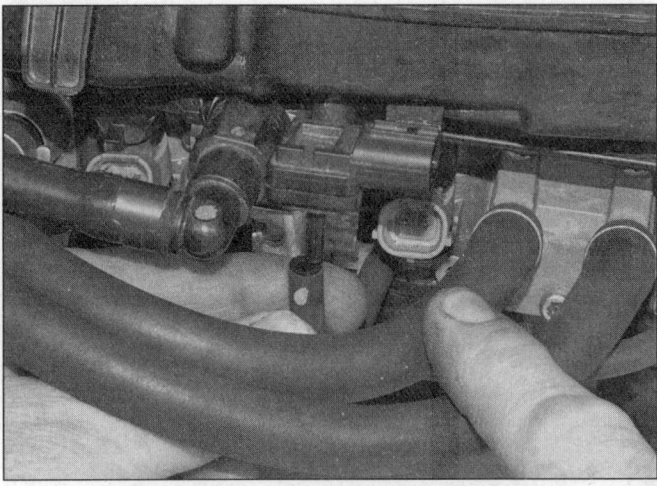

3.27a Disconnect the hose from the sensor

3.27b Undo the screws (arrowed) and remove the funnels . . .

3.27c . . . and detach the lower section from the throttle bodies

3.27d Remove the seals and fit new ones on reassembly

4•10 Engine management system

3.28a Pull the rubber restrictor out of the retainer...

3.28b ...then press the retainer tabs in and pull the connector off

3.28c Remove the retainer from the union

restrictor from the connector retainer, noting how it seats **(see illustration)**. Press the retainer tabs in and pull the connector off the fuel rail union and remove the hose **(see illustration)**. Remove the retainer **(see illustration)** – note that Honda specify to replace it with a new one whenever the fuel hose is disconnected. Also check the condition of the restrictor and replace it with a new one if necessary. Seal the union and the connector with a piece from a plastic bag or the finger from a latex glove, secured with an elastic band, to prevent dirt getting in.

29 If required detach the throttle cables (see Section 15).

30 If required remove the fuel rail and injectors (see Section 4).

31 If required remove the idle speed control valve (see Section 11).

Caution: The throttle body assembly must be treated as a sealed unit. NEVER loosen any of the white-painted nuts/bolts/screws on the assembly as these are pre-set at the factory to ensure correct synchronisation of the throttle valves.

Caution: NEVER use a solvent-based cleaner to clean the throttle body components. The throttle bores are covered with a molybdenum coating which could be removed by the cleaner.

Inspection

32 Check the throttle body hoses for signs of damage or deterioration and replace any suspect hoses with new ones **(see illustration)**. Make sure all hoses are securely connected.

33 Check the intake rubbers for signs of damage or deterioration. If required slacken the clamp screws and remove the rubbers from the throttle bodies and cylinder head, noting their orientation and the position of the clamps **(see illustration)**. When refitting the rubbers locate the ribs on each side of the lug on the throttle body, and seat the hole in each clamp over the peg on the rubber. Tighten the clamps so that the gap between the ends is 6 to 8 mm.

Reassembly

34 Reassembly is the reverse of removal, referring to the relevant Sections where directed, and noting the following:

- When fitting the fuel hose, if removed fit the rubber restrictor onto the pipe union. Fit a new retainer into the connector, aligning the tabs with the holes **(see illustration 3.34a)**. Fit the connector onto the pipe and push it until both retainer tabs click into place, then try to pull the connector off to make sure it has locked **(see illustration 3.34b)**. Fit the rubber restrictor into the retainer, so the tabs cannot be pushed in.
- New throttle body seals must be used **(see illustration 3.27d)**. Check the condition of the housing and air duct seals and replace them with new ones if they are damaged or deformed or have deteriorated **(see illustrations 3.26a and e)**. Make sure the seals seat properly in the grooves.
- Check the condition of all hoses and replace them with new ones if they are in any way damaged or deteriorated **(see illustration 3.32)**.
- The centre screw in the recessed hole in the upper section of the air filter housing is shorter than the perimeter screws **(see illustration 3.26c)**.
- Make sure all wiring connectors are securely connected.
- Make sure all cables, hoses and wiring are correctly routed.

3.32 Check all hoses for cracks, splits, kinks and any other signs of damage or deterioration

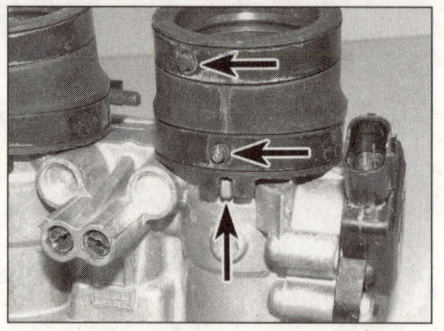

3.33 Make sure the rubbers and clamps are positioned as described

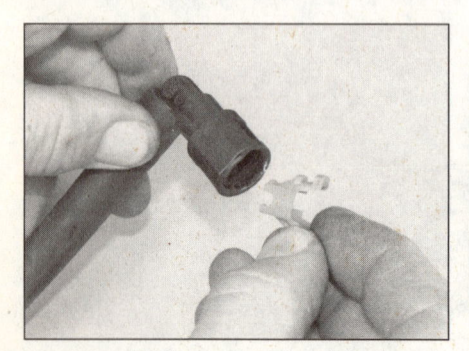

4 Fuel rails and injectors

Warning: Refer to the precautions given in Section 1 before starting work.

Check

1 If the engine runs, start it and allow it to idle. Check the operation of each injector using

3.34a Fit the new retainer into the connector...

3.34b ...and push the connector on so it clicks into place

Engine management system 4•11

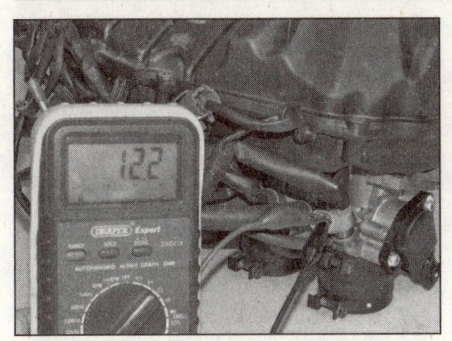

4.3 Check the resistance of an injector

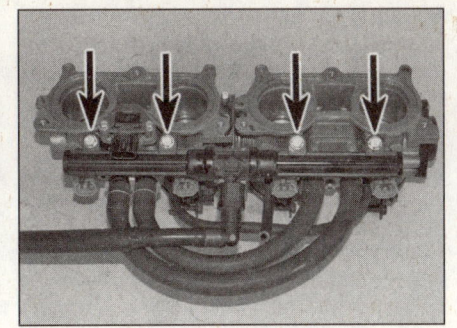

4.7a Unscrew the bolts (arrowed) ...

4.7b ... and lift the fuel rail and injector assembly off

sounding rod held against it; an injector will emit a 'clicking' noise when functioning. If any injector is silent, either the injector or its wiring harness is faulty.

2 If the engine does not run, remove the fuel tank (see Section 2). Disconnect the wiring connector from the injector **(see illustration 3.23)**.

3 Connect an ohmmeter between the injector terminals and measure the resistance **(see illustration)**. Compare the reading for the injector to that given in the Specifications. If the resistance differs greatly replace the injector with a new one.

4 Check for battery voltage at the black/white wire terminal in the wiring connector with the ignition ON and the kill switch set to RUN. If there is no voltage, check the wiring between the injector and the engine stop relay, then check the relay.

5 Check for continuity in the other wire to the ECM connector.

Removal

6 Remove the air filter housing and throttle body assembly, then separate them (see Section 3).

7 Unscrew the fuel rail bolts **(see illustration)**. Carefully lift off the fuel rail assembly and injectors **(see illustration)**. Remove the seals from the injector nozzles, or from the injector seat if they stayed in the throttle body **(see illustrations)**. Discard them as new ones must be used.

8 If required pull the injectors out of the fuel rail **(see illustration)**. Remove the O-rings and discard them **(see illustration)** – new ones must be used.

9 If required pull each fuel rail off the centre joint piece **(see illustration)**. Remove the O-rings and discard them – new ones must be used **(see illustration)**.

Installation

10 If the fuel rails have been separated from the joint piece, fit a new O-ring lubricated with clean engine oil into the groove in the end of each rail **(see illustration 4.9b)**. Push each rail onto the joint, making sure the O-ring stays in place **(see illustration 4.9a)**.

11 If the injectors have been removed from their rail, fit a new O-ring lubricated with clean engine oil into the groove in the top of each injector **(see illustration 4.8b)**.

12 Align the injector connector with the raised tab on the rail and ease it into place, taking care not to dislodge the O-ring **(see illustration 4.8a)**.

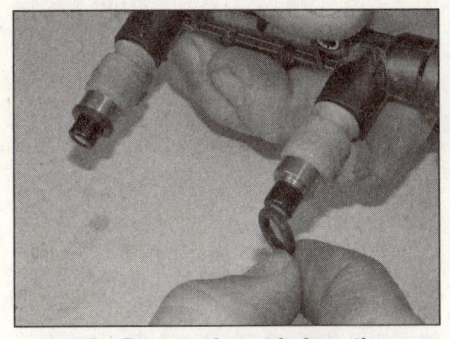

4.7c Remove the seals from the nozzles ...

4.7d ... or the injector seats

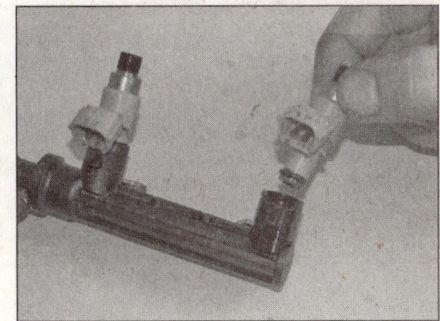

4.8a Pull each injector out ...

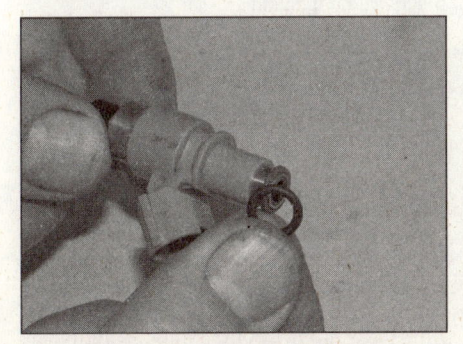

4.8b ... and remove its O-ring

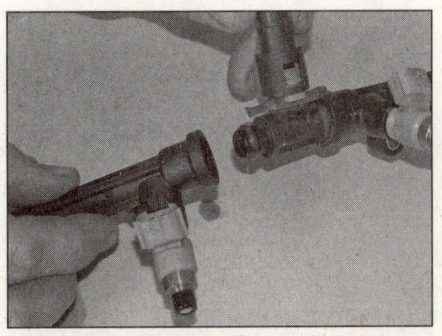

4.9a Separate the rails and joint piece if required ...

4.9b ... then remove the O-rings

13 Fit a new seal lubricated with clean engine oil onto each injector nozzle **(see illustration 4.7c)**.
14 Fit the fuel rail assembly, making sure each injector enters its seat and the seals stay in place and locates correctly **(see illustration 4.7b)**. Fit the fuel rail bolts and tighten them to the torque setting specified at the beginning of the Chapter **(see illustration 4.7a)**.
15 Install the throttle bodies and air filter housing (see Section 3). Run the engine and check that the fuel system is working correctly before taking the machine out on the road.

5 Fuel injection system description

1 All models are equipped with Honda's programmed fuel injection (PGM-FI) system. It is controlled by a management system with an engine control module (ECM) that operates both the injection and ignition systems.
2 The engine control module (ECM) monitors signals from the following sensors.
- Throttle position (TP) sensor – informs the ECM of the throttle position, and the rate of throttle opening or closing.
- Engine coolant temperature (ECT) sensor – informs the ECM of engine temperature. It also actuates the temperature display or warning light (see Chapter 3).
- Manifold absolute pressure (MAP) sensor – informs the ECM of the engine load by monitoring the pressure in the throttle body intake tracts.
- Intake air temperature (IAT) sensor – informs the ECM of the temperature of the air entering the throttle body.
- Crankshaft position (CKP) sensor – informs the ECM of engine speed and crankshaft position.
- Speed sensor – informs the ECM of the motorcycle's road speed (see Chapter 8).
- Oxygen sensor – informs the ECM of the oxygen content of the exhaust gases.
- Lean angle sensor – cuts the ignition and fuel pump if the bike falls over.

3 All the information from the sensors is analysed by the ECM, and from that it determines the appropriate ignition and fuelling requirements of the engine. The ECM controls each fuel injector by varying its pulse width – the length of time the injector is held open – to provide more or less fuel, as appropriate for cold starting, warm up, idle, cruising, and acceleration. The injection system is fully sequential, with each injector receiving its own signal from the ECM. The injectors are mounted in the throttle bodies on the engine side of the throttle valve.
4 Cold starting, warm up and idle speed are controlled by an automatic idle control system, which basically takes the place of a manual choke lever. A control valve, actuated by the ECM, allows additional air to bypass the throttle valves when the throttle is closed, and this increases the engine idle speed.
5 If there is an abnormality in any of the readings obtained from any sensor, the ECM enters its back-up mode. In this event, the ECM ignores the abnormal sensor signal, and assumes a pre-programmed value that will allow the engine to continue running (albeit at reduced efficiency). If the ECM enters this back-up mode, or when any faults occur, the fuel injection system (FI) warning light in the instrument cluster will come on or flash (depending on circumstances), and the relevant fault code will be stored in the ECM memory. The fault can be identified using the fault codes that can be accessed using the self-diagnosis function (see Section 6). However if there are certain faults detected in the injectors or the crankshaft position sensor, the back-up mode becomes ineffective and the ECM will not allow the engine to run at all.
6 All UK models have an immobiliser system (HISS – Honda Ignition Security System) that will not allow the engine to be started unless the correct key is used. A fault in this system should not be confused with a fuel injection system fault. The immobiliser system has its own warning light and fault diagnosis function (see Section 22).

6 Fuel injection system fault diagnosis

1 If the fuel injection system (FI) warning light on the instrument cluster illuminates when the motorcycle is running, a fault has occurred in the fuel injection/ignition system. The engine control module (ECM) will store the relevant fault code in its memory and this code can be read as follows using the self-diagnostic mode of the ECM. While the engine is running above 5000 rpm and the motorcycle is being ridden, the light will come on and stay on. When the motorcycle is on its sidestand and the engine is idling, the light will flash, the pattern of the flashes indicating the code for the fault the ECM has identified.
2 If the engine can be started, place the motorcycle on its sidestand then start the engine and allow it to idle. Whilst the engine is idling, observe the FI warning light on the instrument cluster.
3 If the engine cannot be started, place the motorcycle on its sidestand. With the kill switch in the run position turn the engine over on the starter motor for more than ten seconds and observe the FI warning light on the instrument cluster.
4 Alternatively, and to check for any stored fault codes even though the warning light has not illuminated, raise the fuel tank (Section 2). Locate the engine management system data link connector (DLC), which is a red blanked single-sided 4-pin connector near the ECM **(see illustrations)**. Remove the blanking cap from the connector **(see illustration)**. Either fit the Honda SCS service connector (Part No. 070PZ-ZY30100, available from your dealer), or bridge the brown and green wire terminals of the connector with a piece of electrical wire **(see illustration)**. With the terminals connected, make sure the kill switch is in the RUN position then turn the ignition ON and

6.4a Data link connector (arrowed) – CB and CBR models

6.4b Data link connector (arrowed) – CBF models

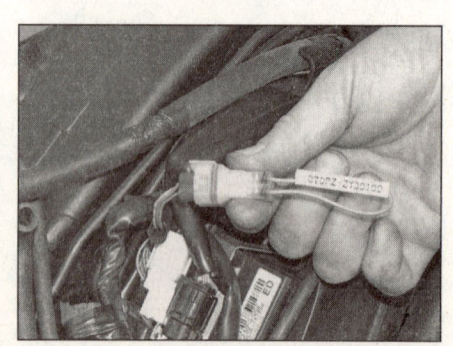

6.4c Remove the blanking cap . . .

6.4d . . . and connect the special tool or a jumper wire

Engine management system 4•13

observe the FI warning light. If there are stored fault codes, the light will flash.

5 The FI warning light emits long (1.3 second) and short (0.5 second) flashes to give out the fault code. A long flash is used to indicate the first digit of a double digit fault code (i.e. 10 and above). If a single digit fault code is being displayed (i.e. 0 – 9), there will be a number of short flashes equivalent to the code being displayed. For example, two long (1.3 sec) flashes followed by five short (0.5 sec) flashes indicates the fault code number 25. If there is more than one fault code, there will be a gap before the other codes are revealed (the codes will be revealed in order, starting with the lowest and finishing with the highest). Once all codes have been revealed, the ECM will continuously run through the code(s) stored in its memory, revealing each one in turn with a short gap between them. The fault codes are shown in the table.

Fault code (No. of flashes)	Symptoms	Possible causes
No code; warning light off	Engine cranks but does not start. Fuel pump does not pressurise when ignition turned on.	Blown fuse (FI 20A fuse or starter 10A fuse)
		Faulty power supply to or from engine control module (ECM)
		Faulty engine stop relay or wiring
		Faulty engine stop switch or wiring
		Faulty ignition switch
		Faulty lean angle sensor or wiring
		Faulty engine control module (ECM)
No code; warning light off	Engine cranks but does not start, or is hard to start, stalls, or has rough idle	Fuel supply contaminated or restricted
		Fuel tank breather blocked (creating vacuum in tank)
		Intake air leak (loose clamp, split intake rubber)
		Faulty idle speed control system
		Faulty ignition system
No code; warning light off	Engine backfires when throttling off	Faulty PAIR system
No code; warning light off	Engine backfires when accelerating	Faulty ignition system
No code; warning light off	Poor performance and economy	Fuel supply problem (pump, pressure regulator, filter, hose)
		Faulty MAP sensor
		Faulty injector
		Faulty ignition system
No code; warning light off	Low idle and fast idle speeds	Faulty idle speed control system – valve stuck closed
		Fuel supply problem (pump, pressure regulator, filter, hose)
		Faulty ignition system
No code; warning light off	High idle and fast idle speeds	Faulty idle speed control system – valve stuck open
		Intake air leak (loose clamp, split intake rubber)
		Throttle sticking, cable freeplay adjustment incorrect
		Faulty ignition system
No code; warning light off	Engine runs normally	Open or short circuit in FI warning light wiring
		Faulty engine control module (ECM)
No code; warning light constantly on	Engine runs normally	Short circuit in data link connector or wiring
		Faulty engine control module (ECM)
1	Engine runs normally	Faulty manifold absolute pressure (MAP) sensor or wiring
2	Engine runs normally	Manifold absolute pressure (MAP) sensor vacuum hose disconnected/broken
7	Engine difficult to start at low temperatures	Faulty engine coolant temperature (ECT) sensor or wiring
8	Poor throttle response	Faulty throttle position (TP) sensor or wiring
9	Engine runs normally	Faulty intake air temperature (IAT) sensor or wiring
11	Engine operates normally	Faulty speed sensor or wiring
12	Engine does not start	Faulty No. 1 injector or wiring
13	Engine does not start	Faulty No. 2 injector or wiring
14	Engine does not start	Faulty No. 3 injector or wiring
15	Engine does not start	Faulty No. 4 injector or wiring
21	Engine operates normally	Faulty oxygen sensor or wiring
23	Engine operates normally	Faulty oxygen sensor heating element
29	Engine stalls, hard to start, rough idle	Faulty idle speed control valve

Once all the codes have been revealed, switch off the ignition and (where necessary) remove the auxiliary wire or SCS connector from the data link connector. Identify the fault using the table above, then refer to the following (see overleaf) for checking procedures.

4•14 Engine management system

6 Once the fault has been identified and corrected, it will be necessary to reset the system by removing the fault code from the ECM memory. To do this, ensure the ignition is switched OFF, then bridge the brown and green wire terminals of the data link connector (DLC) (see Step 4). Make sure the kill switch is in the RUN position, then turn the ignition switch ON. Disconnect the auxiliary wire or tool from the DLC. When the wire is disconnected the warning light should come on for about five seconds, during which time the auxiliary wire must be reconnected. The light should start to flash when it is reconnected, indicating that all fault codes have been erased. Turn off the ignition then remove the auxiliary wire. Check the FI warning light (in some cases it may be necessary to repeat the erasing procedure more than once).

7 If a fault appears, use the diagnostic function and fault code system described above to work out which component is faulty. First ensure that the relevant system wiring connectors are securely connected and free of corrosion – poor connections are the cause of the majority of problems. Also check the wiring itself for any obvious faults or breaks, and use a continuity tester to check the wiring between the component, its connectors and the ECM, referring to the wiring diagrams at the end of Chapter 8. Next refer to Section 7 to see if there are any other specific checks that can be made on that particular component using home equipment. If this fails to reveal the cause of the problem, the motorcycle should be taken to a Honda dealer for testing. They will have the special tools that should locate the fault quickly and simply.

8 Also ensure that any fault is not due to poor maintenance – i.e. check that the air filter element is clean, that the spark plugs are in good condition, that the valve clearances are correctly adjusted, the cylinder compression pressures are correct, and the ignition timing is correct (refer to Chapters 1 and 2, and to Section 19). It is also worth removing the sensor(s) in question (see Section 7) and checking that the sensing tip or head is clean and not obstructed by anything. Where there is a vacuum hose to a sensor, make sure it is securely connected at both ends and has no cracks or splits.

7 Fuel injection system sensors

Caution: *Ensure the ignition is switched OFF before disconnecting/reconnecting any fuel injection system wiring connector. If a connector is disturbed with the ignition switched ON the engine control module (ECM) could be damaged.*

Special tool: *Honda specify a peak voltage adapter (Honda pt. no. 07HGJ-0020100) plus an aftermarket digital multimeter having an impedance of 10 M-ohm/DCV minimum for the crankshaft position sensor test (see Step 32).*

Manifold absolute pressure (MAP) sensor

Check

1 The MAP sensor is mounted on the air filter housing **(see illustration)**. Raise the fuel tank (see Section 2). Make sure that the vacuum hoses to it are securely fixed at both ends, and have no cracks or splits.

2 To check the input circuit connect the positive (+) lead of a voltmeter to the yellow/red terminal of the sensor wiring connector, then connect the negative (–) lead to a good earth. Turn the ignition switch ON and set the kill switch to RUN and check that a voltage of 4.75 to 5.25 volts is present. If it isn't, check for continuity in the yellow/red wire to the ECM. If there is no continuity locate the break and repair it. If the wiring is good, the ECM could be faulty. If the voltage was good, check for continuity in the light green/yellow wire to earth. If there is continuity locate the short circuit and repair it. If the wiring is good, the MAP sensor is faulty.

3 To check the output circuit check there is a voltage of 2.7 to 3.1 V between the light green/yellow and green/orange wire terminals of the connector. If there is voltage, the MAP sensor is faulty. If there is no voltage, check for continuity to the ECM in the each of the wires. If there is none, trace the fault in the wire and repair it. If all the wiring is good the ECM could be faulty.

Removal and installation

4 Raise the fuel tank (see Section 2).

5 Disconnect the wiring connector **(see illustration 7.1)**. Detach the vacuum hose **(see illustration)**. Undo the screw and remove the sensor – access is restricted, so an angled screwdriver is required. If access is too restricted for the tools available, remove the air filter housing and throttle body assembly (see Section 3).

6 Installation is the reverse of removal.

Engine coolant temperature (ECT) sensor

Note: *The sensor also operates the coolant temperature display – refer to Chapter 3 to check this aspect of its function.*

Check

7 The ECT sensor is mounted in the thermostat housing **(see illustration)**.

8 Disconnect the wiring connector from the sensor. With the engine cold, connect an ohmmeter between the pink/white and green/orange wire terminals on the sensor and measure its resistance. Compare the reading obtained to that given in the Specifications, noting that the specified value is valid at 20°C (68°F); the sensor resistance will increase at lower temperatures and decrease at higher temperatures. If the resistance reading differs greatly from that specified, the sensor is probably faulty.

9 If the sensor resistance is good, check its power supply. Connect the positive (+) lead of a voltmeter to the pink/white wire terminal in the sensor wiring connector, then connect the negative (–) lead to a good earth. Turn the ignition switch ON and check that a voltage of 4.75 to 5.25 volts is present. If it isn't, check for continuity in the pink/white wire to the ECM. If there is no continuity locate the break and repair it. If the wiring is good, the ECM could be faulty. If voltage was present, now connect the negative lead to the green/orange terminal of the connector and check that the same voltage is present. If it isn't, there is a break in the green/orange wire or a fault in the ECM. If there is voltage, the ECM is probably faulty.

7.1 MAP sensor (arrowed)

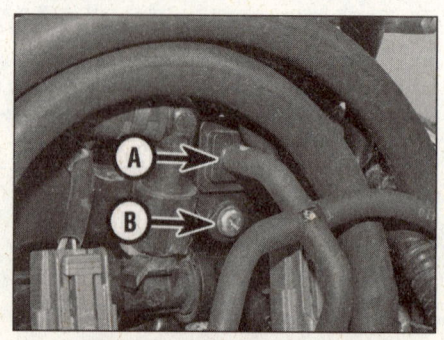

7.5 MAP sensor vacuum hose (A) and screw (B)

7.7 ECT sensor (arrowed)

Engine management system 4•15

7.11 TP sensor (arrowed)

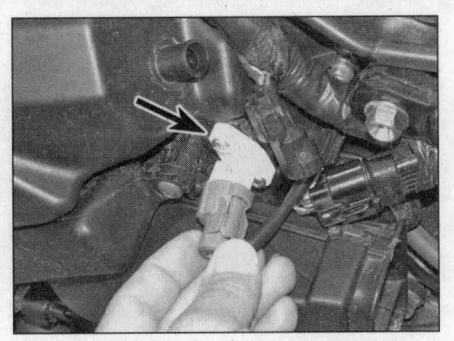

7.13 IAT sensor (arrowed)

Removal and installation

⚠ *Warning: The engine must be completely cool before carrying out this procedure.*

10 see Chapter 3, Section 3.

Throttle position (TP) sensor

Check

11 The sensor is on the left-hand end of the throttle body assembly (see illustration). Disconnect the wiring connector from the sensor. Connect the positive (+) lead of a voltmeter to the yellow/red terminal of the sensor wiring connector, then connect the negative (–) lead to a good earth. Turn the ignition switch ON and check that a voltage of 4.75 to 5.25 volts is present. If it isn't, there is a break in the yellow/red wire or a fault in the ECM. If voltage was present, now connect the negative lead to the green/orange wire terminal of the connector and check that the same voltage is present. If it isn't, there is a break in the green/orange wire or a fault in the ECM. If there is voltage, check for continuity to the ECM in the red/yellow wire. If all the wiring is good have the sensor output voltage checked by a Honda dealer. If that is good, then the ECM is faulty.

Removal and installation

12 The throttle sensor is an integral part of the throttle body assembly and is not available separately (see illustration 7.11). If the sensor is faulty, a complete new throttle body assembly will have to be installed, though it is worth checking with your Honda dealer or parts specialist whether anything can be done to avoid this.

Intake air temperature (IAT) sensor

Check

13 The sensor is mounted in the left-hand side of the air filter housing – remove the left-hand side cover to access it (see Chapter 7). Disconnect the wiring connector from the sensor (see illustration).

14 With the sensor cold, connect an ohmmeter across the sensor terminals and measure its resistance. Compare the reading obtained to that given in the Specifications noting that the specified value is valid between 20 to 30°C (68 to 86°F); the sensor resistance will increase at lower temperatures and decrease at higher temperatures. If the resistance reading differs greatly from that specified, the sensor is probably faulty.

15 If the sensor appears to be functioning correctly, check its power supply. Connect the positive (+) lead of a voltmeter to the grey/blue terminal of the sensor wiring connector, then connect the negative (–) lead to a good earth. Turn the ignition switch ON and check that a voltage of 4.75 to 5.25 volts is present. If it isn't, there is a break in the grey/blue wire or a fault in the ECM. If voltage was present, now connect the negative lead to the green/orange terminal of the connector and check that the same voltage is present. If it isn't, there is a break in the green/orange wire or a fault in the ECM. If all the wiring is good have the sensor output voltage checked by a Honda dealer. If that is good, then the ECM is faulty.

Removal and installation

16 The sensor is mounted in the left-hand side of the air filter housing – remove the left-hand side cover to access it (see Chapter 7).

17 Disconnect the wiring connector from the sensor (see illustration 7.13).

18 Undo the screws and remove the sensor. Remove the O-ring – a new one should be used.

19 Installation is the reverse of removal – use a new O-ring.

Vehicle speed sensor

20 See Chapter 8, Section 16.

Oxygen sensor

Check

21 Apart from the wiring and connector checks that are outlined in Section 6, the operation of the oxygen sensor itself cannot be checked – if the sensor circuit is good (have this checked by a dealer for confirmation) and the sensor is thought to be faulty, replace it with a new one.

22 To check the sensor heater remove the right-hand side cover (see Chapter 7). Disconnect the sensor wiring connector (see illustrations). Connect an ohmmeter between the white wire terminals on the sensor side of the connector and check that the resistance is between 10 and 40 ohms. Also check that there is no continuity to earth (ground) in each

7.22a Oxygen sensor wiring connector (arrowed) – CB and CBR models

7.22b Oxygen sensor wiring connector – CBF models

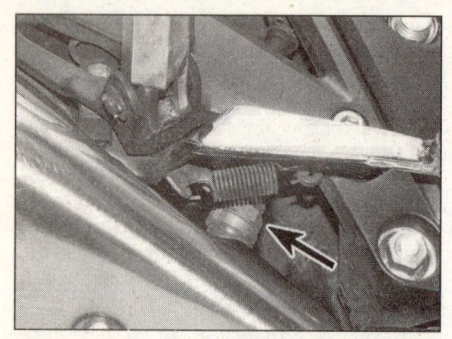

4•16 Engine management system

7.25a Oxygen sensor (arrowed) – CB and CBR models

7.25b Oxygen sensor (arrowed) – CBF models

7.26 Release the connector

white wire. If the resistance is not as specified or if there is continuity to earth, replace the sensor with a new one.

23 Check for battery voltage between the black/white (+) wire terminal and earth with the ignition ON. If there is no voltage, check the black/white wire for continuity to the engine stop relay, then check the relay.

24 If there is voltage check for continuity between the connector and the ECM in the black/green, orange/white and green/orange wires. If all the wiring is good the ECM could be faulty.

Removal and installation

Note: *The oxygen sensor is delicate and will not work if dropped or knocked, or if any cleaning materials are used on it. Ensure the exhaust system is cold before proceeding. A special socket to accommodate the sensor wiring can be bought from Honda, part No.* 07LAA-PT50101 *if required. Otherwise use an open-ended 22 mm spanner.*

25 On CB600F/FA and CBR600F/FA models the sensor is in the centre section of the exhaust system, between the downpipes and the silencer, on the right-hand side **(see illustration)**. On CBF600N/NA/S/SA models the sensor is located in the rear of the exhaust downpipe assembly **(see illustration)**.

26 Remove the right-hand side cover (see Chapter 7). Disconnect the sensor wiring connector **(see illustration 7.22a or b)**. Release the connector from the retainer **(see illustration)**. Feed the wiring down to the sensor, noting its routing.

27 On CB600F/FA and CBR600F/FA models unscrew the nut on the silencer mounting bolt, then withdraw the bolt **(see illustration)**. Unscrew the right-hand footrest bracket bolts then position and secure it as required for access to the sensor.

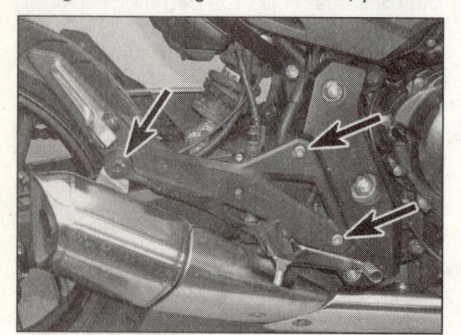

28 Unscrew the oxygen sensor and remove it from the exhaust system.

29 Installation is the reverse of removal. On CB600F/FA and CBR600F/FA models tighten the footrest bracket and silencer bolts to the torque settings specified at the beginning of the Chapter.

Crankshaft position (CKP) sensor

Check

Special tool: *Honda specify a peak voltage adapter (Honda part No. 07HGJ-0020100) plus an aftermarket digital multimeter having an impedance of 10 M-ohm/DCV minimum for a complete test of the sensor (see Step 32).*

29 Raise the fuel tank (Section 2).

30 The sensor is in the clutch cover on the right-hand side of the engine. Trace the wiring from the sensor and disconnect it at the red wiring connector **(see illustration)**.

31 Using an ohmmeter check for continuity between each wire terminal in the sensor side of the connector and earth (ground). If there is continuity in either wire the sensor is faulty. Measure the resistance of the sensor by connecting the meter, set to the ohms x 100 scale, to the terminals and compare the reading to that specified at the beginning of the chapter **(see illustration)**. If the value obtained differs greatly or is zero or infinity the sensor is faulty.

32 If a peak voltage adapter is available (see **Special tool** note) connect the positive (+) lead of the voltmeter and peak voltage adapter arrangement to the yellow wire terminal on the sensor and the negative (–) lead to the white/yellow wire terminal. Turn the engine over on the starter motor and note the voltage reading obtained. If this reading is below the specified minimum, the sensor is faulty.

33 If the sensor functions correctly check both wires to the ECM for continuity. If the wiring is good the ECM could be faulty.

Removal

34 Remove the clutch cover (see Chapter 2, Section 14, Steps 1 to 4). The sensor is mounted inside it.

35 Undo the sensor mounting bolts, then free the wiring grommet from the cover and remove the sensor **(see illustration)**.

7.27 Unscrew the bolts (arrowed) and displace the bracket

7.30 CKP sensor wiring connector (arrowed)

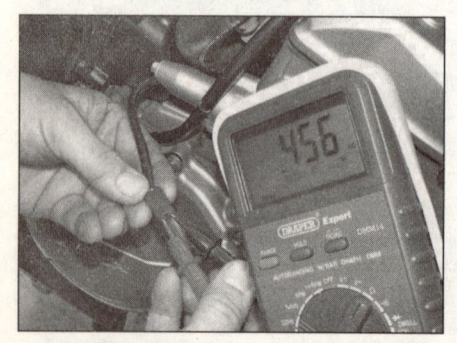

7.31 Checking CKP sensor resistance

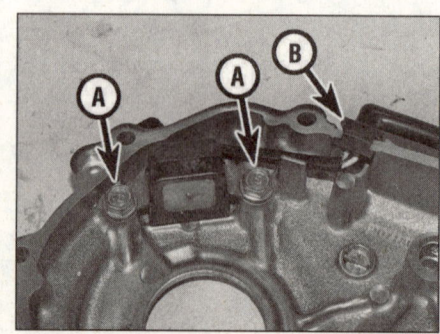

7.35 Unscrew the sensor bolts (A) and free the wiring grommet (B)

Engine management system 4•17

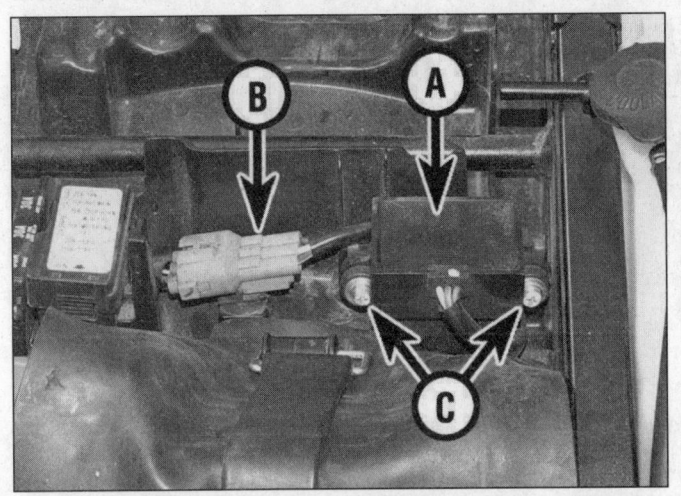

7.39a Lean angle sensor (A) and its wiring connector (B) and mounting screws (C) – CB and CBR models

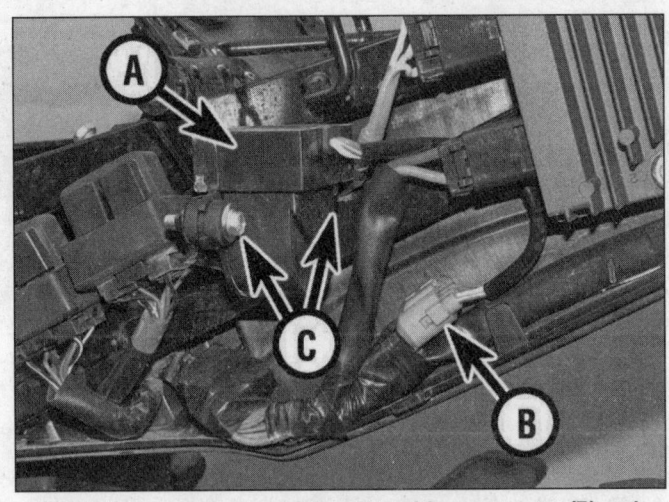

7.39b Lean angle sensor (A) and its wiring connector (B) and mounting screws (C) – CBF models

Installation

36 Remove all traces of sealant from the sensor wiring grommet and clutch cover and apply a smear of fresh sealant to the grommet.
37 Locate the grommet and sensor in the cover and tighten the sensor bolts (see illustration 7.35). Clean the sensor tip.
38 Install the clutch cover (see Chapter 2, Section 14, Steps 29 to 32).

Lean angle sensor

Check

39 On CB600F/FA and CBR600F/FA models remove the seat (see Chapter 7) – the sensor is behind the battery on the left (see illustration). On CBF600N/NA/S/SA models remove the left-hand seat cowl (see Chapter 7) – the sensor is mounted between the relays and the regulator/rectifier (see illustration).
40 With the ignition switch ON and the kill switch set to run, connect the positive (+) lead of a voltmeter to the white/black wire terminal of the lean angle sensor connector and the negative (-) lead to the green wire terminal and check that battery voltage (approximately 12 volts) is present. If not check the lean angle sensor fuse (see Chapter 8). If that is good check the white/black wire from the fuse to the connector for continuity, then check the green wire for continuity to earth.
41 If the voltage and wiring are good, undo the screws, noting the washers, and displace the sensor. Hold the sensor horizontal and switch the ignition ON – the engine stop relay (behind the seat cowl on the right-hand side on CB600F/FA and CBR600F/FA models and just ahead of the lean angle sensor on CBF600N/NA/S/SA models (see illustration 9.5a or b) should click, indicating the power supply is closed (on). Slowly tilt the sensor to the left whilst listening to the engine stop relay; once the sensor reaches an angle of approximately 60° the relay should be heard to click, indicating the power supply is open (off). Switch the ignition OFF and return the sensor to the horizontal, then switch the ignition back ON again (engine stop relay should click again) and tilt the sensor to the right. The engine stop relay should be heard to click again once the sensor reaches an angle of around 60°.
42 If the relay does not click, first check the red/blue wire between the sensor and the relay, and if that is good check the relay. If all is good, it is likely the sensor is faulty.

Removal and installation

43 On CB600F/FA and CBR600F/FA models remove the seat (see Chapter 7) – the sensor is behind the battery on the left (see illustration 7.39a). CBF600N/NA/S/SA models remove the left-hand seat cowl (see Chapter 7) – the sensor is mounted between the relays and the regulator/rectifier (see illustration 7.39b).
44 Disconnect the sensor wiring connector. Undo the screws, noting the washers, and remove the sensor.
45 Installation is the reverse of removal. Make sure the sensor is fitted with the UP arrow pointing up.

8 Engine control module (ECM)

Check

1 The engine control module (ECM) itself cannot be checked, but a process of elimination of other possible faulty components can point to it being faulty. First check the FI system fuse (see Chapter 8). Next disconnect the ECM wiring connectors (see Steps 2-on) and check for loose or broken terminal pins in the connectors or ECM sockets, then check for continuity in each wire to/from the ECM and to its related component or connector, or to earth (ground) as appropriate, according to the wiring diagram for your model at the end of Chapter 8, and referring to the electrical system fault finding at the beginning of Chapter 8 – start with the wires to/from the engine stop relay, fuel cut-off relay and lean angle sensor, and the green and green/white wires to earth (ground). If any wire does not show continuity check the connectors and terminals in the circuit before assuming there is a break in the wire. Alternatively take the bike to a Honda dealer for checking on their diagnostic tester.

Removal and installation

Note: *Some countries require the fitting of a security bracket to the ECM that has to be removed before the connectors can be disconnected. The bracket is fitted with security bolts that will have to be driven around using a cold chisel, or if necessary the heads have to be drilled off.*

2 Make sure the ignition is OFF. Raise the fuel tank (Section 2).
3 On CB600F/FA and CBR600F/FA models displace the rear brake fluid reservoir (see illustration). Undo the ECM retainer screws and displace the retainer, moving the vacuum

8.3a Unscrew the reservoir bolt and move it clear

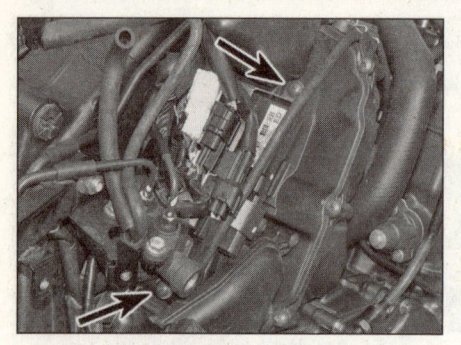

8.3b Undo the screws (arrowed) . . .

8.3c . . . then release the connectors . . .

8.3d . . . and draw the ECM out

hose aside **(see illustration)**. Release the throttle body sub-loom and oxygen sensor wiring connectors from the retainer, noting which fits where **(see illustration)**. Draw the ECM out and disconnect the wiring connectors **(see illustration)** (see **Note**).

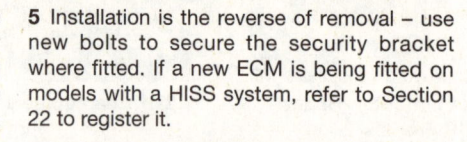

4 On CBF600N/NA/S/SA models release the throttle body sub-loom and oxygen sensor wiring connectors from the ECM retainer, noting which fits where **(see illustration and 7.26)**. Move the vacuum hose aside **(see illustration)**. Undo the screws and remove the retainer **(see illustration)**. Draw the ECM out and disconnect the wiring connectors **(see illustration)** (see **Note**).

5 Installation is the reverse of removal – use new bolts to secure the security bracket where fitted. If a new ECM is being fitted on models with a HISS system, refer to Section 22 to register it.

9 Fuel injection system relays

Engine stop relay

Check

1 Remove the relay (see below).

2 Set a multimeter to the ohms x 1 scale and connect it across the relay's A and B terminals **(see illustration)**. There should be no continuity (infinite resistance). Using a fully-charged 12 volt battery and two insulated jumper wires, connect the positive (+) terminal of the battery to the C terminal on the relay, and the negative (–) terminal to the D terminal on the relay. At this point the relay should be heard to click and the multimeter read 0 ohms (continuity). If this is the case the relay is proved good. If the relay does not click when battery voltage is applied and still indicates no continuity (infinite resistance) across its terminals, it is faulty and must be replaced with a new one.

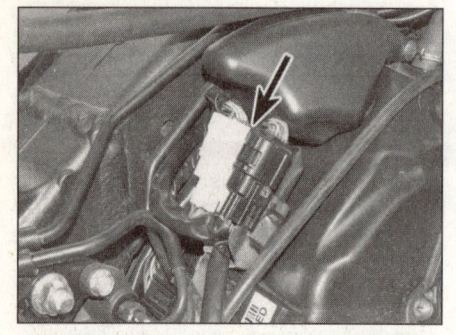

8.4a Throttle body sub-loom connectors (arrowed)

8.4b Move the hose aside . . .

8.4c . . . then undo the screws (arrowed)

8.4d Draw the ECM out and disconnect the wiring

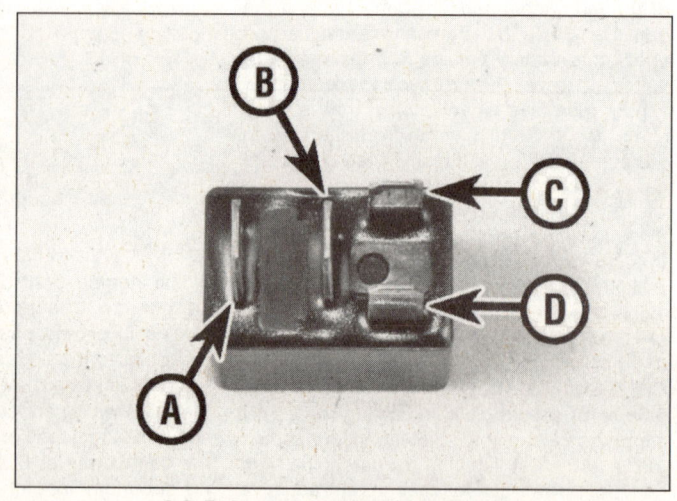

9.2 Relay test terminal identification

Engine management system 4•19

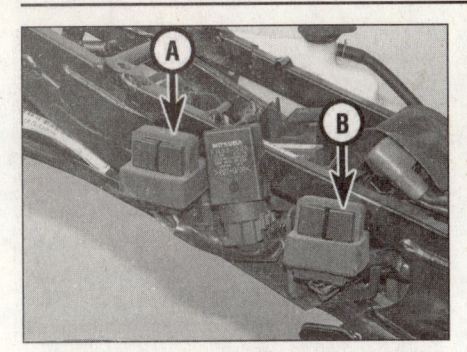

9.5a Engine stop relay (A), fuel cut-off relay (B) – 2007 to 2010 CB models

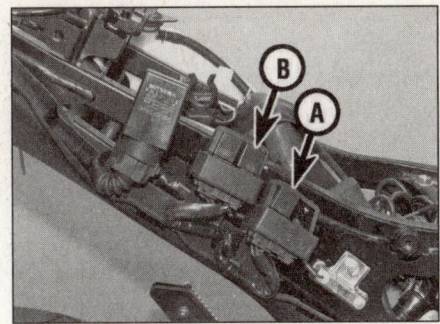

9.5b Engine stop relay (A), fuel cut-off relay (B) – 2011-on CB and CBR models

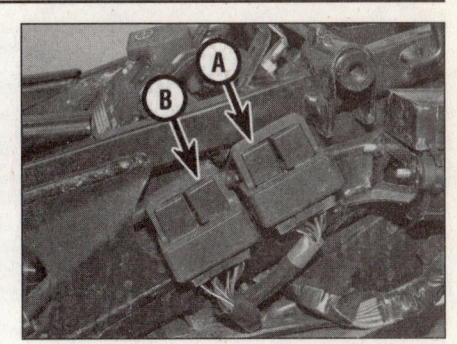

9.5c Engine stop relay (A), fuel cut-off relay (B) – CBF models

3 If the relay is good refer to the wiring diagrams at the end of Chapter 8 and check the wiring and connectors in the circuit to and from the relay.

Removal and installation

4 On CB600F/FA and CBR600F/FA models remove the seat cowl (see Chapter 7). On CBF600N/NA/S/SA models remove the left-hand seat cowl (see Chapter 7).
5 Move the rubber retainer aside then pull the relay off the connector **(see illustrations)**.
6 Installation is the reverse of removal.

Fuel cut-off relay

Check

7 Remove the relay (see below).
8 Set a multimeter to the ohms x 1 scale and connect it across the relay's A and B terminals **(see illustration 9.2)**. There should be no continuity (infinite resistance). Using a fully-charged 12 volt battery and two insulated jumper wires, connect the positive (+) terminal of the battery to the C terminal on the relay, and the negative (–) terminal to the D terminal on the relay. At this point the relay should be heard to click and the multimeter read 0 ohms (continuity). If this is the case the relay is proved good. If the relay does not click when battery voltage is applied and still indicates no continuity (infinite resistance) across its terminals, it is faulty and must be replaced with a new one.
9 If the relay is good refer to the wiring diagrams at the end of Chapter 8 and check the wiring and connectors in the circuit to and from the relay.

Removal and installation

10 On CB600F/FA and CBR600F/FA models remove the seat cowl (see Chapter 7). On CBF600N/NA/S/SA models remove the left-hand seat cowl (see Chapter 7).
11 Move the rubber retainer aside then pull the relay off the connector **(see illustration 9.5a, b or c)**.
12 Installation is the reverse of removal.

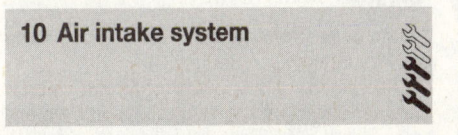

10 Air intake system

Air intake diaphragm valve

Removal

1 Remove the left-hand side cover (see Chapter 7).
2 Undo the air intake duct screws and displace the duct, then disconnect the vacuum hose from the diaphragm valve **(see illustrations)**.
3 Turn the diaphragm valve anti-clockwise, then unhook the rod from the flap in the duct and remove the valve **(see illustration)**.

Inspection

4 Make sure the vacuum hoses between the diaphragm valve, the control valve, the vacuum chamber, the one-way valve and the throttle bodies are all in good condition, are securely connected at each end, and are not kinked, split or cracked **(see illustration 10.9)**. If a hose has a split the system will not work as it relies on vacuum. Replace the hoses with new ones if necessary.
5 Make sure the flap opens and closes – if not repair it, or replace the duct with a new one **(see illustration)**. Check that the rod moves in and out of the diaphragm valve – if not replace the valve with a new one.
6 Check the diaphragm valve by applying a vacuum of 250 mm Hg to its union using a vacuum tool to see whether the rod moves. If the rod does not move the diaphragm may be split.

Installation

7 Installation is the reverse of removal. Make sure the vacuum hose is securely connected at each end. Make sure the air duct rubber seal is in good condition and seated in its groove – fit a new seal if necessary.

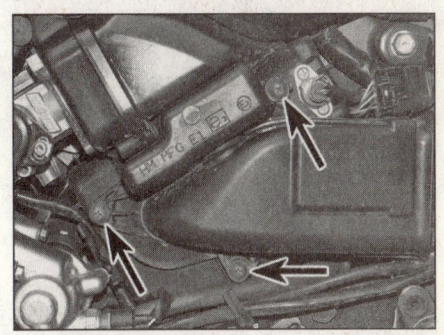

10.2a Undo the screws (arrowed) . . .

10.2b . . . then displace the duct and disconnect the hose

10.3 Release the valve and unhook the rod

10.5 Check the action of the flap in the duct

4•20 Engine management system

10.9 Air intake control valve (A), vacuum chamber (B), one-way valve (C)

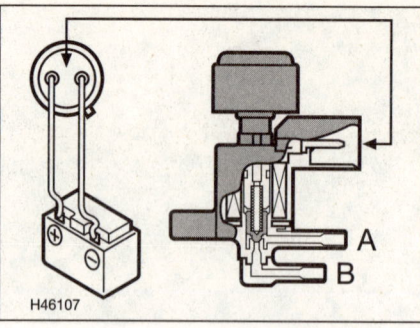

10.11 Control valve operation test

Air intake control valve

Removal

8 Remove the air filter housing and throttle body assembly (see Section 3).
9 Disconnect the wiring connector then detach the vacuum hoses, noting which fits where **(see illustration)**. Undo the screw and remove the valve.

Inspection

10 Refer to Step 4 and check the air intake system vacuum hoses.
11 Check the operation of the control valve by blowing through the union A; no air should flow through the valve and out of union B **(see illustration)**. Now connect a 12 volt battery, positive (+) to the black/white wire terminal, negative (-) to the yellow/black terminal, and repeat the check; air should now flow freely through the valve.
12 Check the resistance of the control valve windings by connecting an ohmmeter between its connector terminals and compare the reading obtained to that given in the Specifications. Replace the valve with a new one if faulty.

Installation

13 Installation is the reverse of removal. Make sure the vacuum hoses and wiring connector are securely connected.

Air intake one-way valve and vacuum chamber

Removal

14 Remove the air filter housing and throttle body assembly (see Section 3).
15 To remove the vacuum chamber detach the vacuum hoses, noting which fits where, then undo the screw and remove the chamber, noting how it locates on the air filter housing **(see illustration 10.9)**.
16 To remove the one-way valve note which way round it fits, then detach the hoses and remove the valve **(see illustration 10.9)**.

Inspection

17 Refer to Step 4 and check the air intake system vacuum hoses.
18 Check the operation of the one-way valve by blowing through the union A – air should flow through the valve and out of unions B and C **(see illustration)**. Now blow through union B; no air should flow through the valve and out of unions A and C.
19 Check the vacuum chamber for signs of damage and replace it with a new one if necessary.

Installation

20 Installation is the reverse of removal. Make sure the one-way valve is fitted with its wide end as shown in illustration 10.9. Make sure the hoses are securely connected at each end.

11 Idle speed control system

Warning: Refer to the precautions given in Section 1 before starting work.

Check

1 Idle speed is controlled automatically by a valve that adjusts a flow of air that by-passes the throttle valves in the throttle bodies. The valve is actuated by the ECM and adjusts according to information received from sensors on engine and air temperature and throttle position. When the ignition is switched ON the valve self-checks by turning through its range of movement, and should emit a beep. If there is a fault, a code should be indicated by the FI warning light in the instrument cluster (see Section 6).
2 If the engine idle speed is not as specified at the beginning of the Chapter, and there is no fault indicated, check the throttle cable freeplay, spark plugs, air filter and the valve clearances (see Chapter 1).
3 Next raise the fuel tank (see Section 2). Inspect the intake rubbers between the throttle bodies and the cylinder head for loose clamps or splits that could cause an air leak, causing a weak mixture. Make sure the idle air distribution hoses are in good condition and are securely connected at each end **(see illustration)**. The air hose unions on the right-hand end have an O-ring, which

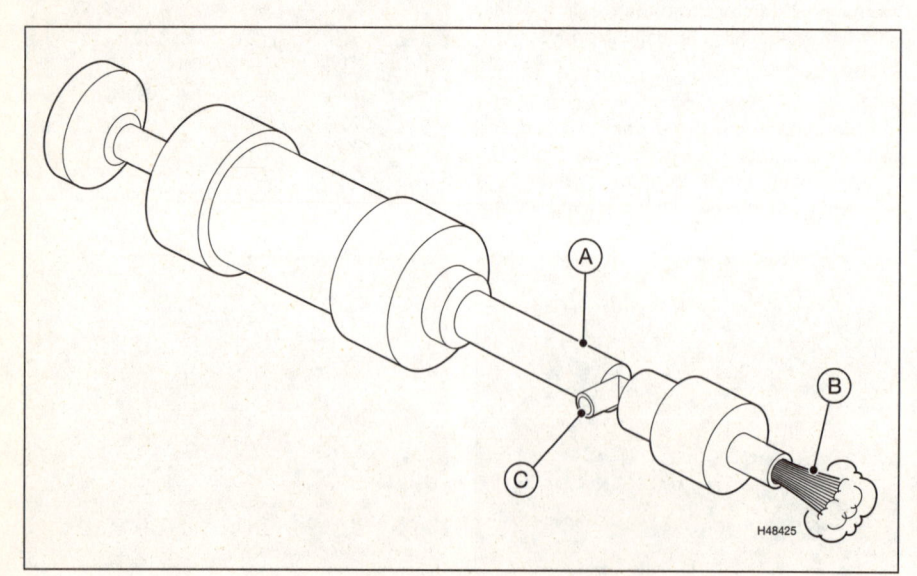

10.18 Test the one-way valve as described

11.3a Make sure the hoses are in good condition and securely connected

Engine management system 4•21

11.3b Detach the hoses

11.3c Undo the screw (arrowed) and remove the plate . . .

11.3d . . . and each union . . .

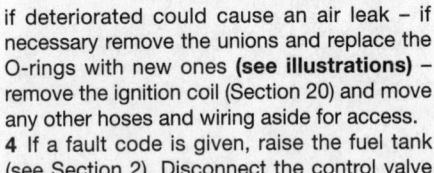

if deteriorated could cause an air leak – if necessary remove the unions and replace the O-rings with new ones **(see illustrations)** – remove the ignition coil (Section 20) and move any other hoses and wiring aside for access.

4 If a fault code is given, raise the fuel tank (see Section 2). Disconnect the control valve wiring connector **(see illustration)**. Check the connector wires and terminals are secure and clean. Check each wire between the connector and the ECM for continuity.

5 If necessary remove the valve (Steps 7 to 9), then reconnect the wiring, turn the ignition ON and check the valve moves and beeps.

6 If all is good the ECM could be faulty.

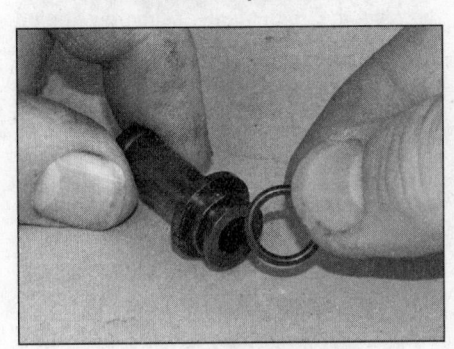

Removal

7 Remove the air filter housing and throttle body assembly, then separate the throttle bodies from the housing (see Section 3).

11.3e . . . and fit new O-rings

8 Clean the area around the valve to prevent any dirt entering the air passages.

9 Undo the control valve screws and remove the plate, then draw the valve out **(see**

11.4 Control valve wiring connector (arrowed) is recessed

illustration). Remove the O-ring – a new one must be used **(see illustration)**. Check the action of the valve by turning it **(see illustration)**.

Installation

10 Fit a new O-ring onto the valve and smear it with clean oil **(see illustration)**. Turn the valve clockwise until lightly seated **(see illustration 11.9c)**. Align the groove in the valve with the pin in its housing, turning the valve back if required, then insert the valve **(see illustration)**. Fit the plate, seating the cut-out over the lug, and tighten the screws **(see illustration 11.9a)**.

11 Install the throttle bodies and air filter housing (see Section 3).

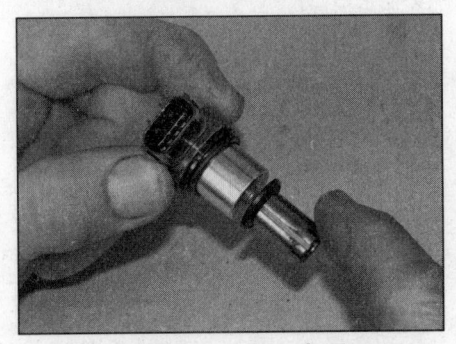

11.9a Undo the screws (arrowed) and remove the plate . . .

11.9b . . . then draw the valve out. Remove and discard the O-ring (arrowed)

11.9c Make sure the valve turns

11.10a Fit a new O-ring . . .

11.10b . . . then align the groove with the pin (arrowed) and insert the valve

12 Fuel pressure check

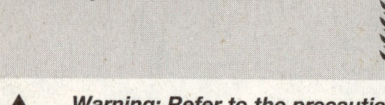

Warning: *Refer to the precautions given in Section 1 before starting work.*

Note: *A pressure gauge along with some adapters and hoses that are compatible with the quick-release fittings of the bike's fuel hose are required for this check. Honda can supply the various parts required, but it may be cheaper to get a dealer to perform the check, especially as hopefully you will not need the equipment more than once.*

1 Raise the fuel tank (see Section 2, Steps 1 to 4). Disconnect the fuel pump wiring connector **(see illustration 2.7)**. To eliminate any residual pressure in the fuel system start the engine and let it idle until it stops.
2 Disconnect the battery negative (–) lead (see Chapter 8).
3 Disconnect the fuel hose (see Section 2, Step 10).
4 Connect the fuel gauge assembly between the fuel tank and the disconnected fuel hose.
5 Reconnect the fuel pump wiring connector and battery negative (–) lead. Start the engine and allow it to idle at the specified speed. Note the pressure present in the fuel system by reading the gauge, then turn the engine off. Compare the reading obtained to that given in the Specifications.
6 If the fuel pressure is higher than specified, the pressure regulator in the fuel pump or the pump itself is faulty and must be replaced with a new one (see Section 13).
7 If the fuel pressure is lower than specified, first check for a leak, which should be obvious from the smell of fuel. If there are no leaks check for a pinched or blocked tank breather hose or fuel hose. Next remove the pump (see Section 13), and check the strainer for a blockage (though this is unlikely). Otherwise the fuel filter or pressure regulator, both of which are integral components of the pump assembly, or the pump itself, are faulty, and so the pump must be replaced with a new one.
8 On completion, repeat Step 1, then disconnect the battery negative (–) lead again. Remove the fuel gauge assembly, being prepared to catch any residual fuel, then reconnect the bike's fuel hose and lower the tank, referring to Section 2, Steps 19-on.
9 Reconnect the battery. Start the engine and check that there is no sign of fuel leakage.

13 Fuel pump

Warning: *Refer to the precautions given in Section 1 before starting work.*

Check

1 The fuel pump is located inside the fuel tank. The fuel pump should run for a few seconds when the ignition is switched ON to pressurise the fuel system, and then cut out until the engine is started. Check that it does this – you can hear it run. If it doesn't, first check the FI fuse and the lean angle sensor fuse (see Chapter 8).
2 If the fuses are good raise the fuel tank (see Section 2).
3 Make sure the ignition is switched OFF then disconnect the fuel pump wiring connector **(see illustration)**. Connect the positive (+) lead of a voltmeter to the brown wire terminal on the loom side of the connector and the negative (–) lead to the green wire terminal. Switch the ignition ON whilst noting the reading obtained on the meter.

4 If battery voltage is present for a few seconds, the fuel pump circuit is operating correctly and the fuel pump itself is faulty and must be replaced with a new one.
5 If no reading is obtained, check the fuel pump circuit wiring for continuity and make sure all the connectors are free from corrosion and are securely connected. Repair/replace the wiring as necessary and clean the connectors using electrical contact cleaner. If this fails to reveal the fault, check the following components.
- Engine kill switch (see Chapter 8, Section 19).
- Fuel cut-off relay (see Section 9).
- Engine stop relay (see Section 9).
- Lean angle sensor (see Section 7).
- Engine control module (ECM) (see Section 8).

Removal

6 Remove the fuel tank (see Section 2). Drain or siphon as much fuel as possible from the tank. Make sure the fuel cap is secure, then place the tank upside down on plenty of rag.
7 Unscrew the fuel pump mounting plate nuts **(see illustration 13.13)**. Carefully lift the pump assembly from the tank along with the mounting plate seal **(see illustration)**.
8 Remove the seal, noting how it fits, and discard it **(see illustration)** – a new one must be used on installation.
9 Remove the rubber cover from the fuel strainer, noting how it locates **(see illustration)**. Check the strainer for signs of dirt and clean it if necessary – note that the strainer is part of the fuel pump and is not available separately. Refit the rubber cover, hooking the peg into the hole.

Installation

10 Make sure the wiring terminal screws, nuts and connectors are tight, both on the pump and the base.
11 Ensure the mounting plate and tank surfaces are clean and dry. Fit the new seal onto the plate, aligning the rubber locating pegs with the holes **(see illustration 13.8)**.

13.3 Fuel pump wiring connector (arrowed)

13.7 Carefully draw the pump out ...

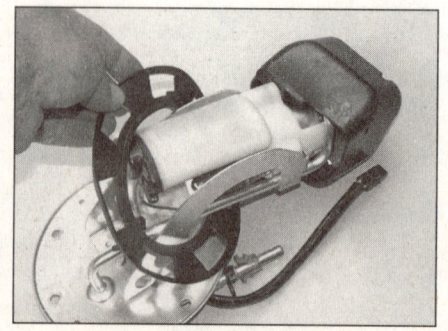

13.8 ... and remove the seal

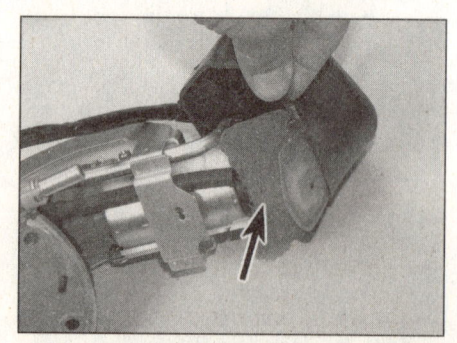

13.9 Displace the rubber cover to reveal the strainer (arrowed)

Carefully pull the pegs through so the ribs are past the holes **(see illustration)**.

12 Carefully manoeuvre the pump assembly into the tank, making sure it is correctly positioned as shown, and seat the seal and plate over the studs **(see illustration 13.7)**.

13 Fit the nuts and tighten them finger-tight. Now tighten them evenly and a little at a time in the numerical sequence shown to the torque setting specified at the beginning of the Chapter **(see illustration)**.

14 Install the fuel tank (see Section 2).

14 Fuel gauge and level sensor

Check

CB600F/FA and CBR600F/FA

1 The circuit consists of the level sensor in the fuel tank and the fuel gauge, which is part of the instrument cluster LCD display. Under normal circumstances with the tank full all segments of the gauge will show, and when there are only about 3.5 litres left the final segment will flash. The system performs its own self diagnosis when the ignition is turned ON, and if an open circuit is detected in the wiring the display will operate as follows – it starts with the centre two segments coming on, then the adjacent two segments also come on, followed by the outer segments, then the segments will go out, and this pattern will repeat until the fault is repaired.

2 If a fault is indicated, raise the fuel tank (see Section 2). Disconnect the level sensor wiring connector **(see illustration 14.7)**. Connect a jumper wire between the terminals in the loom side of the connector then turn the ignition ON – if all the segments come on the circuit is good, in which case go to Step 4 and check the sensor. If the segments are still performing their routine check for continuity in the grey/black wire between the pump connector and the instrument cluster connector, and in the green wire to earth, referring to Chapter 8. If the wiring is good the instrument PCB is faulty (see Chapter 8).

3 If all the gauge segments are on when there is less than a full tank, raise the fuel tank (see Section 2). Disconnect the level sensor wiring connector **(see illustration 14.7)**. If the segments remain lit check for a short circuit to earth in the grey/black wire between the instrument cluster connector and the level sensor connector. If the wire is good the PCB is faulty (see Chapter 8). If the segments display as in Step 1 for an open circuit go to Step 4 and check the sensor

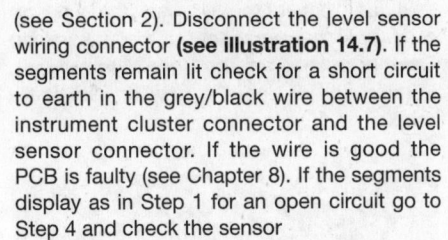

4 To check the sensor connect an ohmmeter or multimeter set to the ohms scale to the terminals in the sensor side of the wiring connector and measure the resistance. Compare the reading obtained to those given for a full and empty tank at the beginning of the Chapter, adjusting for the amount of fuel you estimate is there.

5 To accurately check the sensor, remove it from the tank (see below). Check the float arm for damage and look for fuel inside the float, and check that the arm moves up and down smoothly and freely. Also check the wiring. Connect the meter to the sensor connector as above, then manually move the float up and down to simulate movement between the full and empty positions, and compare the resistance readings to those given **(see illustrations 14.8a and b)**. If they are not as specified replace the sensor with a new one.

CBF600N/NA/S/SA

6 The circuit consists of the level sensor in the fuel tank and the fuel gauge, which is part of the instrument cluster. Under normal circumstances with the tank full the needle should point to F, and when the needle enters the red zone there are only about 4 litres left.

7 If the gauge does not work, check the amount of fuel in the tank, then raise the tank (see Section 2). Disconnect the level sensor wiring connector **(see illustration)**. Connect an ohmmeter or multimeter set to the ohms scale to the terminals in the sensor side of the wiring connector and measure the resistance. Compare the reading obtained to those given at the beginning of the Chapter for a full and empty tank, adjusting for the amount of fuel you estimate is there.

8 To accurately check the sensor remove it from the tank (see below). Check the float arm for damage and look for fuel inside the float, and check that the arm moves up and down smoothly and freely. Also check the wiring. Connect the meter to the sensor connector as above, then manually move the float up and down to simulate movement between the full and empty positions, and compare the resistance readings to those given **(see illustrations)**. If they are not as specified replace the pump assembly with a new one.

9 If the level sensor appears to be functioning correctly, check for continuity in the grey/black wire between the pump connector and the instrument cluster connector, and in the green wire to earth, referring to Chapter 8. If the wiring is good connect the sensor wiring connector, turn the ignition ON and manually move the float up and down – if the gauge needle does not move in response to the movement of the float there is a fault in the instrument cluster (see Chapter 8).

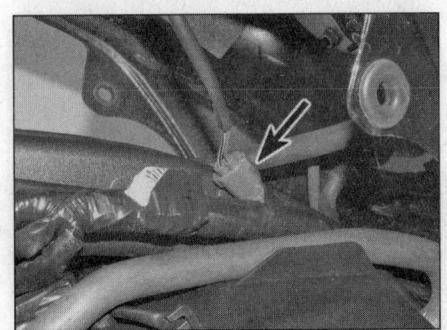

13.11 Fit a new seal and pull the legs through

13.13 Fuel pump nut tightening sequence

14.7 Fuel level sensor wiring connector (arrowed)

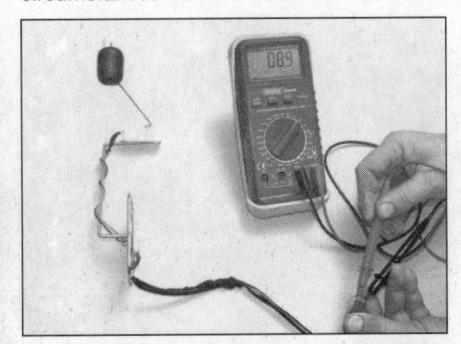

14.8a Check the resistance with the float arm in the full position . . .

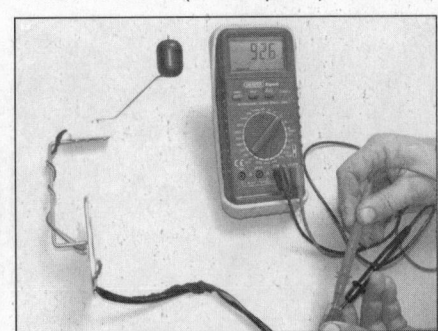

14.8b . . . and the empty position

4•24 Engine management system

14.11a Unscrew the nuts (arrowed) . . .

14.11b . . . then draw the sensor out

14.12 Fit a new O-ring into the groove

Removal and installation

10 If the gauge is faulty refer to Chapter 8.
11 If the sensor is faulty remove the fuel tank (see Section 2). Drain or siphon as much fuel as possible from the tank. Make sure the fuel cap is secure, then place the tank upside down on plenty of rag. Unscrew the nuts and carefully lift the sensor out of the tank, taking care not to snag the float **(see illustrations)**. Remove the O-ring – a new one must be used.
12 Fit a new O-ring into the groove in the tank **(see illustration)**. Manoeuvre the sensor float into the tank and seat the plate over the studs with the wiring pointing to the left-hand side of the tank. Fit the nuts and tighten them evenly and a little at a time in a criss-cross sequence. Install the tank and check for leakage around the sensor plate.

15 Throttle cables

> **Warning:** *Refer to the precautions given in Section 1 before proceeding.*

Removal

1 Remove the fuel tank (Section 2).
2 Slacken the cable adjuster locknut, then thread the adjuster fully in to get maximum freeplay in the cable **(see illustration)**.
3 Unscrew the hex holding the closing (front) cable in the bracket on the throttle bodies by enough to free the captive nut, then release the cable from the bracket **(see illustration)**. Slacken the locknut holding the rear cable in the bracket, then unscrew the adjuster and slip the cable out of the bracket.
4 Unscrew the cable elbow nuts at the throttle pulley housing **(see illustration)**. Remove the housing screws and separate the halves **(see illustrations)**. Detach the closing cable end from the pulley, then withdraw the cable from the housing **(see illustrations)**.
5 Detach the opening cable end from the pulley. Thread the cable adjuster fully off the

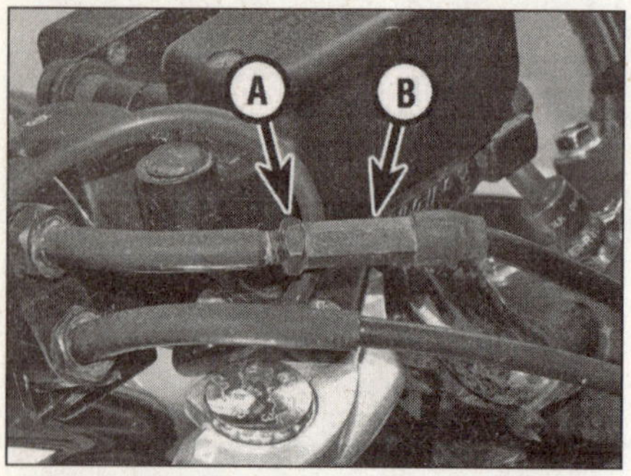

15.2 Slacken the locknut (A) and turn the adjuster (B) in

15.3 Release the cables from the bracket as described

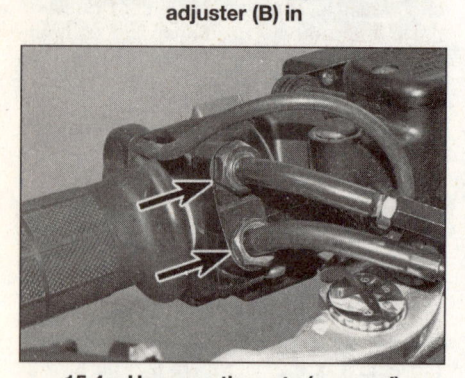

15.4a Unscrew the nuts (arrowed)

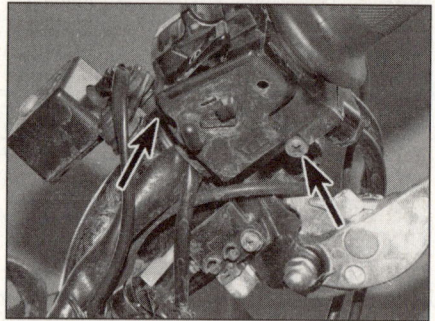

15.4b Undo the screws (arrowed) . . .

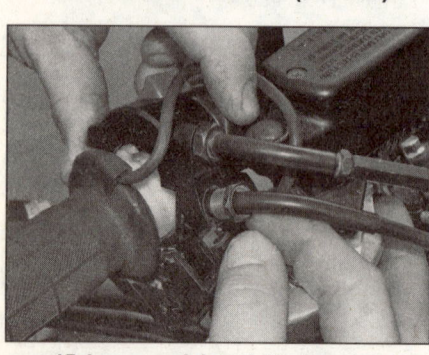

15.4c . . . and detach the housing

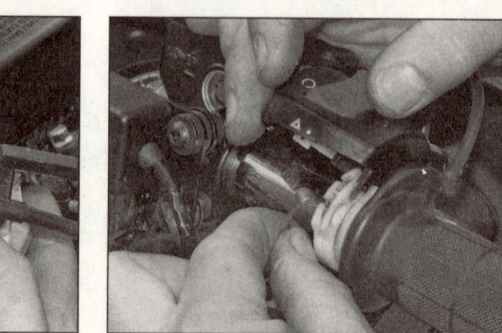

15.4d Detach the cable from the pulley . . .

15.4e . . . and withdraw it

Engine management system 4•25

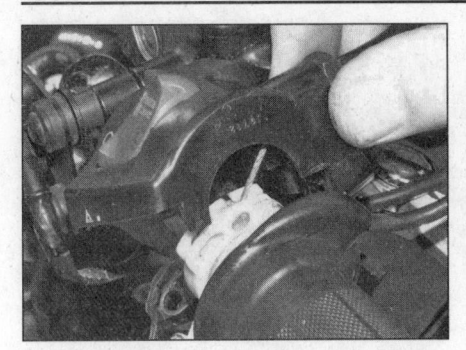

15.5a Detach the cable from the pulley

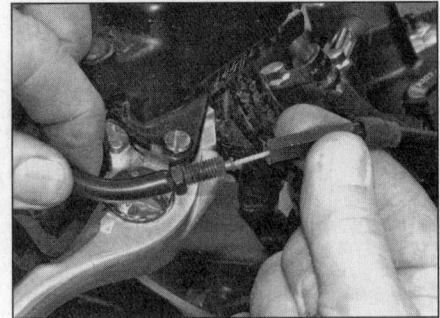

15.5b Thread the adjuster off the elbow . . .

15.5c . . . then thread the elbow out of the housing

throttle opening cable elbow, then thread the cable elbow out of the housing **(see illustrations)**. Withdraw the cable from the housing **(see illustration)**.
6 Remove the air filter housing and throttle body assembly (see Section 3). Mark each cable according to its location.
7 Detach the cable ends from the throttle cam **(see illustrations 15.8c, b and a)**.

Installation

Note: *If a new opening cable is being fitted, thread the cable adjuster fully off the elbow beforehand* **(see illustration 15.5b)**.
8 Fit the opening cable end into the rear socket in the throttle body cam **(see illustrations)**. Fit the closing cable end into the front of the throttle cam **(see illustration)**.

9 Install the throttle body and air filter housing assembly (see Section 3).
10 Fit the throttle opening cable into the upper socket of the throttle pulley housing and thread the elbow in without it becoming tight on the bottom of the threads **(see illustration)** – the elbow must stay loose so that it aligns itself. Thread the adjuster fully on to the elbow **(see illustration)**. Lubricate the cable end with multi-purpose grease and fit it into the throttle pulley **(see illustration 15.5a)**.
11 Fit the closing cable into the lower socket **(see illustration 15.4e)**. Lubricate the cable end with multi-purpose grease and fit it into the throttle pulley **(see illustration 15.4d)**. Thread the lower cable nut into the housing, leaving it loose.
12 Assemble the housing onto the handlebar, making sure the pin locates in the hole, then fit

the screws and tighten them **(see illustration)**. Align the cable elbows and tighten the nuts **(see illustration 15.4a)**.
13 Fit the opening cable into the rear of the bracket on the throttle bodies and lightly tighten the locknut **(see illustration 15.3)**. Fit the closing cable into the front of the bracket and fully tighten the hex. Operate the throttle to check that it opens and closes freely.
14 Check and adjust the throttle cable freeplay (see Chapter 1). Turn the handlebars back-and-forth to make sure the cables don't cause the steering to bind.
15 Install the fuel tank.
16 Start the engine and check that the idle speed does not rise as the handlebars are turned. If it does, the throttle cables are routed incorrectly. Correct the problem before riding the motorcycle.

15.8a Fit the opening cable down the back . . .

15.8b . . . and into the rear socket

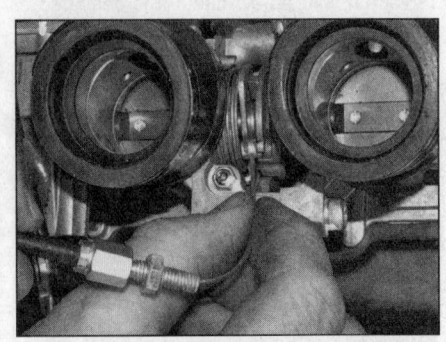

15.8c Fit the closing cable into the front socket

15.10a Thread the elbow into the housing . . .

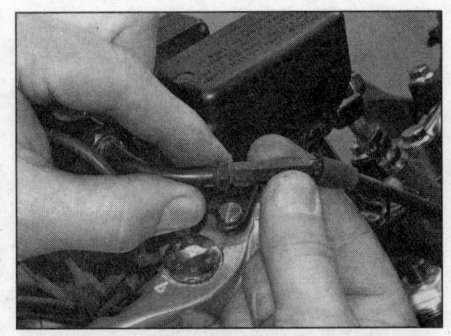

15.10b . . . then thread the adjuster onto the elbow

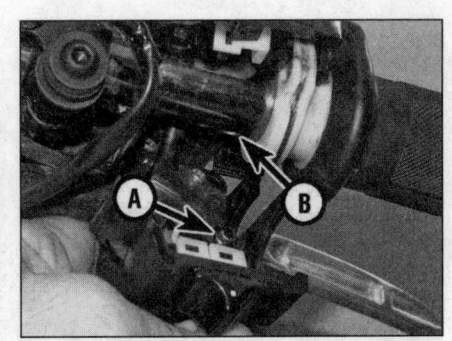

15.12 Locate the pin (A) in the hole (B)

16 Exhaust system

Warning: *If the engine has been running the exhaust system will be very hot. Allow the system to cool before carrying out any work.*

HAYNES HINT: *Exhaust system clamp bolts tend to become corroded and seized. It is advisable to spray them with WD40 or a similar product before attempting to slacken them.*

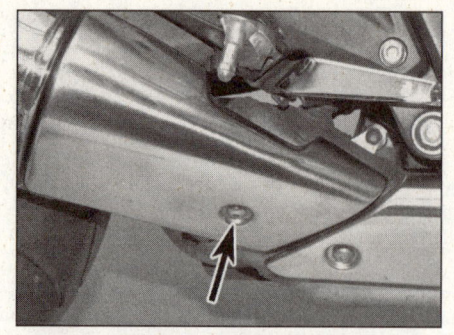

16.1a Unscrew the bolt (arrowed)...

16.1b ...and draw the cover off the tabs

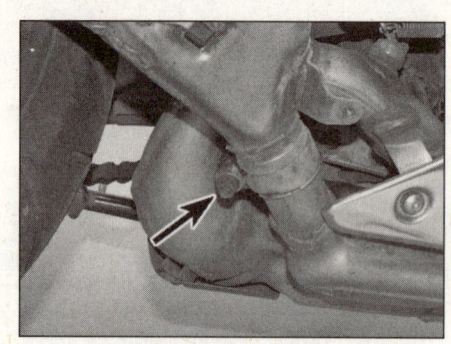

16.2 Slacken the clamp (arrowed)

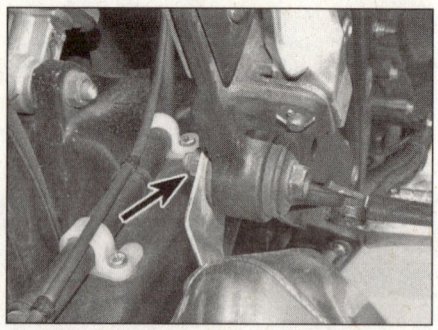

16.3 Unscrew the nut (arrowed), withdraw the bolt and remove the silencer

Removal – CB600F/FA and CBR600F/FA

Silencer

1 Unscrew the silencer cover bolt **(see illustration)**. Draw the cover forwards to release it from the tabs **(see illustration)**.
2 Slacken the silencer clamp bolt **(see illustration)**.
3 Unscrew the nut on the silencer mounting bolt **(see illustration)**. Support the silencer, then withdraw the bolt, noting the washer, and ease the silencer off the downpipe assembly. Note the collar in the mount and remove it safekeeping if required.
4 Check the condition of the sealing ring and replace it with a new one if it is damaged or deformed or no longer sealing correctly. If you do fit a new one, remove the clamp and expand the tangs on the end of the pipe slightly to make it easier to fit.
5 Check the condition of the nut and bolts, washer, collar and rubbers and replace them with new ones if necessary.

16.8a Front mounting (arrowed)

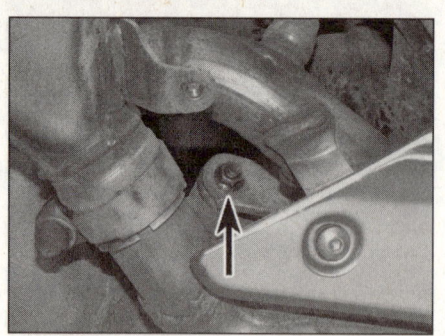

16.8b Rear mounting (arrowed)

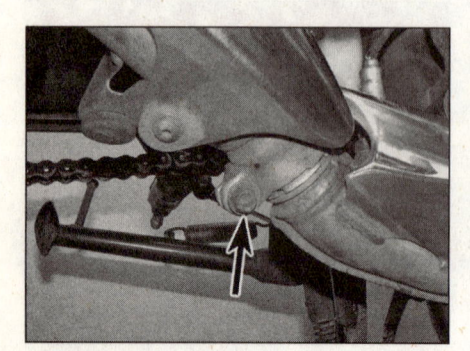

16.12 Slacken the clamp (arrowed)

16.13a Unscrew the nut

Downpipe assembly

6 Remove the silencer (see above).
7 Remove the right-hand side cover (see Chapter 7). Disconnect the oxygen sensor wiring connector and free the connector from the retainer **(see illustration 7.22a)**. Feed the wiring down to the sensor, releasing it from the clamp and noting its routing.
8 Unscrew the nuts on the chamber mounting bolts and remove the washers where fitted **(see illustrations)**. Unscrew the nuts securing the downpipe flanges to the cylinder head **(see illustration 16.18b)**. Support the assembly, then withdraw the mounting bolts, noting the washers where fitted, draw the flanges off the studs and manoeuvre the downpipe assembly off.
9 Remove the sealing ring from each port in the cylinder head and discard them as new ones must be used **(see illustration 16.19)**.
10 If required remove the shields from the chamber, noting the collars in the rubbers.
11 Note the collars in the chamber mounts and remove them for safekeeping if required. Check the condition of the nuts and bolts, washers, collars and rubbers and replace them with new ones if necessary.

Removal – CBF600N/NA/S/SA

Silencer

12 If required remove the shield. Slacken the clamp bolt **(see illustration)**.
13 Unscrew the nut on the silencer mounting bolt **(see illustration)**. Support the silencer, then withdraw the bolt, noting the collar

Engine management system 4•27

16.13b Note the collar fitted in the bush

16.18a Unscrew the mounting bolt nut . . .

16.18b . . . and the downpipe nuts . . .

16.18c . . . withdraw the bolt and remove the system

and washer, and ease the silencer out of the downpipe assembly. Note the collar in the mount and remove it for safekeeping if required **(see illustration)**.

14 Check the condition of the sealing ring and replace it with a new one if it is damaged

16.19 Remove and discard the sealing rings

or deformed or no longer sealing correctly. If you do fit a new one, remove the clamp and expand the tangs on the end of the pipe slightly to make it easier to fit.

15 Check the condition of the nut and bolt, washer, collars and mounting rubber and replace them with new ones if necessary.

Downpipe assembly

16 Remove the silencer (see above).

17 Remove the right-hand side cover (see Chapter 7). Disconnect the oxygen sensor wiring connector and free the connector from the retainer **(see illustrations 7.22b and 7.26)**. Feed the wiring down to the sensor, releasing it from the guides and noting its routing.

18 Unscrew the nut on the mounting bolt **(see illustration)**. Unscrew the nuts securing the downpipe flanges to the cylinder head **(see illustration)**. Support the assembly, then withdraw the bolt, noting the washer, draw the flanges off the studs and manoeuvre the downpipe assembly off **(see illustration)**.

19 Remove the sealing ring from each port in the cylinder head and discard them as new ones must be used **(see illustration)**.

20 Note the collar in the rear mount and remove it for safekeeping if required **(see illustration 16.13b)**. Check the condition of the nuts and bolt, washer, collar and mounting rubbers and replace them with new ones if necessary.

Installation – all models

21 Installation is the reverse of removal, noting the following:

- Replace any damaged, deformed or deteriorated mounting rubbers with new ones. Replace any badly corroded clamp, collars, nuts bolts and washers with new ones. Make sure the collars are fitted in the rubbers.
- Check that the amount of protrusion of each stud from the cylinder head is

4•28 Engine management system

16.21a Measure stud protrusion as shown

16.21b Fit a new sealing ring into each port

45 to 46 mm when measured as shown **(see illustration 16.21a)**.
- Use a new sealing ring in each cylinder head port, and dab them with grease to stick them in place **(see illustration 16.21b)**.
- Apply a smear of copper grease to all nuts and bolts to prevent them from seizing up. Fit and secure all mounts finger-tight before fully tightening them. On the downpipe assembly tighten the flange nuts before the mounting bolt(s). Tighten the nuts/bolts to the torque settings specified at the beginning of the Chapter.
- Do not forget to reconnect the oxygen sensor wiring connector, and make sure the wiring is correctly routed and secured.
- Run the engine and check the system for leaks.

17 Pulse secondary air (PAIR) system

General information

1 To reduce the amount of unburned hydrocarbons released in the exhaust gases, a pulse secondary air (PAIR) system is fitted. The system consists of the control valve (mounted under the fuel tank), the reed valves (fitted in the valve cover) and the hoses linking them. The control valve is actuated electronically by the ECM.
2 Under normal operating conditions the valve is open allowing filtered air to be drawn through the reed valves and cylinder head passages and into the exhaust ports. The air mixes with the exhaust gases, causing any unburned particles of the fuel in the mixture to be burnt in the exhaust port/pipes. This process changes a considerable amount of hydrocarbons and carbon monoxide into relatively harmless carbon dioxide and water. The reed valves in the valve cover are fitted to prevent the flow of exhaust gases back up the cylinder head passages and into the air filter housing.

Testing

3 Start the engine and warm it up normal temperature, then stop it.
4 Raise the fuel tank (see Section 2). Detach the PAIR hose from the air filter housing **(see illustration 3.14a)**. Check that the hose is clean – the presence or carbon deposits indicates a faulty system. Start the engine again and open the throttle slightly, and check air is being sucked into the detached hose. If not, stop the engine, then perform the following checks.
5 Disconnect the control valve wiring connector **(see illustration 3.14b)**. Clean the end of the air filter housing hose. Manually check the operation of the system by blowing through the hose – air should flow through the control valve and reed valves **(see illustration)**. Using a pair of auxiliary wires apply battery voltage (12 volts) across the control valve terminals and repeat the check **(see illustration)** – no air should flow through the control valve. Disconnect the battery. If the valve does not behave as described check its resistance (Step 7).
6 Now suck on the air filter hose union; you should not be able to suck air back up the hose, indicating the reed valves are closing and sealing correctly. If you can suck air through, first identify which reed valve is faulty by blocking one hose from the valve cover, then the other. Having identified the faulty valve, remove it for cleaning (see below), then test it again. Replace the valve with a new one if necessary.
7 Check the resistance of the control valve solenoid by connecting an ohmmeter between its connector terminals and compare the reading obtained to that given in the Specifications **(see illustration)**. Replace the valve with a new one if faulty.

Component renewal

Control valve

8 Raise the fuel tank (see Section 2).
9 Detach the PAIR hoses from the reed valves **(see illustration)**. Detach the hose from the air filter housing **(see illustration 3.14a)**.
10 Disconnect the control valve wiring connector **(see illustration 3.14b)**.
11 Displace the control valve from its mount and remove it along with the hoses, noting their routing. Detach the hoses from the valve if required, noting which fits where **(see illustration 17.5a)**.
12 Installation is the reverse of removal.

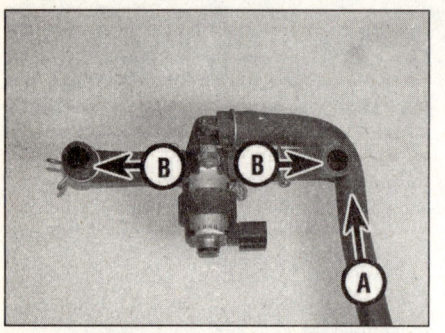

17.5a When blowing into hose (A) air should flow out of hoses (B)

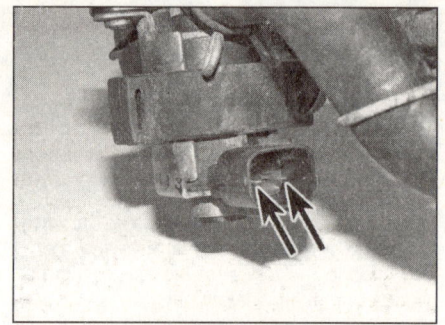

17.5b Apply battery voltage to the terminals

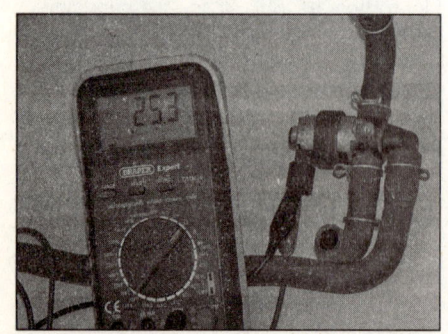

17.7 Check the resistance of the control valve

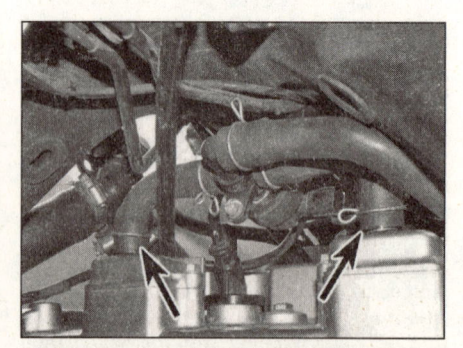

17.9 Detach the hoses (arrowed) from the reed valve housings

Engine management system 4•29

Reed valves

13 Raise, or for better access remove, the fuel tank (see Section 2).
14 Release the clamps and detach the air hoses **(see illustration 17.9)**. Unscrew the bolts and remove the covers. Remove the reed valves and the base plates, noting which way around they fit.
15 Installation is the reverse of removal. Make sure the reed valve components and housings are clean and free of carbon deposits, and that the base plates and valves seat correctly. Tighten the cover bolts to the torque setting specified at the beginning of the Chapter.

18 Catalytic converter

General information

1 There is a catalytic converter incorporated in the exhaust system to minimise the level of exhaust pollutants released into the atmosphere.
2 A catalytic converter consists of a canister containing a fine mesh impregnated with a catalyst material, over which the hot exhaust gases pass. The catalyst speeds up the oxidation of harmful carbon monoxide, unburned hydrocarbons and soot, effectively reducing the quantity of harmful products released into the atmosphere via the exhaust gases.
3 The catalytic converter is of the closed-loop type with exhaust gas oxygen content information being fed back to the engine control module (ECM) by the oxygen sensor.
4 The oxygen sensor contains a heating element which is controlled by the ECM. When the engine is cold, the ECM switches on the heating element which warms the exhaust gases as they pass over the sensor. This brings the catalytic converter quickly up to its normal operating temperature and decreases the level of exhaust pollutants emitted whilst the engine warms up. Once the engine is sufficiently warmed up, the ECM switches off the heating element.
5 Refer to Section 16 for exhaust system removal and installation, and Section 7 for oxygen sensor removal and installation information.

Precautions

6 A catalytic converter is a reliable and simple device which needs no maintenance in itself, but there are some facts of which an owner should be aware if the converter is to function properly for its full service life.

- DO NOT use leaded or lead replacement petrol (gasoline) – the additives will coat the precious metals, reducing their converting efficiency and will eventually destroy the catalytic converter.
- Always keep the ignition and fuel systems well-maintained in accordance with the manufacturer's schedule – if the fuel/air mixture is suspected of being incorrect have it checked on an exhaust gas analyser.
- If the engine develops a misfire, do not ride the bike at all (or at least as little as possible) until the fault is rectified.
- DO NOT use fuel or engine oil additives – these may contain substances harmful to the catalytic converter.
- DO NOT continue to use the bike if the engine burns oil to the extent of leaving a visible trail of blue smoke.
- Remember that the catalytic converter and oxygen sensor are FRAGILE – do not strike them with tools during servicing work.

19 Ignition system check

Warning: The energy levels in electronic systems can be very high. On no account should the ignition be switched on whilst the plugs or caps are being held. Shocks from the HT circuit can be most unpleasant. Secondly, it is vital that the engine is not turned over or run with any of the plug caps removed, and that the plugs are soundly earthed (grounded) when the system is checked for sparking. The ignition system components can be seriously damaged if the HT circuit becomes isolated.

1 As no means of adjustment is available, any failure of the system can be traced to failure of a system component or a simple wiring fault. Of the two possibilities, the latter is by far the most likely. In the event of failure, check the system in a logical fashion, as described below.
2 Raise the fuel tank (see Section 2).
3 Make sure the ignition is OFF. Working on one cylinder at a time, pull the cap off the spark plug **(see illustration)**. Connect the cap to a spare spark plug (preferably use a new plug). Earth the plug against the cylinder head – do not earth the plug against the valve cover itself. If necessary, hold the spark plug with an insulated tool.

Warning: Do not remove any of the spark plugs from the engine to perform this check – atomised fuel being pumped out of the open spark plug hole could ignite, causing severe injury! Make sure the plugs are securely held against the engine – if they are not earthed when the engine is turned over, the ECM could be damaged.

4 Having observed the above precautions, check that the kill switch is in the RUN position and the transmission is in neutral, then turn the ignition switch ON and turn the engine over on the starter motor. If the system is in good condition a regular, fat blue spark should be evident at the plug electrode. If the spark appears thin or yellowish, or is non-existent, further investigation is necessary. Turn the ignition OFF and repeat the check for each coil.
5 The ignition system must be able to produce a spark which is capable of jumping at least a 6 mm gap. Simple ignition spark gap testing tools are commercially available – follow the manufacturer's instructions **(see illustration)**.
6 If the test results are good the entire ignition system can be considered good. If the spark appears thin or yellowish, or is non-existent, further investigation is necessary.
7 Ignition faults can be divided into two categories, namely those where the ignition system has failed completely, and those which are due to a partial failure. The likely faults are listed below, starting with the most probable source of failure. Work through the list systematically, referring to the subsequent sections for full details of the necessary checks and tests. **Note:** *Before checking the following items ensure that the battery is fully charged and that all fuses are in good condition.*

- Loose, corroded or damaged wiring connections, broken or shorted wiring between any of the component parts of the ignition system.
- Loose spark plug cap or lead connection, faulty spark plug cap or HT lead, faulty spark plug, dirty, worn or corroded plug electrodes.
- Faulty neutral, clutch or sidestand switch (see Chapter 8).
- Faulty ignition coil(s) (Section 20).
- Faulty ignition switch or engine kill switch (see Chapter 8).
- Faulty crankshaft position (CKP) sensor (Section 7) or damaged triggers on timing rotor (Chapter 2).
- Faulty engine stop relay (Section 9).
- Faulty ECM (Section 8).

8 If the above checks don't reveal the cause of the problem, have the ignition system tested by a Honda dealer.

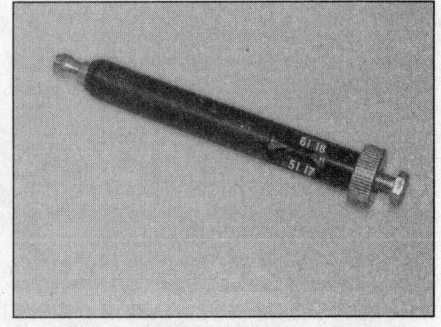

19.3 Pull the cap off the spark plug

19.5 An ignition spark gap tester

4•30 Engine management system

20.2a Ignition coil (arrowed) for cylinders 1 and 4

20.2b Unscrew the bolt and move the filler neck aside

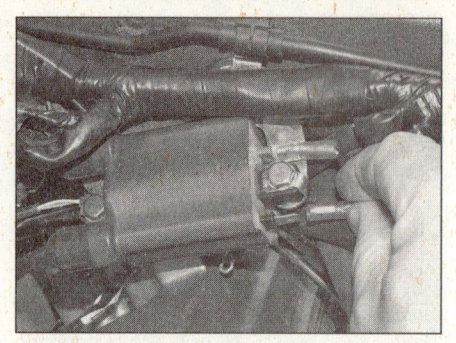

20.4 Disconnect the primary wiring connectors

20 Ignition coils

Special tool: *Honda specify a peak voltage adapter (Honda pt. no. 07HGJ-0020100) plus an aftermarket digital multimeter having an impedance of 10 M-ohm/DCV minimum for a complete test of the coils (see Step 7).*

Check

1 Disconnect the battery negative (–) lead (see Chapter 8).
2 Raise the fuel tank (see Section 2). There are two coils, one on the right-hand side of the frame for cylinders 1 and 4, the other on the left for cylinders 2 and 3 **(see illustration)**. To test the right-hand coil, displace the cooling system filler neck **(see illustration)**. To test the left-hand coil, remove the PAIR system control valve along with its hoses (Section 17).
3 Check each coil visually for loose or damaged connectors and terminals, cracks and other damage.
4 Disconnect the primary circuit wiring connectors from the coil **(see illustration)**. Pull the caps off the spark plugs **(see illustration 19.3)**.
5 To check the condition of the primary windings, set a multimeter to the ohms x 1 scale. Connect the meter probes to the primary terminals on the coil and measure the resistance **(see illustration)**. If the reading obtained is not as given in the Specifications, it is likely that the coil is defective.
6 To check the resistance of the secondary windings, set the meter to the K-ohm scale. Connect the meter probes to the contacts in the spark plug caps and measure the resistance **(see illustration)**. If the reading obtained is not as given in the Specifications, unscrew the plug caps and test the coil again, this time inserting the probes into the ends of the HT leads **(see illustrations)**. If the reading obtained is not as given in the Specifications (resistance with no caps) unscrew the leads from the coil and test the coil again, this time connecting the probes to the sockets in the coil **(see illustration)**. If the reading obtained is not as given in the Specifications (resistance without plug caps) it is likely the coil is defective. If the reading is good check the resistance of each plug cap, and if that is as specified replace the HT leads with new ones, otherwise replace the plug caps with new ones **(see illustration)**.
7 If a peak voltage adapter is available (see **Special tool** note) the coil's primary peak voltage can be checked. Disconnect the plug

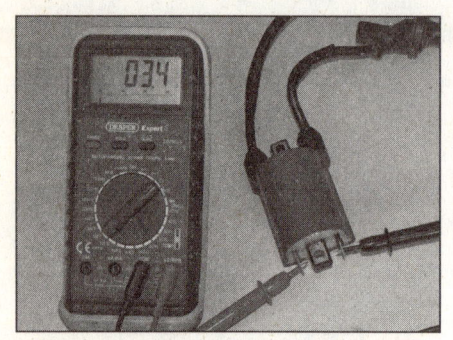

20.5 To test the coil primary resistance, connect the multimeter leads to the primary wiring terminals

20.6a To test the coil secondary resistance, connect the multimeter probes to the spark plug sockets

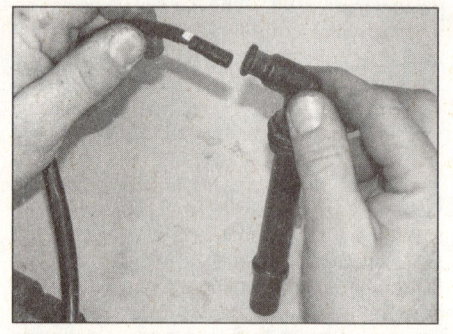

20.6b Unscrew the caps from the leads . . .

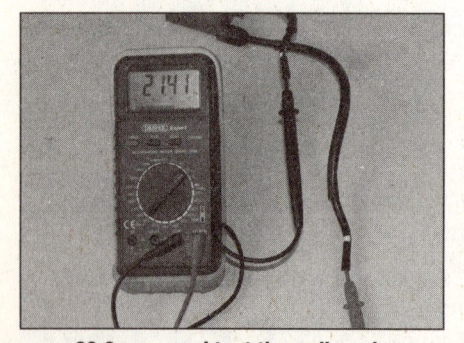

20.6c . . . and test the coil again

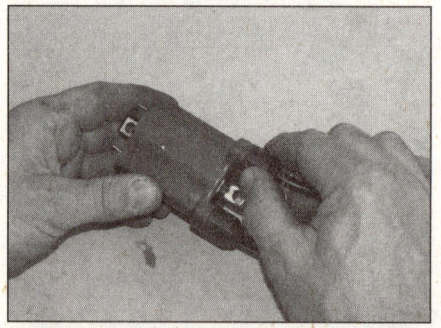

20.6d Unscrew the leads from the coil

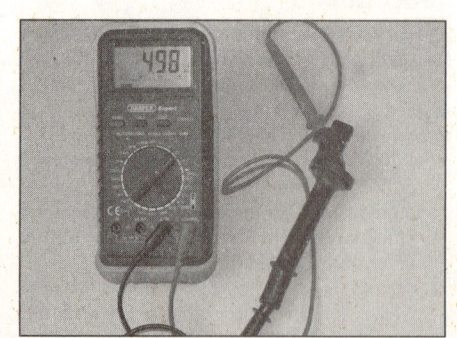

20.6e Checking a spark plug cap resistance

Engine management system 4•31

20.11 Note the shaped double-washer fitted with each bolt

21.4 Unscrew the timing inspection cap

caps from all four cylinders and earth spare plugs against the cylinder head as described in Section 19. Leaving the primary wires connected, connect the peak voltage adaptor positive probe to the yellow/blue wire primary terminal of the coil when checking the coil for cylinders 1 and 4, and to the blue/yellow wire primary terminal when checking the coil for cylinders 2 and 3. Connect the negative probe to earth. With the ignition ON, battery voltage should be shown on the meter. Crank the engine over on the starter motor and note the peak voltage registered on the meter – it should be above the minimum given in the Specifications at the beginning of this Chapter.

> **HAYNES HiNT**
> Note if a fault exists in the ignition circuit for one pair of cylinders (e.g. 1 and 4), you can swap the coils over to check if the fault then appears on the other pair of cylinders (e.g. 2 and 3). If so, the coil is confirmed faulty.

Removal and installation

8 Disconnect the battery negative (–) lead (see Chapter 8).
9 Raise the fuel tank (see Section 2). To remove the right-hand coil, displace the cooling system filler neck **(see illustration 20.2b)**. To remove the left-hand coil, remove the PAIR system control valve along with its hoses (Section 17).

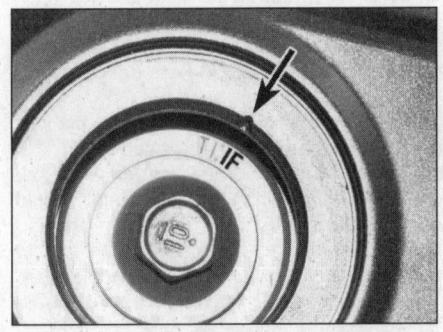

10 Disconnect the primary circuit wiring connectors from the coil, making a note of which fits where **(see illustration 20.4)**. Pull the caps off the spark plugs **(see illustration 19.3)**.
11 Unscrew the coil mounting bolts and remove the coil, noting the shaped double-washer **(see illustration)**.
12 Installation is the reverse of removal – the leads are numbered according to their cylinder.

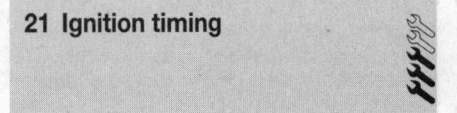

21 Ignition timing

General information

1 Since no provision exists for adjusting the ignition timing and since no component is subject to mechanical wear, there is no need for regular checks; only if investigating a fault such as a loss of power or a misfire should the ignition timing be checked.
2 The ignition timing is checked dynamically (engine running) using a stroboscopic lamp. The inexpensive neon lamps should be adequate in theory, but in practice may produce a pulse of such low intensity that the timing mark remains indistinct. If possible, one of the more precise xenon tube lamps should be used, powered by an external source of the appropriate voltage. **Note:** *Do not use the machine's own battery as an incorrect reading may result from stray impulses within the machine's electrical system.*

Check

3 Warm the engine up to normal operating temperature then stop it. On CBR600F/FA models remove the left-hand fairing side and upper panels (see Chapter 7).
4 Unscrew the timing inspection cap from the crankcase cover **(see illustration)**. Check the condition of its O-ring and obtain a new one if necessary.
5 The dynamic timing mark on the rotor which indicates the firing point at idle speed for the No. 1 cylinder is the line next to the F mark **(see illustration)**. The static timing mark with which this should align is a notch or pointer in the inspection hole rim.

> **HAYNES HiNT**
> *The timing marks can be highlighted with white paint to make them more visible under the stroboscope light.*

6 Connect the timing light to the No. 1 cylinder coil HT lead.
7 Start the engine and aim the light at the static timing mark.
8 With the machine idling, the timing mark should align with the notch. Now increase engine speed above 3000 rpm. The dynamic timing mark should move anti-clockwise in relation to the static mark. This confirms the ignition is advancing.
9 As already stated, there is no means of adjusting the ignition timing. If the ignition timing is incorrect, or suspected of being incorrect, one of the ignition system components is at fault, and the system must be tested as described in the preceding Sections of this Chapter.
10 When the check is complete, fit the timing inspection cap using a new O-ring, and smear the O-ring with oil and the cap threads with grease **(see illustration)**. Tighten the cap to the torque setting specified at the beginning of the Chapter.

21.5 'F' mark and static timing mark (arrowed)

21.10 Fit the cap using a new O-ring

22 Immobiliser system

General information

1 An immobiliser system (known as HISS – Honda Ignition Security System) is fitted either as standard or as an option (depending on market) as an anti-theft device. The system will only allow the machine to be started if the correct registered key is used to turn the ignition ON. The system consists of a transponder in the ignition key, a receiver fitted around the ignition switch, and the engine control module (ECM).

2 When the ignition is switched ON, the ECM sends power through the receiver to the transponder. The transponder sends a coded signal back through the receiver to the ECM. If the signal sent by the transponder matches the signal stored in the ECM memory, the HISS immobiliser indicator light in the instrument cluster comes on for two seconds then goes out, and the ECM allows the engine to be started. If the key code signal is not recognised, or if there is a fault in the system, the indicator light stays on. If the light stays on, or if the light does not come on at all, refer to the fault diagnosis and troubleshooting Sections below.

3 The ECM can store the codes for up to four registered keys. These keys should be kept separately (i.e. not on the same key-ring) as the proximity of another key to the one being used in the switch can lead to the signal from it being jammed, and the bike will not start. The key has a built in transponder which can be damaged if the key is dropped or knocked, gets too hot, is too close to a magnetic object, or is submerged in water for too long. If all the keys are lost, the ECM must be replaced with a new one, so always make sure you have at least one spare key. If a new key is obtained, it must be registered into the system before the bike can be started with the key.

Key registration procedure

With old ignition switch

Special tool: *The following procedures refer to the Honda special tools (part nos. 07XMZ-MBW0101 and 070MZ-MEC0100) – these are wiring loom adapters to connect a battery into the loom side of the crankshaft position (CKP) sensor wiring connector.*

4 Obtain a new key from a Honda dealer, and have it cut to match the original key.

5 Raise the fuel tank (Section 2). Disconnect the crankshaft position (CKP) sensor wiring connector **(see illustration 7.30)**. Connect the special tools together at the connector, then connect the wiring connector end to the loom side of the CKP sensor connector, and connect the red clip of the tool to the battery positive (+) terminal and the green clip to the battery negative (–) terminal.

6 Turn the ignition switch ON using your original key. The immobiliser indicator light should come on and stay on – if it starts to flash after ten seconds, then there is a fault in the system, which will have gone into fault diagnosis, and the pattern of the flashes it emits should be matched with the fault code (see below). Now disconnect the red clip from the battery positive terminal and leave it disconnected for at least two seconds, then reconnect it. The indicator should now come on for two seconds, then begin to flash repeatedly four times. This indicates that the system is in registration mode. At this point the registrations of all keys except the one in the switch will have been cancelled, so if you have another spare apart from the new one you want to register, this will also have to be registered.

7 Turn the ignition OFF and remove the original key, placing it well away from the receiver.

8 Insert the new key into the switch and turn it ON. The indicator should now come on for two seconds, then begin to flash repeatedly four times. This indicates that the system has registered the new key. If the indicator starts to flash after ten seconds, then there is a fault in the system, which will have gone into fault diagnosis, and the pattern of the flashes it emits should be matched with the fault code (see below). Turn the ignition OFF and remove the key.

9 To register any other spare keys that will have been cancelled, repeat Step 8. Up to four keys can be registered.

10 On completion turn the ignition OFF, then remove the special tool and reconnect the crankshaft position (CKP) sensor wiring connector. Now turn the ignition ON using any of the registered keys to return the system to normal mode.

11 Check that all registered keys can start the motorcycle.

With a new ignition switch

12 Obtain a new switch and two (or more) new keys.

13 Remove the faulty switch (see Chapter 8), but retain the HISS receiver to fit with the new switch.

14 Raise the fuel tank (Section 2). Disconnect the crankshaft position (CKP) sensor wiring connector **(see illustration 7.30)**. Connect the special tools together at the connector, then connect the wiring connector end to the loom side of the CKP sensor connector, and connect the red clip of the tool to the battery positive (+) terminal and the green clip to the battery negative (–) terminal.

15 Place one of the original registered keys for the faulty switch next to the receiver.

16 Connect the new ignition switch to its connector in the wiring loom, but keep it away from the receiver. Turn the new switch ON with one of the new keys. The immobiliser indicator light should come on and stay on, which means the ECM recognises the old key that is next to the receiver – if it starts to flash after ten seconds, then there is a fault in the system, which will have gone into fault diagnosis, and the pattern of the flashes it emits should be matched with the fault code (see below). Now disconnect the red clip from the battery positive terminal and leave it disconnected for at least two seconds, then reconnect it. The indicator should now come on for two seconds, then begin to flash repeatedly four times. This indicates that the system is in registration mode. At this point the registrations of all keys except the one near the receiver will have been cancelled.

17 Turn the ignition OFF and remove the new key.

18 Install the new ignition switch, then fit the receiver onto it (see Chapter 8).

19 Insert the new key into the switch and turn it ON. The indicator should now come on for four seconds, then begin to flash repeatedly four times. This indicates that the system has registered the new key. If the indicator starts to flash after ten seconds, then there is a fault in the system, which will have gone into fault diagnosis, and the pattern of the flashes it emits should be matched with the fault code (see below). Turn the ignition OFF and disconnect the red clip of the special tool from the battery positive terminal.

20 Turn the ignition ON using the newly registered key. The indicator light should come on for two seconds, then go off.

21 Turn the ignition OFF and reconnect the red clip to the battery positive terminal.

22 Turn the ignition ON using the newly registered key. The indicator light should come on and stay on – if it starts to flash after ten seconds, then there is a fault in the system, which will have gone into fault diagnosis, and the pattern of the flashes it emits should be matched with the fault code (see below). Now disconnect the red clip from the battery positive terminal and leave it disconnected for at least two seconds, then reconnect it. The indicator should now come on for two seconds, then begin to flash repeatedly four times. This indicates that the system is in registration mode. At this point the registrations of all old keys (for the faulty switch) are cancelled.

23 Turn the ignition OFF and remove the key, placing it well away from the receiver.

24 Insert the second new unregistered key and turn the ignition ON. The indicator should now come on for four seconds, then begin to flash repeatedly four times. This indicates that the system has registered the second new key. Turn the ignition OFF and remove the key.

25 To register any other new spare keys, repeat Step 24. Up to four keys can be registered.

26 On completion turn the ignition OFF, then remove the special tool and reconnect the CKP sensor wiring connector. Now turn the ignition ON using any of the registered keys to return the system to normal mode.
27 Check that all newly registered keys can start the motorcycle.

With a new ECM (engine control module)

28 Obtain a new ECM along with two new keys. Install the new ECM (see Section 8). Have the keys cut to match the original key for your ignition switch.
29 Insert a new key into the switch and turn it ON. The indicator should now come on for two seconds, then begin to flash repeatedly four times. This indicates that the system has registered the new key. If the indicator stays on for ten seconds then starts to flash, then there is a fault in the system, which will have gone into fault diagnosis, and the pattern of the flashes it emits should be matched with the fault code (see below).
30 Turn the ignition OFF and remove the key.
31 Insert the second new key and turn the ignition ON. The indicator should now come on for two seconds, then begin to flash repeatedly four times. This indicates that the system has registered the second new key.
32 Turn the ignition OFF and remove the key.
33 The new ECM will only register two new keys at this stage. If you have a third key to register, refer to Steps 4 to 10 to register it, noting that you will need the special tool mentioned therein.
34 Check that both newly registered keys can start the motorcycle.

Fault diagnosis

35 There are two fault diagnosis modes, one for faults that occur during normal use, and one for a fault that occurs when registering a new key. Make sure you refer to the correct table below when matching the fault code pattern.
36 If the indicator light has come on and stayed on during normal use, raise the fuel tank (Section 2). Disconnect the crankshaft position (CKP) sensor wiring connector (see illustration 7.30). Connect the special tools together at the connector, then connect the wiring connector end to the loom side of the CKP sensor connector, and connect the red clip of the tool to the battery positive (+) terminal and the green clip to the battery negative (–) terminal.
37 Turn the ignition switch ON. The indicator light will come on for ten seconds, then start to flash. This means it has entered diagnostic mode, and the pattern of the flashes indicates the fault that has occurred. The pattern repeats continuously. Match the pattern with the fault codes below, making sure you refer to the relevant table. If the indicator stays on after ten seconds and does not flash, then there is no fault logged in the system.

If fault is indicated during normal use		
Flash pattern	Fault	Solution
Two short, one long, one short	Faulty ECM	Install new ECM
Two short, two long	Faulty receiver or wiring	Follow Troubleshooting procedure below
One long, three short	Signal jammed by other key	Place other key well away from receiver
One long, two short, one long	Signal jammed by other key	Place other key well away from receiver

If fault is indicated during key registration		
Flash pattern	Fault	Solution
One short, one long, one short, one long	Key already registered	Use a new or cancelled key
Two short, two long	Faulty receiver or wiring	Follow Troubleshooting procedure below
One short, one long, two short	Key already registered on old ECM	Use a new key

Troubleshooting procedure

Indicator light does not come on when ignition switched ON

38 Check the instrument fuse (see Chapter 8).
39 If the fuse is good, make sure the engine is in neutral then turn the ignition ON and check whether the neutral light has come on.
40 If the light has not come on, on CB600F/FA and CBR600F/FA models remove the instrument cover (see Chapter 7), on CBF600N/NA models remove the headlight beam unit (see Chapter 8), and on CBF600S/SA models remove the fairing (see Chapter 7). On all except CBF600N/NA models pull back the rubber boot on the instrument cluster wiring connector. On CBF600N/NA models locate the instrument 9-pin black wiring connector. Using a voltmeter, connect the positive (+) probe to the black/brown wire terminal (connector still connected) and the negative (–) probe to the green/black wire terminal in the connector. With the ignition ON there should be battery voltage. If voltage is present, the instrument cluster is faulty (see Chapter 8). If there is no voltage, check for continuity in the wiring, referring to the wiring diagrams at the end of Chapter 8. The green/black wire goes to earth (ground).
41 If the light has come on, refer to Section 8 to access the ECM and disconnect the grey wiring connector. Using a voltmeter, connect the positive (+) probe to the white/red wire terminal on the loom side of the ECM connector and the negative (–) probe to earth (ground). Turn the ignition ON – there should be battery voltage.
42 If there was no voltage, using a voltmeter, connect the positive (+) probe to the white/red wire terminal in the instrument cluster connector and the negative (–) probe to earth. Turn the ignition ON – there should be no voltage for two seconds, then there should be battery voltage. If no voltage after two seconds, check for continuity in the white/red wire, and also in the green or green/black wire to earth, referring to the wiring diagrams at the end of Chapter 8. If voltage is present, the instrument cluster is faulty (see Chapter 8).
43 If there is voltage in Step 41, using a voltmeter, connect the positive (+) probe to the black/white (ECM) wire terminal on the loom side of the ECM black connector and the negative (–) probe to earth (ground). Turn the ignition ON – there should be battery voltage. If there is no voltage, check for continuity in the black/white wire. If voltage is present, check for continuity to earth (ground) in the green and green/white wires. If the wiring is good, check the ECM connector for loose, damaged or corroded terminals. If the connector is good, then the ECM could be faulty, and should be checked by a Honda dealer.

Indicator light stays on when ignition switched ON

44 Check that none of the other registered keys are close to the receiver. If they are, remove them and try the ignition again.
45 Turn the ignition ON with a spare key and check the indicator light, which should come on for two seconds, then go out. If it does, the first key is faulty. If it doesn't, perform the fault diagnosis procedure described above. If a fault code is displayed, use the appropriate table to determine the fault and the solution.
46 If no fault code is displayed, or the system does not go into fault diagnosis mode, refer to Section 8 to access the ECM and disconnect the grey wiring connector. Using a voltmeter, connect the positive (+) probe to the white/red wire terminal on the loom side of the connector and the negative (–) probe to earth (ground). Turn the ignition ON – there should be battery voltage. If there is no voltage, check for continuity in the white/red wire between the ECM and the instrument connector.
47 If there is voltage, check for continuity in the yellow and white/yellow wires between the ECM and the crankshaft position (CKP) sensor, referring to the wiring diagrams at

4•34 Engine management system

22.52a HISS receiver wiring connector (arrowed) – 2007 to 2010 CB models

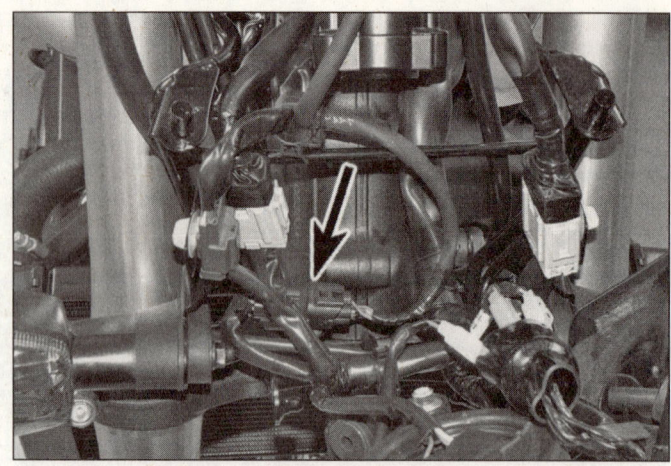

22.52b HISS receiver wiring connector (arrowed) – 2011-on CB models

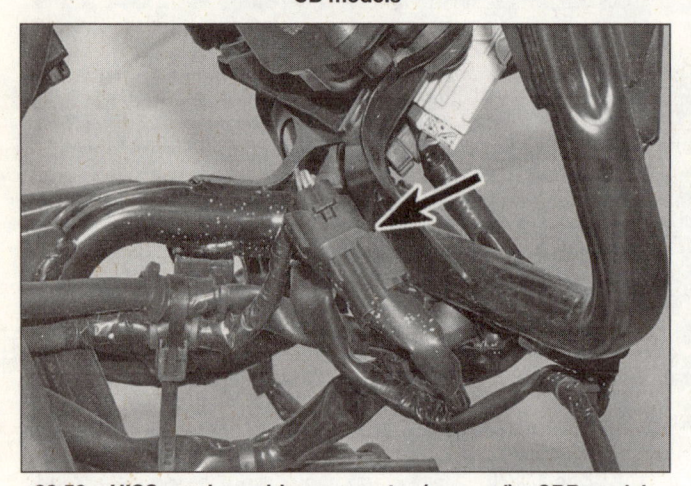

22.52c HISS receiver wiring connector (arrowed) – CBR models

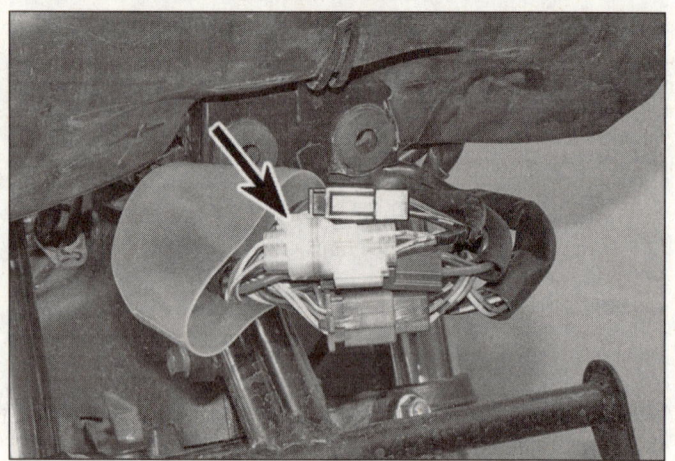

22.52d HISS receiver wiring connector (arrowed) – CBF-S/SA models

the end of Chapter 8. If there is no continuity, trace the fault and repair or replace the wiring as necessary. If there is continuity, the ECM could be faulty and should be taken to a Honda dealer for assessment.

Fault code indicated by flash pattern

48 If the 'two short, two long' flash pattern has been indicated during the fault diagnosis procedure, on CB600F/FA and CBR600F/FA models remove the headlight (see Chapter 8) and then on 2007 to 2010 CB600F/FA models the instrument cover (see Chapter 7), on CBF600N/NA models remove the headlight beam unit (see Chapter 8), and on CBF600S/SA models remove the fairing (see Chapter 7). Trace the wiring from the receiver on the ignition switch and disconnect it at the 4-pin connector **(see illustration 22.52)**. Using a voltmeter, connect the positive (+) probe to the yellow/red wire terminal on the loom side of the receiver connector and the negative (–) probe to earth (ground). Turn the ignition ON – there should be approximately 5 volts present. If there is no voltage, check for continuity in the yellow/red wire between the ECM and the

receiver, and repair or replace the wiring if there is no continuity.

49 If there is 5 volts present, check for continuity to earth (ground) in the green/orange wire on the loom side of the connector, and repair or replace the wiring if there is no continuity.

50 If the wiring is good, using a voltmeter, connect the positive (+) probe to the pink wire terminal on the loom side of the receiver connector and the negative (–) probe to earth (ground). Turn the ignition ON – there should be approximately 5 volts present. If there is, the receiver is faulty.

51 If there is no voltage, check for continuity in the yellow/blue or orange/blue (according to model) and pink wires between the ECM and the receiver, and repair or replace the wiring if there is no continuity between the connectors, or if there is continuity in either to earth (ground). If the wiring is good, the receiver is faulty.

Replacement

52 To replace the receiver, on CB600F/FA and CBR600F/FA models remove the headlight (see Chapter 8) and then on 2007 to 2010 CB600F/FA models the instrument cover (see

Chapter 7), on CBF600N/NA models remove the instrument assembly (see Chapter 8), and on CBF600S/SA models remove the fairing (see Chapter 7). Trace the wiring from the receiver on the ignition switch and disconnect it at the 4-pin connector **(see illustrations)**. Feed the wiring back to the receiver, freeing it from any ties and noting its routing. Undo the screws and remove the receiver, turning the handlebars as required for best access **(see illustration)**.

53 To replace the ECM see Section 8.

22.52e HISS receiver screws (arrowed)

Chapter 5
Frame and suspension

Contents

	Section number		Section number
Footrests, brake pedal and gearchange lever	3	Sidestand and centrestand	4
Fork oil change	7	Sidestand switch	see Chapter 8
Fork overhaul	8	Stand lubrication	see Chapter 1
Fork removal and installation	6	Steering head bearing check and adjustment	see Chapter 1
Frame inspection and repair	2	Steering head bearings	10
General information	1	Steering stem	9
Handlebar switches	see Chapter 8	Suspension adjustment	13
Handlebars and levers	5	Suspension check	see Chapter 1
Rear shock absorber	11	Swingarm	12

Degrees of difficulty

Easy, suitable for novice with little experience	**Fairly easy,** suitable for beginner with some experience	**Fairly difficult,** suitable for competent DIY mechanic	**Difficult,** suitable for experienced DIY mechanic	**Very difficult,** suitable for expert DIY or professional

Specifications

Front forks
Fork oil type .... 10W fork oil (Honda Ultra Cushion 10W)
Fork oil capacity (per fork)
   CB600F/FA .... 494 ± 2.5 cc
   CBR600F/FA .... 538 ± 2.5 cc
   CBF600N/NA/S/SA .... 457 ± 2.5 cc
Fork oil level*
   CB600F/FA .... 70 mm
   CBR600F/FA .... 64 mm
   CBF600N/NA/S/SA .... 149 mm
Fork spring free length (min)
   CB600F/FA 2007 and 2008
      Standard .... 245.7 mm
      Service limit .... 240.8 mm
   CB600F/FA 2009-on
      Standard .... 266.0 mm
      Service limit .... 260.7 mm
   CBR600F/FA
      Standard .... 266.0 mm
      Service limit .... 260.7 mm
   CBF600N/NA/S/SA
      Standard .... 328.5 mm
      Service limit .... 321.9 mm
Fork tube runout limit .... 0.2 mm

*Oil level is measured from the top of the tube with the fork spring removed and the leg fully compressed.

Steering head bearings
Bearing pre-load (see text) .... 8.8 to 13.7 N (0.9 to 1.4 kgf; 2.0 to 3.1 lbf)

Torque settings

Footrest bracket bolts	37 Nm
Fork damper cartridge/rod bolt	20 Nm
Fork clamp bolts	
Top yoke	22 Nm
Bottom yoke	39 Nm
Fork top bolt	34 Nm
Front brake master cylinder clamp bolts	12 Nm
Gearchange lever pivot bolt	27 Nm
Handlebar clamp bolts (CB600F/FA and CBF600N/NA/S/SA)	27 Nm
Levers	
Pivot screw	1 Nm
Pivot screw locknut	6 Nm
Rear shock absorber bolts/nuts	42 Nm
Sidestand pivot bolt	15 Nm
Sidestand pivot bolt nut	39 Nm
Silencer mounting bolt/nut	22 Nm
Steering head bearing adjuster nut	
CB600F/FA and CBR600F/FA	26 Nm
CBF600N/NA/S/SA	25 Nm
Steering stem nut	103 Nm
Swingarm	
Pivot bolt nut	98 Nm
Pivot bracket bolt nuts	69 Nm

1 General information

All models have an aluminium mono-backbone frame that uses the engine as a stressed member.

On CB600F/FA and CBR600F/FA models front suspension is by a pair of 41 mm upside-down oil-damped telescopic forks with cartridge dampers. The forks have adjustable spring pre-load and rebound damping on CB models from 2009-on and on all CBR models. Rear suspension is by an aluminium box-section swingarm and a single shock absorber, with adjustable spring pre-load on all models, and adjustable rebound damping on CBR models and on CB models from 2009-on.

On CBF600N/NA/S/SA models front suspension is by a pair of 41 mm oil-damped telescopic forks with adjustable spring pre-load. Rear suspension is by an aluminium box-section swingarm and a single shock absorber with adjustable spring pre-load.

The swingarm pivots through the frame.

2 Frame inspection and repair

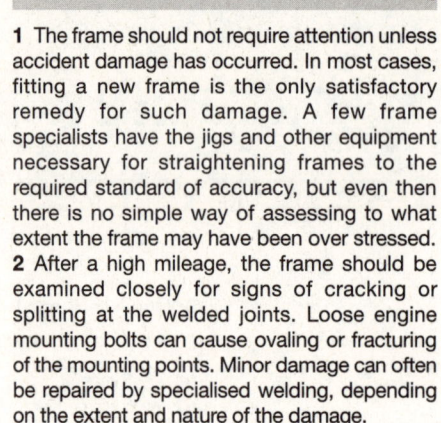

1 The frame should not require attention unless accident damage has occurred. In most cases, fitting a new frame is the only satisfactory remedy for such damage. A few frame specialists have the jigs and other equipment necessary for straightening frames to the required standard of accuracy, but even then there is no simple way of assessing to what extent the frame may have been over stressed.

2 After a high mileage, the frame should be examined closely for signs of cracking or splitting at the welded joints. Loose engine mounting bolts can cause ovaling or fracturing of the mounting points. Minor damage can often be repaired by specialised welding, depending on the extent and nature of the damage.

3 Remember that a frame that is out of alignment will cause handling problems. If, as the result of an accident, misalignment is suspected, it will be necessary to strip the machine completely so the frame can be thoroughly checked.

3 Footrests, brake pedal and gearchange lever

Footrests

Removal

1 To remove the rider's footrests remove the split pin and washer from the bottom of the footrest pivot pin, then withdraw the pivot pin and remove the footrest **(see illustration)**. Note the fitting of the return spring.

2 To remove the passenger footrests, remove the split pin from the bottom of the footrest pivot pin, then undo the pivot pin screw, withdraw the pin and remove the footrest **(see illustrations)**. On CB600F/FA and CBR600F/FA models note the fitting of the detent plate, ball and spring, and take care not to let the ball and spring ping away when removing the footrest. On CBF600N/NA/S/SA models note the washer against the inner end of the rubber.

3 You can replace the footrest rubbers with new ones – for the rider's footrests unscrew

3.1 Remove the split pin (arrowed) and washer, then draw the pivot pin out the top

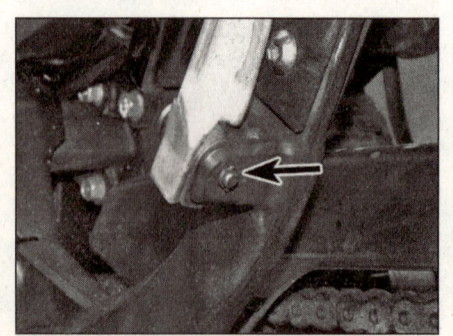

3.2a Remove the split pin (arrowed) . . .

3.2b . . . then undo the screw (arrowed) and draw the pivot pin out the top

Frame and suspension 5•3

3.3 Unscrew the bolts (arrowed) to release the rubber

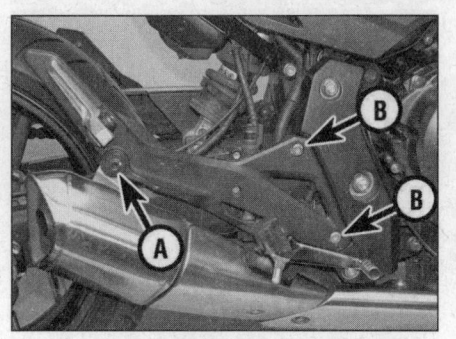

3.5 Silencer bolt (A), footrest bracket bolts (B)

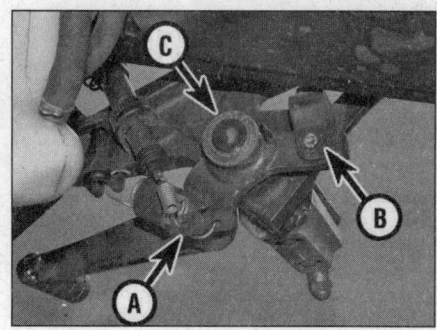

3.6 Springs (A), split pin (B), circlip and washer (C)

the bolts on the underside to release the rubber, and note the arrangement of the setting plate and rubber (where fitted) **(see illustration)**. On CBF600N/NA/S/SA models the passenger footrest rubbers are a sliding fit on the peg, with the outer end locating around the plate.

Installation

4 Installation is the reverse of removal. Apply a small amount of grease to the pivot pin.

Brake pedal

Removal

5 On CB600F/FA and CBR600F/FA models unscrew the nut on the silencer mounting bolt, then withdraw the bolt, noting the washer **(see illustration)**. Unscrew the footrest bracket bolts and displace the bracket so you have access to the back of it – take care not to strain the brake hoses and the brake light switch wiring, and if necessary displace them from the bracket (see Chapters 6 and 8).

6 Unhook the brake pedal return spring and the brake light switch spring from the pedal **(see illustration)**.

7 Straighten the ends of the split pin and withdraw it from the master cylinder pushrod clevis pin **(see illustration 3.6)**.

8 Release the circlip securing the brake pedal and remove the washer **(see illustration 3.6)**. Slide the pedal part-way off its pivot until the clevis pin is clear of the bracket, then withdraw the pin, detach the pushrod from the pedal and remove the pedal **(see illustrations)**.

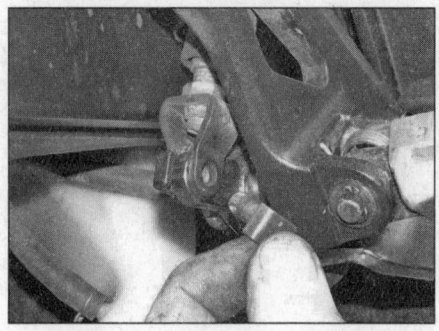

3.8a Move the pedal to withdraw the clevis . . .

Installation

9 Installation is the reverse of removal, noting the following:
- Clean any old grease off the pedal and pivot, then apply fresh grease.
- Slide the pedal part-way onto the pivot, then locate the pushrod and insert the clevis pin **(see illustrations 3.8b and a)**. Slide the pedal all the way on and fit the washer. Make sure the circlip locates correctly in the groove, and use a new one if the old one deformed when removed **(see illustration 3.6)**. Connect the springs.
- Use a new split pin on the master cylinder pushrod clevis pin **(see illustration)**.
- On CB600F/FA and CBR600F/FA models tighten the footrest bracket bolts and the silencer mounting bolt nut to the torque settings specified at the beginning of the Chapter **(see illustration 3.5)**.

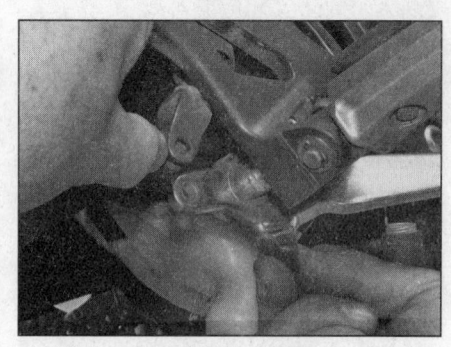

3.8b . . . then detach the pushrod and remove the pedal

- Check the operation of the rear brake light switch (see Chapter 1).

Gearchange lever and linkage

Removal

10 Note the alignment of the existing punch marks between the gearchange linkage arm and shaft, or mark the alignment of the shaft with the slit in the linkage arm if they are not clear **(see illustration)**. Unscrew the linkage arm bolt and slide the arm off the shaft

11 Unscrew the gearchange lever pivot bolt, noting the washer behind the lever, and remove the lever and linkage assembly **(see illustration)**.

12 If you want to separate the lever from the linkage rod note how far the rod is threaded into the lever and arm as this determines the height of the lever relative to the footrest. Slacken the linkage rod locknuts, then

3.9 Use a new split pin

3.10 Mark the alignment then unscrew the bolt and slide the arm off the shaft

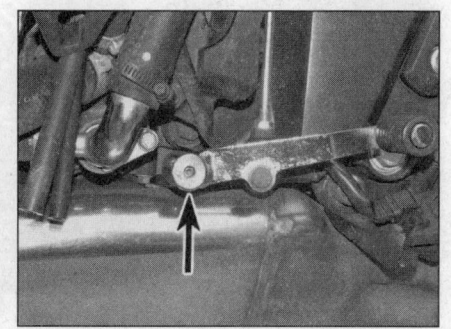

3.11 Lever pivot bolt (arrowed)

5•4 Frame and suspension

4.2 Stand springs (arrowed)

4.3 Sidestand switch bolt (arrowed)

4.4 Sidestand pivot bolt nut (arrowed)

unscrew the rod and separate it from the lever and the arm – the rod is reverse-threaded on one end and will simultaneously unscrew from both lever and arm when turned in the one direction.

Installation

13 Installation is the reverse of removal, noting the following:
- Clean off all old grease from the pivot components and apply fresh grease. Fit new pivot seals if necessary.
- Tighten the lever pivot bolt to the torque setting specified at the beginning of the Chapter.
- Align the slit in the linkage arm clamp with the mark made on the gearchange shaft.
- Adjust the gear lever height as required by screwing the linkage rod in or out of the lever and arm. Tighten the locknuts on completion.

4 Sidestand and centrestand

Sidestand

Removal

1 Support the bike on the centrestand on CBF600N/NA/S/SA models, or using an auxiliary stand on all other models.

2 Carefully unhook and remove the stand springs **(see illustration)**.
3 Unscrew the sidestand switch bolt and displace the switch, noting how it locates **(see illustration)** – there is no need to disconnect its wiring connector or remove it completely, just let it hang from its wiring.
4 Unscrew the nut from the pivot bolt **(see illustration)**. Unscrew the pivot bolt and remove the stand.

Installation

5 Apply grease to the pivot bolt shank and tighten the bolt to the torque setting specified at the beginning of the Chapter. Fit the nut finger-tight, then counter-hold the bolt and tighten the nut to the specified torque **(see illustration 4.4)**.
6 Fit the sidestand switch **(see illustration 4.3)**.
7 Reconnect the springs and check that they hold the stand securely up when not in use – an accident is almost certain to occur if the stand extends while the machine is in motion **(see illustration 4.2)**.
8 Check the operation of the stand and switch (see Chapter 1).

Centrestand (CBF600N/NA/S/SA)

9 Remove the silencer (see Chapter 4).
10 Support the bike on the sidestand.

Carefully unhook and remove the stand springs **(see illustration)**.
11 Unscrew the pivot bolt nut and remove the washer. Withdraw the pivot bolt with its washers and remove the stand. Note the collars and remove them for safekeeping if required.
12 Installation is the reverse of removal. Apply grease to the pivot bolt, collars and mounts.

5 Handlebars and levers

Handlebar removal – CB600F/FA and CBF600N/NA/S/SA

Note: *The handlebars can be displaced from the top yoke without detaching any of the assemblies from them – follow Step 9 only. Rest the assembly on some rag.*

1 As a precaution, raise and support the fuel tank (see Chapter 4) – though not actually necessary, this will prevent the possibility of any damage in case a tool slips or you drop something.
2 On CB600F/FA and CBF600N/NA models remove the mirrors (see Chapter 7).
3 Undo the handlebar end-weight retaining screws and remove the weights from the ends of the handlebar **(see illustration)**.

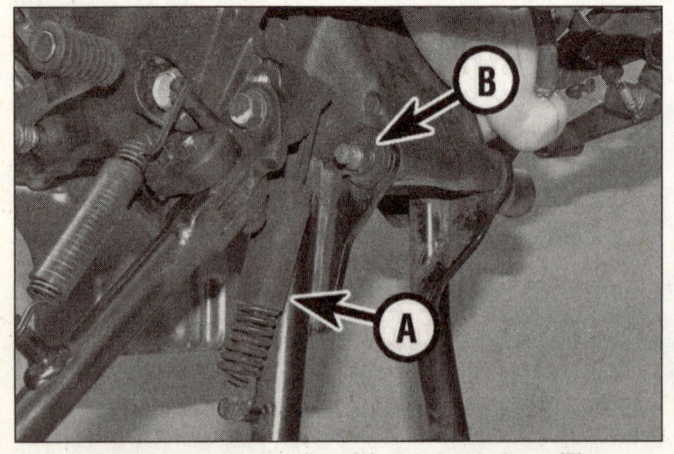

4.10 Centrestand springs (A) and pivot bolt nut (B)

5.3 Handlebar end-weight screw (arrowed)

Frame and suspension 5•5

5.4a Disconnect the wiring connectors (arrowed)

5.4b Unscrew the brake master cylinder clamp bolts (arrowed) and displace the assembly

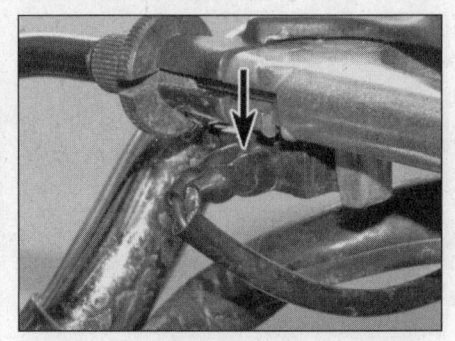

5.5a Disconnect the wiring connectors (arrowed)

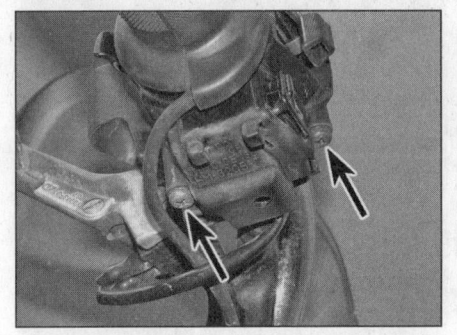

5.5b Switch housing screws (arrowed)

5.7 Clutch lever bracket bolt (arrowed)

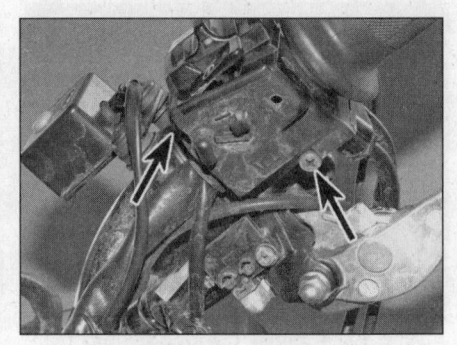

5.8 Switch housing screws (arrowed)

4 Disconnect the wires from the brake light switch (see illustration). Unscrew the two master cylinder assembly clamp bolts and position the assembly clear of the handlebar, making sure no strain is placed on the hydraulic hose (see illustration). Keep the master cylinder reservoir upright to prevent possible fluid leakage.

5 Where fitted release the cable-ties from the handlebars. Disconnect the wires from the clutch switch (see illustration). Unscrew the left-hand switch housing screws and detach the housing (see illustration).

6 Slide the grip off the left-hand end – you may need to insert a suitable tool (that won't scratch the handlebar) between the grip and the top of the handlebar from the inner end, then squirt some lubricant (such as WD40) in the gap (shield your eyes from any sprayback) and allow it to work its way round by moving the tool around. If the grip has been glued on, you will probably have to slit it with a knife to remove it, which means replacing it with a new one. Also slide the switch housing plate off.

7 Remove the clutch lever (see below). Align the slots in the adjuster and lockring with that in the bracket and slip the cable out. Slacken the clutch lever bracket bolt and slide the bracket off (see illustration).

8 Unscrew the right-hand switch housing screws and detach the housing (see illustration).

9 Unscrew the handlebar clamp bolts, remove the clamps and slide the handlebar out of the throttle pulley (see illustration).

Handlebar removal – CBR600F/FA

Note: *Each handlebar can be displaced from the top yoke without detaching any of the assemblies from them – follow Step 14 and/or 19 only. Rest the assembly on some rag.*

10 As a precaution, raise and support the fuel tank (see Chapter 4) – though not actually necessary, this will prevent the possibility of any damage in case a tool slips or you drop something.

5.9a Unscrew the bolts (arrowed) . . .

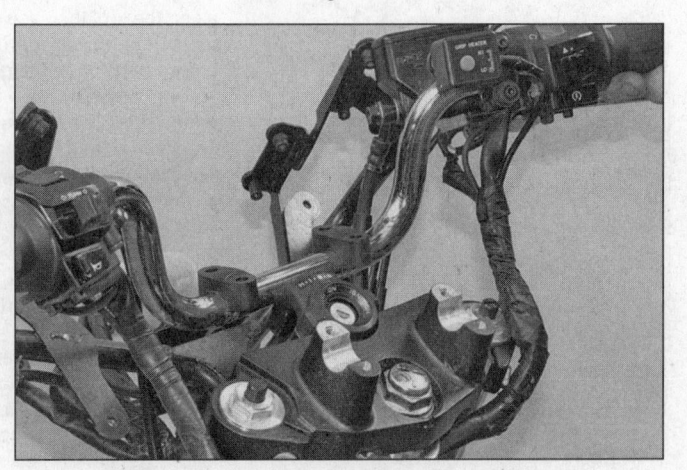

5.9b . . . and displace or remove the handlebars

5•6 Frame and suspension

5.14a Remove the stopper ring

5.14b Slacken the bolt (arrowed) . . .

5.14c . . . and lift the handlebar off

5.19a Remove the stopper ring

5.19b Slacken the bolt (arrowed) . . .

5.19c . . . and lift the handlebar off

Right handlebar

11 Disconnect the wires from the brake light switch **(see illustration 5.4a)**. Unscrew the two master cylinder assembly clamp bolts and position the assembly clear of the handlebar, making sure no strain is placed on the hydraulic hose **(see illustration 5.4b)**. Keep the master cylinder reservoir upright to prevent possible fluid leakage.

12 Undo the handlebar end-weight retaining screw and remove the weight **(see illustration 5.3)**.

13 Undo the handlebar switch housing screws and separate the halves **(see illustration 5.8)**.

5.20 Removing the handlebar inner weight

1 End-weight	5 Hole in handlebar
2 Retainer	6 Retainer tab
3 Rubbers	7 Screwdriver
4 Inner weight	

14 Remove the stopper ring from its groove in the top of the fork **(see illustration)**. Unscrew the handlebar clamp bolt **(see illustration)**. Ease the handlebar up and off the fork and slide the throttle twistgrip off **(see illustration)**.

Left handlebar

15 Undo the handlebar end-weight retaining screw and remove the weight **(see illustration 5.3)**.

16 Undo the handlebar switch housing screws and separate the halves **(see illustration 5.5b)**.

17 Slide the grip off the handlebar – you may need to insert a small screwdriver between the grip and the handlebar from the inner end along the top, then squirt some lubricant (such as WD40) in the gap (shield your eyes from any sprayback). If the grip has been glued on, you will probably have to slit it with a knife to remove it, which means replacing it with a new one. Also slide the switch housing plate off.

18 Disconnect the wires from the clutch switch **(see illustration 5.5a)**. Remove the clutch lever (see below). Align the slots in the adjuster and lockring with that in the bracket and slip the cable out. Slacken the clutch lever bracket bolt and slide the bracket off **(see illustration 5.7)**.

19 Remove the stopper ring from its groove in the top of the fork **(see illustration)**. Slacken the handlebar clamp bolt **(see illustration)**. Ease the handlebar up and off the fork and slide the clutch lever assembly off **(see illustration)**.

Handlebar weights

20 If a new handlebar is being installed, you need to transfer the inner weights from the old bar to the new one – to do this, reinstall the end-weight and tighten its screw **(see illustration 5.3)**. Squirt some lubricant (such as WD40) into the inner weight retainer tab hole, then press down on the tab using a screwdriver, then twist and pull on the end-weight, drawing the inner weight assembly out **(see illustration)**. Remove the end-weight and discard the retainer as a new one should be used. Check the condition of the rubbers on the inner weight and fit new ones if they are damaged, deformed or deteriorated.

Installation

21 Installation is the reverse of removal, noting the following.

- When fitting the handlebar inner weights, locate the tab on the retainer in the hole in the handlebar.
- Smear some grease onto the throttle twistgrip sliding surface. Slide the throttle pulley housing onto the handlebar before fitting the handlebar onto the yoke.
- On CB600F/FA and CBF600N/NA/S/SA models align the punch mark on the back of the handlebar with the clamp/holder mating surfaces **(see illustration 5.21a)**. Fit the handlebar clamps with the punch marks to the front **(see illustration 5.21b)**. Tighten the handlebar clamp bolts to the torque setting specified at the beginning of the Chapter, tightening the front bolts first, then the rear, so that any gap is at the back.

Frame and suspension 5•7

5.21a Align the clamp mating surfaces with the punch mark (arrowed)

5.21b Fit the clamps with the punch mark (arrowed) to the front

5.21c Seat the lug (arrowed) in the gap

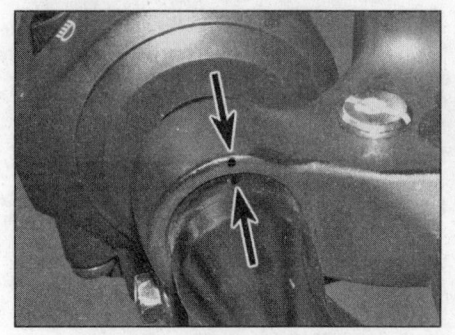

5.21d Align the punch marks

5.21e Align clamp mating surfaces with the punch mark (arrowed)

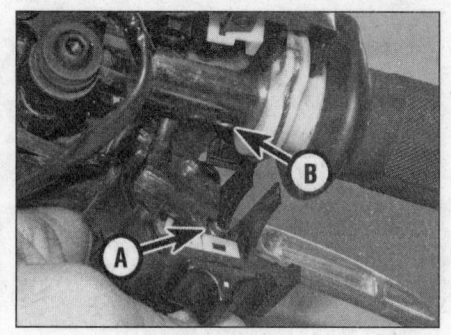

5.21f Locate the pin (A) in the hole (B)

- On CBR600F/FA models seat the lug on the bottom of each handlebar clamp in the gap in the top yoke clamp *(see illustration 5.21c)*. Push the handlebar forwards and tighten the handlebar clamp bolt. Fit the stopper ring into its groove *(see illustration 5.14a or 5.19a)*.
- Align the punch mark on the clutch lever bracket with the punch mark on the top of the handlebar *(see illustration 5.21d)*.
- Slide the left-hand switch housing plate on after the clutch lever bracket and before fitting the grip.
- To fit new grips onto the throttle twistgrip and left handlebar, apply a suitable glue (Pro Honda handgrip cement or equivalent) to each, making sure they are clean, then rotate the grip when in place to evenly distribute the glue. Allow the glue to fully dry before riding the bike.
- When fitting the handlebar end-weights, align the boss with the cut-out on the inner weight inside the handlebar.
- Make sure the front brake master cylinder clamp is installed with the UP mark facing up and with the clamp mating surfaces aligned with the punch mark on the top of the handlebar *(see illustration 5.21e)*. Tighten the master cylinder clamp bolts to the specified torque setting, tightening the top bolt first.
- Make sure the pin in the bottom half of each switch housing locates in its hole in the handlebar and the housing seats correctly around the twistgrip on the right and the housing plate on the left *(see illustration 5.21f)*. Tighten the front housing screw first, then the rear. Secure the wiring with new cable-ties where removed.
- Do not forget to reconnect the front brake light switch and clutch switch wiring connectors *(see illustrations 5.4a and 5.5a)*.
- Check the operation of the throttle and clutch, and adjust cable freeplay as required (see Chapter 1).

Levers

22 To remove the front brake lever, undo the lever pivot screw locknut, then undo the pivot screw and remove the lever *(see illustration)*.
23 To remove the clutch lever loosen the cable adjuster lockring then thread the adjuster into the bracket to provide freeplay in the cable *(see illustration)*. Undo the lever pivot screw locknut, then undo the pivot screw and remove the lever, detaching the cable nipple as you do *(see illustration)*.
24 Installation is the reverse of removal. Apply silicone grease to the contact area

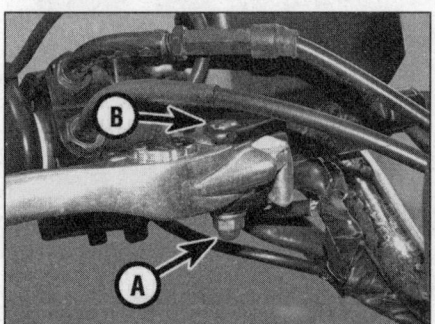

5.22 Front brake lever locknut (A) and pivot screw (B)

5.23a Loosen the lockring (A) and thread the adjuster (B) in

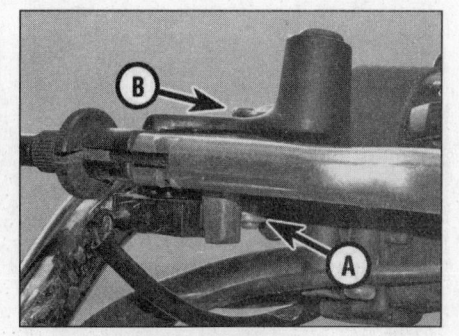

5.23b Clutch lever locknut (A) and pivot screw (B)

5•8 Frame and suspension

between the front brake master cylinder pushrod tip and the brake lever and to the pivot screw shaft. Apply multi-purpose grease to the clutch lever pivot screw shaft, cable end, and the contact areas between the lever and its bracket. Tighten each pivot screw lightly, then hold it and tighten the locknut – torque settings are given at the beginning of the Chapter if the correct torque wrench is available. Apply a spray lubricant such as WD40, or a dry-film Teflon lubricant to the brake lever span adjuster mechanism. Adjust clutch cable freeplay (see Chapter 1).

6 Fork removal and installation

Removal

1 If the fork oil is being changed, or if the fork is to be disassembled, where applicable adjust spring pre-load to its minimum setting, noting the number of turns made so it can be reset the same (see Section 13).
2 On CBR600F/FA and CBF600S/SA models remove the fairing side panels (see Chapter 7).
3 Remove the front wheel (see Chapter 6). Tie the front brake calipers and hoses back so that they are out of the way.
4 Remove the front mudguard (see Chapter 7). Note the routing of all cables, hoses and wiring around the forks.
5 On CBR600F/FA models displace the handlebar from the fork and top yoke (Section 5).

6.6 Fork clamp bolt (arrowed) – CBF model shown

6 Working on one fork at a time, slacken the fork clamp bolt in the top yoke **(see illustration)**.
7 If the fork oil is being changed, or if the fork is to be disassembled, slacken the fork top bolt **(see illustration)**.
8 Slacken the fork clamp bolt in the bottom yoke, and remove the fork by twisting it and pulling it downwards **(see illustrations)**.

> **HAYNES HINT** If the fork legs are seized in the yokes, spray the area with penetrating oil and allow time for it to soak in before trying again.

Installation

9 Remove all traces of corrosion from the fork tube and the yokes. As you fit each fork make sure all cables, hoses and wiring are routed on the correct side of the fork.

6.7 Slacken the top bolt now if required

10 On CB600F/FA and CBF600N/NA/S/SA models slide the fork up through the bottom yoke and into the top yoke and set the top of the fork tube (not the top bolt) flush with the upper surface of the yoke, then tighten the fork clamp bolt in the bottom yoke to the torque setting specified at the beginning of the Chapter **(see illustration)**.
11 On CBR600F/FA models slide the fork up through the bottom yoke and the top yoke, and set it so the top of the tube (not the top bolt) is 31.5 mm above the upper surface of the top yoke, then tighten the fork clamp bolt in the bottom yoke to the torque setting specified at the beginning of the Chapter **(see illustration)**.
12 If the fork oil was changed or if the fork has been dismantled, tighten the fork top bolt to the specified torque setting **(see illustration)**.
13 Now tighten the fork clamp bolt in the top yoke to the specified torque **(see illustration 6.6)**.
14 On CBR600F/FA models fit the handlebar (Section 5).
15 Install the front mudguard (see Chapter 7) and the front wheel (see Chapter 6).
16 Check the operation of the front forks and brakes before taking the machine out on the road.
17 On CBR600F/FA and CBF600N/NA/S/SA models install the fairing side panels (see Chapter 7).
18 Reset the spring pre-load adjuster as noted or required according to model (see Section 13).

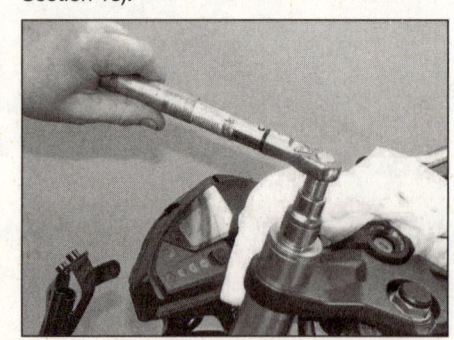

6.8a Slacken the bottom clamp bolt (arrowed) . . .

6.8b . . . and draw the fork down and out of the yokes

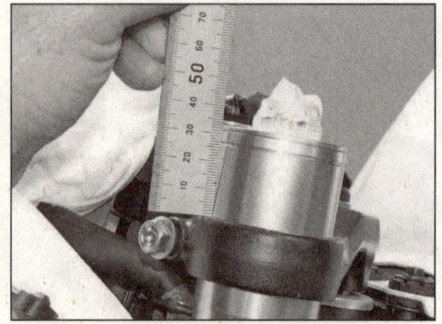

6.10 Set the top of the fork flush with the top of the yoke

6.11 Set the fork at the specified height above the top yoke

6.12 Tighten the top bolt to the specified torque

Frame and suspension 5•9

7.3 Thread the top bolt out of the tube

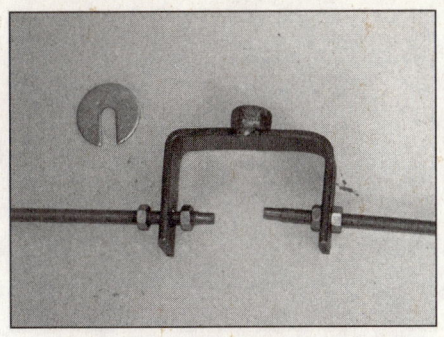

7.4a Spacer holding tool and slotted washer – home-made equivalent to the Honda tools

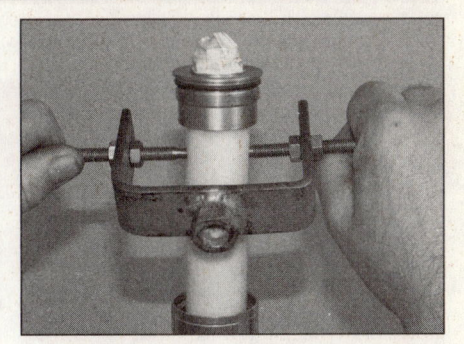

7.4b Fit the holder onto the spacer as shown

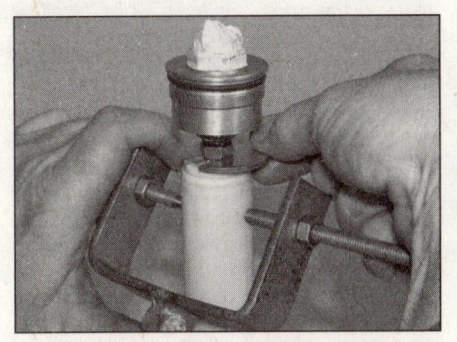

7.4c Push down on the holder and slip the washer under the nut

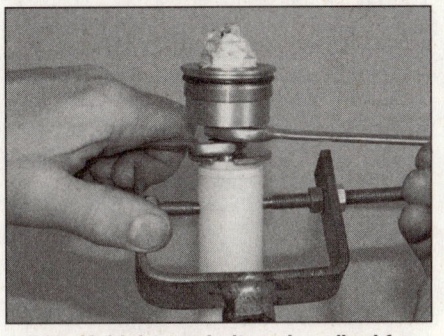

7.5a Hold the top bolt as described for your model (CBR shown) and loosen the locknut . . .

7.5b . . . then unscrew the top bolt, and where applicable draw the adjuster rod out

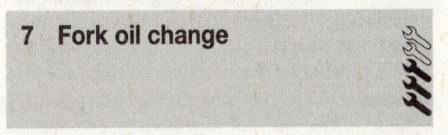

7 Fork oil change

1 After a high mileage the fork oil will deteriorate and its damping and lubrication qualities will be impaired. Always change the oil in both fork legs.

2 Remove the fork – as applicable make sure you adjust the pre-load damping to its minimum (see Section 13), and on all models loosen the top bolt while the leg is still clamped in the bottom yoke (see Section 6).

CB600F/FA and CBR600F/FA

3 Unscrew the fork top bolt from the top of the outer tube (see illustration). The bolt will remain on the damper rod, held by the locknut on its top. Slide the outer tube down gently until it seats on the bottom.

4 Next you need either the Honda service tools (spacer holder part No. 070MF-MBZC110 and stopper plate part No. 070MF-MBZC130), or an equivalent home-made set-up as shown (see illustration). Fit the holder onto the fork spacer as shown (see illustration). Now with the aid of an assistant, pull up on the fork top bolt and press down on the spacer using the holding tool to compress the spring and expose the locknut on the damper rod, and insert the stopper plate or slotted washer under the locknut and on top of the spacer, where fitted keeping the spacer seat above it (see illustration). Carefully release the pressure on the spacer and allow the plate or slotted washer to rest against the underside of the locknut under spring pressure.

5 On 2007 and 2008 CB models, counter-hold the locknut using one spanner and loosen the top bolt assembly using another spanner, fitting it on the top bolt hex, then thread the top bolt off. On 2009-on CB models and all CBR models, counter-hold the locknut using one spanner and loosen the top bolt assembly using another spanner, fitting it on the pre-load adjuster flats, then thread the top bolt off drawing the damping adjuster rod out (see illustrations). Note: *The top bolt assembly should not be disassembled.*

6 Push down on the spacer and remove the plate or slotted washer, then carefully allow the spring to relax (see illustration). On 2009-on CB models and all CBR models remove the spacer seat (see illustration). Remove the spacer (see illustration). Withdraw the spring from the tube, noting which way up it

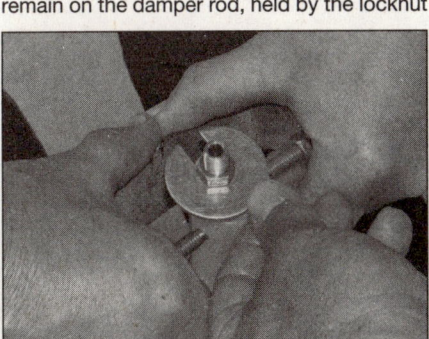

7.6a Remove the slotted washer . . .

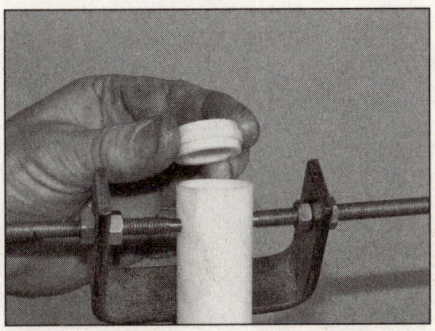

7.6b . . . the spacer seat where fitted . . .

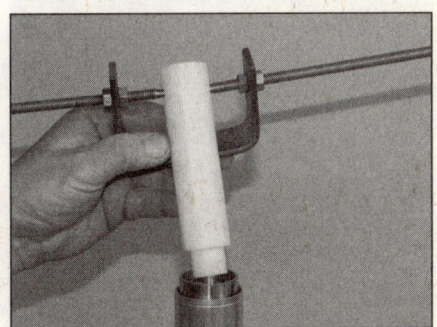

7.6c . . . the spacer . . .

5•10 Frame and suspension

7.6d ... and the spring

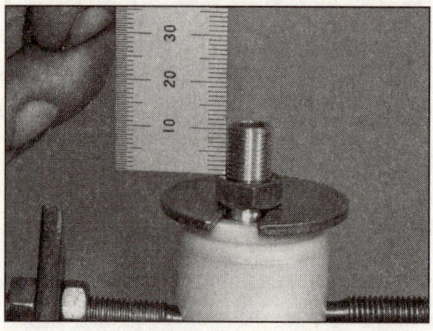

7.6e Record the position of the locknut on the damper rod

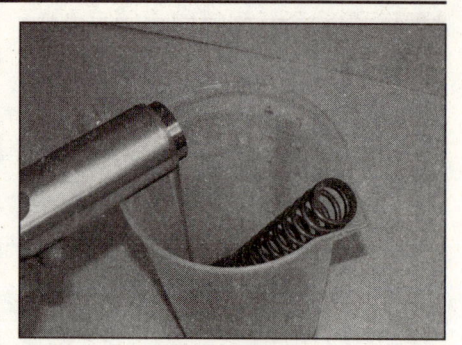

7.7a Drain the oil ...

fits **(see illustration)**. Mark or measure and note the position of the locknut on the damper rod **(see illustration)** – it must be set in the same position when the fork is reassembled.

7 Invert the fork leg over a suitable container and pump the fork and damper rod several times to expel as much fork oil as possible **(see illustrations)**. Support the fork upside down in the container for a while to allow as much oil as possible to drain, then pump the fork and rod again. If the fork oil contains metal particles inspect the fork bushes for wear (see Section 8). Wipe any excess oil off the spring and spacer.

8 Stand the fork upright. Slowly pour in the specified quantity of the specified grade of fork oil **(see illustration)**. Draw the outer tube fully up, then cover the top with your hand and slowly push it down. Remove your hand and draw it up, and repeat two or three times. Now pump the damper rod slowly at least ten times – this distributes the oil and expels all air from the damper. Slide the inner tube down gently until it seats on the bottom, and leave to stand for five minutes. Then measure the oil level from the top of the tube **(see illustration)**. Add or subtract oil until it is at the level specified at the beginning of this Chapter.

9 Check the locknut is correctly positioned on the damper rod (see illustration 7.6e). Fit a piece of thin wire around the rod under the locknut to help keep it extended **(see illustration)**. Pull the damper rod out as far as possible, then fit the spring with the tapered end at the top **(see illustration)**. Fit the spacer, sliding it down over the wire **(see illustration)**. On 2009-on CB models and all CBR models fit the spacer seat **(see illustration)**.

10 Keeping the damper rod extended, push down on the spacer to compress the spring (see Step 4), then insert the stopper plate

7.7b ... and pump the rod as described

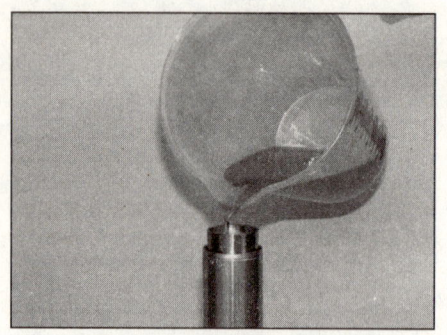

7.8a Fill the fork slowly to prevent air bubbles and overfilling

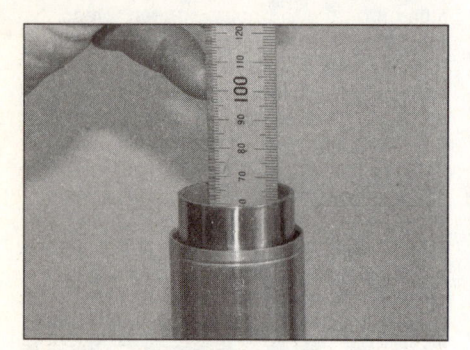

7.8b Measure the distance from the top of the tube to the oil

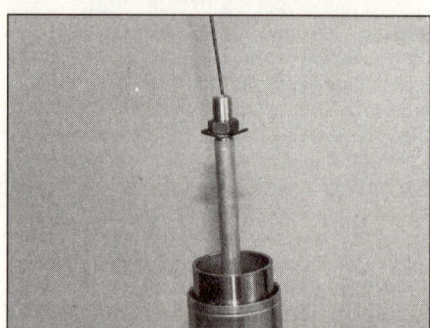

7.9a Tie some wire under the locknut

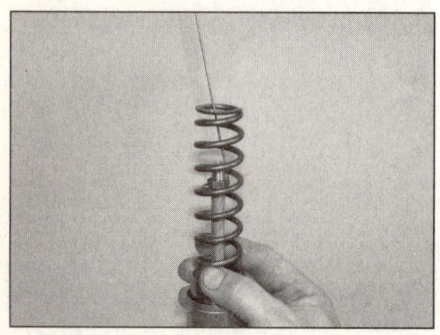

7.9b Make sure the tapered end is at the top

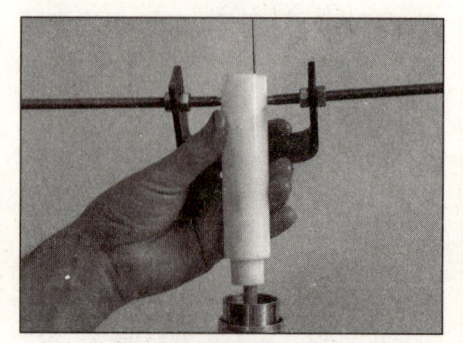

7.9c Fit the spacer ...

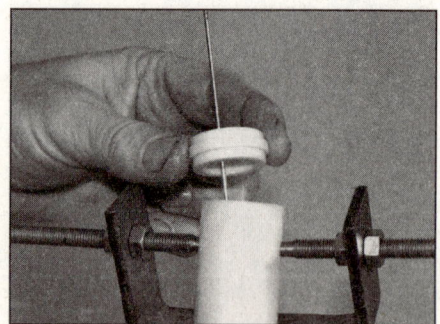

7.9d ... and the spacer seat, where used

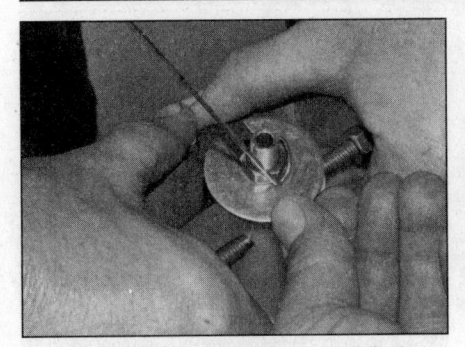

Frame and suspension 5•11

7.10 Push the spacer down and fit the washer under the nut

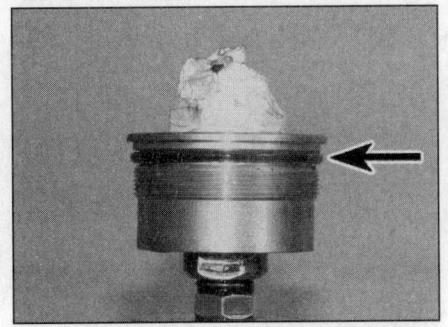

7.14 Check the O-ring (arrowed), then thread the top bolt into the tube

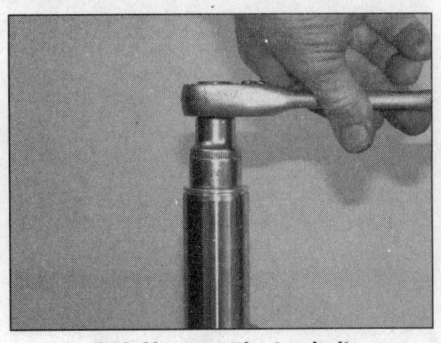

7.16 Unscrew the top bolt

or slotted washer under the locknut **(see illustration)**. Remove the wire.

11 On CB600F/FA 2007 and 2008 models thread the top bolt onto the damper rod. Counter-hold the locknut and tighten the top bolt securely against it.

12 On 2009-on CB600F/FA models and all CBR600F/FA models insert the damping adjuster rod and thread the top bolt onto the damper rod **(see illustration 7.5b)**. Counter-hold the pre-load adjuster using a spanner as before and tighten the locknut securely against it **(see illustration 7.5a)**.

13 Press down on the spacer to compress the spring and remove the plate or slotted washer, then carefully release the spring pressure **(see illustration 7.4c)**. Remove the holding tool.

14 If the top bolt O-ring is damaged or deteriorated fit a new one **(see illustration)**. Smear some fork oil onto the O-ring. Extend the outer tube and thread the top bolt into it, making sure it does not cross-thread, and tighten it as much as possible holding the inner tube by hand **(see illustration 7.3)**. Note: *Tighten the top bolt to the specified torque setting when the fork has been installed in the bike and is held in the bottom yoke, but before the top yoke clamp bolt or handlebar clamp bolt is tightened.*

15 Install the fork (see Section 6). Set the spring pre-load adjuster as noted or required (see Section 13).

CBF600N/NA/S/SA models

16 Unscrew the fork top bolt from the top of the inner tube – the bolt is under pressure from the fork spring, so use a ratchet tool so it does not need to be removed from the bolt as you unscrew it, and maintain some downward pressure on it, particularly as you come to the end of the threads, or alternatively hold the tool still and twist the fork tube to unthread it from the bolt **(see illustration)**.

17 Slide the inner tube down gently until it seats on the bottom. Remove the spacer, then hook the spacer seat and spring out of the tube **(see illustrations)**.

18 Invert the fork leg over a suitable container and pump the fork several times to expel as much fork oil as possible **(see illustration)**. Support the fork upside down in the container for a while to allow as much oil as possible to drain, then pump the fork again. If the fork oil contains metal particles inspect the fork bushes for wear (see Section 8). Wipe any excess oil off the spring and spacer.

19 Stand the fork upright. Slowly pour in the specified quantity of the specified grade of fork oil **(see illustration)**. Now pump the fork slowly at least ten times each to distribute the oil evenly and expel all air from the damper. Slide the inner tube down gently until it seats on the bottom. Measure the oil level from the top of the tube **(see illustration)**. Add or

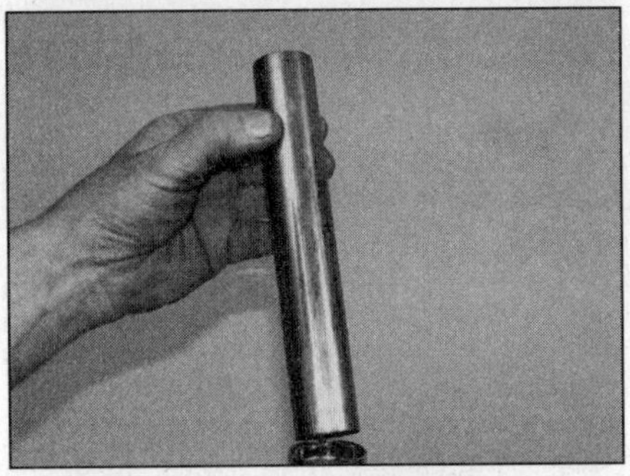

7.17a Remove the spacer . . .

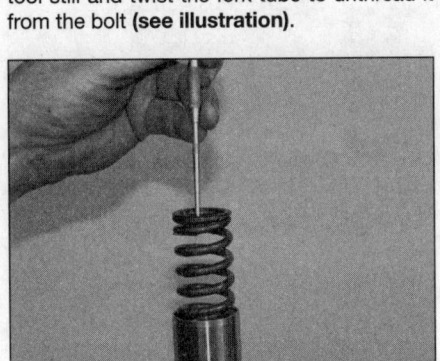

7.17b . . . then hook the spring up . . .

7.17c . . . noting the spacer seat . . .

7.18 Drain the oil as described

7.19a Fill the fork slowly to prevent air bubbles and overfilling

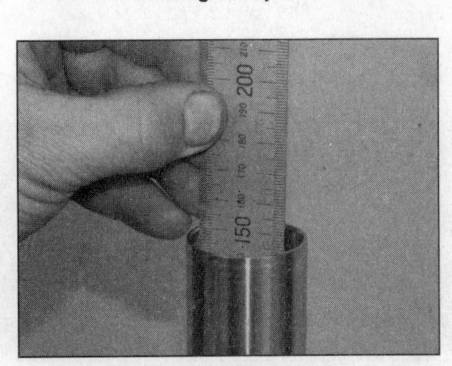

7.19b Measure the distance from the top of the tube to the oil

5•12 Frame and suspension

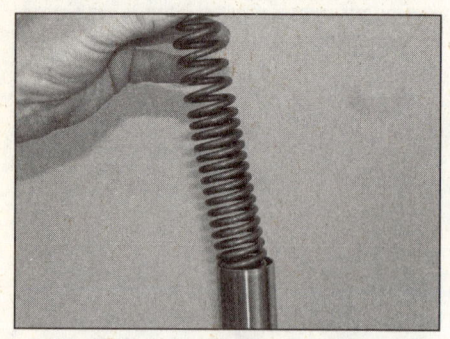

7.20a Make sure the closer-wound coils are at the bottom

7.20b Fit the spacer seat . . .

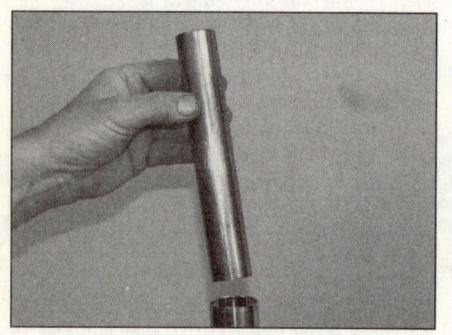

7.20c . . . and the spacer

7.21 Check the O-ring (arrowed)

8.2 Slacken the damper cartridge bolt

8.4 Remove the bolt . . .

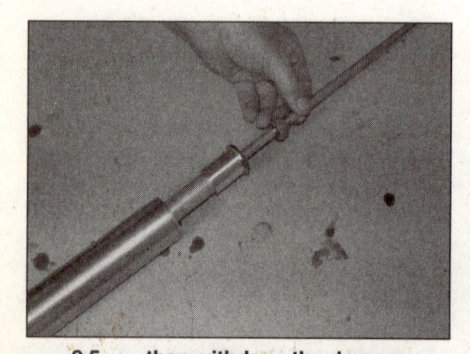

8.5 . . . then withdraw the damper cartridge

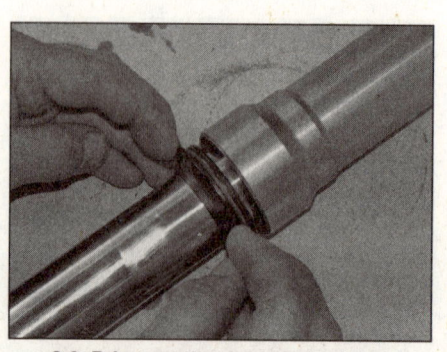

8.6 Prise out the dust seal using a flat-bladed screwdriver

subtract oil until it is at the level specified at the beginning of this Chapter.

20 Pull the inner tube out, then fit the spring with the closer-wound coils at the bottom **(see illustration)**. Fit the spacer seat and spacer **(see illustrations)**.

21 If the top bolt O-ring is damaged or deteriorated fit a new one **(see illustration)**. Smear some fork oil onto the O-ring. Extend the inner tube and fit the top bolt into it, compressing the spring as you do, and thread it in, making sure it does not cross-thread, keeping downward pressure on the spring, using a ratchet tool or by turning the tube while holding the bolt still, and tighten it as much as possible holding the inner tube by hand **(see illustration 7.16)**. **Note:** *Tighten the top bolt to the specified torque setting when the fork has been installed in the bike and is held in the bottom yoke, but before the top yoke clamp bolt is tightened.*

22 Install the fork (see Section 6). Set the spring pre-load adjuster as noted or required (see Section 13).

8 Fork overhaul

Special tools: *A fork bush and seal driver is referred to in Steps 18 and 48. An alternative method is also described.*

1 Remove the fork – as applicable make sure you adjust the pre-load and/or damping to its minimum (see Section 13), and on all models loosen the top bolt while the leg is still clamped in the bottom yoke (see Section 6). Always dismantle the fork legs separately to avoid interchanging parts and thus causing an accelerated rate of wear. Store all components in separate, clearly marked containers.

CB600F/FA and CBR600F/FA

Disassembly

2 Lay the fork flat on the bench with the caliper mounting lugs to the left. Remove the wheel axle clamp bolt **(see illustration 8.29)**. Hold the fork down and slacken then lightly retighten the damper cartridge bolt in the base of the fork **(see illustration)**. If the damper cartridge rotates inside the fork whilst attempting to unscrew the bolt, compress the fork so that the spring exerts pressure on the cartridge body whilst the bolt is unscrewed. Alternatively, if available use an air wrench.

3 Refer to Section 7, Steps 3 to 7 and drain the oil from the fork.

4 Remove the damper cartridge bolt and its sealing washer from the bottom of the fork **(see illustration)**. A new sealing washer must be used on reassembly.

5 Withdraw the damper cartridge from inside the fork tube **(see illustration)**. Pump the damper a few times over the oil drain tray to expel any residual oil.

6 Carefully prise out the dust seal from the bottom of the outer tube **(see illustration)**.

Frame and suspension 5•13

7 Carefully prise out the oil seal retaining clip, taking care not to scratch the surface of the inner tube (see illustration).
8 To separate the inner and outer tubes it is necessary to displace the bottom bush and oil seal from the bottom of the outer tube. The top bush on the inner tube will not pass through the bottom bush, and this can be used to good effect. Grasp the inner tube in one hand and the outer tube in the other and compress them slightly, then pull them apart so that the top bush strikes the bottom bush (see illustration). Repeat this operation until the bottom bush and seal are tapped out (see illustration).
9 To remove the bottom bush carefully lever its ends apart using a screwdriver and slide it over the top bush (see illustration). Slide the oil seal washer, the oil seal, the retaining ring and the dust seal over the top bush and off the inner tube, noting which way up they fit (see illustration). Discard the oil seal and the dust seal as new ones must be used. Note that Honda specify to use a new top bush if it is removed from its recess – if required remove it by levering its ends apart until it clears its recess (see illustration).

Inspection

10 Clean all parts in solvent and blow them dry with compressed air, if available.
11 Check the fork inner tube for score marks, dents, pitting, scratches, flaking of its surface and excessive or abnormal wear. Fit a new tube if any are found. Check the inner tube for runout using V-blocks and a dial gauge. If the amount of runout exceeds the service limit specified, a new tube should be fitted.

⚠ **Warning: If the inner tube is bent or exceeds the runout limit, it should not be straightened; replace it with a new one.**

12 Check the fork outer tube for cracks. Check the fork seal seat and housing for nicks, gouges and scratches. If damage is evident, leaks will occur. Also check the oil seal washer for damage or distortion and fit a new one if necessary.
13 Check the spring for cracks and other damage. Measure the spring free length and compare the measurement to the specifications at the beginning of the Chapter (see illustration). If it is defective or sagged below the service limit, replace the springs in both forks with new ones. Never renew only one spring.
14 Examine the working surfaces of the two bushes (i.e. the inner surface of the bottom bush and the outer surface of the top bush) (see illustration); if the grey Teflon outer surface has been worn away to reveal the copper inner surface over more than 75% of the surface area, or if the bushes are scored or badly scuffed, they must be replaced with new ones. Note that it is a good idea to replace the bushes with new ones as a matter of course as part of a fork overhaul.
15 Check the damper cartridge and rod, and

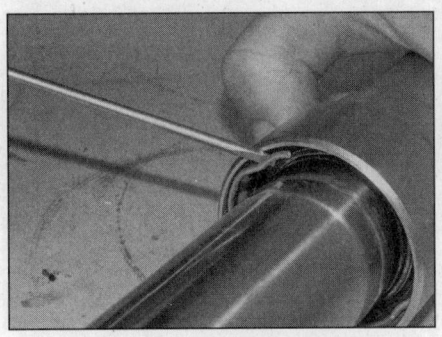

8.7 Prise out the retaining clip using a flat-bladed screwdriver

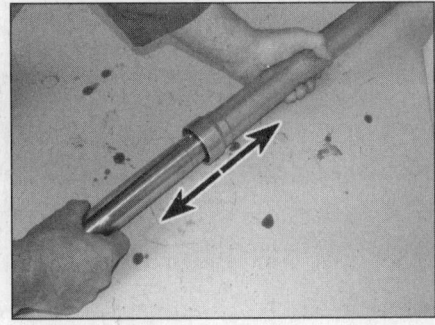

8.8a To separate the tubes pull them apart firmly several times . . .

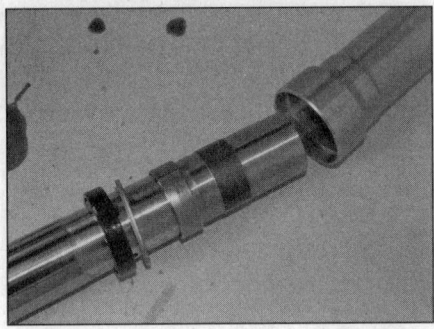

8.8b . . . the slide-hammer effect will displace the oil seal, washer and top bush

8.9a Carefully lever the ends apart to expand it over the top bush

8.9b Slide the remaining components off

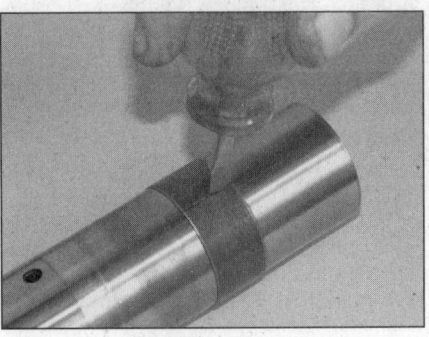

8.9c Only remove the top bush if you are replacing it with a new one

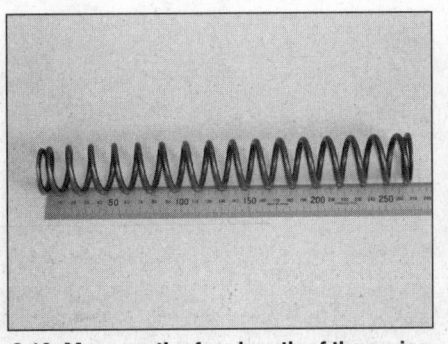

8.13 Measure the free length of the spring

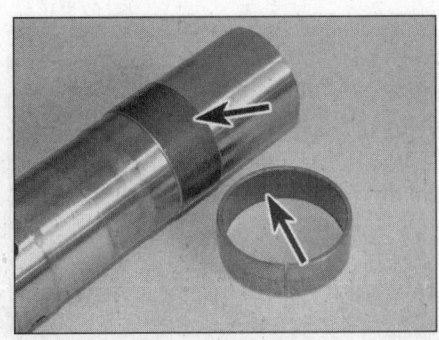

8.14 Check the working surface (arrowed) of each bush for wear

5•14 Frame and suspension

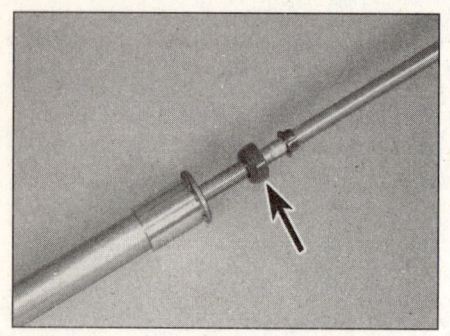

8.15 Check the damper and oil lock valve (arrowed)

8.16a Use insulating tape to cover sharp edges . . .

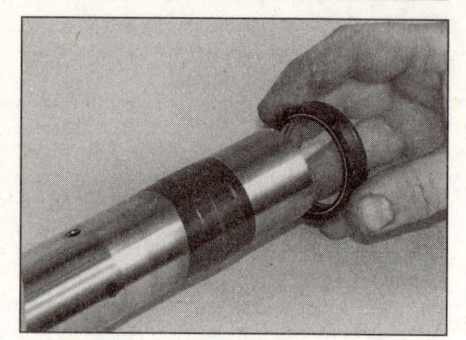

8.16b . . . then slide the specified components over it

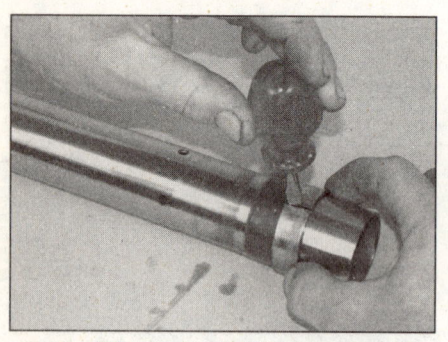

8.16c If the top bush is in place expand the ends of the bottom bush to fit over it

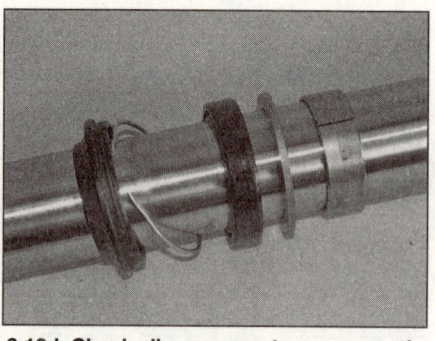

8.16d Check all components are correctly in place

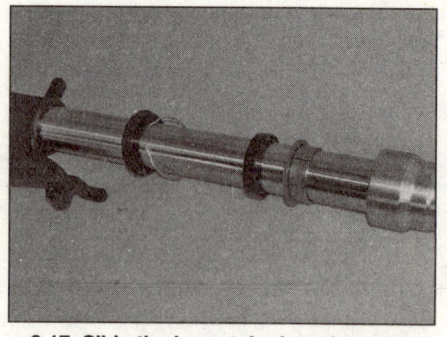

8.17 Slide the inner tube into the outer tube

the oil lock valve fitted on it, for damage and wear **(see illustration)**. Hold the body of the cartridge and pump the rod in and out. If any wear or damage is found, or if the rod does not move smoothly in the damper, a new damper must be installed.

Reassembly

16 Wrap one layer of thin insulating tape over the edges of the recess for the top bush in the inner tube, or over the bush itself if not removed, to protect the seal lips **(see illustration)**. Smear some oil over the tape, and also over the oil seal lips. Slide the new dust seal, retaining clip, new oil seal, and oil seal washer onto the inner tube, making sure they are the correct way round – the marked side of the oil seal must face to the bottom of the fork **(see illustration)**. Remove the tape, then lubricate the inner surface of the bottom bush and slide it on, over the top bush if in place **(see illustration)**. Make sure all components are correctly fitted **(see illustration)**. If removed fit the new top bush into its recess in the inner tube **(see illustration 8.9c)**. Apply a smear of the specified clean fork oil to the bushes.

17 Slide the inner tube fully into the outer tube **(see illustration)**. Support the fork upside down, and have an assistant hold the inner tube and the components on it up. Slide the bottom bush into the bottom of the outer tube, then fit the washer on top.

18 Using either the special service tools (part Nos. 07KMD-KZ30100 and 07RMD-MW40100) or a suitable drift, carefully drive the bottom bush fully into its recess – the oil seal washer prevents damaging the edges of the bush **(see illustration)**. If using a drift, wrap tape around it to prevent scratching the inner tube. Make sure the bush enters the recess squarely. It is best to make sure that the inner tube is withdrawn as much as possible from the outer tube so that any accidental scratching is confined to the area that does not affect the oil seal. Lift the washer to check the bush is seated fully and squarely in its recess in the outer tube, then wipe the recess clean **(see illustration)**.

19 Slide the oil seal washer back onto the bush **(see illustration)**.

20 Slide the new oil seal down and into the

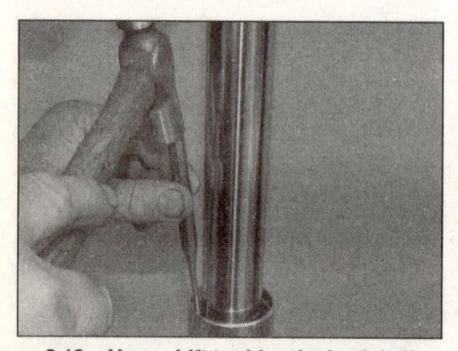

8.18a Use a drift to drive the bush in if necessary, using the washer as an interface

8.18b Check the bush is fully seated . . .

8.19 . . . then fit the washer onto it

Frame and suspension 5•15

8.20a Slide the new seal down and into the outer tube

8.20b Cut the old seal in half . . .

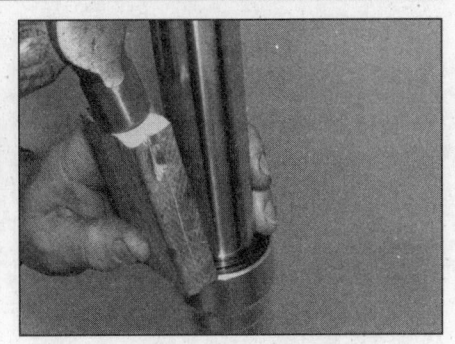

8.20c . . . and use it to push the new seal in, or to protect it if driving it in

8.20d Make sure the retaining clip groove (arrowed) is fully exposed

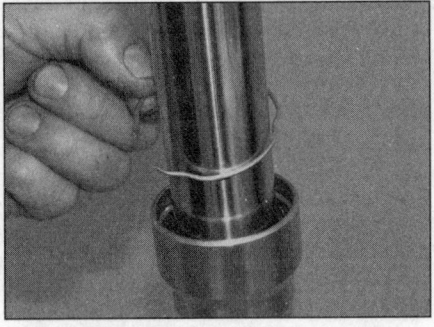

8.21 Fit the retaining clip in its groove . . .

8.22 . . . then press the dust seal in

outer tube **(see illustration)**. Push the seal into place and drive it in as in Step 18 until the retaining clip groove is visible – to avoid damaging the seal if a drift is being used, remove the springs from the old seal then cut it in half and use it as an interface between the drift and the new seal, moving it around as required **(see illustrations)**. The new seal is seated when the old seal is just about flush with the rim of the outer tube. Remove the old seal – it can be easily lifted out.

21 Fit the retaining clip, making sure it is correctly located in its groove **(see illustration)**.

22 Press the dust seal into the top of the outer tube **(see illustration)**.

23 Clean the threads of the damper cartridge bolt. Lay the fork flat on the bench with the caliper mounting lugs to the right. Slide the damper cartridge fully into the fork tube **(see illustration)**. Fit a new sealing washer onto the cartridge bolt and apply a few drops of a suitable non-permanent thread locking compound **(see illustration)**. Fit the bolt into the bottom of the tube and thread it into the cartridge, tightening it to the torque setting specified at the beginning of the Chapter. If the cartridge rotates inside the tube as you tighten the bolt, wait until the fork is fully reassembled and tighten it then (the pressure of the spring on the cartridge will prevent it from turning).

24 Refer to Section 7, Steps 8 to 14 and fill the fork with oil and finish reassembly.

25 If the damper cartridge bolt requires tightening (see Step 23) place the fork upside down on the floor, using a rag to protect it, then have an assistant compress the fork so that maximum spring pressure is placed on the damper cartridge head while tightening the bolt to the specified torque setting.

26 Fit the axle clamp bolt **(see illustration 8.29)**.

27 Install the fork (see Section 6). Set the spring pre-load adjuster as noted or required (see Section 13).

CBF600N/NA/S/SA

Disassembly

28 Remove the fork protector, noting how it locates **(see illustration)**.

29 Lay the fork flat on the bench with the

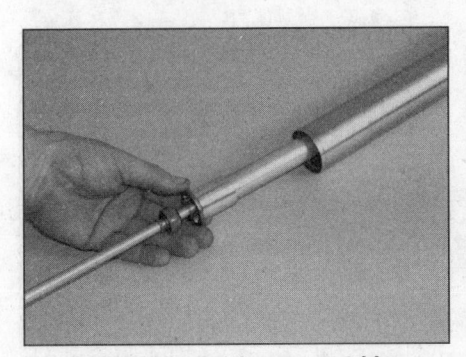

8.23a Insert the damper cartridge

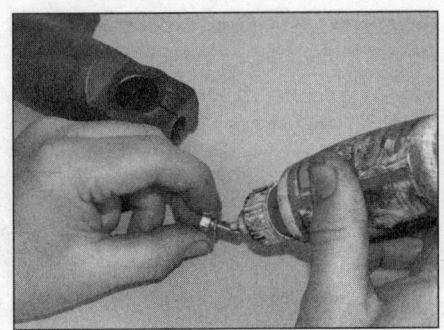

8.23b Fit a new sealing washer and apply threadlock

8.28 Remove the protector, using a soft drift if necessary

8.29 Remove the clamp bolt

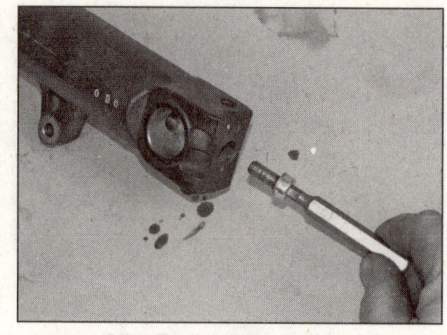

8.31 Remove the bolt . . .

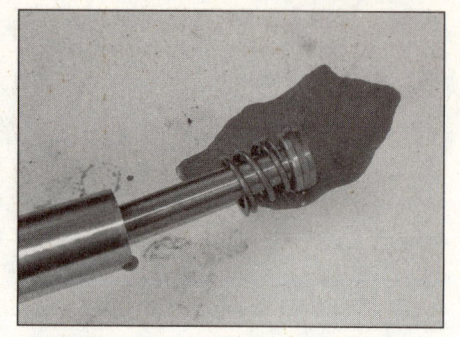

8.32 . . . then tip the damper rod out

caliper mounting lugs to the left. Remove the wheel axle clamp bolt **(see illustration)**. Hold the fork down and slacken then lightly retighten the damper rod bolt in the base of the fork **(see illustration 8.2)**. If the damper rod rotates inside the fork whilst attempting to unscrew the bolt, compress the fork so that the spring exerts pressure on the rod whilst the bolt is unscrewed. Alternatively, if available use an air wrench.

30 Refer to Section 7, Steps 16 to 18 and drain the oil from the fork.

31 Remove the damper rod bolt and its sealing washer from the bottom of the fork **(see illustration)**. A new sealing washer must be used on reassembly.

32 Tip the damper rod out of the fork **(see illustration)**.

33 Carefully prise out the dust seal from the top of the outer tube **(see illustration)**.

34 Carefully prise out the oil seal retaining clip, taking care not to scratch the surface of the inner tube **(see illustration)**.

35 To separate the inner and outer tubes it is necessary to displace the top bush and oil seal from the top of the outer tube. The bottom bush on the inner tube will not pass through the top bush, and this can be used to good effect. Grasp the inner tube in one hand and the outer tube in the other and compress them slightly, then pull them apart so that the bottom bush strikes the top bush **(see illustration)**. Repeat this operation until the top bush and seal are tapped out **(see illustration)**.

36 Tip the oil lock piece out of the outer tube **(see illustration)** – if it is not there it will be in the bottom of the inner tube. Slide the oil seal, the oil seal washer and top bush off the inner tube, noting which way up they fit **(see illustration**

8.35b). Discard the oil seal and the dust seal as new ones must be used. Do not remove the bottom bush from the inner tube unless it is being replaced with a new one – to remove it carefully lever its ends apart using a screwdriver and slide it out of its recess **(see illustration)**.

Inspection

37 Clean all parts in solvent and blow them dry with compressed air, if available.

38 Check the fork inner tube for score marks, dents, pitting, scratches, flaking of its surface and excessive or abnormal wear. Fit a new tube if any are found. Check the inner tube for runout using V-blocks and a dial gauge. If the amount of runout exceeds the service limit specified, a new tube should be fitted.

⚠️ *Warning: If the inner tube is bent or exceeds the runout limit, it should not be straightened; replace it with a new one.*

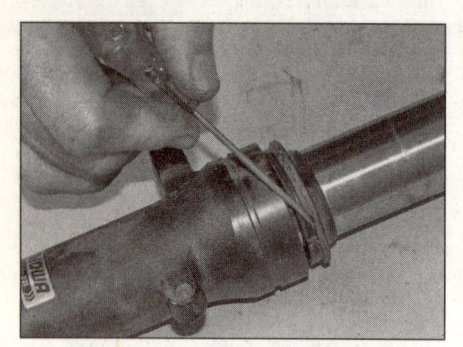

8.33 Prise out the dust seal using a flat-bladed screwdriver

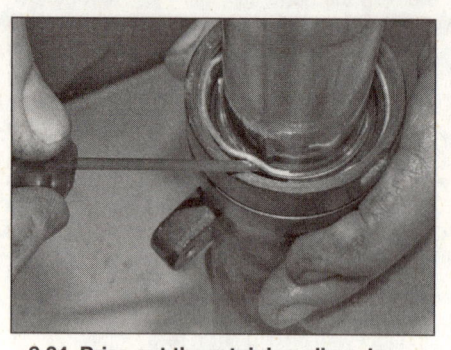

8.34 Prise out the retaining clip using a flat-bladed screwdriver

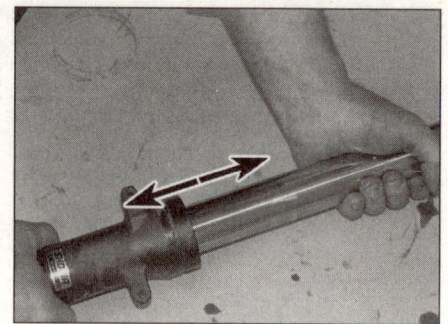

8.35a To separate the tubes pull them apart firmly several times . . .

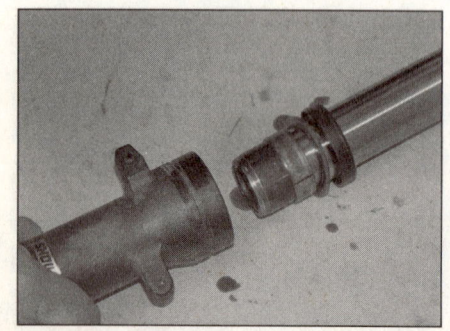

8.35b . . . the slide-hammer effect will displace the oil seal, washer and top bush

8.36a Tip the oil lock piece out

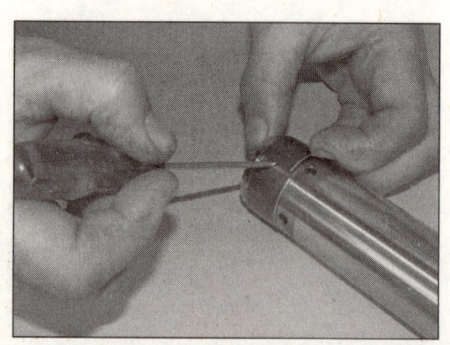

8.36b Carefully lever the ends apart to expand it

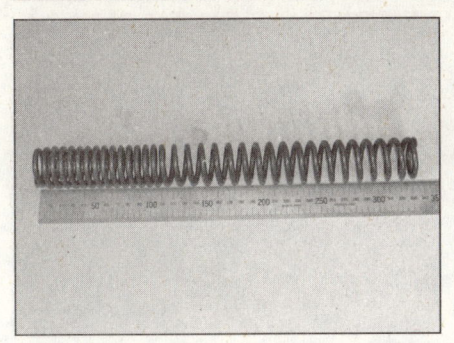

Frame and suspension 5•17

8.40 Check the free length of the spring

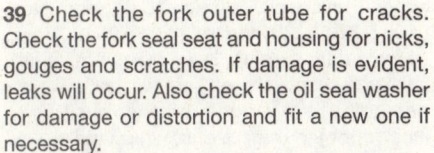

8.41 Check the working surface (arrowed) of each bush for wear

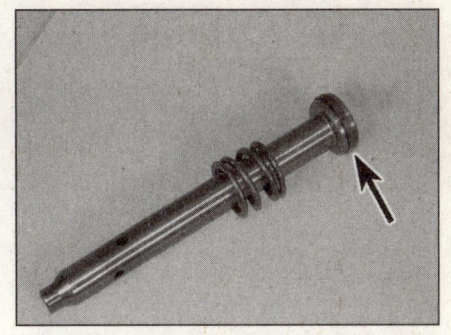

8.42 Check the damper, rebound spring and piston ring (arrowed)

39 Check the fork outer tube for cracks. Check the fork seal seat and housing for nicks, gouges and scratches. If damage is evident, leaks will occur. Also check the oil seal washer for damage or distortion and fit a new one if necessary.

40 Check the spring for cracks and other damage. Measure the spring free length and compare the measurement to the specifications at the beginning of the Chapter **(see illustration)**. If it is defective or sagged below the service limit, replace the springs in both forks with new ones. Never renew only one spring.

41 Examine the working surfaces of the two bushes (i.e. the outer surface of the bottom bush and the inner surface of the top bush) **(see illustration)**; if the grey Teflon outer surface has been worn away to reveal the copper inner surface over more than 75% of the surface area, or if the bushes are scored or badly scuffed, they must be replaced with new ones. Note that it is a good idea to replace the bushes with new ones as a matter of course as part of a fork overhaul.

42 Check the damper rod, the rebound spring fitted on it, and the piston ring in the head for damage and wear **(see illustration)**. If the piston ring is removed it must be replaced with a new one.

Reassembly

43 If necessary, fit a new bottom bush into its recess in the bottom of the inner tube **(see illustration 8.36b)**.

44 If removed, fit a new piston ring into the groove in the head of the damper rod **(see illustration 8.42)**. Fit the rebound spring onto the rod. Slide the damper rod into the top of the inner tube and all the way down so it protrudes from the bottom **(see illustration)**. Fit the oil lock piece onto the bottom of the rod, then push the rod back into the tube so the oil lock piece fits into the bottom **(see illustrations)**.

45 Apply a smear of the specified clean fork oil to the surface of the bottom bush. Slide the inner tube fully into the outer tube **(see illustration)**.

46 Clean the threads of the damper rod bolt. Lay the fork flat on the bench with the caliper mounting lugs to the right. Fit a new sealing washer onto the bolt and apply a few drops of a suitable non-permanent thread locking compound **(see illustration)**. Fit the bolt into the bottom of the outer tube and thread it into the damper rod, tightening it to the torque setting specified at the beginning of the Chapter **(see illustration)**. If the rod rotates inside the tube as you tighten the bolt, wait

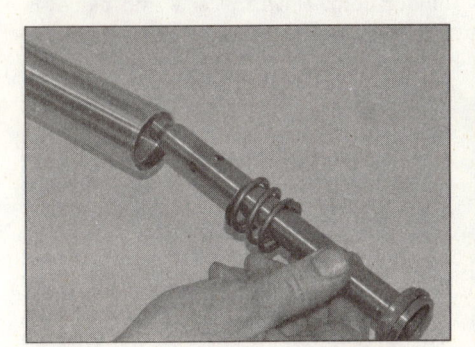

8.44a Fit the damper rod into the tube . . .

8.44b . . . then fit the oil lock piece onto the protruding end . . .

8.44c . . . and push it into the tube

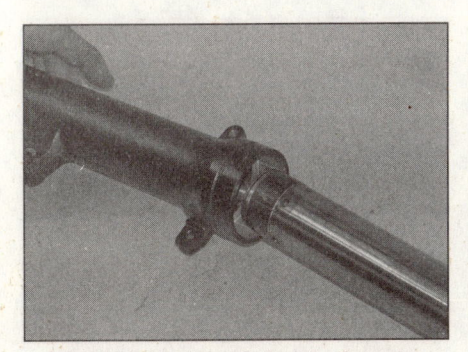

8.45 Slide the inner tube into the outer tube

8.46a Fit a new sealing washer and apply threadlock . . .

8.46b . . . and tighten the bolt to the specified torque

5•18 Frame and suspension

8.47a Slide the top bush down and into the outer tube . . .

8.47b . . . then seat the washer on the bush . . .

8.48 . . . and drive the bush in and onto its seat

until the fork is fully reassembled and tighten it then (the pressure of the spring on the rod will prevent it from turning).

47 Apply a smear of the specified clean fork oil to the inner surface of the top bush. Slide the bush down the inner tube and seat it in the top of the outer tube **(see illustration)**. Slide the oil seal washer onto the bush **(see illustration)**.

48 Support the fork upright. Using either the special service tools (part Nos. 07947-KA50100 and 07947-KF00100) or a suitable drift, carefully drive the top bush fully into its recess – the oil seal washer prevents damaging the edges of the bush **(see illustration)**. If using a drift, wrap tape around it to prevent scratching the inner tube. Make sure the bush enters the recess squarely. It is best to make sure that the inner tube is withdrawn as much as possible from the outer tube so that any accidental scratching is confined to the area that does not affect the oil seal.

49 Lift the washer to check the bush is seated fully and squarely in its recess in the outer tube, then wipe the recess clean and re-seat the washer **(see illustration)**.

50 Apply a smear of clean fork oil to the lips of the new oil seal. Slide the seal onto the tube with its marked side facing up **(see illustration)**. Drive the seal into place as described in Step 48 until the retaining clip groove is visible – to avoid damaging the seal, fit the old seal above it and use it as an interface between the drift and the new seal **(see illustrations)**. The new seal is seated when the old seal is just about flush with the rim of the outer tube – at this point lift it and check that the retaining clip groove is fully exposed **(see illustration)**. Remove the old seal.

51 Fit the retaining clip, making sure it is correctly located in its groove **(see illustration)**.

52 Press the dust seal into the top of the outer tube **(see illustration)**.

8.49 Make sure the bush (arrowed) has been fully driven in

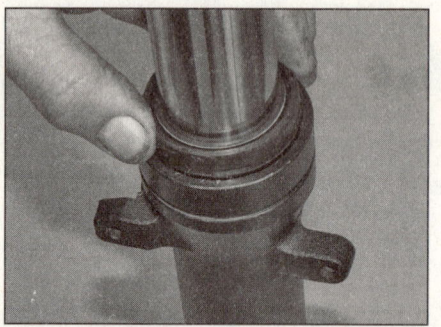

8.50a Slide the new seal down and into the outer tube . . .

8.50b . . . then fit the old seal on top . . .

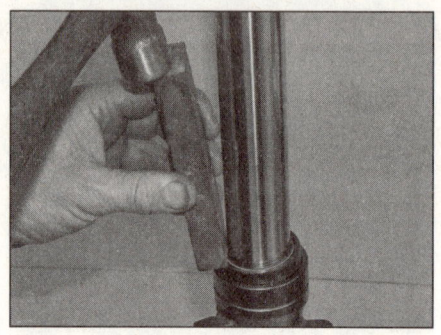

8.50c . . . and drive the new seal in and onto its seat using the old seal as an interface

8.50d Lift the old seal and make sure the retaining clip groove (arrowed) is fully exposed

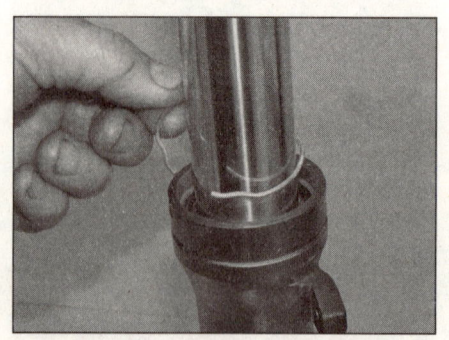

8.51 Fit the retaining clip in its groove . . .

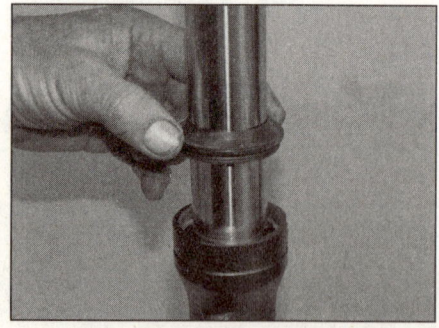

8.52 . . . then press the dust seal in

Frame and suspension 5•19

53 Refer to Section 7, Steps 19 to 21 and fill the fork with oil and finish reassembly.

54 If the damper rod bolt requires tightening (see Step 46), place the fork upside down on the floor, using a rag to protect it, then have an assistant compress the fork so that maximum spring pressure is placed on the damper rod head while tightening the bolt to the specified torque setting.

55 Fit the axle clamp bolt **(see illustration 8.29)**. Fit the fork protector, aligning the tab with the cut-out **(see illustration)**.

56 Install the fork (see Section 6). Set the spring pre-load adjuster as noted or required (see Section 13).

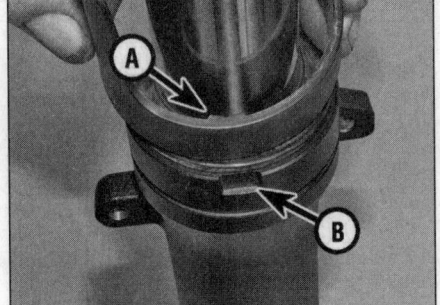

9 Steering stem

Special tool: *Either the Honda special tool (part No. 07916-3710101), equivalent peg spanner, or a suitably sized C-spanner is necessary for this procedure – see Step 8.*

Removal

1 As a precaution, remove the fuel tank (see Chapter 4) – though not actually essential, this will prevent the possibility of damage should a tool slip.

2 On CB600F/FA 2007 to 2010 models remove the headlight and the instrument cluster (see Chapter 8). On CB600F/FA 2010 and 2011 models remove the instrument cluster and the headlight (see Chapter 8). On CBR600F/FA models remove the headlight (see Chapter 8). On CBF600N/NA models remove the headlight and the instrument cluster (see Chapter 8), then remove the headlight bracket, noting the rubber on each locating prong – the procedure involves displacing the handlebars and the top yoke, so ignore references to doing so in the next Steps. On CBF600S/SA models remove the fairing (see Chapter 7).

3 Remove the front forks (see Section 6).

4 Displace the handlebars (Section 5), headlight bracket, instrument bracket and all cables, wiring and hoses from the top and bottom yokes as required according to model and tie or support them so they do not interfere with yoke removal – as far as possible keep everything together to avoid unnecessary disconnection of wiring and cables. If possible take some pictures of the routing of everything as an aid to installation. On C-ABS models unscrew the bolt securing the brake pipe/hose joint pieces together to the bracket on the frame under the bottom yoke and move them aside, taking care not to bend the pipes **(see illustration)**. The bracket can stay on the frame.

5 Unscrew the steering stem nut **(see illustration)**. Lift the top yoke up off the steering stem and support it clear, using a rag to protect the yoke and other components **(see illustration)**.

6 Bend the lockwasher tabs out of the notches in the locknut **(see illustration)**. Unscrew the locknut using your fingers **(see illustration)** – it shouldn't be tight. If it is tight use a C-spanner located in one of the notches. Remove the lockwasher **(see illustration)**. Inspect the tabs for cracks or signs of fatigue. If there is any sign of damage, discard the lockwasher and use a new one; otherwise the old one can be re-used, but note that Honda recommend using a new one as a matter of course.

7 If the peg spanner or socket mentioned above is not available, make an alignment mark between the adjuster nut and the frame – this can serve as a rough guide for the tightness of the adjuster nut on installation. As you unscrew the nut count the number of turns.

8.55 Align the tab (A) with the cut-out (B)

9.4 Unscrew the brake pipe joint bolt so the pipes/hoses are free of the bracket

9.5a Unscrew the steering stem nut . . .

9.5b . . . and lift the top yoke off

9.6a Bend down the lockwasher tabs . . .

9.6b . . . then unscrew the locknut . . .

9.6c . . . and remove the lockwasher

9.8a Unscrewing the nut using a C-spanner

9.8b Remove the grease seal

9.9a Remove the inner race and upper bearing from the head . . .

8 Support the bottom yoke and unscrew the adjuster nut using a peg-spanner, socket or a C-spanner located in one of the notches **(see illustration)**. Remove the grease seal **(see illustration)**. Gently lower the bottom yoke and steering stem out of the frame **(see illustration 9.12a)**.

9 Remove the inner race and bearing from the top of the steering head **(see illustration)**. Remove the bearing from the base of the steering stem **(see illustration)**.

10 Remove all traces of old grease from the bearings and races and check them for wear or damage as described in Section 10. **Note:** *Do not attempt to remove the races from the steering head or the steering stem unless they are to be replaced with new ones (see Section 10).*

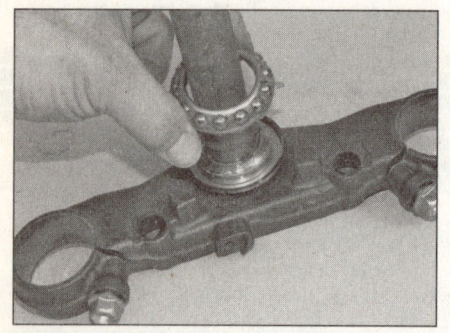

Installation

11 Smear a liberal quantity of Urea based multi-purpose grease with EP2 rating onto the bearing races, and work some grease well into both the upper and lower bearings. Also smear the grease seal lip, using a new seal if necessary. Fit the lower bearing onto the steering stem **(see illustration 9.9b)**.

12 Carefully lift the steering stem/bottom yoke up through the steering head and support it there **(see illustration)**. Fit the upper bearing and its inner race into the top of the steering head **(see illustrations)**. Fit the grease seal **(see illustration)**. Apply clean oil to the adjuster nut threads and thread it onto the steering stem **(see illustration)**.

13 Using the Honda service tool (part No. 07916-3710101) or a suitable peg spanner, which can be made by cutting castellations into an old socket **(see illustration)**, tighten

9.9b . . . and the lower bearing from the stem

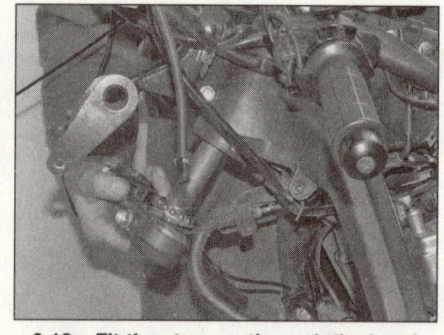

9.12a Fit the stem up through the head

9.12b Fit the upper bearing . . .

9.12c . . . the inner race . . .

9.12d . . . and the grease seal . . .

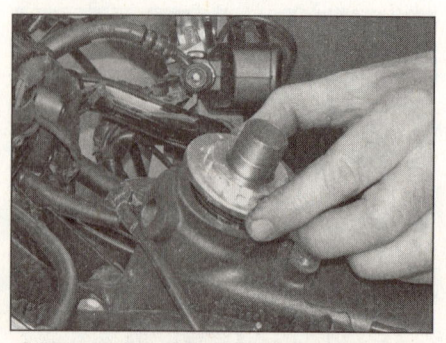

9.12e . . . then thread the adjuster nut on

9.13 Home-made peg spanner

Frame and suspension 5•21

9.14 Tightening the nut using a C-spanner

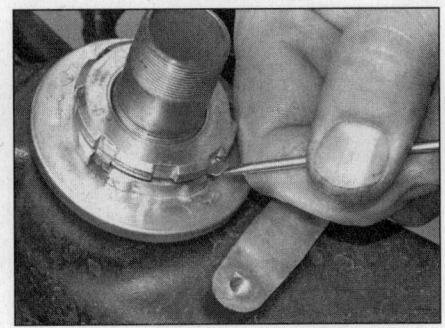

9.16 Bend the lockwasher tabs up into the notches in the lockwasher

9.18 Tighten the stem nut to the specified torque

the adjuster nut to the torque setting specified at the beginning of the Chapter, then turn the steering from lock-to-lock five times, then reapply the specified torque setting to the nut. Check that the steering stem is able to move smoothly (though it may feel a bit tight, but this is normal as the weight of the forks and wheel is not influencing the feel) from lock-to-lock following adjustment – note that it is best to check and if necessary reset the bearing adjustment as described in Chapter 1 after the forks and front wheel and all other components have been installed.

14 If the correct tools are not available, tighten the nut the number of turns recorded on removal using a C-spanner until the marks align **(see illustration)**. Turn the steering from lock-to-lock five times, then slacken the nut, and tighten it again until the marks align. Install the forks and wheel, then refer to the procedure in Chapter 1 and check the feel of the bearings as described, and adjust if necessary.

Caution: Take great care not to apply excessive pressure because this will cause premature failure of the bearings.

15 With the bearings correctly adjusted, fit the lockwasher, using a new one if the tabs are weakened or cracked, onto the adjuster nut and fit the two short tabs into the notches in the adjuster nut **(see illustration 9.6c)**.

16 Fit the locknut and tighten it finger-tight (see illustration 9.6b). Tighten the locknut further (but no more than 90°) until its notches align with the remaining lockwasher tabs, making sure the adjuster nut does not turn as well (though that is unlikely). Secure the locknut in position by bending up the long lock washer tabs into its notches **(see illustration)**.

17 On CBF600N/NA models make sure the rubbers are fitted onto each locating prong of the headlight bracket, then fit the bracket into the holes in the bottom yoke.

18 Fit the top yoke onto the steering stem **(see illustration 9.5b)** – on CBF600N/NA models make sure the rubbers on the top prongs on the headlight bracket locate in the holes in the underside of the yoke. Fit the steering stem nut and tighten it finger-tight **(see illustration 9.5a)**. Temporarily install one of the forks to align the top and bottom yokes, and secure it by tightening the bottom yoke clamp bolts only (see Section 6). Now tighten the steering stem nut to the torque setting specified at the beginning of the Chapter **(see illustration)**.

19 Install the remaining components in a reverse of the removal procedure, referring to the relevant Sections or Chapters, and to the torque settings specified at the beginning of the Chapter.

20 Carry out a final check of the steering head bearing freeplay as described in Chapter 1, and if necessary re-adjust.

10 Steering head bearings

Inspection

1 Remove the steering stem (see Section 9).
2 Remove all traces of old grease from the bearings and races and check them for wear or damage.
3 The outer races in the top and bottom of the steering head should be polished and free from indentations **(see illustration)**. Inspect the bearing balls for signs of wear, damage or discoloration, and examine the ball retainer cage for signs of cracks or splits. If there are any signs of wear on any of the above components both upper and lower bearing assemblies must be renewed as a set. Only remove the outer races in the steering head and the lower bearing inner race on the steering stem if they need to be replaced with new ones – do not re-use them once they have been removed.

Replacement

4 The outer races are an interference fit in the steering head – tap them from position using a suitable drift located in the recesses provided in the steering head that expose the lip of the race **(see illustrations)**. Tap firmly and evenly between the recesses to ensure the race is driven out squarely. Curve the end of the drift slightly to improve access if necessary.

10.3 Check the outer races in the top and bottom of the steering head

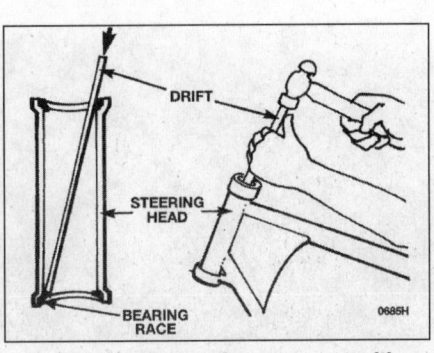

10.4a Drive the bearing races out with a brass drift . . .

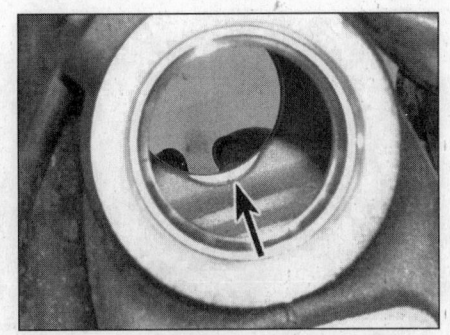

10.4b . . . locating it in the cut-outs (arrowed)

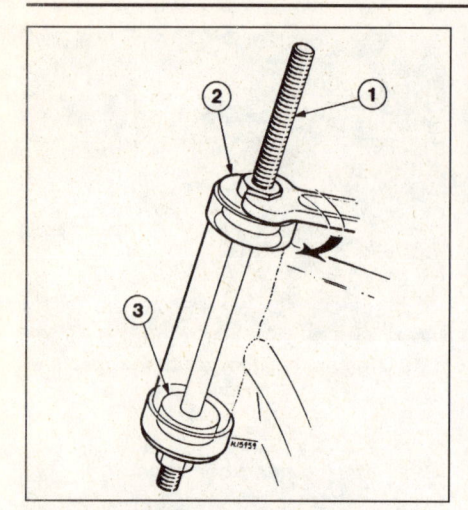

5•22 Frame and suspension

10.5 Drawbolt arrangement for fitting steering stem bearing races

1 Long bolt or threaded bar
2 Thick washer
3 Guide for lower race

5 Press the new outer races into the head using a drawbolt arrangement **(see illustration)**, or drive them in using a large diameter tubular drift. Ensure that the drawbolt washer or drift (as applicable) bears only on the outer edge of the race and does not contact the working surface. Alternatively, have the races installed by a Honda dealer equipped with the bearing race installation tools.

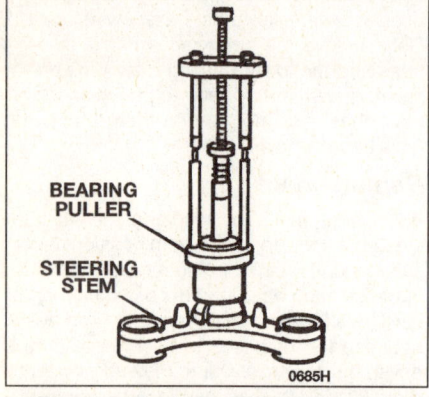

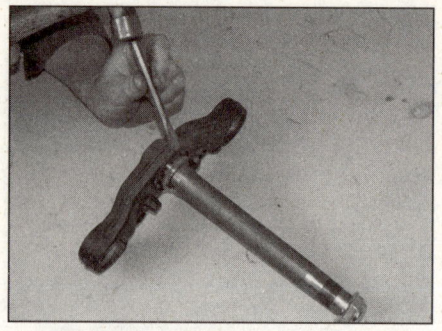

10.6a Remove the lower bearing race using a cold chisel . . .

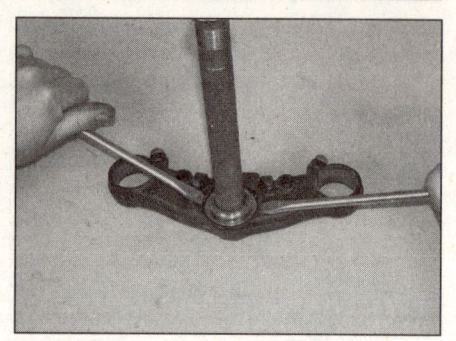

10.6b . . . and/or screwdrivers . . .

HAYNES HiNT *Installation of new bearing outer races is made much easier if the races are left overnight in the freezer. This causes them to contract slightly making them a looser fit. Alternatively, use a freeze spray.*

6 Only remove the lower bearing inner race from the steering stem if a new one is being fitted. To remove the race, first thread the steering stem nut onto the top then position the yoke on its front for stability – the nut will protect the threads from the transmitted force of the impact of the chisel. Tap under the race using a cold chisel to displace it, and if required use two screwdrivers placed on opposite sides to work it free, using blocks of wood to improve leverage and protect the yoke **(see illustrations)**. If the race is firmly in place it will be necessary to use a puller **(see illustration)**. Take the steering stem to a Honda dealer if required.

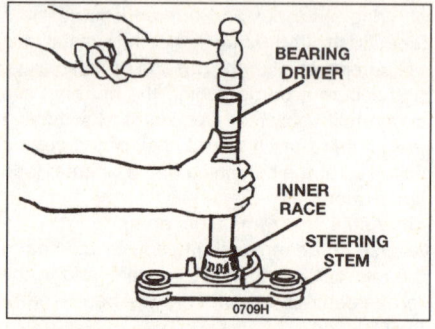

7 Remove the dust seal from the bottom of the stem and replace it with a new one. Smear the new one with grease.

8 Fit the new lower race onto the steering stem. Drive the new race into position using a length of tubing with an internal diameter slightly larger than the steering stem **(see illustration)** – heating the race and cooling the steering stem will make installation easier, or use an hydraulic press if necessary.

9 Install the steering stem (see Section 9).

10.6c . . . or using a puller if necessary

10.8 Drive the new inner race on using a suitable bearing driver or a length of pipe that bears only against the inner rim and not the bearing surface

11 Rear shock absorber

⚠ **Warning: Do not attempt to disassemble the shock absorber in the home workshop. It is nitrogen-charged under high pressure. Improper disassembly could result in serious injury.**

Removal

1 On CB600F/FA and CBR600F/FA models support the motorcycle on an auxiliary stand so that no weight is transmitted through any part of the rear suspension. On CBF600N/NA/S/SA models support the motorcycle on the centrestand. Tie the front brake lever to the handlebar to ensure the bike can't roll forward. Position a support under the rear wheel so that it does not drop when the shock absorber is removed, but also making sure that the weight of the machine is off the rear suspension so that the shock is not compressed.

2 Remove the seat(s) and side covers.

3 On CB600F/FA and CBR600F/FA models displace the rear brake fluid reservoir **(see illustration)**. Release the chainguard from its boss on the swingarm **(see illustration)**.

4 On CBF600N/NA/S/SA models release the wiring loom from the left-hand side of the rear

11.3a Unscrew the bolt and move the reservoir aside to access the top bolt

11.3b Release the chainguard from its boss (arrowed) to withdraw the bottom bolt

Frame and suspension 5•23

11.4a Release the catch . . .

11.4b . . . and draw the loom holder off its peg

11.5 Unscrew the nut and withdraw the bolt

11.6a Unscrew the nut . . .

11.6b . . . withdraw the bolt and remove the shock absorber

11.8 Check the bush (arrowed)

sub-frame **(see illustrations)**. Release the fuel tank drain and breather hose joint from the clamp on the right-hand side.

5 Unscrew the nut and withdraw the bolt securing the bottom of the shock absorber **(see illustration)** – depending on the tools you are using you may want to displace the brake hose guide from the swingarm **(see illustration 11.13)**. Remove the support from under the wheel and lower it to the ground.

6 Unscrew the nut on the bolt securing the top of the shock absorber **(see illustration)**. Support the shock and withdraw the bolt, then remove the shock absorber **(see illustration)**.

Inspection

7 Check the shock absorber for obvious physical damage and oil leakage, and the spring for looseness, cracks or signs of fatigue.

8 Check the bush in the top of the shock absorber for wear or damage **(see illustration)**.

9 Withdraw the sleeve from the bottom mount **(see illustration)**. Clean off old grease and dirt. Check the condition of the grease seals and bearing. If required lever out the grease seals **(see illustration)**. Fit the spacer back in and check for play between it and the bearing. Refer to *Tools and Workshop Tips* (Section 5) in the Reference section for more information on bearings.

10 If the bearing is worn, drive it out of the bore using a suitable driver or socket or draw it out using a drawbolt (one can be made up as described in *Tools and Workshop Tips* in the Reference section) – do not re-use the bearing after removing it. The new bearing should be pressed or drawn in, not driven in. When fitting the new bearing make sure it is central in the bore – the gap between the outer end and the rim of the bore should be 5.0 to 5.5 mm.

11 Press the new seals squarely into place **(see illustration)**. Fit the sleeve **(see illustration 11.9a)**. Lubricate the bearing, spacer and new seals with the specified grease (see Chapter 1). If the pre-load adjuster ring is hard to turn lubricate it with molybdenum paste.

12 Parts are not available for the shock absorber itself. If it is worn or damaged, it must be replaced with a new one. Before disposing of an old shock absorber, you should release the nitrogen gas from the top. To do this, make a drill point 35 mm below the middle of the top mount using a centre punch. Mount the shock in a vice. Drill a hole using a sharp 2 or 3 mm drill bit to release the gas – it is best to cover the shock and drill and avert

11.9a Withdraw the sleeve and check the seals and bearing

11.9b If necessary lever the seals out using a screwdriver

11.11 You can fit the seals in using thumb pressure

5•24 Frame and suspension

your face to prevent the possibility of injury, making sure the material used does not get caught in the chuck as it spins.

⚠️ **Warning:** *Wear protective eyewear and be very careful when releasing the gas pressure – it is possible for fine debris particles to be released with it, and as the pressure is high these could damage your eyes if done carelessly. If in doubt, ask a dealer to dispose of the shock absorber.*

Installation

13 Installation is the reverse of removal, noting the following:
- Apply the recommended grease (see Step 10) to the shock absorber pivot points.
- On CB600F/FA 2009-on and CBR600F/FA models install the shock absorber with the damping adjuster screw facing to the right.
- Tighten the nuts/bolts to the torque setting specified at the beginning of the Chapter **(see illustration)**.

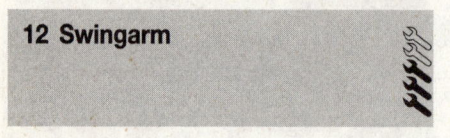

12 Swingarm

Removal

1 On CB600F/FA and CBR600F/FA models support the motorcycle on an auxiliary stand so that no weight is transmitted through any part of the rear suspension. On CBF600N/NA/S/SA models support the motorcycle on the centrestand. Tie the front brake lever to the handlebar to ensure the bike can't roll forward.
2 On CBF600N/NA/S/SA models remove the side covers (see Chapter 7).
3 Remove the rear wheel (see Chapter 6).
4 Remove the chainguard from the swingarm, noting how it locates **(see illustration)**.
5 Unscrew the brake hose guide screws **(see illustration)**. Displace the brake caliper from the swingarm and tie the assembly up out of the way.
6 Unscrew the nut and withdraw the bolt securing the shock absorber to the swingarm **(see illustration 11.5)**.
7 Slacken the nuts on the right-hand ends of the pivot bracket bolts, counter-holding the bolt heads if necessary **(see illustration)**. Unscrew the swingarm pivot bolt nut and remove the washer **(see illustration)**. Draw the left-hand pivot bracket out slightly.
8 Withdraw the swingarm pivot bolt and manoeuvre the swingarm back out of the frame **(see illustrations)**.
9 Remove the chain slider from the swingarm if necessary, noting the collars **(see illustration)**. If it is badly worn or damaged, it should be replaced with a new one – look for the wear limit arrows on the front (see Chapter 1, Section 1).

Inspection

10 Remove the sleeve from the left-hand

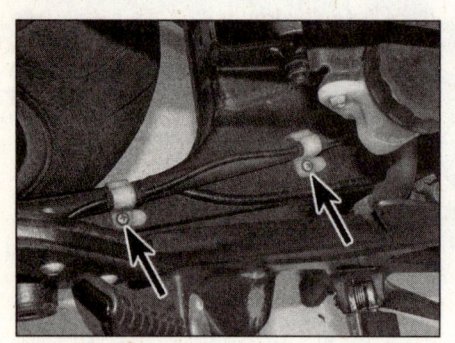

11.13 Depending on your model you may need to displace the hose guide to get a socket extension on the bolt

12.4 Unscrew the bolts (arrowed) and remove the chainguard

12.5 Hose guide screws (arrowed)

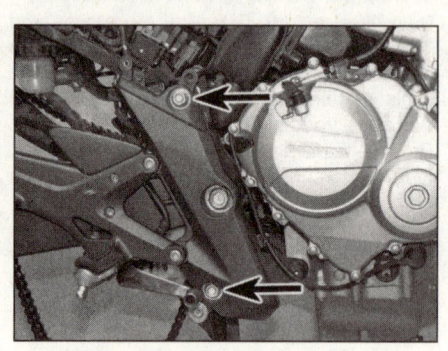

12.7a Slacken the pivot bracket nuts (arrowed)

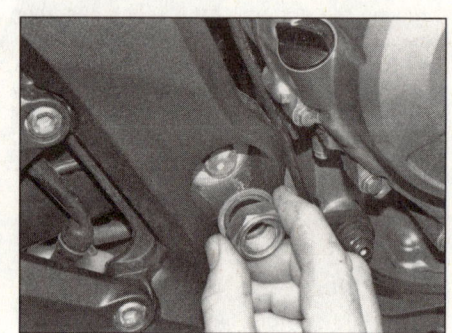

12.7b Unscrew the nut and remove the washer

12.8a Withdraw the bolt . . .

12.8b . . . and remove the swingarm

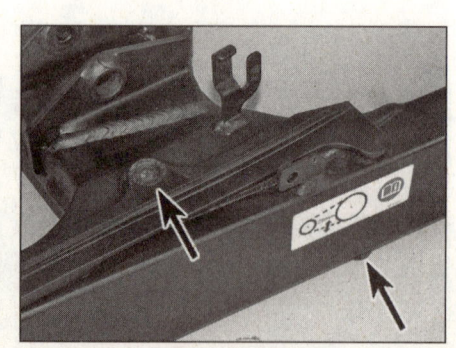

12.9 Chain slider screws (arrowed) – CBF model shown

Frame and suspension 5•25

pivot and the spacers from the right-hand one **(see illustrations)**.

11 Thoroughly clean all pivot components, removing all traces of dirt, corrosion and grease.

12 Check the swingarm closely, looking for obvious signs of wear such as heavy scoring, or for damage such as cracks or distortion.

13 Check the condition of the grease seals and bearings – there are two ball bearings in the right-hand pivot and a needle bearing in the left **(see illustrations)**. Check the ball bearings run smoothly. Fit the sleeve back in the needle bearing and check for play between them. Refer to *Tools and Workshop Tips* (Section 5) in the Reference section for more information on bearings. Inspect all components closely, looking for obvious signs of wear such as heavy scoring, or for damage such as cracks or distortion. Replace worn or damaged components with new ones as required.

14 If required lever out the grease seals using a seal hook or screwdriver **(see illustration)**. Discard them – new ones must be used.

15 Worn bearings can be driven or pressed out of their bores, but note that removal will destroy them – remove the circlip from the right-hand pivot before removing the ball bearings **(see illustration 12.13a)**. New bearings should be obtained before work commences. The new bearings should be pressed or drawn into their bores rather than driven into position. In the absence of a press, a suitable drawbolt tool can be made up as described in *Tools and Workshop Tips* in the Reference section. When fitting the new ball bearings pack them with grease and make sure their marked side faces out and that they are against the seat. Secure them with a new circlip. When fitting the needle bearing make sure the marked side faces out and the set depth of the outer end below the rim of the bore is 5 to 6 mm on CB600F/FA and CBR600F/FA models and 8 to 9 mm on CBF600N/NA/S/SA models.

16 Lubricate the needle bearings, sleeves and seals with the grease specified in Chapter 1.

17 Press the new seals squarely into place, with the marked flat side facing out, and fitting the smaller seal to the inner side of the right-hand pivot **(see illustration)**. Fit the sleeve and spacers – on the right-hand pivot the short spacer fits to the inner side, the long to the outer **(see illustrations 12.10a and b)**.

Installation

18 If removed, fit the chain slider, making sure it locates correctly over the lug at the front, and the mounting bosses fit in the holes **(see illustration)**.

19 Clean the swingarm pivot bolt and smear it with grease.

20 Offer up the swingarm, making sure the drive chain is looped over the front **(see illustration 12.8b)**. Slide the pivot bolt through from the left-hand side **(see illustration 12.8a)**. Push the pivot bracket in.

21 Fit the nut and washer onto the end of the pivot bolt **(see illustration 12.7b)**. Tighten the bracket bolt nuts to the torque setting specified at the beginning of the Chapter, counter-holding the bolt heads if necessary **(see illustration 12.7a)**. Now tighten the swingarm pivot bolt nut to the specified torque. Check the swingarm moves up and down smoothly and freely.

22 Install the remaining components in reverse order. Tighten the shock absorber bolt/nut to the specified torque setting **(see illustration 11.13)**. Make sure the chain guide locates correctly on its inner side **(see illustration or 11.3b)**.

12.10a Remove the sleeve . . .

12.10b . . . and the spacers

12.13a Right-hand pivot ball bearings – a circlip (arrowed) secures them

12.13b Left-hand pivot needle bearing

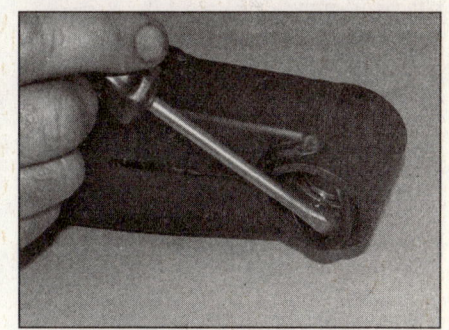

12.14 Lever the seals out

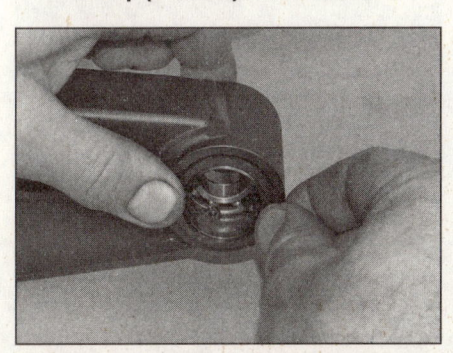

12.17 Press the new seals in so they are flush

12.18 The slot fits over the lug (arrowed)

12.22 Make sure the guard seats correctly on the swingarm

5•26 Frame and suspension

23 Check and adjust the drive chain slack (see Chapter 1). Check the operation of the rear suspension and brake before taking the machine on the road.

13 Suspension adjustment

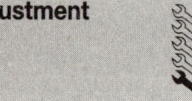

CB600F/FA and CBR600F/FA

Front forks

1 On 2007 and 2008 CB600F/FA models the forks are not adjustable.
2 On 2009-on models the forks have adjustable spring pre-load and rebound damping. Always make sure both forks are set equally.
3 Spring pre-load is adjusted using a 19 mm spanner on the adjuster flats (see illustration) – a spanner should be provided in the toolkit. Turn the adjuster clockwise to increase pre-load and anti-clockwise to decrease it. To set the standard position, turn the adjuster fully anti-clockwise until it stops, then turn it clockwise 8 full turns.
4 Rebound damping is adjusted using a screwdriver in the slot in the top of the damper rod protruding from the pre-load adjuster (see illustration 13.3). Turn it clockwise to increase damping and anti-clockwise to decrease it. To set the standard position, turn the adjuster fully clockwise until it stops, then turn it anti-clockwise 2 turns until the punch mark on the adjuster aligns with the index mark below the directional arrow.

Rear shock absorber

5 On 2007 and 2008 CB600F/FA models the shock absorber has adjustable spring pre-load. On 2009-on models the shock absorber has adjustable spring pre-load and rebound damping.
6 Spring pre-load is adjusted using a suitable C-spanner (one is provided in the toolkit) to turn the spring seat on the bottom of the shock absorber (see illustrations 13.11a and b). There are seven positions. Position 1 is the lowest setting for light loads, position 2 the standard, and position 7 the highest, for heavy loads. Align the setting required with the adjustment stopper.
7 Rebound damping adjustment is made by turning the adjuster on the bottom of the shock absorber on the right-hand side using a flat-bladed screwdriver (see illustration). To increase the damping, turn the adjuster clockwise. To decrease the damping, turn the adjuster anti-clockwise. To set the standard position, turn the adjuster clockwise until it stops, then turn it anti clockwise 1½ turns until the punch mark on the adjuster aligns with the index mark on the shock absorber.

CBF600N/NA/S/SA models

Front forks

8 The front forks have adjustable spring pre-load.
9 Pre-load is adjusted using a screwdriver in the slot in the top of the adjuster protruding from the top bolt (see illustration). Turn it clockwise to increase pre-load and anti-clockwise to decrease it. To set the standard position, turn the adjuster so the third line is level with the top of the top bolt hex.

Rear shock absorber

10 The shock absorber has adjustable spring pre-load.
11 Spring pre-load is adjusted using a suitable C-spanner (one is provided in the toolkit) to turn the spring seat on the bottom of the shock absorber (see illustrations). There are seven positions. Position 1 is the lowest setting for light loads, position 3 the standard, and position 7 the highest, for heavy loads. Align the setting required with the adjustment stopper.

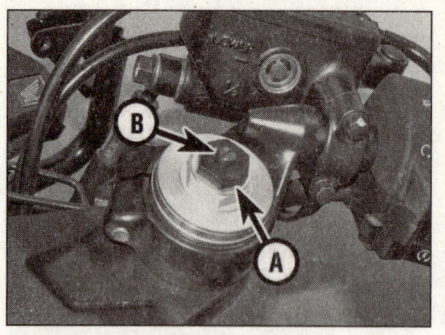

13.3 Spring pre-load adjuster (A), rebound damping adjuster (B)

13.7 Rebound damping adjuster (arrowed)

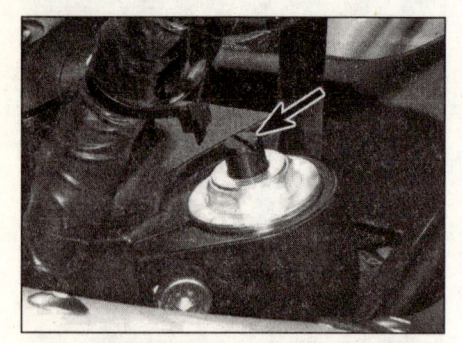

13.9 Spring pre-load adjuster (arrowed)

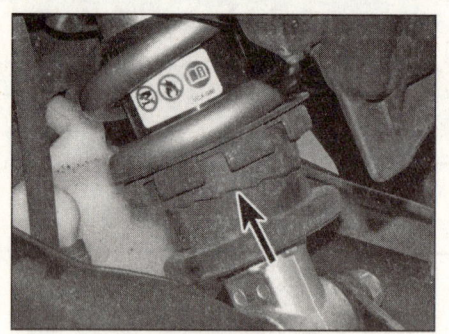

13.11a Spring pre-load adjuster (arrowed) . . .

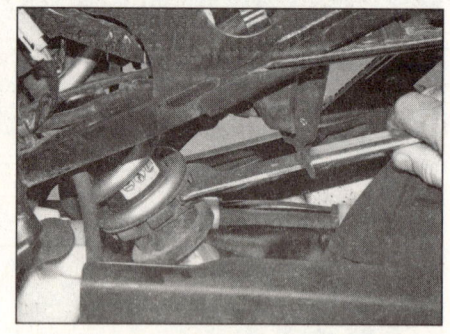

13.11b . . . a C-spanner is provided for adjusting it

Chapter 6
Brakes, wheels and final drive

Contents

	Section number
Brake fluid level check	see *Pre-ride checks*
Brake hoses and fittings	10
Brake light switches	see Chapter 8
Brake pad wear check	see Chapter 1
Brake system bleeding and fluid change	11
Brake system check	see Chapter 1
C-ABS components	14
C-ABS fault diagnosis	13
C-ABS operation	12
Drive chain maintenance	see Chapter 1
Drive chain removal and installation	21
Front brake calipers	3
Front brake discs	4
Front brake master cylinder	5
Front brake pads	2
Front wheel	17

	Section number
General information	1
Rear brake caliper	7
Rear brake disc	8
Rear brake master cylinder	9
Rear brake pads	6
Rear sprocket coupling/rubber dampers	23
Rear wheel	18
Sprockets	22
Tyres	20
Tyre pressure, tread depth and condition	see *Pre-ride checks*
Wheel alignment check	16
Wheel bearing check	see Chapter 1
Wheel bearings	19
Wheel check	see Chapter 1
Wheel inspection and repair	15

Degrees of difficulty

Easy, suitable for novice with little experience	**Fairly easy,** suitable for beginner with some experience	**Fairly difficult,** suitable for competent DIY mechanic	**Difficult,** suitable for experienced DIY mechanic	**Very difficult,** suitable for expert DIY or professional

Specifications

Brake fluid
Brake fluid type .... DOT 4

Front brake calipers
Caliper bore ID
  CB600F, CBR600F and CBF600N/S
    Standard .... 25.400 to 25.450 mm
    Service limit .... 25.460 mm
  CB600FA, CBR600FA and CBF600NA/SA
    Standard .... 22.650 to 22.700 mm
    Service limit .... 22.710 mm
Caliper piston OD
  CB600F, CBR600F and CBF600N/S
    Standard .... 25.318 to 25.368 mm
    Service limit .... 25.310 mm
  CB600FA, CBR600FA and CBF600NA/SA
    Standard .... 22.585 to 22.618 mm
    Service limit .... 22.560 mm

Front brake master cylinder
Master cylinder bore ID
    Standard...12.700 to 12.743 mm
    Service limit ....12.755 mm
Master cylinder piston OD
    Standard...12.657 to 12.684 mm
    Service limit ....12.645 mm

Front brake discs
Disc thickness
    Standard...4.5 mm
    Service limit ....3.5 mm
Disc maximum runout ....0.3 mm

Rear brake caliper
Caliper bore ID
  CB600F and CBR600F
    Standard...30.230 to 30.280 mm
    Service limit ....30.290 mm
  CB600FA, CBR600FA and CBF600N/NA/S/SA
    Standard...38.180 to 38.230 mm
    Service limit ....38.240 mm
Caliper piston OD
  CB600F and CBR600F
    Standard...30.148 to 30.198 mm
    Service limit ....30.140 mm
  CB600FA, CBR600FA and CBF600N/NA/S/SA
    Standard...38.098 to 38.148 mm
    Service limit ....38.090 mm

Rear brake master cylinder
Master cylinder bore ID
  CB600F and CBR600F
    Standard...12.700 to 12.743 mm
    Service limit ....12.755 mm
  CB600FA and CBR600FA
    Standard...17.460 to 17.503 mm
    Service limit ....17.515 mm
  CBF600N/S
    Standard...14.000 to 14.043 mm
    Service limit ....14.055 mm
  CBF600NA/SA
    Standard...15.870 to 15.913 mm
    Service limit ....15.925 mm
Master cylinder piston OD
  CB600F and CBR600F
    Standard...12.657 to 12.684 mm
    Service limit ....12.645 mm
  CB600FA and CBR600FA
    Standard...17.417 to 17.444 mm
    Service limit ....17.405 mm
  CBF600N/S
    Standard...13.954 to 13.984 mm
    Service limit ....13.945 mm
  CBF600NA/SA
    Standard...15.827 to 15.854 mm
    Service limit ....15.815 mm

Rear brake disc
Disc thickness
    Standard...5.0 mm
    Service limit ....4.0 mm
Disc maximum runout ....0.3 mm

ABS system
Wheel speed sensor air gap.................................... 0.2 to 1.2 mm

Wheels
Maximum wheel runout (front and rear)
    Axial (side-to-side) .... 2.0 mm
    Radial (out-of-round) .... 2.0 mm
Maximum axle runout (front and rear) .... 0.2 mm

Tyres
Tyre pressures .... see *Pre-ride* checks
Tyre sizes*
  CB600F/FA and CBR600F/FA
    Front 120/70-ZR17M/C (58W)
    Rear 180/55-ZR17M/C (73W)
  CBF600N/NA/S/SA
    Front 120/70-ZR17M/C (58W)
    Rear 160/60-ZR17M/C (69W)

Refer to the owners handbook or the tyre information label for approved tyre brands.

Final drive
Drive chain slack and lubricant .... see Chapter 1
Drive chain type
  CB600F/FA and CBR600F/FA
    DID DID525VM2-118LE
    REGINA.. REG525ZRPB-118L
  CBF600N/NA/S/SA
    DID DID525VM2-124LE
Joining link pin projection from side plate (unstaked)
  CB600F/FA and CBR600F/FA .... 1.15 to 1.55 mm
  CBF600N/NA/S/SA .... 1.30 to 1.50 mm
Joining link staked ends diameter .... 5.50 to 5.80 mm
Sprocket sizes (No. of teeth)
  Front (engine) sprocket................................... 16
  Rear (wheel) sprocket
    CB600F/FA and CBR600F/FA 43
    CBF600N/NA/S/SA...................................... 42

Torque settings
Brake caliper bleed valves................................... 5.5 Nm
Brake disc bolts
  Front .... 20 Nm
  Rear .... 42 Nm
Brake hose banjo bolts....................................... 34 Nm
Brake pipe nuts .... 14 Nm
Delay valve bolts .... 12 Nm
Footrest bracket bolts .... 37 Nm
Front axle bolt .... 59 Nm
Front axle clamp bolts .... 22 Nm
Front brake caliper mounting bolts .... 30 Nm
Front brake master cylinder clamp bolts .... 12 Nm
Front brake pad retaining pin .... 17 Nm
Front brake pad retaining pin plug .... 2.5 Nm
Front sprocket bolt.. 54 Nm
Front wheel pulse ring screws .... 7 Nm
Proportional control valve bolts .... 12 Nm
Rear axle nut .... 98 Nm
Rear brake caliper mounting bolt/slider pin (CB600FA, CBR600FA,
  and CBF600N/NA/S/SA) .... 22 Nm
Rear brake pad retaining pin .... 17 Nm
Rear brake master cylinder mounting bolts .... 12 Nm
Rear sprocket nuts.. 108 Nm
Rear wheel pulse ring screws............................... 7 Nm
Silencer mounting bolt/nut.................................. 22 Nm

1 General information

All models covered in this manual are fitted with cast alloy wheels designed for tubeless tyres only. Both front and rear brakes are hydraulically operated disc brakes.

CB600F, CBR600F and CBF600N and S models have a conventional braking system with two twin piston sliding calipers acting on 296 mm discs at the front, and one single piston sliding caliper acting on a 240 mm disc at the rear.

CB600FA, CBR600FA and CBF600NA and SA models have a combined anti-lock braking system (C-ABS), with two triple piston sliding calipers acting on 296 mm discs at the front, and one single piston sliding caliper acting on a 240 mm disc at the rear.

C-ABS system

The combined part of the system (C-) links the rear brake with part of the front, actuating the centre piston in the right-hand caliper via a proportional control valve, whenever the pedal is depressed.

The anti-lock part of the system (ABS) prevents the wheels from locking up under hard braking or on uneven road surfaces. A sensor on each wheel transmits information about the speed of rotation to the control unit in the ABS modulator; if the unit senses that a wheel is about to lock, it releases brake pressure to that wheel momentarily, preventing a skid.

Caution: Disc brake components rarely require disassembly. Do not disassemble components unless absolutely necessary. If an hydraulic brake hose is loosened or disconnected, the banjo union sealing washers must be replaced with new ones and the system must be bled upon reassembly. Do not use solvents on internal brake components. Solvents will cause the seals to swell and distort. Use only clean DOT 4 brake fluid for cleaning. Use care when working with brake fluid as it can injure your eyes and it will damage painted surfaces and plastic parts.

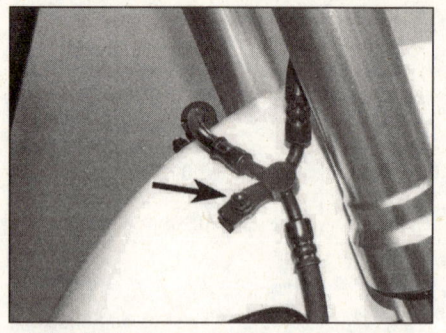

2.1a Brake hose guide nut (arrowed) – standard model

2.1b Brake hose guide bolt (arrowed) – C-ABS model

2 Front brake pads

Note: *Honda recommend using new caliper mounting bolts. This is because the bolts are pre-treated with a locking compound. If they are not available it is possible, however, to clean up the old bolts and reinstall them using a suitable non-permanent thread locking compound that is commercially available.*

Caution: Do not operate the front brake (or either brake on C-ABS models) while a caliper is off the disc.

1 For greater freedom of movement displace the brake hose guides and where fitted the wheel sensor wire from the mudguard as required according to model **(see illustrations)**. Lay some rag over the mudguard to prevent the loose guides scratching it.

2 On CB600F, CBR600F and CBF600N/S models unscrew the pad retaining pin plug **(see illustration)**. Slacken the pad pin. Unscrew the caliper mounting bolts and slide the caliper assembly off the disc **(see illustration)**. Unscrew and remove the pad pin, then remove the pads, noting how they locate **(see illustrations)**.

3 On CB600FA, CBR600FA and CBF600NA/SA models slacken the pad retaining pin **(see illustration)**. Unscrew the caliper mounting bolts and slide the caliper assembly off the

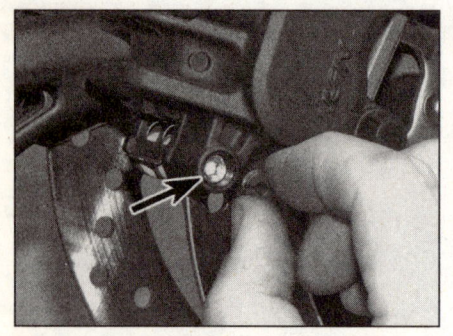

2.2a Unscrew the plug and slacken the pin (arrowed)

2.2b Unscrew the bolts (arrowed) and slide the caliper off

2.2c Remove the pad pin . . .

2.2d . . . then remove the pads

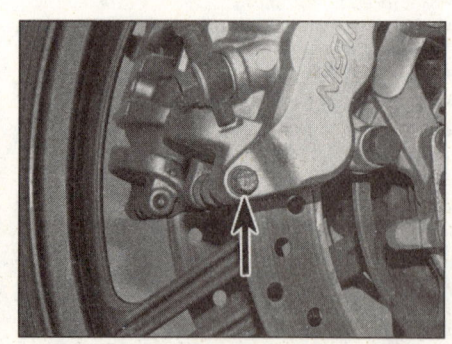

2.3a Slacken the pad pin (arrowed)

Brakes, wheels and final drive 6•5

2.3b Unscrew the bolts (arrowed) and slide the caliper off

2.3c Remove the pad pin . . .

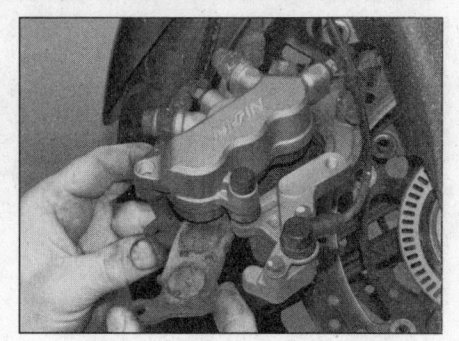

2.3d . . . then remove the pads

disc **(see illustration)**. Unscrew and remove the pad pin, then remove the pads, noting how they locate **(see illustrations)**.

4 Slide the caliper and bracket apart **(see illustrations)**. Clean all old grease off the slider pins. Check the condition of the rubber boots and replace them with new ones if necessary.

5 Where fitted and if required remove the shim from the back of each pad, noting how it fits – note that new pads should come with new shims where applicable, but make sure they do, especially if fitting after-market pads, before discarding the old ones.

6 Inspect the surface of each pad for contamination and check that the friction material has not worn to or beyond its service limit (see Chapter 1, Section 3). If any pad is worn, fouled with oil or grease, or heavily scored or damaged, fit a complete set of new pads. Also check that wear is even across each pad – uneven wear is indicative of a sticking or seized piston (see Steps 7 and 8). **Note:** *It is not possible to degrease the friction material; if the pads are contaminated in any way they must be replaced with new ones.*

7 If the pads are in good condition clean them carefully, using a fine wire brush that is completely free of oil and grease to remove all traces of road dirt and corrosion. Using a pointed instrument, dig out any embedded particles of foreign matter. Spray with a dedicated brake cleaner.

8 Remove the pad spring from the caliper if required, noting which way round it fits **(see illustration 2.12a or b)**. Clean around the exposed section of each piston to remove any dirt or debris that could cause the seals to be damaged. If new pads are being fitted, now push the pistons all the way back into the caliper to create room for them; if the old pads are still serviceable push the pistons in a little way. To push the pistons back use finger pressure or a piece of wood as leverage, or place the old pads back in the caliper and use a metal bar or a screwdriver inserted between them (but take care not to damage the friction surface if the pads are being re-used), or use grips and a piece of wood, with rag or card to protect the caliper body **(see illustration)**. Alternatively obtain a proper piston-pushing tool from a good tool supplier **(see illustration)**. It may be necessary to remove the master cylinder reservoir cover, plate and diaphragm and siphon out some fluid (Section 5). If the pistons are difficult to push back, remove the bleed valve cap, then attach a length of clear hose to the bleed valve and place the open end in a suitable container, then open the valve and try again (see Section 11). Take great care not to draw any air into the system. If in doubt, bleed the brakes afterwards.

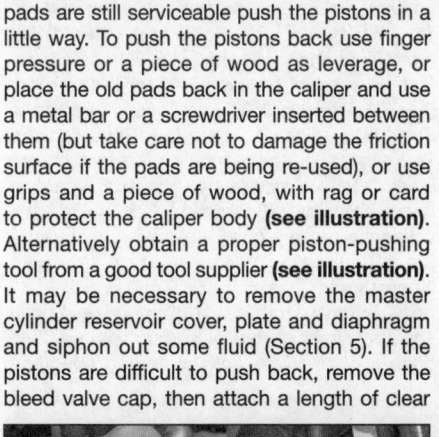

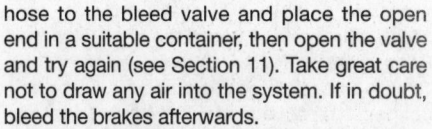

9 If a piston appears seized, first block or hold the other piston(s) using wood or cable-ties, then apply the brake lever and check whether the piston in question moves at all. If it moves out but can't be pushed back in the chances are there is some hidden corrosion stopping it. If it doesn't move at all, or to fully clean and inspect the pistons, disassemble the caliper and overhaul it (see Section 3).

10 Remove all traces of corrosion from the pad pin and check for wear and damage. On CB600FA, CBR600FA and CBF600NA/SA models check the condition of the stopper ring on the pin and replace it with a new one if it is damaged or deformed **(see illustration)**.

2.4a Sliding the caliper and bracket apart – standard model. Clean and check the pins and the boots (arrowed)

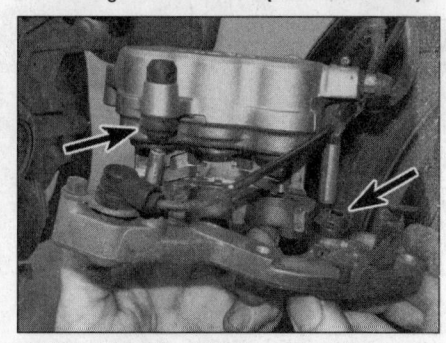

2.4b Sliding the caliper and bracket apart – C-ABS model. Clean and check the pins and the boots (arrowed)

2.8a Press the pistons in as described to make clearance for new pads

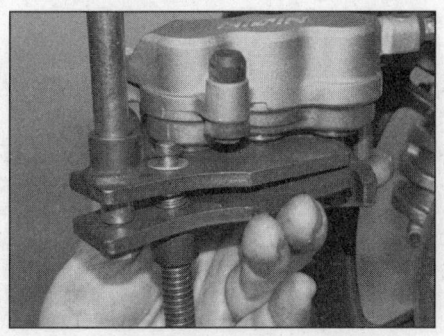

2.8b This is a commercially available piston pushing tool

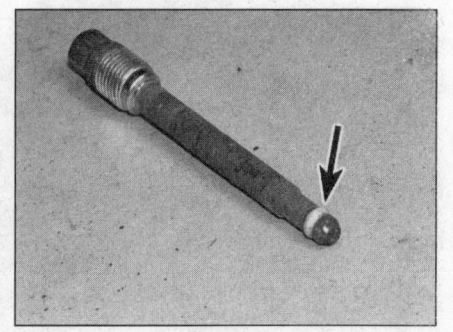

2.10 Check the condition of the stopper ring (arrowed)

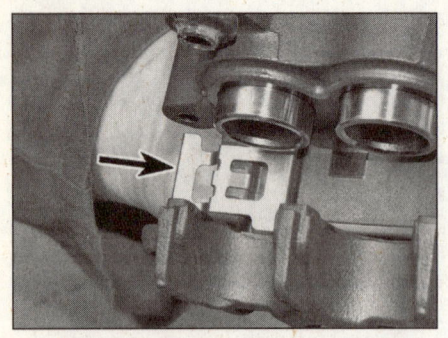

6•6 Brakes, wheels and final drive

2.12a Pad spring (arrowed) – standard models

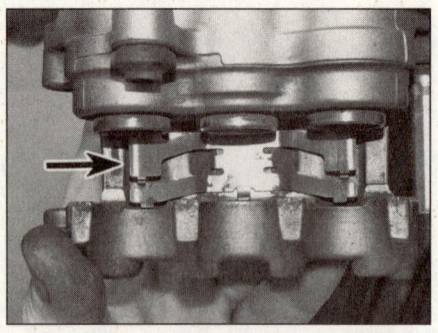

2.12b Pad spring (arrowed) – C-ABS models

2.12c Make sure the guide (arrowed) is clean and correctly fitted – standard model shown

11 Check the condition of the brake disc (see Section 4).

12 Clean the pad spring and fit it into the caliper if removed, making sure it locates correctly **(see illustrations)**. Clean the pad guide on the bracket and check it is correctly fitted **(see illustration)**.

13 Make sure the slider pins are tight. Smear the slider pins and inside the rubber boots with silicone grease. Slide the caliper and bracket together, making sure each boot lip locates correctly in the groove in the pin **(see illustration 2.4a or b)**.

14 Where fitted and if removed fit the shim onto the back of each pad, making sure it locates correctly. Clean the outer face of each shim so it is shiny.

15 On pads without shims lightly smear the back of the pad backing material with copper-based grease, making sure that none gets on the friction material. Also smear the pad pin, but not the stopper ring where fitted.

16 On CB600F, CBR600F and CBF600N/S models fit the pads into the caliper so the friction material on each pad faces the other **(see illustration 2.2d)**, and seat the pads in the guide on the bracket **(see illustration)**. Press them up against the spring to align the holes, then insert the pad pin and tighten it finger-tight **(see illustration 2.2c)**. Slide the caliper assembly onto the disc making sure the pads locate correctly on each side **(see illustration)**. Either fit the new caliper mounting bolts, or clean the threads of the original bolts and apply fresh thread locking compound, then tighten them to the torque setting specified at the beginning of the Chapter. Tighten the pad pin to the torque setting specified at the beginning of this Chapter. Fit the pad pin plug **(see illustration 2.2a)**.

17 On CB600FA, CBR600FA and CBF600NA/SA models apply a smear of silicone grease to the stopper ring on the pad pin **(see illustration 2.10)**. Fit the pads into the caliper so the friction material on each pad faces the other **(see illustration 2.3d)**, and seat the pads in the guide on the bracket **(see illustration)**. Press them up against the spring to align the holes, then insert the pad pin and tighten it finger-tight **(see illustration 2.3c)**. Slide the caliper assembly onto the disc making sure the pads locate correctly on each side **(see illustration)**. Either fit the new caliper mounting bolts, or clean the threads of the original bolts and apply fresh thread locking compound, then tighten them to the torque setting specified at the beginning of the Chapter. Tighten the pad pin to the torque setting specified at the beginning of this Chapter **(see illustration 2.3a)**.

18 Fit the brake hose guides onto the mudguard **(see illustration 2.1a or b)**.

19 Operate the brake lever until the pads contact the disc. On CB600FA, CBR600FA and CBF600NA/SA models also operate the brake pedal until the centre piston in the right-hand caliper contacts the pads. Check the level of fluid in each reservoir and top-up if necessary (see *Pre-ride checks*).

20 Check the operation of the brakes before riding the motorcycle.

2.16a Fit the pads making sure the shaped ends locate correctly in the pad guide

2.16b Slide the caliper onto the disc and fit the bolts

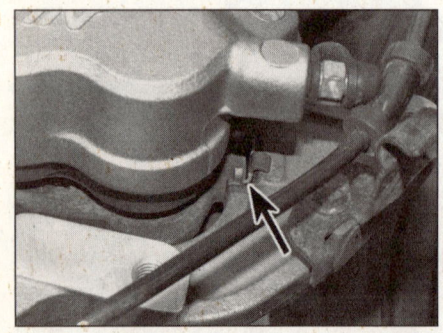

2.17a Fit the pads making sure the shaped ends locate correctly in the pad guide

2.17b Slide the caliper onto the disc and fit the bolts

3 Front brake calipers

⚠️ **Warning:** *Overhaul of the brake calipers must be done in a spotlessly clean work area to avoid contamination and possible failure of the brake hydraulic system components. Do not, under any circumstances, use petroleum-based solvents to clean brake parts. Use clean DOT 4 brake fluid, dedicated brake cleaner or denatured alcohol only, as described. To prevent*

# Brakes, wheels and final drive 6•7

3.2a Brake hose banjo bolt (arrowed) – standard models

3.2b Brake hose banjo bolts (arrowed) – right-hand caliper on C-ABS models

3.2c Seal the banjo using a nut and bolt and the sealing washers

damage from spilled brake fluid, always cover paintwork when working on the braking system.

Note: *If a caliper is in need of an overhaul it is best to drain all old brake fluid from the system, then fill with new fluid after the overhaul (see Section 11).*

Removal

Note: *Honda recommend using new caliper mounting bolts. This is because the bolts are pre-treated with a locking compound. If they are not available it is possible, however, to clean up the old bolts and reinstall them using a suitable non-permanent thread locking compound that is commercially available.*

Note: *If the caliper is being overhauled (usually due to sticking pistons or fluid leaks) read through the entire procedure first and make sure that you have obtained all the new parts required, including some new DOT 4 brake fluid.*

Caution: *Do not operate the front brake (or either brake on C-ABS models) while a caliper is off the disc.*

1 If you just want to displace the calipers for front wheel removal, displace the brake hose guides and where fitted the wheel sensor wire from the mudguard as required according to model **(see illustration 2.1a or b)**. Lay some rag over the mudguard to prevent the loose guides scratching it. Unscrew the caliper mounting bolts and slide the caliper assembly off the disc **(see illustrations 2.2b or 2.3b)**. Tie the front brake calipers and hoses back so that they are out of the way.

2 If the caliper is being completely removed or overhauled, unscrew the brake hose banjo bolt(s) and detach the banjo union(s), noting the alignment with the caliper **(see illustrations)**. If the brake fluid has not been drained seal the banjo unions – one way of doing this is to fit a suitable bolt and nut with the old sealing washers **(see illustration)**. Note that new sealing washers will be required later.

3 If the caliper is being overhauled, follow the procedure for your model in Section 2, Steps 1 to 4, and remove the brake pads – this involves removing the caliper from the disc and sliding the caliper and bracket apart.

Overhaul

4 Clean the exterior of the caliper and the bracket with denatured alcohol or brake system cleaner. Have some clean rag ready to catch any spilled brake fluid.

5 Place the caliper piston-side down and insert some rag or a piece of wood between the pistons and the inner side of the caliper **(see illustration)**.

6 Apply compressed air gradually and progressively, starting with a fairly low pressure, to the fluid passage and allow the pistons to ease out of their bores **(see illustration)**. Make sure the pistons are displaced evenly, using pressure to block one while another moves if necessary.

7 If a piston is stuck in its bore due to corrosion the caliper should be replaced with a new one. Do not try to remove a piston by levering it out or by using pliers or other grips.

8 Mark each piston and the caliper body to ensure that the pistons can be matched to their original bores on reassembly.

9 Remove the dust seals and the piston seals from the bores using a plastic tool to avoid scratching the bores **(see illustrations)**. Discard the seals – new ones must be fitted on reassembly.

10 Clean the pistons and bores with clean brake fluid. If compressed air is available, blow it through the fluid passages to ensure they are clear (make sure it is filtered and unlubricated).

Caution: *Do not, under any circumstances, use a petroleum-based solvent to clean brake parts.*

3.5 Use rag or a piece of wood to protect the pistons and caliper . . .

3.6 . . . then apply compressed air to force the pistons out

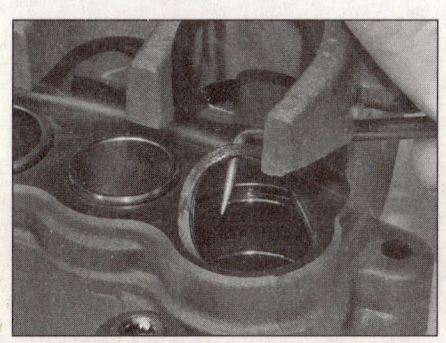

3.9a Remove the dust seal . . .

3.9b . . . and the piston seal

6•8 Brakes, wheels and final drive

3.11 Check the surfaces of the pistons and bores

3.12a Lubricate the new piston seals with brake fluid . . .

3.12b . . . then fit them into their grooves

3.13a Lubricate the new dust seals with silicone grease . . .

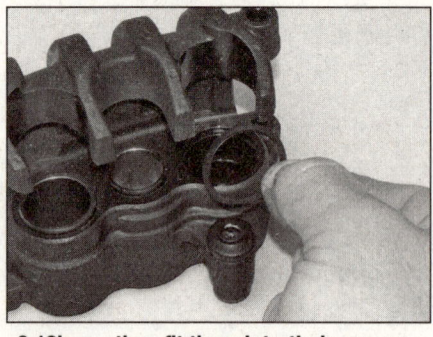

3.13b . . . then fit them into their grooves

11 Inspect the caliper bores and pistons for signs of corrosion, nicks and burrs and loss of plating **(see illustration)**. If surface defects are present, the pistons and/or the caliper assembly must be replaced with new ones. If the necessary measuring equipment is available, compare the dimensions of the caliper bores and pistons to those specified at the beginning of this Chapter, and obtain new pistons or a new caliper if necessary. If one caliper is in poor condition, the other front caliper and the master cylinder should also be checked.

12 Lubricate the new piston seals with clean brake fluid and fit them into the inner grooves in the caliper bores **(see illustrations)**.

13 Lubricate the new dust seals with silicone grease and fit them into the outer grooves in the caliper bores **(see illustrations)**.

14 Lubricate the pistons with clean brake fluid and fit them, closed-end first, into the caliper bores, taking care not to displace the seals **(see illustration)**. Using your thumbs, push the pistons all the way in, making sure they enter the bore squarely.

Installation

15 If the caliper was overhauled refer to Section 2 and if not already done clean and check the pads, pad pin, spring and guide, and the caliper slider pins and rubber boots, then join the caliper and bracket together. Fit the brake pads into the caliper and the caliper onto the disc following the procedure for your model in Section 2.

16 If the caliper was just displaced slide it onto the disc making sure the pads locate correctly on each side **(see illustrations 2.16b or 2.17b)**. Either fit the new caliper mounting bolts, or clean the threads of the original bolts and apply fresh thread locking compound, then tighten them to the torque setting specified at the beginning of the Chapter.

17 If detached, connect the brake hose(s) to the caliper, using new sealing washers on each side of the banjo fitting(s) **(see illustration)**. Align the fittings as noted on removal **(see illustration 3.2a or b)**. Tighten the banjo bolts to the specified torque setting.

18 Secure the brake hoses and wiring on the mudguard as required according to model **(see illustration 2.1a or b)**.

19 Refer to Section 11 and fill and/or bleed the system as required.

20 Operate the brake lever until the pads contact the disc. On CB600FA, CBR600FA and CBF600NA/SA models also operate the brake pedal until the centre piston in the

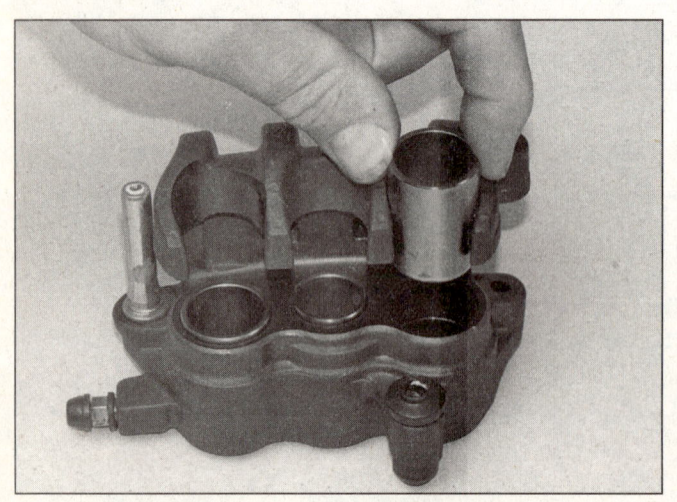

3.14 Fit the pistons and push them all the way in

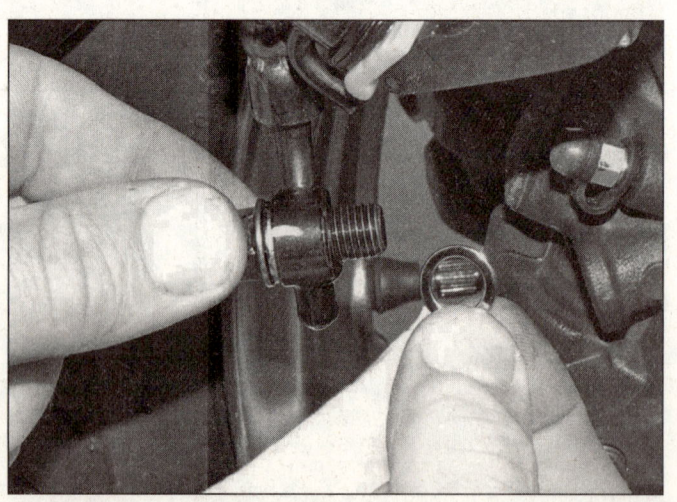

3.17 Use a new sealing washer on each side of the banjo union

Brakes, wheels and final drive 6•9

right-hand caliper contacts the pads. Check the level of fluid in each reservoir and top-up if necessary (see *Pre-ride checks*).

21 Check that there are no fluid leaks and test the operation of the brakes before riding the motorcycle.

4 Front brake discs

Inspection

1 Inspect the surface of the disc for score marks and other damage. Light scratches are normal after use and won't affect brake operation, but deep grooves and heavy score marks will reduce braking efficiency and accelerate pad wear. If a disc is badly grooved it must be replaced with a new one.

2 The disc must not be allowed to wear down to a thickness less than the service limit listed in this Chapter's Specifications. The minimum thickness is also stamped on the disc **(see illustration)**. Check the thickness of the disc in the middle of the pad contact area using a micrometer **(see illustration)** – do not measure across the rim of the disc with a ruler. Replace the disc with a new one if necessary.

3 To check if the disc is warped, position the bike on an auxiliary stand with the front wheel raised off the ground (on CBF600N/NA/S/SA models use the bike's centrestand). Mount a dial gauge to the fork leg, with the gauge plunger touching the surface of the disc about 10 mm from its outer edge **(see illustration)**. Rotate the wheel and watch the gauge needle, comparing the reading with the limit listed in the Specifications at the beginning of this Chapter. If the runout is greater than the service limit, check the wheel bearings for play (see Chapter 1). If the bearings are worn, install new ones (see Section 19) and repeat this check. If the disc runout is still excessive, remove the disc (Steps 4 and 5) and check for corrosion where it seats on the hub and clean it up if necessary. You can also try moving the disc around the wheel one bolt hole at a time and after each movement rechecking for runout. In most cases a new disc will have to be fitted.

Removal

Note: *Honda recommend using new disc mounting bolts. This is because the bolts are pre-treated with a locking compound. If they are not available it is possible, however, to clean up the old bolts and reinstall them using a suitable non-permanent thread locking compound that is commercially available.*

4 Remove the wheel (see Section 17). On CB600FA, CBR600FA and CBF600NA/SA models remove the pulse ring from the right-hand side of the wheel (see Section 14).

Caution: Don't lay the wheel down and allow it to rest on either disc – the disc could become warped. Set the wheel on

4.2a The minimum thickness is marked on the disc

4.2b Check the thickness using a micrometer

4.3 Checking disc runout with a dial gauge

4.5 Brake disc bolts (arrowed)

wood blocks so the wheel rim supports the weight of the wheel.

5 If you are not replacing the disc with a new one, mark the relationship of the disc to the wheel, so it can be installed in the same position and on the same side as originally fitted. Unscrew the disc bolts, loosening them evenly and a little at a time in a criss-cross pattern to avoid distorting the disc, then remove the disc **(see illustration)**.

Installation

6 Before fitting the disc, make sure there is no dirt or corrosion where the disc seats on the hub. If the disc does not sit flat when it is bolted down, it will appear to be warped when checked or when the front brake is used.

7 Fit the disc on the wheel with its marked side facing out, aligning the previously applied matchmarks (if you're reinstalling the original disc), and making sure the arrow points in the direction of normal rotation.

8 Either fit the new bolts, or clean the threads of the original bolts and apply fresh thread locking compound, and tighten them evenly and a little at a time in a criss-cross pattern to the torque setting specified at the beginning of this Chapter. Clean the disc using acetone or brake system cleaner. If a new disc has been installed, remove any protective coating from its working surfaces and fit new brake pads.

9 On CB600FA, CBR600FA and CBF600NA/SA models fit the pulse ring onto the right-hand side of the wheel (see Section 14). Install the front wheel (see Section 17).

10 Operate the brake lever until the pads contact the disc. On CB600FA, CBR600FA and CBF600NA/SA models also operate the brake pedal until the centre piston in the right-hand caliper contacts the pads. Check the level of fluid in each reservoir and top-up if necessary (see *Pre-ride checks*).

11 Check the operation of the brakes before riding the motorcycle.

5 Front brake master cylinder

Warning: Overhaul must be done in a spotlessly clean work area to avoid contamination and possible failure of the brake hydraulic system components. Do not, under any circumstances, use petroleum-based solvents to clean brake parts. Use clean DOT 4 brake fluid, dedicated brake cleaner or denatured alcohol only, as described. To prevent damage from spilled brake fluid, always cover paintwork when working on the braking system.

Note: *If the master cylinder is in need of an overhaul it is best to drain all old brake fluid from the system, then fill with new fluid after the overhaul (see Section 11).*

Removal

Note: *If the master cylinder is being overhauled (usually due to sticking or poor action, or fluid leaks) read through the entire procedure first and make sure that you have obtained all the new parts required, including some new DOT 4 brake fluid.*

6•10 Brakes, wheels and final drive

5.1 Disconnect the brake light switch wires (arrowed)

5.2 Unscrew the bolts (arrowed) and remove the master cylinder and its clamp

5.4 Slacken the cover screws

1 Disconnect the brake light switch wiring connectors **(see illustration)**. On CB600F/FA and CBF600N/NA models remove the mirror (see Chapter 7).

2 If the master cylinder is just being displaced unscrew the clamp bolts and remove the back of the clamp, noting how it fits, then cover the master cylinder and reservoir in rag and position it clear of the handlebar **(see illustration)**. Ensure no strain is placed on the hydraulic hose. Keep the reservoir upright to prevent air entering the system.

3 If the master cylinder is being overhauled, remove the brake lever (see Chapter 5).

4 If the brake fluid wasn't drained, slacken the reservoir cover screws **(see illustration)**.

5 Unscrew the brake hose banjo bolt and detach the banjo union, noting its alignment with the master cylinder **(see illustration)**. If the brake fluid has not been drained seal the banjo unions – one way of doing this is to fit a suitable bolt and nut with the old sealing washers **(see illustration 3.2c)**. Note that new sealing washers will be required later.

6 Unscrew the master cylinder clamp bolts and remove the back of the clamp, noting how it fits, then lift the master cylinder away from the handlebar **(see illustration 5.2)**.

7 Remove the reservoir cover, diaphragm plate and the diaphragm. If the brake fluid wasn't drained tip the fluid from the master cylinder and reservoir into a suitable container. Wipe any remaining fluid out of the reservoir with a clean rag.

8 If required, undo the screw securing the brake light switch to the bottom of the master cylinder and remove the switch.

Overhaul

9 Remove the rubber boot from the master cylinder **(see illustration)**. Depress the piston and use circlip pliers to remove the circlip, then slide out the piston assembly and spring, noting how they fit **(see illustrations)**. If they are difficult to remove, apply low pressure compressed air to the brake fluid outlet. Lay the parts out in the proper order to prevent confusion during reassembly.

10 Clean the master cylinder and reservoir with clean brake fluid. If compressed air is available, blow it through the fluid galleries to ensure they are clear (make sure the air is filtered and unlubricated).

Caution: Do not, under any circumstances, use a petroleum-based solvent to clean brake parts.

11 Check the master cylinder bore for corrosion, scratches, nicks and score marks. If the necessary measuring equipment is available, compare the dimensions of the piston and bore to those given in the Specifications at the beginning of this Chapter. If damage or wear is evident, the master cylinder must be replaced with a new one. If the master cylinder is in poor condition, then the calipers should be checked as well.

12 The dust boot, circlip, piston and its cup and seal, and the spring are all included in a master cylinder rebuild kit, and all other components are available individually. Use all of the new parts, regardless of the apparent condition of the old ones. Lubricate the master cylinder bore with new brake fluid.

13 Smear the cup and seal with new brake fluid and if not already in place fit them into their grooves in the piston so their wider ends will fit into the master cylinder first **(see illustration)**.

14 Fit the spring onto the piston (see

5.5 Brake hose banjo bolt (arrowed)

5.9a Remove the boot from the end of the master cylinder piston . . .

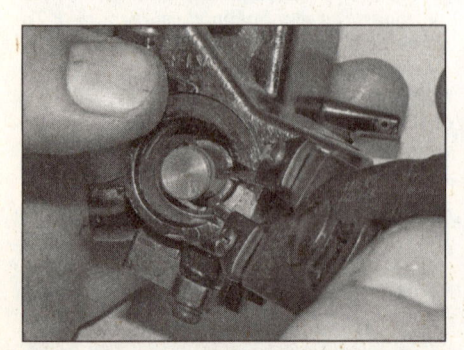

5.9b . . . then depress the piston, remove the circlip . . .

5.9c . . . and draw out the piston and spring

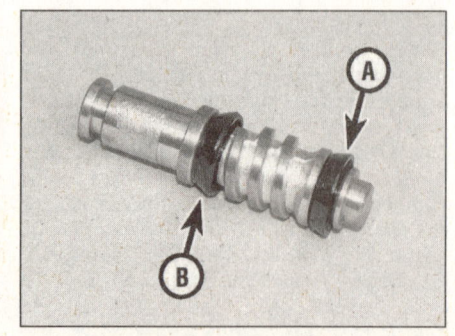

5.13 Make sure the cup (A) and seal (B) are correctly installed

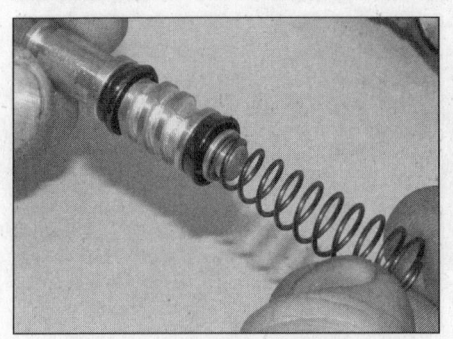

Brakes, wheels and final drive 6•11

5.14a Fit the spring onto the piston

5.14b Fit the assembly into the cylinder . . .

5.14c . . . making sure the lips do not turn inside out

5.14d Fit the circlip . . .

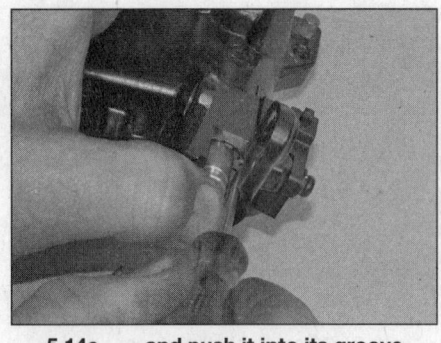

5.14e . . . and push it into its groove

5.15a Fit the rubber boot . . .

illustration). Lubricate the piston, cup and seal with clean brake fluid and slide the spring and piston assembly into the master cylinder. Make sure the lips on the cup and seal do not turn inside out. Push the piston in to compress the spring and fit the new circlip, making sure it locates in the groove (see illustrations).

15 Smear the outer end of the piston and the inside of the boot with silicone grease. Carefully push the wide rim of the boot onto its seat in the master cylinder and locate the narrow end lips in the groove in the piston (see illustrations).

16 Inspect the reservoir diaphragm and fit a new one if it is damaged or deteriorated.

Installation

17 If removed, fit the brake light switch onto the bottom of the master cylinder, making sure the pin locates in the hole, and tighten the screw.

18 Attach the master cylinder to the handlebar, aligning the clamp joint with the punch mark on the top of the handlebar, then fit the back of the clamp with its UP mark facing up (see illustration). Tighten the upper bolt to the torque setting specified at the beginning of this Chapter, followed by the lower bolt.

19 If detached connect the brake hose to the master cylinder, using new sealing washers on each side of the banjo fitting. Align the hose as noted on removal (see illustration 5.5). Tighten the banjo bolt to the torque setting specified at the beginning of this Chapter.

20 Install the brake lever (see Chapter 5).

21 Connect the brake light switch wiring (see illustration 5.1). On CB600F/FA and CBF600N/NA models install the mirror (see Chapter 7).

22 Refer to Section 11 and fill and/or bleed the system as required. Check that there are no fluid leaks and test the operation of the brakes before riding the motorcycle.

6 Rear brake pads

Caution: *Do not operate the brake pedal with the pads removed or the caliper off the disc.*

Note: *On CB600FA, CBR600FA and CBF600N/NA/S/SA models Honda recommend using new caliper mounting bolts. This is because the bolts are pre-treated with a locking compound. If they are not available it is possible, however, to clean up the old bolts and reinstall them using a suitable non-permanent thread locking compound that is commercially available.*

1 Push the caliper against the disc, as far as it will go if new pads are being fitted so the piston is pushed all the way back into the caliper to create room for them (see illustration). It may

5.15b . . . locating it as shown

5.18 Align the mating surface with the punch mark (arrowed)

6.1 Push the caliper against the disc to force the piston in

6•12 Brakes, wheels and final drive

6.3a Unscrew the pin (arrowed) . . .

6.3b . . . and remove the pads

6.4a Slacken the pin (A) and unscrew the bolt (B)

6.4b Remove the pin . . .

6.4c . . . then pivot the caliper up and remove the pads

be necessary to remove the master cylinder reservoir cover, plate and diaphragm and siphon out some fluid (see Section 9). If the piston is difficult to push back, remove the bleed valve cap, then attach a length of clear hose to the bleed valve and place the open end in a suitable container, then open the valve and try again (see Section 11). Take great care not to draw any air into the system. If in doubt, bleed the brakes afterwards.

2 If the caliper is difficult to push in the chances are there is some hidden corrosion stopping it. If it doesn't move at all, or to fully clean and inspect the piston, remove the caliper and overhaul it (see Section 7).

3 On CB600F and CBR600F models unscrew and remove the pad pin, then draw the pads out (see illustrations).

4 On CB600FA, CBR600FA and CBF600N/NA/S/SA models slacken the pad retaining pin (see illustration). Unscrew the caliper rear mounting bolt/slider pin. Unscrew the retaining pin then pivot the back of the caliper up off the disc and remove the pads, noting how they fit (see illustrations).

5 Where fitted and if required remove the shim from the back of each pad, noting how it fits (see illustration) – note that new pads should come with new shims where applicable, but make sure they do, especially if fitting after-market pads, before discarding the old ones.

6 Inspect the surface of each pad for contamination and check that the friction material has not worn beyond its service limit (see Chapter 1, Section 3). If either pad is worn, is fouled with oil or grease, or heavily scored or damaged, fit a set of new pads. **Note:** *It is not possible to degrease the friction material; if the pads are contaminated in any way they must be replaced with new ones.*

7 If the pads are in good condition clean them carefully, using a fine wire brush that is completely free of oil and grease to remove all traces of road dirt and corrosion. Using a pointed instrument, dig out any embedded particles of foreign matter. Spray with a dedicated brake cleaner to remove any dust.

8 Remove all traces of corrosion from the pad pin and check it for wear and damage. Check the condition of the stopper ring on the pin and replace it with a new one if it is damaged or deformed (see illustration 2.10).

9 Check the condition of the brake disc (see Section 8).

10 Where fitted and if removed fit the shim onto the back of each pad, making sure it locates correctly (see illustration 6.5). Clean the outer face of each shim so it is shiny.

11 On pads without shims lightly smear the back of the pad backing material with copper-based grease, making sure that none gets on the friction material. Also smear the pad pin, but not the stopper ring.

12 Apply a smear of silicone grease to the stopper ring on the pad pin (see illustration 2.10).

13 On CB600F and CBR600F models fit the pads into the caliper so the friction material on each pad faces the other (see illustration 6.3b), and seat the pads in the guide on the bracket (see illustration). Press them up against the spring to align the holes, then insert the pad pin and tighten it to the torque setting specified at the beginning of this Chapter (see illustration).

14 On CB600FA, CBR600FA and CBF600N/NA/S/SA models fit the pads so the friction material on each pad faces the other (see

6.5 Remove the shim from the back if required

6.13a Make sure the pads seat correctly against the guide . . .

6.13b . . . then press them up against the spring and insert the pin

Brakes, wheels and final drive 6•13

6.14a Make sure the pads seat correctly against the guide

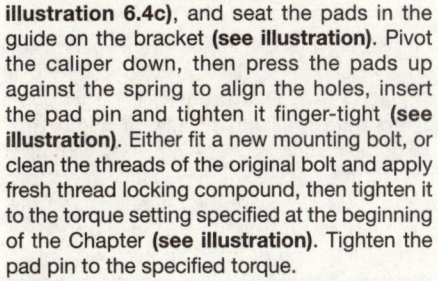

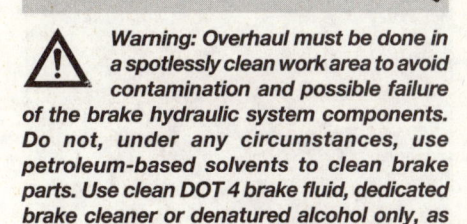

6.14b Press the pads up against the spring and insert the pin

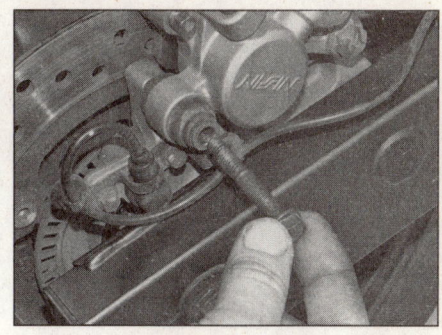

6.14c Fit the bolt and tighten to the specified torque

illustration 6.4c), and seat the pads in the guide on the bracket **(see illustration)**. Pivot the caliper down, then press the pads up against the spring to align the holes, insert the pad pin and tighten it finger-tight **(see illustration)**. Either fit a new mounting bolt, or clean the threads of the original bolt and apply fresh thread locking compound, then tighten it to the torque setting specified at the beginning of the Chapter **(see illustration)**. Tighten the pad pin to the specified torque.

15 Operate the brake pedal until the pads contact the disc. Check the level of fluid in each reservoir and top-up if necessary (see *Pre-ride checks*).

16 Check the operation of the brakes before riding the motorcycle.

7 Rear brake caliper

⚠ **Warning:** *Overhaul must be done in a spotlessly clean work area to avoid contamination and possible failure of the brake hydraulic system components. Do not, under any circumstances, use petroleum-based solvents to clean brake parts. Use clean DOT 4 brake fluid, dedicated brake cleaner or denatured alcohol only, as described. To prevent damage from spilled brake fluid, always cover paintwork when working on the braking system.*

Note: *If the caliper is in need of an overhaul it is best to drain all old brake fluid from the system, then fill with new fluid after the overhaul (see Section 11).*

Removal

Note: *On CB600FA, CBR600FA and CBF600N/NA/S/SA models Honda recommend using new caliper mounting bolts. This is because the bolts are pre-treated with a locking compound. If they are not available it is possible, however, to clean up the old bolts and reinstall them using a suitable non-permanent thread locking compound that is commercially available.*

Note: *If the caliper is being overhauled (usually due to a sticking piston or fluid leak) read through the entire procedure first and make sure that you have obtained all the new parts required, including some new DOT 4 brake fluid.*

Caution: *Do not operate the brake pedal while the caliper is off the disc.*

1 If the caliper is being completely removed or overhauled, unscrew the brake hose banjo bolt and detach the banjo union, noting its alignment with the caliper **(see illustration)**. If the brake fluid has not been drained seal the banjo union – one way of doing this is to fit a suitable bolt and nut with the old sealing washers **(see illustration 3.2c)**. Note that new sealing washers will be required later.

2 Remove the brake pads (see Section 6).

3 On CB600F and CBR600F models remove the rear wheel (see Section 18). Slide the caliper and bracket apart **(see illustration)**.

4 On CB600FA, CBR600FA and CBF600N/NA/S/SA models, if the brake hose has been detached pivot the caliper up and slide it off the bracket. If the hose has not been detached, or if you want to remove the caliper bracket, displace the wheel sensor (see Section 14), then remove the rear wheel (see Section 18), displace the bracket from the swingarm, noting how it locates, and if the hose has not been detached slide the caliper and bracket apart **(see illustration)**.

7.1 Brake hose banjo bolt (arrowed)

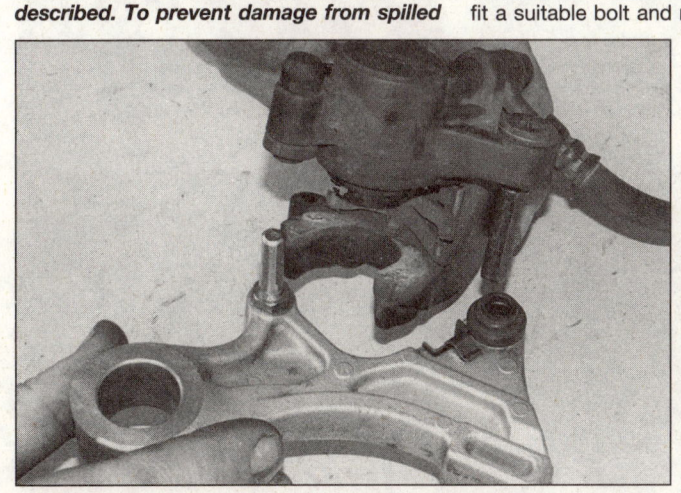

7.3 Slide the caliper and bracket apart – CB600F and CBR600F models

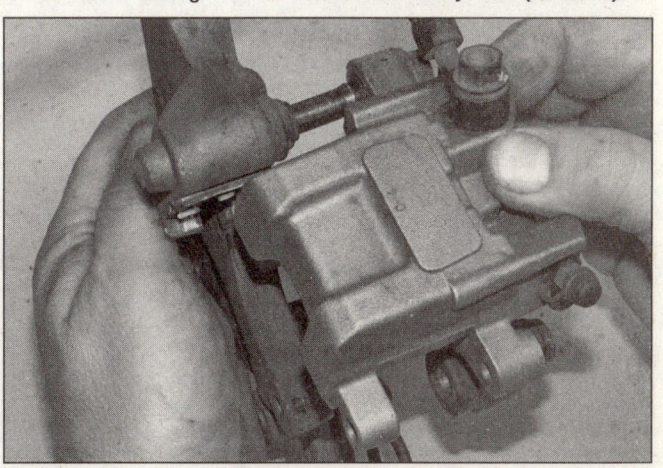

7.4 Slide the caliper and bracket apart – CB600FA, CBR600FA and CBF models

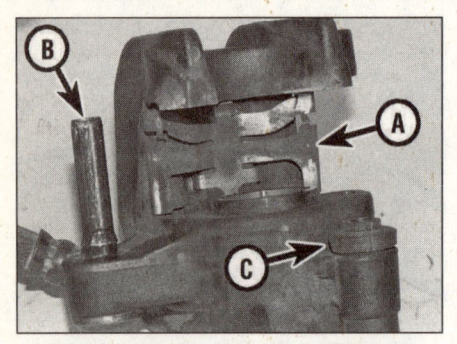

6•14 Brakes, wheels and final drive

7.5a Pad spring (A), slide pin (B) and rubber boot (C) – CB600F and CBR600F models

7.5b Pad spring (arrowed) – CB600FA, CBR600FA and CBF models

7.5c Pad guide (A), slider pin (B) and rubber boot (C) – CB600F and CBR600F models

5 Remove the pad spring from the caliper and the guide from the bracket if required **(see illustrations)**. Clean all old grease off the slider pins and rubber boots. Check the condition of the rubber boots and replace them with new ones if necessary. Note the sleeve in the caliper boot on CB600FA, CBR600FA and CBF600N/NA/S/SA models.

Overhaul

6 Clean the exterior of the caliper with denatured alcohol or brake system cleaner. Have some clean rag ready to catch any spilled brake fluid.

7 Place the caliper piston-side down and insert some rag or a piece of wood between the piston and the inner side of the caliper. Apply compressed air gradually and progressively, starting with a fairly low pressure, to the fluid passage and allow the piston to ease out of the bore, controlling it with hand pressure on the caliper **(see illustrations)**.

8 If the piston is stuck in its bore due to corrosion the caliper should be replaced with a new one. Do not try to remove the piston by levering it out or by using pliers or other grips.

9 Remove the dust seal and the piston seal from the piston bore using a plastic tool to avoid scratching **(see illustration)**. Discard the seals as new ones must be fitted on reassembly.

10 Clean the piston and bore with clean brake fluid. If compressed air is available, blow it through the fluid passages to ensure they are clear (make sure it is filtered and unlubricated).

Caution: Do not, under any circumstances, use a petroleum-based solvent to clean brake parts.

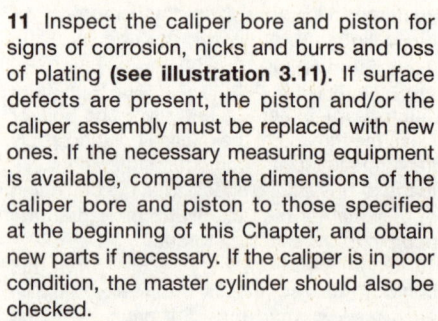

11 Inspect the caliper bore and piston for signs of corrosion, nicks and burrs and loss of plating **(see illustration 3.11)**. If surface defects are present, the piston and/or the caliper assembly must be replaced with new ones. If the necessary measuring equipment is available, compare the dimensions of the caliper bore and piston to those specified at the beginning of this Chapter, and obtain new parts if necessary. If the caliper is in poor condition, the master cylinder should also be checked.

12 Lubricate the new piston seal with clean brake fluid and fit it into the inner groove in the caliper bore **(see illustrations)**.

13 Lubricate the new dust seal with silicone grease and fit it into the outer groove in the caliper bore **(see illustration)**.

14 Lubricate the piston with clean brake fluid

7.7a Use compressed air to force the piston out . . .

7.7b . . . and remove it

7.9 Remove the seals

7.12a Lubricate the new piston seal with brake fluid . . .

7.12b . . . then fit it into the lower groove

7.13 Lubricate the new dust seal with silicone grease and fit it into the upper groove

Brakes, wheels and final drive 6•15

7.14a Fit the piston . . .

7.14b . . . and push it all the way in

and fit it, closed-end first, into the caliper bore, taking care not to displace the seals **(see illustration)**. Using your thumbs, push the piston all the way in, making sure it enters the bore squarely **(see illustration)**.

Installation

15 If the pad spring was removed, make sure it is clean then fit it into the caliper, making sure it locates correctly **(see illustration 7.5a or b)**. Make sure the pad guide on the bracket is clean and correctly fitted **(see illustration 7.5c)**. Make sure the slider pins are tight. Smear the slider pins and inside the rubber boots with silicone grease. On CB600FA, CBR600FA and CBF600N/NA/S/SA models make sure the sleeve is in the caliper boot

16 On CB600F and CBR600F models slide the caliper and bracket together, making sure each boot lip locates correctly in the groove in the pin **(see illustration 7.3)**. Install the wheel (see Section 18).

17 On CB600FA, CBR600FA and CBF600N/NA/S/SA models, if the hose was not detached slide the caliper onto the bracket and locate the bracket on the swingarm, then install the wheel (see Section 18) and the wheel sensor (see Section 14). If the hose was detached and the bracket was removed locate the bracket on the swingarm, then install the wheel (see Section 18) and the wheel sensor (see Section 14). Slide the caliper onto the bracket.

18 If detached connect the brake hose to the caliper, using new sealing washers on each side of the banjo fitting **(see illustration 3.17)**. Align the fitting as noted on removal **(see illustration 7.1)**. Tighten the banjo bolt to the specified torque setting.

19 Install the brake pads (see Section 6).

20 Refer to Section 11 and fill and/or bleed the system as required. Check that there are no fluid leaks and test the operation of the brakes before riding the motorcycle.

8 Rear brake disc

Inspection

1 Refer to Section 4 of this Chapter, noting that the dial gauge should be attached to the swingarm.

Removal

Note: *Honda recommend using new disc mounting bolts. This is because the bolts are pre-treated with a locking compound. It is possible, however, to clean up the old bolts and reinstall them using a suitable non-permanent thread locking compound that is commercially available.*

2 Remove the rear wheel (see Section 18).

3 On CB600FA, CBR600FA and CBF600NA/SA models remove the pulse ring from the wheel (see Section 14).

4 If you are not replacing the disc with a new one, mark the relationship of the disc to the wheel or stub axle so it can be installed in the same position. Unscrew the disc bolts, loosening them evenly and a little at a time in a criss-cross pattern to avoid distorting the disc, then remove the disc **(see illustration)**.

Installation

5 Before fitting the disc, make sure there is no dirt or corrosion where the disc seats on the hub. If the disc does not sit flat when it is bolted down, it will appear to be warped when checked or when the rear brake is used.

6 Fit the disc on the wheel with its marked side facing out, aligning the previously applied matchmarks (if you're reinstalling the original disc).

7 Either fit the new bolts, or clean the threads of the original bolts and apply fresh thread locking compound. Tighten the bolts evenly and a little at a time in a criss-cross pattern to the torque setting specified at the beginning of this Chapter. Clean the disc using acetone or brake system cleaner. If a new disc has been installed, remove any protective coating from its working surfaces and fit new brake pads.

8 On CB600FA, CBR600FA and CBF600NA/SA models fit the pulse ring onto the wheel (see Section 14).

9 Install the rear wheel (see Section 18).

10 Operate the brake pedal several times to bring the pads into contact with the disc. Check the operation of the brakes before riding the motorcycle.

9 Rear brake master cylinder

⚠ **Warning: Overhaul must be done in a spotlessly clean work area to avoid contamination and possible failure of the brake hydraulic system components. Do not, under any circumstances, use petroleum-based solvents to clean brake parts. Use clean DOT 4 brake fluid, dedicated brake cleaner or denatured alcohol only, as described. To prevent damage from spilled brake fluid, always cover paintwork when working on the braking system.**

Note: *If the master cylinder is in need of an overhaul it is best to drain all old brake fluid from the system, then fill with new fluid after the overhaul (see Section 11).*

Removal

Note: *If the master cylinder is being overhauled (usually due to sticking or poor action, or fluid leaks) read through the entire procedure first and make sure that you have obtained all the new parts required, including some new DOT 4 brake fluid.*

1 On CB600F/FA and CBR600F/FA models remove the right-hand side cover (see Chapter 7).

2 Unscrew the reservoir bolt and displace the reservoir **(see illustration)**.

8.4 Rear brake disc bolts (arrowed)

9.2 Unscrew the reservoir bolt

6•16 Brakes, wheels and final drive

9.3a Brake hose banjo bolt (arrowed) – CB and CBR

9.3b Brake hose banjo bolt (arrowed) – CBF

9.4 Unscrew the bolts (arrowed) and displace the bracket

9.5 Straighten and remove the split pin

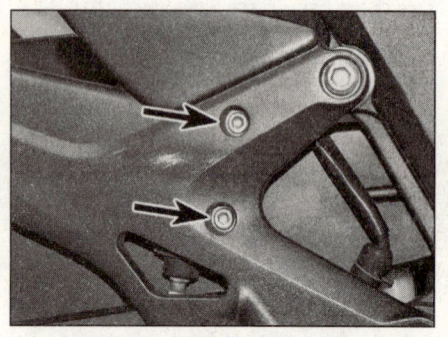

9.6a Unscrew the bolts (arrowed – CBF shown), displace the master cylinder . . .

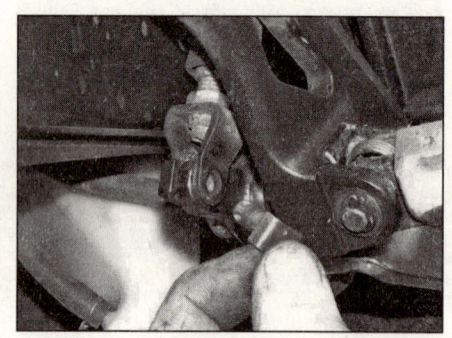

9.6b . . . and withdraw the clevis pin

3 Unscrew the brake hose banjo bolt and detach the banjo union, noting its alignment with the master cylinder **(see illustrations)**. If the brake fluid has not been drained seal the banjo unions – one way of doing this is to fit a suitable bolt and nut with the old sealing washers **(see illustration 3.2c)**. Note that new sealing washers will be required later.

4 On CB600F/FA and CBR600F/FA models unscrew the nut on the silencer mounting bolt, then withdraw the bolt, noting the washer **(see illustration)**. Unscrew the footrest bracket bolts and displace the bracket so you have access to the back of it – take care not to strain the brake light switch wiring.

5 Straighten the ends of the split pin and withdraw it from the master cylinder pushrod clevis pin **(see illustration)**.

6 Unscrew the master cylinder bolts and lower it until the clevis pin is clear of the bracket, then withdraw the pin, detach the pushrod from the pedal and remove the master cylinder along with the reservoir **(see illustrations)**.

Overhaul

7 If the system wasn't drained undo the reservoir cap and remove the diaphragm plate and diaphragm, and tip the fluid out. Release the clip securing the reservoir hose to the union on the master cylinder and detach the hose, being prepared to catch any residual fluid **(see illustration)**.

8 If required, undo the reservoir hose union screw and detach it from the master cylinder **(see illustration)**. Remove the O-ring – a new one must be used. Check the reservoir hose for cracks or splits and replace it with a new one if necessary.

9 If required (doing so will give extra clearance for your circlip pliers in the next step), note how far the clevis is threaded up the pushrod, then slacken its locknut and thread it off, followed by the locknut.

10 Dislodge the rubber dust boot from the base of the master cylinder and from around the pushrod, noting how it locates **(see illustration)**. Push the pushrod in and, using circlip pliers, remove the circlip from its

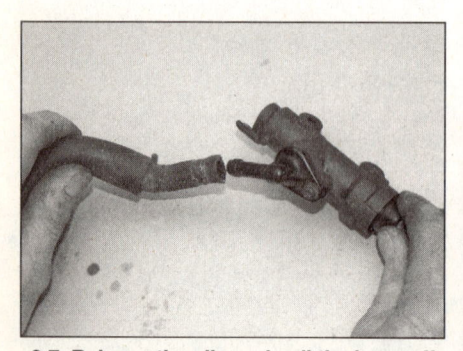

9.7 Release the clip and pull the hose off its union

9.8 Undo the screw and remove the union

9.10a Remove the rubber boot . . .

Brakes, wheels and final drive 6•17

9.10b . . . then release the circlip . . .

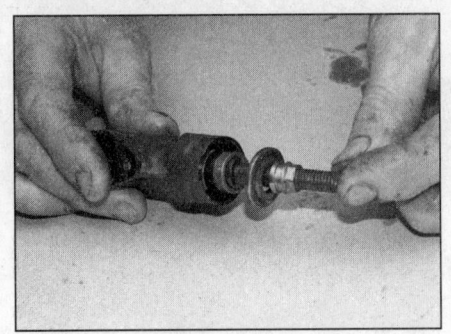

9.10c . . . and remove the pushrod, piston and spring

groove in the master cylinder and slide out the pushrod, piston and spring noting how they fit **(see illustrations)**. Lay the parts out in order as you remove them to prevent confusion during reassembly.

11 Clean the master cylinder with clean brake fluid. If compressed air is available, blow it through the fluid galleries to ensure they are clear (make sure the air is filtered and unlubricated).

Caution: Do not, under any circumstances, use a petroleum-based solvent to clean brake parts.

12 Check the master cylinder bore for corrosion, scratches, nicks and score marks. If the necessary measuring equipment is available, compare the dimensions of the piston and bore to those given in the Specifications at the beginning of this Chapter.

If damage or wear is evident, the master cylinder must be replaced with a new one. If the master cylinder is in poor condition, then the caliper should be checked as well.

13 The dust boot, circlip, piston, seal, cup and spring are all included in the master cylinder rebuild kit. Use all of the new parts, regardless of the apparent condition of the old ones.

14 On CB600F and CBR600F models, if the cup and seal are not already on the piston, fit them into their grooves so the wider ends will fit into the master cylinder first, with the cup on the inner end and the seal on the outer **(see illustration 5.13)**. Fit the spring onto the lug on the end of the piston **(see illustration 5.14a)**. Fit the new circlip onto the pushrod if not already in place **(see illustration 9.16f)**. Lubricate the piston, cup, seal and master

cylinder bore with new brake fluid. Fit the piston/spring assembly, spring-end first, into the master cylinder and push the cup and seal in, making sure their lips do not turn inside out. Smear some silicone grease onto the rounded end of the pushrod and around the lips of the boot. Push the piston in using the pushrod until the washer is beyond the circlip groove, then locate the circlip in the groove **(see illustration 9.16g)**. Fit the rubber boot, making sure the lips are seated correctly in the master cylinder and around the pushrod **(see illustrations 9.16h, i and j)**.

15 On CB600FA and CBR600FA models, if the seal is not already on the piston, fit it into its groove so the wider end will fit into the master cylinder first **(see illustrations 9.16a and b)**. Fit the cup onto the narrow end of the spring, locating the peg in the hole **(see illustration 9.16c)**. Fit the new circlip onto the pushrod between the rubber boot and the washer if not already in place. Lubricate the piston, cup, seal and master cylinder bore with new brake fluid. Fit the spring wide-end first into the master cylinder and push the cup in, making sure its lips do not turn inside out **(see illustration 9.16d)**. Fit the piston/pushrod assembly in and up against the cup and spring. Make sure the lips on the seal do not turn inside out. Push the assembly in until the washer is beyond the circlip groove, then locate the circlip in the groove **(see illustration 9.16g)**. Fit the rubber boot, making sure the lips are seated correctly in the master cylinder and around the pushrod **(see illustrations 9.16h, i and j)**.

16 On CBF600N/NA/S/SA models, if the seal is not already on the piston, fit it into its groove so the wider end will fit into the master cylinder first **(see illustrations)**. Fit the cup onto the narrow end of the spring, locating the peg in the hole **(see illustration)**. Fit the new circlip onto the pushrod between the rubber boot and the washer if not already in place. Lubricate the piston, cup, seal and master cylinder bore with new brake fluid. Fit the spring wide-end first into the master cylinder and push the cup in, making sure its lips do not turn inside out **(see illustration)**. Slide the piston into the master cylinder and up against the cup and spring **(see illustration)**. Make sure the lips on

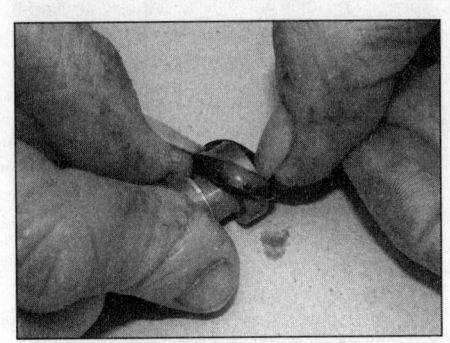

9.16a Fit the seal onto the piston . . .

9.16b . . . as shown

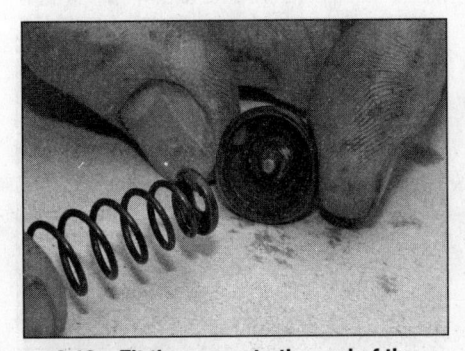

9.16c Fit the cup onto the end of the spring, locating the peg in the hole

9.16d Fit the spring making sure the cup locates correctly in the bore . . .

9.16e . . . then push the piston in

6•18 Brakes, wheels and final drive

9.16f Position the circlip on the washer . . .

9.16g . . . then depress the pushrod and fit the circlip into the groove

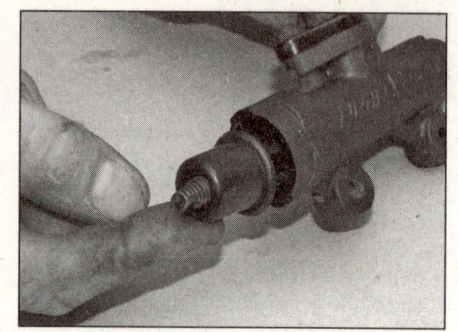

9.16h Fit the new boot . . .

9.16i . . . then press it into the cylinder . . .

9.16j . . . and make sure it is correctly located around the pushrod

the seal do not turn inside out. Smear some silicone grease onto the rounded end of the pushrod and around the lips of the boot. Push the piston in using the pushrod until the washer is beyond the circlip groove, then locate the circlip in the groove **(see illustration)**. Fit the rubber boot, making sure the lips are seated correctly in the master cylinder and around the pushrod **(see illustrations)**.

17 If not already in place thread the locknut and clevis onto the pushrod, setting them as noted on removal – Honda specify the distance between the centre of the clevis pin hole and the lower mounting bolt hole measured parallel to the pushrod should be 67.5 mm. Tighten the locknut securely against the clevis.

18 If removed fit a new fluid reservoir hose union O-ring smeared with brake fluid, then press the union into the master cylinder and secure it with the screw **(see illustrations)**.

19 Connect the hose to the union on the master cylinder and secure it with the clip **(see illustration)**. Check that the hose is secured with a clip at the reservoir end as well. If the clips have weakened, use new ones.

Installation

20 Align the clevis on the pushrod with the brake pedal, then insert the pin **(see illustration 9.6b)**. Locate the master cylinder on the footrest bracket and tighten the bolts to the torque setting specified at the beginning of this Chapter **(see illustration 9.6a)**.
21 Secure the clevis with a new split pin **(see illustration 9.5)**. Bend the ends of the pin round to lock it.
22 On CB600F/FA and CBR600F/FA models fit the footrest bracket onto the frame and tighten the bolts to the torque setting specified at the beginning of the Chapter **(see illustration 9.4)**. Fit the silencer bolt with its washer, and tighten the nut to the specified torque.
23 Fit the fluid reservoir onto the frame **(see illustration 9.2)**.
24 Connect the brake hose to the master cylinder, using new sealing washers on each side of the banjo fitting **(see illustration 3.17)**. Align the fitting as noted on removal **(see illustration 9.3a or b)**. Tighten the banjo bolt to the specified torque setting.
25 Refer to Section 11 and fill and/or bleed the system as required. Check that there are no fluid leaks and test the operation of the brakes before riding the motorcycle.

10 Brake hoses and fittings

Inspection

1 To fully inspect all the brake hoses and pipes on models with C-ABS raise and support the fuel tank (see Chapter 4).
2 Check brake hose condition according to the brake system check interval in the service schedule (see Chapter 1). Twist and flex the hoses while looking for cracks, bulges and seeping hydraulic fluid. Check extra carefully around the areas where the hoses connect with the banjo fittings, as these are common areas for hose failure.
3 On models with C-ABS also check the brake pipes, the hose and pipe joints, the proportional control valve, and the modulator, referring to the relevant Sections of this

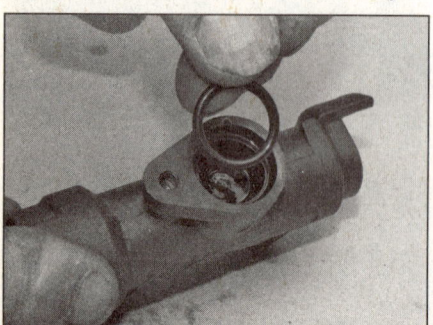

9.18a Fit a new O-ring . . .

9.18b . . . then press the union into place

9.19 Fit the reservoir hose onto its union

Chapter, for signs of fluid leakage and for any dents or cracks in the pipes.

4 Inspect the banjo fittings connected to the brake hoses and the pipe joints on C-ABS models. If the fittings are rusted, scratched or cracked, fit new ones.

Removal and installation

5 Drain all old brake fluid from the system (see Section 11).

6 The brake hoses have banjo fittings on each end. Cover the surrounding area with plenty of rags and unscrew the banjo bolt at each end of the hose, noting the alignment of the fitting with the master cylinder or brake caliper **(see illustrations 3.2a or b, 5.5, 7.1, and 9.3a or b)**. Free the hose from any clips or guides and remove it, noting its routing. Discard the sealing washers. **Note:** *Do not operate the brake lever or pedal while a brake hose is disconnected.*

7 Position the new hose, making sure it isn't twisted or otherwise strained, and ensure that it is correctly routed through any clips or guides and is clear of all moving components.

8 Check that the fittings align correctly, then install the banjo bolts, using new sealing washers on both sides of the fittings **(see illustration 3.17)**. Tighten the banjo bolts to the torque setting specified at the beginning of this Chapter.

9 The brake pipes are held by nuts **(see illustration 14.20)**. There are no sealing washers. Unscrew the nuts and detach the pipes. Make sure the pipe is correctly positioned, fitted into any clips, and with any joint blocks secured, before tightening the nuts. If the correct tools are available tighten the nuts to the torque setting specified at the beginning of this Chapter for your model.

10 Refill the system with new DOT 4 brake fluid (see *Pre-ride checks*) and bleed the air from it (see Section 11).

11 Check the operation of the brakes before riding the motorcycle.

11 Brake system bleeding and fluid change

Special tool: *Honda recommend using a vacuum-type brake bleeding tool (see illustration 11.20). If bleeding the system using the conventional method does not work sufficiently well, it is advisable to obtain this tool and repeat the procedure detailed below, following the manufacturer's instructions for using the tool.*

Bleeding

1 Bleeding a brake is the process of removing aerated brake fluid from the master cylinder, the hose(s) and the brake caliper(s). Bleeding is necessary whenever a brake system hydraulic connection is loosened, after a component or hose is replaced with a new one, when a master cylinder or caliper is overhauled, or when there is a spongy feel to the lever and it travels all the way back to the handlebar, and where braking force is less than it should be, and it is not due to any mechanical fault in the system (i.e. a sticking piston in the caliper, or a pad that is not moving as it should due to corrosion, for example on the pad pin). Leaks in the system may also allow air to enter, but leaking brake fluid will reveal their presence and warn you of the need for repair.

2 Brake bleeding is considered by some as a bit of a black art – seasoned professionals sometimes have trouble getting a good firm feel in the brake lever, while a first timer may have no trouble at all. One of the problems, particularly with the front brakes, is that you are working against natural principles – science dictates that air bubbles in a liquid will rise to the top, but the process entails pumping the brake fluid and any air bubbles it contains down, from the master cylinder at the top to the bleed valve in the caliper at the bottom, so while the fluid is moving down the air bubbles will want to rise. Air bubbles can also get trapped, particularly where there are high points in its path, and when there are extra components and pipes such as on models with C-ABS.

3 To bleed the brakes using the conventional method, you will need some new DOT 4 brake fluid, a length of clear flexible hose, a small container partially filled with clean brake fluid, some rags, and a spanner to fit the brake caliper bleed valve. Bleeding kits that include the hose, a one-way valve and a container are available relatively cheaply from a good auto store, and simplify the task.

4 Cover painted components to prevent damage in the event that brake fluid is spilled. **Caution:** *Brake fluid attacks painted finishes and plastics – to prevent damage from spilled fluid, always cover paintwork when working on the braking system, and clean up any spills immediately using brake cleaner.*

Front brake system

5 Turn the handlebars so the reservoir is level. Undo the reservoir cover screws and remove the cover, diaphragm plate and diaphragm **(see illustrations)**. Slowly pump the brake lever a few times to dislodge any air bubbles from the holes in the bottom of the reservoir.

6 Pull the dust cap off the bleed valve on the left-hand caliper **(see illustration)**. If using a ring spanner (which is preferable to an open-ended one) fit it onto the valve **(see illustration)**. Attach one end of the bleeding hose to the bleed valve and, if not using a kit, submerge the other end in the clean brake fluid in the container **(see illustration)**.

11.5a Undo the screws . . .

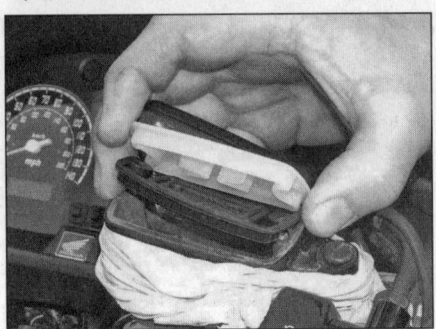

11.5b . . . and remove the cover, diaphragm plate and diaphragm

11.6a Pull the dust cap off the bleed valve (arrowed)

11.6b Fit a ring spanner onto the valve hex . . .

11.6c . . . then connect the bleed hose

6•20 Brakes, wheels and final drive

11.7 Keep the reservoir topped up

7 Check the fluid level in the reservoir – keep it topped up and do not allow the level to drop below the bottom of the window during the procedure **(see illustration)**.

8 Slowly pump the brake lever three or four times, then hold it in and open the bleed valve a quarter turn **(see illustration)**. When the valve is opened, brake fluid will flow out of the master cylinder into the clear tubing, and the lever will move toward the handlebar. If there is air in the system there will be air bubbles in the brake fluid coming out of the caliper.

9 Tighten the bleed valve, then slowly release the brake lever. Repeat the process until no air bubbles are visible in the brake fluid leaving the caliper, and the lever is firm when applied, topping the reservoir up when necessary. On completion tighten the bleed valve.

10 Now transfer the equipment to the bleed valve on the right-hand caliper – on models with C-ABS fit it onto the upper of the two bleed valves **(see illustration)**. Repeat the bleeding procedure.

Rear brake system

11 On CB600F/FA and CBR600F/FA models remove the right-hand side cover (see Chapter 7).

12 Unscrew the reservoir bolt and displace the reservoir so the cap is clear **(see illustration 9.2)**. Unscrew the reservoir cap, and remove the diaphragm plate and diaphragm **(see illustration)**. Refit the reservoir. Slowly pump the brake pedal a few times to dislodge any air bubbles from the holes in the bottom of the reservoir.

13 On models with C-ABS bleed the front portion of the system first using the centre bleed valve on the right-hand caliper **(see illustration 11.10)**, then bleed the rear portion using the bleed valve on the rear caliper. Note that the rear brake pedal may have some resistance to it as you push it down – this is due to the proportional control valve and is normal, but make sure you push the pedal all the way down

14 Pull the dust cap off the caliper bleed valve **(see illustration)**. If using a ring spanner (which is preferable to an open-ended one) fit it onto the valve **(see illustration)**. Attach one end of the bleeding hose to the bleed valve and, if not using a kit, submerge the other end

11.8 Bleeding the front brake system

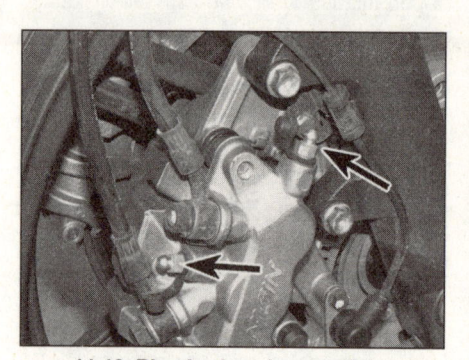

11.10 Bleed valves (arrowed) on right-hand caliper – models with C-ABS

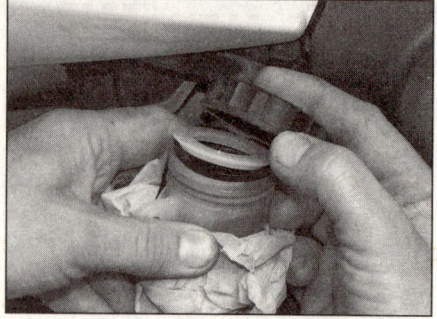

11.12 Unscrew the cap and remove the diaphragm plate and diaphragm

11.14a Pull the dust cap off the bleed valve (arrowed)

11.14b Fit a ring spanner onto the valve hex . . .

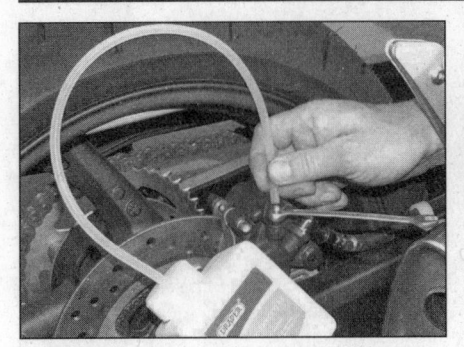

11.14c ... then connect the bleed hose

11.15 Keep the reservoir topped up

in the clean brake fluid in the container **(see illustration)**.
15 Check the fluid level in the reservoir – keep it topped up and do not allow the level to drop below the bottom of the window during the procedure **(see illustration)**.
16 On models with a standard braking system slowly pump the brake pedal three or four times, then hold it down and open the bleed valve a quarter turn **(see illustration)**. When the valve is opened, brake fluid will flow out of the master cylinder into the clear tubing, and the pedal will move down. If there is air in the system there will be air bubbles in the brake fluid coming out of the caliper. Tighten the bleed valve, then slowly release the brake pedal. Repeat the process until no air bubbles are visible in the brake fluid leaving the caliper, and the pedal is firm when applied, topping the reservoir up when necessary. On completion tighten the bleed valve.
17 On models with C-ABS quickly pump the brake pedal five to ten times, then hold it down and open the bleed valve a quarter turn **(see illustration 11.16)**. When the valve is opened, brake fluid will flow out of the master cylinder into the clear tubing, and the pedal will move down. If there is air in the system there will be air bubbles in the brake fluid coming out of the caliper. Keep the pedal held down for a few seconds. Tighten the bleed valve, then slowly release the brake pedal. Wait a few seconds, then repeat the process, doing so until no air bubbles are visible in the brake fluid leaving the caliper, and the pedal is firm when applied, topping the reservoir up when necessary. On completion tighten the bleed valve.

Both systems

18 If it is not possible to produce a firm feel to the lever or pedal, remove body panels as required (see Chapter 7) and look for any high point in the system in which a pocket of air may become trapped. Displace and agitate the hose or pipe so the bubble can be dislodged (but take care not to bend a pipe on C-ABS models) – tapping it may help. If necessary displace the master cylinder and/or the caliper(s), and free the brake hose(s) from its guides and move the parts around to dislodge the air and encourage it towards a bleed valve – refer to the relevant Sections as required to displace components. On C-ABS models it is not practical to disturb the modulator, proportional control valve or delay valve as the pipes have to be detached, allowing more air to enter the system – if you cannot get the system to bleed correctly take the bike to a Honda dealer.
19 If you are still having trouble the fluid may be full of many tiny air bubbles rather than a few big ones. To remedy this apply some pressure to the system, for the front brake by tying the front brake lever lightly back to the handlebar, and for the rear by tying a weight to the brake pedal – do not apply too much pressure or the cup and seals in the master cylinder and caliper may fail. Let the fluid stabilise for a few hours, after which the tiny bubbles should either have risen to the top in the reservoir, or have formed into one or more big bubbles that can be more easily bled out by repeating the bleeding procedure.
20 If bleeding the system using the conventional tools and methods stated does not give satisfactory results, or if otherwise preferred, you can use a commercially available vacuum-type brake bleeding tool, such as the Mity-vac shown, following the manufacturer's instructions **(see illustration)**. This type of tool literally sucks the fluid out by creating a vacuum at the bleed valve. Users of such tools often get confused by the amount of air that appears to be in the brake fluid – more often than not this is caused by the vacuum sucking air past the bleed valve threads (air provides less resistance to the vacuum than the brake fluid) where it mixes with the fluid being drawn out. If this is the case the vacuum applied may be too great, or the bleed valve may have been loosened too much. One way to get round this is to remove the bleed valve and thread some PTFE tape around its threads, but note that doing so will be a bit messy, so have some rag to hand.
21 When the system has been successfully bled there should be a good and progressively firm feel as the lever or pedal is applied, and the lever or pedal should not be able to travel all the way back to the handlebar or down to its stop.
22 On completion remove the equipment used and make sure the bleed valve is tight (to the torque setting specified at the beginning of the Chapter if you have a suitable torque wrench), then fit the dust cap. Top-up the reservoir, then fit the diaphragm, diaphragm plate, and cover or cap **(see illustrations 11.5b and 11.12)**.

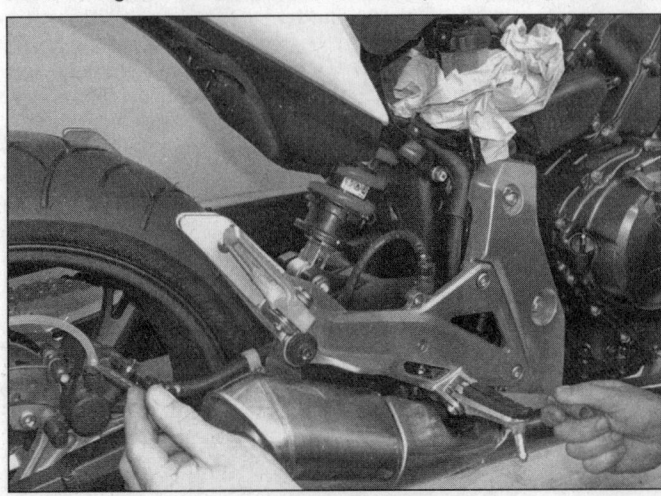

11.16 Bleeding the rear brake system

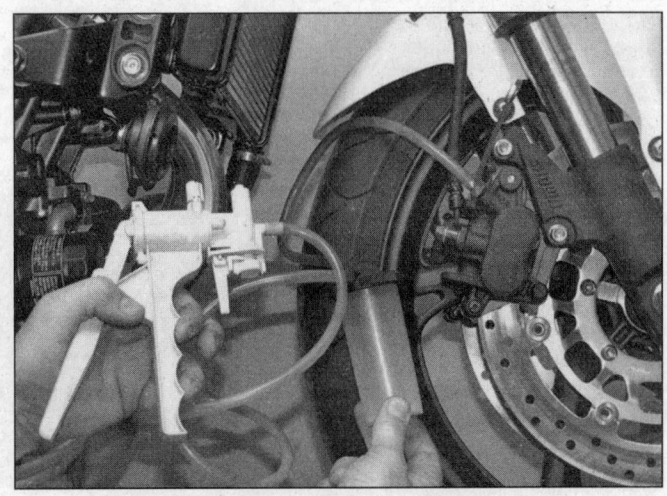

11.20 A vacuum-operated brake bleeding tool

6•22 Brakes, wheels and final drive

Check for spilled brake fluid and clean up as required. Check the entire system for fluid leaks.
23 Check the operation of the brake before riding the motorcycle.

Fluid change

24 Changing the brake fluid is a similar process to bleeding the brakes and requires the same materials plus a suitable tool (such as a syringe, or alternatively lots of absorbent rag or paper) for siphoning the fluid out of the reservoir.
25 Cover painted components and fit the equipment to the relevant caliper following the appropriate Steps in the bleeding procedure given above. Remove the reservoir cover or cap, diaphragm plate and diaphragm and siphon the old fluid out of the reservoir **(see illustrations 11.5a and b or 11.12)**. Wipe the reservoir clean. Fill the reservoir with new brake fluid **(see illustration 11.7 or 11.15)**. Pump the brake lever or pedal as described above then hold it in or down and open the bleed valve **(see illustrations 11.8 and 11.16)**. When the valve is opened, brake fluid will flow out of the caliper into the clear tubing, and the lever will move toward the handlebar, or the pedal will move down.
26 Tighten the bleed valve, then slowly release the brake lever or pedal. Keep the reservoir topped-up with new fluid at all times or air may enter the system and greatly increase the length of the task. Repeat the process until new fluid can be seen emerging from the caliper bleed valve.

> **HAYNES HiNT** *Old brake fluid is invariably much darker in colour than new fluid, making it easy to see when all old fluid has been expelled from the system.*

27 On completion remove the equipment used and make sure the bleed valve is tight (to the torque setting specified at the beginning of the Chapter if you have a suitable torque wrench), then fit the dust cap. Top-up the reservoir, then fit the diaphragm, diaphragm plate, and cover or cap. Check for spilled brake fluid and clean up as required. Check the entire system for fluid leaks.
28 Check the operation of the brakes before riding the motorcycle.

Draining the system for overhaul

29 Draining the brake fluid is again a similar process to bleeding the brakes. The quickest and easiest way is to use a commercially available vacuum-type brake bleeding tool (see Step 20) – follow the manufacturer's instructions. Otherwise follow the procedure described above for changing the fluid, but quite simply do not put any new fluid into the reservoir – the system fills itself with air instead.
30 When it comes to refilling the system start by adding new fluid from a sealed container to the reservoir, then perform the bleeding procedure as described above until the fluid comes out of the bleed valve, and keep at it. On models with a conventional braking system, and when doing the front brake system via the front brake lever on models with C-ABS, continue until you are certain there is no more air left in the system. When doing the linked circuit via the rear brake pedal on models with C-ABS, start with the centre bleed valve on the right-hand front caliper, and transfer to the rear when it is obvious that there is mostly fluid coming out, even though there may still be some air – this is normal as the rear portion of the circuit is still full of air and some may be working its way to the front. When the rear portion is mostly filled with fluid bleed the system as described above, front portion first.

12 C-ABS operation

1 The combined part of the system (C-) links the rear brake with part of the front, actuating the centre piston in the right-hand caliper via a proportional control valve, whenever the pedal is depressed. The anti-lock part of the system (ABS) prevents the wheels from locking up under hard braking or on uneven road surfaces. A sensor on each wheel transmits information about the speed of rotation to the control unit in the ABS modulator; if the unit senses that a wheel is about to lock, it releases brake pressure to that wheel momentarily, preventing a skid.
2 The anti-lock system is self-checking and is activated when the ignition switch is turned on – the ABS indicator light in the instrument cluster will come on and will remain on until road speed increases above 6 mph (10 kmh) at which point, if the ABS is normal, the light will go off. **Note:** *If the ABS indicator light does not come on initially there is a fault in the system – see Section 13.*
3 If the indicator light remains on, or starts flashing while the machine is being ridden, there is a fault in the system and the ABS function will be switched off – the brakes will still function but in normal mode. If you turn the ignition OFF while the light is flashing, the fault code will not be displayed again if the ignition is switched on again, but will be stored in the system's memory.
4 The warning light emits long (1.3 second) and short (0.3 second) flashes to give out the fault code. A long flash is used to indicate the first digit of the double-digit fault code. For example, two long (1.3 sec) flashes followed by three short (0.3 sec) flashes indicates the fault code number 23. If there is more than one fault code, there will be a 3.6 sec gap before the next code is revealed (the codes are revealed in ascending numerical order). Once all codes have been revealed, the display will continuously run through the code(s) stored in its memory, revealing each one in turn with a short gap between them. The fault codes are shown in the table in Section 13. To check the ABS components see Section 14.
5 To retrieve any stored fault codes, on CB600FA and CBR600FA models remove the seat, and on CBF600NA/SA models remove the left-hand side cover (see Chapter 7) to gain access to the service check connector, which is a blanked 3-pin connector coming out of the wiring loom **(see illustrations)**. Ensure the ignition is switched OFF. Remove the blanking cap from the connector. Using a short jumper wire, connect between the brown/white and green wire terminals in the connector. With the terminals connected, turn the ignition ON and observe the ABS warning light. If there are stored fault codes, the light will come on for 2 seconds, then go out for 3.6 seconds, then start to flash the fault code. If the light comes on and stays on without flashing after the 3.6 second gap no fault codes are stored. Do not apply the brake lever or pedal during code retrieval.
6 Turn the ignition switch OFF and remove the jumper wire when the code or codes have been recorded.
7 Once the fault has been corrected, erase the fault code(s) as follows. Follow Step 5 to connect the terminals in the service check connector. Hold the front brake lever on and turn the ignition switch on – the ABS light should come on for two seconds, then go out. When the light goes out immediately release the brake lever – the light should come on.

12.5a ABS service check connector (arrowed) – CB and CBR models

12.5b ABS service check connector (arrowed) – CBF models

Brakes, wheels and final drive 6•23

When the light comes on immediately apply the brake lever – the light should go out. When the light goes out immediately release the brake lever. The code(s) should now be erased, in which case the light will flash twice, then come on and stay on.

8 Turn the ignition switch OFF and remove the jumper wire when the code or codes have been erased. Check that the ABS is operating normally (see Step 2).

9 If necessary, repeat the reset procedure.

Caution: The C-ABS indicator may diagnose a fault if tyre sizes other than those specified by Honda are fitted, if the tyre pressures are incorrect, if the machine has been run continuously over bumpy roads, if the front wheel comes off the ground whilst riding (wheelie) or if the machine is on an auxiliary stand with the engine running and the rear wheel turning.

13 C-ABS fault diagnosis

1 If a fault is indicated in the ABS, first check that the battery is fully charged, then check the ABS fuses (see Chapter 8).

2 Unless specified otherwise, carry out all checks with the ignition switch OFF.

3 Refer to Chapter 8, Section 2, for general electrical fault finding procedures and equipment.

4 If after a thorough check, the source of a fault has not been identified, have the system tested by a Honda dealer.

Fault codes 11, 12, 21, 41 and 42

Note: *Before carrying out any of the checks, follow the procedure in Section 12 to reset the control unit memory, then activate the self-checking procedure. If the fault code is the result of unusual riding or conditions and the ABS is normal, the indicator light will go off. Otherwise perform the following checks.*

5 Measure the air gap between the front wheel speed sensor and the pulse ring with a feeler gauge, then compare the result with the Specification at the beginning of this Chapter **(see illustration)**. The gap is not adjustable –

Fault codes	Faulty component or system	Possible causes
No code displayed	ABS light does not come on with ignition ABS light on all the time	Blown ABS 10A main fuse Faulty wiring or wiring connector Faulty modulator Faulty ABS indicator light
11, 12, 21	Front wheel speed sensor circuit Front wheel speed sensor Front wheel pulse ring	Faulty wiring or wiring connector Faulty sensor Damaged pulse ring
13, 14, 23	Rear wheel speed sensor circuit Rear wheel speed sensor Rear wheel pulse ring	Faulty wiring or wiring connector Faulty sensor Damaged pulse ring
31, 32, 33, 34, 37 and 38	Modulator solenoid valve	Faulty modulator
41 and 42	Front wheel lock – riding conditions Front wheel speed sensor circuit Front wheel speed sensor Front wheel pulse ring	Faulty sensor Faulty wiring or wiring connector Damaged pulse ring
43	Rear wheel lock – riding conditions Rear wheel speed sensor circuit Rear wheel speed sensor Rear wheel pulse ring	Faulty wiring or wiring connector Faulty sensor Damaged pulse ring
51	Modulator motor lock	Faulty modulator
52	Modulator motor stuck OFF	Faulty modulator
53	Modulator motor stuck ON	Faulty modulator
54	Fail-safe relay circuit	ABS 30A fail-safe relay fuse Faulty relay circuit Faulty modulator
61	Power supply voltage low	ABS 10A main fuse Faulty wiring or wiring connector Faulty modulator
62	Power supply voltage high	ABS 10A main fuse Faulty wiring or wiring connector Faulty modulator
71	Incorrect tyre size	Incorrect tyre
81	CPU in modulator control unit	Faulty modulator

if it is outside the specification, check that the sensor and pulse ring fixings are tight. Also check that the components are not damaged and that there is no dirt or anything else on the sensor tip or between the slots in the pulse ring. If any of the components are damaged they must be replaced with new ones.

6 Raise the fuel tank (see Chapter 4). Disconnect the ABS modulator wiring connector **(see illustration)**. Trace the wheel sensor wiring to the connector and disconnect it **(see illustration)**. Check for continuity first in the yellow/black or pink/black wire (according to model) between the control unit wiring connector and the sensor wiring connector and then in the green/orange wire – there should be continuity in each wire between the connectors, and no continuity to earth. If not locate and repair the break.

7 If there is continuity in the wiring next check for continuity between each terminal in the sensor side of the sensor connector and earth (ground). If there is continuity in either

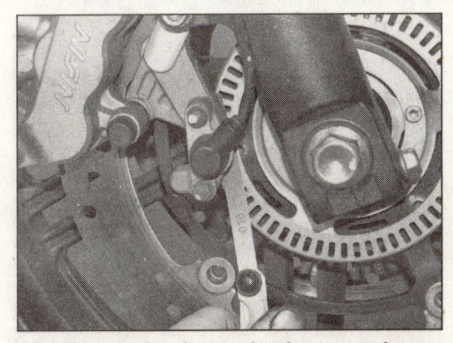

13.5 Measuring front wheel sensor air gap

13.6a Pull the security clip up to release the connector

13.6b Front wheel sensor connector (arrowed)

6•24 Brakes, wheels and final drive

13.9 Measuring rear wheel sensor air gap

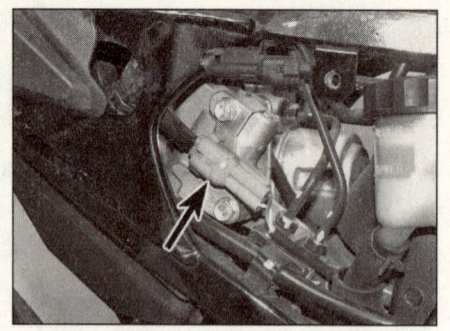

13.10a Rear wheel sensor connector (arrowed) – CB and CBR models

13.10b Rear wheel sensor connector (arrowed) – CBF models

of the wires the sensor is faulty and must be replaced with a new one.

8 If all the checks have failed to identify the fault, replace the wheel sensor with a known good one. Connect all wiring connectors then follow the procedure in Section 12 to reset the control unit memory, then activate the self-checking procedure. If the indicator light is no longer flashing, the original sensor was faulty. If the fault code reappears have the ABS modulator checked by a Honda dealer.

Fault codes 13, 14, 23 and 43

Note: Before carrying out any of the checks, follow the procedure in Section 12 to reset the control unit memory, then activate the self-checking procedure. If the fault code is the result of unusual riding or conditions and the ABS is normal, the indicator light will go off. Otherwise perform the following checks.

9 Measure the air gap between the rear wheel speed sensor and the pulse ring with a feeler gauge, then compare the result with the Specification at the beginning of this Chapter **(see illustration)**. The gap is not adjustable – if it is outside the specification, check that the sensor and pulse ring fixings are tight. Also check that the components are not damaged and that there is no dirt or anything else on the sensor tip or between the slots in the pulse ring. If any of the components are damaged they must be replaced with new ones.

10 Remove the seat(s) and the right-hand side cover (see Chapter 7). Disconnect the ABS modulator wiring connector **(see illustration 13.6a)**. Trace the wheel sensor wiring to the connector and disconnect it **(see illustrations)**. Check for continuity first in the pink/white wire between the control unit wiring connector and the sensor wiring connector and then in the green/red wire – there should be continuity in each wire between the connectors, and no continuity to earth. If not locate and repair the break.

11 If there is continuity in the wiring next check for continuity between each terminal in the sensor side of the sensor connector and earth (ground). If there is continuity in either of the wires the sensor is faulty and must be replaced with a new one.

12 If all the checks have failed to identify the fault, replace the wheel sensor with a known good one. Connect all wiring connectors then follow the procedure in Section 12 to reset the control unit memory, then activate the self-checking procedure. If the indicator light is no longer flashing, the original sensor was faulty. If the fault code reappears have the ABS modulator checked by a Honda dealer.

Fault codes 31, 32, 33, 34, 37 and 38

13 Erase the fault code (see Section 12). Start the engine and go for a short ride so the ABS system performs its self-diagnosis. If the ABS indicator light stays off, the fault was temporary.

14 If the ABS indicator light still flashes fault code 31, 32, 33, 34, 37 or 38 the ABS modulator is faulty.

Fault codes 51, 52 and 53

15 Check the ABS 30A motor fuse (see Chapter 8). If the fuse has blown, on CBF600NA/SA models remove the seats (see Chapter 7). Disconnect the ABS modulator wiring connector **(see illustration 13.6a)**. Check for continuity in the red wire terminal in the connector to earth. If there is continuity, repair the wire. If not replace the blown fuse with a new one. Connect all wiring connectors then follow the procedure in Section 12 to reset the control unit memory, then activate the self-checking procedure. If the fault code is no longer shown there was a temporary fault.

16 If the fuse has not blown refit it. On CBF600NA/SA models remove the seats (see Chapter 7). Disconnect the ABS modulator wiring connector **(see illustration 13.6a)**. Check for battery voltage at the red wire terminal in the connector at all times (i.e. with the ignition on or off). If there is no voltage check the red wire from the connector to the fusebox for continuity, and if that is good check the red/blue (CB600FA and CBR600FA) or red/green (CBF600NA/SA) wire for continuity to the battery, and repair the circuit as required.

17 If there is voltage erase the fault code (see Section 12). Start the engine and go for a short ride so the ABS system performs its self-diagnosis. If the ABS indicator light stays off, the fault was temporary.

18 If the ABS indicator light still flashes the same fault code, the ABS modulator is faulty.

Fault code 54

19 Check the ABS 30A fail safe relay fuse (see Chapter 8). If the fuse has blown, on CBF600NA/SA models remove the seats (see Chapter 7). Disconnect the ABS modulator wiring connector **(see illustration 13.6a)**. Check for continuity in the black wire terminal in the connector to earth. If there is continuity, repair the wire. If not replace the blown fuse with a new one. Connect all wiring connectors then follow the procedure in Section 12 to reset the control unit memory, then activate the self-checking procedure. If the fault code is no longer shown there was a temporary fault.

20 If the fuse has not blown refit it. On CBF600NA/SA models remove the seats (see Chapter 7). Disconnect the ABS modulator wiring connector **(see illustration 13.6a)**. Check for battery voltage at the black wire terminal in the connector at all times (i.e. with the ignition on or off). If there is no voltage check the black wire from the connector to the fusebox for continuity, and if that is good check the red/blue (CB600FA and CBR600FA) or red/green (CBF600NA/SA) wire for continuity to the battery, and repair the circuit as required.

21 If there is voltage erase the fault code (see Section 12). Start the engine and go for a short ride so the ABS system performs its self-diagnosis. If the ABS indicator light stays off, the fault was temporary.

22 If the ABS indicator light still flashes the same fault code, the ABS modulator is faulty.

Fault codes 61 and 62

23 Check the ABS 10A main fuse (see Chapter 8). If the fuse has blown on CBF600NA/SA models remove the seats (see Chapter 7). Disconnect the ABS modulator wiring connector **(see illustration 13.6a)**. Check for continuity in the red/brown wire terminal in the connector to earth. If there is continuity, repair the wire. If not replace the blown fuse with a new one. Connect all wiring connectors then follow the procedure in Section 12 to reset the control unit memory, then activate the self-checking procedure. If

Brakes, wheels and final drive 6•25

the fault code is no longer shown there was a temporary fault.

24 If the fuse has not blown refit it. On CBF600NA/SA models remove the seats (see Chapter 7). Disconnect the ABS modulator wiring connector **(see illustration 13.6a)**. Check for battery voltage at the red/brown wire terminal in the connector with the ignition on. If there is no voltage check the red/brown wire from the connector to the fusebox for continuity, and if that is good check the red/black wire for continuity to the ignition switch, and repair the circuit as required.

25 If there is voltage erase the fault code (see Section 12). Start the engine and go for a short ride so the ABS system performs its self-diagnosis. If the ABS indicator light stays off, the fault was temporary.

26 If the ABS indicator light still flashes the same fault code, the ABS modulator is faulty.

Fault code 71

27 First check the tyre pressure (see *Pre-ride checks*). Next make sure the correct tyres are fitted, comparing the tyre size codes on the sidewall to the Specifications at the beginning of the Chapter. Also check the tyres and wheels for deformations. Correct any problems found.

28 Erase the fault code (see Section 12). Start the engine and go for a short ride so the ABS system performs its self-diagnosis. If the ABS indicator light stays off, the fault was temporary.

29 If the ABS indicator light still flashes the same fault code, the ABS modulator is faulty.

Fault code 81

30 Erase the fault code (see Section 12). Start the engine and go for a short ride so the ABS system performs its self-diagnosis. If the ABS indicator light stays off, the fault was temporary.

31 If the ABS indicator light still flashes the same fault code, the ABS modulator is faulty.

No fault code detected

32 If the ABS indicator light stays on the whole time, check the ABS 10A main fuse (see Chapter 8). If the fuse has blown, remove it. On CBF600NA/SA models remove the seats (see Chapter 7). Disconnect the ABS modulator wiring connector **(see illustration 13.6a)**. Check for continuity in the red/brown wire terminal in the connector to earth. If there is continuity, repair the wire. If not replace the blown fuse with a new one. Connect all wiring connectors then follow the procedure in Section 12 to reset the control unit memory, then activate the self-checking procedure. If the fault code no longer shown there was a temporary fault.

33 If the fuse has not blown refit it. On CBF600NA/SA models remove the seats (see Chapter 7). Disconnect the ABS modulator wiring connector **(see illustration 13.6a)**. Check for battery voltage at the red/brown wire terminal in the connector with the ignition on. If there is no voltage check the red/brown wire from the connector to the fusebox for continuity, and if that is good check the red/black wire for continuity to the ignition switch, and repair the circuit as required.

34 If there is voltage check for continuity in the brown/white wire terminal in the connector to earth. If there is continuity, repair the wire.

35 If there is no continuity, refer to Chapter 8 to access the instrument wiring connector. Using a suitable probe and jumper wire short the red/black wire in the instrument cluster wiring connector to earth with the connector still connected and the ignition ON. If the ABS indicator light stays on, the instrument cluster PCB is faulty (see Chapter 8).

36 If the ABS indicator light goes out check the red/black wire between the modulator and instrument cluster wiring connectors for continuity, and if there is none repair the wire.

37 If there is continuity short between the red/black and No. 1 green/orange wire terminals in the modulator connector using a jumper wire with the ignition on. If the ABS light goes out the modulator is faulty. If the light stays on check the green/orange wire for continuity to earth – if there is none repair the wire.

38 If the ABS indicator light does not come on with the ignition switch, check the instrument cluster power and earth wires (see Chapter 8).

39 If all is good, remove the seat(s) (see Chapter 7). Disconnect the ABS modulator wiring connector **(see illustrations 13.6a)**. Turn the ignition on – if the light is on, the modulator is faulty.

40 If the light does not come on, disconnect the instrument wiring connector. Check for continuity in the red/black wire in the instrument cluster wiring connector to earth. If there is, repair the wire. If there is no continuity the instrument cluster is faulty.

14 C-ABS components

Front wheel sensor

1 Raise and support the fuel tank (see Chapter 4). Trace the wheel sensor wiring to the connector and disconnect it **(see illustration 13.6b)**.

2 Release the sensor wiring guides and feed the wire down to the sensor, noting its routing. Unscrew the sensor bolts and remove the sensor and wiring guide where fitted **(see illustration)**.

3 Make sure the tip of the sensor, its mounting surfaces, and the pulse ring are clean. Fit the sensor, with the guide where fitted, and tighten the bolts. Feed the wiring up to the connector, routing and securing it as noted on removal.

4 Check the air gap (see Section 13, Step 5). Lower the fuel tank (see Chapter 4).

Front pulse ring

5 Remove the front wheel (see Section 17).

6 Undo the screws securing the ring and lift it off **(see illustration)**.

7 Ensure there is no dirt or corrosion where the ring seats on the hub – if the ring does not sit flat when it is installed the sensor air gap will be incorrect. Clean the threads of the bolts and apply a non-permanent thread locking compound (or alternatively use new bolts from Honda which come pre-treated) and tighten them to the torque setting specified at the beginning of the Chapter.

8 Install the front wheel (see Section 17). Check the speed sensor air gap (see Section 13, Step 5).

Rear wheel sensor

9 Remove the right-hand side cover (see Chapter 7). Trace the wheel sensor wiring to the connector and disconnect it **(see illustration 13.10a or b)**.

10 Release the sensor wiring guides and feed the wire down to the sensor, noting its routing. Unscrew the sensor bolts and remove the sensor and wiring guide **(see illustration)**.

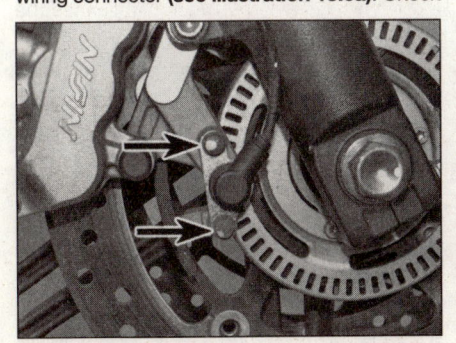

14.2 Front wheel sensor bolts (arrowed)

14.6 Front pulse ring screws (arrowed)

14.10 Rear wheel sensor and wiring guide bolts (arrowed)

6•26 Brakes, wheels and final drive

14.14 Rear pulse ring screws (arrowed)

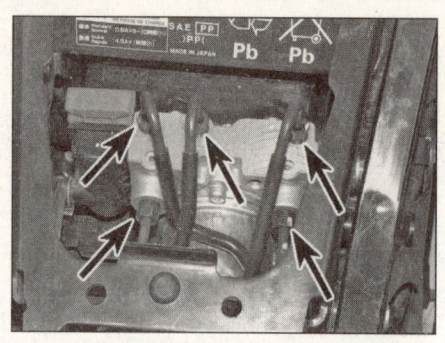

14.20 Brake pipe nuts (arrowed)

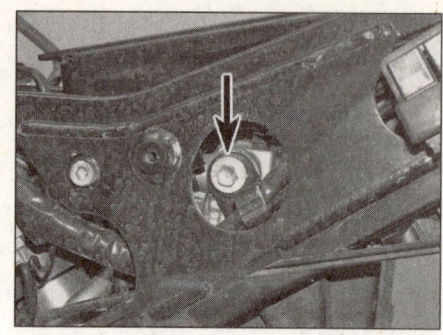

14.21a Side mounting bolt (arrowed) . . .

11 Make sure the tip of the sensor, its mounting surfaces, and the pulse ring are clean. Fit the sensor and wiring guide and tighten the bolts. Feed the wiring up to the connector, routing and securing it as noted on removal.

12 Check the air gap (see Section 13, Step 9). Install the side cover (see Chapter 7).

Rear pulse ring

13 Remove the rear wheel (see Section 18).
14 Undo the screws securing the ring and lift it off (see illustration).
15 Ensure there is no dirt or corrosion where the ring seats on the hub – if the ring does not sit flat when it is installed the sensor air gap will be incorrect. Clean the threads of the bolts and apply a non-permanent thread locking compound (or alternatively use new bolts from Honda which come pre-treated) and tighten them to the torque setting specified at the beginning of the Chapter.
16 Install the rear wheel (see Section 18). Check the sensor air gap (see Section 13, Step 9).

Modulator

Note: *Before removing the modulator it is best to drain all old brake fluid from the brake system, then fill with new fluid on installation (see Section 11). The modulator cannot be dismantled for overhaul, and no component parts are available. If it fails, it must be replaced with a new one.*

17 Remove the rear mudguard (see Chapter 7).
18 Disconnect the modulator wiring connector (see illustration 13.6a).
19 Cover the area around the modulator with clean rag to prevent damage to paintwork in the event that brake fluid is spilled.
20 Unscrew the brake pipe nuts and detach the pipes (see illustration). Plug the ends of the pipes or wrap something tightly around them to minimise fluid loss if the system wasn't drained, and to prevent dirt entering the system.
21 Unscrew the mounting bolts and remove the modulator, taking care not to snag the brake pipes (see illustration).
22 Note the sleeves in the rubber mounts – replace the rubbers with new ones if cracked or hardened.
23 Installation is the reverse of removal, noting the following:
- Smear the pipe nut threads with clean brake fluid, and fit them all finger-tight before finally tightening any of them. If the correct tools are available tighten them to the torque setting specified at the beginning of the Chapter for your model.
- Make sure the wiring connector is secure.
- Follow the procedure in Section 11 to refill and bleed the brake system. Check that there are no fluid leaks and test the operation of the brakes before riding the motorcycle.

Caution: *Brake fluid attacks painted finishes and plastics – to prevent damage from spilled fluid, always cover paintwork when working on the braking system, and clean up any spills immediately using brake cleaner.*

Proportional control valve

Note: *The valve cannot be dismantled for overhaul, and no component parts are available. If the valve fails, it must be replaced with a new one.*

Removal – CB600FA and CBR600FA

24 Remove the modulator (see above). Cover the area around the PCV with clean rag to prevent damage to paintwork in the event that brake fluid is spilled.
25 Unscrew the pipe joint nuts and detach the pipes from the valve (see illustrations). Plug the ends of the pipes or wrap something tightly around them to minimise fluid loss if the system wasn't drained, and to prevent dirt entering the system.
26 Unscrew the bolts and remove the valve.

Removal – CBF600NA/SA

27 Remove the right-hand side cover (see Chapter 7).
28 Either drain the brake fluid (Section 11) or prepare to plug the pipe ends.

14.21b . . . and lower mounting bolts (arrowed) – CBF model shown

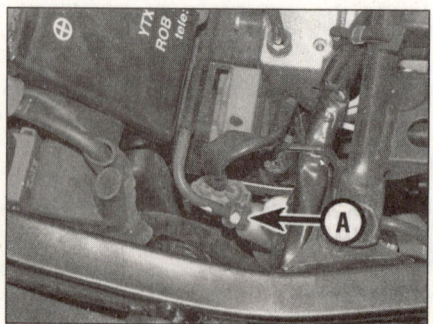

14.25a Proportional control valve pipe nuts (A) . . .

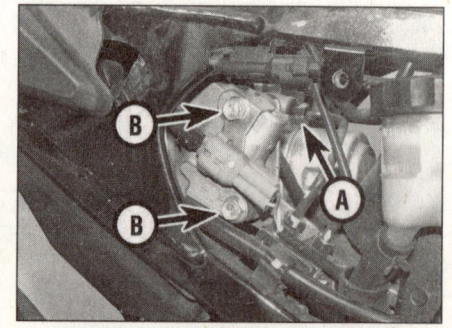

14.25b . . . and mounting bolts (B)

Brakes, wheels and final drive 6•27

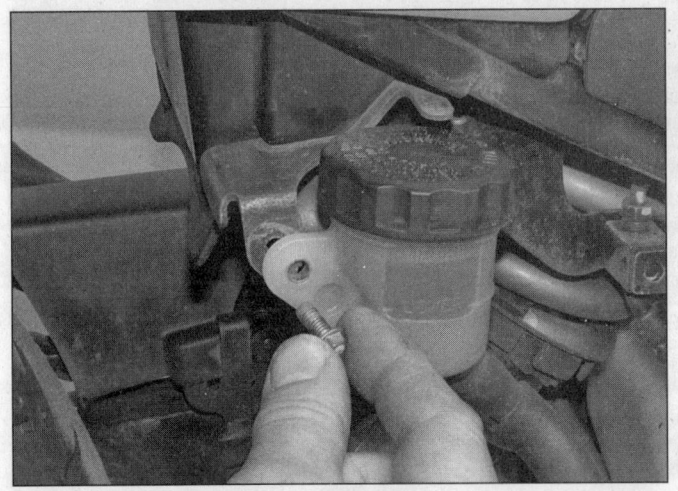

14.29 Remove the reservoir bolt

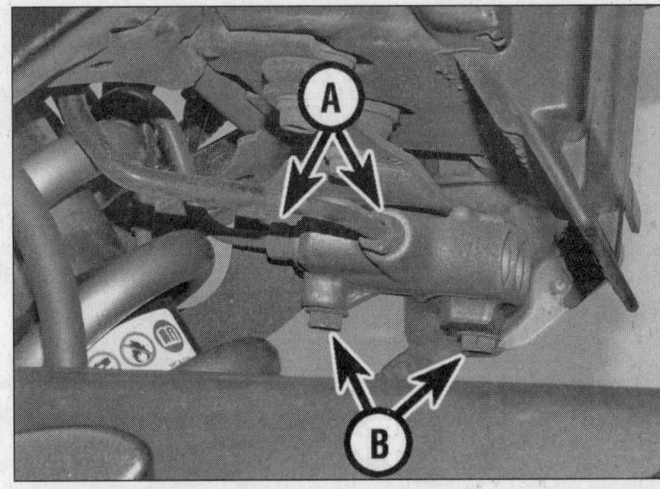

14.30 Proportional control valve pipe nuts (A) and mounting bolts (B)

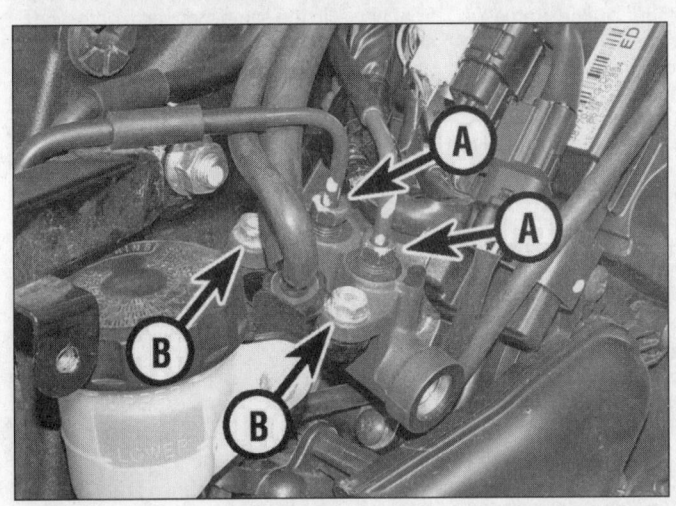

14.35a Delay valve pipe nuts (A) and mounting bolts (B) – CB and CBR models

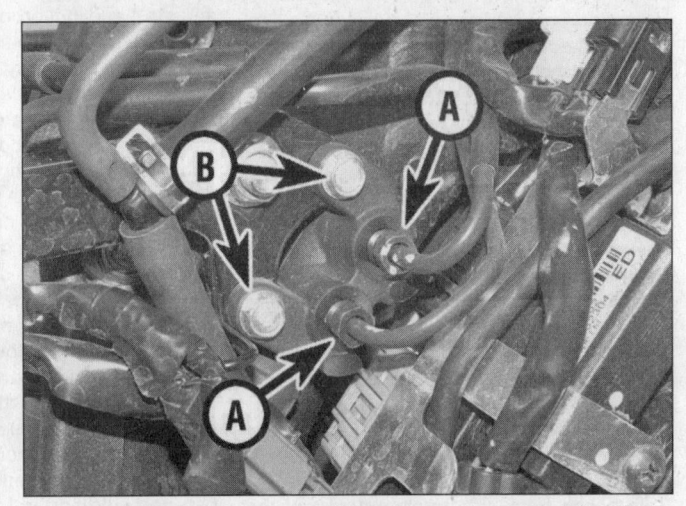

14.35b Delay valve pipe nuts (A) and mounting bolts (B) – CBF models

29 Unscrew the reservoir bolt and displace the reservoir **(see illustration)**.
30 Unscrew the pipe joint nuts and detach the pipes from the valve **(see illustration)**. Plug the ends of the pipes or wrap something tightly around them to minimise fluid loss if the system wasn't drained, and to prevent dirt entering the system.
31 Unscrew the bolts and remove the valve.

Installation

32 Installation is the reverse of removal, noting the following:
- Tighten the mounting bolts to the torque setting specified at the beginning of the Chapter.
- Smear the pipe nut threads with clean brake fluid, and fit them all finger-tight before finally tightening any of them. If the correct tools are available tighten them to the torque setting specified at the beginning of the Chapter for your model.
- Refer to Section 11 and fill and/or bleed the system as required. Check that there are no fluid leaks and test the operation of the brakes before riding the motorcycle.

Delay valve

Note: *The valve cannot be dismantled for overhaul, and no component parts are available. If the valve fails, it must be replaced with a new one.*

Removal

33 Remove the right-hand side cover (see Chapter 7).
34 Either drain the brake fluid (Section 11) or prepare to plug the pipe ends.
35 Unscrew the pipe joint nuts and detach the pipes from the valve **(see illustrations)**. If the brake fluid hasn't been drained plug the ends or wrap something tightly around them to minimise fluid loss and prevent dirt entering the system.
36 Unscrew the bolts and remove the valve.

Installation

37 Installation is the reverse of removal, noting the following:
- Tighten the mounting bolts to the torque setting specified at the beginning of the Chapter.
- Smear the pipe nut threads with clean brake fluid, and fit them all finger-tight before finally tightening any of them. If the correct tools are available tighten them to the torque setting specified at the beginning of the Chapter for your model.
- Refer to Section 11 and fill and/or bleed the system as required. Check that there are no fluid leaks and test the operation of the brakes before riding the motorcycle.

15 Wheel inspection and repair

1 In order to carry out a proper inspection of the wheels, support the bike on the centrestand on CBF600N/NA/S/SA models, and on an auxiliary stand on all other models. Clean the wheels thoroughly to remove mud

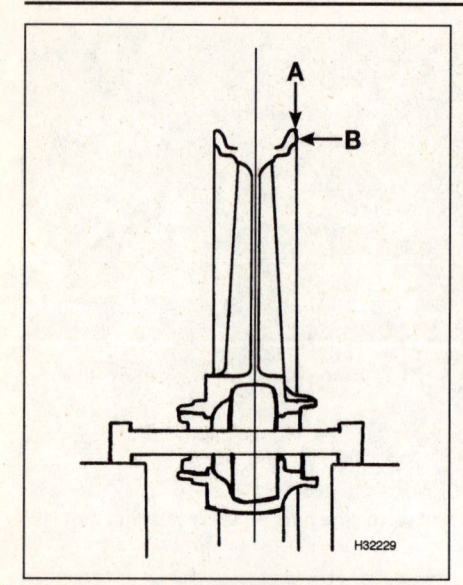

6•28 Brakes, wheels and final drive

15.3 Check the wheel for radial (out-of-round) runout (A) and axial (side-to-side) runout (B)

and dirt that may interfere with the inspection procedure or mask defects. Make a general check of the wheels (see Chapter 1) and tyres (see *Pre-ride checks*).

2 Inspect the wheels for cracks, flat spots on the rim and other damage. Look very closely for dents in the area where the tyre bead contacts the rim. Dents in this area may prevent complete sealing of the tyre against the rim, which leads to deflation of the tyre over a period of time. If damage is evident, or if runout in either direction is excessive, the wheel will have to be renewed. Never attempt to repair a damaged alloy wheel.

3 To check axial (side-to-side) runout of the wheel rim attach a dial gauge to the fork or the swingarm and position its tip against the side of the wheel rim. Spin the wheel slowly and check the amount of run-out, comparing it to the specification listed at the beginning of the Chapter **(see illustration)**.

4 In order to accurately check radial (out of round) runout with the dial gauge, remove the wheel from the machine, and the tyre from the wheel. With the axle clamped in a vice and the dial gauge positioned on the top of the rim, the wheel can be rotated to check the runout **(see illustration 15.3)**.

5 An easier, though slightly less accurate, method is to attach a stiff wire pointer to the fork or the swingarm and position the end a fraction of an inch from the wheel rim where the wheel and tyre join. If the wheel is true, the distance from the pointer to the rim will be constant as the wheel is rotated. **Note:** *If wheel runout is excessive, check the wheel bearings very carefully before renewing the wheel.*

16 Wheel alignment check

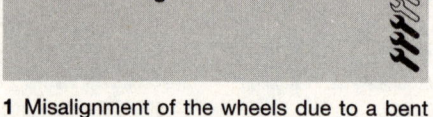

1 Misalignment of the wheels due to a bent frame or forks can cause strange and possibly serious handling problems. If the frame or forks are at fault, repair by a frame specialist or renewal are the only options.

2 To check wheel alignment you will need an assistant, a length of string or a perfectly straight piece of wood and a ruler. A plumb bob or spirit level for checking that the wheels are vertical will also be required.

3 Support the bike on the centrestand on CBF600N/NA/S/SA models, and on an auxiliary stand on all other models. Measure the width of both tyres at their widest points. Subtract the smaller measurement from the larger measurement, then divide the difference by two. The result is the amount of offset that should exist between the front and rear tyres on both sides of the machine.

4 If the string method is used, have your assistant hold one end of it about halfway between the floor and the rear axle, with the string touching the back edge of the rear tyre sidewall.

5 Run the other end of the string forward and pull it tight so that it is roughly parallel to the floor **(see illustration)**. Slowly bring the string into contact with the front edge of the rear tyre sidewall, then turn the front wheel until it is parallel with the string. Measure the distance from the front tyre sidewall to the string.

6 Repeat the procedure on the other side of the motorcycle. The distance from the front tyre sidewall to the string should be equal on both sides.

7 As previously mentioned, a perfectly straight length of wood or metal bar may be substituted for the string **(see illustration)**.

8 If the distance between the string and tyre is greater on one side, or if the rear wheel appears to be out of alignment, have your machine checked by a Honda dealer or frame specialist.

9 If the front-to-back alignment is correct, the wheels still may be out of alignment vertically.

10 Using a plumb bob or spirit level, check the rear wheel to make sure it is vertical. To do this, hold the string of the plumb bob against the tyre upper sidewall and allow the weight to settle just off the floor. If the string touches both the upper and lower tyre sidewalls and is perfectly straight, the wheel is vertical. If it is not, adjust the stand until it is.

11 Once the rear wheel is vertical, check the front wheel in the same manner. If both wheels are not perfectly vertical, the frame and/or major suspension components are bent.

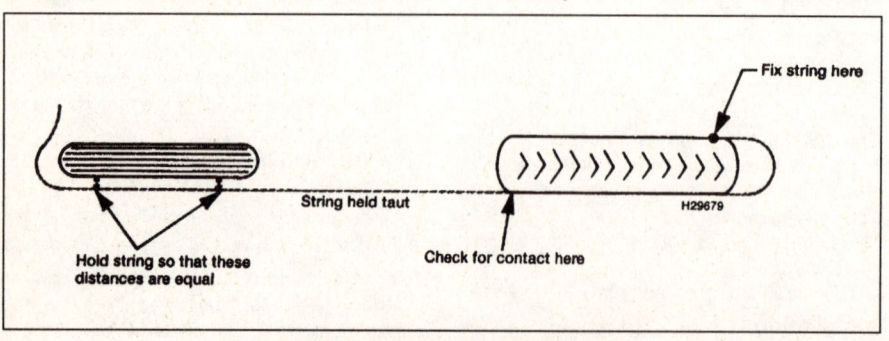

16.5 Wheel alignment check using string

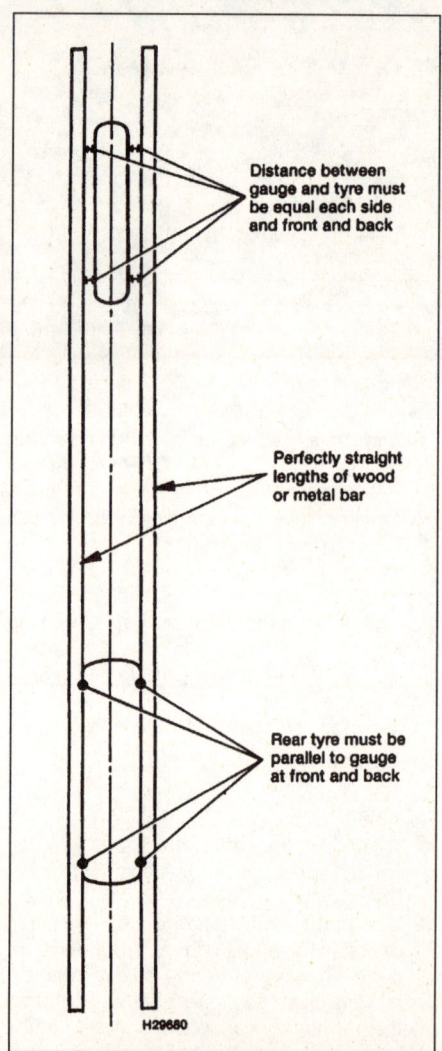

16.7 Wheel alignment check using a straight-edge

Brakes, wheels and final drive 6•29

17.3 Slacken the axle clamp bolt (A), then unscrew the axle bolt (B)

17.5a Slacken the axle clamp bolt (arrowed) . . .

17 Front wheel

Removal

1 Position the motorcycle on the centrestand on CBF600N/NA/S/SA models and on an auxiliary stand on all other models, and support it so that the front wheel is off the ground. If a jack is being placed under the engine place a piece of wood between the jack head and the sump to spread the load. Do not support the bike on the exhaust system. Always make sure the motorcycle is properly supported.
2 Displace the front brake calipers (see Section 3). Support the calipers with a cable-tie or a bungee cord so that no strain is placed on the hydraulic hoses. There is no need to disconnect the hoses from the calipers. **Note:** *Do not operate the front brake lever (or either brake on C-ABS models) with the calipers removed.*
3 Slacken the axle clamp bolt on the bottom of the right-hand fork **(see illustration)**.
4 Unscrew the axle bolt most of the way out of the right-hand end of the axle.
5 Slacken the axle clamp bolt on the bottom of the left-hand fork **(see illustration)**. Take the weight of the wheel, then push the axle through from the right using the axle bolt, then remove the bolt and withdraw the axle from the left – there is a hole in the end of the axle that can be used to hook a tool in to ease withdrawal if required **(see illustration)**. Carefully lower the wheel and draw it forwards.
6 Remove the long spacer from the right-hand side of the wheel and the short spacer from the left-hand side **(see illustrations)**. Clean all old grease off the spacers, axle and seals.
Caution: *Don't lay the wheel down and allow it to rest on a disc – the disc could become warped. Set the wheel on wood blocks so the disc doesn't support the weight of the wheel.*
7 Check the axle is straight by rolling it on a flat surface such as a piece of plate glass (first wipe off all old grease and remove any corrosion using steel wool). If the equipment is available, place the axle in V-blocks and measure the runout using a dial gauge. If the axle is bent or the runout exceeds the limit specified, replace it with a new one.
8 Check the condition of the grease seals and wheel bearings (see Section 19).

Installation

9 Apply a smear of grease to the inside of the wheel spacers, and also to the outside where

17.5b . . . then withdraw the axle and remove the wheel

they fit into the seals. Fit the long spacer into the right-hand side of the wheel and the short spacer into the left-hand side **(see illustrations 17.6a and b)**. Each side of the wheel can be identified using the directional arrow (denoting the normal direction of wheel rotation) on the tyre and cast into one of the spokes and on the brake disc, or by the pulse ring fitted on the right-hand side on C-ABS models **(see illustration 17.10)**.
10 Manoeuvre the wheel into position between the forks – check it is the correct way round using the directional arrows **(see illustration)**. Apply a thin coat of grease to the axle.

17.6a Remove the long right-hand spacer . . .

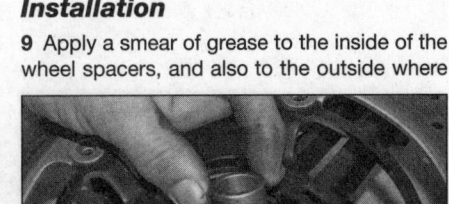

17.6b . . . and the short left-hand spacer

17.10 Make sure the wheel is the correct way round

6•30 Brakes, wheels and final drive

17.12a Fit the axle bolt . . .

17.12b . . . and tighten it to the specified torque

17.12c Counter-hold the axle head using a hex bit on CB and CBR models

11 Lift the wheel into place, making sure the spacers remain in position. Slide the axle all the way in from the left-hand side **(see illustration 17.5b)**.
12 Fit the axle bolt and tighten it to the torque setting specified at the beginning of the Chapter **(see illustrations)**. If the axle turns when tightening the bolt counter-hold it using a large hex key on CB600F/FA and CBR600F/FA models **(see illustration)**, or a screwdriver through the holes in the left-hand end on CBF600N/NA/S/SA models.
13 Tighten the axle clamp bolt on the bottom of the right-hand fork to the specified torque setting **(see illustration 17.3)**.
14 Lower the front wheel to the ground. Install the brake calipers (see Section 3, and the Note therein regarding the mounting bolts).

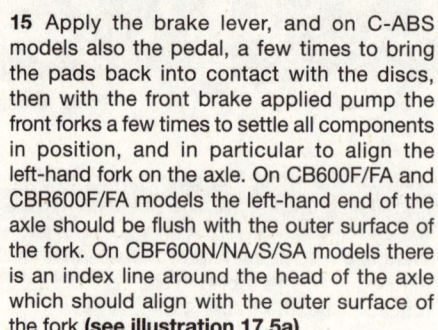

15 Apply the brake lever, and on C-ABS models also the pedal, a few times to bring the pads back into contact with the discs, then with the front brake applied pump the front forks a few times to settle all components in position, and in particular to align the left-hand fork on the axle. On CB600F/FA and CBR600F/FA models the left-hand end of the axle should be flush with the outer surface of the fork. On CBF600N/NA/S/SA models there is an index line around the head of the axle which should align with the outer surface of the fork **(see illustration 17.5a)**.
16 Tighten the axle clamp bolt on the bottom of the left-hand fork to the specified torque **(see illustration 17.5a)**.
17 Clean the discs using brake system cleaner. Check for correct operation of the brakes before riding the motorcycle.

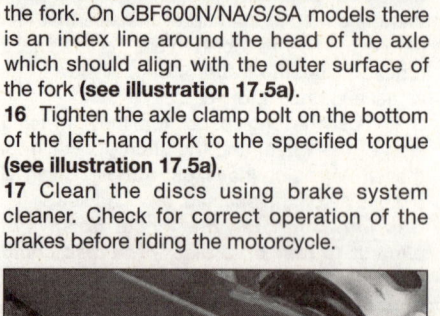

18 Rear wheel

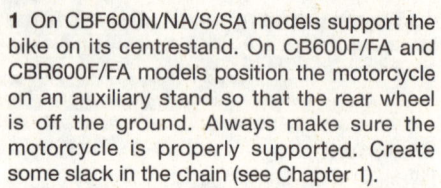

Removal

1 On CBF600N/NA/S/SA models support the bike on its centrestand. On CB600F/FA and CBR600F/FA models position the motorcycle on an auxiliary stand so that the rear wheel is off the ground. Always make sure the motorcycle is properly supported. Create some slack in the chain (see Chapter 1).
2 Unscrew the axle nut and remove the washer, and on CBF600N/NA/S/SA models the slide plate **(see illustration)**.
3 Take the weight of the wheel, then withdraw the axle from the left-hand side, on CBF600N/NA/S/SA models bringing the side plate with it, and lower the wheel to the ground **(see illustration)**. If the axle is difficult to withdraw, drive it out using a soft-faced mallet to prevent damage to the threads.
4 Disengage the chain from the sprocket **(see illustration)**. Draw the wheel back until the caliper bracket is clear of its guide on the swingarm, then lift it out from between the swingarm and the wheel and support it clear **(see illustration)** – on models with C-ABS take care not to knock the head of the wheel sensor. Remove the wheel. Fit the caliper bracket back onto the swingarm if required, and secure it using a cable tie. On CBF600N/NA/S/SA models remove the chain adjuster from each side of the swingarm if required **(see illustration)**.

18.2 Unscrew the axle nut and remove the washer and the plate (arrowed) – CBF model shown

18.3 Withdraw the axle and lower the wheel

18.4a Slip the chain off the sprocket

18.4b Draw the wheel back and displace the caliper bracket when clear

18.4c Remove the chain adjuster from each side

18.5a Remove the shouldered left-hand spacer . . .

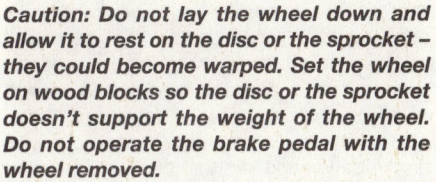

18.5b . . . and the plain right-hand spacer

19.3 Lever out the bearing seals

Caution: Do not lay the wheel down and allow it to rest on the disc or the sprocket – they could become warped. Set the wheel on wood blocks so the disc or the sprocket doesn't support the weight of the wheel. Do not operate the brake pedal with the wheel removed.

5 Remove the shouldered spacer from the left-hand side of the wheel and the plain spacer from the right-hand side **(see illustrations)**. Clean all old grease off the spacers, axle and seals.

6 Check the axle is straight by rolling it on a flat surface such as a piece of plate glass (if the axle is corroded, first remove the corrosion with steel wool). If the equipment is available, place the axle in V-blocks and check the runout using a dial gauge. If the axle is bent or the runout exceeds the limit specified at the beginning of the Chapter, replace it with a new one.

7 Check the condition of the grease seals and wheel bearings (see Section 19).

Installation

8 Apply a smear of grease to the inside of the wheel spacers, and also to the outside where they fit into the wheel. Fit the shouldered spacer into the left-hand side of the wheel and the plain spacer into the right-hand side **(see illustrations 18.5a and b)**. Apply a thin coat of grease to the axle. If the caliper bracket is located on the swingarm displace it and support it clear.

9 On CBF600N/NA/S/SA models slide the chain adjusters into the swingarm if removed (see illustration 18.4c). Fit the side plate onto the axle with the angled section facing away from the head **(see illustration 18.3)**.

10 Manoeuvre the wheel into position between the ends of the swingarm. Slide the brake caliper bracket between the wheel and the swingarm **(see illustration 18.4b)** and locate it on its guide – on models with C-ABS take care not to knock the head of the wheel sensor. Engage the drive chain with the sprocket **(see illustration 18.4a)**.

11 Lift the wheel into position and slide the axle in from the left **(see illustration 18.3)**, making sure the spacers and caliper bracket remain correctly installed. On CBF600N/NA/S/SA models locate the bottom edge of the side plate under the swingarm. Check that everything is correctly aligned. On CBF600N/NA/S/SA models fit the side plate onto the right-hand end of the axle. Fit the washer and axle nut but leave it loose **(see illustration 18.2)**. Check and adjust the drive chain slack (see Chapter 1). On completion tighten the axle nut to the torque setting specified at the beginning of the Chapter.

12 Operate the brake pedal several times to bring the pads into contact with the disc. Check the operation of the rear brake carefully before riding the bike.

19 Wheel bearings

Note: Always renew the wheel bearings in sets, never individually. Avoid using a high pressure cleaner on the wheel bearing area.

Front wheel bearings

1 Remove the wheel (see Section 17). If required remove the discs (see Section 4) to prevent them being damaged or distorted during bearing removal – if you do leave them in place, take care to support the wheel on wood blocks so that the wheel rim supports the weight of the wheel.

2 Inspect the seals and bearings – check that the bearing inner race turns smoothly and that the outer race is a tight fit in the hub (see *Tools and Workshop Tips* (Section 5) in the Reference Section). **Note:** *Do not remove the bearings unless they are going to be replaced with new ones.*

3 If new components are needed lever out the bearing seal from each side of the hub using a flat-bladed screwdriver or a seal hook **(see illustration)**. Take care not to damage the hub. Discard the seals as new ones must be fitted on reassembly.

4 Move the centre spacer to one side to expose the inner race of the bearing, then locate a drift on it and drive the bearing out **(see illustrations)**. If you can't get sufficient purchase, remove the bearings using an internal expanding puller with slide-hammer attachment, which can be obtained commercially – select the correct attachment and locate it between the inner race of the bearing and the spacer, then tighten the inner bolt to expand and lock the puller **(see illustration)**. Attach the slide-hammer, hold

19.4a Drive the bearing out using a drift . . .

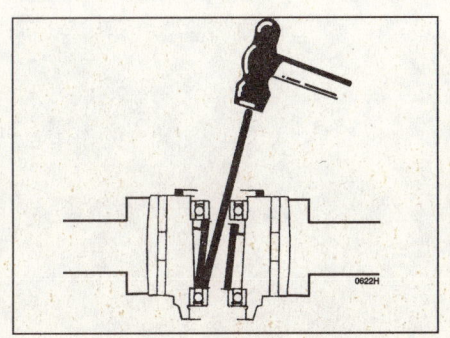

19.4b . . . locating it as shown

19.4c Fit the attachment under the bearing . . .

19.4d ... then fit the slide-hammer and jar the bearing out

19.7 Using a socket to drive the bearing in

19.9 Fit the seal, setting it flush with the rim

the wheel firmly down and jar the bearing out **(see illustration)**. Having removed the first bearing remove the spacer which fits between the bearings.
5 Remove the other bearing using a suitable drift (such as a socket on an extension) inserted from the opposite side to the bearing.
6 Thoroughly clean the hub area of the wheel with a suitable solvent and inspect the bearing housing for scoring and wear.
7 Drive the new bearings into the hub using a bearing driver or suitable socket **(see illustration)**. Fit the right-hand bearing first, with its marked side facing outwards. Make sure that the driver or socket bears only on the outer race and the bearing fits squarely and all the way into its seat.
8 Turn the wheel over and fit the bearing spacer. Fit the second bearing in the same way as the first.
9 Fit the new seals into the hub using finger pressure or a suitable driver that bears on the outer rim, setting them flush with the hub **(see illustration and 19.19)**. Smear the seal lips with grease.
10 Install the brake discs if removed (see Section 4). Clean the discs using brake system cleaner, then install the wheel (see Section 17).

Rear wheel bearings

11 Remove the wheel (see Section 18). If required remove the disc (see Section 8) to prevent it being damaged or distorted during bearing removal – if you do leave it in place, take care to support the wheel on wood blocks so that the wheel rim supports the weight of the wheel. Lift the sprocket coupling out of the hub **(see illustration)**.
12 Inspect the seal and the bearings in both sides of the hub – check that the bearing inner race turns smoothly and that the outer race is a tight fit in the hub (see *Tools and Workshop Tips* (Section 5) in the Reference section). **Note:** *Do not remove the bearings unless they are going to be replaced with new ones.*
13 If new components are needed lever out the bearing seal from the right-hand side of the hub using a flat-bladed screwdriver or a seal hook **(see illustration)**. Take care not to damage the hub. Discard the seal as a new one should be fitted on reassembly.
14 Move the centre spacer to one side to expose the inner race of the bearing, then locate a drift on it and drive the bearing out **(see illustrations 19.4 and b)**. If you can't get sufficient purchase, remove the bearings using an internal expanding puller with slide-hammer attachment, which can be obtained commercially – select the correct attachment and locate it behind the inner race of the bearing, then tighten the inner bolt to expand and lock the puller **(see illustration 19.4c)**. Attach the slide-hammer, hold the wheel firmly down and jar the bearing out **(see illustration 19.4d)**. Having removed the first bearing remove the spacer which fits between the bearings.
15 Remove the other bearing using a suitable drift (such as a socket on an extension) inserted from the opposite side to the bearing.
16 Thoroughly clean the hub area of the wheel with a suitable solvent and inspect the bearing housing for scoring and wear.
17 Drive the new bearings into the hub using a bearing driver or suitable socket **(see illustration 19.7)**. Fit the right-hand bearing first, with its marked side facing outwards. Make sure that the driver or socket bears only on the outer race and the bearing fits squarely and all the way into its seat.
18 Turn the wheel over and fit the bearing spacer. Fit the second bearing in the same way as the first.
19 Fit the new seal into the right-hand side of the hub using finger pressure or a suitable driver that bears on the outer rim, setting it flush with the hub **(see illustration)**. Smear the seal lips with grease.
20 Check the sprocket coupling/rubber dampers (see Section 23). Check the condition of the hub O-ring and clean it or replace it with a new one if necessary **(see illustration)**.

19.11 Lift the sprocket coupling off the wheel

19.13 Lever out the bearing seal

19.19 Using a piece of wood across the rim as shown automatically sets the seal flush

19.20 Fit a new O-ring if necessary

Brakes, wheels and final drive 6•33

19.23 Lever out the bearing seal

19.24 Drive the spacer out of the bearings from the outside

Smear the O-ring with oil. Fit the sprocket coupling into the wheel **(see illustration 19.11)**. Clean the brake disc using acetone or brake system cleaner. Install the wheel (see Section 18).

Sprocket coupling bearing

21 Remove the wheel (see Section 18). Lift the sprocket coupling out of the hub **(see illustration 19.11)**.
22 Inspect the seal and bearing – check that the bearing inner races turn smoothly and that the outer race is a tight fit in the coupling (see *Tools and Workshop Tips (Section 5)* in the Reference Section). **Note:** *Do not remove the bearing unless it is being replaced with a new one.*
23 If new components are needed lever out the bearing seal using a flat-bladed screwdriver or a seal hook **(see illustration)**. Take care not to damage the rim of the coupling. Discard the seal – a new one must be fitted.

24 Remove the bearing spacer from inside the coupling – if it is tight place the coupling on the work surface, sprocket side up, and drive it out using a suitably sized socket **(see illustration)**.
25 Support the coupling on blocks of wood, sprocket side down, and drive the bearing out from the inside using a bearing driver or socket **(see illustration)**.
26 Thoroughly clean the coupling with a suitable solvent and inspect the bearing housing for scoring and wear.
27 Place the new bearing marked side down on a hard flat surface, then drive the spacer fully in until its rim seats on the inner race of the bearing.
28 Drive the bearing and spacer as one squarely into the coupling, with the spacer innermost, using a driver or suitable socket on the outer race of the bearing until the bearing seats (see *Tools and Workshop Tips*) **(see illustration)**.

19.25 Drive the bearings out from the inside

29 Fit the new seal into the coupling **(see illustration)**. Level the seal with the rim of the coupling with a small block of wood **(see illustration 19.19)**. Smear the seal lip with grease.
30 Check the sprocket coupling/rubber

19.28 Drive the bearing and spacer assembly in from the outside

19.29 Press the new seal into the hub

6•34 Brakes, wheels and final drive

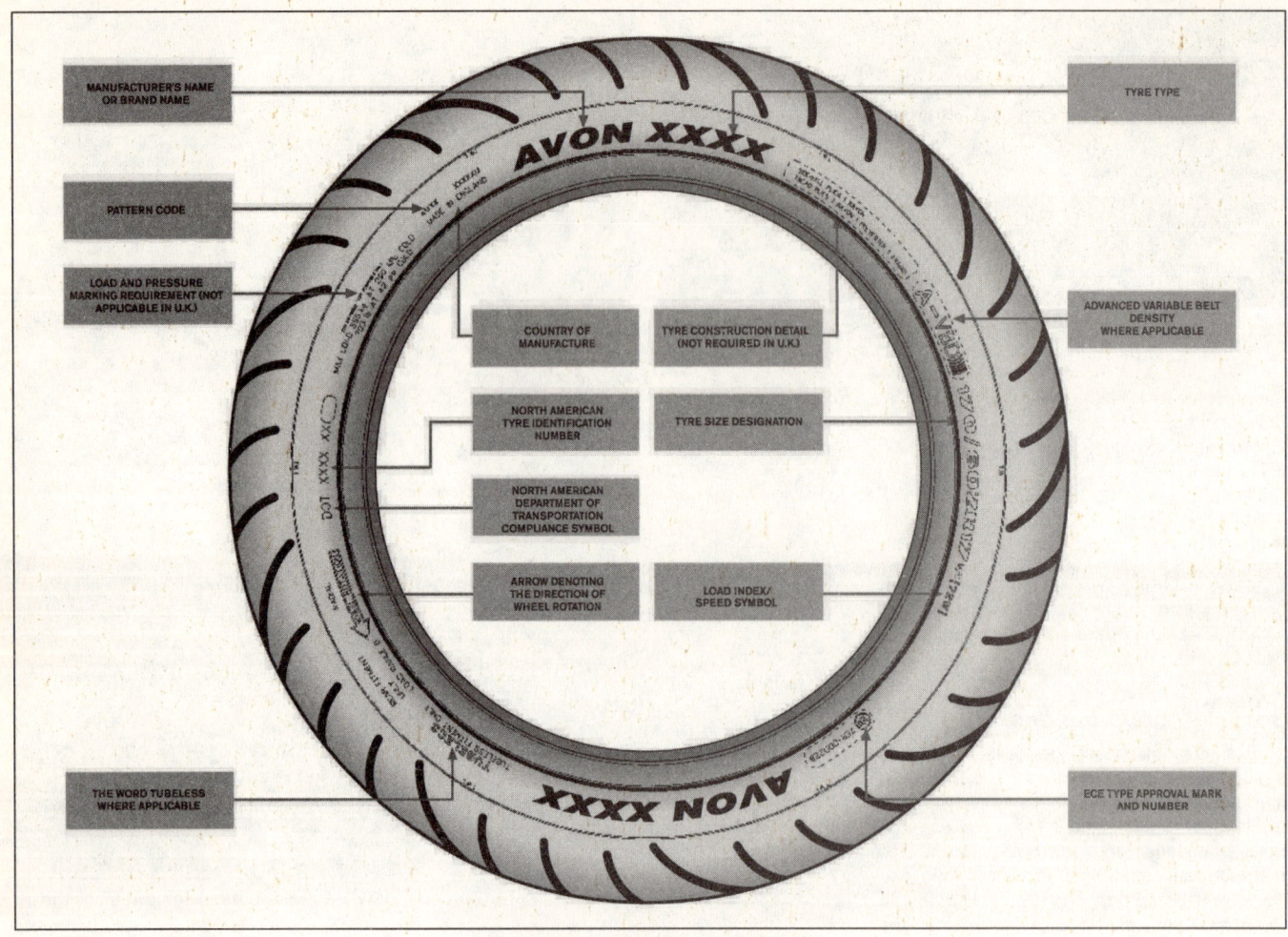

20.3 Common tyre sidewall markings

Labels around the tyre:
- MANUFACTURER'S NAME OR BRAND NAME
- PATTERN CODE
- LOAD AND PRESSURE MARKING REQUIREMENT (NOT APPLICABLE IN U.K.)
- COUNTRY OF MANUFACTURE
- NORTH AMERICAN TYRE IDENTIFICATION NUMBER
- NORTH AMERICAN DEPARTMENT OF TRANSPORTATION COMPLIANCE SYMBOL
- ARROW DENOTING THE DIRECTION OF WHEEL ROTATION
- THE WORD TUBELESS WHERE APPLICABLE
- TYRE TYPE
- TYRE CONSTRUCTION DETAIL (NOT REQUIRED IN U.K.)
- ADVANCED VARIABLE BELT DENSITY WHERE APPLICABLE
- TYRE SIZE DESIGNATION
- LOAD INDEX/SPEED SYMBOL
- ECE TYPE APPROVAL MARK AND NUMBER

dampers (see Section 23). Check the condition of the hub O-ring and clean it or replace it with a new one if necessary **(see illustration 19.20)**. Smear the O-ring with oil. Fit the sprocket coupling into the wheel. Install the wheel (see Section 18).

20 Tyres

General information

1 The wheels are designed to take tubeless tyres only. Tyre sizes are given in the Specifications at the beginning of this chapter.
2 Refer to the *Pre-ride checks* listed at the beginning of this manual for tyre maintenance.

Fitting new tyres

3 When selecting new tyres, refer to the tyre information in the Owner's Handbook. Ensure that front and rear tyre types are compatible, the correct size and correct speed rating; if necessary seek advice from a Honda dealer or tyre fitting specialist **(see illustration)**.
4 It is recommended that tyres are fitted by a motorcycle tyre specialist rather than attempted in the home workshop. This is particularly relevant in the case of tubeless tyres because the force required to break the seal between the wheel rim and tyre bead is substantial, and is usually beyond the capabilities of an individual working with normal tyre levers. Additionally, the specialist will be able to balance the wheels after tyre fitting.
5 Note that punctured tubeless tyres can in some cases be repaired. External repairs made using a repair kit should only ever be considered as a temporary measure to get you to a dealer for a new tyre, and riding at speed or with any extra load should be avoided. Internal repairs carried out by a motorcycle tyre fitting specialist are better. Make sure a wheel with a repaired tyre is balanced before it is fitted back on the bike. Honda advise that a repaired tyre should not be used at speeds above 50 mph (80 kmh) for the first 24 hours, and not above 80 mph (130 kmh) thereafter, and carrying heavy loads should be avoided.

21 Drive chain

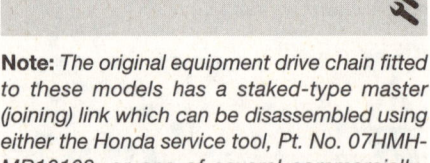

Note: *The original equipment drive chain fitted to these models has a staked-type master (joining) link which can be disassembled using either the Honda service tool, Pt. No. 07HMH-MR10103, or one of several commercially-available drive chain cutting/staking tools (but the cheap ones are best avoided). Such chains can be recognised by the master joining link side plate's identification marks (and usually its different colour), as well as by the staked ends of the link's two pins which look as if they have been deeply centre-punched, instead of peened over as with all the other pins.*

Removal

1 Support the motorcycle on the centrestand on CBF600N/NA/S/SA models, and on an auxiliary stand so that the rear wheel is off the ground on all other models. Locate the joining link in a suitable position to work on by rotating

Brakes, wheels and final drive 6•35

21.1 Soft link can be easily identified by its different pin ends

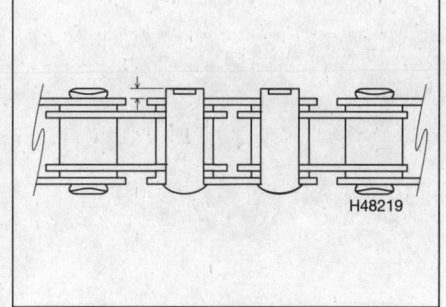

21.8 Measure the joining link pin projection from the sideplate

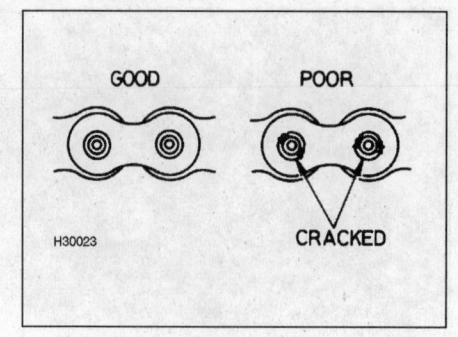

21.9a Check staking for any signs of cracking

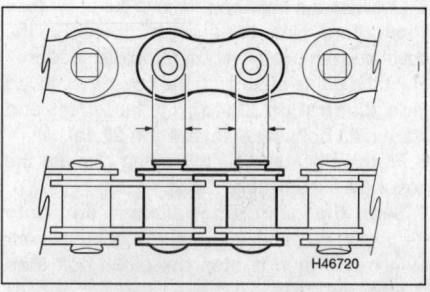

21.9b Check the diameter of the staked pin ends

the back wheel (see illustration). Slacken the drive chain as described in Chapter 1.
2 If required, remove the chainguard.
3 Remove the front sprocket cover (see Section 22).
4 Split the chain at the joining link using the chain tool, following carefully the manufacturer's operating instructions (see also Section 8 in *Tools and Workshop Tips* in the Reference Section). Remove the chain from the bike, noting its routing around the swingarm.

Cleaning

5 Refer to Chapter 1, Section 1, for details of routine cleaning with the chain installed on the sprockets.
6 If the chain is extremely dirty remove it from the motorcycle and soak it in paraffin (kerosene) for approximately five or six minutes, then clean it using a soft brush.
Caution: *Don't use gasoline (petrol), solvent or other cleaning fluids which might damage its internal sealing properties. Don't use high-pressure water. Remove the chain, wipe it off, then blow dry it with compressed air immediately. The entire process shouldn't take longer than ten minutes – if it does, the O-rings in the chain rollers could be damaged.*

Installation

⚠️ **Warning:** *NEVER install a drive chain which uses a clip-type master (split) link. Use ONLY the correct service tools to secure the staked-type of master link – if you do not*

have access to such tools, have the chain replaced by a Honda dealer.
Note: *The specifications referred to in Steps 8 and 9 only apply to the DID and Regina drive chain types fitted as original equipment (see Specifications).*
7 Route the drive chain around the sprockets leaving the two ends mid-way between the sprockets along the bottom run.
8 Referring to Section 8 in *Tools and Workshop Tips* in the Reference Section, install the new joining link from the inside using new O-rings. Fit the new side plate using new O-rings and with its identification marks facing out. Measure the amount that the joining link pins project from the sideplate and check they are within the measurements specified at the beginning of the Chapter (see illustration). Stake the new link using the chain tool, following carefully the instructions of both the chain manufacturer and the tool manufacturer. DO NOT re-use old joining link components.
9 After staking, check the joining link and staking for any signs of cracking (see illustration). If there is any evidence of cracking, the joining link, O-rings and sideplate must be replaced. Measure the diameter of the staked ends in two directions and check that it is evenly staked and within the measurements specified at the beginning of the Chapter (see illustration). Check that the link pivots freely.
10 Install the sprocket cover (see Section 22).
11 Install the chainguard if removed.
12 On completion, adjust and lubricate the chain following the procedures described in Chapter 1.

22 Sprockets

Front sprocket cover removal and installation

1 Carefully pull the outer cover away from the engine to release its pegs from the grommets (see illustration). Check the condition of the grommets and replace them with new ones if cracked or hardened. Clean all old chain grease and road dirt from the inside of the cover, sprocket and surrounding area.
2 Note the alignment of the existing punch marks between the gearchange linkage arm and shaft, or mark the alignment of the shaft with the slit in the linkage arm if they are not clear (see illustration). Unscrew the linkage arm bolt and slide the arm off the shaft.
3 Release the sidestand switch wiring clip from the cover (see illustration).

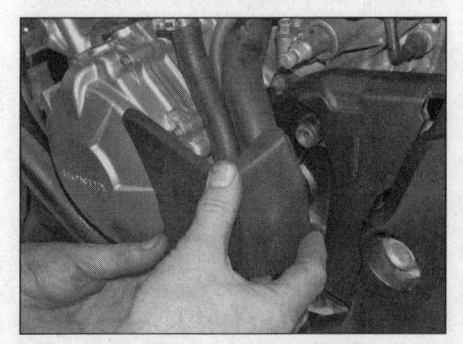

22.1 Pull the outer cover off

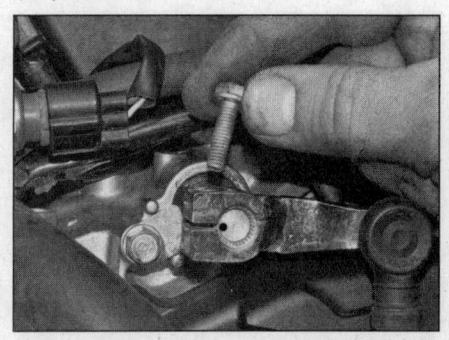

22.2 Note the alignment then unscrew the bolt and slide the arm off the shaft

22.3 Release the wiring clip

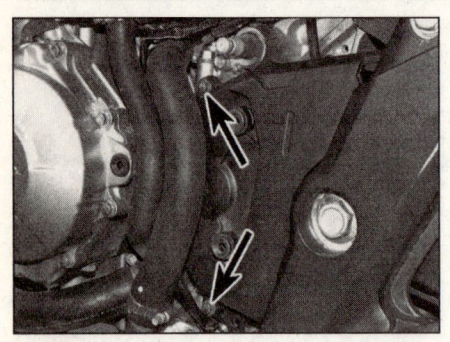

6•36 Brakes, wheels and final drive

22.4a Sprocket cover bolts (arrowed)

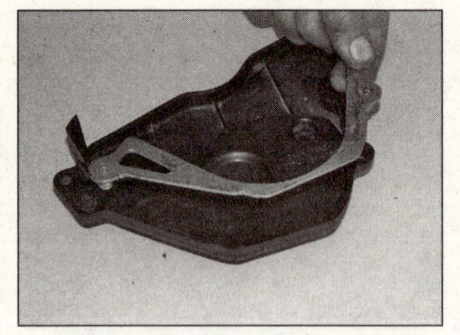

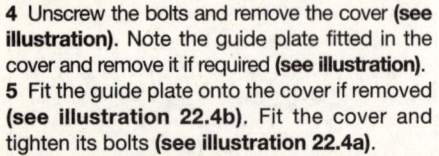

22.4b Remove the guide if required

22.12 Unscrew the bolt and remove the washer

4 Unscrew the bolts and remove the cover **(see illustration)**. Note the guide plate fitted in the cover and remove it if required **(see illustration)**.
5 Fit the guide plate onto the cover if removed **(see illustration 22.4b)**. Fit the cover and tighten its bolts **(see illustration 22.4a)**.
6 Fit the sidestand switch wiring clip into the cover **(see illustration 22.3)**.
7 Slide the gearchange linkage arm onto the shaft, aligning the punch marks, or your own mark, then tighten the pinch bolt **(see illustration 22.2)**.
8 Carefully push the outer cover pegs into the grommets **(see illustration 22.1)**.

Sprocket check

9 Check the wear pattern on both sprockets (see Chapter 1, Section 1). If the sprocket teeth are worn excessively, replace the chain and both sprockets as a set. Whenever the sprockets are inspected, the drive chain should be inspected also (see Chapter 1). Always renew the chain and sprockets as a set – worn sprockets can ruin a new drive chain and *vice versa*.
10 Adjust and lubricate the chain following the procedures described in Chapter 1.

Sprocket removal and installation

Front sprocket

11 Remove the front sprocket cover (see Steps 1 to 4).
12 Have an assistant apply the rear brake, then unscrew the sprocket bolt and remove the washer **(see illustration)**.
13 Fully slacken the drive chain as described in Chapter 1. If the rear sprocket is being removed as well, remove the rear wheel now to give full slack (see Section 18). Otherwise disengage the chain from the rear sprocket if required to provide more slack.
14 Slide the chain and sprocket off the shaft, then slip the sprocket out of the chain **(see illustration)**.
15 Engage the new sprocket with the chain, making sure the marked side is facing out, and slide it on the shaft **(see illustration 22.14)**.
16 If removed, fit the rear sprocket now, and install the wheel (see Section 18). If the chain was merely disengaged, fit it back onto the rear sprocket. Take up the slack in the chain.
17 Fit the sprocket bolt with its washer **(see illustration 22.12)**. Tighten the bolt to the torque setting specified at the beginning of the Chapter, holding the rear brake on to prevent the sprocket turning.
18 Fit the sprocket covers (see Steps 5 to 8). Adjust and lubricate the chain following the procedures described in Chapter 1.

Rear sprocket

19 Remove the rear wheel (see Section 18). Rest it sprocket side up on some blocks of wood.
20 Unscrew the sprocket nuts and lift the sprocket off the studs, noting which way round it fits **(see illustration)**.
21 Fit the sprocket over the studs and onto the hub with the marked side facing out. Fit the nuts and tighten them evenly and in a criss-cross sequence to the torque setting specified at the beginning of the Chapter.
22 Install the rear wheel (see Section 18).

23 Rear sprocket coupling/ rubber dampers

1 Remove the rear wheel (see Section 18). Check for play between the sprocket coupling and the wheel hub by turning the sprocket. Any play indicates worn rubber damper segments.
Caution: Do not lay the wheel down on the disc as it could become warped. Lay the wheel on wooden blocks so that the disc is off the ground.
2 Lift the sprocket coupling off the wheel leaving the rubber dampers in position **(see illustration 19.11)**. Note the spacer inside the coupling – it should be a tight fit. Check the coupling for cracks or any obvious signs of damage.
3 Lift the rubber damper segments from the wheel and check them for cracks, hardening and general deterioration **(see illustration)**. Replace them with a new set if necessary.
4 Check the condition of the hub O-ring and clean it or replace it with a new one if necessary **(see illustration 19.20)**. Smear the O-ring with oil.
5 Checking and replacement procedures for the sprocket coupling bearing are in Section 19.
6 Installation is the reverse of removal. Make sure the spacer is correctly installed in the coupling. Align the coupling correctly with the rubber dampers and press it fully into the hub.
7 Install the rear wheel (see Section 18).

22.14 Draw the sprocket off the shaft and disengage the chain

22.20 Unscrew the nuts (arrowed) and remove the sprocket

23.3 Check the rubber dampers as described

Chapter 7
Bodywork

Contents

	Section number		Section number
CB600F/FA – 2007 to 2010	3	CBR600F/FA	5
CB600F/FA – 2011-on	4	General information	1
CBF600N/NA	6	Trim clips	2
CBF600S/SA	7		

Degrees of difficulty

Easy, suitable for novice with little experience	Fairly easy, suitable for beginner with some experience	Fairly difficult, suitable for competent DIY mechanic	Difficult, suitable for experienced DIY mechanic	Very difficult, suitable for expert DIY or professional

Specifications

Torque settings

Front mudguard bolts	12 Nm
Mirror bolts	14 Nm
Passenger grab-rail bolts	27 Nm
Seat bracket bolts (CBF600N/NA/S/SA)	22 Nm

1 General information

This Chapter covers the procedures necessary to remove and install the bodywork. Since many service and repair operations on these motorcycles require the removal of the body panels, the procedures are grouped here and referred to from other Chapters.

In the case of damage to the bodywork, it is usually necessary to remove the broken component and replace it with a new (or used) one. Note that there are however some companies that specialise in 'plastic welding' and there are a number of bodywork repair kits now available for motorcycles.

When attempting to remove any body panel, first study it closely, noting any fasteners and associated fittings, to be sure of returning everything to its correct place on installation. Refer to Section 2 for more information on the types of trim clip used and how to release and refit them. In some cases the aid of an assistant will be required when removing panels, to help avoid the risk of damage to paintwork. Once the evident fasteners have been removed, try to withdraw the panel as described but DO NOT FORCE IT – if it will not release, check that all fasteners have been removed and try again.

When installing a body panel, first study it closely, noting any fasteners and associated fittings removed with it, to be sure of returning everything to its correct place. Check that all fasteners are in good condition, including the trim clips and damping/rubber mounts; replace any faulty fasteners with new ones before the panel is reassembled. Check also that all mounting brackets are straight and repair them or replace them with new ones if necessary before attempting to install the panel.

Tighten the fasteners securely, but be careful not to overtighten any of them or the panel may break (not always immediately) due to the uneven stress.

2 Trim clips

1 Three types of plastic trim clip may be used, so carefully note which fits where when removing the body panels.
2 The first and most widely used type has a centre pin that you push into the body of the clip to allow the clip to be drawn out of the panel **(see illustrations)**. To install the clip,

2.2a Push the centre pin (arrowed) . . .

2.2b . . . into the body to release the clip

2.2c Push the centre pin out before installing the clip, then push it in when installed to lock it

7•2 Bodywork

2.3 Pull the centre pin (arrowed) out to release the clip, and push it back in to lock it

first expand the pawls of the clip body and push the centre pin back out **(see illustration)**. Now fit the clip body into its hole, then push the centre pin in so that it is flush with the clip head. The clip should now be locked in place.

3 The second type has a protruding centre pin that you pull out of the body of the clip to allow the clip to be drawn out of the panel **(see illustration)**. To install the clip, fit the clip body into its hole, then push the centre pin in. The clip should now be locked in place.

4 The third type of trim clip has a Phillips screw head in the centre that you unscrew, then pull the body of the clip out of the panel **(see illustration)**. When installing them, insert it in the panel then push the centre fully into the body **(see illustration)**. As they are made of plastic, the threads easily become worn in which case the centres may not unscrew. If this happens, lever the centre out of the body using a small screwdriver and replace the trim clip with a new one.

3 CB600F/FA – 2007 to 2010

Seat

1 Unlock the seat using the ignition key, turning it clockwise, then draw the seat up and back to remove it, noting how the hooks locate **(see illustration)**.

2 Installation is the reverse of removal – make sure the hooks locate correctly. Push down on the back of the passenger seat to engage the latch.

Side covers

3 Unscrew the bolt **(see illustration)**.
4 Carefully release the tabs from the grommets in the fuel tank and swingarm pivot bracket and remove the cover **(see illustrations)**.
5 Installation is the reverse of removal. Make sure the grommets are in good condition and correctly seated.

Headlight covers

6 Remove the two trim clips securing the upper cover (see Section 2), then release the tabs from the side covers and the headlight **(see illustrations)**.
7 To remove the side covers first remove the upper cover. Remove the right-hand cover first – unscrew the bolt on the side, then carefully

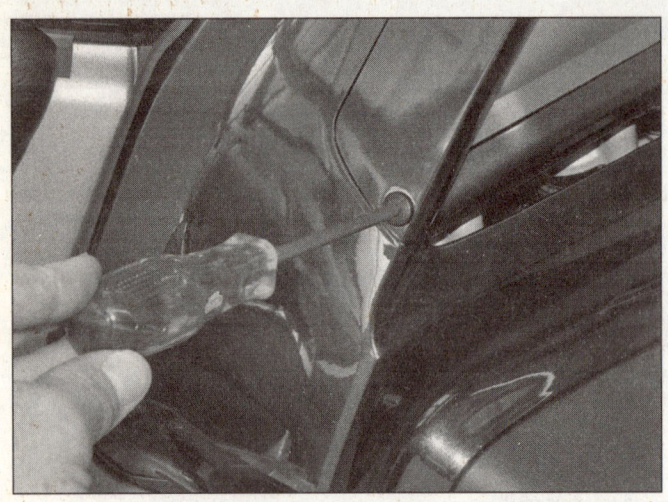

2.4a Undo the centre screw then pull the clip out

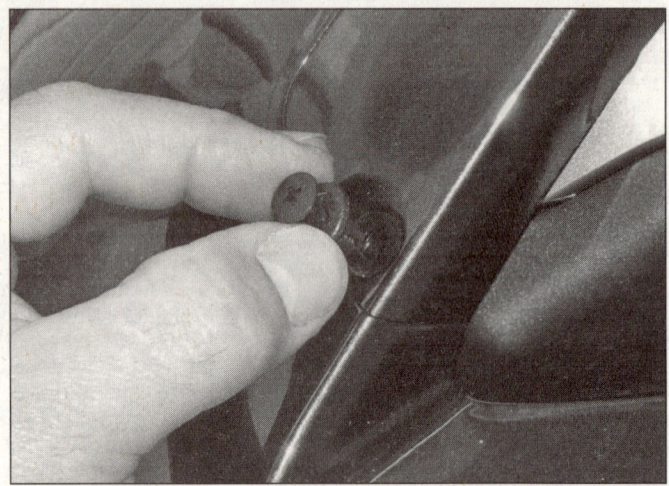

2.4b Fit the clip in the hole then push the centre in to lock it

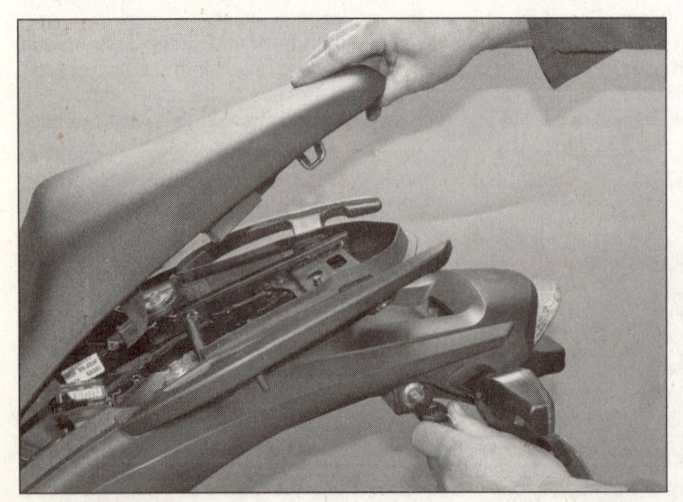

3.1 Unlock the seat and lift it up noting how the hooks locate

3.3 Side cover bolt (arrowed)

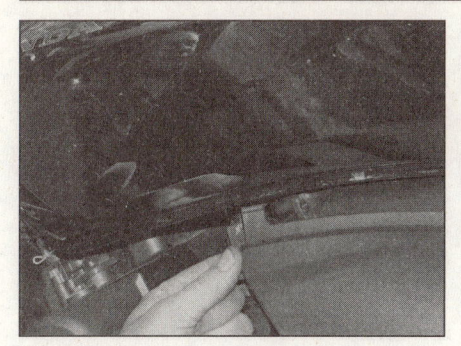

Bodywork 7•3

3.4a Release the cover from the tank . . .

3.4b . . . and the pivot bracket

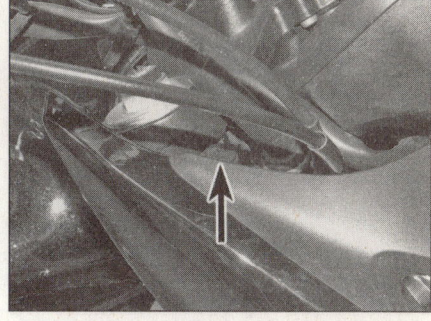

3.6a Release the trim clip (arrowed) on each side . . .

pull the cover away to release the peg from the grommet in the headlight and the tabs on the underside from the left-hand cover **(see illustrations)**. Release the wiring connector retainer and move the connector aside **(see illustration)**. Disconnect both turn signal wiring connectors and remove the right-hand cover, drawing the connector through the guide hole **(see illustrations)**. After removing the right-hand cover release the wiring clip from the bracket on the underside, then release the left-hand turn signal wire from the clip **(see illustration)**. Remove the left-hand cover – unscrew the bolt on the side, then carefully pull the cover away to release the peg from the grommet in the headlight and remove the cover, drawing the turn signal connector through the guide hole.

8 Installation is the reverse of removal –

3.6b . . . then release the tabs

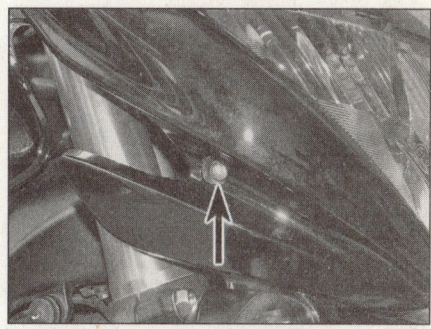

install the left-hand cover first. Make sure the grommets are in good condition and correctly seated, and smear them with oil.

3.7a Unscrew the bolt (arrowed) . . .

Instrument cover

9 Remove the headlight covers (see above) and the headlight (see Chapter 8).

3.7b . . . pull the peg out of the grommet . . .

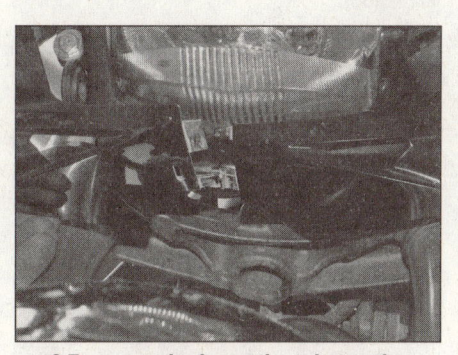

3.7c . . . and release the tabs on the underside

3.7d Release the retainer and move the connector aside

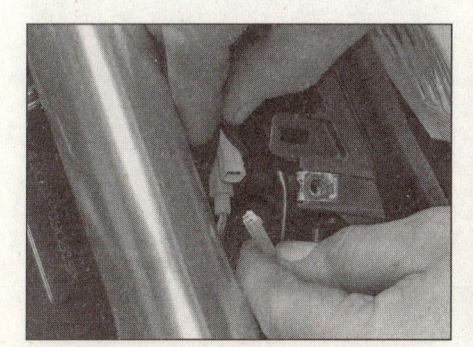

3.7e Disconnect the turn signal connectors . . .

3.7f . . . and draw the connector through the hole

3.7g Release the clip (arrowed) from the bracket and the wire from the clip

7•4 Bodywork

3.10 Instrument cover screws (arrowed)

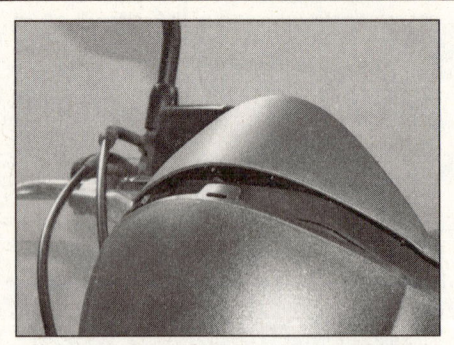

3.11 Make sure the tab locates correctly

3.13 Remove the grab-rails . . .

3.14 . . . then the upper section

10 Undo the screws and remove the cover, noting how the tab at the top locates **(see illustration)**.
11 Installation is the reverse of removal. Make sure the tab locates correctly **(see illustration)**.

Seat cowl

Removal

12 Remove the seat.
13 Unscrew the grab-rail bolts, noting the washers with the rear bolts and the collars with the front, and remove the rails **(see illustration)**.
14 Unscrew the two bolts and remove the upper rear section of the seat cowl **(see illustration)**.
15 Unscrew the bolt on each side, noting the collar with the rear bolt **(see illustration)**. Release the tabs on each underside and at the back and displace the cowl, then disconnect the tail light wiring connector **(see illustrations)**.

16 If required remove the tail light (see Chapter 8).
17 If required separate the side sections from the lower rear section by undoing the screws and releasing the tabs (see Chapter 8).

Installation

18 Installation is the reverse of removal. Make sure the tabs locate correctly. Tighten the grab-rail bolts to the torque setting specified at the beginning of the Chapter.

Front mudguard

19 Unscrew the nut on each side and release the brake hoses and wheel sensor wiring and guide according to model **(see illustration)**.
20 Unscrew the bolts on each side, noting the washers with the front bolts, then carefully

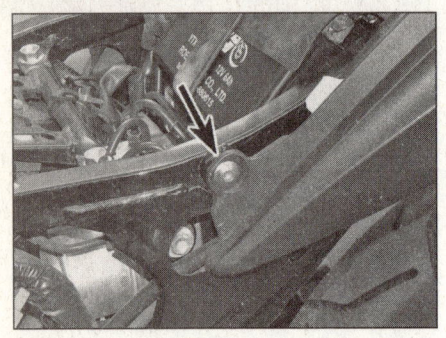

3.15a Unscrew the bolt (arrowed) on each side

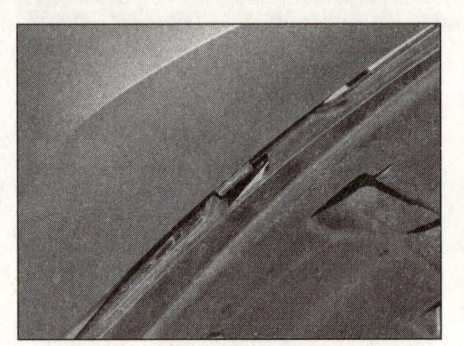

3.15b Release the tabs on the underside . . .

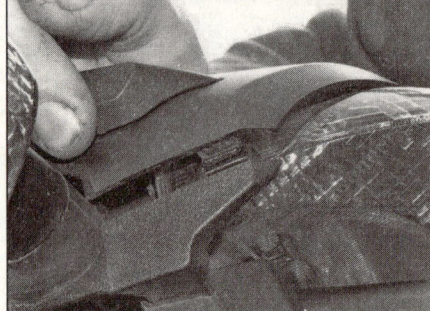

3.15c . . . and at the back

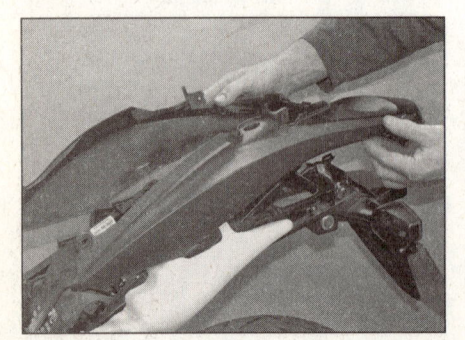

3.15d Displace the cowl . . .

3.15e . . . and disconnect the wiring connector

3.19 Brake hose bracket nut (arrowed)

Bodywork 7•5

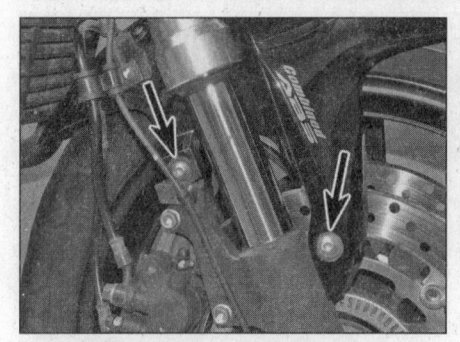

3.20 Mudguard bolts (arrowed)

3.26a Displace the fuseboxes (arrowed) ...

3.26b ... and the relays

3.27a Disconnect the wiring (arrowed) ...

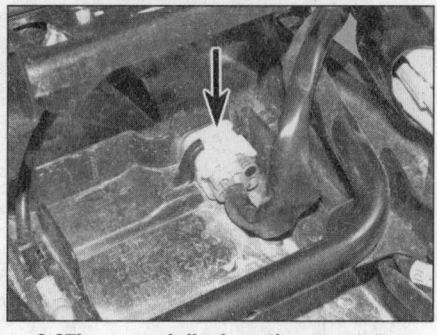

3.27b ... and displace the connector (arrowed)

3.28a Detach the cable (arrowed) ...

draw the mudguard forwards and remove it **(see illustration)**.
21 Note the collar fitted into the inner side of each rubber grommet. Check the grommets and replace them with new ones if cracked or hardened.
22 Installation is the reverse of removal. Tighten the bolts to the torque setting specified at the beginning of the Chapter.

Rear mudguard

23 Remove the seat cowl.
24 Remove the battery and the starter relay (see Chapter 8).
25 Remove the lean angle sensor (see Chapter 4).
26 Displace the fuseboxes and relay holders from the mudguard **(see illustrations)**.
27 Disconnect the licence plate light and rear turn signal wiring connectors **(see illustration)**. Release the auxiliary connector from its holder **(see illustration)**.
28 Release and detach the seat lock cable from the lock barrel **(see illustration)**. If required release the barrel catch and remove the barrel **(see illustration)**. Release the battery lead clip.
29 Unscrew the bolt on each side at the back and the bolts on the underside and lower the mudguard **(see illustrations)**. Release the hook from the frame and remove the mudguard, taking care not to snag the wiring.
30 Installation is the reverse of removal.

Mirrors

31 Pull the rubber boot up off the base of the mirror stem.
32 Slacken the top nut, then unscrew the mirror from the base bolt, turning it clockwise **(see illustration)**. If required unscrew the base bolt.

3.28b ... and remove the barrel (arrowed) by lifting the catch

33 Installation is the reverse of removal.
34 To adjust the position of the mirror stem slacken the locknut, adjust the mirror, then tighten the locknut.

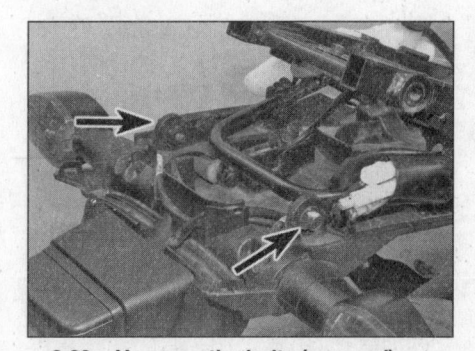

3.29a Unscrew the bolts (arrowed) ...

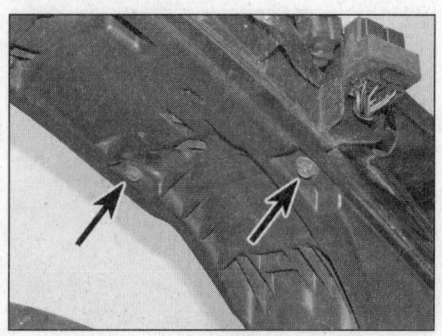

3.29b ... and the bolts (arrowed)

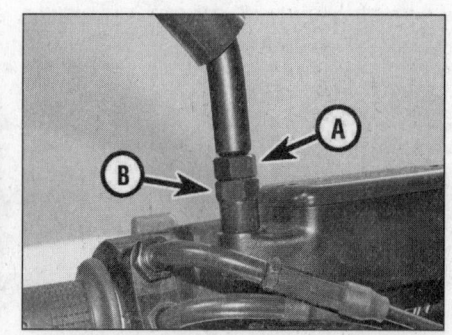

3.32 Mirror top nut (A) and base bolt (B)

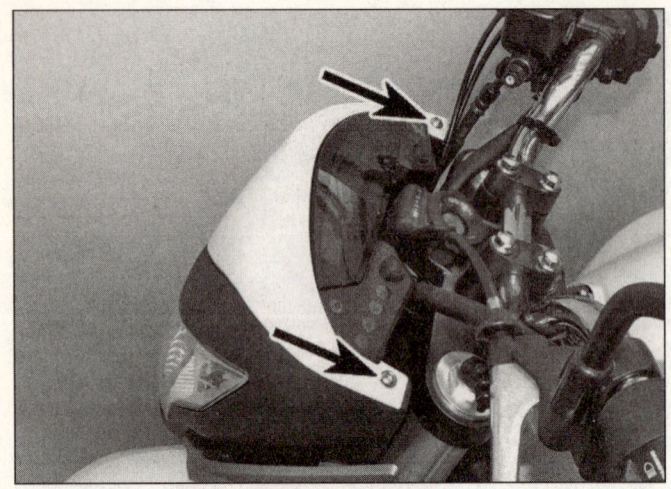

7•6 Bodywork

4.3a Undo the screws (arrowed) . . .

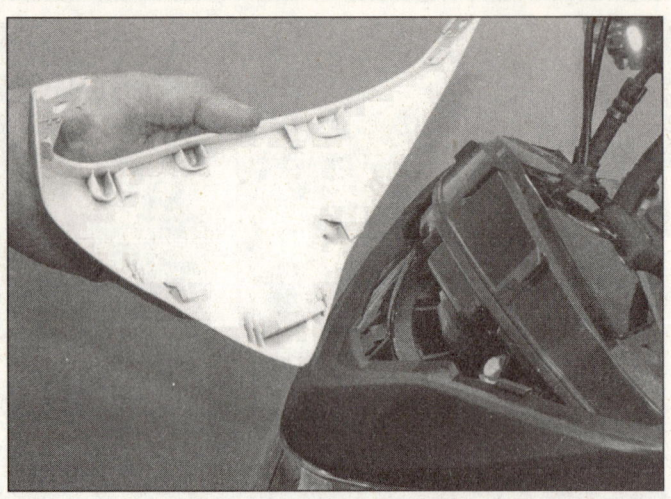

4.3b . . . and release the tabs

4.7 Seat cowl screws and bolts (arrowed)

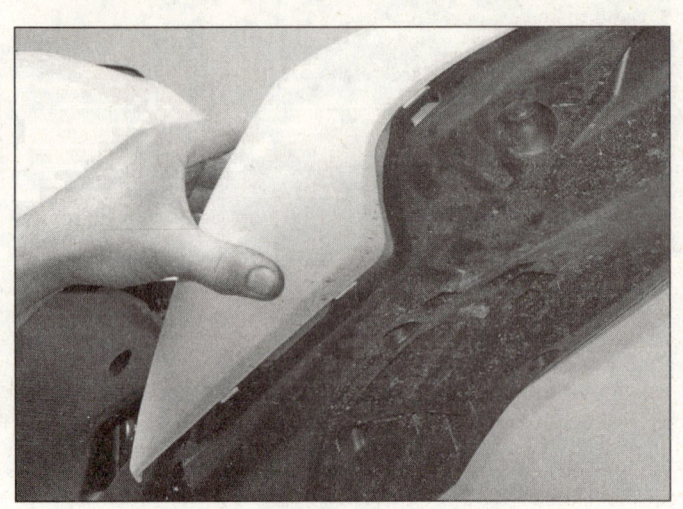

4.8a Release the tabs on the underside . . .

4 CB600F/FA – 2011-on

Seat

1 See Section 3

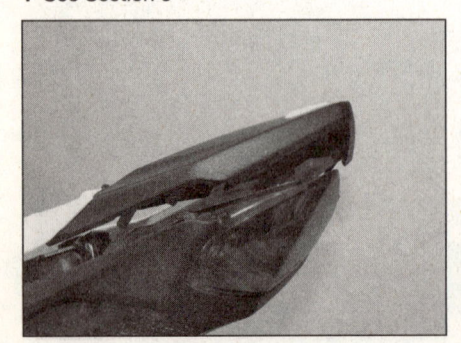

4.8b . . . and from the tail light . . .

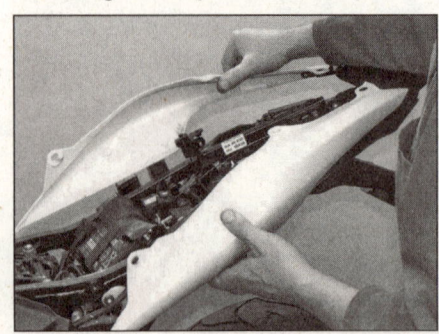

4.8c . . . and remove the cowl

Side covers

2 See Section 3

Instrument and headlight covers

3 Undo the two screws securing the instrument cover, then release the tabs from the headlight cover **(see illustrations)**.

4 To remove the headlight covers first remove the headlight assembly from the bike, then remove the headlight from the covers (see Chapter 8). Undo the screws and release the tabs joining the side sections to the main section.

5 Installation is the reverse of removal.

Seat cowl

6 Remove the seat.

7 Undo the rear screws, noting the washers, and the two bolts on each side **(see illustration)**.

8 Carefully release the tabs on each underside, then draw the cowl back to release it from the tail light and remove the cowl **(see illustrations)**.

9 If required separate the side sections from the lower rear section by undoing the screws and releasing the tabs (see Chapter 8).

10 Installation is the reverse of removal. Make sure the hook and tabs locate correctly.

Bodywork 7•7

4.13a Undo the screw (arrowed) . . .

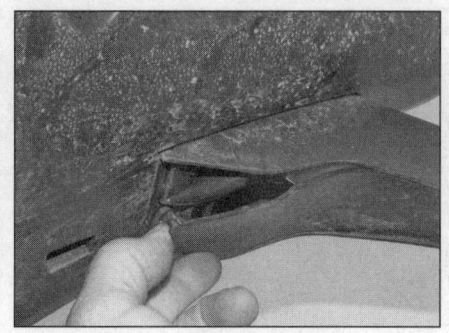

4.13b . . . release the tabs . . .

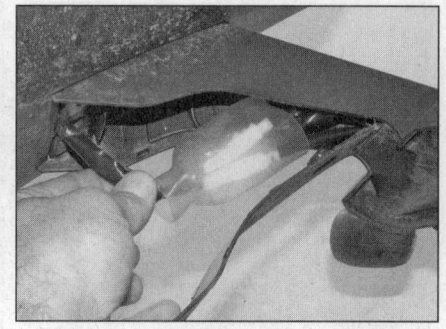

4.13c . . . and disconnect the wiring

Front mudguard
11 See Section 3.

Rear mudguard
12 Remove the seat cowl.
13 Undo the screw on the underside of the licence plate/turn signal holder, then release the cover tabs **(see illustrations)**. Disconnect the tail light, turn signal and licence plate light wiring connectors **(see illustration)**. Release the auxiliary connector from its holder.
14 Unscrew the licence plate/turn signal holder bolts and remove the assembly **(see illustration)**. If required undo the screws and detach the licence plate holder from the turn signal holder, then remove the turn signals and licence plate light (see Chapter 8).
15 Remove the battery (see Chapter 8).
16 Remove the lean angle sensor (see Chapter 4).
17 Displace the starter relay, fuseboxes and relays from the mudguard.
18 Release and detach the seat lock cable from the lock barrel **(see illustration)**. If required release the barrel catch and remove the barrel.
19 Release the wiring loom clip from the underside, just behind the shock absorber. Unscrew the bolts on the underside and lower the mudguard **(see illustration 3.29b)**.

Release the hooks from the frame and remove the mudguard, taking care not to snag the wiring.
20 Installation is the reverse of removal.

Mirrors
21 See Section 3.

5 CBR600F/FA

Seat
1 See Section 3.

Side covers
2 Remove the seat.
3 Unscrew the bolt **(see illustration)**.
4 Carefully release the tabs and peg from the grommets in the fuel tank, fairing side panel and swingarm pivot bracket and remove the cover **(see illustration)**.
5 Installation is the reverse of removal. Make sure the grommets are in good condition and correctly seated. Smear the peg grommet with oil.

Seat cowl
6 See Section 4.

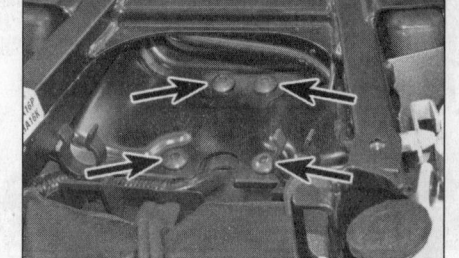

4.14 Licence plate/turn signal holder bolts (arrowed)

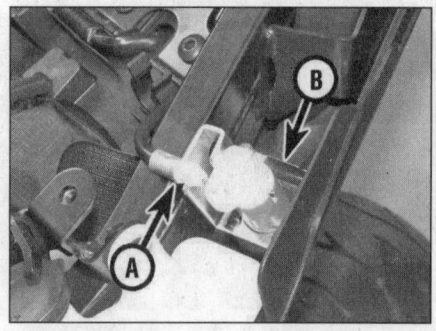

4.18 Detach the cable (A) and remove the barrel by lifting the catch (B)

5.3 Unscrew the bolt (arrowed) . . .

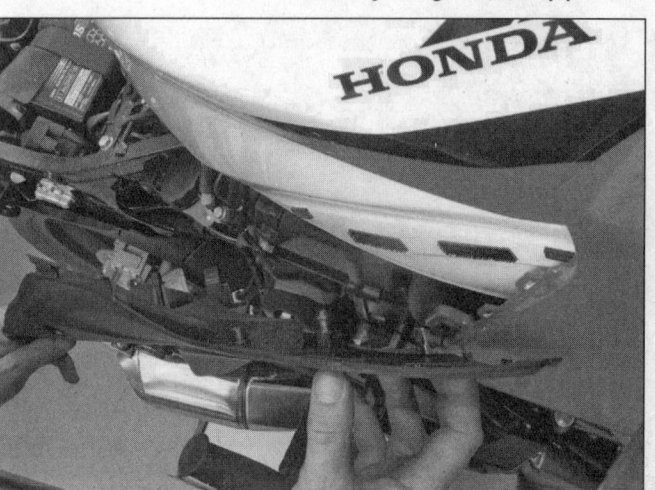

5.4 . . . then release the tabs and peg

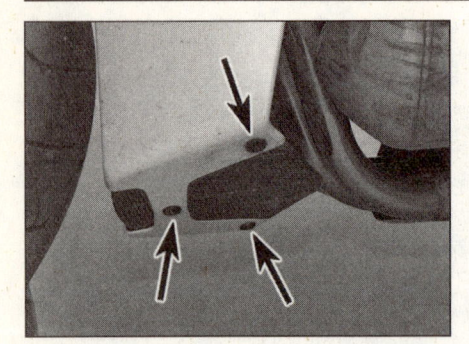

5.7a Release the trim clips (arrowed) . . .

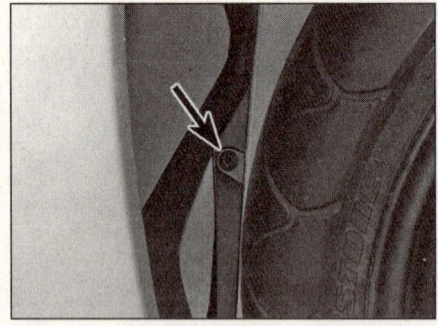

5.7b . . . and undo the screw (arrowed) on each side

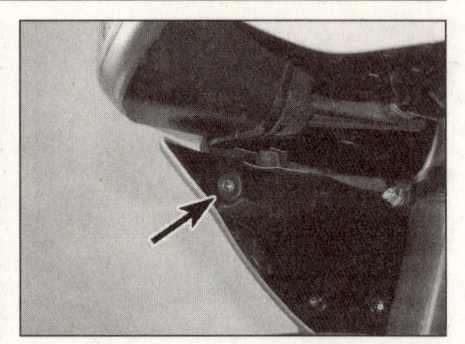

5.8a Undo the screw (arrowed) . . .

Fairing side panels

7 Release the trim clips (see Section 2) on the underside of the centre section, then undo the two screws, free the tabs and remove the centre section **(see illustrations)**.

8 Undo the four screws, then carefully pull the panel away to release the clip, and disconnect the turn signal wiring connector **(see illustrations)**.

9 If required remove the turn signal (see Chapter 8). Undo the screws and detach the inner section of the side panel **(see illustration)**.

10 Installation is the reverse of removal.

Fairing upper panels

11 Remove the side covers and fairing side panels.

5.8b . . . and the screws (arrowed) . . .

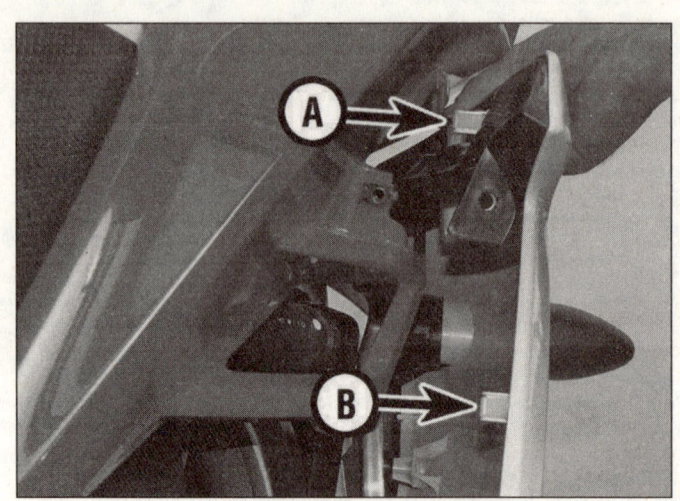

5.8c . . . release the clip (A) and hook (B) . . .

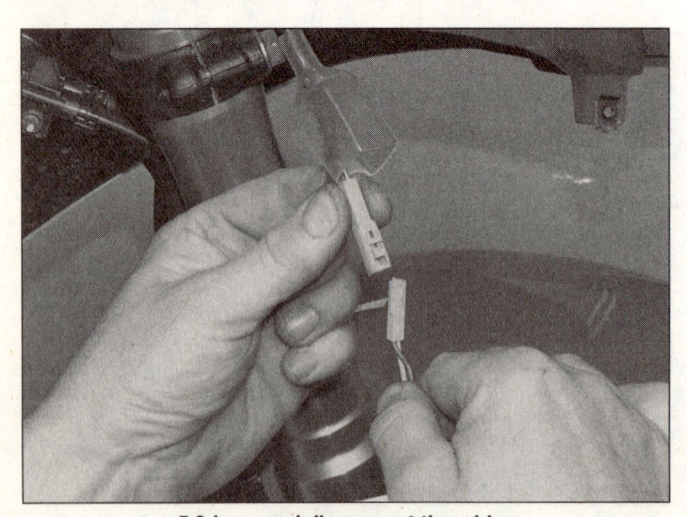

5.8d . . . and disconnect the wiring

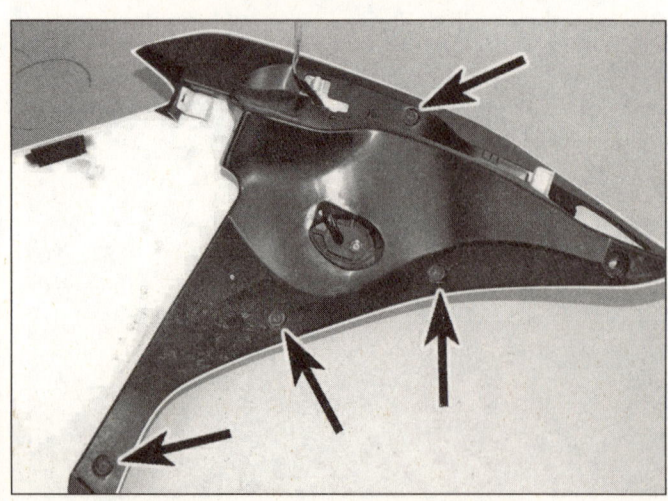

5.9 Inner panel screws (arrowed)

Bodywork 7•9

5.12a Undo the screw (arrowed) . . .

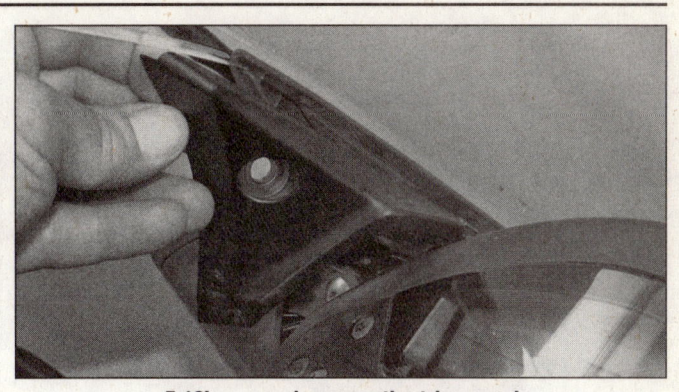

5.12b . . . and remove the trim panel

12 Remove the cockpit trim panel screw, then release the tabs and remove the panel **(see illustrations)**.

13 Undo the three screws **(see illustration)**. Carefully pull the panel away at the back to release the peg from the grommet on the tank, then release the tabs from the fairing and remove the panel **(see illustrations)**.

14 Installation is the reverse of removal.

Fairing

15 Remove the headlight assembly (see Chapter 8).

16 Undo the screws and detach the fairing sections from the headlight **(see illustration)**.

5.13a Undo the screws (arrowed) . . .

5.13b . . . pull the peg from the grommet . . .

5.13c . . . and release the tabs

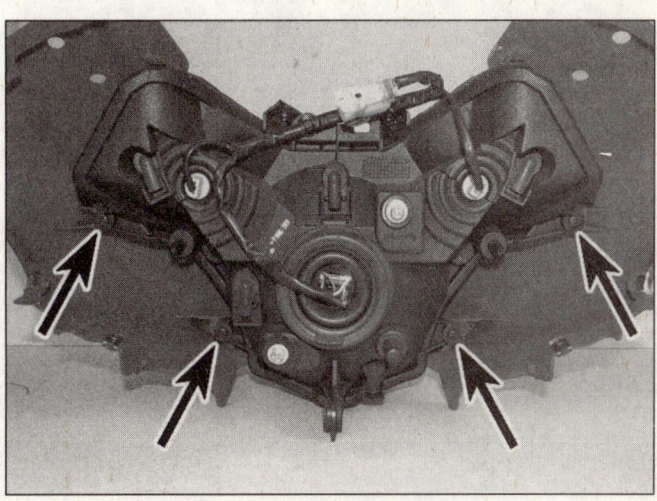

5.16 Fairing section screws (arrowed)

7•10 Bodywork

5.20a Release the front tabs . . .

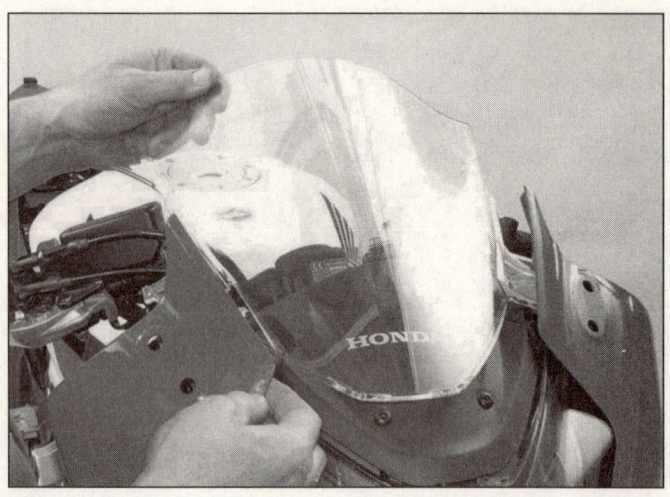

5.20b . . . then lift the fairing sections and remove the windshield

17 Installation is the reverse of removal.

Windshield

18 Remove the cockpit trim panel screw, then release the tabs and remove the panel **(see illustrations 5.12a and b)**.
19 Remove the mirrors.
20 Release the tabs at the front of the windshield by drawing it down, then carefully lift each side of the fairing and remove the windshield **(see illustrations)**.
21 Installation is the reverse of removal.

Instrument cover

22 Remove the windshield.
23 Remove the fairing side and upper panels.
24 Undo the two screws **(see illustration)**.
25 Carefully lift each side of the fairing and lift the cockpit surround off the headlight stay, noting how the peg locates in the grommet **(see illustrations)**.
26 Installation is the reverse of removal.

Front mudguard

27 See Section 3.

Rear mudguard

28 See Section 4.

Mirrors

29 Unscrew the bolts and remove the mirrors **(see illustration)**.

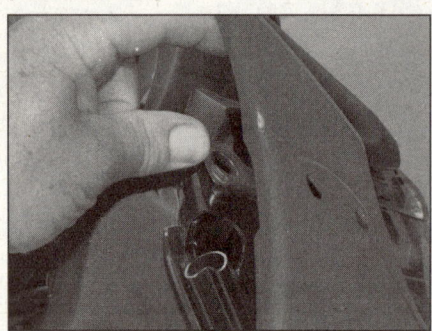

30 Installation is the reverse of removal. Tighten the bolts to the torque setting specified at the beginning of the Chapter.

6 CBF600N/NA

Seats

Passenger seat removal

1 Unlock the seat using the ignition key, turning it clockwise **(see illustration)**. Draw the seat up and back to remove it, noting how the hooks at the front locate **(see illustration)**.

Rider's seat removal

2 Remove the passenger seat.
3 Unscrew the bolts securing the back of the seat **(see illustration)**. Draw the seat up and back, noting how the hook at the front locates **(see illustration)**.

Rider's seat bracket removal

4 Remove the rider's seat.
5 Before removing the brackets note their position – there are three height options, determined by which bolt holes are used.
6 Unscrew the bolts and remove the brackets **(see illustrations)**.

5.24 Undo the screws (arrowed)

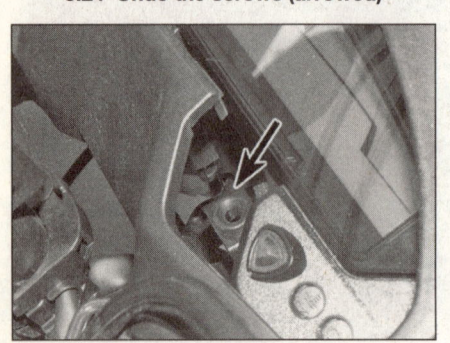

5.25a Lift the sides . . .

5.25b . . . free the peg from the grommet . . .

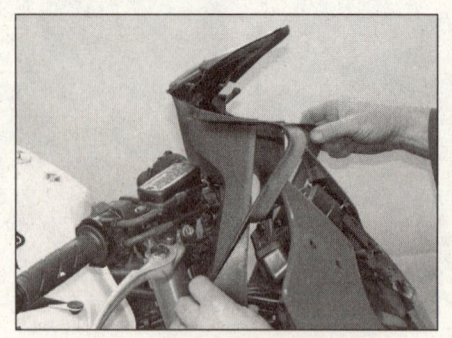

5.25c . . . and remove the cover

5.29 Mirror bolts (arrowed)

Bodywork 7•11

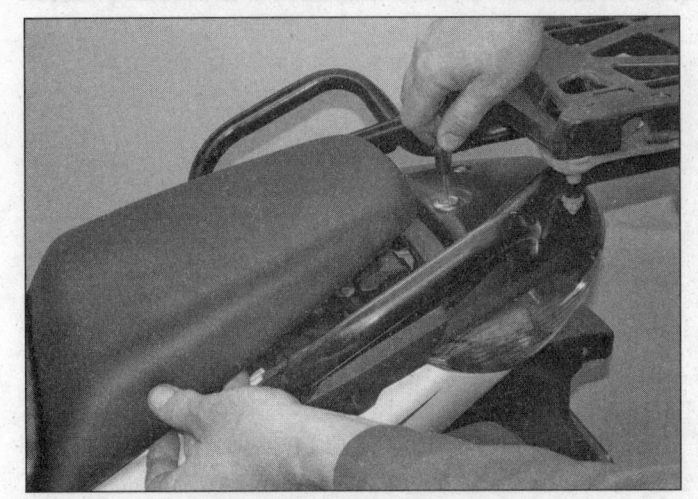

6.1a Unlock and lift the seat . . .

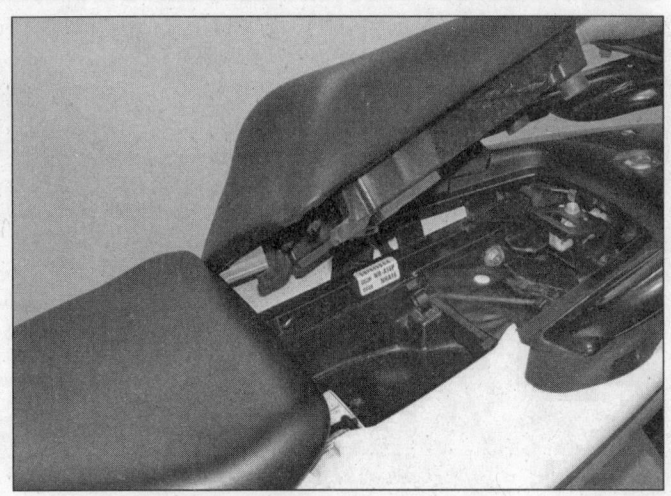

6.1b . . . noting how the hooks locate

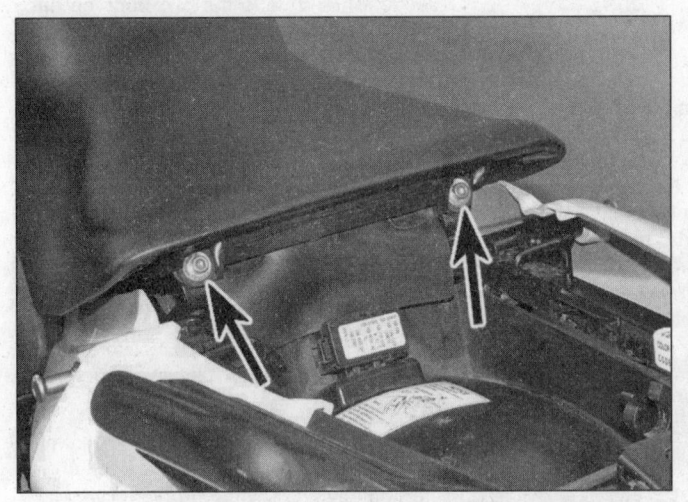

6.3a Unscrew the bolts (arrowed) . . .

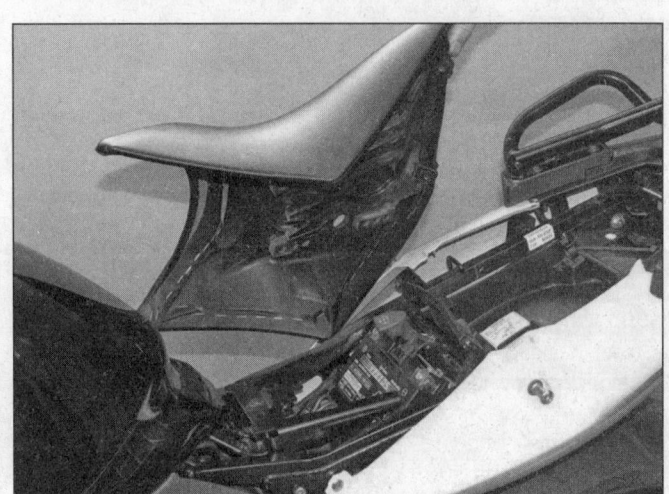

6.3b . . . and remove the seat

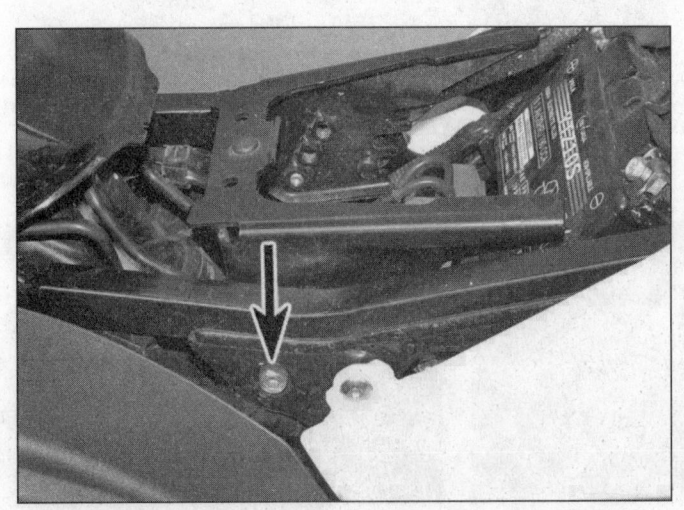

6.6a To remove the front bracket unscrew the bolt (arrowed) on each side

6.6b To remove the rear bracket unscrew the bolts (arrowed)

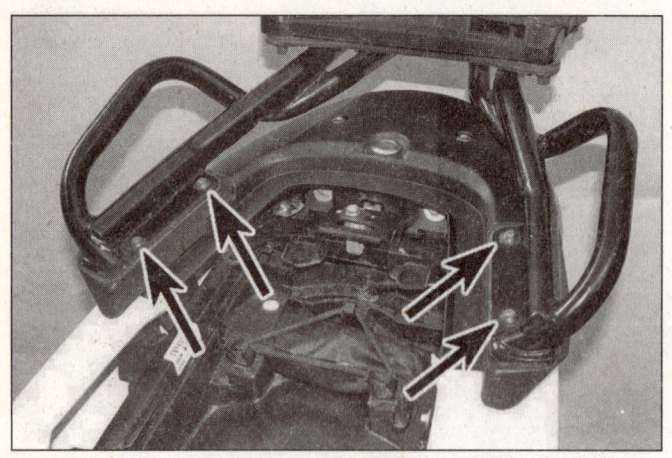

7•12 Bodywork

6.10 Grab-rail bolts (arrowed)

6.11 Rear section bolts (arrowed)

Installation

7 Installation is the reverse of removal, noting the following:
- To adjust the height of the rider's seat re-position the brackets as required using the different mounting holes – there are three positions, but make sure each bracket is set to the same position as the other **(see illustrations 6.6a and b)**. Tighten the bracket bolts to the torque setting specified at the beginning of the Chapter.
- Make sure the hook(s) on each seat locate(s) correctly.
- Push down on the back of the passenger seat to engage the latch.

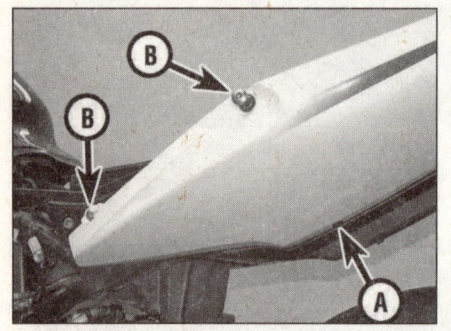

Side covers

8 See Section 7.

Seat cowl

Removal

9 If you only want to remove the rear section of the cowl, remove the passenger seat, but if you are removing either or both side sections remove both seats and the side covers.
10 Carefully prise the blanking caps out of the grab-rail bolt heads. Unscrew the bolts and remove the grab-rails **(see illustration)**.
11 To remove the rear section of the seat cowl unscrew the two bolts **(see illustration)**.

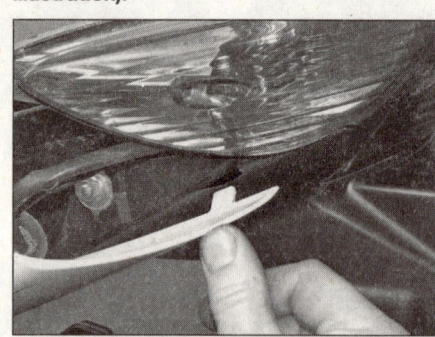

12 To remove either of the side sections release the trim clip on the underside (see Section 2) and undo the two bolts on each side, noting the collar with the rear bolt **(see illustration)**. Release the tab at the rear and remove the cowl **(see illustration)**.

Installation

13 Installation is the reverse of removal. Make sure the rear tab on each side section locates correctly. The upper rims of the grommets for the rear section must be above the surface of the cowl, so the cowl is seated in the grommet recess – use a small screwdriver to do this **(see illustration)**. Tighten the grab-rail bolts to the torque setting specified at the beginning of the Chapter.

Front mudguard

14 Remove the front wheel (see Chapter 6).
15 Unscrew the retaining bolt on each side, then carefully draw the mudguard forwards and remove it **(see illustration)**.
16 Installation is the reverse of removal.

Rear mudguard

17 Remove the seat cowl.
18 Disconnect the tail light assembly and licence plate light wiring connectors **(see illustration)**.
19 Unscrew the tail light/licence plate

6.12a Release the trim clip (A) and undo the bolts (B) . . .

6.12b . . . then release the tab

6.13 Ease the rim of each grommet above the surface of the cowl

6.15 Unscrew the bolts and remove the mudguard

6.18 Disconnect the wiring in the boot (arrowed)

Bodywork 7•13

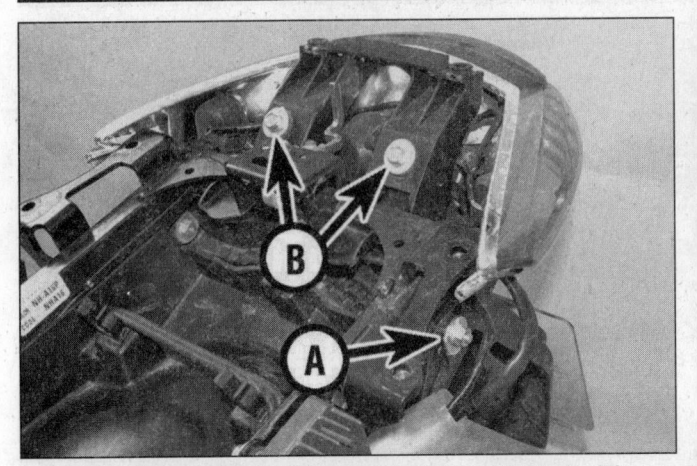

6.19 Unscrew the nut (A) on each side and the bolts (B)

6.21 Reservoir bolt (arrowed)

6.22 Release the fusebox (arrowed)

6.23a Remove the bolt (arrowed) on each side

6.23b Unscrew the bolts (arrowed)

assembly nuts and remove the washers, then unscrew the bolts and remove the assembly **(see illustration)**. If required remove the tail light and licence plate.
20 Remove the battery (see Chapter 8).
21 Unscrew the brake fluid reservoir bolt and support the reservoir clear, keeping it upright **(see illustration)**.
22 Displace the fusebox from the mudguard **(see illustration)**. Release the wiring from the guides on the right-hand side.
23 Remove the bolt, washer and collar on each side **(see illustration)**. Unscrew the bolts on the underside and remove the mudguard, noting how the tabs at the front locate **(see illustration)**.
24 Installation is the reverse of removal.

Mirrors
25 See Section 3.

7 CBF600S/SA

Seats
1 See Section 6.

Side covers
2 Unscrew the bolt **(see illustration)**.
3 Carefully pull the cover away from the tank and swingarm pivot bracket to free the pegs from the grommets **(see illustration)**.
4 Installation is the reverse of removal. Make sure the grommet is in good condition and correctly seated. Smear the grommet with oil. Make sure the peg locates fully in the grommet.

Seat cowl
5 See Section 6.

7.2 Unscrew the bolt (arrowed) . . .

7.3 . . . then release the pegs from the grommets

7•14 Bodywork

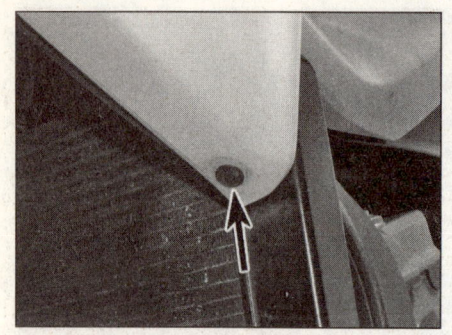

7.6a Release the trim clip (arrowed)

7.6b Unscrew the bolt (arrowed) . . .

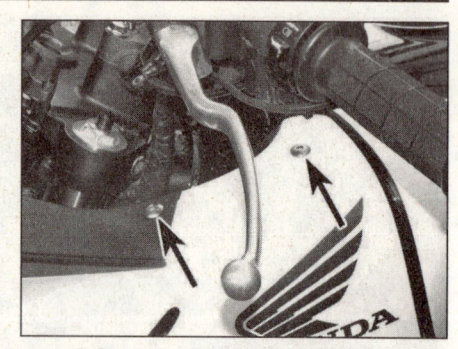

7.6c . . . and the bolts (arrowed)

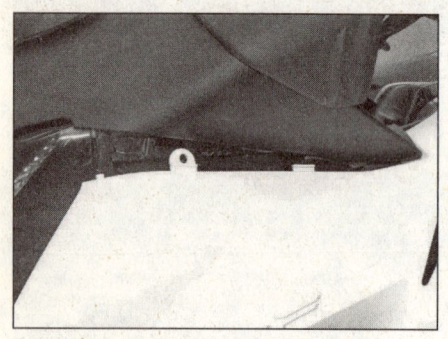

7.6d Free the tabs along the side . . .

7.6e . . . and at the front . . .

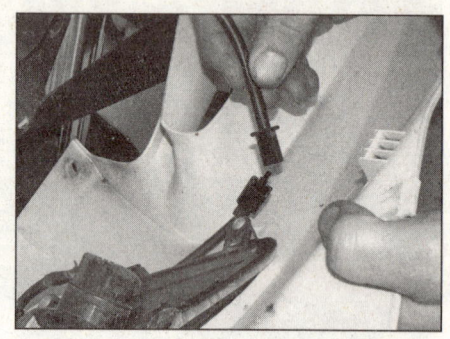

7.6f . . . and disconnect the wiring connector

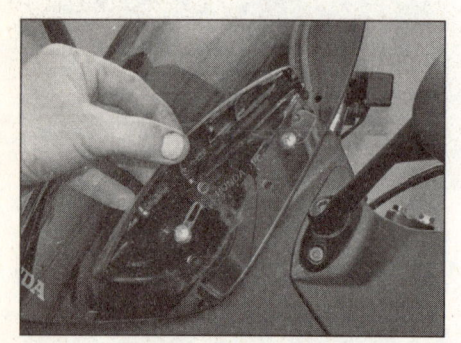

7.9 Remove the covers

Fairing side panels

6 Release the trim clip (see Section 2) on the underside, then unscrew the three bolts, noting which fits where and the collar with the front bolt **(see illustrations)**. Free the tabs from the fairing and disconnect the turn signal wiring connector **(see illustrations)**.
7 If required remove the turn signal (see Chapter 8).
8 Installation is the reverse of removal.

Windshield

9 Carefully pull the windshield screw covers off **(see illustration)**.

10 Undo the screws, noting the spacers, and lift the windshield off, noting which mounting holes were used **(see illustration)** – there are two different positions for height adjustment.
11 Installation is the reverse of removal. Set the windshield at the desired height **(see illustration)**.

Cockpit surround

12 Remove the windshield.
13 Remove the fairing side panels.
14 Undo the four screws, release the

7.10 Windshield screws (arrowed)

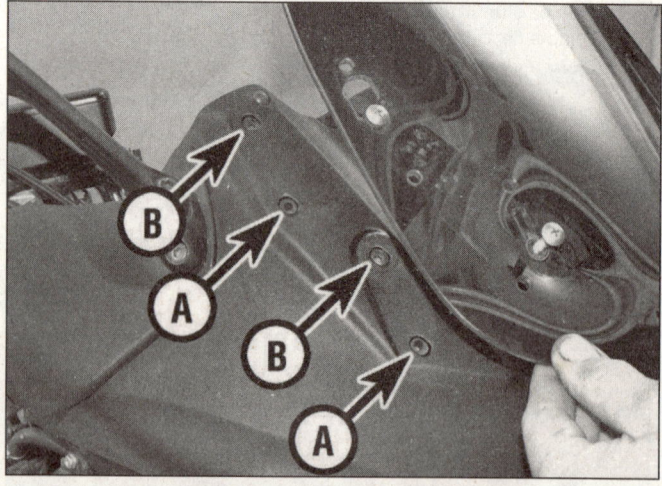

7.11 Low position screw holes (A), high position holes (B)

Bodywork 7•15

7.14a Undo the screw on each side and retrieve the clip nut

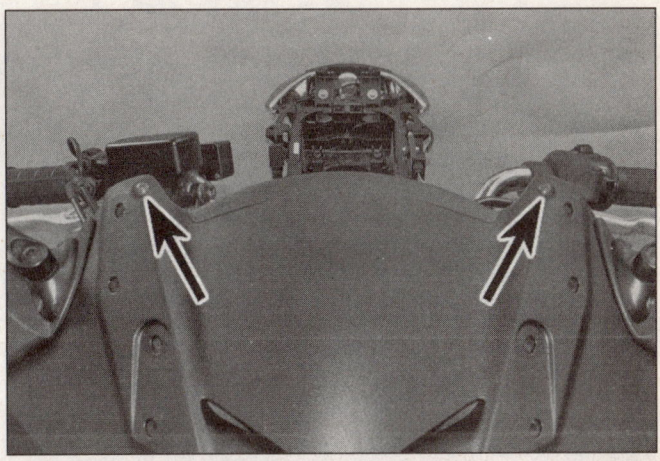

7.14b Undo the screws (arrowed) . . .

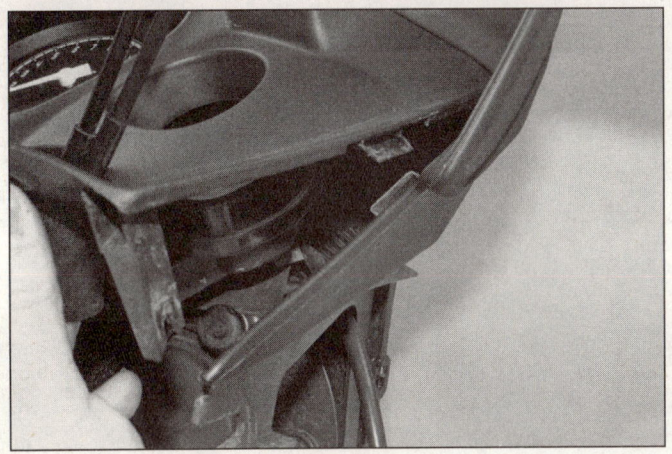

7.14c . . . release the tabs . . .

7.14d . . . and remove the surround

tabs, and lift the cockpit surround off **(see illustrations)**.

15 Installation is the reverse of removal.

Fairing

16 Remove the fairing side panels.
17 Remove the windshield.
18 Remove the cockpit surround.
19 Remove the mirrors.
20 Disconnect the headlight wiring connector **(see illustration)**.
21 Release the fairing from the mirror mounts and draw it forwards, noting how the pegs locate in the grommets **(see illustration)**.
22 If required remove the headlight (see Chapter 8).
23 Installation is the reverse of removal.

7.20 Disconnect the connector

7.21 Release and remove the fairing

7•16 Bodywork

7.26a Mirror bolts (arrowed)

7.26b Remove the spacers if loose

Front mudguard
24 See Section 6.

Rear mudguard
25 See Section 6.

Mirrors
26 Unscrew the bolts and remove the mirrors **(see illustration)**. Retrieve the spacers if loose **(see illustration)**.
27 Installation is the reverse of removal. Tighten the bolts to the torque setting specified at the beginning of the Chapter.

Chapter 8
Electrical system

Contents

	Section number		Section number
Alternator	29	Ignition system components	see Chapter 4
Battery charging	4	Instrument check and replacement	16
Battery removal and maintenance	3	Instrument removal and installation	15
Brake light switches	14	Lighting system check	6
Brake/tail/licence plate light bulbs	9	Neutral switch	20
Charging system testing	28	Oil pressure switch	17
Clutch switch	22	Regulator/rectifier	30
Diode block	23	Sidestand switch	21
Electrical system fault finding	2	Starter motor overhaul	27
Fuses	5	Starter motor removal and installation	26
General information	1	Starter relay	25
Handlebar switches	19	Tail light	10
Headlight	8	Turn signal assemblies	13
Headlight and sidelight bulbs	7	Turn signal bulbs	12
Horn	24	Turn signal circuit check	11
Ignition switch	18	Vehicle speed sensor	16

Degrees of difficulty

Easy, suitable for novice with little experience	**Fairly easy,** suitable for beginner with some experience	**Fairly difficult,** suitable for competent DIY mechanic	**Difficult,** suitable for experienced DIY mechanic	**Very difficult,** suitable for expert DIY or professional

Specifications

Battery
Capacity	12 V, 8.6 Ah
Voltage	
Fully-charged	13.0 to 13.2 V
Discharged	below 12.3 V
Charging rate	
Normal	0.8 A for 5 to 10 hrs
Quick	4.5 A for 1 hr

Charging system
Alternator stator coil resistance	0.1 to 1.0 ohms
Output	
CB600F/FA 2007 to 2010 and CBF600N/NA/S/SA	333 W @ 5000 rpm
CB600F/FA 2011-on and CBR600F/FA	316 W @ 5000 rpm
Regulated voltage	15.5 V @ 5000 rpm
Current leakage	2 mA (max)

Starter motor
Brush length
   Standard... 12.0 mm
   Service limit (min) .... 6.5 mm

Fuses
See Wiring Diagrams at the end of this Chapter or label on fusebox lid for fuse identification
Main 30A
Others .... 20A x 3, 10A x 4
C-ABS system (FA/NA/SA models) .... 30A x 2, 10A x 1

Resistor
Resistance .... 38 to 42 ohms

Bulbs
CB600F/FA 2007 to 2010
   Headlight
      High beam .... 55 W
      Low beam.. 55 W
   Sidelight .... 5 W x 2
   Brake/tail light... LED
   Licence plate light .... 5 W
   Turn signal lights.. 21 W x 4 amber
   Instrument and warning lights .... LED
CB600F/FA 2011-on
   Headlight (high beam/low beam)........................ 60/55 W
   Sidelight .... 5 W
   Brake/tail light... LED
   Licence plate light .... 5 W
   Turn signal lights.. 21 W x 4 amber
   Instrument and warning lights .... LED
CBR600F/FA
   Headlight (high beam/low beam)........................ 60/55 W
   Sidelight .... 5 W x 2
   Brake/tail light... LED
   Licence plate light .... 5 W
   Turn signal lights.. 21 W x 4 amber
   Instrument and warning lights .... LED
CBF600N/NA
   Headlight (high beam/low beam)........................ 60/55 W
   Sidelight .... 5 W
   Brake/tail light... 21/5 W
   Licence plate light .... 5 W
   Turn signal lights.. 21 W x 4 amber
   Instrument illumination lights .... 1.7 W x 2
   Instrument warning lights
      Turn signals.. 1.7 W x 2
      All others... LED
CBF600S/SA
   Headlight
      High beam .... 55 W
      Low beam.. 55 W
   Sidelight .... 5 W x 2
   Brake/tail light... 21/5 W
   Licence plate light .... 5 W
   Turn signal lights.. 21 W x 4 amber
   Instrument and warning lights .... LED

Torque settings
Alternator rotor bolt .... 113 Nm
Alternator stator bolts....................................... 12 Nm
Footrest bracket bolts .... 37 Nm
Fork clamp bolts (top yoke) .... 22 Nm
Ignition switch bolts .... 25 Nm
Neutral switch... 12 Nm
Oil pressure switch.. 12 Nm
Steering stem nut... 103 Nm

Electrical system 8•3

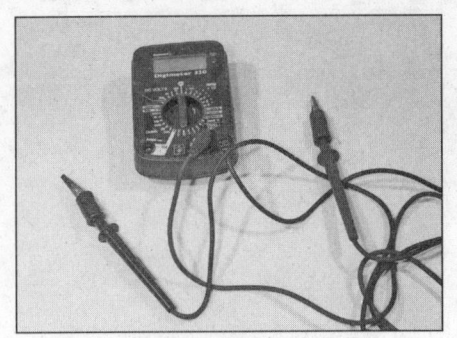

2.4a A digital multimeter can be used for all electrical tests

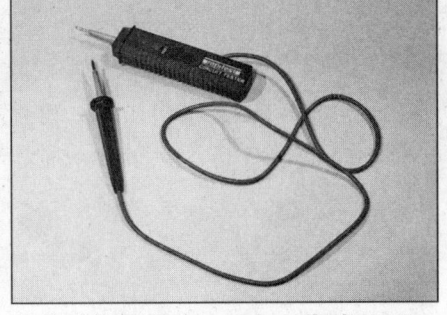

2.4b A battery-powered continuity tester

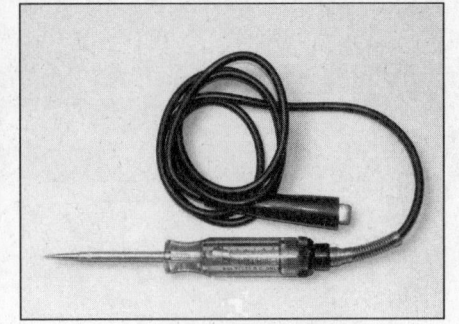

2.4c A simple test light is useful for voltage tests

1 General information

All models have a 12 volt electrical system charged by a three-phase alternator with a separate regulator/rectifier.

The regulator maintains the charging system output within the specified range to prevent overcharging, and the rectifier converts the ac (alternating current) output of the alternator to dc (direct current) to power the lights and other components and to charge the battery. The alternator rotor is mounted on the left-hand end of the crankshaft.

The starter motor is mounted on the top of the crankcase behind the cylinders. The starting system includes the motor, the battery, the relay and the various wires and switches. Some of the switches are part of a starter interlock system that prevents the engine from being started if the sidestand is down and the engine is in gear. The engine can be started with the sidestand up when it is in gear as long as the clutch lever is pulled in. The system will also cut the engine should the sidestand extend while the engine is running and in gear – see Chapter 1 for further information and checks on the system.

Note: *Keep in mind that electrical parts, once purchased, often cannot be returned. To avoid unnecessary expense, make very sure the faulty component has been positively identified before buying a replacement part.*

2 Electrical system fault finding

1 A typical electrical circuit consists of an electrical component, the switches, relays, etc, related to that component and the wiring and connectors that link the component to the battery and the frame.

2 Before tackling any troublesome electrical circuit, first study the wiring diagram thoroughly to get a complete picture of what makes up that individual circuit. Trouble spots, for instance, can often be narrowed down by noting if other components related to that circuit are operating properly or not. If several components or circuits fail at one time, chances are the fault lies either in the fuse or in a common earth (ground) connection, as several circuits are often routed through the same fuse and earth (ground) connections.

3 Electrical problems often stem from simple causes, such as loose or corroded connections or a blown fuse. Prior to any electrical fault finding, always visually check the condition of the fuse, wires and connections in the problem circuit. Intermittent failures can be especially frustrating, since you can't always duplicate the failure when it's convenient to test. In such situations, a good practice is to clean all connections in the affected circuit, whether or not they appear to be good – where possible use a dedicated electrical cleaning spray along with sandpaper, wire wool or other abrasive material to remove corrosion, and a dedicated electrical protection spray to prevent further problems. All of the connections and wires should also be wiggled to check for looseness which can cause intermittent failure.

4 If you don't have a multimeter it is highly advisable to obtain one – they are not expensive and will enable a full range of electrical tests to be made **(see illustration)**. Go for a modern digital one with LCD display as they are easier to use. A continuity tester and/or test light are useful for certain electrical checks as an alternative, though are limited in their usefulness compared to a multimeter **(see illustrations)**.

Continuity checks

5 The term continuity describes the uninterrupted flow of electricity through an electrical circuit. Continuity can be checked with a multimeter set either to its continuity function (a beep is emitted when continuity is found), or to the resistance (ohms / Ω) function, or with a dedicated continuity tester. Both instruments are powered by an internal battery, therefore the checks are made with the ignition OFF. As a safety precaution, always disconnect the battery negative (-) lead before making continuity checks, particularly if ignition switch checks are being made.

6 If using a multimeter, select the continuity function if it has one, or the resistance (ohms) function. Touch the meter probes together and check that a beep is emitted or the meter reads zero, which indicates continuity. If there is no continuity there will be no beep or the meter will show infinite resistance. After using the meter, always switch it OFF to conserve its battery.

7 A continuity tester can be used in the same way – its light should come on or it should beep to indicate continuity in the switch ON position, but should be off or silent in the OFF position.

8 Note that the polarity of the test probes doesn't matter for continuity checks, although care should be taken to follow specific test procedures if a diode or solid-state component is being checked.

Switch continuity checks

9 If a switch is at fault, trace its wiring to the wiring connectors. Separate the connectors and inspect them for security and condition. A build-up of dirt or corrosion here will most likely be the cause of the problem – clean up and apply a water dispersant such as WD40, or alternatively use a dedicated contact cleaner and protection spray.

10 If using a multimeter, select the continuity function if it has one, or the resistance (ohms) function, and connect its probes to the terminals in the connector **(see illustration)**. Simple ON/OFF type switches, such as brake light switches, only have two wires whereas combination switches, like the handlebar

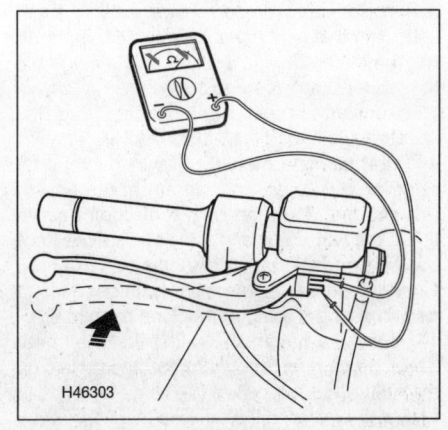

2.10 Continuity should be indicated across switch terminals when lever is operated

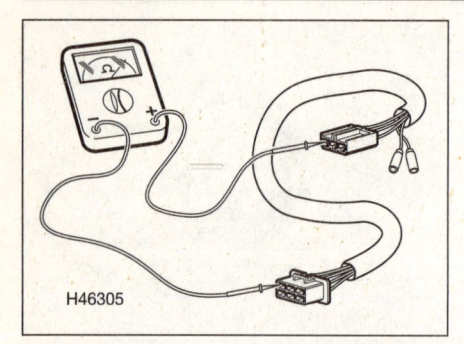

8•4 Electrical system

2.12 Wiring continuity check. Connect the meter probes across each end of the same wire

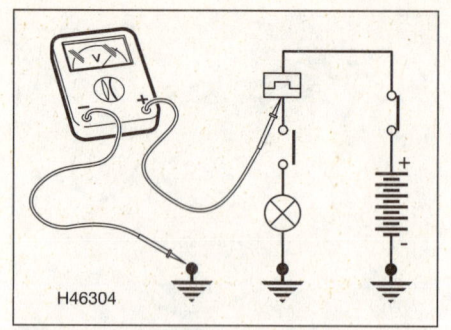

2.15 Voltage check. Connect the meter positive probe to the component and the negative probe to earth

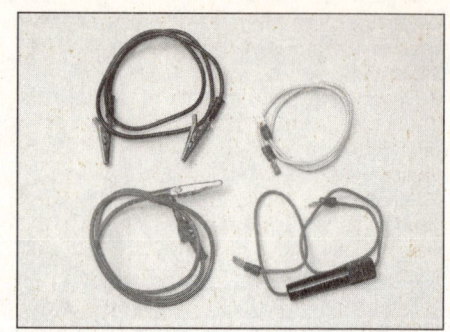

2.23 A selection of insulated jumper wires

switches, have many wires. Study the wiring diagram to ensure that you are connecting to the correct pair of wires. Continuity should be indicated with the switch ON and no continuity with it OFF.

Wiring continuity checks

11 Many electrical faults are caused by damaged wiring, often due to incorrect routing or chaffing on frame components. Loose, wet or corroded wire connectors can also be the cause of electrical problems.

12 A continuity check can be made on a single length of wire by disconnecting it at each end and connecting the meter or continuity tester probes to each end of the wire **(see illustration)**. Continuity (low or no resistance – 0 ohms) should be indicated if the wire is good. If no continuity (high resistance) is shown, suspect a broken wire.

13 To check for continuity to earth in any earth wire connect one probe of your meter or tester to the earth wire terminal in the connector and the other to the frame, engine, or battery earth (-) terminal. Continuity (low or no resistance – 0 ohms) should be indicated if the wire is good. If no continuity (high resistance) is shown, suspect a broken wire or corroded or loose earth point (see below).

Voltage checks

14 A voltage check can determine whether power is reaching a component. Use a multimeter set to the dc voltage scale, or a test light. The test light is the cheaper component, but the meter has the advantage of being able to give a voltage reading.

15 Connect the meter or test light in parallel, i.e. across the load **(see illustration)**.

16 First identify the relevant wiring circuit by referring to the wiring diagram at the end of this manual. If other electrical components share the same power supply (i.e. are fed from the same fuse), take note whether they are working correctly – this is useful information in deciding where to start checking the circuit.

17 If using a meter, check first that the meter leads are plugged into the correct terminals on the meter (red to positive (+), black to negative (-). Set the meter to the dc volts function, where necessary at a range suitable for the battery voltage – 0 to 20 vdc. Connect the meter red probe (+) to the power supply wire and the black probe to a good metal earth (ground) on the bike's frame or directly to the battery negative terminal. Battery voltage should be shown on the meter with the ignition switch, and if necessary any other relevant switch, ON.

18 If using a test light, connect its positive (+) probe to the power supply terminal and its negative (-) probe to a good earth (ground) on the bike's frame. With the switch, and if necessary any other relevant switch, ON, the test light should illuminate.

19 If no voltage is indicated, work back towards the fuse continuing to check for voltage. When you reach a point where there is voltage, you know the problem lies between that point and your last check point.

Earth (ground) checks

20 Earth connections are made either directly to the engine or frame via the mounting of the component, or by a separate wire into the earth circuit of the wiring harness. Alternatively a short earth wire is sometimes run from the component directly to the bike's frame.

21 Corrosion is a common cause of a poor earth connection, as is a loose earth terminal fastener.

22 If total or multiple component failure is experienced, check the security of the main earth lead from the negative (-) terminal of the battery, the earth lead bolted to the engine, and the main earth point(s) on the frame. If corroded, dismantle the connection and clean all surfaces back to bare metal. Remake the connection and prevent further corrosion from forming by smearing battery terminal grease over the connection.

23 To check the earth of a component, use an insulated jumper wire to temporarily bypass its earth connection **(see illustration)** – connect one end of the jumper wire to the earth terminal or metal body of the component and the other end to the bike's frame. If the circuit works with the jumper wire installed, the earth circuit is faulty.

24 To check an earth wire first check for corroded or loose connections, then check the wiring for continuity (Step 13) between each connector in the circuit in turn, and then to its earth point, to locate the break.

3 Battery removal and maintenance

Caution: Be extremely careful when handling or working around the battery. The electrolyte is very caustic and an explosive gas (hydrogen) is given off when the battery is charging.

Removal and installation

CB600F/FA and CBR600F/FA

1 Make sure the ignition is switched OFF.
2 Remove the seat (see Chapter 7).
3 Release the retaining strap and remove the rubber cover **(see illustration)**.
4 Unscrew the negative (–) terminal bolt first and disconnect the lead from the battery **(see illustration 3.8a)**. Lift up the red insulating cover to access the positive (+) terminal, then unscrew the bolt and disconnect the lead **(see illustration 3.8b)**. Lift the battery out.
5 Installation is the reverse of removal. Clean the battery terminals and lead ends with a wire brush, emery paper or steel wool. Reconnect the leads, connecting the positive (+) terminal first.

CBF600N/NA/S/SA models

6 Make sure the ignition is switched OFF.
7 Remove the seats and the front seat bracket (see Chapter 7).
8 Unscrew the negative (–) terminal bolt first and disconnect the lead from the battery **(see illustration)**. Lift up the red insulating

3.3 Unhook the strap (arrowed)

Electrical system 8•5

cover to access the positive (+) terminal, then unscrew the bolt and disconnect the lead **(see illustration)**.

9 Unscrew the battery holder bolt and remove the holder, noting the position of the washer **(see illustration)**. Lift the battery out **(see illustration)**.

10 Installation is the reverse of removal. If you have an FTZ10S battery fit the holder bolt washer between the holder and the bolt head. If you have a YTZ10S battery fit the holder bolt washer between the bracket and the holder **(see illustration 3.9a)**. Clean the battery terminals and lead ends with a wire brush, emery paper or steel wool. Reconnect the leads, connecting the positive (+) terminal first.

HAYNES HiNT *Battery corrosion can be kept to a minimum by applying a layer of battery terminal grease or petroleum jelly (Vaseline) to the terminals after the leads have been connected. DO NOT use a mineral based grease.*

Inspection and maintenance

11 The battery on all models is of the maintenance free (sealed) type, therefore requiring no regular maintenance. However, the following checks should still be performed.
Note: *Do not attempt to remove the battery caps to check the electrolyte level or battery specific gravity. Removal will damage the caps, resulting in electrolyte leakage and battery damage.*

12 Check the state of charge by measuring the voltage at the battery terminals **(see illustration)**. Connect the voltmeter positive (+) probe to the battery positive (+) terminal, and the negative (−) probe to the battery negative (−) terminal. When fully-charged there should be 13.0 to 13.2 volts present. If the voltage falls below 12.3 volts remove the battery (see above), and recharge it as described below in Section 4.

13 Check the battery terminals and leads are tight and free of corrosion. If corrosion is evident, clean the terminals as described above, then protect them from further corrosion (see **Haynes Hint**).

14 Keep the battery case clean to prevent current leakage, which can discharge the battery over a period of time (especially when it sits unused). Wash the outside of the case with a solution of baking soda and water. Rinse the battery thoroughly, then dry it.

15 Look for cracks in the case and replace the battery with a new one if any are found. If acid has been spilled on the frame or battery box, neutralise it with a baking soda and water solution, dry it thoroughly, then touch up any damaged paint.

16 If the motorcycle sits unused for long periods of time, disconnect the leads from the battery terminals, negative (−) terminal first. Refer to Section 4 and charge the battery once every month to six weeks.

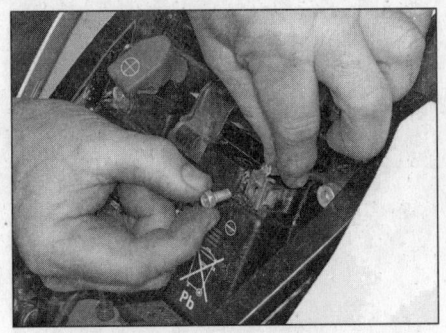

3.8a Disconnect the negative lead first ...

3.8b ... then disconnect the positive lead

3.9a Remove the battery holder ...

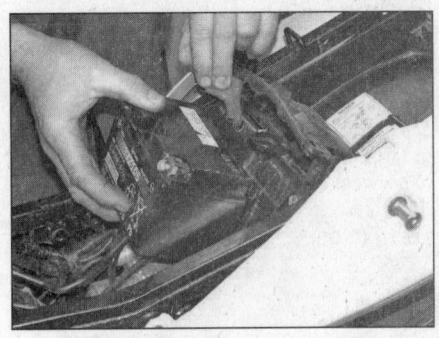

3.9b ... then remove the battery

4 Battery charging

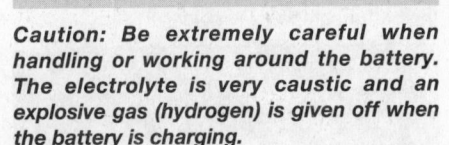

Caution: *Be extremely careful when handling or working around the battery. The electrolyte is very caustic and an explosive gas (hydrogen) is given off when the battery is charging.*

1 Remove the battery (see Section 3). Connect the charger to the battery, making sure that the positive (+) lead on the charger is connected to the positive (+) terminal on the battery, and the negative (−) lead is connected to the negative (−) terminal.

2 Honda recommend that the battery is charged at the normal rate specified at the beginning of the Chapter. A higher 'quick charge' rate that can be used if absolutely necessary is also specified, but note that exceeding this could cause the battery to overheat, buckling the plates and rendering it useless. If a normal domestic charger is used check that after a possible initial peak, the charge rate falls to a safe level **(see illustration)**. If the battery becomes hot during charging **stop**. Further charging will cause damage. Note that there are many bike-specific chargers available from good suppliers that are designed for the maintenance and recovery of motorcycle batteries, in particular catering for the requirements of heavily discharged MF batteries. They are not expensive, and are a worthwhile investment, especially if the bike is not used over winter. Follow the manufacturer's instructions.

3 If the recharged battery discharges rapidly if left disconnected it is likely that an internal short caused by physical damage or

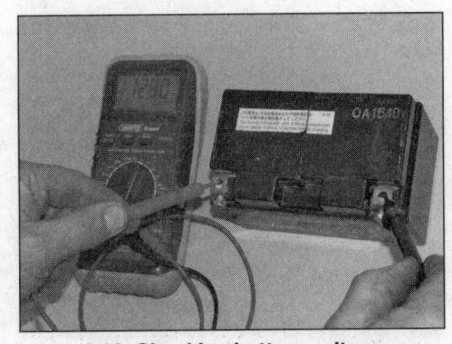

3.12 Checking battery voltage

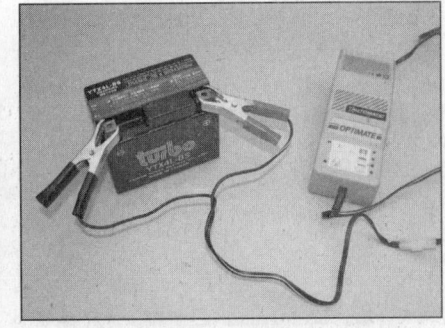

4.2 Battery connected to a charger

8•6 Electrical system

5.2a Disconnect the wiring connector . . .

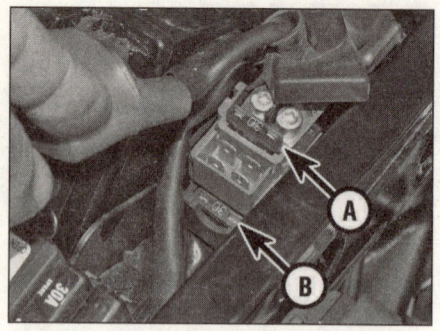

5.2b . . . to access the main fuse (A) and spare fuse (B)

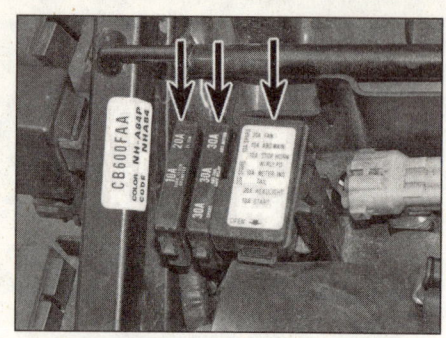

5.3a Fusebox and holders (arrowed)

sulphation has occurred. A new battery will be required. A sound item will tend to lose its charge at about 1% per day.

4 Install the battery (see Section 3).

5 If the motorcycle sits unused for long periods of time, charge the battery once every month to six weeks and leave it disconnected.

5 Fuses

1 The electrical system as a whole is protected by the main fuse, and individual circuits are protected by other fuses of different ratings.

CB600F/FA and CBR600F/FA

2 The main fuse is integral with the starter relay – to access it remove the seat (see Chapter 7). Disconnect the wiring connector – the fuse is under it **(see illustrations)**. A spare main fuse is housed in the back of the relay holder.

3 All other fuses are housed in the fusebox, located under the seat, or in the fuse holder(s) next to the box **(see illustration)**. Remove the seat for access (see Chapter 7). The location, identity and rating of each fuse is marked on the box or holder lid. Unclip the lid to access the fuses **(see illustration)**.

4 A spare fuse of each rating is provided, either in the fusebox or the fuse holder next to it, according to model and fuse rating.

CBF600N/NA/S/SA

5 The main fuse is integral with the starter relay – to access it remove the right-hand side cover (see Chapter 7). Disconnect the wiring connector – the fuse is under it **(see illustration)**. A spare main fuse is housed in the bottom of the relay holder.

6 The fuel injection system/ignition fuse, and on C-ABS models the ABS fuses, are housed in separate holders next to the starter relay **(see illustration)**. Remove the right-hand side cover for access (see Chapter 7). Unclip the lid(s) to access the fuse(s).

7 All other fuses are housed in the fusebox, located under the passenger seat **(see illustration)**. Remove the seat for access (see Chapter 7). The location, identity and rating of each fuse is marked on the box lid. Unclip the lid to access the fuses **(see illustration)**.

8 A spare fuse of each rating is provided, either in the fusebox or the fuse holder next to it, according to model and fuse rating.

All models

9 The fuses can be removed and checked visually – use the tool provided in the toolkit, your fingers, or a suitable pair of pliers **(see illustration)**. A blown fuse is easily identified

5.3b Unclip the lids to access the fuses

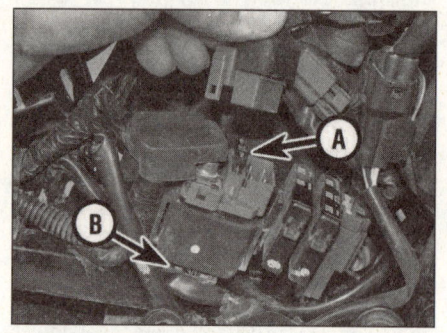

5.5 Disconnect the wiring connector to access the main fuse (A) and spare fuse (B)

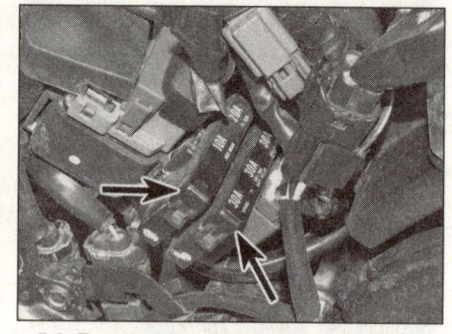

5.6 Fuse holders (arrowed) – unclip the lids to access the fuses

5.7a Fusebox (arrowed)

5.7b Unclip the lid to access the fuses

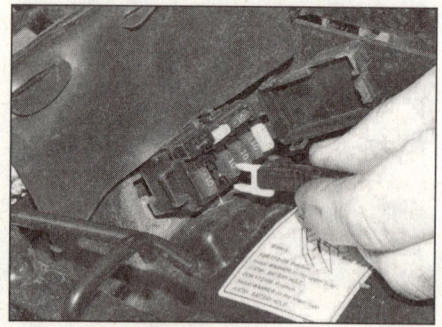

5.9a Pull the fuse out

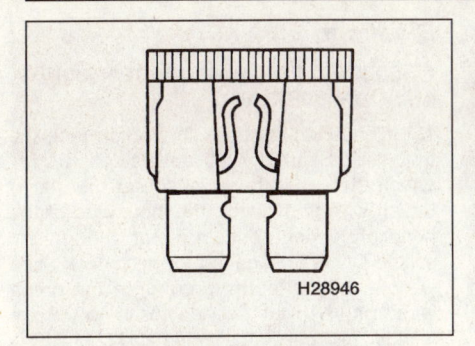

5.9b A blown fuse can be identified by a break in its element

by a break in the element **(see illustration)**, but if there is any doubt check the fuse for continuity (see Section 2). Each fuse is clearly marked with its rating and must only be replaced by a fuse of the correct rating. If a spare fuse is used, always replace it with a new one so that a spare of each rating is carried on the bike at all times.

⚠️ *Warning: Never put in a fuse of a higher rating or bridge the terminals with any other substitute, however temporary it may be. Serious damage may be done to the circuit, or a fire may start.*

10 If the new fuse blows immediately check the wiring circuit very carefully for evidence of a short-circuit. Look for bare wires and chafed, melted or burned insulation.

11 Occasionally a fuse will blow or cause an open-circuit for no obvious reason. Corrosion of the fuse ends and fusebox terminals may occur and cause poor fuse contact. If this happens, remove the corrosion with a wire brush or emery paper, then spray the fuse end and terminals with electrical contact cleaner.

6 Lighting system check

Note: *Refer to electrical system fault finding in Section 2 and to the wiring diagram for your model at the end of this Chapter.*

1 If a light fails, first check the bulb (see relevant Section), and the bulb terminals in the holder. If none of the lights work, check the battery (see Section 3). Low battery voltage indicates either a faulty battery or a defective charging system. Refer to Section 3 for battery checks and Section 28 for charging system tests. Also check the fuses (Section 5) – if there is more than one problem at the same time, it is likely to be a fault relating to a multi-function component, such as one of the fuses governing more than one circuit, or the ignition switch. When checking for a blown filament in a bulb, it is advisable to back up a visual check with a continuity test of the filament as it is not always apparent that a bulb has blown.

Headlight

CB600F/FA 2007 to 2010 and CBF600S/SA

2 These models have two single filament bulbs – the left-hand bulb works on LO beam and both bulbs work on HI beam. If one headlight beam fails to work, first check the bulb (see Section 7). If both headlight beams fail to work, first check the fuse (see Section 5), and then the bulbs (see Section 7). If they are good, the problem lies in the wiring or connectors, the HI beam relay or the dimmer switch. Refer to Section 19 for the switch testing procedures, and also to the wiring diagrams at the end of this Chapter.

3 If the HI beam does not work and the relay is suspected of being faulty, on CB600F/FA models remove the seat cowl, and on CBF600S/SA models remove the left-hand seat cowl (see Chapter 7). Pull the relay off its connector and test it as follows **(see illustrations)**: set a multimeter to the ohms x 1 scale and connect it across the relay's A and B terminals. There should be no continuity (infinite resistance). Using a fully-charged 12 volt battery and two insulated jumper wires, connect the positive (+) terminal of the battery to the C terminal on the relay, and the negative (–) terminal to the D terminal. At this point the relay should be heard to click and the meter read 0 ohms (continuity). If this is the case the relay is good. If the relay does not click when battery voltage is applied and indicates no continuity (infinite resistance) across its terminals, it is faulty and must be replaced with a new one.

4 If the relay is good, check there is battery voltage at the black/red wire terminal on the relay wiring connector with the ignition ON. If there is no voltage, check the wiring between the relay wiring connector and the ignition switch, via the fusebox. If voltage is present, refer to Section 7 (CBF models) or 8 (CB models) and check the blue/black wire between the relay connector and the headlight connector, and the blue wire between the relay connector and the dimmer switch for continuity, and check there is continuity to earth (ground) in the green/black (CB600F/FA models) or green (CBF600S/SA models) wire from the headlight connector, and in the green wire from the relay connector. Repair or renew the wiring or connectors as necessary.

5 If the LO beam does not work, refer to Section 7 (CBF models) or 8 (CB models) and check for battery voltage at the blue/white wire terminal on the headlight wiring connector with the ignition ON. If voltage is present, check for continuity to earth (ground) in the green/black (CB600F/FA models) or green (CBF600S/SA models) wire from the wiring connector. If no voltage is present check the blue/white wire from the connector to the starter button and the dimmer switch, and then check the switches themselves, and then the wiring between them and the fusebox. Repair or renew the wiring or connectors as necessary.

CB600F/FA 2011-on, CBF600N/NA and CBR600F/FA

6 These models have one twin filament bulb. If both headlight beams fail to work, check the fuse (see Section 5). If either the LO beam or the HI beam fails to work check the bulb (see Section 7). If all seems good, the problem lies in the wiring or connectors, or the dimmer switch. Refer to Section 19 for the switch testing procedures.

7 If the HI beam does not work, refer to Section 7 and check for battery voltage at the blue wire terminal on the headlight wiring

6.3a Headlight relay (arrowed) – CB models

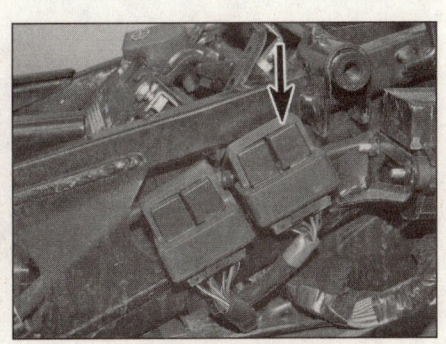

6.3b Headlight relay (arrowed) – CBF models

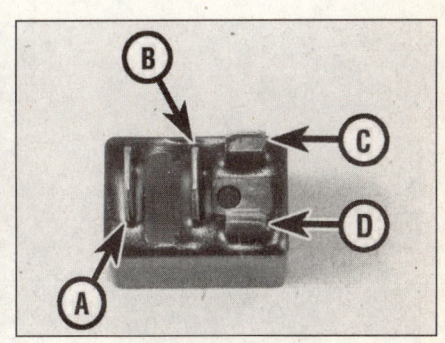

6.3c Relay test set-up

8•8 Electrical system

connector with the ignition ON. If voltage is present, check for continuity to earth (ground) in the green wire from the wiring connector. Repair or renew the wiring or connectors as necessary. If no voltage is present check the blue wire to the dimmer switch and then the blue/white wire from the switch to the starter button, and then check the switches themselves, and then the wiring between them and the fusebox. Repair or renew the wiring or connectors as necessary.

8 If the LO beam does not work, refer to Section 7 and check for battery voltage at the white wire terminal on the headlight wiring connector with the ignition ON. If voltage is present, check for continuity to earth (ground) in the green wire from the wiring connector. Repair or renew the wiring or connectors as necessary. If no voltage is present check the white wire to the dimmer switch and then the blue/white wire from the switch to the starter button, and then check the switches themselves, and then the wiring between them and the fusebox. Repair or renew the wiring or connectors as necessary.

Tail light

CB600F/FA and CBR600F/FA

9 If the tail light fails to work, refer to Section 10 and disconnect the tail light wiring connector, and check for battery voltage at the black/brown wire terminal on the loom side of the connector with the ignition switch ON. If voltage is present, check for continuity to earth (ground) in the green wire from the wiring connector. If no voltage is indicated, check the wiring and connectors between the tail light and the fusebox.

10 If the power, wiring and connectors are good, or if only one or some of the tail light LEDs have failed leaving others working, then the tail light unit is faulty and must be replaced with a new one – individual LEDs are not available.

CBF600N/NA/S/SA

11 If the tail light fails to work, check the bulb (see Section 9). If it is good, check there is battery voltage at the black/brown wire terminal in the bulbholder with the ignition switch ON. If voltage is present, check there is continuity to earth (ground) in the green wire from the wiring connector. If no voltage is indicated, check the wiring and connectors between the tail light and the fusebox.

Brake light

CB600F/FA and CBR600F/FA

12 If the brake light fails to work, refer to Section 10 and disconnect the tail light wiring connector, and check for battery voltage at the green/yellow wire terminal on the loom side of the connector, first with the front brake lever on, then with the rear brake pedal on. If voltage is present with one brake on but not the other, then the switch or its wiring is faulty. If voltage is present in both cases, check for continuity to earth (ground) in the green wire from the wiring connector. If no voltage is indicated, check the wiring and connectors between the brake light and the brake switches, and the fusebox, then check the switches themselves. Refer to Section 14 for the switch testing procedures.

13 If the power, wiring and connectors are good, or if only one or some of the brake light LEDs have failed leaving others working, then the tail light unit is faulty and must be replaced with a new one – individual LEDs are not available.

CBF600N/NA/S/SA

14 If the brake light fails to work, check the bulb (see Section 9). If it is good, check there is battery voltage at the green/yellow wire terminal in the bulbholder with the ignition ON, and first with the front brake lever on, then with the rear brake pedal on. If voltage is present with one brake on but not the other, then the switch or its wiring is faulty. If voltage is present in both cases, check there is continuity to earth (ground) in the green wire from the wiring connector. If no voltage is indicated, check the wiring and connectors between the brake light and the brake switches, and the fusebox, then check the brake light switches themselves. Refer to Section 14 for the switch testing procedures.

Sidelight

CB600F/FA 2007 to 2010, CBR600F/FA and CBF600S/SA

15 If one sidelight fails to work, check the bulb (see Section 7); if both sidelights fail check there is battery voltage at the black/brown wire terminal on the loom side of the headlight wiring connector with the ignition switch ON. If voltage is present, check there is continuity to earth (ground) in the green wire from the wiring connector. If no voltage is indicated, check the wiring and connectors between the sidelight and the fusebox.

CB600F/FA 2011-on and CBF600N/NA

16 If the sidelight fails to work, check the bulb (see Section 7). If it is good, check there is battery voltage at the black/brown wire terminal on the loom side of the headlight wiring connector with the ignition switch ON. If voltage is present, check there is continuity to earth (ground) in the green wire from the wiring connector. If no voltage is indicated, check the wiring and connectors between the sidelight and the fusebox.

Licence plate light

17 If the light fails to work, check the bulb (see Section 9). If the bulb is good, check there is battery voltage at the black/brown wire terminal on the loom side of the wiring connector with the ignition switch ON. If voltage is present, check there is continuity to earth (ground) in the green wire from the wiring connector. If no voltage is indicated, check the wiring and connectors between the tail light and the fusebox.

Turn signals

18 See Section 11.

Instrument and warning lights

19 See Section 16.

7 Headlight and sidelight bulbs

Note: *The headlight bulbs are of the quartz-halogen type. Do not touch the bulb glass as skin acids will shorten the bulb's service life. If the bulb is accidentally touched, it should be wiped carefully when cold with a rag soaked in methylated spirit and dried before fitting. Always use a paper towel or dry cloth when handling new bulbs to prevent injury if the bulb should break and to increase bulb life.*

CB600F/FA 2007 to 2010

Headlights

1 Remove the headlight (see Section 8).
2 Remove the relevant rubber dust cover (see illustration).
3 Disconnect the wiring connector from the bulb (see illustration).

7.2 Dislodge the cover . . .

7.3 . . . then disconnect the wiring connector

Electrical system 8•9

7.4a Release the clip . . .

7.4b . . . and remove the bulb

7.10 Pull the bulbholder out . . .

4 Release the bulb retaining clip and remove the bulb (see illustrations).
5 Fit the new bulb into the headlight bearing in mind the information in the Note above. Make sure the bulb locates correctly and secure it with the retaining clip (see illustrations 7.4b and a).
6 Connect the wiring connector (see illustration 7.3).
7 Fit the dust cover, locating the tabs in the cut-outs (see illustration 7.2).
8 Install the headlight and check it works.

Sidelights

9 Remove the headlight covers (see Chapter 7).
10 Carefully pull the relevant bulbholder out of the headlight (see illustration).
11 Carefully pull the bulb out of the holder (see illustration).
12 Fit the new bulb in the bulbholder, then fit the bulbholder into the headlight – make sure the rubber seal is in good condition and correctly seated.

13 Install the headlight covers and check the sidelight works.

CB600F/FA 2011-on

Headlight

14 Lay some rag or a towel on the front mudguard. Unscrew the bolt on each side of the headlight, noting the washer (see illustration).
15 Slightly raise the headlight to free the grommets from their locating pegs, then draw it forwards and disconnect the wiring connector (see illustrations).
16 If required lay the headlight on the front mudguard, making sure it is secure.
17 Remove the rubber dust cover, noting how it fits (see illustration 7.30).
18 Release the bulb retaining clip and remove the bulb (see illustrations 7.31a and b).
19 Fit the new bulb into the headlight bearing in mind the information in the Note above. Make sure the bulb locates correctly

and secure it with the retaining clip (see illustrations 7.31b and a).
20 Fit the dust cover with the tab at the top (see illustration 7.30).
21 Connect the wiring connector (see illustration 7.15b).
22 Fit the headlight onto its bracket, locating the grommets over the pegs (see illustration 7.15a). Fit the bolts with their washers (see illustration 7.14).
23 Check the operation of the headlight.

Sidelight

24 Carefully pull the bulbholder out of the headlight (see illustration).
25 Carefully pull the bulb out of the holder (see illustration).
26 Fit the new bulb in the bulbholder, then fit the bulbholder into the headlight – make sure the rubber seal is in good condition and correctly seated.
27 Check the sidelight works.

7.11 . . . then pull the bulb out of the holder

7.14 Unscrew the bolt (arrowed) on each side

7.15a Displace the headlight unit as described . . .

7.15b . . . and disconnect the wiring connector (arrowed)

7.24 Pull out the sidelight bulbholder . . .

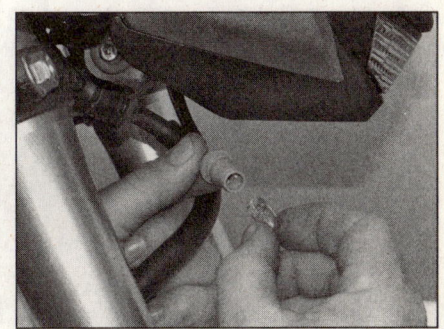

7.25 . . . and pull the bulb out of the holder

8•10 Electrical system

7.29 Disconnect the wiring connector

7.30 Remove the dust cover

CBR600F/FA

Headlight

28 Remove the instrument surround (see Chapter 7), and if required for better access remove the headlight (see Section 8).
29 Disconnect the wiring connector from the bulb **(see illustration)**.
30 Remove the rubber dust cover **(see illustration)**.
31 Release the bulb retaining clip and remove the bulb **(see illustrations)**.
32 Fit the new bulb into the headlight bearing in mind the information in the **Note** above. Make sure the bulb locates correctly and secure it with the retaining clip **(see illustrations 7.31b and a)**.
33 Fit the dust cover with the tab at the bottom **(see illustration 7.30)**.
34 Connect the wiring connector **(see illustrations 7.29)**.
35 Install the headlight and check it works.

Sidelights

36 Remove the instrument surround (see Chapter 7).
37 Carefully pull the relevant bulbholder out of the headlight **(see illustration)**.
38 Carefully pull the bulb out of the holder **(see illustration)**.
40 Fit the new bulb in the bulbholder, then fit the bulbholder into the headlight – make sure the rubber seal is in good condition and correctly seated.
41 Install the headlight and check the sidelight works.

CBF600N/NA

Headlight

42 Undo the three headlight rim screws and draw the beam unit out of the shell **(see illustration)**.
43 Disconnect the headlight and sidelight wiring connectors and remove the shell to a bench.

44 Remove the rubber dust cover.
45 Release the bulb retaining clip and remove the bulb.
46 Fit the new bulb into the headlight bearing in mind the information in the **Note** above. Make sure the bulb locates correctly and secure it with the retaining clip.
47 Fit the dust cover, aligning the cut-outs with the bulb terminals.
48 Connect the wiring connectors.
49 Fit the beam unit into the shell and tighten the screws. Check the headlight works.

Sidelight

50 Undo the three headlight rim screws and draw the beam unit out of the shell **(see illustration 7.42)**.
51 Disconnect the headlight and sidelight wiring connectors and remove the shell to a bench.
52 Carefully pull the bulbholder out of the headlight.
53 Carefully remove the bulb from the holder.
54 Fit the new bulb in the bulbholder, then fit the bulbholder into the headlight – make sure the rubber seal is in good condition and correctly seated.
55 Connect the wiring connectors.
56 Fit the beam unit into the shell and tighten the screws. Check the headlight works.

CBF600S/SA

Headlights

57 Remove the fairing side panel on the side of the bulb being changed (see Chapter 7).
58 Remove the rubber dust cover **(see illustration)**.

7.31a Release the clip . . .

7.31b . . . and remove the bulb

7.37 Pull the bulbholder out . . .

7.38 . . . then pull the bulb out of the holder

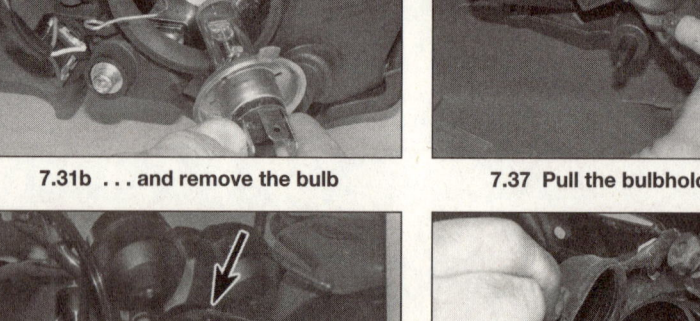

7.42 Headlight rim screws (arrowed)

7.58 Dislodge the cover . . .

Electrical system 8•11

7.59 ... then disconnect the wiring connector

7.60a Release the clip ...

7.60b ... and remove the bulb

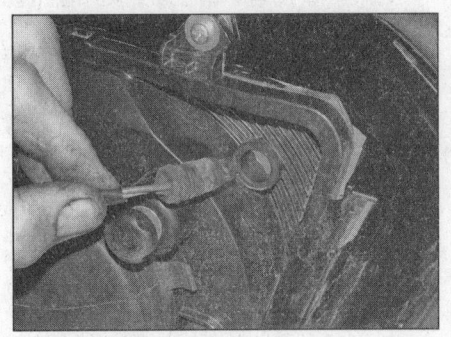

7.66 Pull the bulbholder out ...

7.67 ... then pull the bulb out of the holder

8.2 Release the wiring connector

59 Disconnect the wiring connector from the bulb (see illustration).
60 Release the bulb retaining clip and remove the bulb (see illustrations).
61 Fit the new bulb into the headlight bearing in mind the information in the Note above. Make sure the bulb locates correctly and secure it with the retaining clip (see illustrations 7.60b and a).
62 Connect the wiring connector (see illustrations 7.59).
63 Fit the dust cover, locating the tabs in the cut-outs (see illustration 7.58).
64 Check the headlight works, then install the fairing side panel.

Sidelights

65 Remove the fairing side panel on the side of the bulb being changed (see Chapter 7).
66 Carefully pull the bulbholder out of the headlight (see illustration).
67 Carefully pull the bulb out of the holder (see illustration).
68 Fit the new bulb in the bulbholder, then fit the bulbholder into the headlight – make sure the rubber seal is in good condition and correctly seated.
69 Check the sidelight works, then install the fairing side panel.

8 Headlight

CB600F/FA 2007 to 2010

1 Remove the headlight covers (see Chapter 7).
2 Free the blue connector from its clip on the left-hand side (see illustration).
3 Unscrew the bolt on each side (see illustration).
4 Support the headlight, then unscrew the top bolt, noting the washer, displace the headlight and disconnect the headlight wiring connector (see illustration).

8.3 Headlight bolts

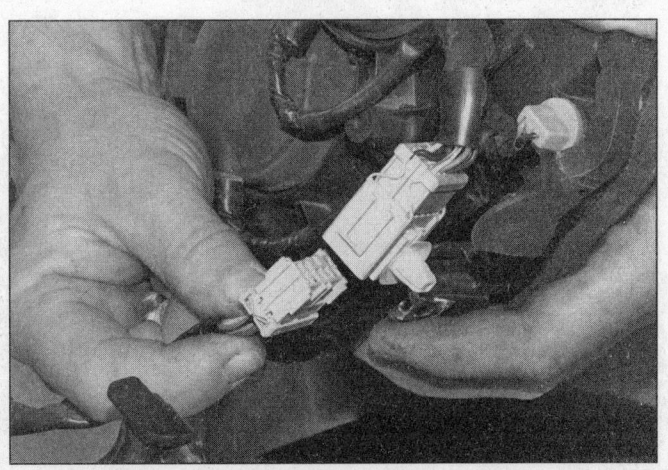

8.4 Displace the headlight and disconnect the wiring

8•12 Electrical system

8.6 Top mount has a collar

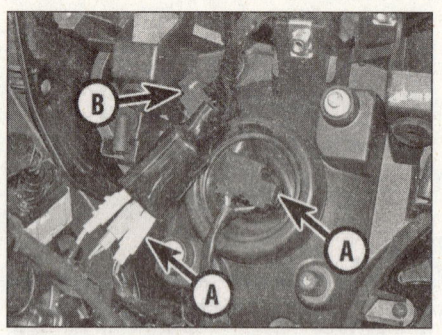

8.9 Disconnect the connectors (A) and free the clip (B)

8.10 Undo the screws (arrowed) and remove the headlight

5 If required remove the headlight and sidelight bulbs (see Section 7).
6 Installation is the reverse of removal. Make sure the collar is in the top mount **(see illustration)**. Check the operation of the headlights and sidelights. Check the headlight aim (see Chapter 1).

CB600F/FA 2011-on

7 Remove the instrument cluster (Section 15).
8 Unscrew the bolt on each side of the headlight, noting the washer **(see illustration 7.14)**. Slightly raise the headlight to free the grommets from their locating pegs, then draw it forwards **(see illustration 7.15a)**.
9 Disconnect the headlight and sidelight wiring connectors and free the wiring clip **(see illustration)**.
10 Undo the screws and remove the headlight from the covers **(see illustration)**.
11 If required remove the headlight and sidelight bulbs (see Section 7).
12 Installation is the reverse of removal. Check the operation of the headlight and sidelight. Check the headlight aim (see Chapter 1).

CBR600F/FA

13 Remove the instrument cover (see Chapter 7).
14 Free the headlight loom wiring connector clip and the turn signal wiring clips **(see illustrations)**.
15 Unscrew the bolt, noting the washer **(see illustration)**. Lift each side of the fairing off the mirror mount and draw the assembly forwards to free the grommets from their locating pegs, and disconnect the wiring connector **(see illustrations)**.

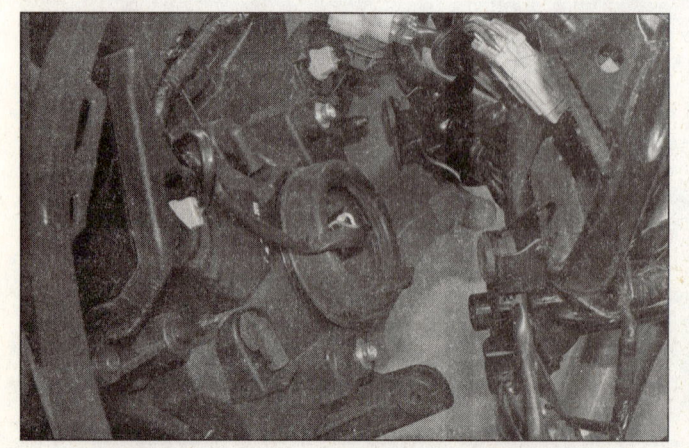

8.14a Release the clip (arrowed) ...

8.14b ... and the clip (arrowed) on each side

8.15a Unscrew the bolt (arrowed) ...

8.15b ... release the fairing ...

8.15c ... draw the pegs out of the grommets ...

8.15d ... and disconnect the wiring

Electrical system 8•13

8.16 Release the screws to free each fairing section

8.22 Unscrew the bolt (arrowed) on each side

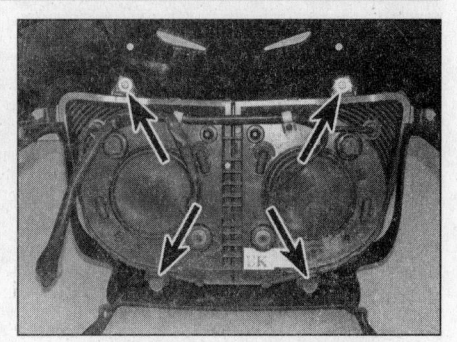

8.25 Headlight screws (arrowed)

16 Undo the screws and detach the fairing sections from the headlight (see illustration).
17 If required remove the headlight and sidelight bulbs (see Section 7), and the wiring loom.
18 Installation is the reverse of removal. Check the operation of the headlight and sidelights. Check the headlight aim (see Chapter 1).

CBF600N/NA

19 Undo the three headlight rim screws and draw the beam unit out of the shell (see illustration 7.42).
20 Disconnect the headlight and sidelight wiring connectors and remove the shell. If required remove the headlight and sidelight bulbs (see Section 7).
21 Disconnect the various wiring connectors in the shell and feed them through the holes in the back.

22 Unscrew the bolt on each side, retrieving the nut on the inside, and remove the shell from the bracket (see illustration).
23 Installation is the reverse of removal. Make sure the shell nuts are correctly located. Check the operation of the headlight and sidelight. Check the headlight aim (see Chapter 1).

CBF600S/SA

24 Remove the fairing (see Chapter 7).
25 Undo the screws securing the headlight assembly to the fairing and lift it out (see illustration).
26 If required remove the headlight and sidelight bulbs (see Section 7).
27 Installation is the reverse of removal – the black screws are for the bottom mounts, the silver for the top. Check the operation of the headlights and sidelights. Check the headlight aim (see Chapter 1).

9 Brake/tail/licence plate light bulbs

Note: *It is a good idea to use a paper towel or dry cloth when handling bulbs to prevent injury if it breaks, and to increase bulb life.*

Brake/tail light

CB600F/FA and CBR600F/FA

1 The tail light contains LEDs rather than a conventional bulb. If one or more of the LEDs within the brake or tail light unit has failed, replace the entire tail light assembly with a new one – individual LEDs are not available (see Section 10).

CBF600N/NA/S/SA models

2 Undo the screws and remove the lens (see illustration).
3 Carefully push the bulb in and turn it anti-clockwise to release it (see illustration).
4 Check the socket terminals for corrosion and clean them if necessary.
5 Line up the pins of the new bulb with the slots in the socket, then push the bulb in and turn it clockwise until it locks into place. Fit the lens – do not overtighten the screws as the lens and threads are easily damaged.

Licence plate light

6 Undo the screws and remove the lens (see illustration).
7 Carefully pull the bulb out (see illustration).
8 Check the socket terminals for corrosion and clean them if necessary.
9 Fit the new bulb, then fit the lens – do not overtighten the screws as the lens and threads are easily damaged.

9.2 Undo the screws (arrowed) and remove the lens

9.3 Push the bulb in and turn it anti-clockwise to release it

9.6 Undo the screws (arrowed) and remove the lens

9.7 Pull the bulb out

10 Tail light

CB600F/FA 2007 to 2010

1 Remove the seat cowl (see Chapter 7).
2 Release the wiring from its guides.
3 Undo the screws and remove the tail light

8•14 Electrical system

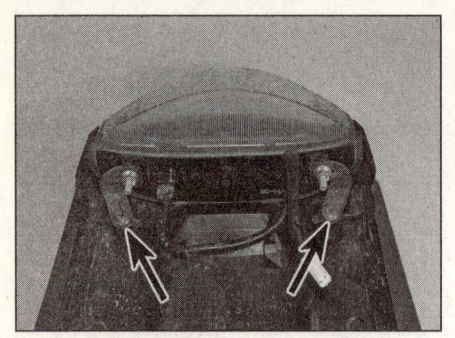

10.3 Tail light screws (arrowed)

10.6a Undo the screw (arrowed) . . .

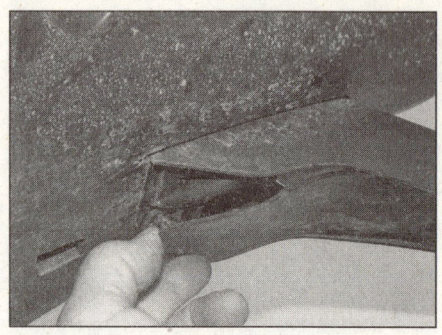

10.6b . . . release the tabs . . .

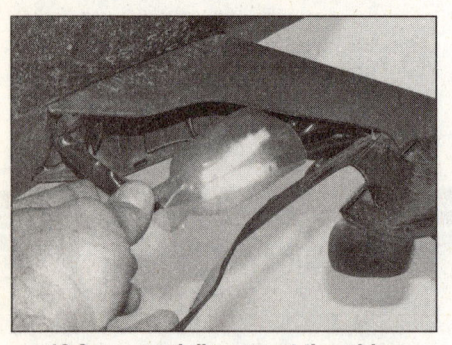

10.6c . . . and disconnect the wiring

10.7 Tail light bolts (arrowed)

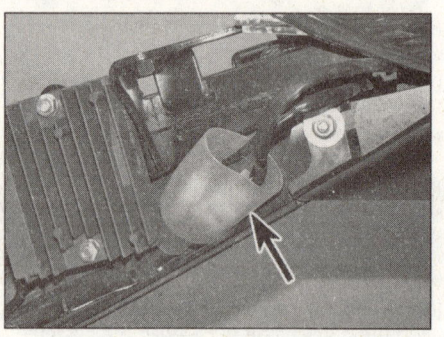

10.10 Connector is inside the boot (arrowed)

(see illustration). If required undo the nuts and remove the brackets.

4 Installation is the reverse of removal. Check the operation of the tail and brake lights.

CB600F/FA 2011-on and CBR600F/FA

5 Remove the seat cowl (see Chapter 7).
6 Undo the screw on the underside of the licence plate/turn signal holder, then release the cover tabs **(see illustrations)**. Disconnect the tail light wiring connector **(see illustration)**.
7 Undo the bolts, noting the collars, and remove the tail light, taking care not to snag the wiring **(see illustration)**.
8 Installation is the reverse of removal. Check the operation of the tail and brake lights.

CBF600N/NA/S/SA

9 Remove the rear and left-hand sections of the seat cowl (see Chapter 7).
10 Disconnect the tail light wiring connector **(see illustration)**.
11 Undo the screws and remove the tail light **(see illustration)**.
12 Installation is the reverse of removal. Check the operation of the tail and brake lights and the turn signals.

11 Turn signal circuit check

1 Most turn signal problems are the result of a burned out bulb or corroded socket. This is especially true when the turn signals function properly in one direction (although possibly too quickly), but fail to flash in the other direction. If this is the case, first check the bulbs, the sockets and the wiring connectors (see Sections 12 and 13). If all the turn signals fail to work, check the fuse (see Section 5), and then the relay (see Steps 2 to 4). If they are good, the problem lies in the wiring or connectors, or the switch. Refer to Section 19 for the switch testing procedures, and also to the wiring diagrams at the end of this Chapter.
2 To check the relay, on CB600F/FA and CBR600F/FA models remove the seat cowl, and on CBF600S/SA models remove the right-hand seat cowl (see Chapter 7).
3 Displace the relay and disconnect the wiring connector **(see illustrations)**. Check for battery voltage at the white/green wire

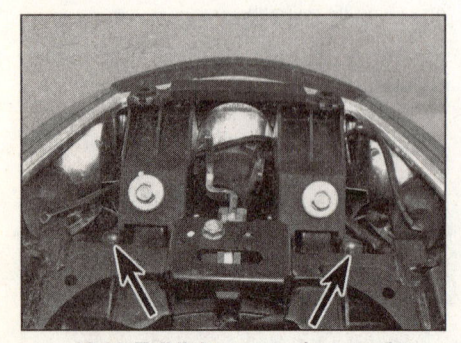

10.11 Tail light screws (arrowed)

11.3a Turn signal relay (arrowed) – early CB models

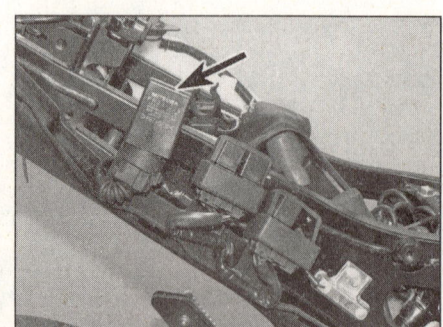

11.3b Turn signal relay (arrowed) – late CB and CBR models

Electrical system 8•15

11.3c Turn signal relay (arrowed) – CBF models

terminal on the loom side of the connector with the ignition ON. If no voltage is present, check the white/green wire from the relay to the fuse for continuity. Refer to electrical system fault finding in Section 2 and to the wiring diagrams at the end of this Chapter. If voltage was present check the green wire for continuity to earth, and repair or renew the wiring or connectors as required.

4 If voltage was present, short between the white/green and grey wire terminals on the loom side of the connector using a jumper wire. Turn the ignition ON and operate the turn signal switch. If the lights come on (they won't flash), the relay is faulty and must be replaced with a new one.

5 If the lights do not come on, check the grey wire for continuity to the left-hand switch housing and repair or renew the wiring or connectors as required.

6 If all is good so far, or if the lights came on one side but not the other, check the wiring between the left-hand switch housing and the turn signals themselves. Repair or renew the wiring or connectors as necessary.

7 Note that the red/green wire connection to the turn signal relay is a power feed for the hazard switch and is not wired through the ignition switch.

12 Turn signal bulbs

Note: *It is a good idea to use a paper towel or dry cloth when handling bulbs to prevent injury if the bulb should break and to increase bulb life.*

Front turn signals

CBF600S/SA

1 The bulbs can be removed with the fairing side panel in place but it is fiddly and you can't see what you are doing, so for best access remove the relevant panel (see Chapter 7).
2 Turn the bulbholder anti-clockwise to release it **(see illustration)**.
3 Carefully push the bulb in and turn it anti-clockwise to release it **(see illustration)**. Check the socket terminals for corrosion and clean them if necessary.
4 Line up the pins of the new bulb with the slots in the socket, then push the bulb in and turn it clockwise until it locks into place. Note that the pin slots in the bulbholder are off-set to allow only the fitting of an amber bulb. Fit the bulbholder and turn it clockwise.
5 Install the fairing side panel if removed.

All other models

6 See Steps 7 to 10.

Rear turn signals

CB600F/FA and CBR600F/FA

7 Undo the screw securing the lens and detach it from the housing, noting how it fits **(see illustration)**. Remove the rubber seal if it is loose, and replace it with a new one if it is damaged, deformed or deteriorated.
8 Push the bulb in and twist it anti-clockwise to release it **(see illustration)**. Check the socket terminals for corrosion and clean them if necessary.
9 Line up the pins of the new bulb with the slots in the socket, then push the bulb in and turn it clockwise until it locks into place. Note that the pin slots in the bulbholder are off-set to allow only the fitting of an amber bulb.
10 Fit a new rubber seal if required, and make sure it is properly seated and does not get pinched. Fit the lens onto the housing, locating the tab in the cut-out in the housing, and fit the screw **(see illustration)** – do not overtighten it as it is easy to strip the threads or crack the lens.

CBF600N/NA/S/SA

11 Undo the tail/brake light lens screws and remove the lens **(see illustration 9.2)**.
12 Undo the turn signal lens screw and remove the lens **(see illustration)**.

12.2 Release the bulbholder . . .

12.3 . . . then remove the bulb from it

12.7 Undo the screw and remove the lens

12.8 Push the bulb in and turn it anti-clockwise to release it

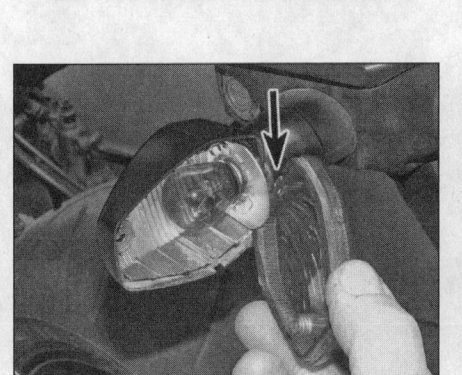

12.10 Make sure the tab (arrowed) locates correctly

12.12 Undo the screw and remove the lens

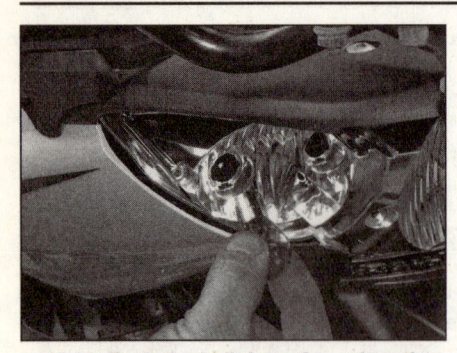

8•16 Electrical system

12.13 Push the bulb in and turn it anti-clockwise to release it

13 Carefully push the bulb in and turn it anti-clockwise to release it **(see illustration)**. Check the socket terminals for corrosion and clean them if necessary.

14 Line up the pins of the new bulb with the slots in the socket, then push the bulb in and turn it clockwise until it locks into place. Note that the pin slots in the bulbholder are off-set to allow only the fitting of an amber bulb.

15 Fit the lenses – do not overtighten the screws as the lens and threads are easily damaged.

13 Turn signal assemblies

CB600F/FA 2007 to 2010

Front turn signals

1 Remove the headlight covers (see Chapter 7).
2 Unscrew the nut, remove the plate and remove the turn signal, taking care as you draw the wire through **(see illustration)**.
3 Installation is the reverse of removal. Check the operation of the turn signal.

Rear turn signals

4 Remove the seat cowl (see Chapter 7).
5 Disconnect the turn signal wiring connector(s) **(see illustration)**.
6 Unscrew the nut, remove the plate and remove the turn signal, taking care as you draw the wire through **(see illustration)**.
7 Installation is the reverse of removal. Check the operation of the turn signal.

CB600F/FA 2011-on

Front turn signals

8 Remove the headlight (see Section 8).

9 Disconnect the turn signal wiring connector(s) **(see illustration)**. When removing the right-hand turn signal release the wiring from the tie.
10 Unscrew the nut, remove the plate and remove the turn signal, taking care as you draw the wire through **(see illustration 13.9)**.
11 Installation is the reverse of removal. Check the operation of the turn signal.

Rear turn signals

12 Undo the screw on the underside of the licence plate/turn signal holder, then release the cover tabs **(see illustrations 10.6a and b)**. Disconnect the turn signal wiring connector(s) **(see illustration 10.6c)**.
13 Undo the screws securing the licence plate holder and remove it **(see illustration)**.
14 Unscrew the nut, remove the plate and remove the turn signal, taking care as you draw the wire through.
15 Installation is the reverse of removal. Check the operation of the turn signal.

CBR600F/FA

Front turn signals

16 Remove the relevant fairing side panel (see Chapter 7).
17 Unscrew the nut, remove the plate and

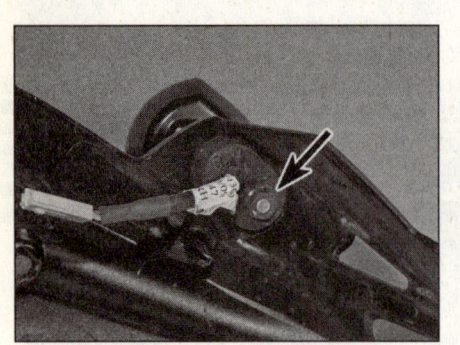

13.2 Turn signal nut (arrowed)

13.5 Wiring connectors are inside the boot (arrowed)

13.6 Turn signal nut (arrowed)

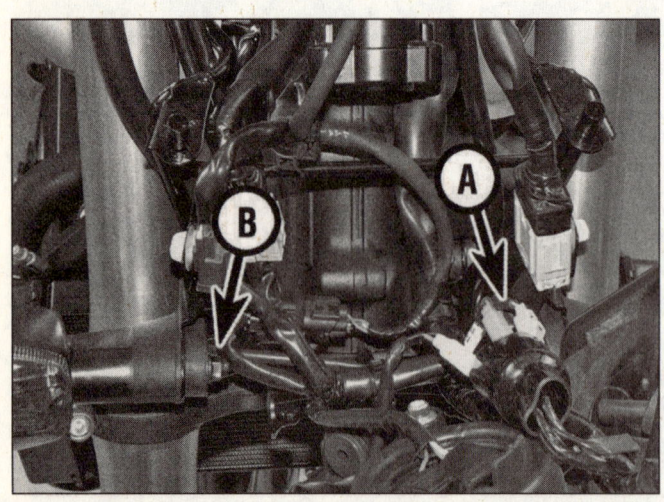

13.9 Turn signal wiring connectors (A) and nut (B)

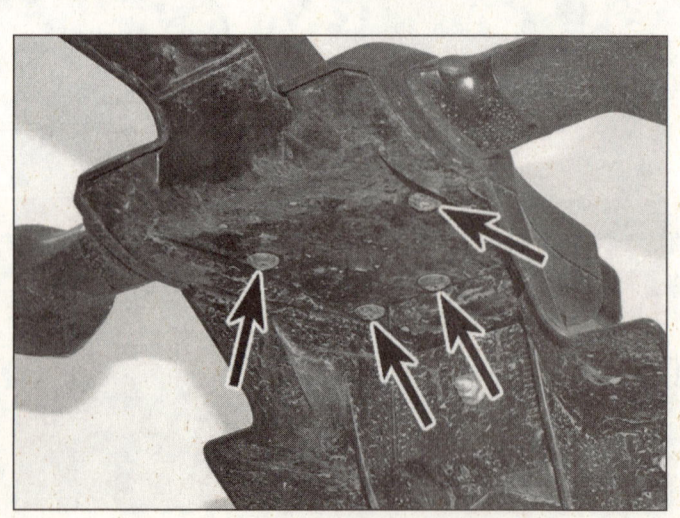

13.13 Licence plate holder screws (arrowed)

Electrical system 8•17

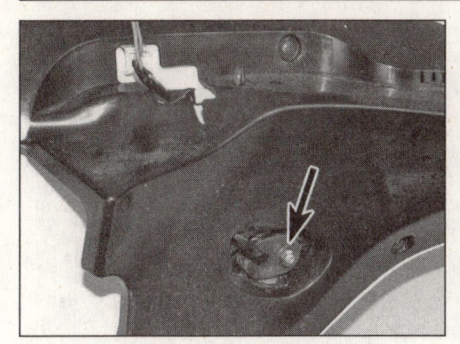

13.17 Turn signal nut (arrowed)

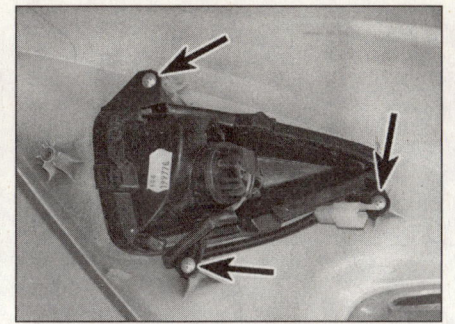

13.27 Turn signal screws (arrowed)

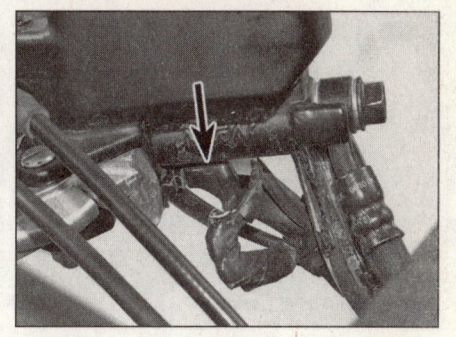

14.2 Front brake switch wiring connectors (arrowed)

remove the turn signal, taking care as you draw the wire through, and note its routing **(see illustration)**.
18 Installation is the reverse of removal. Check the operation of the turn signal.

Rear turn signals
19 See Steps 12 to 15.

CBF600N/NA
Front turn signals
20 Undo the three headlight rim screws and draw the beam unit out of the shell **(see illustration 7.42)**.
21 Disconnect the headlight and sidelight wiring connectors and remove the shell.
22 Disconnect the relevant turn signal wiring connector in the shell and feed it through the hole in the back.
23 Unscrew the nut and remove the turn signal, taking care as you draw the wire through. If you need better access to the nut remove the headlight shell (Section 8).
24 Installation is the reverse of removal. Check the operation of the headlight and turn signal.

Rear turn signals
25 See Section 10.

CBF600S/SA
Front turn signals
26 Remove the relevant fairing side panel (see Chapter 7).
27 Undo the screws and remove the turn signal **(see illustration)**.
28 Installation is the reverse of removal. Check the operation of the turn signal.

Rear turn signals
29 See Section 10.

14 Brake light switches

Circuit check
Note: *Refer to electrical system fault finding in Section 2 and to the wiring diagram for your model at the end of this Chapter.*
1 Before checking the switches, and if not already done, check the brake light circuit (see Section 6).
2 The front brake light switch is mounted on the underside of the brake master cylinder. Disconnect the wiring connectors from the switch **(see illustration)**. Using a continuity tester, connect the probes to the terminals of the switch. With the brake lever at rest, there should be no continuity. With the brake lever applied, there should be continuity. If the switch does not behave as described, replace it with a new one.
3 The rear brake light switch is mounted on the inside of the rider's right-hand footrest bracket **(see illustration 14.9)**. Remove the right-hand side cover (see Chapter 7). Disconnect the wiring connector **(see illustrations)**. Using a continuity tester, connect the probes to the terminals on the switch side of the wiring connector. With the brake pedal at rest, there should be no continuity. With the brake pedal applied, there should be continuity. If the switch does not behave as described, replace it with a new one, although check first that the spring has not become detached or broken, and the switch is adjusted correctly (see Chapter 1).
4 If the switches are good, when checking the front switch check for voltage at one of the wiring connectors, and when checking the rear switch check for voltage at the white/green wire on the loom side of the connector, in each case with the ignition switch ON – there should be battery voltage. If there's no

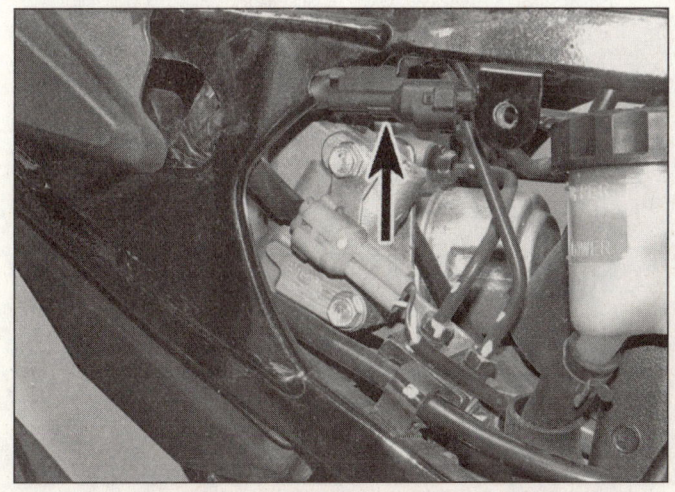

14.3a Rear brake switch wiring connector (arrowed) – CB and CBR models

14.3b Rear brake switch wiring connector – CBF models

8•18 Electrical system

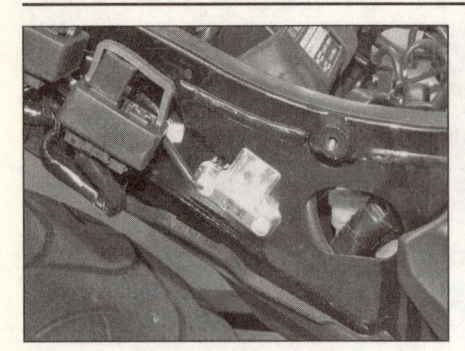

14.5 Resistor location

14.6 Front brake light switch screw (arrowed)

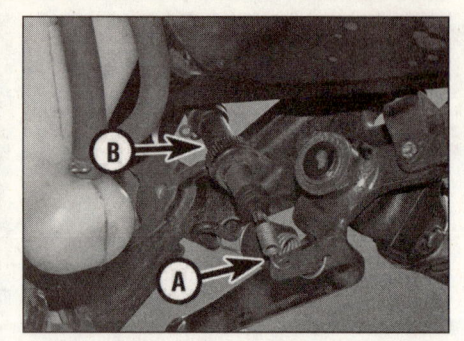

14.9 Detach the spring (A) and remove the switch (B) as described

voltage present, check the wiring between the connector and the fusebox (see the wiring diagrams at the end of this Chapter). If voltage is present, check the other wire for continuity to the brake light, referring to the relevant wiring diagram. Repair or renew the wiring as necessary.

5 Note that there is a resistor in the green/yellow wire circuit from the brake light switches to the brake light on 2011-on CB600F/FA and CBR600F/FA models. The resistor limits current flow through the circuit and protects the LEDs from excessive load. It is mounted on the rear of the frame on the right-hand side **(see illustration)**; remove the seat cowl for access (see Chapter 7). To test the resistor, disconnect its wire at the bullet connector and measure the resistance between the wire end (resistor side) and the mounting screw – it should be as given in the Specifications at the beginning of the Chapter.

Switch replacement

Front brake lever switch

6 The switch is mounted on the underside of the brake master cylinder. Disconnect the wiring connectors from the switch **(see illustration 14.2)**. Undo the single screw securing the switch to the master cylinder and remove the switch **(see illustration)**.

7 Installation is the reverse of removal. Make sure the peg on the switch is correctly located in its hole before tightening the screw. The switch isn't adjustable.

Rear brake pedal switch

8 The rear brake light switch is mounted on the inside of the rider's right-hand footrest bracket. Remove the right-hand side cover (see Chapter 7). Disconnect the wiring connector **(see illustration 14.3a or b)**. Feed the wiring down to the switch, noting its routing and releasing it from any ties.

9 Detach the end of the switch spring from the brake pedal **(see illustration)**. Thread the switch out of its adjuster nut, then pull the nut out of the bracket. For improved access, detach the footrest bracket from the frame (see Chapter 5).

10 Installation is the reverse of removal, noting the following:
- If removed tighten the footrest bracket bolts to the torque setting specified at the beginning of the Chapter.
- Make sure the brake light is activated just before the rear brake pedal takes effect. If adjustment is necessary, refer to Chapter 1, Section 3.

15 Instrument removal and installation

Removal

CB600F/FA 2007 to 2010

1 Remove the headlight (see Section 8).
2 Undo the screws and remove the cover, noting how the tab at the top locates **(see illustrations)**.
3 Disconnect the wiring connector **(see illustration)**.
4 Undo the screws, noting the washers,

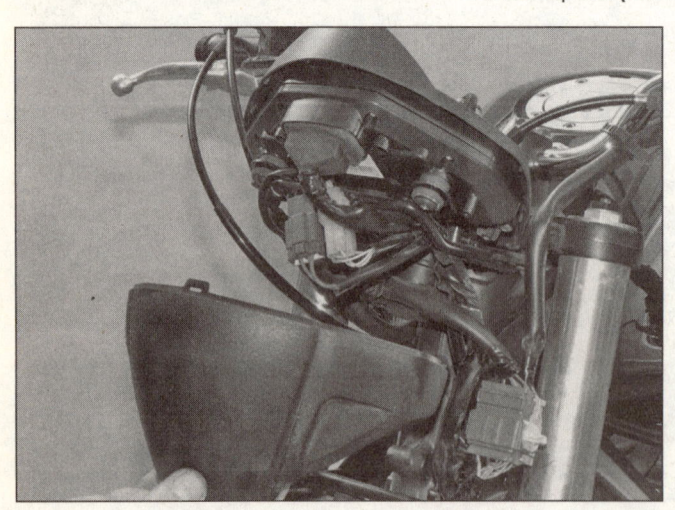

15.2a Undo the screws (arrowed) . . .

15.2b . . . and remove the cover

15.3 Pull the boot back and disconnect the wiring

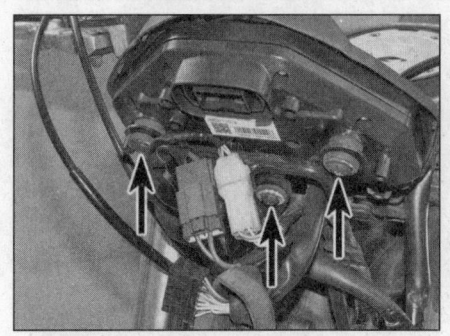

Electrical system 8•19

15.4 Instrument cluster screws (arrowed)

15.6a Unscrew the bolts (arrowed) and lift the instrument cluster . . .

15.6b . . . then pull the boot back and disconnect the wiring

and remove the instrument cluster **(see illustration)**.

CB600F/FA 2011-on

5 Remove the instrument cover (see Chapter 7).
6 Unscrew the bolts and displace the instrument cluster, then disconnect the wiring connector **(see illustrations)**.

CBR600F/FA

7 Remove the headlight (see Section 8).
8 Disconnect the wiring connector **(see illustration)**.
9 Undo the screws, noting the washers, and lift the instrument cluster off the pegs **(see illustration)**.

CBF600N/NA

10 Undo the three headlight rim screws and draw the beam unit out of the shell **(see illustration 7.42)**.
11 Disconnect the headlight and sidelight wiring connectors and remove the beam unit.
12 Disconnect the instrument and ignition switch wiring connectors, and where fitted the HISS receiver wiring connector, and feed them through the hole in the back of the headlight shell.
13 Unscrew the nuts securing the instrument cluster to the headlight bracket **(see illustration)**. Release the wiring tie on the bracket.
14 Displace the handlebars from the top yoke (see Chapter 5).
15 Unscrew the steering stem nut **(see illustration)**. Slacken the fork clamp bolts in the top yoke **(see illustration)**.
16 Gently ease the top yoke/instrument assembly up off the forks.
17 Unscrew the bolts on the underside and remove the instrument cluster. Note the collars in the grommets.

CBF600S/SA

18 Remove the fairing (see Chapter 7). Remove the rubber shroud **(see illustration)**.

15.8 Pull the boot back and disconnect the wiring

15.9 Instrument cluster screws (arrowed)

15.13 Unscrew the nuts (arrowed)

15.15a Unscrew the stem nut

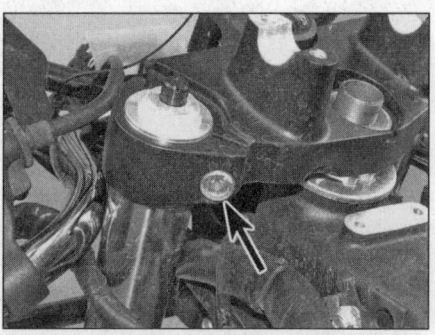

15.15b Slacken the clamp bolt (arrowed) on each side

15.18 Remove the shroud

15.19 Pull the boot back and disconnect the wiring

15.20 Instrument cluster bolts (arrowed)

19 Disconnect the instrument cluster wiring connector **(see illustration)**.
20 Unscrew the bolts and remove the instrument cluster **(see illustration)**. Note the collars in the grommets.

Installation

21 Installation is the reverse of removal, noting the following:
- Where fitted check the rubber grommets and replace them with new ones if necessary, and make sure any collars and washers are fitted.
- On CBF600N/NA models make sure the rubbers on the top prongs on the headlight bracket locate in the holes in the underside of the yoke. Fit the steering stem nut and tighten it to the torque setting specified at the beginning of the Chapter **(see illustration 15.15a)**. Tighten the fork clamp bolts to the specified torque **(see illustration 15.15b)**. Refer to Chapter 5 for installation of the handlebars.
- Make sure all wiring connectors are securely connected.

16 Instrument check and replacement

Check

Note: *Refer to electrical system fault finding in Section 2 and to the wiring diagram for your model at the end of this Chapter.*

Instrument cluster power check

1 If none of the instruments or displays are working, first check the fuse (see Section 5).
2 If the fuse is good, on CB600F/FA 2007 to 2010 models remove headlight (Section 8), then remove the instrument cover (Section 15, Step 2), on CB600F/FA 2011-on models remove the instrument cover (see Chapter 7), on CBR600F/FA models remove the instrument surround, on CBF600N/NA models remove the headlight beam unit (Section 7), and on CBF600S/SA models remove the fairing (see Chapter 7), then remove the rubber shroud **(see illustration 15.18)**. Check the instrument wiring connector(s) for loose or broken connections **(see illustration 15.3, 15.6b, 15.8 or 15.19)**.
3 To check the power input wire, check for battery voltage between the black/brown wire terminal and a good earth (ground) with the ignition switch ON. There should be battery voltage. If there is no voltage, refer to the wiring diagrams and check the wire between the instrument cluster and the fusebox for loose or broken connections or a damaged wire.
4 To check the back-up power wire, check for battery voltage between the red/green wire terminal on the wiring loom side of the connector and a good earth (ground) with the ignition switch OFF. There should be battery voltage. If there is no voltage, refer to the wiring diagrams and check the red/green wire between the instrument cluster and the fusebox for loose or broken connections or a damaged wire, then check the corresponding wire from the fusebox to the main fuse and battery.
5 If there is voltage, and to check the earth (ground) wire, check for continuity between the green/black wire terminal and earth (ground). If there is no continuity, check the circuit for loose or broken connections or a damaged wire and repair as necessary.
6 If all power input and earth wires are good, but there is no display or instrument function, then the printed circuit board (PCB) is faulty. Disassemble the instrument cluster and replace the instrument/PCB with a new one (see the relevant Steps below for your model).

Speedometer and vehicle speed sensor

7 On CB600F/FA 2007 to 2010 models remove headlight (Section 8), then remove the instrument cover (Section 15, Step 2), on CB600F/FA 2011-on models remove the instrument cover (see Chapter 7), on CBR600F/FA models remove the instrument surround, on CBF600N/NA models remove the headlight beam unit (Section 7), and on CBF600S/SA models remove the fairing (see Chapter 7), then remove the rubber shroud **(see illustration 15.18)**. Check the instrument wiring connector(s) for loose or broken connections **(see illustration 15.3, 15.6b, 15.8 or 15.19)**.
8 If the wiring is good, place the bike on the centrestand on CBF600N/NA/S/SA models, and on an auxiliary stand on all other models so the rear wheel is off the ground. Connect a voltmeter between the pink/blue (+) and green/black (-) wire terminals in the connector on CB600F/FA 2007 to 2010 models and CBF600N/NA/S/SA models, and between the pink/green (+) and green/black (-) wire terminals in the connector on CB600F/FA 2011-on models and CBR600F/FA models – make sure the probes make good contact when inserted into the connector. With the ignition switch ON, have an assistant turn the rear wheel by hand and check that a fluctuating voltage reading between 0 and 5 volts is obtained. If the correct reading is obtained the printed circuit board (PCB) is faulty. Disassemble the instrument cluster and replace the instrument/PCB with a new one (see the relevant Steps below for your model). If no reading is obtained, check for continuity in the pink/blue or pink/green wire to the speed sensor wiring connector, which is behind the starter motor, and in the green/black wire to earth. To access the wiring connector remove the air filter housing/throttle body assembly (see Chapter 4).
9 If the wiring is good, remove the air filter housing/throttle body assembly (see Chapter 4). Disconnect the speed sensor 3-pin black wiring connector **(see illustration 16.40)**. Check the connector for loose terminals. With the ignition switch ON, check for battery voltage between the yellow/red (+) and green/black (-) wire terminals on the wiring loom side of the connector. If there is no voltage refer to the wiring diagrams and check the wires for

Electrical system 8•21

continuity to the instrument wiring connector and earth respectively and repair any loose or broken connection or damaged wire.

10 If all is good so far the speed sensor is faulty and must be replaced with a new one (see Steps 39 to 42).

Tachometer

11 On CB600F/FA and CBR600F/FA models when the ignition is switched on the tachometer needle should swing all the way around the dial and back again or the display segments should all come on sequentially from zero to maximum, then go out in the same order, according to model.

12 If the tachometer does not work, on CB600F/FA 2007 to 2010 models remove headlight (Section 8), then remove the instrument cover (Section 15, Step 2), on CB600F/FA 2011-on models remove the instrument cover (see Chapter 7), on CBR600F/FA models remove the instrument surround, on CBF600N/NA models remove the headlight beam unit (Section 7), and on CBF600S/SA models remove the fairing (see Chapter 7), then remove the rubber shroud **(see illustration 15.18)**. Check the instrument wiring connector(s) for loose or broken connections **(see illustration 15.3, 15.6b, 15.8 or 15.19)**.

13 If the wiring is good, check the tachometer input peak voltage using the peak voltage adapter (part No. 07HGJ-0020100) with an aftermarket digital multimeter having an impedance of 10 M-ohm/DCV minimum, for this test. Connect the positive (+) lead of the voltmeter and peak voltage adapter arrangement to the yellow/green wire terminal on the loom side of the instrument wiring connector and the negative (–) lead to a good earth (ground). Start the engine and measure the tachometer input peak voltage, which should be at least 10.5 volts. If the peak voltage is normal, check the instrument cluster earth wire (see Step 5). If it is good then the tachometer is faulty. Disassemble the instrument cluster and replace the instrument/PCB with a new one (see the relevant Steps below for your model).

14 If there is no reading, raise the fuel tank (see Chapter 4), and check there is continuity in the yellow/green wire to the ECM wiring connector. If there is no continuity there is a break in the wire or faulty connector. Refer to the wiring diagrams and trace and rectify the fault. If the wiring is good the ECM could be faulty (see Chapter 4).

All other functions

15 If none of the functions are working, check the instrument cluster power input (see above) and earth wires. If all is good, disassemble the instrument cluster (see below) and check for any obvious internal fault. If none is apparent replace the instrument/PCB with a new one.

16 If an individual function is not working, refer to Chapter 3 for the coolant temperature and warning display, Chapter 4 for the low fuel warning, FI and HISS lights, Chapter 6 for the ABS light, Section 6 for the HI beam light, Section 17 for the oil pressure switch, Section 20 for the neutral switch. If the particular component and its circuit are good the instrument is faulty – on CBF600S/SA models the fuel gauge and FI/HISS/ABS display units are available separately, while on all other models the entire display is one unit.

Instrument and warning lights

17 On CBF600N/NA models the instrument lights and the turn signal warning lights are conventional bulbs that can be replaced with new ones – remove the instrument cluster (Section 15), then remove the rear cover (Step 28). Pull the relevant bulbholder out, then remove the bulb from it and replace it with a new one. All other warning lights are LEDs, which are part of the instrument cluster printed circuit board and are not available individually. If one of the LEDs fails disassemble the instrument cluster and replace the instrument/PCB or indicator board with a new one (see below).

18 On all other models all instrument and warning lights are LEDs, which are part of the instrument cluster printed circuit board and are not available individually. If one of the LEDs fails disassemble the instrument cluster and replace the instrument/PCB with a new one (see below).

Instrument disassembly and replacement

CB600F/FA 2007 to 2010

19 Remove the instrument cluster (see Section 15).

20 Undo the screws on the front and the two bottom screws on the back and remove the outer front cover **(see illustrations)**.

21 Undo the screws on the back and remove the inner front cover **(see illustrations)**.

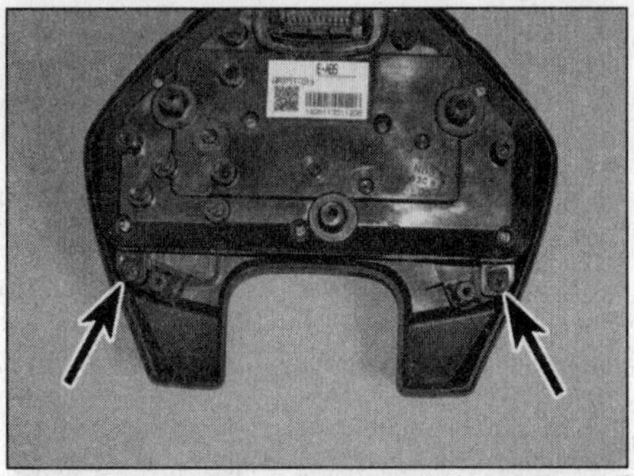

16.20a Undo the screws (arrowed) on the back . . .

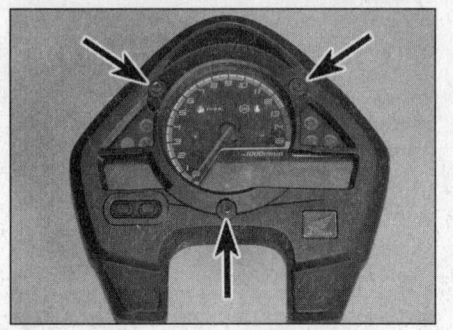

16.20b . . . and on the front . . .

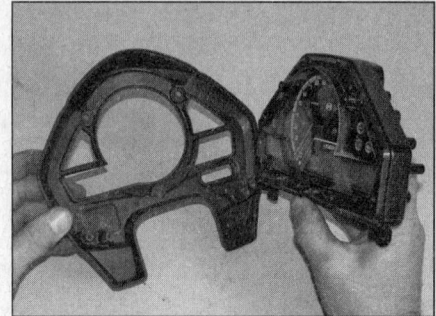

16.20c . . . and remove the cover

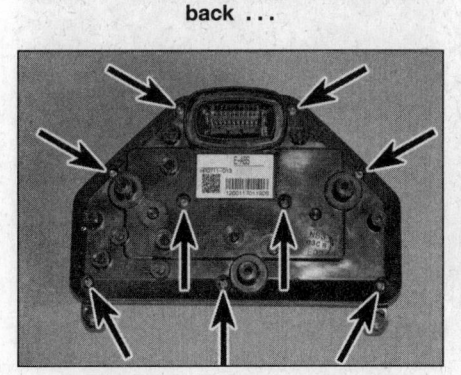

16.21a Undo the screws (arrowed)

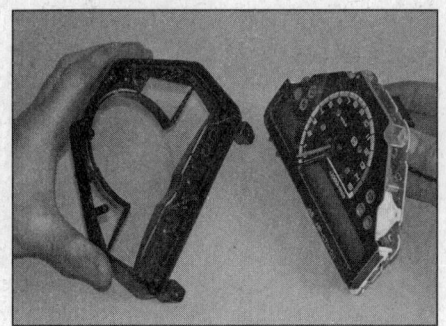

16.21b Remove the inner front cover . . .

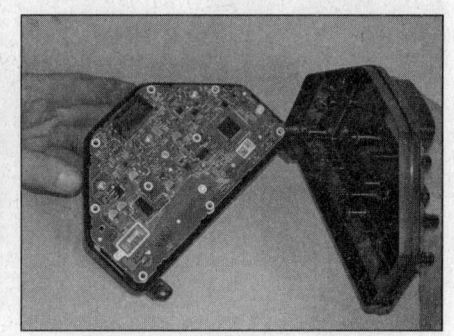

16.21c . . . then lift the PCB out

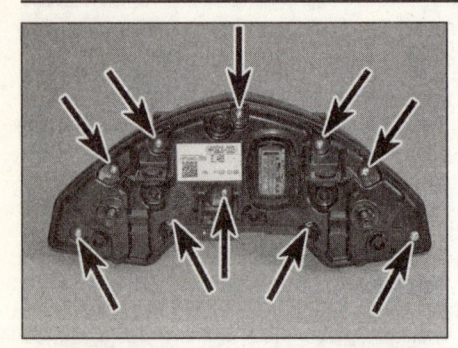

8•22 Electrical system

16.24a Undo the screws (arrowed)

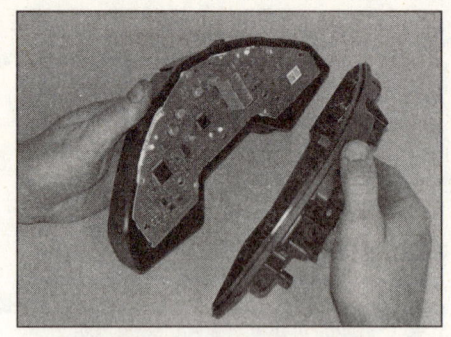

16.24b Remove the rear cover . . .

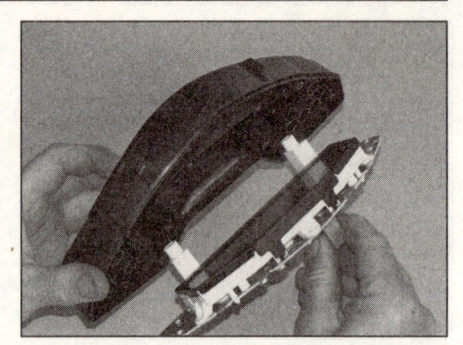

16.24c . . . then lift the PCB out

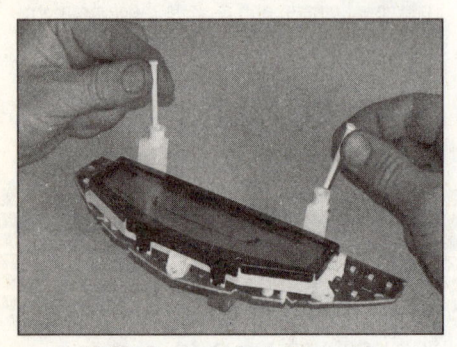

16.25 Remove the button rods

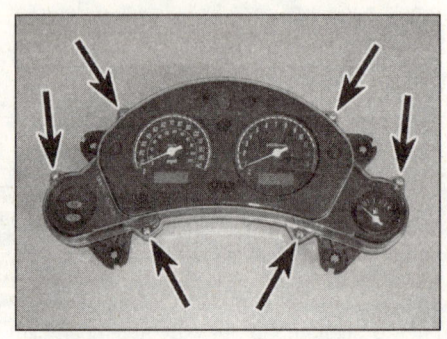

16.34a Undo the screws (arrowed) . . .

16.34b . . . and remove the clear cover . . .

Remove the instrument/PCB **(see illustration)**.

22 Installation is the reverse of removal. Do not over-tighten the screws.

CB600F/FA 2011-on and CBR600F/FA

23 Remove the instrument cluster (see Section 15).
24 Undo the screws on the back and remove the rear cover, then remove the instrument/PCB from the front cover **(see illustrations)**.
25 Remove the button rods from the instrument/PCB **(see illustration)**.

26 Installation is the reverse of removal. Do not over-tighten the screws.

CBF600N/NA

27 Remove the instrument cluster (see Section 15).
28 Undo the screws on the back and remove the rear cover.
29 Undo the screws on the back and remove the front cover.
30 Carefully pull the four bulbholders out. Displace the rubber covers and disconnect the wiring connectors. If required undo the wiring clamp screw and remove the wiring.

31 Undo the screws and remove the instrument/PCB.
32 Installation is the reverse of removal. Do not over-tighten the screws.

CBF600S/SA

33 Remove the instrument cluster (see Section 15).
34 Undo the screws on the front and remove the clear cover and the front cover **(see illustrations)**.
35 To remove the main instrument PCB undo the relevant screws on the back **(see illustration)**. Turn the instrument cluster

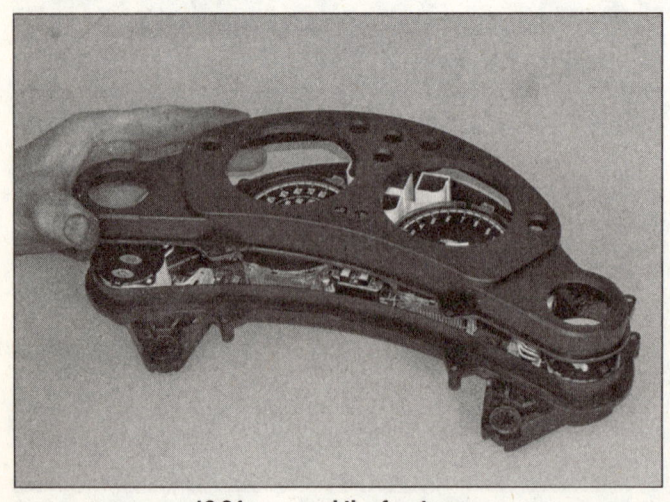

16.34c . . . and the front cover

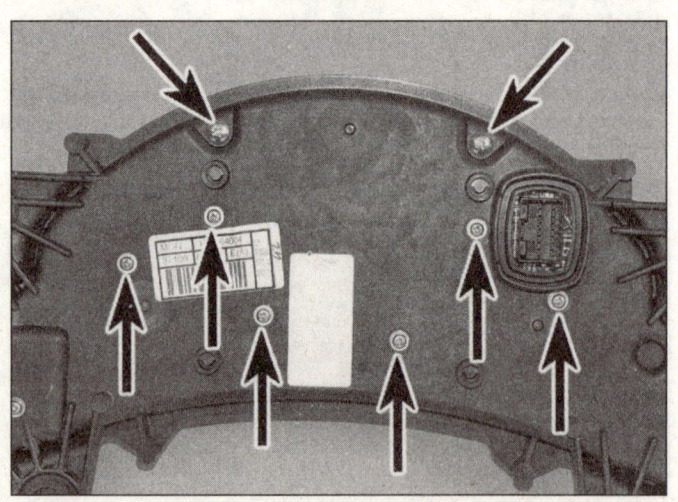

16.35a Undo the screws (arrowed) at the rear . . .

Electrical system 8•23

16.35b . . . and at the front (arrowed) . . .

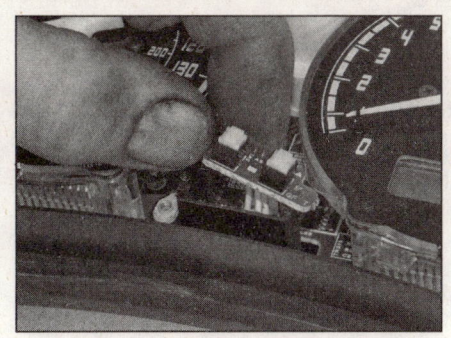

16.35c . . . then displace the button PCB . . .

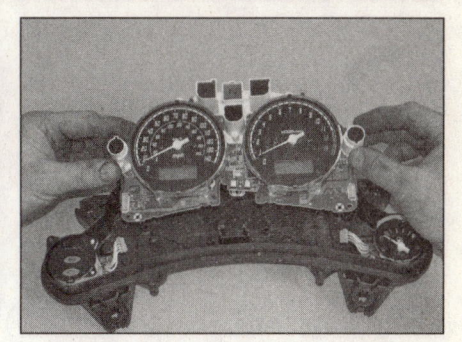

16.35d . . . and lift the main PCB out

16.36a Fuel gauge screws (arrowed)

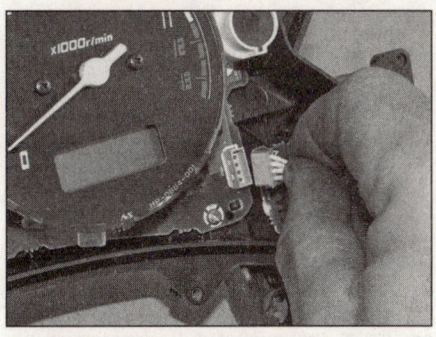

16.36b Disconnect the wiring and remove the gauge

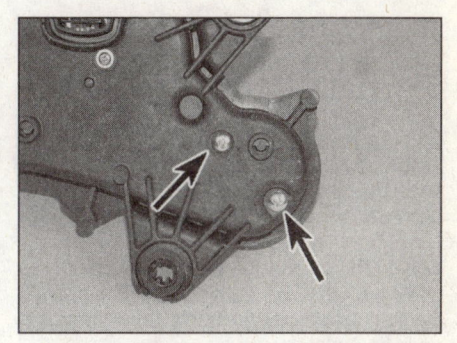

16.37a Fuel gauge screws (arrowed)

over and disconnect the fuel gauge and FI/HISS/ABS display wiring connectors **(see illustrations 16.36b and 16.37b)**. Undo the two main PCB screws, displace the button contact PCB, and lift the main PCB out, noting how it locates **(see illustrations)**.

36 To remove the fuel gauge undo the relevant screws on the back **(see illustration)**. Turn the instrument cluster over and disconnect the fuel gauge wiring connector and remove the gauge **(see illustration)**.

37 To remove the FI/HISS/ABS display undo the relevant screws on the back **(see illustration)**. Turn the instrument cluster over and disconnect the FI/HISS/ABS display wiring connector and remove the display **(see illustration)**.

38 Installation is the reverse of removal. Do not over-tighten the screws. Make sure the wiring connectors are secure.

Vehicle speed sensor

39 The speed sensor is mounted behind the starter motor. To access it remove the air filter housing/throttle body assembly (see Chapter 4).

40 Disconnect the wiring connector **(see illustration)**.

41 Unscrew the bolt and remove the sensor **(see illustration)**. Check the condition of its O-ring and replace it with a new one if it is damaged or there is evidence of leakage around it. While the sensor is removed plug the orifice with clean rag.

42 Installation is the reverse of removal, using a new O-ring if necessary.

17 Oil pressure switch

1 The oil pressure warning light should come on when the ignition switch is turned ON and go out a few seconds after the engine is started. If the oil pressure warning light does not go out or comes on whilst the engine is running, stop the engine immediately and carry out an oil level check (see *Pre-ride checks*), and if the level is correct, an oil pressure check (see Chapter 2).

Check

Note: Refer to electrical system fault finding in Section 2 and to the wiring diagram for your model at the end of this Chapter.

16.37b Disconnect the wiring and remove the gauge

16.40 Speed sensor wiring connector (A) and mounting bolt (B)

16.41 Replace the O-ring with a new one if necessary

8•24 Electrical system

17.2 Pull back the rubber cover then undo the terminal screw (arrowed) and detach the wire

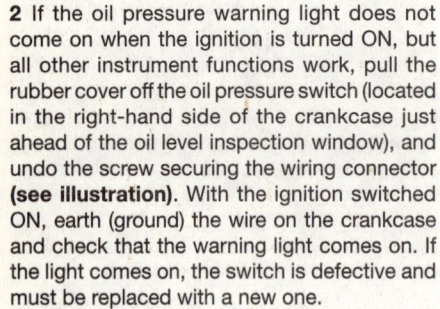

17.7 Counter-hold the base hex (arrowed) when unscrewing the switch

Installation

8 Apply a suitable sealant to the upper portion of the switch threads near the switch body, leaving the bottom 3 to 4 mm of thread clean. Thread the switch into the crankcase, then counter-hold the base hex and tighten the switch to the torque setting specified at the beginning of the Chapter **(see illustration 17.7)**.

9 Attach the wiring connector and secure it with the screw, then fit the rubber cover **(see illustration 17.2)**.

10 Run the engine and check that the switch operates correctly and without leakage.

2 If the oil pressure warning light does not come on when the ignition is turned ON, but all other instrument functions work, pull the rubber cover off the oil pressure switch (located in the right-hand side of the crankcase just ahead of the oil level inspection window), and undo the screw securing the wiring connector **(see illustration)**. With the ignition switched ON, earth (ground) the wire on the crankcase and check that the warning light comes on. If the light comes on, the switch is defective and must be replaced with a new one.

3 If the light still does not come on, check for voltage at the wire terminal with the ignition ON. If there is no voltage present, on CB600F/FA 2007 to 2010 models remove headlight (Section 8), then remove the instrument cover (Section 15, Step 2), on CB600F/FA 2011-on models remove the instrument cover (see Chapter 7), on CBR600F/FA models remove the instrument surround, on CBF600N/NA models remove the headlight beam unit (Section 7), and on CBF600S/SA models remove the fairing (see Chapter 7), then remove the rubber shroud. Check the instrument wiring connector(s) for loose or broken connections **(see illustration 15.3, 15.6b, 15.8 or 15.15)**. Check there is continuity in the blue/red wire between the switch and the instrument cluster connector. Repair the wiring if necessary. If all the wiring is good and the switch is good the instrument/PCB could be faulty (see Section 16).

4 If the warning light does not go out when the engine is started or comes on whilst the engine is running, yet the oil pressure is satisfactory, detach the wire from the oil pressure switch (see above). With the wire detached and the ignition switched ON the light should be out. If it is illuminated, the wire between the switch and instrument cluster is earthed (grounded) at some point. If the wiring is good, the switch must be assumed faulty and replaced with a new one.

Removal

5 The oil pressure switch is screwed into the right-hand side of the crankcase just ahead of the oil level inspection window. On CBF600N/NA/S/SA models put the bike on its sidestand, not the centrestand.

6 Pull the rubber cover off the switch, then undo the screw securing the wiring connector **(see illustration 17.2)**.

7 Counter-hold the base hex and unscrew and remove the switch **(see illustration)** – be prepared to catch any residual oil with a rag.

18 Ignition switch

Warning: To prevent the risk of short circuits, disconnect the battery negative (–) lead before making any ignition switch checks.

Check

Note: *Refer to electrical system fault finding in Section 2 and to the wiring diagram for your model at the end of this Chapter.*

1 The switch can be checked for continuity using an ohmmeter or a continuity test light. Always disconnect the battery negative (–) lead, which will prevent the possibility of a short circuit, before making the checks (see Section 3).

2 To access the connector, on CB600F/FA 2007 to 2010 models remove headlight (Section 8), then remove the instrument cover (Section 15, Step 2), on CB600F/FA 2011-on models and CBR600F/FA models remove the headlight (Section 8), on CBF600N/NA models remove the headlight beam unit (Section 7), and on CBF600S/SA models remove the fairing (see Chapter 7). Trace the wiring from the switch and disconnect it at the brown 2-pin connector **(see illustrations)**. Check for loose or broken connections.

18.2a Ignition switch wiring connector (arrowed) – early CB

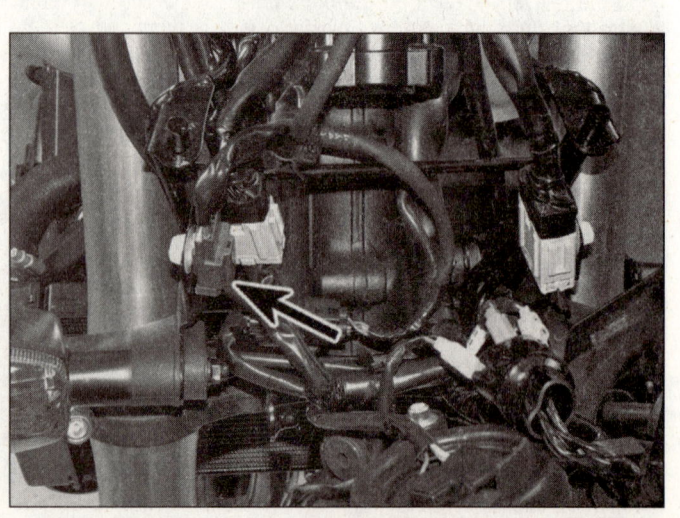

18.2b Ignition switch wiring connector (arrowed) – late CB

Electrical system 8•25

18.2c Ignition switch wiring connector (arrowed) – CBR

18.2d Ignition switch wiring connector (arrowed) – CBF-S/SA

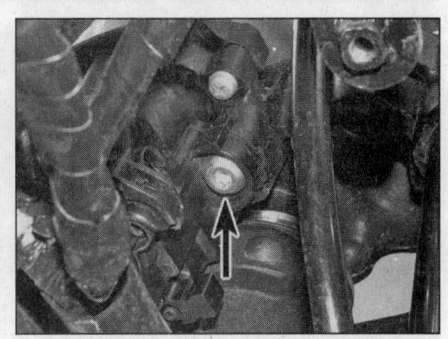

18.9 Remove the shear-head bolt (arrowed) on each side as described

3 Using an ohmmeter or a continuity tester, check the continuity of the connector terminals. Continuity should exist between the terminals when the switch is in the ON position.
4 If the switch fails any of the tests, replace it with a new one.
5 If the switch is good, reconnect the battery. Check there is battery voltage at the red wire terminal in the loom side of the connector. If not, there is a break in the wire between the connector and the battery. If there is voltage check the red/black wire for continuity to the fusebox.

Removal

6 Disconnect the battery negative (–) lead (see Section 3).
7 On CB600F/FA 2007 to 2010 models remove headlight (Section 8), then remove the instrument cover (Section 15, Step 2), on CB600F/FA 2011-on models and CBR600F/FA models remove the headlight, and on CBF600S/SA models remove the fairing (see Chapter 7). Trace the wiring from the switch and disconnect it at the brown 2-pin connector **(see illustration 18.2a, b, c or d)**. Feed the wiring back to the switch, freeing it from any clips and ties and noting the routing

8 On CBF600N/NA models remove the instrument cluster (Section 15).
9 One-way security bolts (which can be done up but not undone using conventional tools) are fitted **(see illustration)** – drive the heads around using a cold chisel. On all except CBF600N/NA models, if you can't move the bolts displace the top yoke for improved access (refer to Chapter 1, Section 14, following the relevant Steps).
10 If required separate the contact plate from the bottom of the switch – it is available separately from the main body of the switch.

Installation

11 Installation is the reverse of removal. Use new ignition switch bolts and tighten them to the torque setting specified at the beginning of the Chapter. On all except CBF600N/NA models refer to Chapter 1 to install the top yoke if removed. Make sure the wiring connector is correctly routed and securely connected.

19 Handlebar switches

1 Generally speaking, the switches are reliable and trouble-free. Most troubles, when they do occur, are caused by dirty or corroded contacts, but wear and breakage of internal parts is a possibility that should not be overlooked. If breakage does occur, the entire switch and related wiring harness will have to be replaced with a new one, as individual parts are not available.

Check

Note: *Refer to electrical system fault finding in Section 2 and to the wiring diagram for your model at the end of this Chapter.*
2 The switches can be checked for continuity using an ohmmeter or a continuity test light. Always disconnect the battery negative (–) lead, which will prevent the possibility of a short circuit, before making the checks (see Section 3).
3 To access the connectors, on CB600F/FA and CBR600F/FA models remove headlight (Section 8), on CBF600N/NA models remove the headlight beam unit (Section 7), and on CBF600S/SA models remove the fairing (see Chapter 7). Trace the wiring from the switch and disconnect it at the connector(s) **(see illustrations)**. Check for loose or broken connections.

19.3a Handlebar switch wiring connectors (arrowed) – early CB

19.3b Handlebar switch wiring connectors (arrowed) – late CB

8•26 Electrical system

19.3c Handlebar switch wiring connectors (arrowed) – CBR

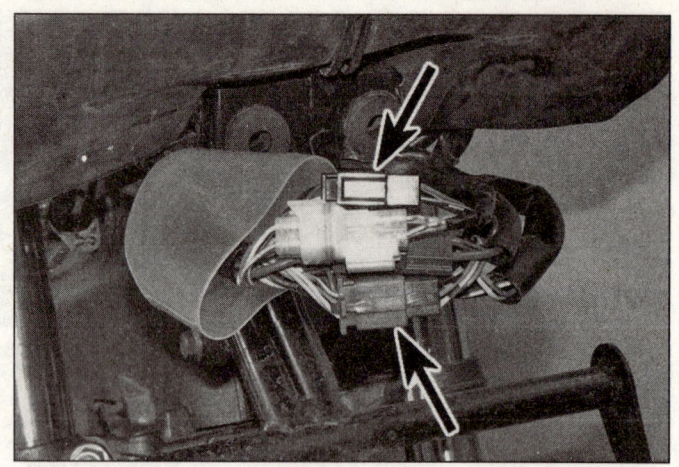

19.3d Handlebar switch wiring connectors (arrowed) – CBF-S/SA

4 Check for continuity between the terminals of the switch connector with the switch in the various positions (i.e. switch off – no continuity, switch on – continuity) – see the wiring diagram for your model at the end of this Chapter. Continuity should exist between the terminals connected by a solid line on the diagram when the switch is in the indicated position.

5 If the continuity check indicates a problem exists, displace the switch housing (Step 8 or 9), and spray the switch contacts with electrical contact cleaner (there is no need to remove the switch completely). If they are accessible, the contacts can be scraped clean with a knife or polished with crocus cloth. If switch components are damaged or broken, it will be obvious when the switch is disassembled.

Removal and installation

6 To access the connectors, on CB600F/FA and CBR600F/FA models remove headlight (Section 8), on CBF600N/NA models remove the headlight beam unit (Section 7), and on CBF600S/SA models remove the fairing (see Chapter 7). Trace the wiring from the switch and disconnect it at the connector(s) (see illustration 19.3a, b, c or d). Feed the wiring back to the switch, freeing it from any clips and ties and noting the routing.

7 If removing the right-hand switch disconnect the wires from the brake light switch (see illustration 14.2). If removing the left-hand switch disconnect the wires from the clutch switch (see illustration 22.2).

8 To remove the left-hand switch housing undo the screws and free the switch from the handlebar by separating the halves (see illustration).

9 To remove the right-hand switch housing refer to Chapter 4 and detach the throttle cables.

10 Installation is the reverse of removal. Make sure the pin in the switch housing locates in the hole in the handlebar (see illustration).

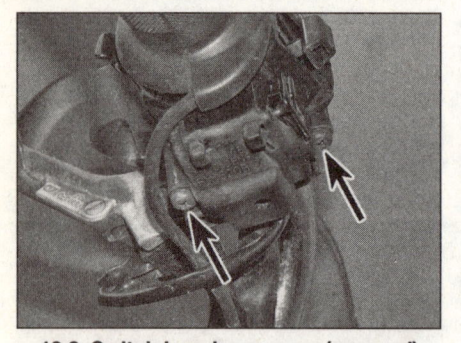

20 Neutral switch

1 The neutral switch is located in the left-hand side of the engine above the front sprocket. The neutral light should come whenever the ignition switch is ON and the transmission is in neutral. The switch is part of the starter interlock safety circuit which prevents or stops the engine running if the transmission is in gear whilst the sidestand is down, and prevents the engine from starting if the transmission is in gear unless the sidestand is up and the clutch is pulled in.

Check

Note: Refer to electrical system fault finding in Section 2 and to the wiring diagram for your model at the end of this Chapter.

2 If the light does not come on when it should, but all other instrument functions work, pull the wiring connector off the switch (see illustration).

3 Check for continuity between the switch terminal and the crankcase. With the transmission in neutral, there should be continuity. With the transmission in gear, there should be no continuity. If not, remove the switch (Step 6) and check whether the plunger is bent or damaged, or just stuck (see illustration). Replace the switch with a new one if necessary.

19.8 Switch housing screws (arrowed)

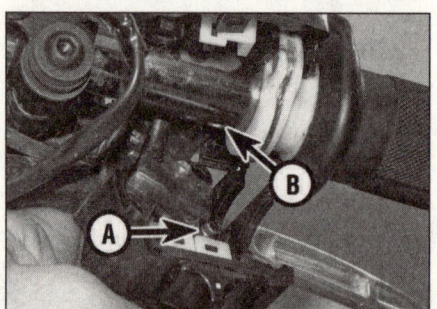

19.10 Locate the pin (A) in the hole (B)

20.2 Disconnect the wire

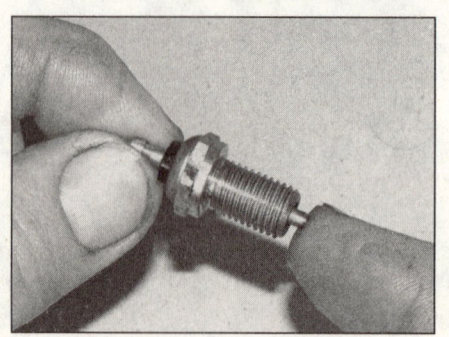

20.3 Make sure the plunger moves in and out smoothly and freely

4 If the switch is good check for continuity in the light green wire from the connector to the diode unit in the fusebox. Next check the other components (clutch switch, sidestand switch, diode block) in the starter safety circuit, and check the wiring between them for continuity, and the connectors for loose or broken connections.

Removal and installation

5 Pull the wiring connector off the switch (see illustration 20.2).
6 Clean the area around the switch, then unscrew it from the crankcase. Remove the sealing washer – a new one should be used.
7 Fit the switch using a new washer and tighten it to the torque setting specified at the beginning of the Chapter.
8 Connect the wiring connector and check the operation of the neutral light.

21 Sidestand switch

1 The sidestand switch is mounted on the stand pivot. The switch is part of the starter interlock safety circuit which prevents or stops the engine running if the transmission is in gear whilst the sidestand is down, and prevents the engine from starting if the transmission is in gear unless the sidestand is up and the clutch is pulled in.

Check

Note: *Refer to electrical system fault finding in Section 2 and to the wiring diagram for your model at the end of this Chapter.*
2 Remove the left-hand side cover (see Chapter 7). Disconnect the sidestand switch 2-pin green wiring connector **(see illustrations)**.
3 Check the operation of the switch using an ohmmeter or continuity test light. Connect the meter between the terminals on the switch side of the connector. With the sidestand up there should be continuity (zero resistance) between the terminals, and with the stand down there should be no continuity (infinite resistance).
4 If the switch does not perform as described, it is faulty and must be replaced with a new one.

21.2a Sidestand switch wiring connector (arrowed) – CB and CBR

21.2b Sidestand switch wiring connector (arrowed) – CBF

5 If the switch is good, check the other components (clutch switch, neutral switch, diode block) in the starter safety circuit, and check the wiring between them for continuity, and the connectors for loose or broken connections.

Removal

6 Carefully pull the outer sprocket cover away from the engine to release its pegs from the grommets **(see illustration)**. Check the condition of the grommets and replace them with new ones if cracked or hardened.
7 Remove the left-hand side cover (see Chapter 7). Trace the wiring from the switch and disconnect at the connector **(see illustration 21.2a or b)**. Feed the wiring back to the switch, freeing it from any clips and ties and noting the routing.
8 Unscrew the switch bolt and remove the switch from the stand, noting how it fits **(see illustration)**. Honda specify that the switch bolt be replaced with a new one every time it is disturbed – the new bolt has a locking compound already applied to its threads. However there is nothing to stop you cleaning up the threads on the old bolt and applying a suitable non-permanent thread locking compound on installation.

Installation

9 Fit the new switch onto the sidestand, making sure the pin locates in the hole, and the lug on the stand bracket locates into the cut-out in the switch body **(see illustration 21.8)**. Secure the switch with a new or cleaned and threadlocked bolt.

10 Feed the wiring up to its connector, making sure it is correctly routed and secured by any clips.
11 Reconnect the wiring connector and check the operation of the sidestand switch. Fit the covers.

22 Clutch switch

1 The clutch switch is mounted on the underside of the clutch lever bracket. The switch is part of the starter interlock safety circuit which prevents or stops the engine running if the transmission is in gear whilst the sidestand is down, and prevents the engine from starting if the transmission is in gear unless the sidestand is up and the clutch lever is pulled in. The switch isn't adjustable.

Check

Note: *Refer to electrical system fault finding in Section 2 and to the wiring diagram for your model at the end of this Chapter.*
2 To check the switch, disconnect the wiring connectors from it **(see illustration)**. Connect the probes of an ohmmeter or a continuity tester to the two switch terminals. With the clutch lever pulled in, continuity should be indicated. With the clutch lever out, no continuity (infinite resistance) should be indicated.
3 If the switch is good, check the other components (sidestand switch, neutral switch, diode block) in the starter safety circuit, and

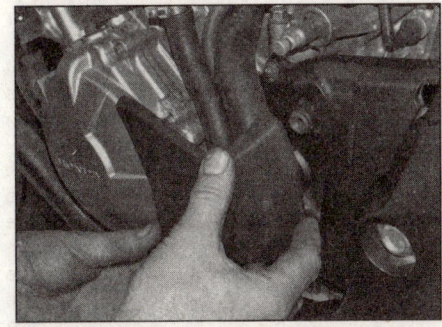

21.6 Remove the outer sprocket cover

21.8 Sidestand switch bolt (arrowed)

22.2 Clutch switch wiring connectors (arrowed)

8•28 Electrical system

22.6 Clutch switch screw (arrowed)

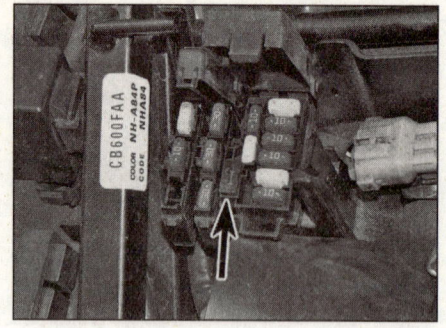

23.2a Diode block (arrowed) – CB and CBR

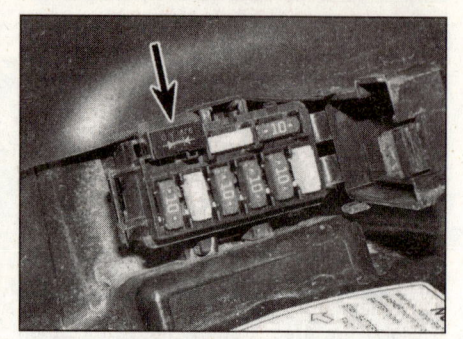

23.2b Diode block (arrowed) – CBF

check the wiring between them for continuity, and the connectors for loose or broken connections.

Removal and installation

4 The clutch switch is mounted on the underside of the lever bracket.
5 Disconnect the wiring connectors from the switch **(see illustration 22.2)**.
6 Undo the single screw securing the switch and remove it, noting how it fits **(see illustration)**.
7 Installation is the reverse of removal. Make sure the switch is correctly located before tightening its screw.

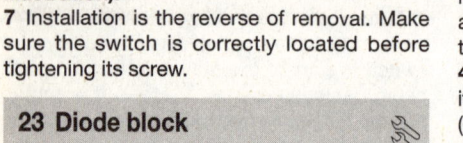

23 Diode block

Note: *Refer to electrical system fault finding in Section 2 and to the wiring diagram for your model at the end of this Chapter.*

1 The diode block plugs into a connector in the fusebox, which is located under the seat on CB600F/FA and CBR600F/FA models and under the passenger seat on CBF600N/NA/S/SA models. The diode block contains two diodes which are part of the starter interlock safety circuit that prevents or stops the engine running if the transmission is in gear whilst the sidestand is down, and prevents the engine from starting if the transmission is in gear unless the sidestand is up and the clutch lever is pulled in.

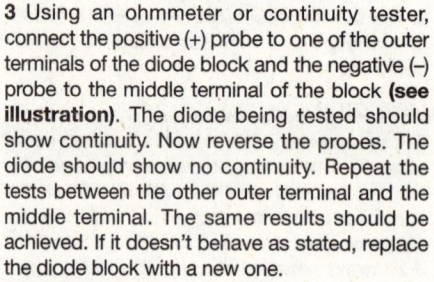

2 Remove the seat(s) (see Chapter 7), then open the fusebox lid and pull the diode block out of its socket **(see illustrations)**.
3 Using an ohmmeter or continuity tester, connect the positive (+) probe to one of the outer terminals of the diode block and the negative (–) probe to the middle terminal of the block **(see illustration)**. The diode being tested should show continuity. Now reverse the probes. The diode should show no continuity. Repeat the tests between the other outer terminal and the middle terminal. The same results should be achieved. If it doesn't behave as stated, replace the diode block with a new one.
4 If the diode block is good, push it back into its socket, then check the other components (sidestand switch, neutral switch, clutch switch) in the starter safety circuit, and check the wiring between them for continuity, and the connectors for loose or broken connections.

24 Horn

Check

Note: *Refer to electrical system fault finding in Section 2 and to the wiring diagram for your model at the end of this Chapter.*

1 The horn is mounted below the radiator on the right-hand side. If it doesn't work first check the fuse (see Section 5).
2 Disconnect the wiring connectors from the horn **(see illustrations)**. Check them for loose

23.3 Test the diode as described

wires. Using two jumper wires, apply voltage from a fully-charged 12V battery directly to the terminals on the horn. If the horn doesn't sound, replace it with a new one.
3 If the horn sounds, check for voltage at the black wire connector with the ignition ON and the horn switch (button) pressed. If voltage is present, check the green wire for continuity to earth. Refer to electrical system fault finding in Section 2 and to the wiring diagrams at the end of this Chapter.
4 If no voltage was present, check the black wire for continuity between the horn and the switch in the left-hand switch housing. Next, with the ignition switch ON, check that there is voltage at the other wire to the horn switch. If there is, check the switch contacts in the switch housing (see Section 19).
5 If there isn't voltage at the other wire, check the wire from the switch to the fusebox.

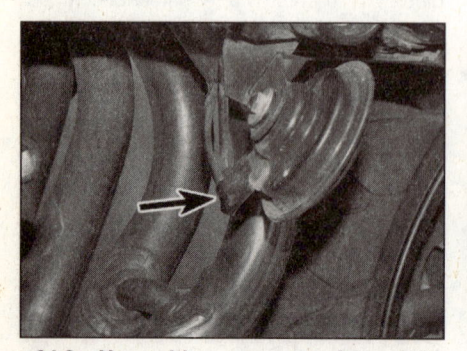

24.2a Horn wiring connectors (arrowed) – CB

24.2b Horn wiring connectors (A) and mounting bolt (B) – CBR

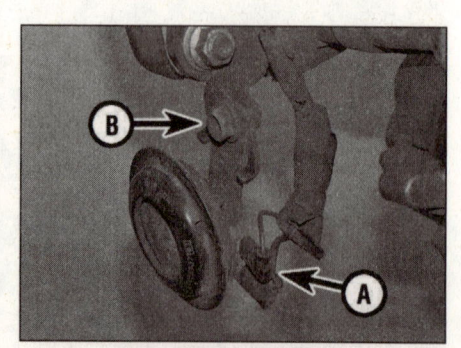

24.2c Horn wiring connectors (A) and mounting bolt (B) – CBF

Electrical system 8•29

24.7 Horn mounting bolt (arrowed) – CB

25.2a Starter relay (arrowed) – CB and CBR

25.2b Starter relay (arrowed) – CBF

Replacement

6 The horn is mounted below the radiator on the right-hand side.
7 Unplug the wiring connectors from the horn (see illustration 24.2a, b or c). Unscrew the bolt securing the horn (see illustration).
8 Fit the horn and tighten the bolt. Connect the wiring to the horn. Check that it works.

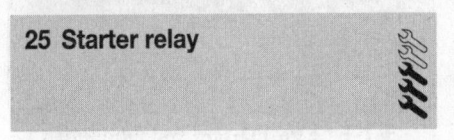

25 Starter relay

Check

1 If the starter circuit is faulty, first check the fuse (see Section 5).
2 To access the relay (and if not already done) on CB600F/FA and CBR600F/FA models remove the seat, and on CBF600N/NA/S/SA models remove the right-hand side cover (see Chapter 7) (see illustrations).
3 Lift the rubber terminal cover and unscrew the bolt securing the starter motor lead, identified by the letter M (the other lead, marked B, is the battery lead) (see illustration); position the lead away from the relay.
4 With the ignition switch ON, the engine kill switch in the RUN position, and the transmission in neutral, press the starter switch. The relay should be heard to click.
5 If the relay doesn't click, switch off the ignition and remove the relay as described below; test it as follows:
6 Set a multimeter to the ohms x 1 scale and connect it across the relay's starter motor and battery lead terminals. There should be no continuity. Using a fully-charged 12 volt battery and two insulated jumper wires, connect the positive (+) terminal of the battery to the yellow/red wire terminal of the relay, and the negative (–) terminal to the green/red wire terminal of the relay (see illustration). At this point the relay should be heard to click and the multimeter read 0 ohms (continuity). If this is the case the relay is proved good. If the relay does not click when battery voltage is applied and indicates no continuity (infinite resistance) across its terminals, it is faulty and must be replaced with a new one.
7 If the relay is good, check for continuity in the main lead from the battery to the relay. Also check that the terminals and connectors at each end of the lead are tight and corrosion-free.
8 Next check for battery voltage at the yellow/red wire terminal on the relay wiring connector with the ignition ON, the kill switch in the RUN position and the starter button pressed. If there is no voltage, check the wiring between the relay wiring connector and the starter button.
9 If voltage is present, check that there is continuity to earth in the green/red wire with the transmission in neutral (note that there will be a very slight resistance due to the diodes in the starter interlock circuit. If not check the wiring and connectors between the relay, the fusebox and the neutral switch, then if that is good check the switch itself and the diode block.
10 Now shift the transmission into gear, raise the sidestand and pull the clutch lever in and check for continuity to earth again. If there is no continuity, check the clutch switch and sidestand switch as described in the relevant sections of this Chapter. If all components are good, check the wiring between the various components (see the wiring diagrams at the end of this Chapter).

Replacement

11 To access the relay on CB600F/FA and CBR600F/FA models remove the seat, and on CBF600N/NA/S/SA models remove the right-hand side cover (see Chapter 7) (see illustration 25.2a or b).
12 Disconnect the battery (see Section 3).
13 Disconnect the relay wiring connector (see illustration). Unscrew the bolts securing the starter motor and battery leads to the relay and detach the leads (see illustration 25.3). If the relay is being replaced with a new one, remove the main fuse and fit it into the new relay (see Section 5). If you are fitting a new rubber sleeve remove the spare main fuse from its pocket and fit it into the new sleeve.
14 Installation is the reverse of removal. Connect the lead from the battery to the terminal marked B and the lead from the starter motor to the terminal marked M, and make sure the terminal bolts are securely tightened (see illustration 25.3). Do not forget to fit the main fuse into the relay and the spare into the rubber sleeve, if removed (see Section 5). Connect the negative (–) lead last when reconnecting the battery.

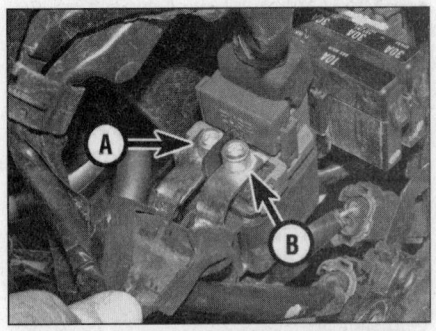

25.3 Lift the rubber cover to access the starter motor lead terminal (A) and battery lead terminal (B) – CBF shown

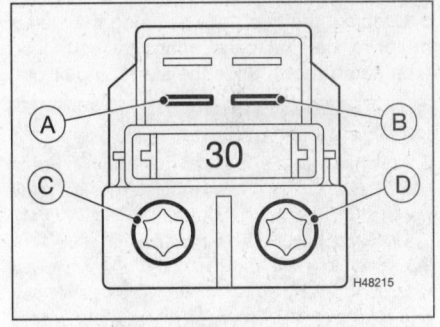

25.6 Starter relay terminal identification

  A Yellow/red wire terminal
  B Green/red wire terminal
  C M terminal
  D B terminal

25.13 Disconnect the wiring connector

8•30 Electrical system

26.4 Pull back the terminal cover then unscrew the nut (arrowed) and detach the lead

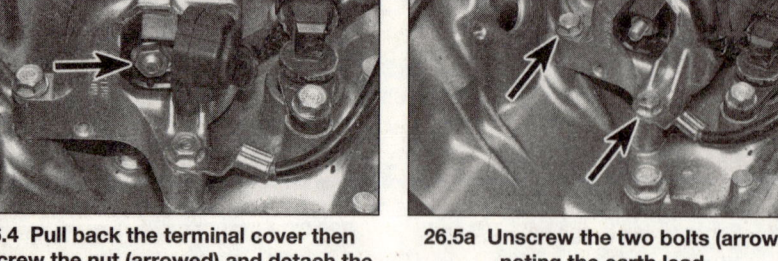

26.5a Unscrew the two bolts (arrowed), noting the earth lead . . .

26.5b . . . and remove the starter motor

26 Starter motor removal and installation

Removal

1 The starter motor is mounted on the crankcase behind the cylinders. Disconnect the battery negative (–) lead (Section 3).
2 Remove the air filter housing/throttle body assembly (see Chapter 4).
3 Remove the thermostat housing and the coolant inlet union (see Chapter 3).
4 Peel back the rubber terminal cover on the starter motor **(see illustration)**. Unscrew the nut and detach the lead.
5 Unscrew the two bolts securing the starter motor to the crankcase, noting the earth lead **(see illustration)**. Slide the starter motor out, using a screwdriver as leverage if required **(see illustration)**.
6 Remove the O-ring on the end of the starter motor – a new one must be used **(see illustration 26.7)**.

Installation

7 Fit a new O-ring onto the end of the starter motor, making sure it is seated in its groove **(see illustration)**. Apply a smear of engine oil to the O-ring.
8 Manoeuvre the motor into position and slide it into the crankcase, meshing starter motor teeth with those of the starter idle/reduction gear **(see illustration 26.5a)**. Fit the mounting bolts, securing the earth lead with the rear bolt, and tighten them **(see illustration 26.5b)**.
9 Connect the starter lead to the motor and secure it with the nut **(see illustration 26.4)**. Fit the rubber cover over the terminal.
10 Install the coolant inlet union and the thermostat housing (see Chapter 3), and the air filter housing/throttle body assembly (see Chapter 4).

27 Starter motor overhaul

Check

1 Remove the starter motor (see Section 26). Cover the body in some rag and clamp the motor in a soft-jawed vice – do not overtighten it.

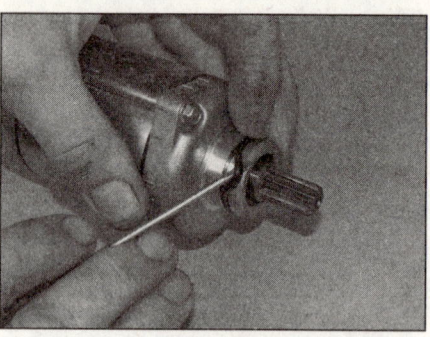

26.7 Fit a new O-ring and lubricate it

2 Using a fully-charged 12 volt battery and two insulated jumper wires, connect the positive (+) terminal of the battery to the protruding terminal on the starter motor, and the negative (–) terminal to one of the motor's mounting lugs. At this point the starter motor should spin. If this is the case the motor is proved good, though it is worth disassembling it and checking it if you suspect it of not working properly under load. If the motor does not spin, disassemble it for inspection.

Disassembly

3 Remove the starter motor (see Section 26).
4 Note any alignment marks between the main housing and the front and rear covers, or make your own if they aren't clear **(see illustration)**.
5 Unscrew the two long bolts and remove the front cover from the motor **(see illustrations)**.
6 Remove the rear cover **(see illustration)**.

27.4 Note the alignment marks (highlighted) between the housing and the covers

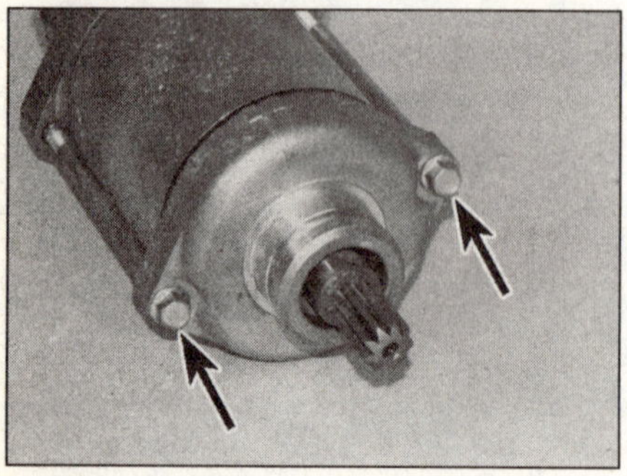

27.5a Unscrew the bolts (arrowed) . . .

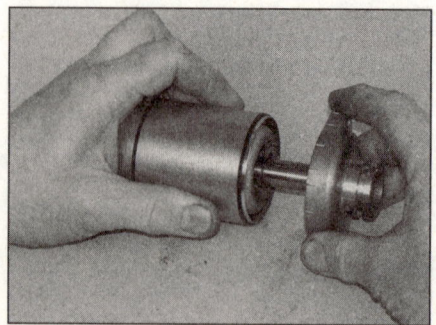

27.5b . . . and remove the front cover . . .

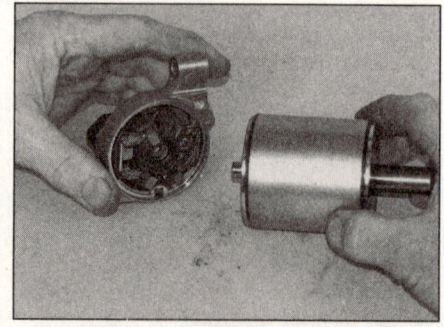

27.6 . . . and the rear cover

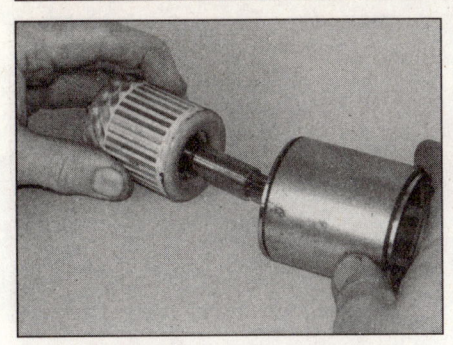

Electrical system 8•31

27.7 Withdraw the armature

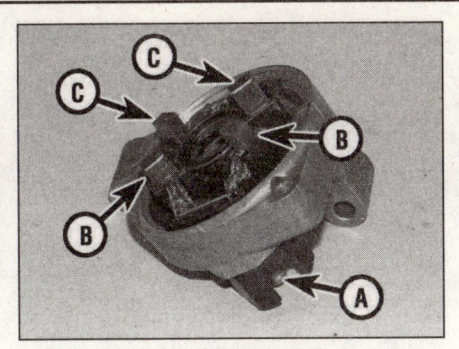

27.8 Terminal bolt (A), positive brushes (B), negative brushes (C)

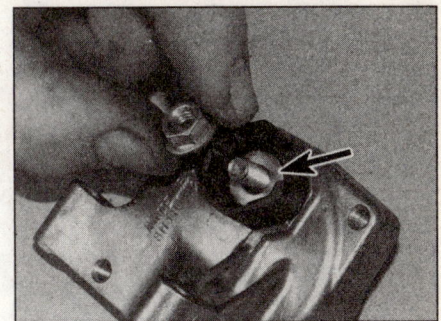

27.9a Undo the nut and remove the plain washer (arrowed) . . .

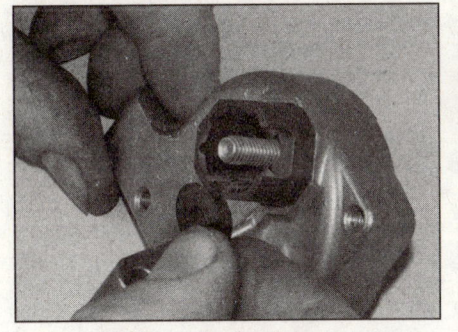

27.9b . . . the insulator . . .

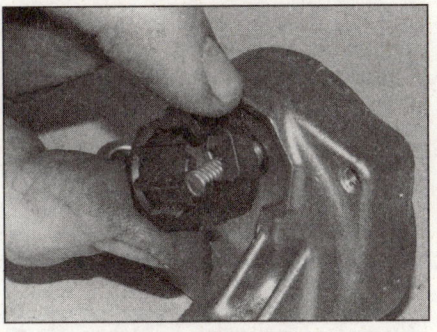

27.9c . . . the shield . . .

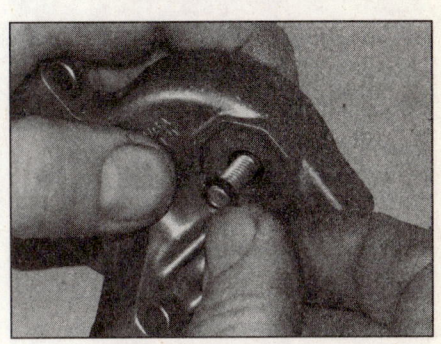

27.9d . . . and the O-ring

7 Withdraw the armature from the main housing **(see illustration)** – it is held in by the attraction of the magnets, so take care not to lose your grip on the armature before the magnets lose theirs.

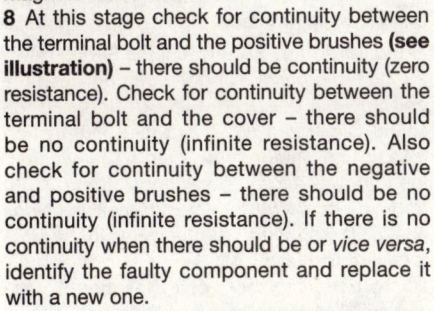

8 At this stage check for continuity between the terminal bolt and the positive brushes **(see illustration)** – there should be continuity (zero resistance). Check for continuity between the terminal bolt and the cover – there should be no continuity (infinite resistance). Also check for continuity between the negative and positive brushes – there should be no continuity (infinite resistance). If there is no continuity when there should be or *vice versa*, identify the faulty component and replace it with a new one.

9 Noting the correct fitted location of each component, unscrew the nut from the terminal bolt and remove the plain washer, the insulator, the terminal shield and the O-ring **(see illustrations)**. Remove the positive brush and terminal bolt assembly, then remove the positive brush springs **(see illustrations)**.

27.9e Withdraw the terminal bolt and brush assembly (arrowed) . . .

27.9f . . . and remove the brush springs

10 Undo the screw and remove the negative brush assembly **(see illustration)**. Remove the brush springs, then remove the holder **(see illustrations)**.

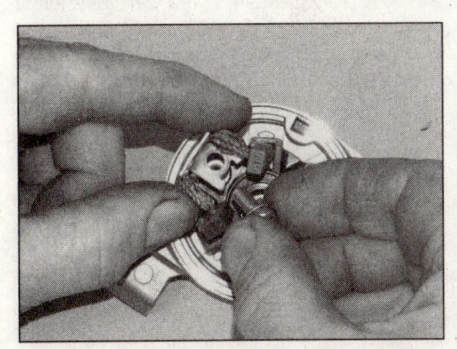

27.10a Undo the screw and remove the negative brush assembly . . .

27.10b . . . and springs . . .

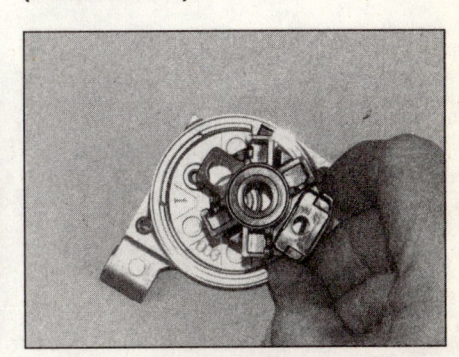

27.10c . . . then remove the brush holder

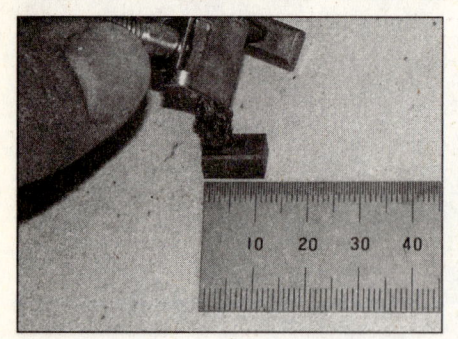

27.11 Measure the length of each brush

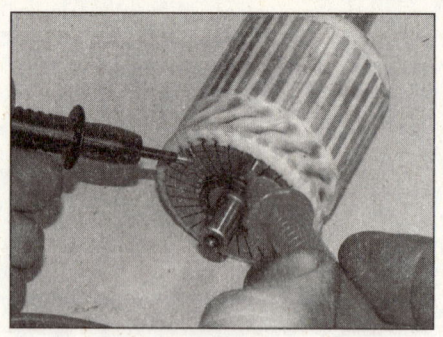

27.13a There should be continuity between the bars . . .

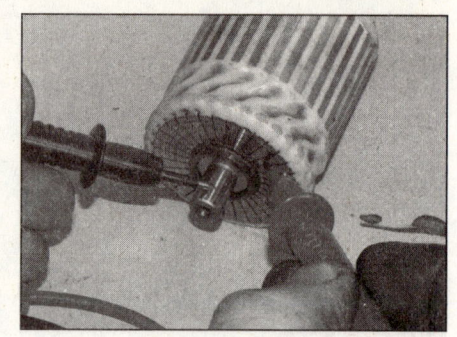

27.13b . . . and no continuity between the bars and the shaft

Inspection

11 The parts of the starter motor that are most likely to require attention are the brushes. Measure the length of each brush and compare the results to the length listed in this Chapter's Specifications **(see illustration)**. If worn replace the brushes with new ones. If the brushes are not worn excessively, nor cracked, chipped, or otherwise damaged, they can be reused.

12 Inspect the commutator bars on the armature for scoring, scratches and discoloration. The commutator can be cleaned and polished with crocus cloth, but do not use sandpaper or emery paper. After cleaning, wipe away any residue with a cloth soaked in electrical system cleaner or denatured alcohol.

13 Using an ohmmeter or a continuity test light, check for continuity between the commutator bars **(see illustration)**. Continuity should exist between each bar and all of the others. Also, check for continuity between the commutator bars and the armature shaft **(see illustration)**. There should be no continuity (infinite resistance) between the commutator and the shaft. If the checks indicate otherwise, the armature is defective and a new starter motor must be obtained – the armature is not available separately.

14 Check the front end of the armature shaft for worn, cracked, chipped and broken teeth. If the shaft is damaged or worn, a new starter motor must be obtained – the armature is not available separately.

15 Inspect the front and rear covers for signs of cracks or wear. Check the oil seal and the needle bearing in the front cover and the bush in the rear cover for wear and damage **(see illustration)** – the seal, bearing, bush and covers are not listed as being available separately so if necessary a new starter motor must be fitted.

16 Inspect the magnets in the main housing and the housing itself for cracks.

17 Inspect the terminal bolt shield, insulator, and O-ring, and the sealing rings on the housing, for signs of damage, deformation and deterioration and replace them with new ones if necessary.

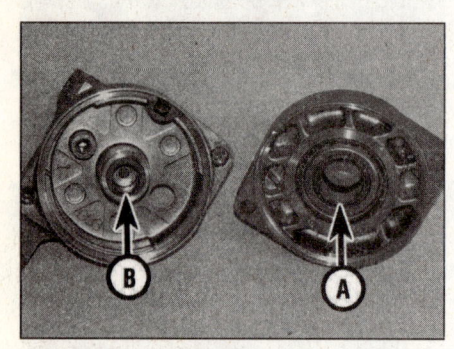

Reassembly

18 Locate the brush holder on the rear cover **(see illustration 27.10c)**. Fit the negative brush springs and brush assembly and secure it and the holder with the screw **(see illustrations 27.10b and a)**.

19 Fit the positive brush springs into their housings **(see illustration 27.9f)**. Fit the terminal bolt through the holder and rear cover **(see illustration 27.9e)**. Roll the O-ring down the bolt and press it into the gap between the bolt and the cover **(see illustration)**. Fit the shield, aligning it as shown **(see illustration 27.9c)**. Fit the insulator and the washer, then tighten the nut **(see illustrations 27.9b and a)**. Locate the brushes in their housings against the springs, with the wires in the slots **(see illustration 27.8)**.

20 To check for correct installation do the continuity checks described in Step 8.

21 If removed fit the sealing rings onto the main housing **(see illustration)**.

22 Grasp the housing and carefully allow the armature to be drawn in, making sure the cut-out in the housing is at the same end as the commutator bars **(see illustration 27.7)**.

23 Apply a smear of grease to the short end of the shaft. Fit the rear cover, aligning the marks, and making sure the brushes remain square and seat against the commutator **(see illustration)**.

24 Apply a smear of grease to the front cover oil seal lip. Slide the front cover on, aligning the marks **(see illustration 27.5b)**.

25 Check the marks made on removal are correctly aligned then fit the long bolts and tighten them **(see illustration 27.5a)**.

26 Install the starter motor (see Section 26).

27.15 Check the bearing and seal (A) and the bush (B)

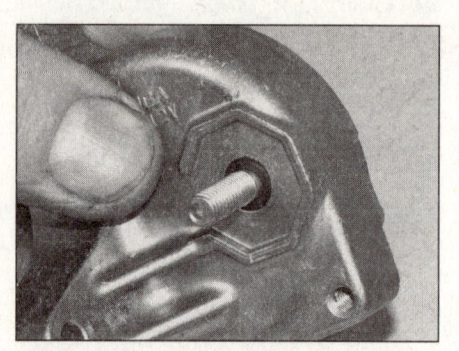

27.19 Fit the O-ring between the bolt and the cover

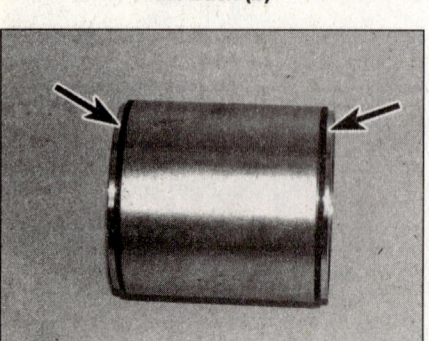

27.21 Main housing sealing rings (arrowed)

27.23 Align the marks when fitting the cover

Electrical system 8•33

28 Charging system testing

1 If the performance of the charging system is suspect, the system as a whole should be checked first, followed by testing of the individual components. **Note:** *Before beginning the checks, make sure the battery is fully charged and that all system connections are clean and tight.*

2 Checking the output of the charging system and the performance of the various components within the charging system requires the use of a multimeter (with voltage, current, resistance checking facilities).

3 When making the checks, follow the procedures carefully to prevent incorrect connections or short circuits resulting in irreparable damage to electrical system components.

Output test

4 Remove the seat(s) (see Chapter 7). Start the engine and warm it up.

5 To check the regulated (DC) voltage output, allow the engine to idle with the headlight main beam (HI) turned ON. Connect a multimeter set to the 0-20 volts DC scale across the terminals of the battery with the positive (+) meter probe to battery positive (+) terminal and the negative (-) meter probe to battery negative (-) terminal (see Section 3) **(see illustration)**.

6 Slowly increase the engine speed to 5000 rpm and note the reading obtained. Compare the result with the Specification at the beginning of this Chapter. If the regulated voltage output is outside the specification, check the alternator and the regulator/rectifier (see Sections 29 and 30).

Leakage test

Caution: *Always connect an ammeter in series, never in parallel with the battery,*

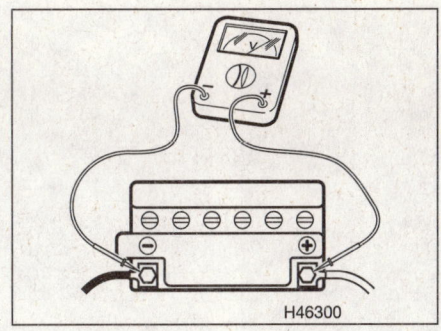

28.5 Checking the charging rate – connect the meter as shown

> **HAYNES HiNT** *Clues to a faulty regulator are constantly blowing bulbs, with brightness varying considerably with engine speed, and battery overheating.*

otherwise it will be damaged. Do not turn the ignition ON or operate the starter motor when the ammeter is connected – a sudden surge in current will blow the meter's fuse.

7 Remove the seat(s) (see Chapter 7). Disconnect the battery negative (-) lead (see Section 3).

8 Set the multimeter to the Amps function and connect its negative (-) probe to the battery negative (-) terminal, and positive (+) probe to the disconnected negative (-) lead **(see illustration)**. Always set the meter to a high amps range initially and then bring it down to the mA (milli Amps) range; if there is a high current flow in the circuit it may blow the meter's fuse.

9 Battery current leakage should not exceed the maximum limit (see Specifications). If a higher leakage rate is shown there is a short circuit in the wiring, although if an after-market immobiliser or alarm is fitted, its current draw should be taken into account. Disconnect the

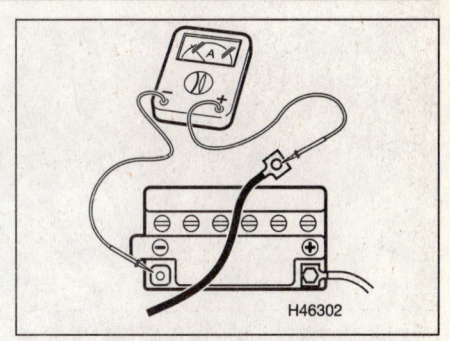

28.8 Checking the charging system leakage rate – connect the meter as shown

meter and reconnect the battery negative (-) lead.

10 If leakage is indicated, refer to Wiring Diagrams at the end of this Chapter to systematically disconnect individual electrical components and repeat the test until the source is identified.

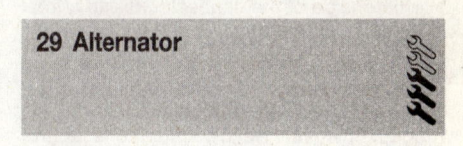

29 Alternator

Check

1 On CB600F/FA and CBR600F/FA models remove the seat and the left hand side cover (see Chapter 7), then unscrew the regulator/rectifier bracket bolts **(see illustration 30.1)**. On CBR600F/FA models also remove the left hand fairing side panel (see Chapter 7). On CBF600N/NA/S/SA models remove the left-hand side cover and left-hand seat cowl (see Chapter 7).

2 Disconnect the 3-pin wiring connector with the three yellow wires from the regulator/rectifier **(see illustrations)**. Check the connector terminals for corrosion and security.

29.2a Alternator wiring connector (arrowed) – CB and CBR models

29.2b Alternator wiring connector (arrowed) – CBF models

8•34 Electrical system

29.8 Alternator cover bolts (arrowed)

29.9 Using a rotor strap to hold the rotor while unscrewing the bolt

3 Using a multimeter set to the ohms x 1 (ohmmeter) scale measure the resistance between each of the yellow wires on the alternator side of the connector, taking a total of three readings, then check for continuity between each terminal and ground (earth). If the stator coil windings are in good condition the three readings should be within the range shown in the Specifications at the start of this Chapter, and there should be no continuity (infinite resistance) between any of the terminals and ground (earth). If not, the alternator stator coil assembly is at fault and should be replaced with a new one. **Note:** *Before condemning the stator coils, check the fault is not due to damaged wiring between the connector and the coils.*

Removal

4 On CBF600N/NA/S/SA models put the bike on its centrestand. On all other models, if you have an auxiliary stand place the bike on it so that it is level – this minimises oil loss. If you do not have an auxiliary stand it is best to drain the oil. Alternatively place a container under the engine to catch the oil that will come out when the alternator cover is removed.
5 On CB600F/FA and CBR600F/FA models remove the seat and the left hand side cover (see Chapter 7), then unscrew the regulator/rectifier bracket bolts **(see illustration 30.1)**. On CBR600F/FA models also remove the left hand fairing side panel (see Chapter 7). On CBF600N/NA/S/SA models remove the left-hand side cover and left-hand seat cowl (see Chapter 7).
6 Carefully pull the outer sprocket cover away from the engine to release its pegs from the grommets **(see illustration 21.6)**. Check the condition of the grommets and replace them with new ones if cracked or hardened.
7 Disconnect the 3-pin wiring connector with the three yellow wires from the regulator/rectifier **(see illustration 29.2a or b)**. Feed the wiring down to the alternator cover, releasing it from the guides and ties and noting its routing.
8 Working in a criss-cross pattern, evenly slacken the alternator cover bolts, on CBR600F/FA models noting the fairing panel bracket **(see illustration)**. Draw the cover off the engine, noting that it will be restrained by the force of the rotor magnets, and be prepared to catch any residual oil. Remove the dowels from either the cover or the crankcase if they are loose.
9 To remove the rotor bolt it is necessary to stop the rotor from turning using either a commercially available rotor strap, or by counter-holding the flats on the rotor boss using a suitable, preferably offset, spanner **(see illustration)**. Unscrew the bolt, noting the washer.
10 To remove the rotor from the shaft it is necessary to use a rotor puller– use either the Honda tool (part No. 07733-0020001) or a commercially available equivalent designed for this bike. Thread the rotor puller into the centre of the rotor and turn it until the rotor is displaced from the shaft, holding the rotor to prevent the engine turning **(see illustrations)**. If the rotor doesn't come off easily tap the end of the tool when it is tight, and if necessary heat the rotor hub using a hot air gun **(see illustration)**.

29.10a Thread the puller into the rotor . . .

29.10b . . . then hold the rotor and turn the puller, using a bar for leverage . . .

Electrical system 8•35

29.10c ... and applying some heat – tap the puller if necessary

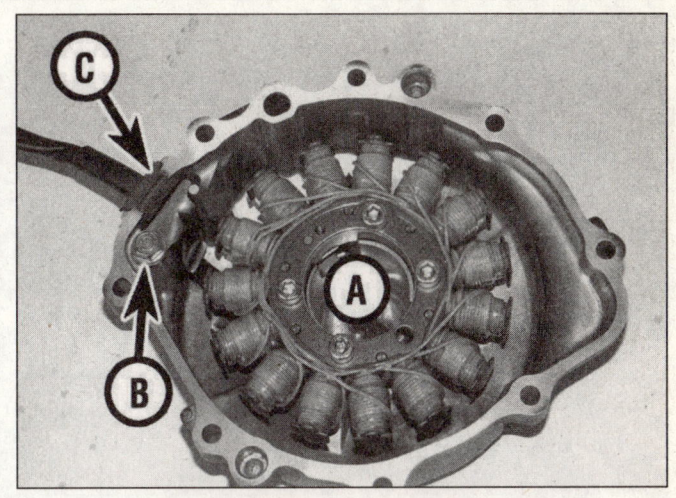

29.11 Stator bolts (A), clamp bolt (B), grommet (C)

11 To remove the stator from the cover, unscrew its bolts, and the bolt securing the wiring clamp, then remove the assembly, noting how the rubber wiring grommet fits **(see illustration)**.

Installation

12 Fit the stator into the cover, aligning the rubber wiring grommet with the groove **(see illustration 29.11)**. Fit the bolts and tighten them to the torque setting specified at the beginning of the Chapter. Apply a suitable sealant to the wiring grommet, then press it into the cut-out in the cover. Secure the wiring with its clamp and tighten the bolt.

13 Clean all old sealant off the cover and crankcase mating surfaces and wipe them with a suitable solvent. Clean the tapered end of the crankshaft and the corresponding mating surface on the inside of the rotor with a suitable solvent **(see illustration)**.

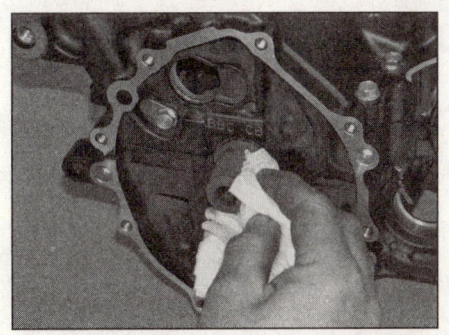

29.13 Clean the end of the crankshaft

29.14 Slide the rotor onto the shaft

14 Make sure that no metal objects have attached themselves to the magnet on the inside of the rotor. Slide the rotor onto the shaft **(see illustration)**.

15 Apply some clean oil to the rotor bolt threads, the underside of the head, and the washer **(see illustration)**. Fit the bolt with its washer and tighten it to the torque setting specified at the beginning of the Chapter, holding the rotor as on removal **(see illustration)**.

16 Apply a smear of suitable sealant to the

29.15a Lubricate the bolt then fit it with its washer ...

29.15b ... and tighten it to the specified torque

8•36 Electrical system

29.16a Apply sealant to the mating surface . . .

29.16b . . . and crankcase joints (A). Make sure the dowels (B) are in place . . .

mating surface of the alternator cover and 10 to 15 mm either side of the crankcase joints **(see illustrations)**. Fit the dowels into the cover or crankcase if removed. Fit the cover, noting that the rotor magnets will forcibly draw the cover/stator on, making sure the dowels locate **(see illustration)**. Fit the cover bolts, on CBR600F/FA models with the bracket, and tighten them evenly in a criss-cross sequence.

17 Reconnect the wiring to the regulator/rectifier, making sure it is correctly routed and secured **(see illustration 29.2a or b)**. On CB600F/FA and CBR600F/FA models fit the regulator/rectifier bracket bolts **(see illustration 30.1)**.

18 Fill the engine with the correct quantity of oil, or top it up to the correct level, as required according to your removal method (see Chapter 1). Install all remaining parts.

30 Regulator/rectifier

Check

1 On CB600F/FA and CBR600F/FA models remove the seat (see Chapter 7), then unscrew the regulator/rectifier bracket bolts **(see illustration)**. On CBF600N/NA/S/SA models remove the left-hand seat cowl (see Chapter 7).
2 Disconnect the regulator/rectifier wiring connectors **(see illustrations)**. Check the connector terminals for corrosion and security.
3 Set the multimeter to the 0 to 20 dc volts setting. Connect the meter positive (+) probe to the red wire terminal on the loom side of the connector and the negative (–) probe to a suitable ground (earth) and check for voltage. Full battery voltage should be present at all times.

4 Switch the multimeter to the resistance (ohms) scale. Check for continuity between the green wire terminal on the loom side of the connector and ground (earth). There should be continuity to earth.
5 Set the multimeter to the ohms x 1 (ohmmeter) scale and measure the resistance between each of the yellow wires on the alternator side of the connector, taking a total of three readings, then check for continuity between each terminal and ground (earth). The three readings should be within the range shown in the Specifications for the alternator stator coil at the start of this Chapter, and there should be no continuity (infinite resistance) between any of the terminals and ground (earth).
6 If the above checks do not provide the expected results check the wiring and connectors between the battery, regulator/rectifier and alternator for shorts, breaks, and loose or corroded terminals (see the wiring diagrams at the end of this chapter).

29.16c . . . then fit the cover

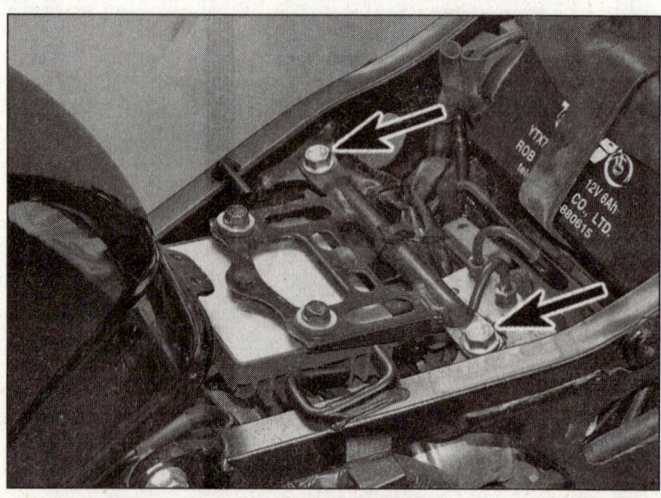

30.1 Unscrew the bracket bolts (arrowed) and flip the assembly over backwards

Electrical system 8•37

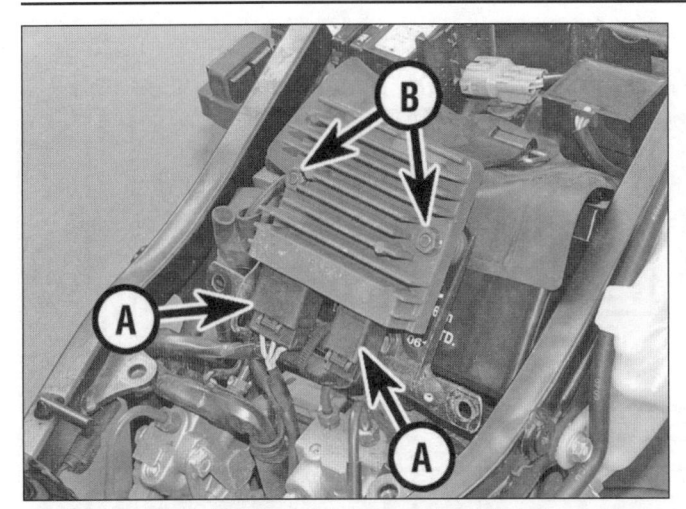

30.2a Regulator/rectifier wiring connectors (A) and mounting nuts/bolts (B) – CB and CBR

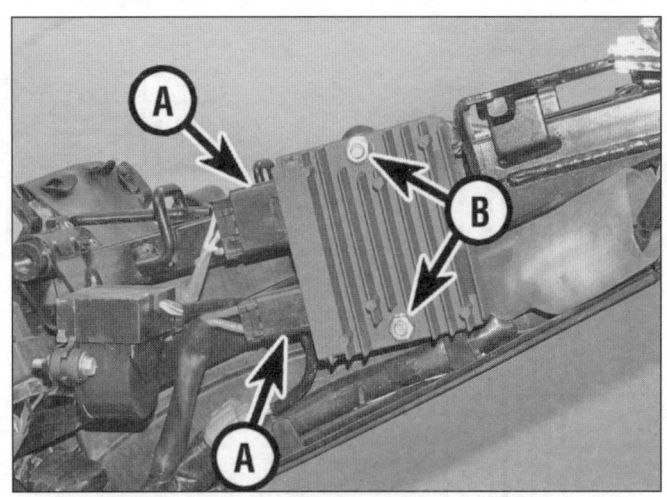

30.2b Regulator/rectifier wiring connectors (A) and mounting nuts/bolts (B) – CBF

7 If the wiring checks out, the regulator/rectifier unit is probably faulty. Honda provide no test data for the unit itself. Take it to a Honda dealer for confirmation of its condition before replacing it with a new one.

> **HAYNES HiNT** *Clues to a faulty regulator are constantly blowing bulbs, with brightness varying considerably with engine speed, and battery overheating.*

Removal and installation

CB600F/FA and CBR600F/FA

8 Remove the seat (see Chapter 7).
9 Unscrew the regulator/rectifier bracket bolts **(see illustration 30.1)**.
10 Disconnect the wiring connectors **(see illustration 30.2a)**.
11 Unscrew the nuts, withdraw the bolts and detach the regulator/rectifier from the bracket, noting the washers and collars.
12 Installation is the reverse of removal. Make sure the rubber grommets are in good condition and the collars are fitted.

CBF600N/NA/S/SA

13 Remove the left-hand seat cowl (see Chapter 7).
14 Disconnect the wiring connectors **(see illustration 30.2b)**.
15 Unscrew the nuts, withdraw the bolts and detach the regulator/rectifier from the bracket, noting the washers and collars.
16 Installation is the reverse of removal. Make sure the rubber grommets are in good condition and the collars are fitted.

8•38 Wiring diagrams

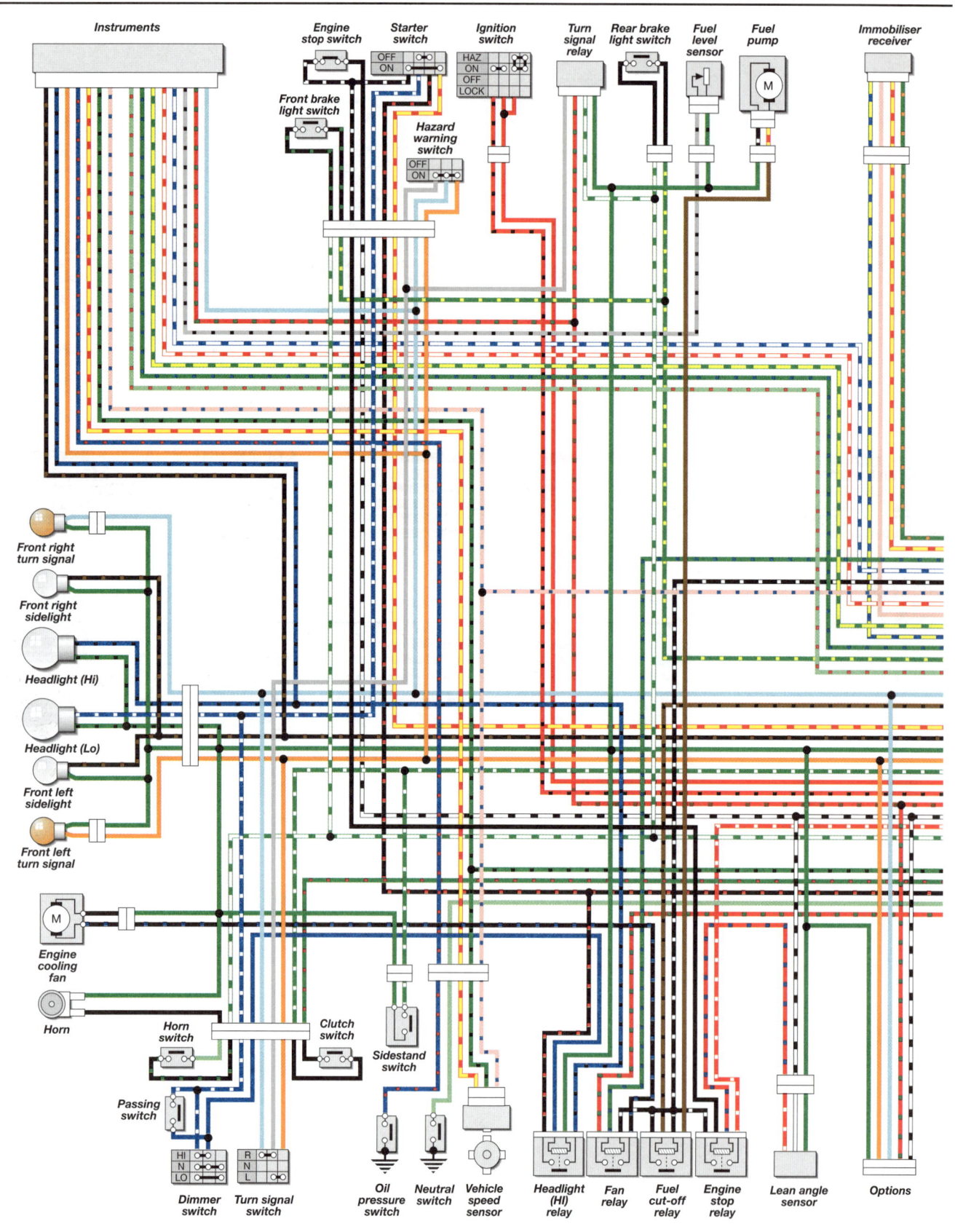

CB600F 2007-2010

Wiring diagrams 8•39

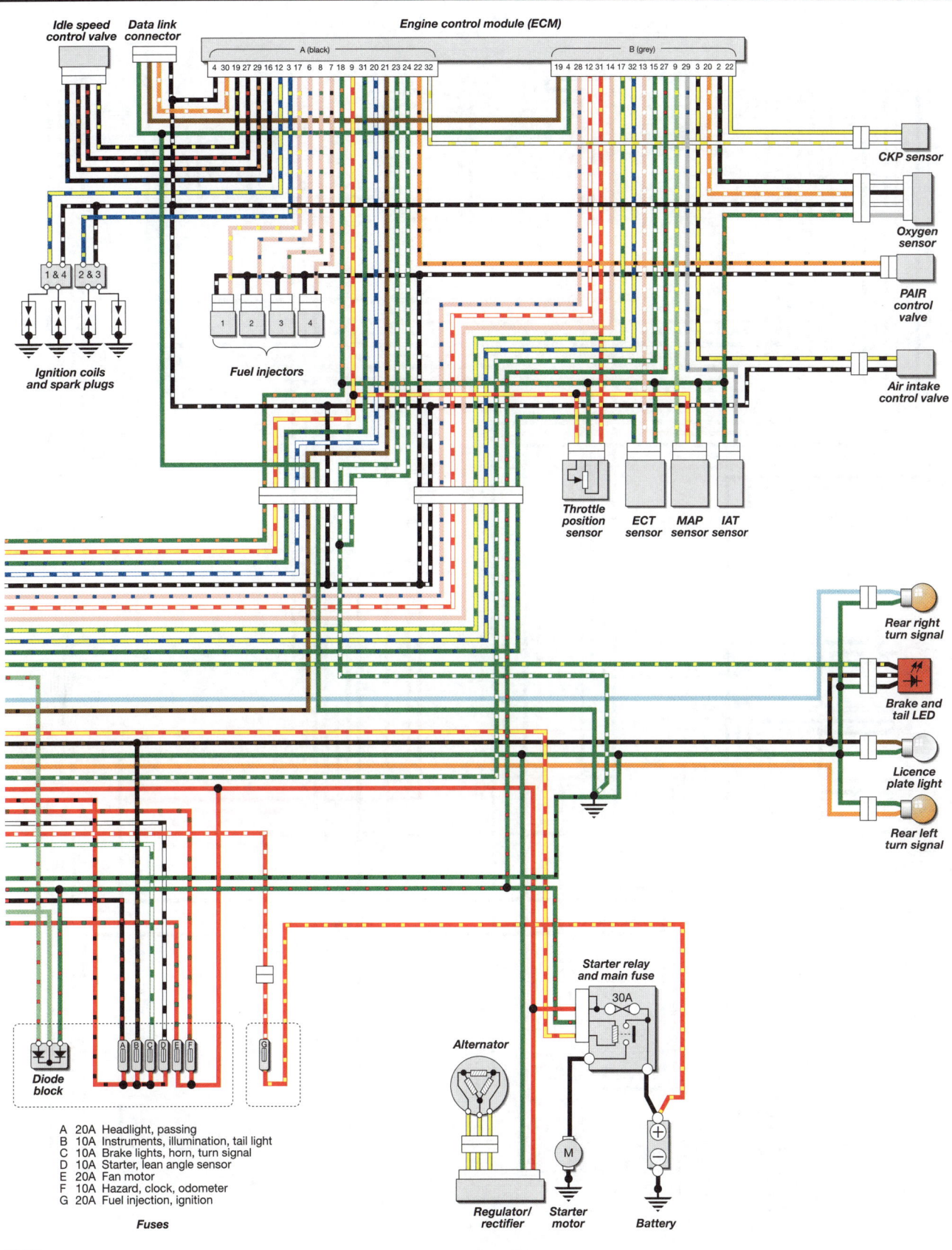

CB600F 2007-2010

Fuses

- A 20A Headlight, passing
- B 10A Instruments, illumination, tail light
- C 10A Brake lights, horn, turn signal
- D 10A Starter, lean angle sensor
- E 20A Fan motor
- F 10A Hazard, clock, odometer
- G 20A Fuel injection, ignition

H47508

8•40 Wiring diagrams

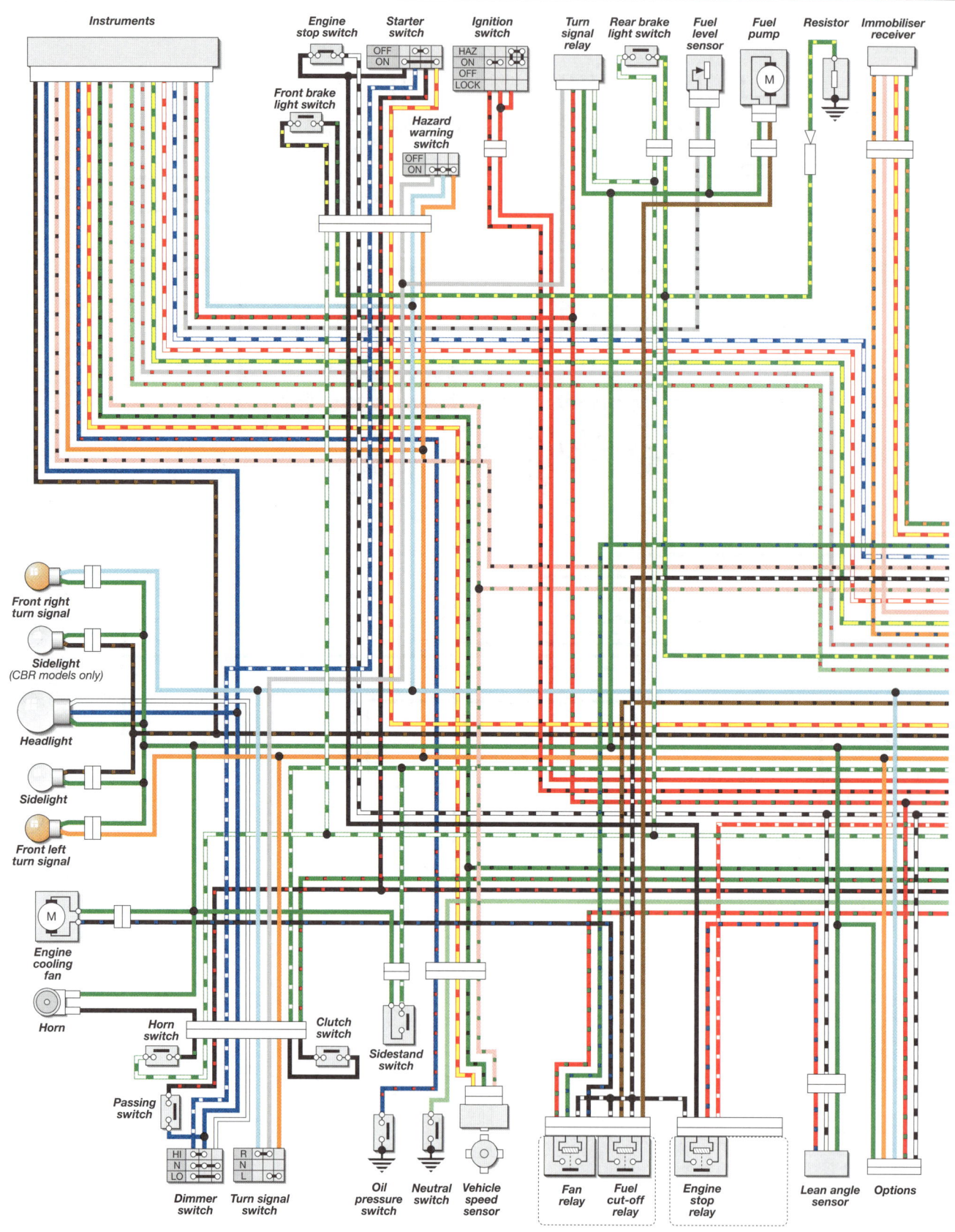

CB600F and CBR600F 2011-on

Wiring diagrams 8•41

Idle speed control valve
Data link connector
Engine control module (ECM)
A (black): 4 30 19 27 29 16 12 3 17 6 8 7 18 9 31 20 21 23 24 22 32
B (grey): 5 19 4 28 12 31 14 17 32 13 15 27 9 29 3 20 2 22

CKP sensor
Oxygen sensor
PAIR control valve
Air intake control valve

Ignition coils and spark plugs (1 & 4, 2 & 3)
Fuel injectors (1, 2, 3, 4)

Throttle position sensor
ECT sensor
MAP sensor
IAT sensor

Rear right turn signal
Brake and tail LED
Licence plate light
Rear left turn signal

Diode block

Alternator
Starter relay and main fuse 30A
Regulator/rectifier
Starter motor
Battery

Fuses
- A 20A Headlight, passing
- B 10A Instruments, illumination, tail light
- C 10A Brake lights, horn, turn signal
- D 10A Starter, lean angle sensor
- E 10A Hazard, clock
- F 20A Fan motor
- G 20A Fuel injection, ignition

H47510

CB600F and CBR600F 2011-on

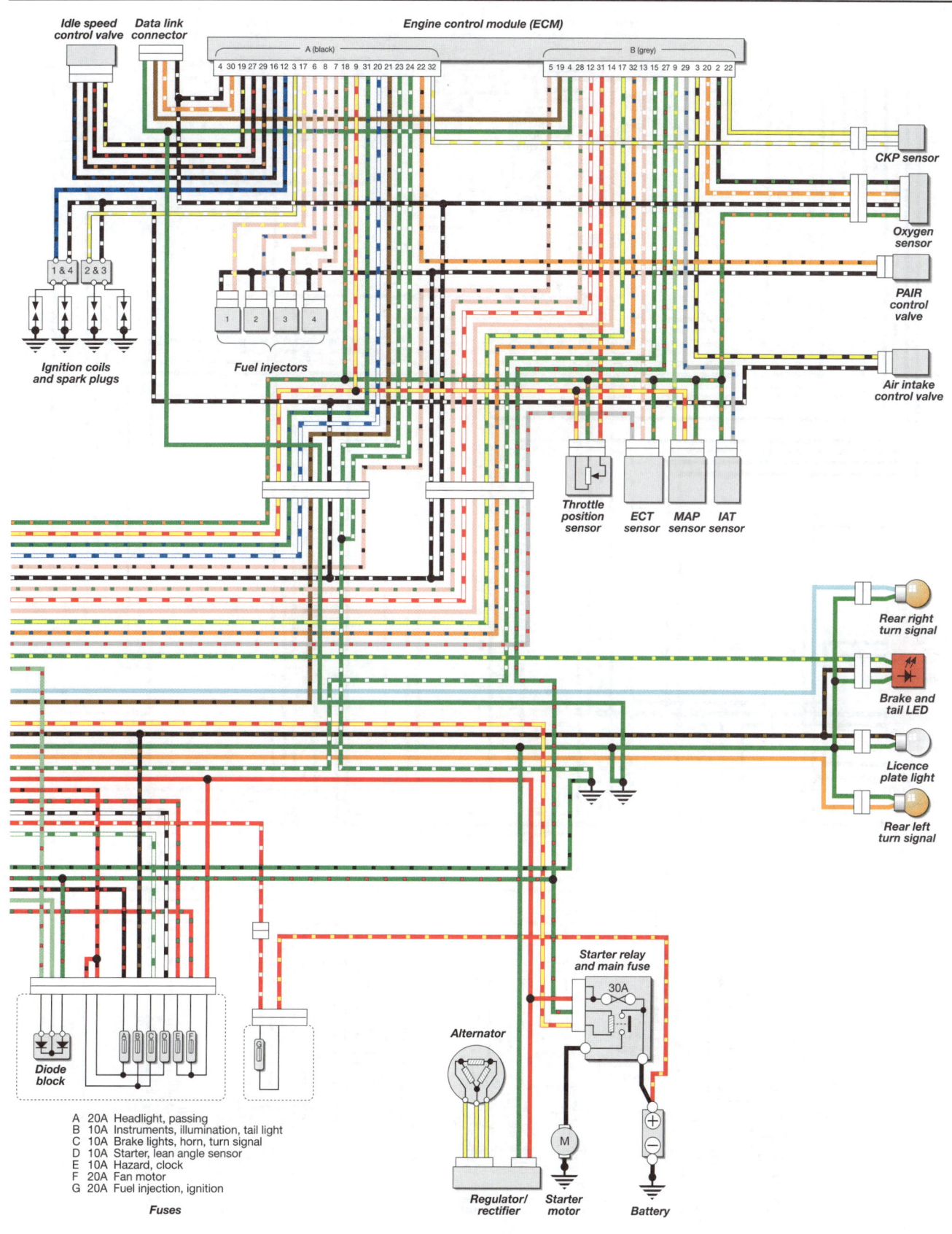

8•42 Wiring diagrams

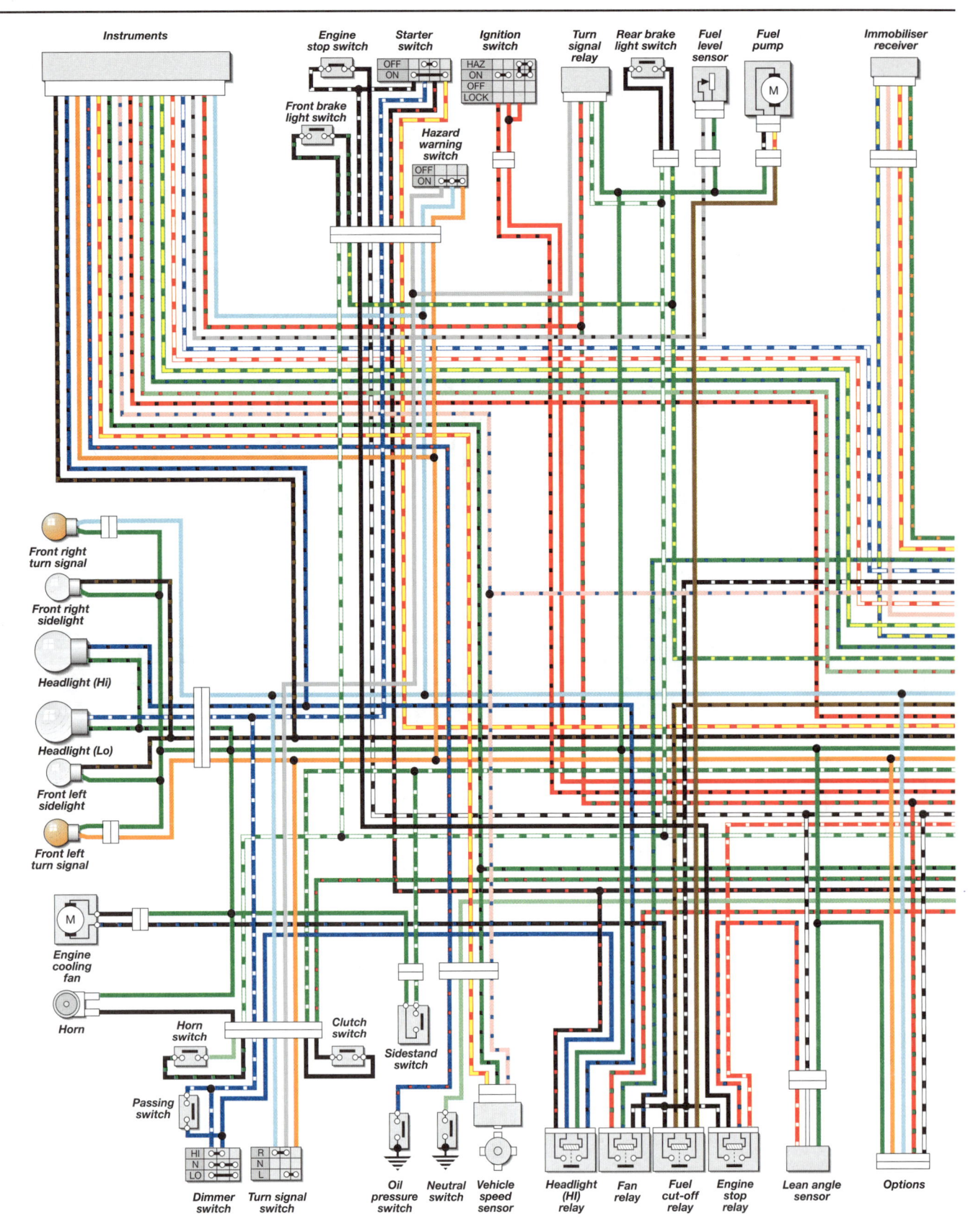

CB600FA 2007-2010

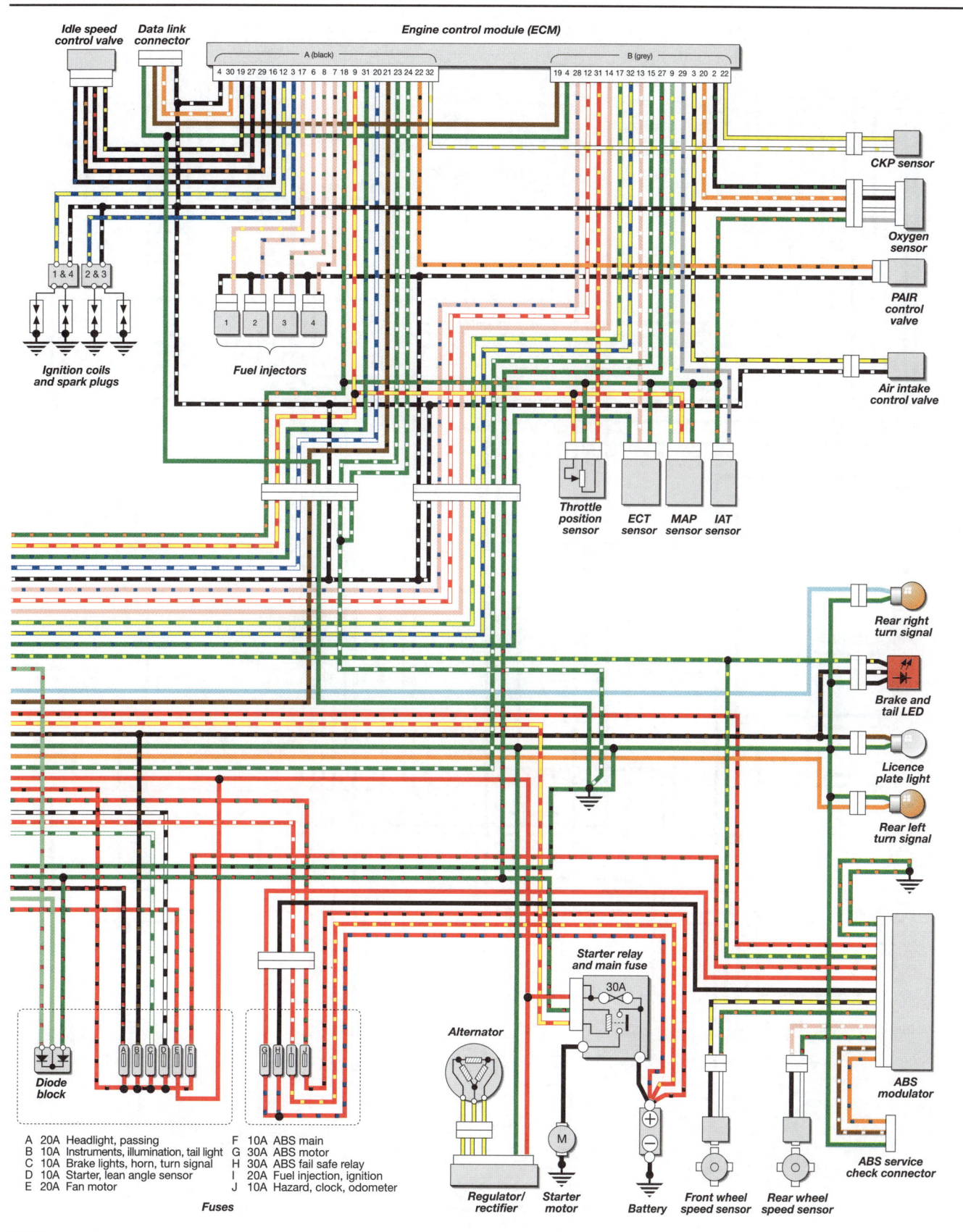

Wiring diagrams 8•43

Idle speed control valve
Data link connector
Engine control module (ECM)
A (black) 4 30 19 27 29 16 12 13 17 6 8 7 18 9 31 20 21 23 24 22 32
B (grey) 19 4 28 12 31 14 17 32 13 15 27 9 29 3 20 2 22

1 & 4   2 & 3
Ignition coils and spark plugs
1 2 3 4
Fuel injectors

CKP sensor
Oxygen sensor
PAIR control valve
Air intake control valve

Throttle position sensor | ECT sensor | MAP sensor | IAT sensor

Rear right turn signal
Brake and tail LED
Licence plate light
Rear left turn signal

Starter relay and main fuse 30A
Alternator
Diode block
Fuses
A B C D E   G H I J

Regulator/rectifier | **Starter motor** | **Battery** | **Front wheel speed sensor** | **Rear wheel speed sensor**

ABS modulator
ABS service check connector

A 20A Headlight, passing
B 10A Instruments, illumination, tail light
C 10A Brake lights, horn, turn signal
D 10A Starter, lean angle sensor
E 20A Fan motor
F 10A ABS main
G 30A ABS motor
H 30A ABS fail safe relay
I 20A Fuel injection, ignition
J 10A Hazard, clock, odometer

H47512

CB600FA 2007-2010

8•44 Wiring diagrams

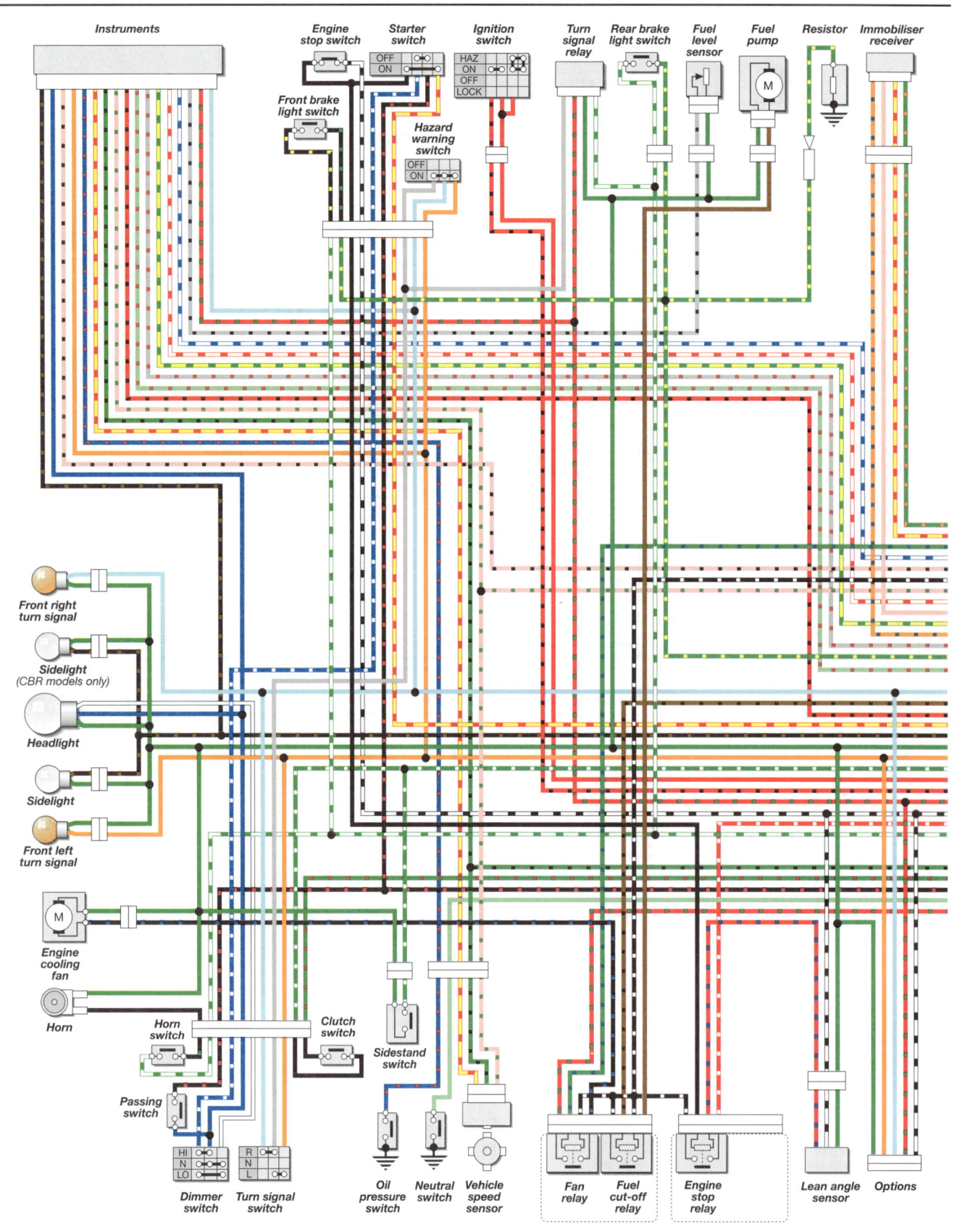

CB600FA and CBR600FA 2011-on

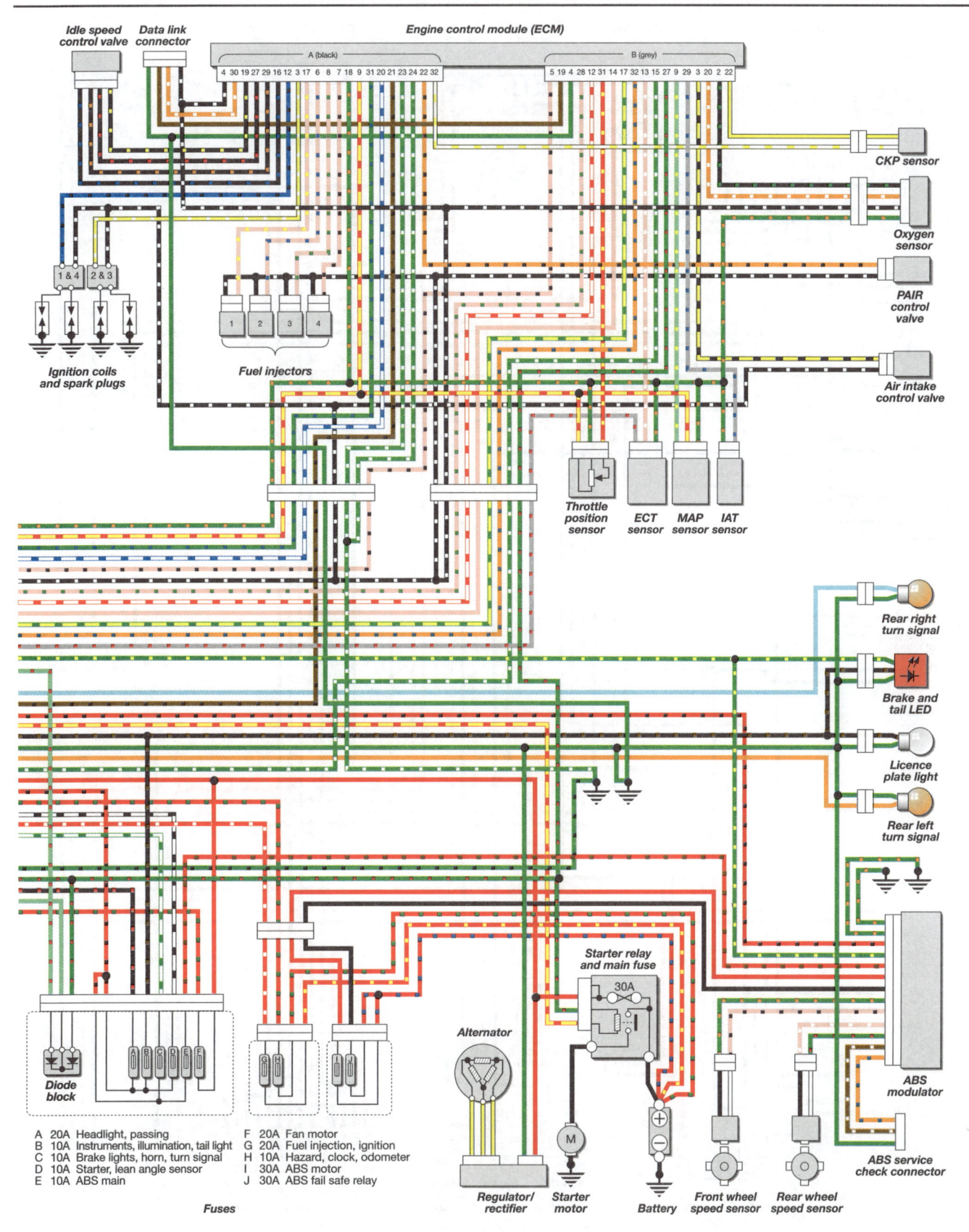

Wiring diagrams 8•45

Idle speed control valve
Data link connector
Engine control module (ECM)
A (black): 4 30 19 27 29 16 12 3 17 6 8 7 18 9 31 20 21 23 24 22 32
B (grey): 5 19 4 28 12 31 14 17 32 18 15 27 29 3 20 2 22

CKP sensor
Oxygen sensor
PAIR control valve
Air intake control valve
Ignition coils and spark plugs (1 & 4, 2 & 3)
Fuel injectors (1, 2, 3, 4)
Throttle position sensor
ECT sensor
MAP sensor
IAT sensor
Rear right turn signal
Brake and tail LED
Licence plate light
Rear left turn signal
Diode block
Fuses
Alternator
Starter relay and main fuse 30A
Starter motor
Regulator/rectifier
Battery
Front wheel speed sensor
Rear wheel speed sensor
ABS modulator
ABS service check connector

A 20A Headlight, passing
B 10A Instruments, illumination, tail light
C 10A Brake lights, horn, turn signal
D 10A Starter, lean angle sensor
E 10A ABS main
F 20A Fan motor
G 20A Fuel injection, ignition
H 10A Hazard, clock, odometer
I 30A ABS motor
J 30A ABS fail safe relay

H47514

CB600FA and CBR600FA 2011-on

8•46 Wiring diagrams

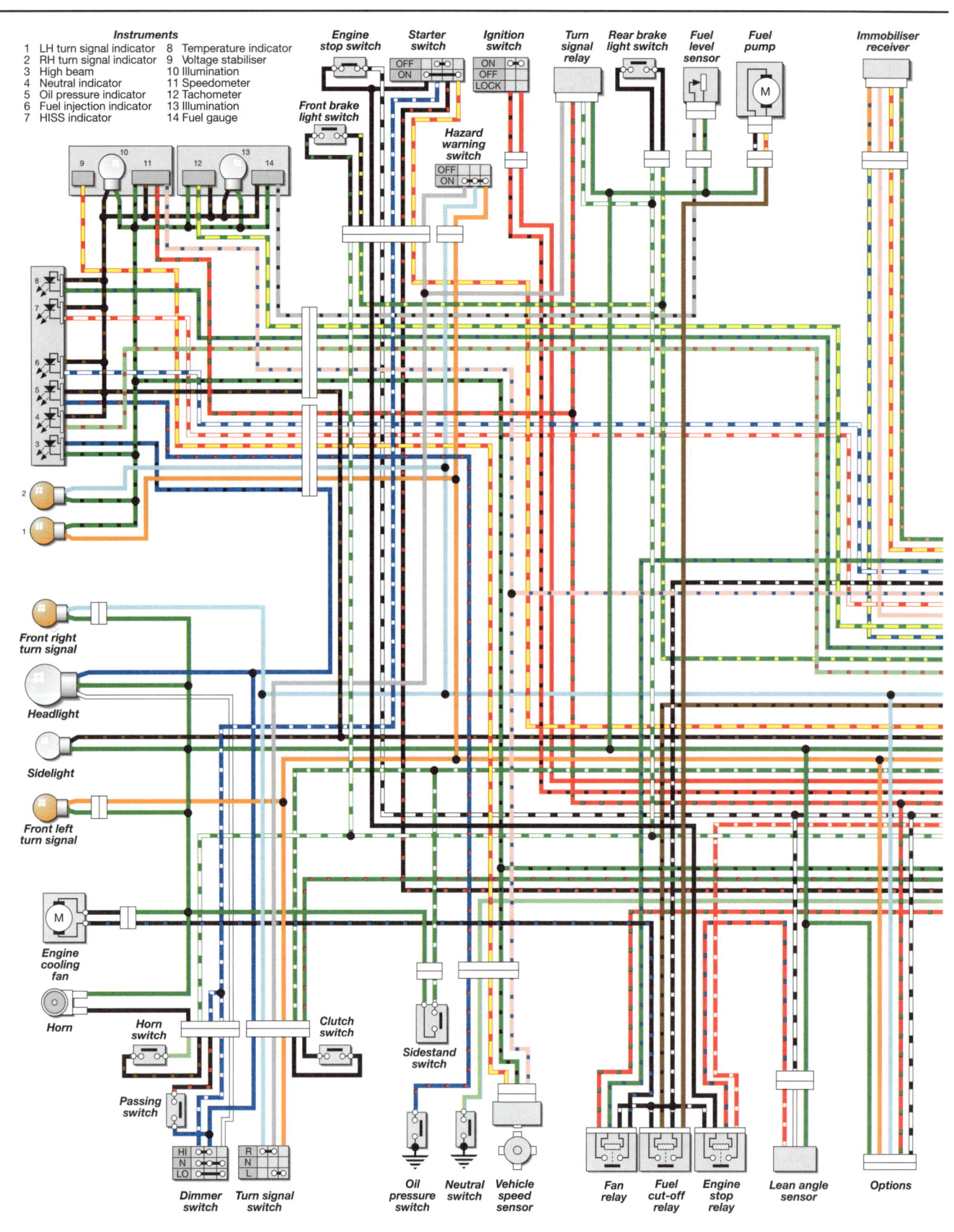

Instruments
1 LH turn signal indicator
2 RH turn signal indicator
3 High beam
4 Neutral indicator
5 Oil pressure indicator
6 Fuel injection indicator
7 HISS indicator
8 Temperature indicator
9 Voltage stabiliser
10 Illumination
11 Speedometer
12 Tachometer
13 Illumination
14 Fuel gauge

CBF600N

H47515

Wiring diagrams 8•47

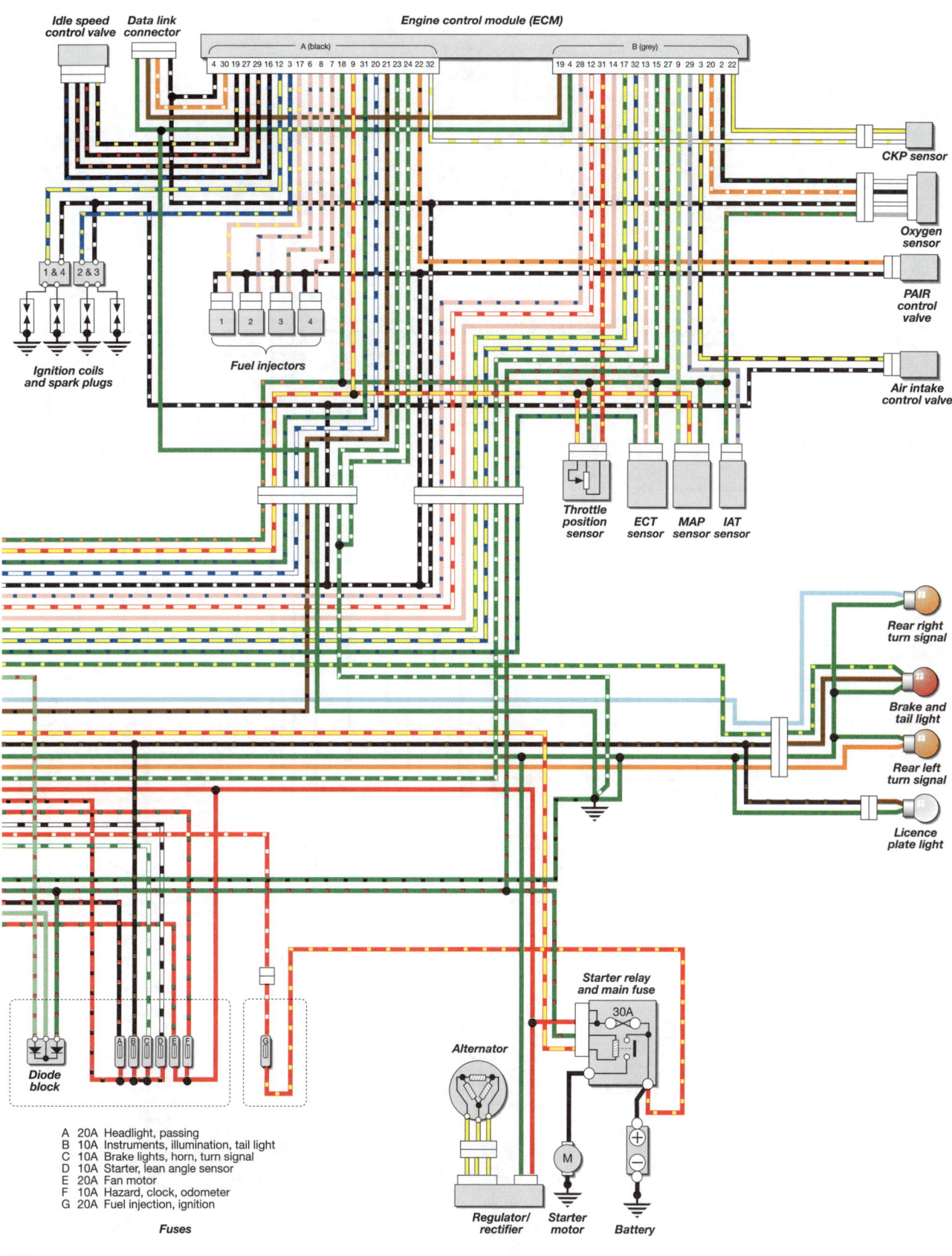

Idle speed control valve
Data link connector
Engine control module (ECM)
A (black) B (grey)

CKP sensor
Oxygen sensor
PAIR control valve
Air intake control valve

Ignition coils and spark plugs (1 & 4, 2 & 3)
Fuel injectors (1, 2, 3, 4)

Throttle position sensor
ECT sensor
MAP sensor
IAT sensor

Rear right turn signal
Brake and tail light
Rear left turn signal
Licence plate light

Diode block

Fuses
A 20A Headlight, passing
B 10A Instruments, illumination, tail light
C 10A Brake lights, horn, turn signal
D 10A Starter, lean angle sensor
E 20A Fan motor
F 10A Hazard, clock, odometer
G 20A Fuel injection, ignition

Alternator
Starter relay and main fuse 30A
Regulator/rectifier
Starter motor
Battery

CBF600N

8•48 Wiring diagrams

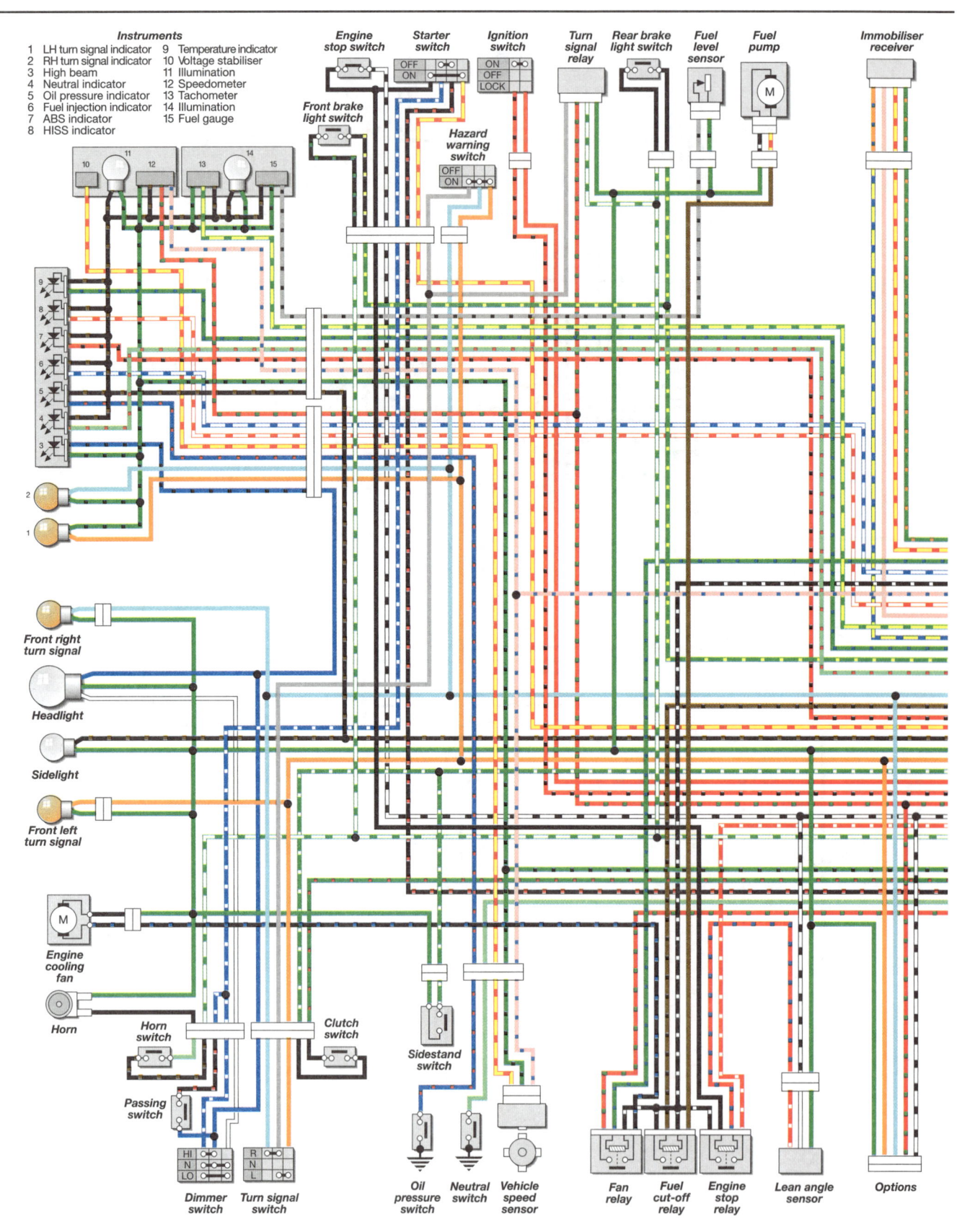

Instruments
1 LH turn signal indicator
2 RH turn signal indicator
3 High beam
4 Neutral indicator
5 Oil pressure indicator
6 Fuel injection indicator
7 ABS indicator
8 HISS indicator
9 Temperature indicator
10 Voltage stabiliser
11 Illumination
12 Speedometer
13 Tachometer
14 Illumination
15 Fuel gauge

CBF600NA

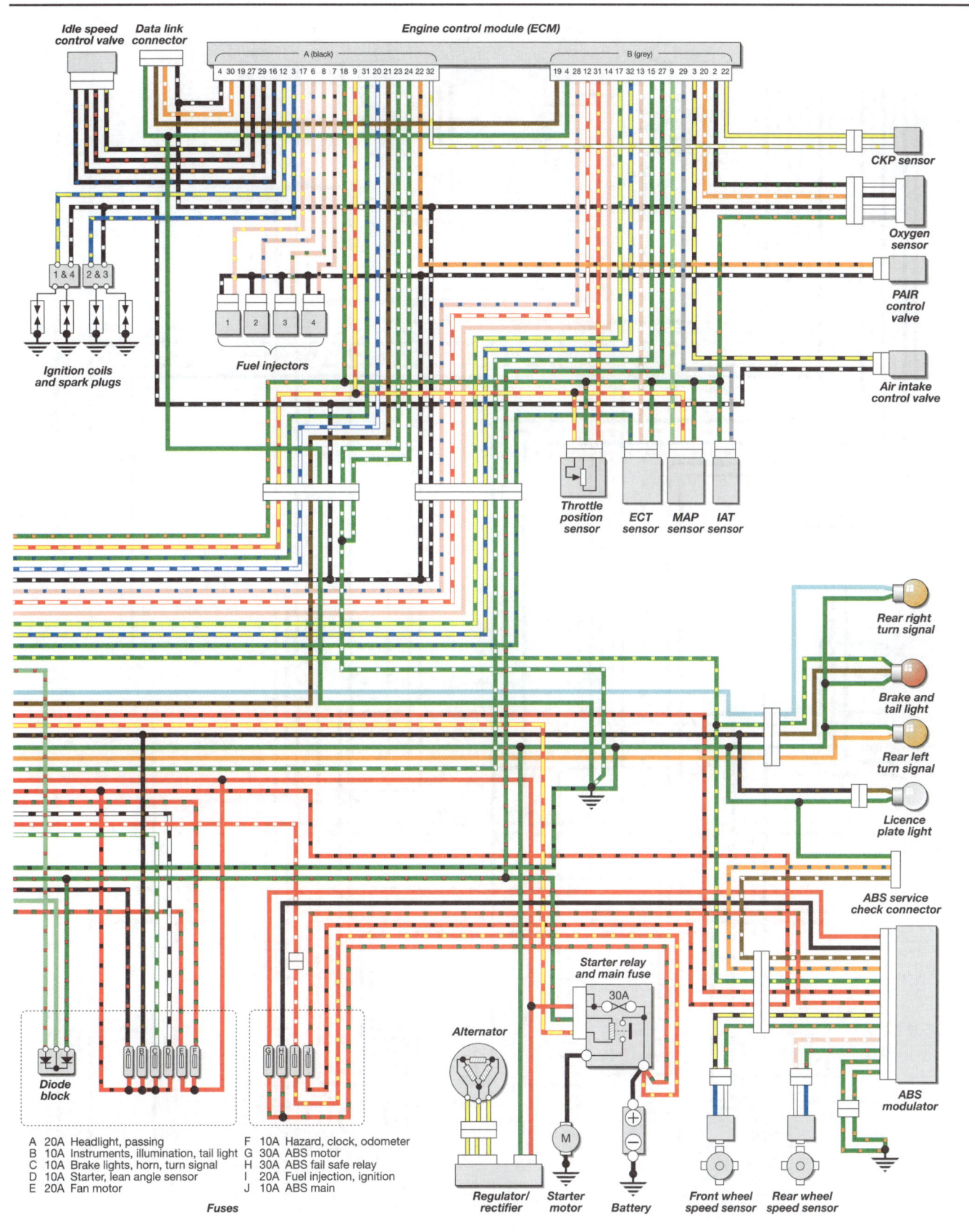

Wiring diagrams 8•49

Idle speed control valve **Data link connector** **Engine control module (ECM)**
A (black): 4 30 19 27 29 16 12 3 17 6 8 7 18 9 31 20 21 23 24 22 32
B (grey): 19 4 28 12 31 14 17 32 13 15 27 9 29 3 20 2 22

- CKP sensor
- Oxygen sensor
- PAIR control valve
- Air intake control valve

Ignition coils and spark plugs (1 & 4, 2 & 3)

Fuel injectors (1, 2, 3, 4)

- Throttle position sensor
- ECT sensor
- MAP sensor
- IAT sensor

- Rear right turn signal
- Brake and tail light
- Rear left turn signal
- Licence plate light
- ABS service check connector
- ABS modulator

Diode block

Starter relay and main fuse (30A)

Alternator — Regulator/rectifier

Starter motor

Battery

Front wheel speed sensor

Rear wheel speed sensor

Fuses
- A 20A Headlight, passing
- B 10A Instruments, illumination, tail light
- C 10A Brake lights, horn, turn signal
- D 10A Starter, lean angle sensor
- E 20A Fan motor
- F 10A Hazard, clock, odometer
- G 30A ABS motor
- H 30A ABS fail safe relay
- I   20A Fuel injection, ignition
- J   10A ABS main

H47518

CBF600NA

8•50 Wiring diagrams

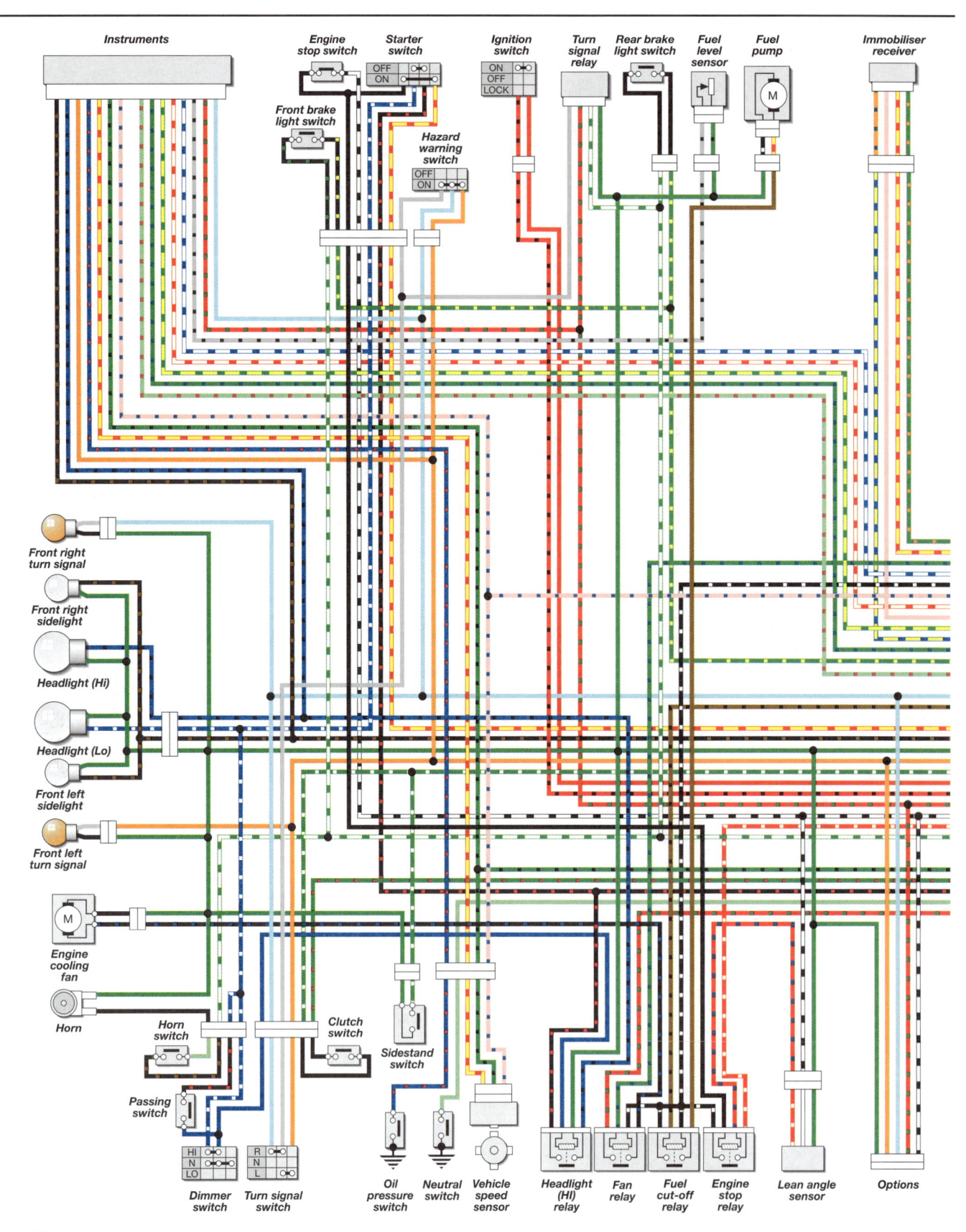

CBF600S

Wiring diagrams 8•51

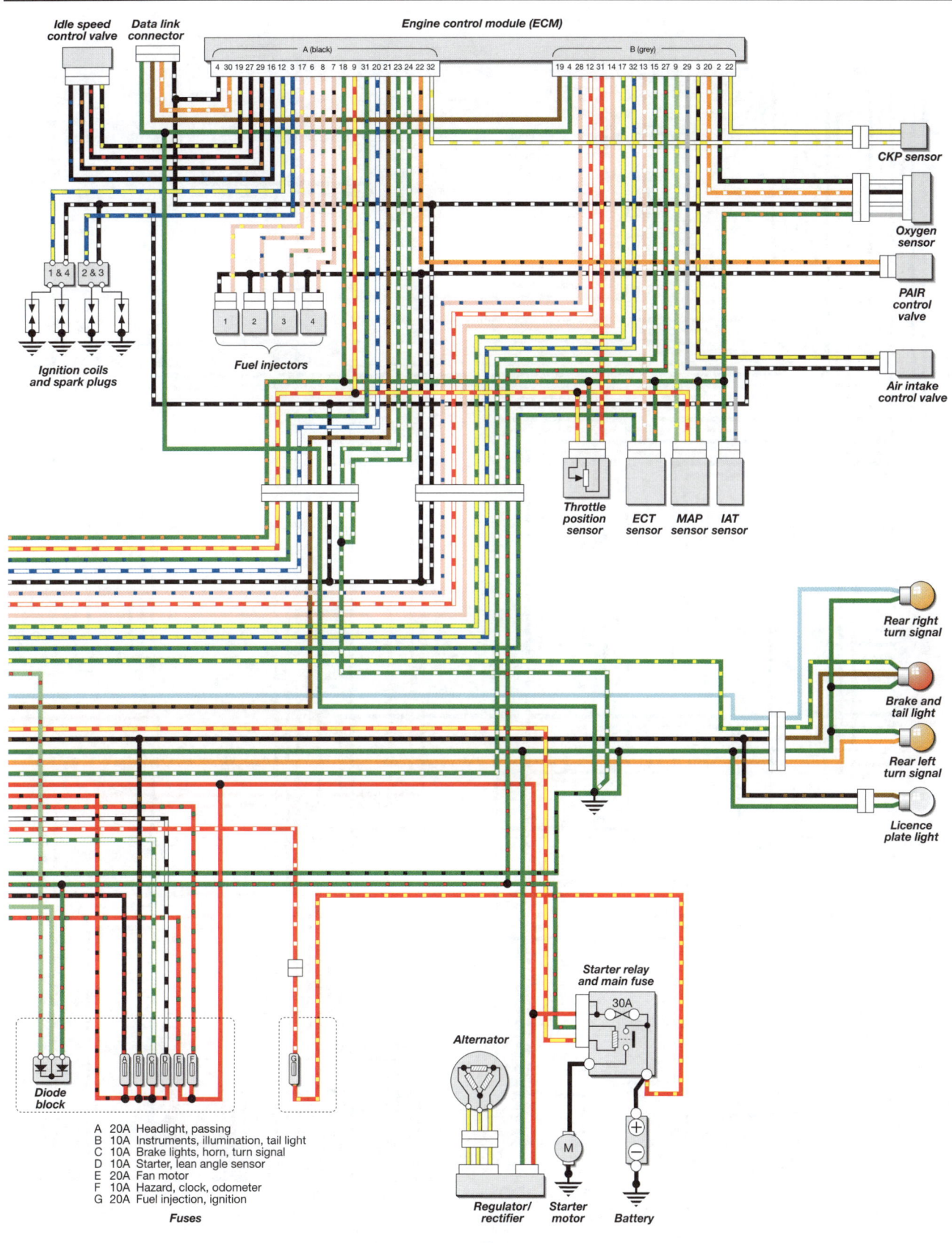

CBF600S

Fuses:
- A 20A Headlight, passing
- B 10A Instruments, illumination, tail light
- C 10A Brake lights, horn, turn signal
- D 10A Starter, lean angle sensor
- E 20A Fan motor
- F 10A Hazard, clock, odometer
- G 20A Fuel injection, ignition

8•52 Wiring diagrams

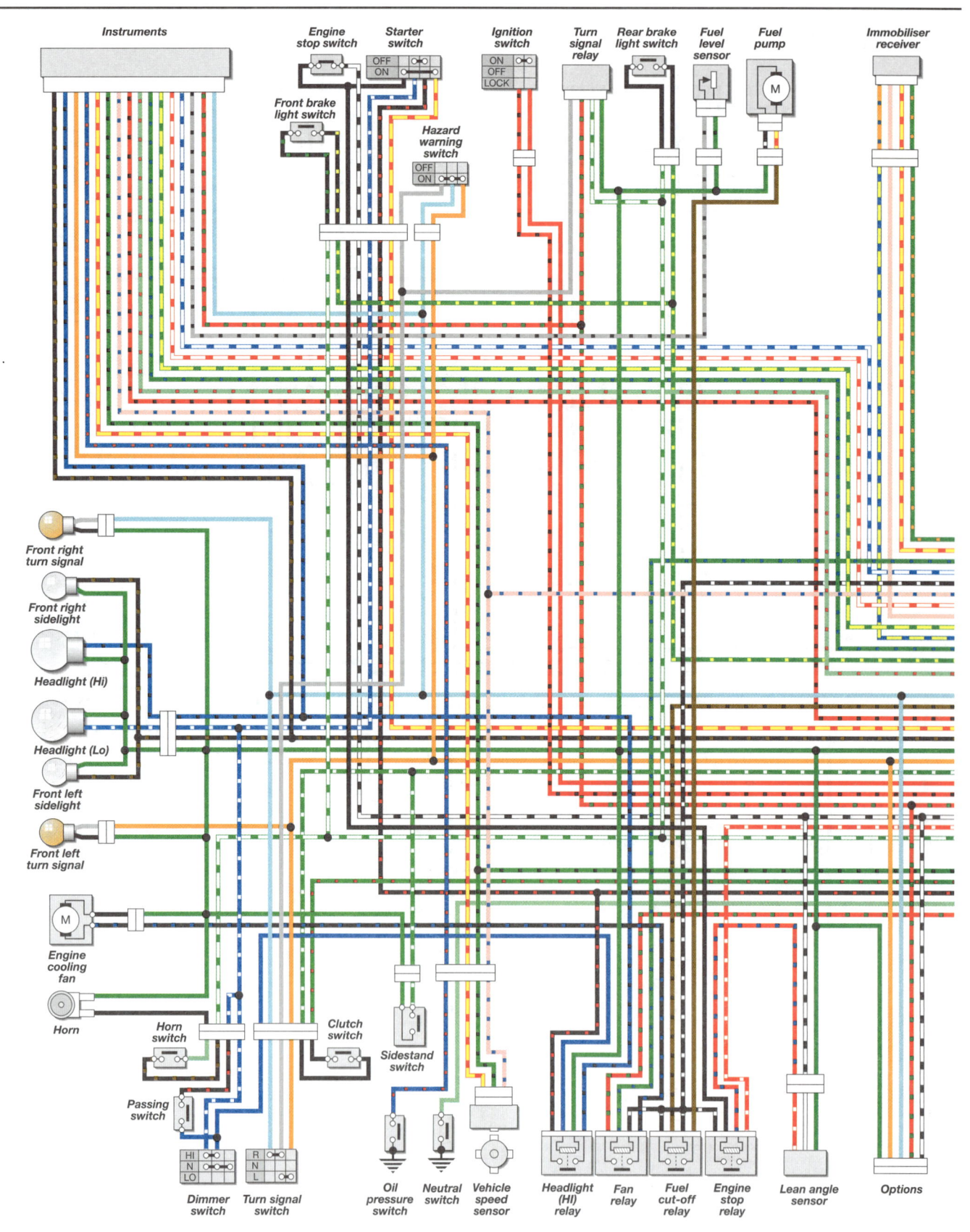

CBF600SA

Wiring diagrams 8•53

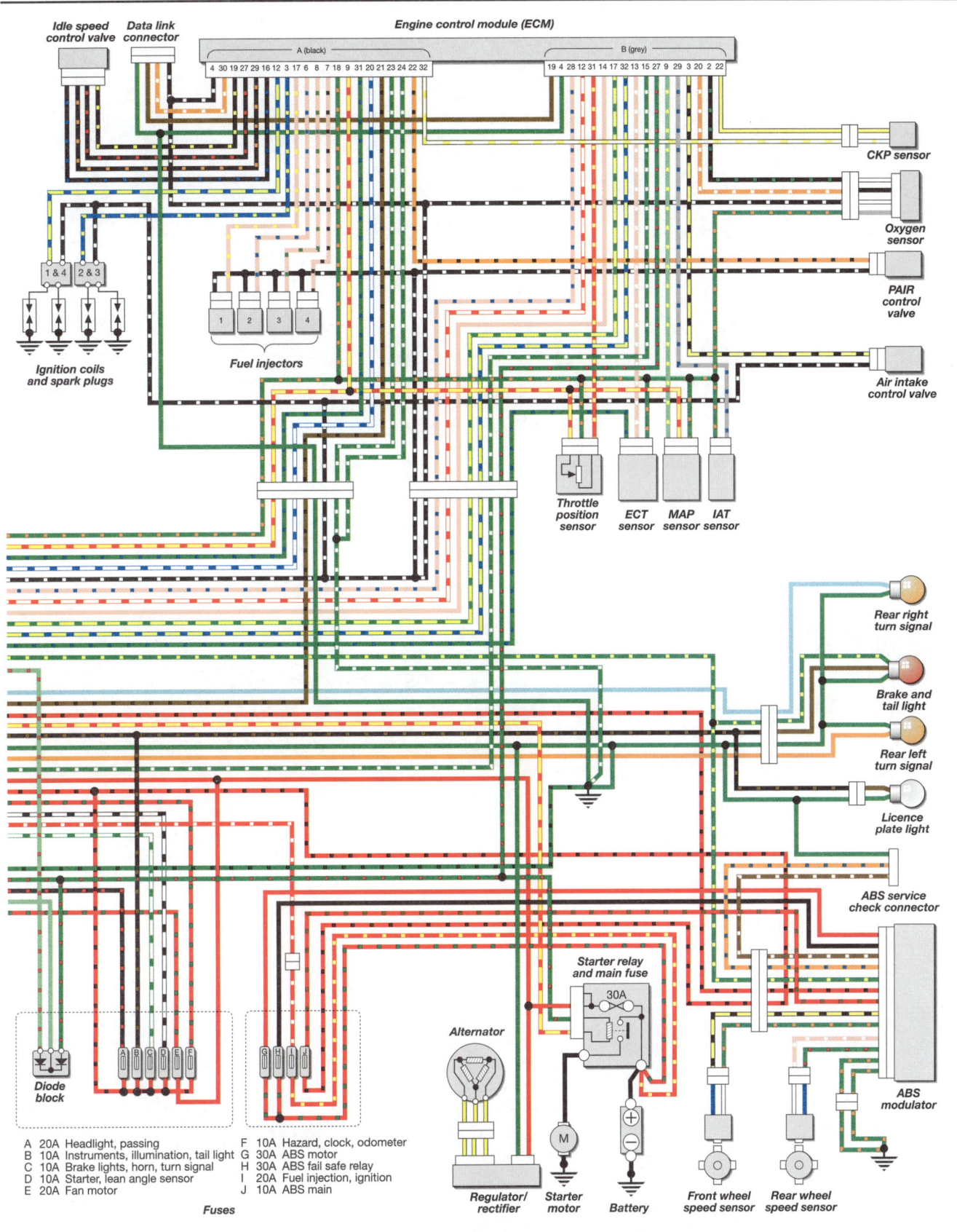

Idle speed control valve
Data link connector
Engine control module (ECM)
A (black)
B (grey)

Ignition coils and spark plugs
Fuel injectors
Throttle position sensor
ECT sensor
MAP sensor
IAT sensor

CKP sensor
Oxygen sensor
PAIR control valve
Air intake control valve

Rear right turn signal
Brake and tail light
Rear left turn signal
Licence plate light
ABS service check connector

Diode block
Fuses
Alternator
Starter relay and main fuse 30A
Regulator/rectifier
Starter motor
Battery
Front wheel speed sensor
Rear wheel speed sensor
ABS modulator

A 20A Headlight, passing
B 10A Instruments, illumination, tail light
C 10A Brake lights, horn, turn signal
D 10A Starter, lean angle sensor
E 20A Fan motor
F 10A Hazard, clock, odometer
G 30A ABS motor
H 30A ABS fail safe relay
I 20A Fuel injection, ignition
J 10A ABS main

H47522

CBF600SA

Notes

Reference REF•1

Reference

Tools and Workshop Tips — REF•2
- Building up a tool kit and equipping your workshop
- Using tools
- Understanding bearing, seal, fastener and chain sizes and markings
- Repair techniques

Security — REF•20
- Locks and chains
- U-locks
- Disc locks
- Alarms and immobilisers
- Security marking systems
- Tips on how to prevent bike theft

Lubricants and fluids — REF•23
- Engine oils
- Transmission (gear) oils
- Coolant/anti-freeze
- Fork oils and suspension fluids
- Brake/clutch fluids
- Spray lubes, degreasers and solvents

Conversion Factors — REF•26

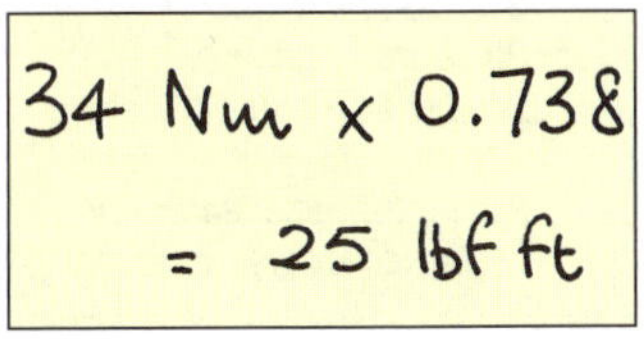

34 Nm × 0.738 = 25 lbf ft

- Formulae for conversion of the metric (SI) units used throughout the manual into Imperial measures

MOT Test Checks — REF•27
- A guide to the UK MOT test
- Which items are tested
- How to prepare your motorcycle for the test and perform a pre-test check

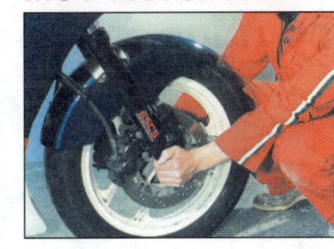

Storage — REF•32
- How to prepare your motorcycle for going into storage and protect essential systems
- How to get the motorcycle back on the road

Fault Finding — REF•35
- Common faults and their likely causes
- Links to main chapters for testing and repair procedures

Technical Terms Explained — REF•46
- Component names, technical terms and common abbreviations explained

Index — REF•50

REF•2 Tools and Workshop Tips

Buying tools

A toolkit is a fundamental requirement for servicing and repairing a motorcycle. Although there will be an initial expense in building up enough tools for servicing, this will soon be offset by the savings made by doing the job yourself. As experience and confidence grow, additional tools can be added to enable the repair and overhaul of the motorcycle. Many of the specialist tools are expensive and not often used so it may be preferable to hire them, or for a group of friends or motorcycle club to join in the purchase.

As a rule, it is better to buy more expensive, good quality tools. Cheaper tools are likely to wear out faster and need to be renewed more often, nullifying the original saving.

> **Warning:** *To avoid the risk of a poor quality tool breaking in use, causing injury or damage to the component being worked on, always aim to purchase tools which meet the relevant national safety standards.*

The following lists of tools do not represent the manufacturer's service tools, but serve as a guide to help the owner decide which tools are needed for this level of work. In addition, items such as an electric drill, hacksaw, files, soldering iron and a workbench equipped with a vice, may be needed. Although not classed as tools, a selection of bolts, screws, nuts, washers and pieces of tubing always come in useful.

For more information about tools, refer to the Haynes *Motorcycle Workshop Practice Techbook* (Bk. No. 3470).

Manufacturer's service tools

Inevitably certain tasks require the use of a service tool. Where possible an alternative tool or method of approach is recommended, but sometimes there is no option if personal injury or damage to the component is to be avoided. Where required, service tools are referred to in the relevant procedure.

Service tools can usually only be purchased from a motorcycle dealer and are identified by a part number. Some of the commonly-used tools, such as rotor pullers, are available in aftermarket form from mail-order motorcycle tool and accessory suppliers.

Maintenance and minor repair tools

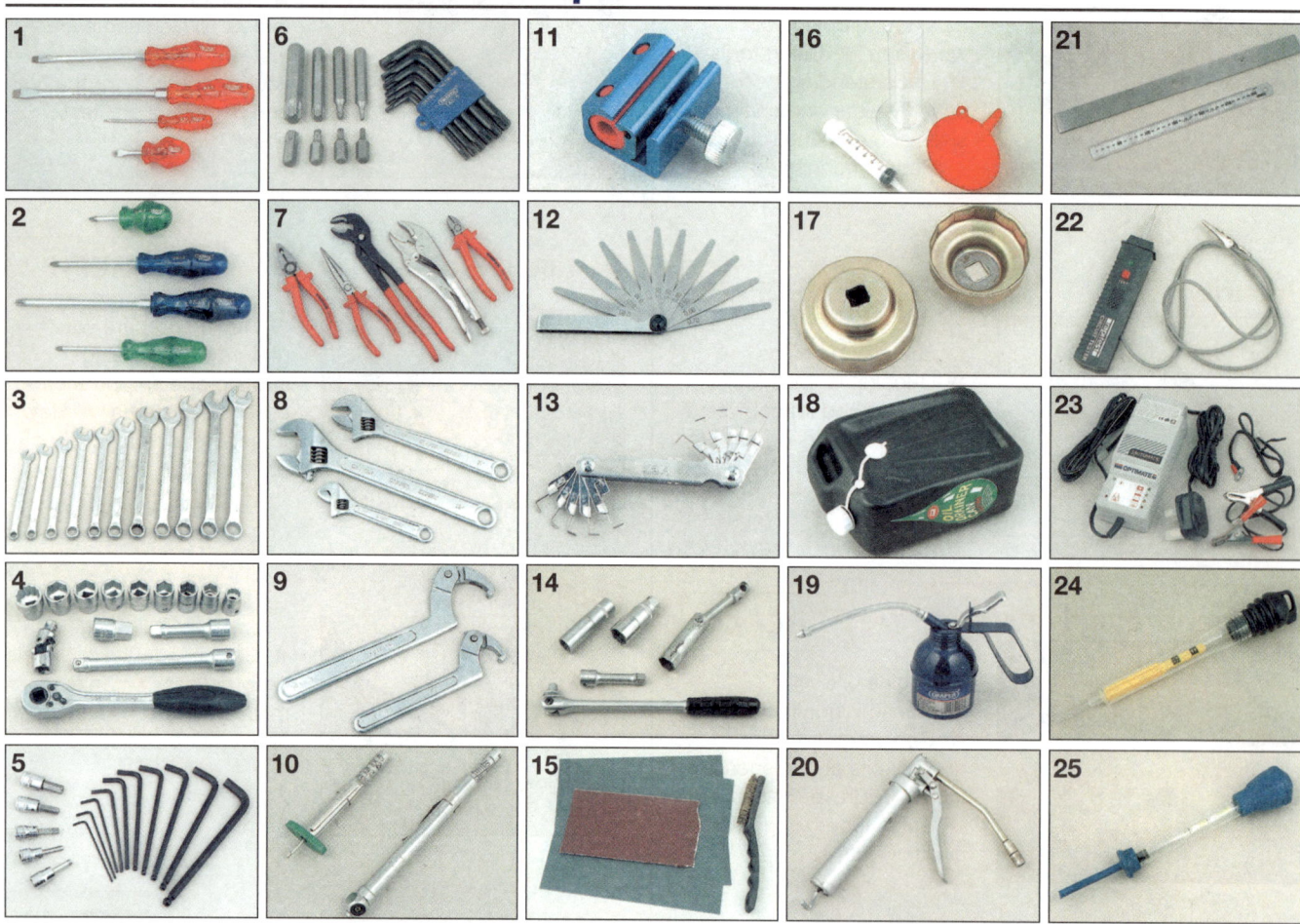

1. *Set of flat-bladed screwdrivers*
2. *Set of Phillips head screwdrivers*
3. *Combination open-end and ring spanners*
4. *Socket set (3/8 inch or 1/2 inch drive)*
5. *Set of Allen keys or bits*
6. *Set of Torx keys or bits*
7. *Pliers, cutters and self-locking grips (Mole grips)*
8. *Adjustable spanners*
9. *C-spanners*
10. *Tread depth gauge and tyre pressure gauge*
11. *Cable oiler clamp*
12. *Feeler gauges*
13. *Spark plug gap measuring tool*
14. *Spark plug spanner or deep plug sockets*
15. *Wire brush and emery paper*
16. *Calibrated syringe, measuring vessel and funnel*
17. *Oil filter adapters*
18. *Oil drainer can or tray*
19. *Pump type oil can*
20. *Grease gun*
21. *Straight-edge and steel rule*
22. *Continuity tester*
23. *Battery charger*
24. *Hydrometer (for battery specific gravity check)*
25. *Anti-freeze tester (for liquid-cooled engines)*

# Tools and Workshop Tips   REF•3

Repair and overhaul tools

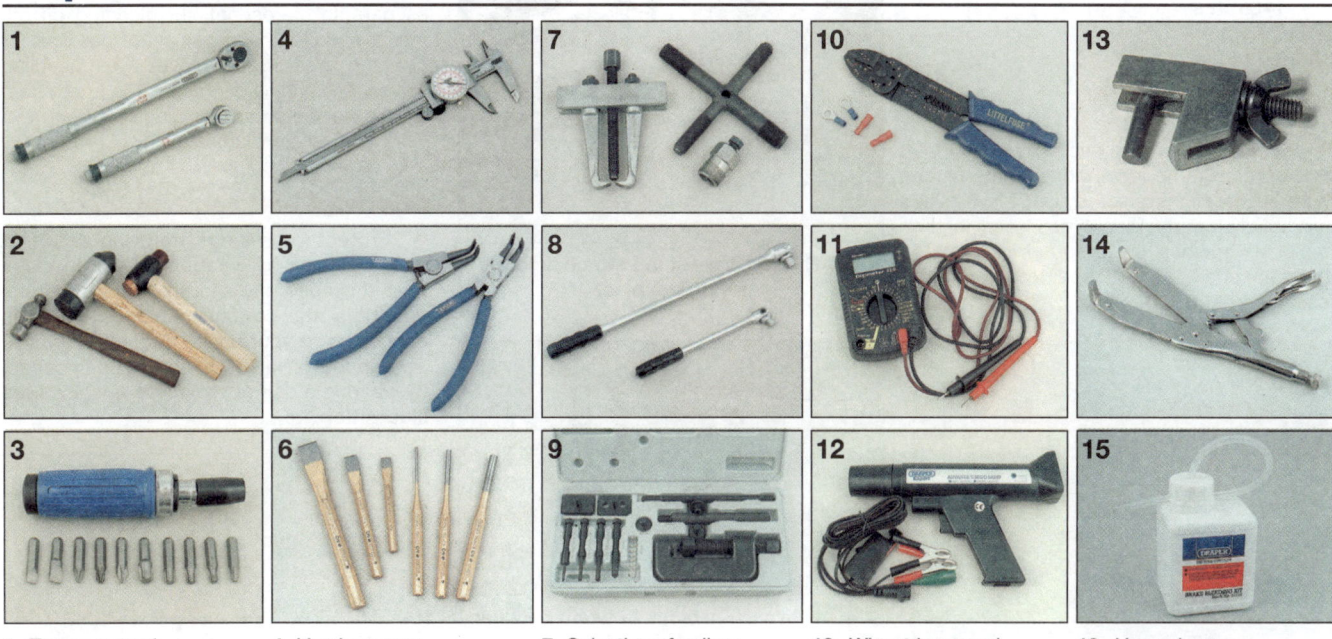

1. Torque wrench (small and mid-ranges)
2. Conventional, plastic or soft-faced hammers
3. Impact driver set
4. Vernier gauge
5. Circlip pliers (internal and external, or combination)
6. Set of cold chisels and punches
7. Selection of pullers
8. Breaker bars
9. Chain breaking/riveting tool set
10. Wire stripper and crimper tool
11. Multimeter (measures amps, volts and ohms)
12. Stroboscope (for dynamic timing checks)
13. Hose clamp (wingnut type shown)
14. Clutch holding tool
15. One-man brake/clutch bleeder kit

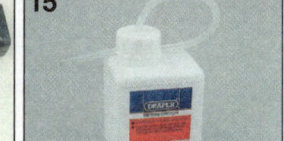

Specialist tools

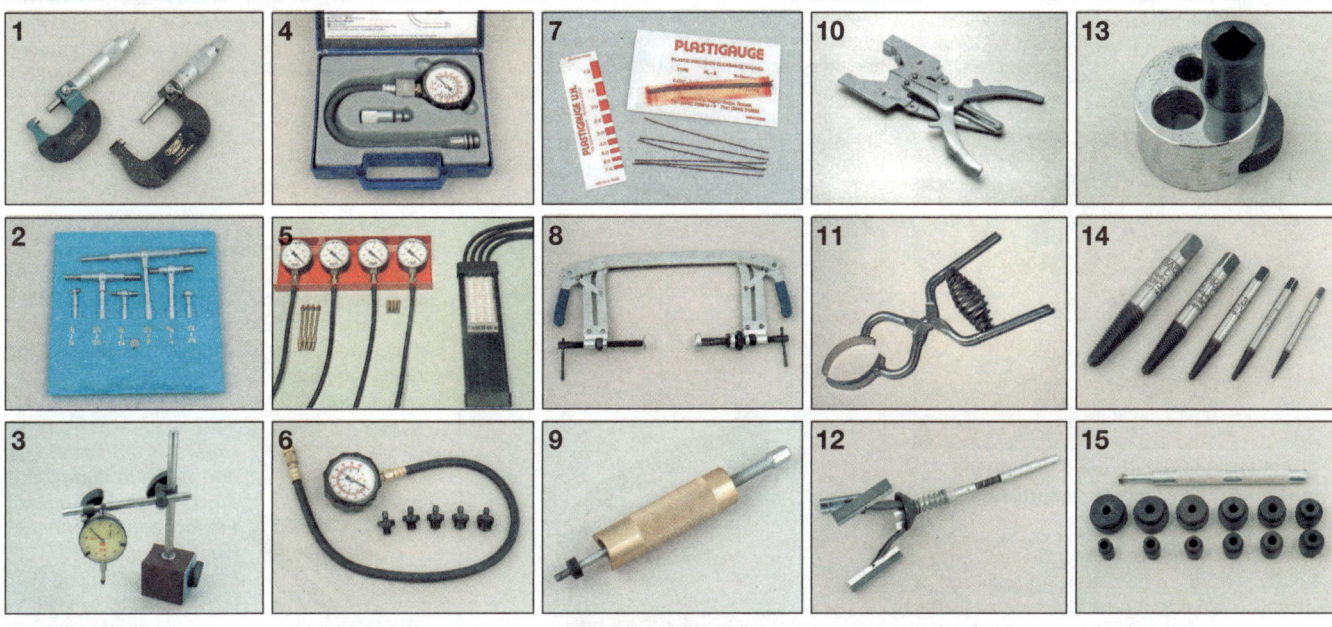

1. Micrometers (external type)
2. Telescoping gauges
3. Dial gauge
4. Cylinder compression gauge
5. Vacuum gauges (left) or manometer (right)
6. Oil pressure gauge
7. Plastigauge kit
8. Valve spring compressor (4-stroke engines)
9. Piston pin drawbolt tool
10. Piston ring removal and installation tool
11. Piston ring clamp
12. Cylinder bore hone (stone type shown)
13. Stud extractor
14. Screw extractor set
15. Bearing driver set

REF•4 Tools and Workshop Tips

1 Workshop equipment and facilities

The workbench

- Work is made much easier by raising the bike up on a ramp - components are much more accessible if raised to waist level. The hydraulic or pneumatic types seen in the dealer's workshop are a sound investment if you undertake a lot of repairs or overhauls **(see illustration 1.1)**.

1.1 Hydraulic motorcycle ramp

- If raised off ground level, the bike must be supported on the ramp to avoid it falling. Most ramps incorporate a front wheel locating clamp which can be adjusted to suit different diameter wheels. When tightening the clamp, take care not to mark the wheel rim or damage the tyre - use wood blocks on each side to prevent this.
- Secure the bike to the ramp using tie-downs **(see illustration 1.2)**. If the bike has only a sidestand, and hence leans at a dangerous angle when raised, support the bike on an auxiliary stand.

1.2 Tie-downs are used around the passenger footrests to secure the bike

- Auxiliary (paddock) stands are widely available from mail order companies or motorcycle dealers and attach either to the wheel axle or swingarm pivot **(see illustration 1.3)**. If the motorcycle has a centrestand, you can support it under the crankcase to prevent it toppling whilst either wheel is removed **(see illustration 1.4)**.

1.3 This auxiliary stand attaches to the swingarm pivot

1.4 Always use a block of wood between the engine and jack head when supporting the engine in this way

Fumes and fire

- Refer to the Safety first! page at the beginning of the manual for full details. Make sure your workshop is equipped with a fire extinguisher suitable for fuel-related fires (Class B fire - flammable liquids) - it is not sufficient to have a water-filled extinguisher.
- Always ensure adequate ventilation is available. Unless an exhaust gas extraction system is available for use, ensure that the engine is run outside of the workshop.
- If working on the fuel system, make sure the workshop is ventilated to avoid a build-up of fumes. This applies equally to fume build-up when charging a battery. Do not smoke or allow anyone else to smoke in the workshop.

Fluids

- If you need to drain fuel from the tank, store it in an approved container marked as suitable for the storage of petrol (gasoline) **(see illustration 1.5)**. Do not store fuel in glass jars or bottles.

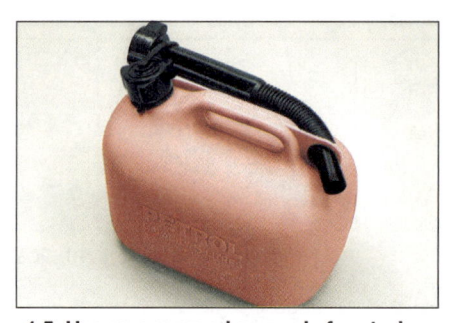

1.5 Use an approved can only for storing petrol (gasoline)

- Use proprietary engine degreasers or solvents which have a high flash-point, such as paraffin (kerosene), for cleaning off oil, grease and dirt - never use petrol (gasoline) for cleaning. Wear rubber gloves when handling solvent and engine degreaser. The fumes from certain solvents can be dangerous - always work in a well-ventilated area.

Dust, eye and hand protection

- Protect your lungs from inhalation of dust particles by wearing a filtering mask over the nose and mouth. Many frictional materials still contain asbestos which is dangerous to your health. Protect your eyes from spouts of liquid and sprung components by wearing a pair of protective goggles **(see illustration 1.6)**.

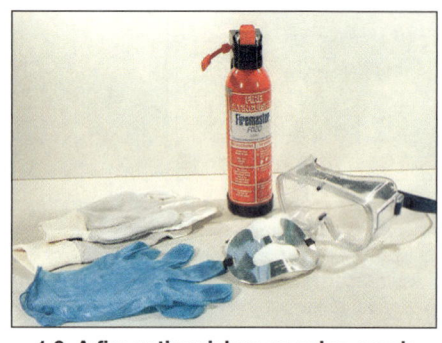

1.6 A fire extinguisher, goggles, mask and protective gloves should be at hand in the workshop

- Protect your hands from contact with solvents, fuel and oils by wearing rubber gloves. Alternatively apply a barrier cream to your hands before starting work. If handling hot components or fluids, wear suitable gloves to protect your hands from scalding and burns.

What to do with old fluids

- Old cleaning solvent, fuel, coolant and oils should not be poured down domestic drains or onto the ground. Package the fluid up in old oil containers, label it accordingly, and take it to a garage or disposal facility. Contact your local authority for location of such sites or ring the oil care hotline.

Note: It is antisocial and illegal to dump oil down the drain. To find the location of your local oil recycling bank in the UK, call 08708 506 506 or visit www.oilbankline.org.uk

In the USA, note that any oil supplier must accept used oil for recycling.

Tools and Workshop Tips REF•5

2 Fasteners - screws, bolts and nuts

Fastener types and applications

Bolts and screws

● Fastener head types are either of hexagonal, Torx or splined design, with internal and external versions of each type **(see illustrations 2.1 and 2.2)**; splined head fasteners are not in common use on motorcycles. The conventional slotted or Phillips head design is used for certain screws. Bolt or screw length is always measured from the underside of the head to the end of the item **(see illustration 2.11)**.

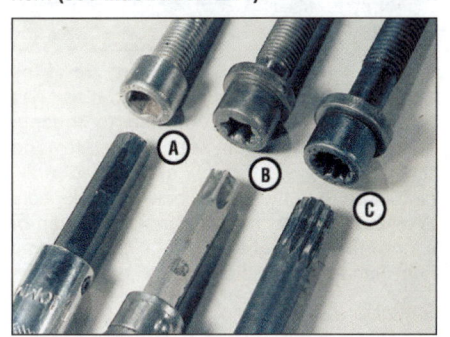

2.1 Internal hexagon/Allen (A), Torx (B) and splined (C) fasteners, with corresponding bits

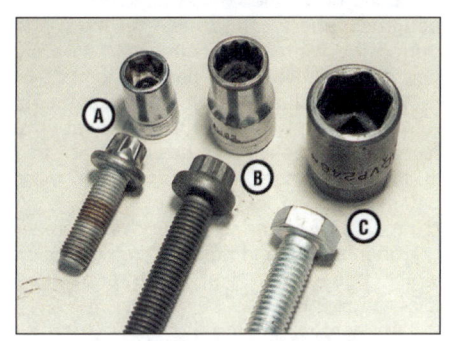

2.2 External Torx (A), splined (B) and hexagon (C) fasteners, with corresponding sockets

● Certain fasteners on the motorcycle have a tensile marking on their heads, the higher the marking the stronger the fastener. High tensile fasteners generally carry a 10 or higher marking. Never replace a high tensile fastener with one of a lower tensile strength.

Washers (see illustration 2.3)

● Plain washers are used between a fastener head and a component to prevent damage to the component or to spread the load when torque is applied. Plain washers can also be used as spacers or shims in certain assemblies. Copper or aluminium plain washers are often used as sealing washers on drain plugs.

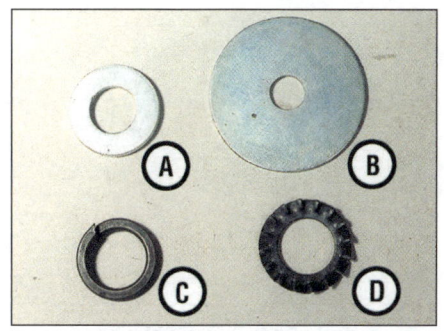

2.3 Plain washer (A), penny washer (B), spring washer (C) and serrated washer (D)

● The split-ring spring washer works by applying axial tension between the fastener head and component. If flattened, it is fatigued and must be renewed. If a plain (flat) washer is used on the fastener, position the spring washer between the fastener and the plain washer.

● Serrated star type washers dig into the fastener and component faces, preventing loosening. They are often used on electrical earth (ground) connections to the frame.

● Cone type washers (sometimes called Belleville) are conical and when tightened apply axial tension between the fastener head and component. They must be installed with the dished side against the component and often carry an OUTSIDE marking on their outer face. If flattened, they are fatigued and must be renewed.

● Tab washers are used to lock plain nuts or bolts on a shaft. A portion of the tab washer is bent up hard against one flat of the nut or bolt to prevent it loosening. Due to the tab washer being deformed in use, a new tab washer should be used every time it is disturbed.

● Wave washers are used to take up endfloat on a shaft. They provide light springing and prevent excessive side-to-side play of a component. Can be found on rocker arm shafts.

Nuts and split pins

● Conventional plain nuts are usually six-sided **(see illustration 2.4)**. They are sized by thread diameter and pitch. High tensile nuts carry a number on one end to denote their tensile strength.

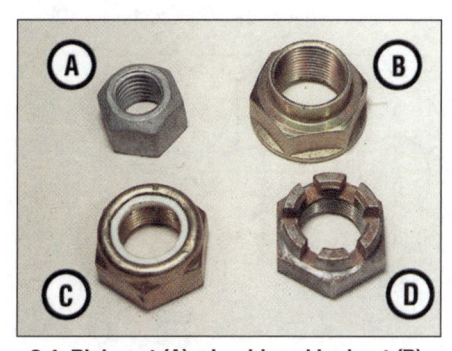

2.4 Plain nut (A), shouldered locknut (B), nylon insert nut (C) and castellated nut (D)

● Self-locking nuts either have a nylon insert, or two spring metal tabs, or a shoulder which is staked into a groove in the shaft - their advantage over conventional plain nuts is a resistance to loosening due to vibration. The nylon insert type can be used a number of times, but must be renewed when the friction of the nylon insert is reduced, ie when the nut spins freely on the shaft. The spring tab type can be reused unless the tabs are damaged. The shouldered type must be renewed every time it is disturbed.

● Split pins (cotter pins) are used to lock a castellated nut to a shaft or to prevent slackening of a plain nut. Common applications are wheel axles and brake torque arms. Because the split pin arms are deformed to lock around the nut a new split pin must always be used on installation - always fit the correct size split pin which will fit snugly in the shaft hole. Make sure the split pin arms are correctly located around the nut **(see illustrations 2.5 and 2.6)**.

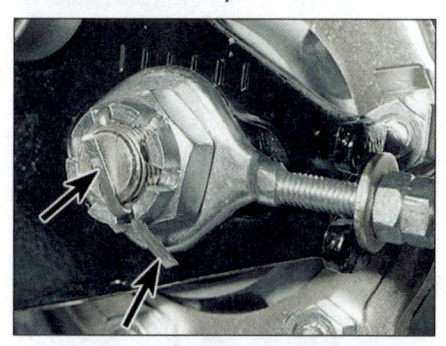

2.5 Bend split pin (cotter pin) arms as shown (arrows) to secure a castellated nut

2.6 Bend split pin (cotter pin) arms as shown to secure a plain nut

> **Caution:** *If the castellated nut slots do not align with the shaft hole after tightening to the torque setting, tighten the nut until the next slot aligns with the hole - never slacken the nut to align its slot.*

● R-pins (shaped like the letter R), or slip pins as they are sometimes called, are sprung and can be reused if they are otherwise in good condition. Always install R-pins with their closed end facing forwards **(see illustration 2.7)**.

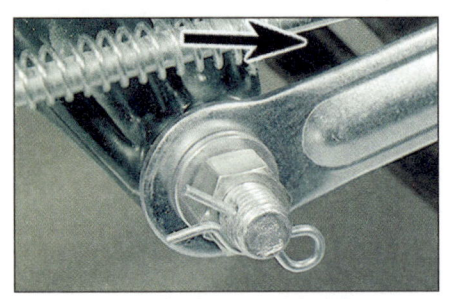

Tools and Workshop Tips

2.7 Correct fitting of R-pin. Arrow indicates forward direction

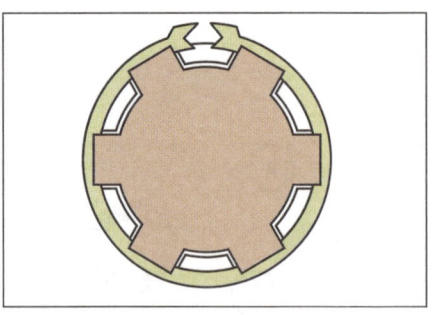

2.10 Align circlip opening with shaft channel

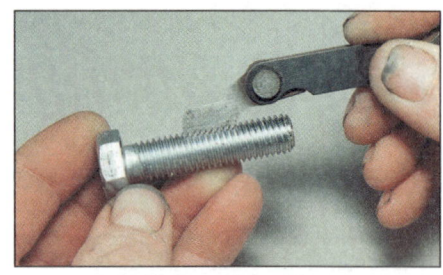

2.12 Using a thread gauge to measure pitch

Circlips (see illustration 2.8)

- Circlips (sometimes called snap-rings) are used to retain components on a shaft or in a housing and have corresponding external or internal ears to permit removal. Parallel-sided (machined) circlips can be installed either way round in their groove, whereas stamped circlips (which have a chamfered edge on one face) must be installed with the chamfer facing away from the direction of thrust load **(see illustration 2.9)**.

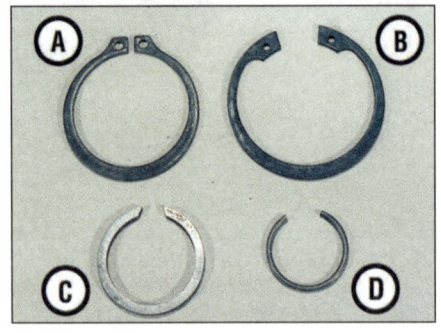

2.8 External stamped circlip (A), internal stamped circlip (B), machined circlip (C) and wire circlip (D)

- Always use circlip pliers to remove and install circlips; expand or compress them just enough to remove them. After installation, rotate the circlip in its groove to ensure it is securely seated. If installing a circlip on a splined shaft, always align its opening with a shaft channel to ensure the circlip ends are well supported and unlikely to catch **(see illustration 2.10)**.

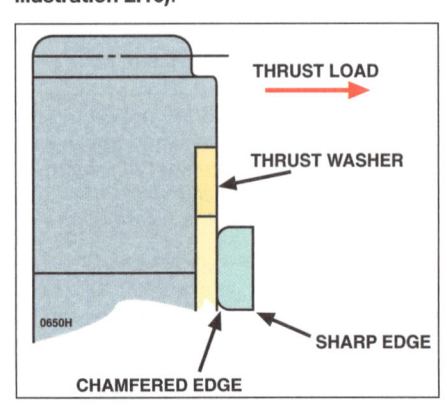

2.9 Correct fitting of a stamped circlip

- Circlips can wear due to the thrust of components and become loose in their grooves, with the subsequent danger of becoming dislodged in operation. For this reason, renewal is advised every time a circlip is disturbed.
- Wire circlips are commonly used as piston pin retaining clips. If a removal tang is provided, long-nosed pliers can be used to dislodge them, otherwise careful use of a small flat-bladed screwdriver is necessary. Wire circlips should be renewed every time they are disturbed.

Thread diameter and pitch

- Diameter of a male thread (screw, bolt or stud) is the outside diameter of the threaded portion **(see illustration 2.11)**. Most motorcycle manufacturers use the ISO (International Standards Organisation) metric system expressed in millimetres, eg M6 refers to a 6 mm diameter thread. Sizing is the same for nuts, except that the thread diameter is measured across the valleys of the nut.
- Pitch is the distance between the peaks of the thread **(see illustration 2.11)**. It is expressed in millimetres, thus a common bolt size may be expressed as 6.0 x 1.0 mm (6 mm thread diameter and 1 mm pitch). Generally pitch increases in proportion to thread diameter, although there are always exceptions.
- Thread diameter and pitch are related for conventional fastener applications and the accompanying table can be used as a guide. Additionally, the AF (Across Flats), spanner or socket size dimension of the bolt or nut **(see illustration 2.11)** is linked to thread and pitch specification. Thread pitch can be measured with a thread gauge **(see illustration 2.12)**.

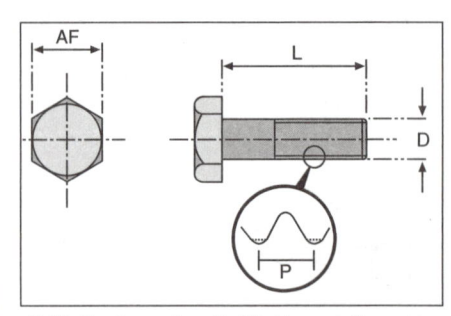

2.11 Fastener length (L), thread diameter (D), thread pitch (P) and head size (AF)

AF size	Thread diameter x pitch (mm)
8 mm	M5 x 0.8
8 mm	M6 x 1.0
10 mm	M6 x 1.0
12 mm	M8 x 1.25
14 mm	M10 x 1.25
17 mm	M12 x 1.25

- The threads of most fasteners are of the right-hand type, ie they are turned clockwise to tighten and anti-clockwise to loosen. The reverse situation applies to left-hand thread fasteners, which are turned anti-clockwise to tighten and clockwise to loosen. Left-hand threads are used where rotation of a component might loosen a conventional right-hand thread fastener.

Seized fasteners

- Corrosion of external fasteners due to water or reaction between two dissimilar metals can occur over a period of time. It will build up sooner in wet conditions or in countries where salt is used on the roads during the winter. If a fastener is severely corroded it is likely that normal methods of removal will fail and result in its head being ruined. When you attempt removal, the fastener thread should be heard to crack free and unscrew easily - if it doesn't, stop there before damaging something.
- A smart tap on the head of the fastener will often succeed in breaking free corrosion which has occurred in the threads **(see illustration 2.13)**.
- An aerosol penetrating fluid (such as WD-40) applied the night beforehand may work its way down into the thread and ease removal. Depending on the location, you may be able to make up a Plasticine well around the fastener head and fill it with penetrating fluid.

2.13 A sharp tap on the head of a fastener will often break free a corroded thread

Tools and Workshop Tips REF•7

• If you are working on an engine internal component, corrosion will most likely not be a problem due to the well lubricated environment. However, components can be very tight and an impact driver is a useful tool in freeing them **(see illustration 2.14)**.

2.14 Using an impact driver to free a fastener

• Where corrosion has occurred between dissimilar metals (eg steel and aluminium alloy), the application of heat to the fastener head will create a disproportionate expansion rate between the two metals and break the seizure caused by the corrosion. Whether heat can be applied depends on the location of the fastener - any surrounding components likely to be damaged must first be removed **(see illustration 2.15)**. Heat can be applied using a paint stripper heat gun or clothes iron, or by immersing the component in boiling water - wear protective gloves to prevent scalding or burns to the hands.

2.15 Using heat to free a seized fastener

• As a last resort, it is possible to use a hammer and cold chisel to work the fastener head unscrewed **(see illustration 2.16)**. This will damage the fastener, but more importantly extreme care must be taken not to damage the surrounding component.

> **Caution: Remember that the component being secured is generally of more value than the bolt, nut or screw - when the fastener is freed, do not unscrew it with force, instead work the fastener back and forth when resistance is felt to prevent thread damage.**

2.16 Using a hammer and chisel to free a seized fastener

Broken fasteners and damaged heads

• If the shank of a broken bolt or screw is accessible you can grip it with self-locking grips. The knurled wheel type stud extractor tool or self-gripping stud puller tool is particularly useful for removing the long studs which screw into the cylinder mouth surface of the crankcase or bolts and screws from which the head has broken off **(see illustration 2.17)**. Studs can also be removed by locking two nuts together on the threaded end of the stud and using a spanner on the lower nut **(see illustration 2.18)**.

2.17 Using a stud extractor tool to remove a broken crankcase stud

2.18 Two nuts can be locked together to unscrew a stud from a component

• A bolt or screw which has broken off below or level with the casing must be extracted using a screw extractor set. Centre punch the fastener to centralise the drill bit, then drill a hole in the fastener **(see illustration 2.19)**. Select a drill bit which is approximately half to three-quarters the diameter of the fastener

2.19 When using a screw extractor, first drill a hole in the fastener . . .

and drill to a depth which will accommodate the extractor. Use the largest size extractor possible, but avoid leaving too small a wall thickness otherwise the extractor will merely force the fastener walls outwards wedging it in the casing thread.

• If a spiral type extractor is used, thread it anti-clockwise into the fastener. As it is screwed in, it will grip the fastener and unscrew it from the casing **(see illustration 2.20)**.

2.20 . . . then thread the extractor anti-clockwise into the fastener

• If a taper type extractor is used, tap it into the fastener so that it is firmly wedged in place. Unscrew the extractor (anti-clockwise) to draw the fastener out.

> ⚠ **Warning: Stud extractors are very hard and may break off in the fastener if care is not taken - ask an engineer about spark erosion if this happens.**

• Alternatively, the broken bolt/screw can be drilled out and the hole retapped for an oversize bolt/screw or a diamond-section thread insert. It is essential that the drilling is carried out squarely and to the correct depth, otherwise the casing may be ruined - if in doubt, entrust the work to an engineer.

• Bolts and nuts with rounded corners cause the correct size spanner or socket to slip when force is applied. Of the types of spanner/socket available always use a six-point type rather than an eight or twelve-point type - better grip

REF•8 Tools and Workshop Tips

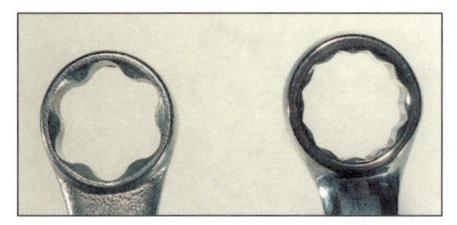

2.21 Comparison of surface drive ring spanner (left) with 12-point type (right)

is obtained. Surface drive spanners grip the middle of the hex flats, rather than the corners, and are thus good in cases of damaged heads **(see illustration 2.21)**.

● Slotted-head or Phillips-head screws are often damaged by the use of the wrong size screwdriver. Allen-head and Torx-head screws are much less likely to sustain damage. If enough of the screw head is exposed you can use a hacksaw to cut a slot in its head and then use a conventional flat-bladed screwdriver to remove it. Alternatively use a hammer and cold chisel to tap the head of the fastener around to slacken it. Always replace damaged fasteners with new ones, preferably Torx or Allen-head type.

> **HAYNES HINT**
>
> *A dab of valve grinding compound between the screw head and screwdriver tip will often give a good grip.*

Thread repair

● Threads (particularly those in aluminium alloy components) can be damaged by overtightening, being assembled with dirt in the threads, or from a component working loose and vibrating. Eventually the thread will fail completely, and it will be impossible to tighten the fastener.

● If a thread is damaged or clogged with old locking compound it can be renovated with a thread repair tool (thread chaser) **(see illustrations 2.22 and 2.23)**; special thread

2.22 A thread repair tool being used to correct an internal thread

2.23 A thread repair tool being used to correct an external thread

chasers are available for spark plug hole threads. The tool will not cut a new thread, but clean and true the original thread. Make sure that you use the correct diameter and pitch tool. Similarly, external threads can be cleaned up with a die or a thread restorer file **(see illustration 2.24)**.

2.24 Using a thread restorer file

● It is possible to drill out the old thread and retap the component to the next thread size. This will work where there is enough surrounding material and a new bolt or screw can be obtained. Sometimes, however, this is not possible - such as where the bolt/screw passes through another component which must also be suitably modified, also in cases where a spark plug or oil drain plug cannot be obtained in a larger diameter thread size.

● The diamond-section thread insert (often known by its popular trade name of Heli-Coil) is a simple and effective method of renewing the thread and retaining the original size. A kit can be purchased which contains the tap, insert and installing tool **(see illustration 2.25)**. Drill out the damaged thread with the size drill specified **(see illustration 2.26)**. Carefully retap the thread **(see illustration 2.27)**. Install the

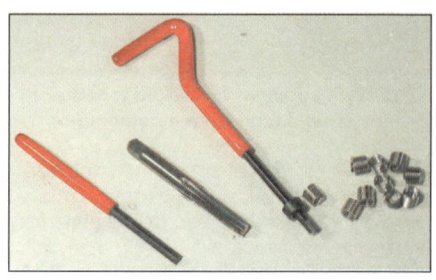

2.25 Obtain a thread insert kit to suit the thread diameter and pitch required

2.26 To install a thread insert, first drill out the original thread . . .

2.27 . . . tap a new thread . . .

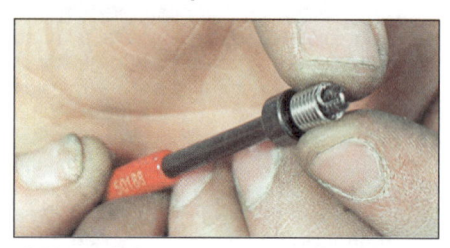

2.28 . . . fit insert on the installing tool . . .

2.29 . . . and thread into the component . . .

2.30 . . . break off the tang when complete

insert on the installing tool and thread it slowly into place using a light downward pressure **(see illustrations 2.28 and 2.29)**. When positioned between a 1/4 and 1/2 turn below the surface withdraw the installing tool and use the break-off tool to press down on the tang, breaking it off **(see illustration 2.30)**.

● There are epoxy thread repair kits on the market which can rebuild stripped internal threads, although this repair should not be used on high load-bearing components.

Tools and Workshop Tips

Thread locking and sealing compounds

● Locking compounds are used in locations where the fastener is prone to loosening due to vibration or on important safety-related items which might cause loss of control of the motorcycle if they fail. It is also used where important fasteners cannot be secured by other means such as lockwashers or split pins.

● Before applying locking compound, make sure that the threads (internal and external) are clean and dry with all old compound removed. Select a compound to suit the component being secured - a non-permanent general locking and sealing type is suitable for most applications, but a high strength type is needed for permanent fixing of studs in castings. Apply a drop or two of the compound to the first few threads of the fastener, then thread it into place and tighten to the specified torque. Do not apply excessive thread locking compound otherwise the thread may be damaged on subsequent removal.

● Certain fasteners are impregnated with a dry film type coating of locking compound on their threads. Always renew this type of fastener if disturbed.

● Anti-seize compounds, such as copper-based greases, can be applied to protect threads from seizure due to extreme heat and corrosion. A common instance is spark plug threads and exhaust system fasteners.

3 Measuring tools and gauges

Feeler gauges

● Feeler gauges (or blades) are used for measuring small gaps and clearances (see illustration 3.1). They can also be used to measure endfloat (sideplay) of a component on a shaft where access is not possible with a dial gauge.

● Feeler gauge sets should be treated with care and not bent or damaged. They are etched with their size on one face. Keep them clean and very lightly oiled to prevent corrosion build-up.

3.1 Feeler gauges are used for measuring small gaps and clearances - thickness is marked on one face of gauge

● When measuring a clearance, select a gauge which is a light sliding fit between the two components. You may need to use two gauges together to measure the clearance accurately.

Micrometers

● A micrometer is a precision tool capable of measuring to 0.01 or 0.001 of a millimetre. It should always be stored in its case and not in the general toolbox. It must be kept clean and never dropped, otherwise its frame or measuring anvils could be distorted resulting in inaccurate readings.

● External micrometers are used for measuring outside diameters of components and have many more applications than internal micrometers. Micrometers are available in different size ranges, eg 0 to 25 mm, 25 to 50 mm, and upwards in 25 mm steps; some large micrometers have interchangeable anvils to allow a range of measurements to be taken. Generally the largest precision measurement you are likely to take on a motorcycle is the piston diameter.

● Internal micrometers (or bore micrometers) are used for measuring inside diameters, such as valve guides and cylinder bores. Telescoping gauges and small hole gauges are used in conjunction with an external micrometer, whereas the more expensive internal micrometers have their own measuring device.

External micrometer

Note: *The conventional analogue type instrument is described. Although much easier to read, digital micrometers are considerably more expensive.*

● Always check the calibration of the micrometer before use. With the anvils closed (0 to 25 mm type) or set over a test gauge

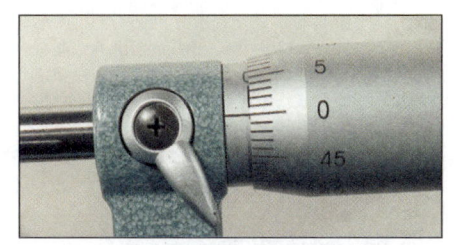

3.2 Check micrometer calibration before use

(for the larger types) the scale should read zero (see illustration 3.2); make sure that the anvils (and test piece) are clean first. Any discrepancy can be adjusted by referring to the instructions supplied with the tool. Remember that the micrometer is a precision measuring tool - don't force the anvils closed, use the ratchet (4) on the end of the micrometer to close it. In this way, a measured force is always applied.

● To use, first make sure that the item being measured is clean. Place the anvil of the micrometer (1) against the item and use the thimble (2) to bring the spindle (3) lightly into contact with the other side of the item (see illustration 3.3). Don't tighten the thimble down because this will damage the micrometer - instead use the ratchet (4) on the end of the micrometer. The ratchet mechanism applies a measured force preventing damage to the instrument.

● The micrometer is read by referring to the linear scale on the sleeve and the annular scale on the thimble. Read off the sleeve first to obtain the base measurement, then add the fine measurement from the thimble to obtain the overall reading. The linear scale on the sleeve represents the measuring range of the micrometer (eg 0 to 25 mm). The annular scale

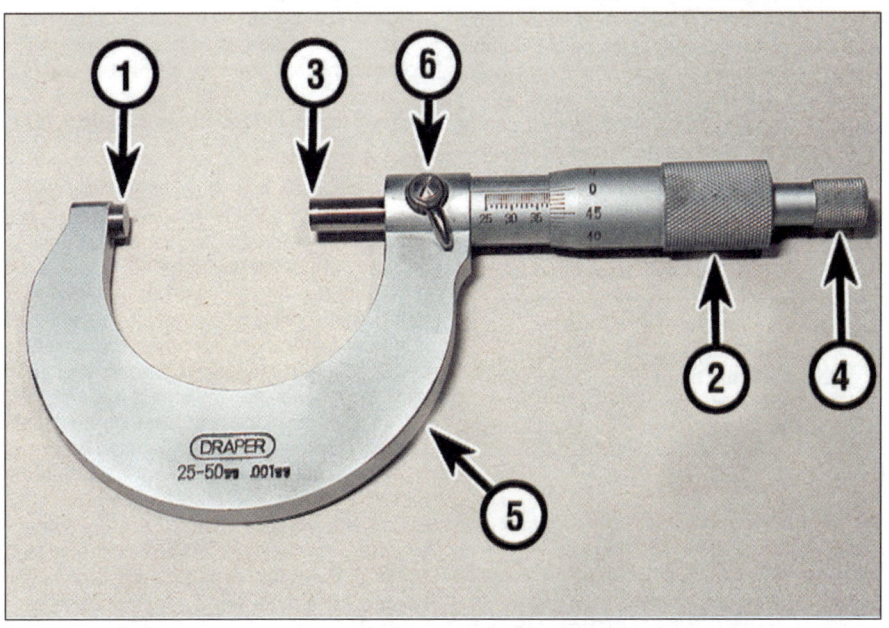

3.3 Micrometer component parts

1 Anvil
2 Thimble
3 Spindle
4 Ratchet
5 Frame
6 Locking lever

REF•10 Tools and Workshop Tips

on the thimble will be in graduations of 0.01 mm (or as marked on the frame) - one full revolution of the thimble will move 0.5 mm on the linear scale. Take the reading where the datum line on the sleeve intersects the thimble's scale. Always position the eye directly above the scale otherwise an inaccurate reading will result.

In the example shown the item measures 2.95 mm **(see illustration 3.4)**:

Linear scale	2.00 mm
Linear scale	0.50 mm
Annular scale	0.45 mm
Total figure	2.95 mm

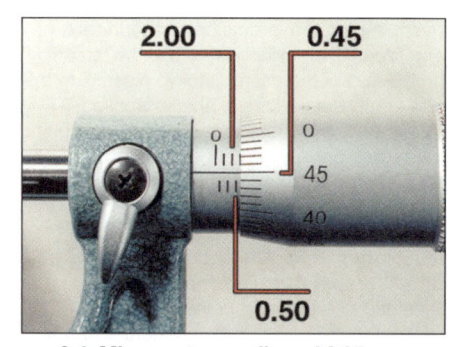

3.4 Micrometer reading of 2.95 mm

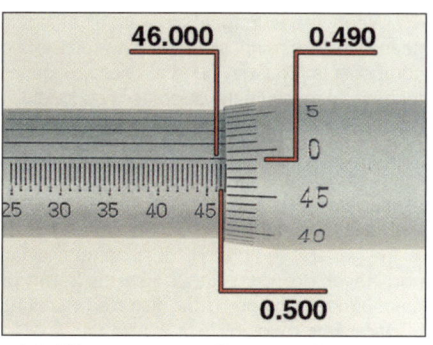

3.5 Micrometer reading of 46.99 mm on linear and annular scales . . .

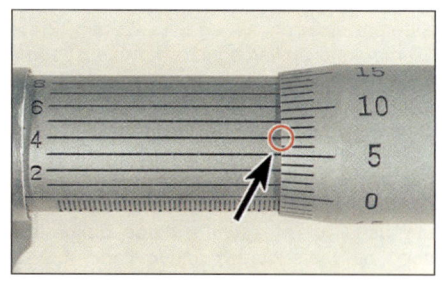

3.6 . . . and 0.004 mm on vernier scale

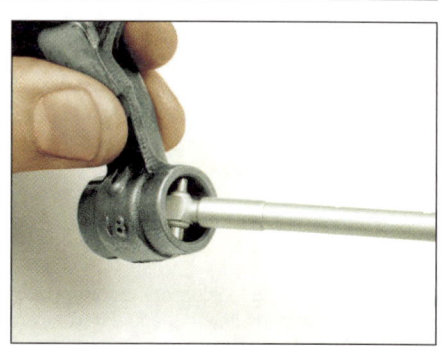

3.7 Expand the telescoping gauge in the bore, lock its position . . .

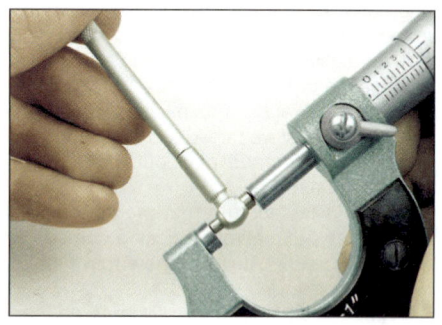

3.8 . . . then measure the gauge with a micrometer

3.9 Expand the small hole gauge in the bore, lock its position . . .

3.10 . . . then measure the gauge with a micrometer

Most micrometers have a locking lever (6) on the frame to hold the setting in place, allowing the item to be removed from the micrometer.

● Some micrometers have a vernier scale on their sleeve, providing an even finer measurement to be taken, in 0.001 increments of a millimetre. Take the sleeve and thimble measurement as described above, then check which graduation on the vernier scale aligns with that of the annular scale on the thimble **Note:** *The eye must be perpendicular to the scale when taking the vernier reading - if necessary rotate the body of the micrometer to ensure this.* Multiply the vernier scale figure by 0.001 and add it to the base and fine measurement figures.

In the example shown the item measures 46.994 mm **(see illustrations 3.5 and 3.6)**:

Linear scale (base)	46.000 mm
Linear scale (base)	00.500 mm
Annular scale (fine)	00.490 mm
Vernier scale	00.004 mm
Total figure	46.994 mm

Internal micrometer

● Internal micrometers are available for measuring bore diameters, but are expensive and unlikely to be available for home use. It is suggested that a set of telescoping gauges and small hole gauges, both of which must be used with an external micrometer, will suffice for taking internal measurements on a motorcycle.

● Telescoping gauges can be used to measure internal diameters of components. Select a gauge with the correct size range, make sure its ends are clean and insert it into the bore. Expand the gauge, then lock its position and withdraw it from the bore **(see illustration 3.7)**. Measure across the gauge ends with a micrometer **(see illustration 3.8)**.

● Very small diameter bores (such as valve guides) are measured with a small hole gauge. Once adjusted to a slip-fit inside the component, its position is locked and the gauge withdrawn for measurement with a micrometer **(see illustrations 3.9 and 3.10)**.

Vernier caliper

Note: *The conventional linear and dial gauge type instruments are described. Digital types are easier to read, but are far more expensive.*

● The vernier caliper does not provide the precision of a micrometer, but is versatile in being able to measure internal and external diameters. Some types also incorporate a depth gauge. It is ideal for measuring clutch plate friction material and spring free lengths.

● To use the conventional linear scale vernier, slacken off the vernier clamp screws (1) and set its jaws over (2), or inside (3), the item to be measured **(see illustration 3.11)**. Slide the jaw into contact, using the thumb-wheel (4) for fine movement of the sliding scale (5) then tighten the clamp screws (1). Read off the main scale (6) where the zero on the sliding scale (5) intersects it, taking the whole number to the left of the zero; this provides the base measurement. View along the sliding scale and select the division which lines up exactly with any of the divisions on the main scale, noting that the divisions usually represents 0.02 of a millimetre. Add this fine measurement to the base measurement to obtain the total reading.

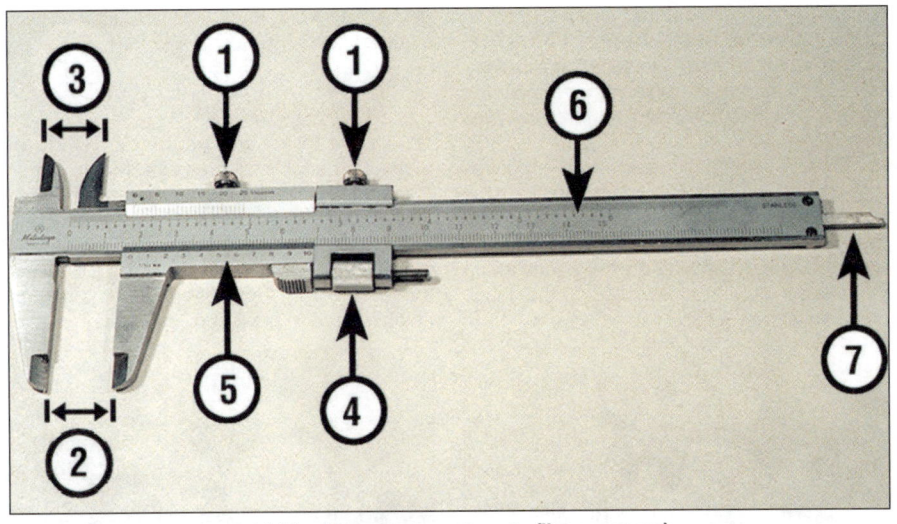

Tools and Workshop Tips REF•11

3.11 Vernier component parts (linear gauge)

1 Clamp screws
2 External jaws
3 Internal jaws
4 Thumbwheel
5 Sliding scale
6 Main scale
7 Depth gauge

In the example shown the item measures 55.92 mm **(see illustration 3.12)**:

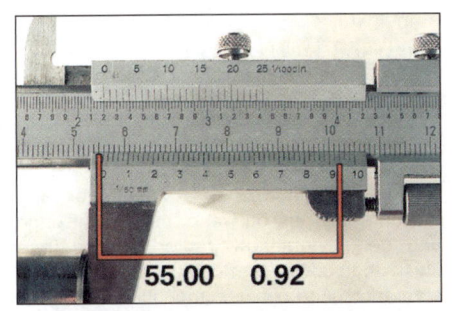

Base measurement	55.00 mm
Fine measurement	00.92 mm
Total figure	55.92 mm

● Some vernier calipers are equipped with a dial gauge for fine measurement. Before use, check that the jaws are clean, then close them fully and check that the dial gauge reads zero. If necessary adjust the gauge ring accordingly. Slacken the vernier clamp screw (1) and set its jaws over (2), or inside (3), the item to be measured **(see illustration 3.13)**. Slide the jaws into contact, using the thumbwheel (4) for fine movement. Read off the main scale (5) where the edge of the sliding scale (6) intersects it, taking the whole number to the left of the zero; this provides the base measurement. Read off the needle position on the dial gauge (7) scale to provide the fine measurement; each division represents 0.05 of a millimetre. Add this fine measurement to the base measurement to obtain the total reading.

In the example shown the item measures 55.95 mm **(see illustration 3.14)**:

Base measurement	55.00 mm
Fine measurement	00.95 mm
Total figure	55.95 mm

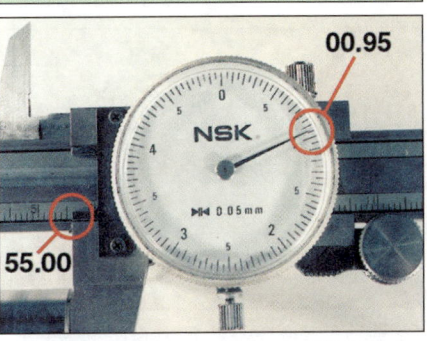

3.12 Vernier gauge reading of 55.92 mm

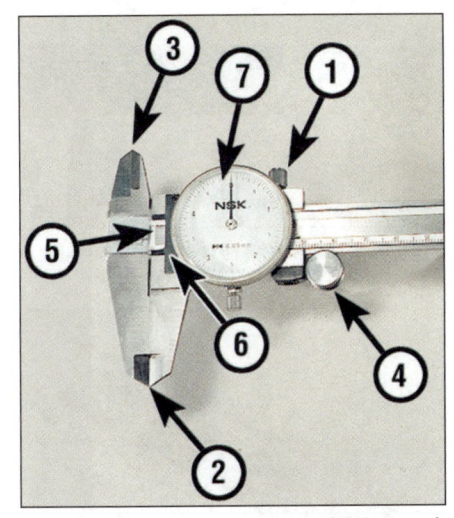

3.13 Vernier component parts (dial gauge)

1 Clamp screw
2 External jaws
3 Internal jaws
4 Thumbwheel
5 Main scale
6 Sliding scale
7 Dial gauge

3.14 Vernier gauge reading of 55.95 mm

Plastigauge

● Plastigauge is a plastic material which can be compressed between two surfaces to measure the oil clearance between them. The width of the compressed Plastigauge is measured against a calibrated scale to determine the clearance.

● Common uses of Plastigauge are for measuring the clearance between crankshaft journal and main bearing inserts, between crankshaft journal and big-end bearing inserts, and between camshaft and bearing surfaces. The following example describes big-end oil clearance measurement.

● Handle the Plastigauge material carefully to prevent distortion. Using a sharp knife, cut a length which corresponds with the width of the bearing being measured and place it carefully across the journal so that it is parallel with the shaft **(see illustration 3.15)**. Carefully install both bearing shells and the connecting rod. Without rotating the rod on the journal tighten its bolts or nuts (as applicable) to the specified torque. The connecting rod and bearings are then disassembled and the crushed Plastigauge examined.

3.15 Plastigauge placed across shaft journal

● Using the scale provided in the Plastigauge kit, measure the width of the material to determine the oil clearance **(see illustration 3.16)**. Always remove all traces of Plastigauge after use using your fingernails.

Caution: Arriving at the correct clearance demands that the assembly is torqued correctly, according to the settings and sequence (where applicable) provided by the motorcycle manufacturer.

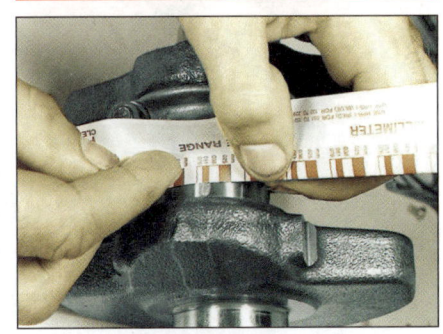

3.16 Measuring the width of the crushed Plastigauge

Tools and Workshop Tips

Dial gauge or DTI (Dial Test Indicator)

● A dial gauge can be used to accurately measure small amounts of movement. Typical uses are measuring shaft runout or shaft endfloat (sideplay) and setting piston position for ignition timing on two-strokes. A dial gauge set usually comes with a range of different probes and adapters and mounting equipment.

● The gauge needle must point to zero when at rest. Rotate the ring around its periphery to zero the gauge.

● Check that the gauge is capable of reading the extent of movement in the work. Most gauges have a small dial set in the face which records whole millimetres of movement as well as the fine scale around the face periphery which is calibrated in 0.01 mm divisions. Read off the small dial first to obtain the base measurement, then add the measurement from the fine scale to obtain the total reading.

In the example shown the gauge reads 1.48 mm (see illustration 3.17):

Base measurement	1.00 mm
Fine measurement	0.48 mm
Total figure	1.48 mm

3.17 Dial gauge reading of 1.48 mm

● If measuring shaft runout, the shaft must be supported in vee-blocks and the gauge mounted on a stand perpendicular to the shaft. Rest the tip of the gauge against the centre of the shaft and rotate the shaft slowly whilst watching the gauge reading (see illustration 3.18). Take several measurements along the length of the shaft and record the maximum gauge reading as the amount of runout in the shaft. **Note:** *The reading obtained will be total runout at that point - some manufacturers specify that the runout figure is halved to compare with their specified runout limit.*

● Endfloat (sideplay) measurement requires that the gauge is mounted securely to the surrounding component with its probe touching the end of the shaft. Using hand pressure, push and pull on the shaft noting the maximum endfloat recorded on the gauge (see illustration 3.19).

3.19 Using a dial gauge to measure shaft endfloat

● A dial gauge with suitable adapters can be used to determine piston position BTDC on two-stroke engines for the purposes of ignition timing. The gauge, adapter and suitable length probe are installed in the place of the spark plug and the gauge zeroed at TDC. If the piston position is specified as 1.14 mm BTDC, rotate the engine back to 2.00 mm BTDC, then slowly forwards to 1.14 mm BTDC.

Cylinder compression gauges

● A compression gauge is used for measuring cylinder compression. Either the rubber-cone type or the threaded adapter type can be used. The latter is preferred to ensure a perfect seal against the cylinder head. A 0 to 300 psi (0 to 20 Bar) type gauge (for petrol/gasoline engines) will be suitable for motorcycles.

● The spark plug is removed and the gauge either held hard against the cylinder head (cone type) or the gauge adapter screwed into the cylinder head (threaded type) (see illustration 3.20). Cylinder compression is measured with the engine turning over, but not running. The gauge will hold the reading until manually released.

Oil pressure gauge

● An oil pressure gauge is used for measuring engine oil pressure. Most gauges come with a set of adapters to fit the thread of the take-off point (see illustration 3.21). If the take-off point specified by the motorcycle manufacturer is an external oil pipe union, make sure that the specified replacement union is used to prevent oil starvation.

3.21 Oil pressure gauge and take-off point adapter (arrow)

● Oil pressure is measured with the engine running (at a specific rpm) and often the manufacturer will specify pressure limits for a cold and hot engine.

Straight-edge and surface plate

● If checking the gasket face of a component for warpage, place a steel rule or precision straight-edge across the gasket face and measure any gap between the straight-edge and component with feeler gauges (see illustration 3.22). Check diagonally across the component and between mounting holes (see illustration 3.23).

3.22 Use a straight-edge and feeler gauges to check for warpage

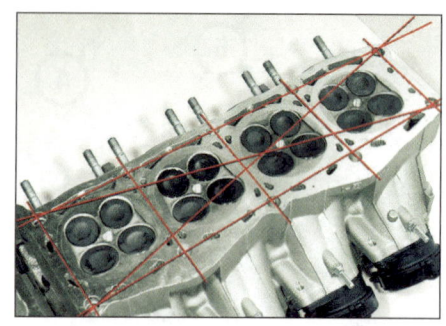

3.18 Using a dial gauge to measure shaft runout

3.20 Using a rubber-cone type cylinder compression gauge

3.23 Check for warpage in these directions

Tools and Workshop Tips REF•13

- Checking individual components for warpage, such as clutch plain (metal) plates, requires a perfectly flat plate or piece or plate glass and feeler gauges.

4 Torque and leverage

What is torque?

- Torque describes the twisting force about a shaft. The amount of torque applied is determined by the distance from the centre of the shaft to the end of the lever and the amount of force being applied to the end of the lever; distance multiplied by force equals torque.
- The manufacturer applies a measured torque to a bolt or nut to ensure that it will not slacken in use and to hold two components securely together without movement in the joint. The actual torque setting depends on the thread size, bolt or nut material and the composition of the components being held.
- Too little torque may cause the fastener to loosen due to vibration, whereas too much torque will distort the joint faces of the component or cause the fastener to shear off. Always stick to the specified torque setting.

Using a torque wrench

- Check the calibration of the torque wrench and make sure it has a suitable range for the job. Torque wrenches are available in Nm (Newton-metres), kgf m (kilograms-force metre), lbf ft (pounds-feet), lbf in (inch-pounds). Do not confuse lbf ft with lbf in.
- Adjust the tool to the desired torque on the scale (see illustration 4.1). If your torque wrench is not calibrated in the units specified, carefully convert the figure (see Conversion Factors). A manufacturer sometimes gives a torque setting as a range (8 to 10 Nm) rather than a single figure - in this case set the tool midway between the two settings. The same torque may be expressed as 9 Nm ± 1 Nm. Some torque wrenches have a method of locking the setting so that it isn't inadvertently altered during use.

- Install the bolts/nuts in their correct location and secure them lightly. Their threads must be clean and free of any old locking compound. Unless specified the threads and flange should be dry - oiled threads are necessary in certain circumstances and the manufacturer will take this into account in the specified torque figure. Similarly, the manufacturer may also specify the application of thread-locking compound.
- Tighten the fasteners in the specified sequence until the torque wrench clicks, indicating that the torque setting has been reached. Apply the torque again to double-check the setting. Where different thread diameter fasteners secure the component, as a rule tighten the larger diameter ones first.
- When the torque wrench has been finished with, release the lock (where applicable) and fully back off its setting to zero - do not leave the torque wrench tensioned. Also, do not use a torque wrench for slackening a fastener.

Angle-tightening

- Manufacturers often specify a figure in degrees for final tightening of a fastener. This usually follows tightening to a specific torque setting.
- A degree disc can be set and attached to the socket (see illustration 4.2) or a protractor can be used to mark the angle of movement on the bolt/nut head and the surrounding casting (see illustration 4.3).

Loosening sequences

- Where more than one bolt/nut secures a component, loosen each fastener evenly a little at a time. In this way, not all the stress of the joint is held by one fastener and the components are not likely to distort.
- If a tightening sequence is provided, work in the REVERSE of this, but if not, work from the outside in, in a criss-cross sequence (see illustration 4.4).

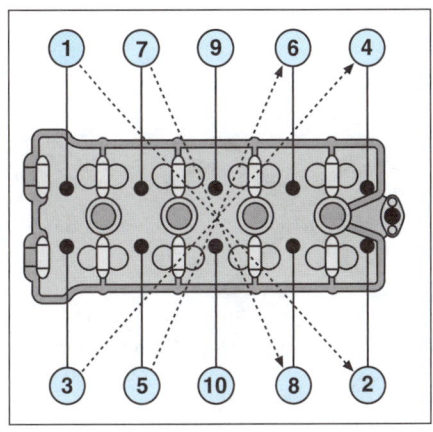

4.4 When slackening, work from the outside inwards

Tightening sequences

- If a component is held by more than one fastener it is important that the retaining bolts/nuts are tightened evenly to prevent uneven stress build-up and distortion of sealing faces. This is especially important on high-compression joints such as the cylinder head.
- A sequence is usually provided by the manufacturer, either in a diagram or actually marked in the casting. If not, always start in the centre and work outwards in a criss-cross pattern (see illustration 4.5). Start off by securing all bolts/nuts finger-tight, then set the torque wrench and tighten each fastener by a small amount in sequence until the final torque is reached. By following this practice,

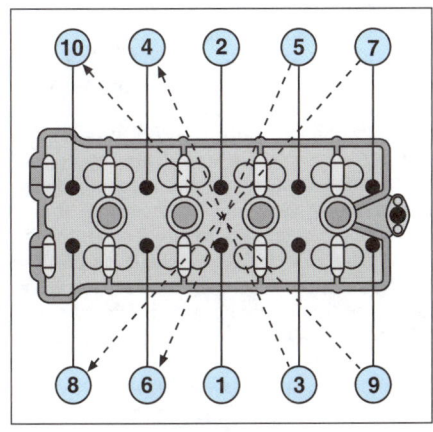

4.1 Set the torque wrench index mark to the setting required, in this case 12 Nm

4.2 Angle tightening can be accomplished with a torque-angle gauge . . .

4.3 . . . or by marking the angle on the surrounding component

4.5 When tightening, work from the inside outwards

REF•14 Tools and Workshop Tips

the joint will be held evenly and will not be distorted. Important joints, such as the cylinder head and big-end fasteners often have two- or three-stage torque settings.

Applying leverage

● Use tools at the correct angle. Position a socket wrench or spanner on the bolt/nut so that you pull it towards you when loosening. If this can't be done, push the spanner without curling your fingers around it **(see illustration 4.6)** - the spanner may slip or the fastener loosen suddenly, resulting in your fingers being crushed against a component.

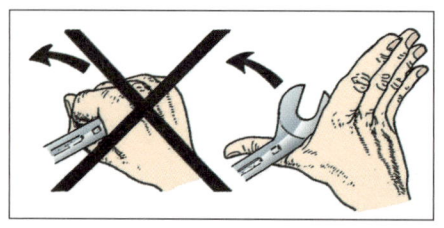

4.6 If you can't pull on the spanner to loosen a fastener, push with your hand open

● Additional leverage is gained by extending the length of the lever. The best way to do this is to use a breaker bar instead of the regular length tool, or to slip a length of tubing over the end of the spanner or socket wrench.
● If additional leverage will not work, the fastener head is either damaged or firmly corroded in place (see Fasteners).

5 Bearings

Bearing removal and installation

Drivers and sockets

● Before removing a bearing, always inspect the casing to see which way it must be driven out - some casings will have retaining plates or a cast step. Also check for any identifying markings on the bearing and if installed to a certain depth, measure this at this stage. Some roller bearings are sealed on one side - take note of the original fitted position.
● Bearings can be driven out of a casing using a bearing driver tool (with the correct size head) or a socket of the correct diameter. Select the driver head or socket so that it contacts the outer race of the bearing, not the balls/rollers or inner race. Always support the casing around the bearing housing with wood blocks, otherwise there is a risk of fracture. The bearing is driven out with a few blows on the driver or socket from a heavy mallet. Unless access is severely restricted (as with wheel bearings), a pin-punch is not recommended unless it is moved around the bearing to keep it square in its housing.

● The same equipment can be used to install bearings. Make sure the bearing housing is supported on wood blocks and line up the bearing in its housing. Fit the bearing as noted on removal - generally they are installed with their marked side facing outwards. Tap the bearing squarely into its housing using a driver or socket which bears only on the bearing's outer race - contact with the bearing balls/rollers or inner race will destroy it **(see illustrations 5.1 and 5.2)**.
● Check that the bearing inner race and balls/rollers rotate freely.

5.1 Using a bearing driver against the bearing's outer race

5.2 Using a large socket against the bearing's outer race

Pullers and slide-hammers

● Where a bearing is pressed on a shaft a puller will be required to extract it **(see illustration 5.3)**. Make sure that the puller clamp or legs fit securely behind the bearing and are unlikely to slip out. If pulling a bearing

5.3 This bearing puller clamps behind the bearing and pressure is applied to the shaft end to draw the bearing off

off a gear shaft for example, you may have to locate the puller behind a gear pinion if there is no access to the race and draw the gear pinion off the shaft as well **(see illustration 5.4)**.

Caution: Ensure that the puller's centre bolt locates securely against the end of the shaft and will not slip when pressure is applied. Also ensure that puller does not damage the shaft end.

5.4 Where no access is available to the rear of the bearing, it is sometimes possible to draw off the adjacent component

● Operate the puller so that its centre bolt exerts pressure on the shaft end and draws the bearing off the shaft.
● When installing the bearing on the shaft, tap only on the bearing's inner race - contact with the balls/rollers or outer race with destroy the bearing. Use a socket or length of tubing as a drift which fits over the shaft end **(see illustration 5.5)**.

5.5 When installing a bearing on a shaft use a piece of tubing which bears only on the bearing's inner race

● Where a bearing locates in a blind hole in a casing, it cannot be driven or pulled out as described above. A slide-hammer with knife-edged bearing puller attachment will be required. The puller attachment passes through the bearing and when tightened expands to fit firmly behind the bearing **(see illustration 5.6)**. By operating the slide-hammer part of the tool the bearing is jarred out of its housing **(see illustration 5.7)**.
● It is possible, if the bearing is of reasonable weight, for it to drop out of its housing if the casing is heated as described opposite.

Tools and Workshop Tips REF•15

5.6 Expand the bearing puller so that it locks behind the bearing . . .

5.7 . . . attach the slide hammer to the bearing puller

If this method is attempted, first prepare a work surface which will enable the casing to be tapped face down to help dislodge the bearing - a wood surface is ideal since it will not damage the casing's gasket surface. Wearing protective gloves, tap the heated casing several times against the work surface to dislodge the bearing under its own weight **(see illustration 5.8)**.

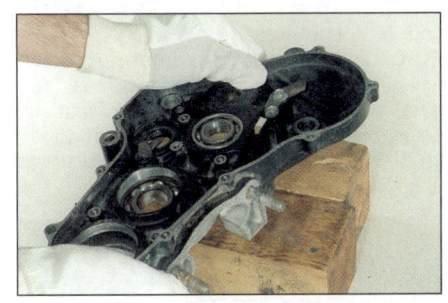

5.8 Tapping a casing face down on wood blocks can often dislodge a bearing

- Bearings can be installed in blind holes using the driver or socket method described above.

Drawbolts

- Where a bearing or bush is set in the eye of a component, such as a suspension linkage arm or connecting rod small-end, removal by drift may damage the component. Furthermore, a rubber bushing in a shock absorber eye cannot successfully be driven out of position. If access is available to a engineering press, the task is straightforward. If not, a drawbolt can be fabricated to extract the bearing or bush.

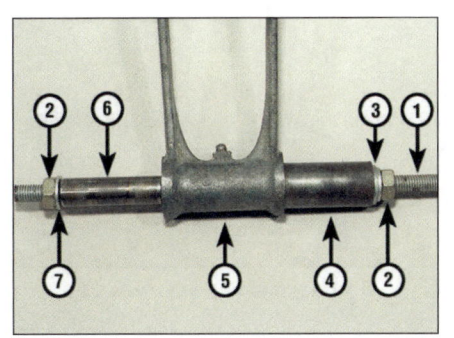

5.9 Drawbolt component parts assembled on a suspension arm

1. Bolt or length of threaded bar
2. Nuts
3. Washer (external diameter greater than tubing internal diameter)
4. Tubing (internal diameter sufficient to accommodate bearing)
5. Suspension arm with bearing
6. Tubing (external diameter slightly smaller than bearing)
7. Washer (external diameter slightly smaller than bearing)

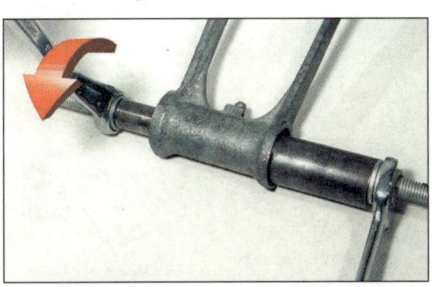

5.10 Drawing the bearing out of the suspension arm

- To extract the bearing/bush you will need a long bolt with nut (or piece of threaded bar with two nuts), a piece of tubing which has an internal diameter larger than the bearing/bush, another piece of tubing which has an external diameter slightly smaller than the bearing/bush, and a selection of washers **(see illustrations 5.9 and 5.10)**. Note that the pieces of tubing must be of the same length, or longer, than the bearing/bush.
- The same kit (without the pieces of tubing) can be used to draw the new bearing/bush back into place **(see illustration 5.11)**.

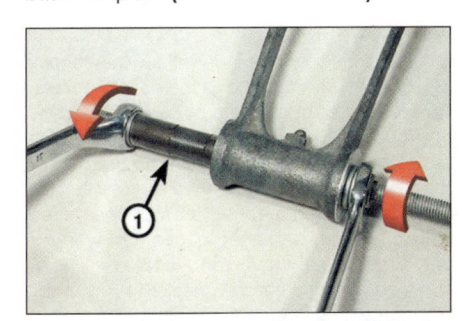

5.11 Installing a new bearing (1) in the suspension arm

Temperature change

- If the bearing's outer race is a tight fit in the casing, the aluminium casing can be heated to release its grip on the bearing. Aluminium will expand at a greater rate than the steel bearing outer race. There are several ways to do this, but avoid any localised extreme heat (such as a blow torch) - aluminium alloy has a low melting point.
- Approved methods of heating a casing are using a domestic oven (heated to 100°C) or immersing the casing in boiling water **(see illustration 5.12)**. Low temperature range localised heat sources such as a paint stripper heat gun or clothes iron can also be used **(see illustration 5.13)**. Alternatively, soak a rag in boiling water, wring it out and wrap it around the bearing housing.

> ⚠ **Warning:** *All of these methods require care in use to prevent scalding and burns to the hands. Wear protective gloves when handling hot components.*

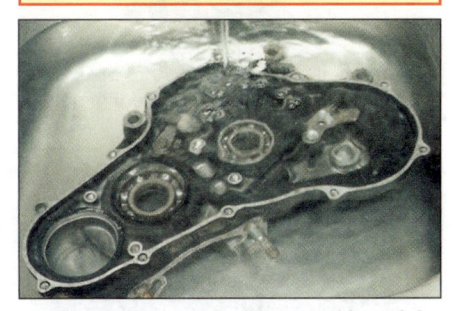

5.12 A casing can be immersed in a sink of boiling water to aid bearing removal

5.13 Using a localised heat source to aid bearing removal

- If heating the whole casing note that plastic components, such as the neutral switch, may suffer - remove them beforehand.
- After heating, remove the bearing as described above. You may find that the expansion is sufficient for the bearing to fall out of the casing under its own weight or with a light tap on the driver or socket.
- If necessary, the casing can be heated to aid bearing installation, and this is sometimes the recommended procedure if the motorcycle manufacturer has designed the housing and bearing fit with this intention.

Tools and Workshop Tips

- Installation of bearings can be eased by placing them in a freezer the night before installation. The steel bearing will contract slightly, allowing easy insertion in its housing. This is often useful when installing steering head outer races in the frame.

Bearing types and markings

- Plain shell bearings, ball bearings, needle roller bearings and tapered roller bearings will all be found on motorcycles (see illustrations 5.14 and 5.15). The ball and roller types are usually caged between an inner and outer race, but uncaged variations may be found.

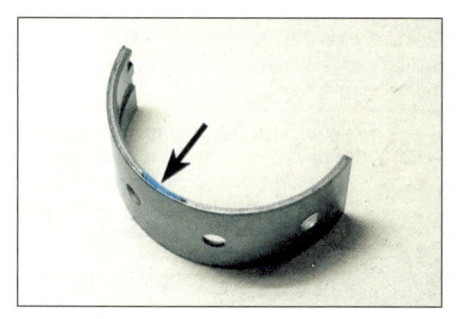

5.16 Typical bearing marking

5.18 Example of ball journal bearing with damaged balls and cages

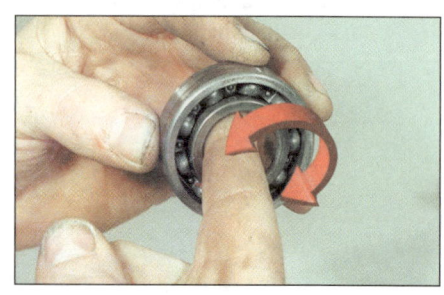

Bearing fault finding

- If a bearing outer race has spun in its housing, the housing material will be damaged. You can use a bearing locking compound to bond the outer race in place if damage is not too severe.
- Shell bearings will fail due to damage of their working surface, as a result of lack of lubrication, corrosion or abrasive particles in the oil (see illustration 5.17). Small particles of dirt in the oil may embed in the bearing material whereas larger particles will score the bearing and shaft journal. If a number of short journeys are made, insufficient heat will be generated to drive off condensation which has built up on the bearings.

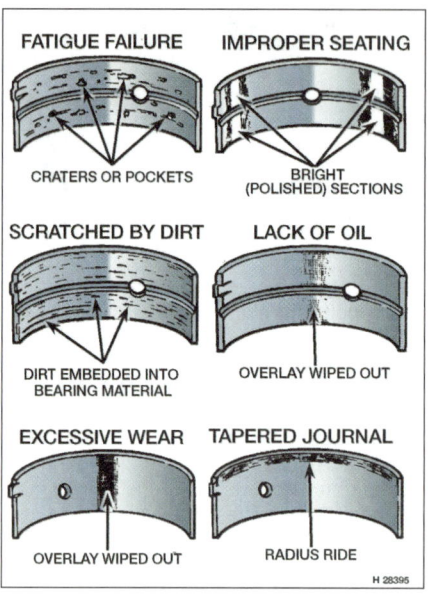

5.14 Shell bearings are either plain or grooved. They are usually identified by colour code (arrow)

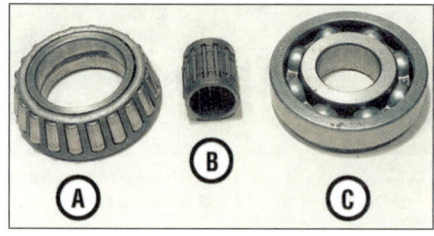

5.19 Hold outer race and listen to inner race when spun

inner race with the other hand (see illustration 5.19). The bearing should be almost silent when spun; if it grates or rattles it is worn.

6 Oil seals

5.15 Tapered roller bearing (A), needle roller bearing (B) and ball journal bearing (C)

5.17 Typical bearing failures

Oil seal removal and installation

- Oil seals should be renewed every time a component is dismantled. This is because the seal lips will become set to the sealing surface and will not necessarily reseal.
- Oil seals can be prised out of position using a large flat-bladed screwdriver (see illustration 6.1). In the case of crankcase seals, check first that the seal is not lipped on the inside, preventing its removal with the crankcases joined.

- Shell bearings (often called inserts) are usually found at the crankshaft main and connecting rod big-end where they are good at coping with high loads. They are made of a phosphor-bronze material and are impregnated with self-lubricating properties.
- Ball bearings and needle roller bearings consist of a steel inner and outer race with the balls or rollers between the races. They require constant lubrication by oil or grease and are good at coping with axial loads. Taper roller bearings consist of rollers set in a tapered cage set on the inner race; the outer race is separate. They are good at coping with axial loads and prevent movement along the shaft - a typical application is in the steering head.
- Bearing manufacturers produce bearings to ISO size standards and stamp one face of the bearing to indicate its internal and external diameter, load capacity and type (see illustration 5.16).
- Metal bushes are usually of phosphor-bronze material. Rubber bushes are used in suspension mounting eyes. Fibre bushes have also been used in suspension pivots.

- Ball and roller bearings will fail due to lack of lubrication or damage to the balls or rollers. Tapered-roller bearings can be damaged by overloading them. Unless the bearing is sealed on both sides, wash it in paraffin (kerosene) to remove all old grease then allow it to dry. Make a visual inspection looking to dented balls or rollers, damaged cages and worn or pitted races (see illustration 5.18).
- A ball bearing can be checked for wear by listening to it when spun. Apply a film of light oil to the bearing and hold it close to the ear - hold the outer race with one hand and spin the

6.1 Prise out oil seals with a large flat-bladed screwdriver

- New seals are usually installed with their marked face (containing the seal reference code) outwards and the spring side towards the fluid being retained. In certain cases, such as a two-stroke engine crankshaft seal, a double lipped seal may be used due to there being fluid or gas on each side of the joint.

Tools and Workshop Tips REF•17

- Use a bearing driver or socket which bears only on the outer hard edge of the seal to install it in the casing - tapping on the inner edge will damage the sealing lip.

Oil seal types and markings

- Oil seals are usually of the single-lipped type. Double-lipped seals are found where a liquid or gas is on both sides of the joint.
- Oil seals can harden and lose their sealing ability if the motorcycle has been in storage for a long period - renewal is the only solution.
- Oil seal manufacturers also conform to the ISO markings for seal size - these are moulded into the outer face of the seal **(see illustration 6.2)**.

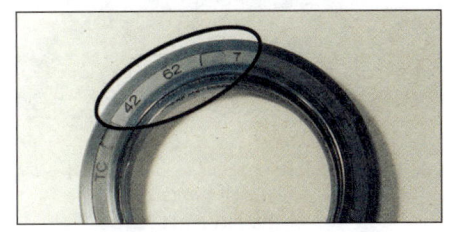

6.2 These oil seal markings indicate inside diameter, outside diameter and seal thickness

7 Gaskets and sealants

Types of gasket and sealant

- Gaskets are used to seal the mating surfaces between components and keep lubricants, fluids, vacuum or pressure contained within the assembly. Aluminium gaskets are sometimes found at the cylinder joints, but most gaskets are paper-based. If the mating surfaces of the components being joined are undamaged the gasket can be installed dry, although a dab of sealant or grease will be useful to hold it in place during assembly.
- RTV (Room Temperature Vulcanising) silicone rubber sealants cure when exposed to moisture in the atmosphere. These sealants are good at filling pits or irregular gasket faces, but will tend to be forced out of the joint under very high torque. They can be used to replace a paper gasket, but first make sure that the width of the paper gasket is not essential to the shimming of internal components. RTV sealants should not be used on components containing petrol (gasoline).
- Non-hardening, semi-hardening and hard setting liquid gasket compounds can be used with a gasket or between a metal-to-metal joint. Select the sealant to suit the application: universal non-hardening sealant can be used on virtually all joints; semi-hardening on joint faces which are rough or damaged; hard setting sealant on joints which require a permanent bond and are subjected to high temperature and pressure. **Note:** *Check first if the paper gasket has a bead of sealant impregnated in its surface before applying additional sealant.*
- When choosing a sealant, make sure it is suitable for the application, particularly if being applied in a high-temperature area or in the vicinity of fuel. Certain manufacturers produce sealants in either clear, silver or black colours to match the finish of the engine. This has a particular application on motorcycles where much of the engine is exposed.
- Do not over-apply sealant. That which is squeezed out on the outside of the joint can be wiped off, whereas an excess of sealant on the inside can break off and clog oilways.

Breaking a sealed joint

- Age, heat, pressure and the use of hard setting sealant can cause two components to stick together so tightly that they are difficult to separate using finger pressure alone. Do not resort to using levers unless there is a pry point provided for this purpose **(see illustration 7.1)** or else the gasket surfaces will be damaged.
- Use a soft-faced hammer **(see illustration 7.2)** or a wood block and conventional hammer to strike the component near the mating surface. Avoid hammering against cast extremities since they may break off. If this method fails, try using a wood wedge between the two components.

Caution: If the joint will not separate, double-check that you have removed all the fasteners.

7.1 If a pry point is provided, apply gently pressure with a flat-bladed screwdriver

7.2 Tap around the joint with a soft-faced mallet if necessary - don't strike cooling fins

Removal of old gasket and sealant

- Paper gaskets will most likely come away complete, leaving only a few traces stuck

HAYNES HINT

Most components have one or two hollow locating dowels between the two gasket faces. If a dowel cannot be removed, do not resort to gripping it with pliers - it will almost certainly be distorted. Install a close-fitting socket or Phillips screwdriver into the dowel and then grip the outer edge of the dowel to free it.

on the sealing faces of the components. It is imperative that all traces are removed to ensure correct sealing of the new gasket.
- Very carefully scrape all traces of gasket away making sure that the sealing surfaces are not gouged or scored by the scraper **(see illustrations 7.3, 7.4 and 7.5)**. Stubborn deposits can be removed by spraying with an aerosol gasket remover. Final preparation of

7.3 Paper gaskets can be scraped off with a gasket scraper tool . . .

7.4 . . . a knife blade . . .

7.5 . . . or a household scraper

REF•18 Tools and Workshop Tips

7.6 Fine abrasive paper is wrapped around a flat file to clean up the gasket face

7.7 A kitchen scourer can be used on stubborn deposits

8.1 Tighten the chain breaker to push the pin out of the link . . .

8.2 . . . withdraw the pin, remove the tool . . .

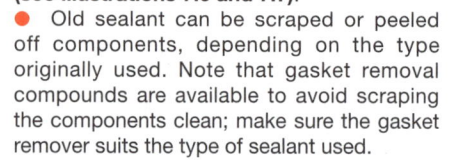

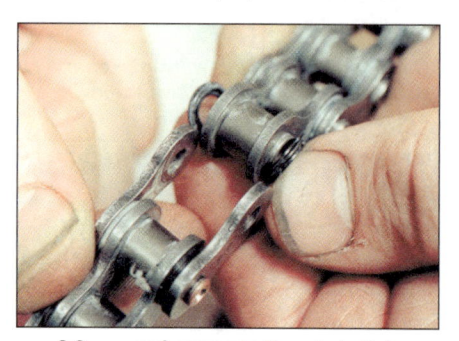

8.3 . . . and separate the chain link

8.4 Insert the new soft link, with O-rings, through the chain ends . . .

8.5 . . . install the O-rings over the pin ends . . .

8.6 . . . followed by the sideplate

8.7 Push the sideplate into position using a clamp

the gasket surface can be made with very fine abrasive paper or a plastic kitchen scourer **(see illustrations 7.6 and 7.7)**.

● Old sealant can be scraped or peeled off components, depending on the type originally used. Note that gasket removal compounds are available to avoid scraping the components clean; make sure the gasket remover suits the type of sealant used.

8 Chains

Breaking and joining final drive chains

● Drive chains for all but small bikes are continuous and do not have a clip-type connecting link. The chain must be broken using a chain breaker tool and the new chain securely riveted together using a new soft rivet-type link. Never use a clip-type connecting link instead of a rivet-type link, except in an emergency. Various chain breaking and riveting tools are available, either as separate tools or combined as illustrated in the accompanying photographs - read the instructions supplied with the tool carefully.

> ⚠ **Warning: The need to rivet the new link pins correctly cannot be overstressed - loss of control of the motorcycle is very likely to result if the chain breaks in use.**

● Rotate the chain and look for the soft link. The soft link pins look like they have been deeply centre-punched instead of peened over like all the other pins **(see illustration 8.9)** and its sideplate may be a different colour. Position the soft link midway between the sprockets and assemble the chain breaker tool over one of the soft link pins **(see illustration 8.1)**. Operate the tool to push the pin out through the chain **(see illustration 8.2)**. On an O-ring chain, remove the O-rings **(see illustration 8.3)**. Carry out the same procedure on the other soft link pin.

> **Caution: Certain soft link pins (particularly on the larger chains) may require their ends to be filed or ground off before they can be pressed out using the tool.**

● Check that you have the correct size and strength (standard or heavy duty) new soft link - do not reuse the old link. Look for the size marking on the chain sideplates **(see illustration 8.10)**.
● Position the chain ends so that they are engaged over the rear sprocket. On an O-ring chain, install a new O-ring over each pin of the link and insert the link through the two chain ends **(see illustration 8.4)**. Install a new O-ring over the end of each pin, followed by the sideplate (with the chain manufacturer's marking facing outwards) **(see illustrations 8.5 and 8.6)**. On an unsealed chain, insert the link through the two chain ends, then install the sideplate with the chain manufacturer's marking facing outwards.

● Note that it may not be possible to install the sideplate using finger pressure alone. If using a joining tool, assemble it so that the plates of the tool clamp the link and press the sideplate over the pins **(see illustration 8.7)**. Otherwise, use two small sockets placed over

Tools and Workshop Tips REF•19

8.8 Assemble the chain riveting tool over one pin at a time and tighten it fully

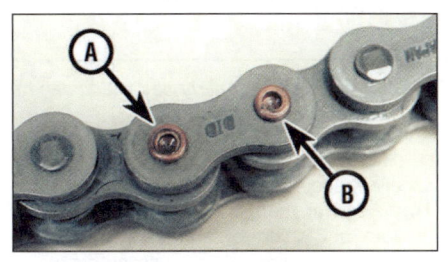

8.9 Pin end correctly riveted (A), pin end unriveted (B)

the rivet ends and two pieces of the wood between a G-clamp. Operate the clamp to press the sideplate over the pins.
● Assemble the joining tool over one pin (following the maker's instructions) and tighten the tool down to spread the pin end securely **(see illustrations 8.8 and 8.9)**. Do the same on the other pin.

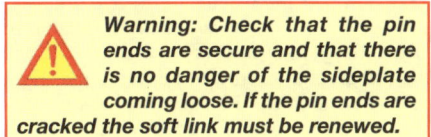

> **Warning:** Check that the pin ends are secure and that there is no danger of the sideplate coming loose. If the pin ends are cracked the soft link must be renewed.

Final drive chain sizing

● Chains are sized using a three digit number, followed by a suffix to denote the chain type **(see illustration 8.10)**. Chain type is either standard or heavy duty (thicker sideplates), and also unsealed or O-ring/X-ring type.
● The first digit of the number relates to the pitch of the chain, ie the distance from the centre of one pin to the centre of the next pin **(see illustration 8.11)**. Pitch is expressed in eighths of an inch, as follows:

8.10 Typical chain size and type marking

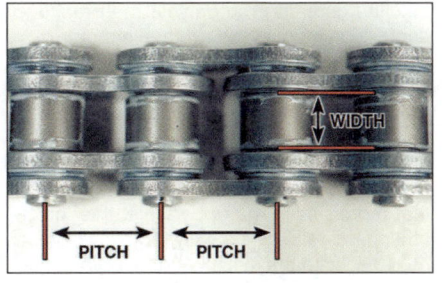

8.11 Chain dimensions

Sizes commencing with a 4 (eg 428) have a pitch of 1/2 inch (12.7 mm)

Sizes commencing with a 5 (eg 520) have a pitch of 5/8 inch (15.9 mm)

Sizes commencing with a 6 (eg 630) have a pitch of 3/4 inch (19.1 mm)

● The second and third digits of the chain size relate to the width of the rollers, again in imperial units, eg the 525 shown has 5/16 inch (7.94 mm) rollers **(see illustration 8.11)**.

9 Hoses

Clamping to prevent flow

● Small-bore flexible hoses can be clamped to prevent fluid flow whilst a component is worked on. Whichever method is used, ensure that the hose material is not permanently distorted or damaged by the clamp.
a) A brake hose clamp available from auto accessory shops **(see illustration 9.1)**.
b) A wingnut type hose clamp **(see illustration 9.2)**.
c) Two sockets placed each side of the hose and held with straight-jawed self-locking grips **(see illustration 9.3)**.
d) Thick card each side of the hose held between straight-jawed self-locking grips **(see illustration 9.4)**.

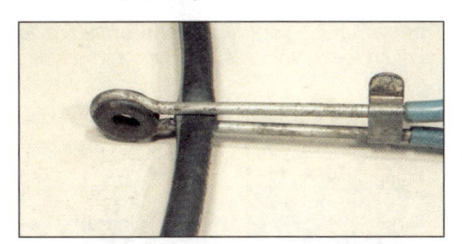

9.1 Hoses can be clamped with an automotive brake hose clamp . . .

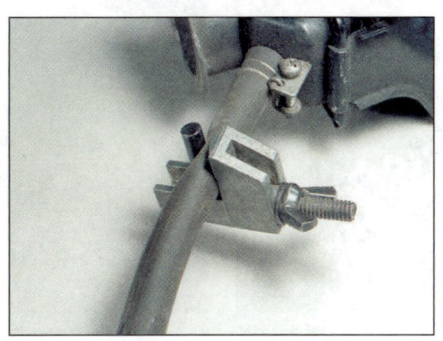

9.2 . . . a wingnut type hose clamp . . .

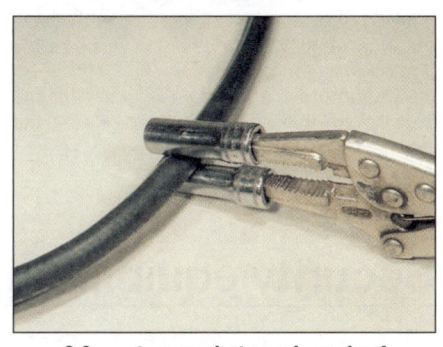

9.3 . . . two sockets and a pair of self-locking grips . . .

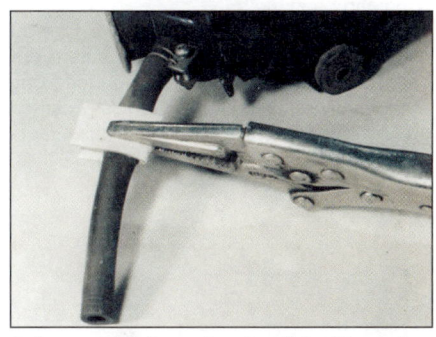

9.4 . . . or thick card and self-locking grips

Freeing and fitting hoses

● Always make sure the hose clamp is moved well clear of the hose end. Grip the hose with your hand and rotate it whilst pulling it off the union. If the hose has hardened due to age and will not move, slit it with a sharp knife and peel its ends off the union **(see illustration 9.5)**.
● Resist the temptation to use grease or soap on the unions to aid installation; although it helps the hose slip over the union it will equally aid the escape of fluid from the joint. It is preferable to soften the hose ends in hot water and wet the inside surface of the hose with water or a fluid which will evaporate.

9.5 Cutting a coolant hose free with a sharp knife

REF•20 Security

Introduction

In less time than it takes to read this introduction, a thief could steal your motorcycle. Returning only to find your bike has gone is one of the worst feelings in the world. Even if the motorcycle is insured against theft, once you've got over the initial shock, you will have the inconvenience of dealing with the police and your insurance company.

The motorcycle is an easy target for the professional thief and the joyrider alike and the official figures on motorcycle theft make for depressing reading; on average a motor-cycle is stolen every 16 minutes in the UK!

Motorcycle thefts fall into two categories, those stolen 'to order' and those taken by opportunists. The thief stealing to order will be on the look out for a specific make and model and will go to extraordinary lengths to obtain that motorcycle. The opportunist thief on the other hand will look for easy targets which can be stolen with the minimum of effort and risk.

Whilst it is never going to be possible to make your machine 100% secure, it is estimated that around half of all stolen motorcycles are taken by opportunist thieves. Remember that the opportunist thief is always on the look out for the easy option: if there are two similar motorcycles parked side-by-side, they will target the one with the lowest level of security. By taking a few precautions, you can reduce the chances of your motorcycle being stolen.

Security equipment

There are many specialised motorcycle security devices available and the following text summarises their applications and their good and bad points.

Once you have decided on the type of security equipment which best suits your needs, we recommended that you read one of the many equipment tests regularly carried out by the motorcycle press. These tests compare the products from all the major manufacturers and give impartial ratings on their effectiveness, value-for-money and ease of use.

No one item of security equipment can provide complete protection. It is highly recommended that two or more of the items described below are combined to increase the security of your motorcycle (a lock and chain plus an alarm system is just about ideal). The more security measures fitted to the bike, the less likely it is to be stolen.

Lock and chain

Pros: *Very flexible to use; can be used to secure the motorcycle to almost any immovable object. On some locks and chains, the lock can be used on its own as a disc lock (see below).*

Cons: *Can be very heavy and awkward to carry on the motorcycle, although some types will be supplied with a carry bag which can be strapped to the pillion seat.*

● Heavy-duty chains and locks are an excellent security measure **(see illustration 1).** Whenever the motorcycle is parked, use the lock and chain to secure the machine to a solid, immovable object such as a post or railings. This will prevent the machine from being ridden away or being lifted into the back of a van.

● When fitting the chain, always ensure the chain is routed around the motorcycle frame or swingarm **(see illustrations 2 and 3).** Never merely pass the chain around one of the wheel rims; a thief may unbolt the wheel and lift the rest of the machine into a van, leaving you with just the wheel! Try to avoid having excess chain free, thus making it difficult to use cutting tools, and keep the chain and lock off the ground to prevent thieves attacking it with a cold chisel. Position the lock so that its lock barrel is facing downwards; this will make it harder for the thief to attack the lock mechanism.

Ensure the lock and chain you buy is of good quality and long enough to shackle your bike to a solid object

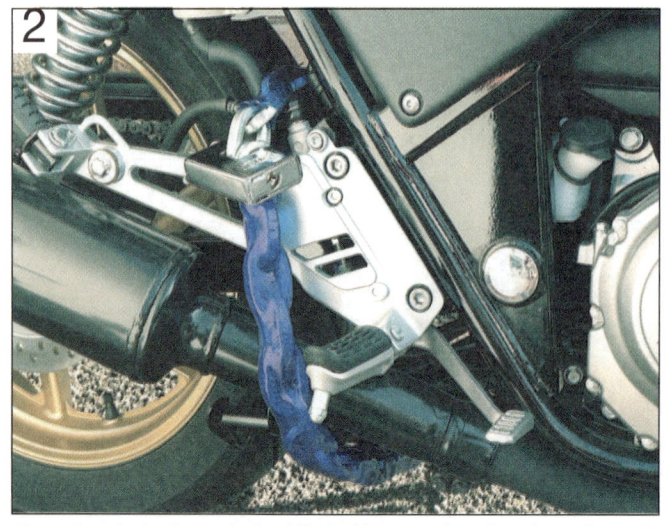

Pass the chain through the bike's frame, rather than just through a wheel . . .

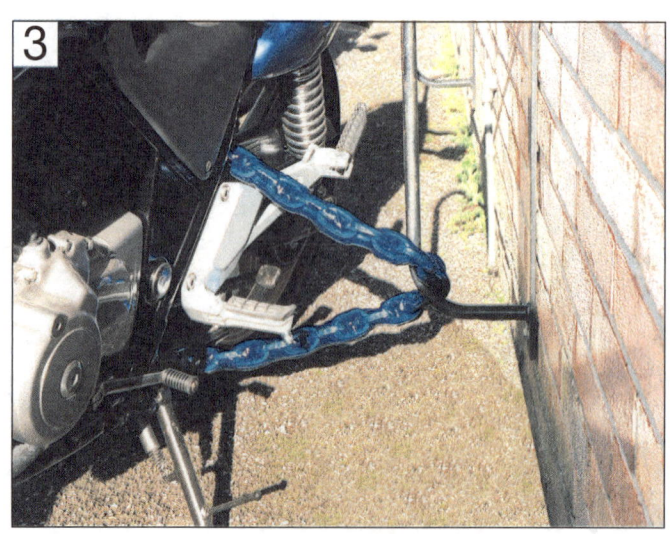

. . . and loop it around a solid object

Security REF•21

U-locks

Pros: *Highly effective deterrent which can be used to secure the bike to a post or railings. Most U-locks come with a carrier which allows the lock to be easily carried on the bike.*

Cons: *Not as flexible to use as a lock and chain.*

- These are solid locks which are similar in use to a lock and chain. U-locks are lighter than a lock and chain but not so flexible to use. The length and shape of the lock shackle limit the objects to which the bike can be secured **(see illustration 4)**.

Disc locks

Pros: *Small, light and very easy to carry; most can be stored underneath the seat.*

Cons: *Does not prevent the motorcycle being lifted into a van. Can be very embarrassing if you forget to remove the lock before attempting to ride off!*

U-locks can be used to secure the bike to a solid object – ensure you purchase one which is long enough

- Disc locks are designed to be attached to the front brake disc. The lock passes through one of the holes in the disc and prevents the wheel rotating by jamming against the fork/brake caliper **(see illustration 5)**. Some are equipped with an alarm siren which sounds if the disc lock is moved; this not only acts as a theft deterrent but also as a handy reminder if you try to move the bike with the lock still fitted.

- Combining the disc lock with a length of cable which can be looped around a post or railings provides an additional measure of security **(see illustration 6)**.

Alarms and immobilisers

Pros: *Once installed it is completely hassle-free to use. If the system is 'Thatcham' or 'Sold Secure-approved', insurance companies may give you a discount.*

Cons: *Can be expensive to buy and complex to install. No system will prevent the motorcycle from being lifted into a van and taken away.*

- Electronic alarms and immobilisers are available to suit a variety of budgets. There are three different types of system available: pure alarms, pure immobilisers, and the more expensive systems which are combined alarm/immobilisers **(see illustration 7)**.

- An alarm system is designed to emit an audible warning if the motorcycle is being tampered with.

- An immobiliser prevents the motorcycle being started and ridden away by disabling its electrical systems.

- When purchasing an alarm/immobiliser system, check the cost of installing the system unless you are able to do it yourself. If the motorcycle is not used regularly, another consideration is the current drain of the system. All alarm/immobiliser systems are powered by the motorcycle's battery; purchasing a system with a very low current drain could prevent the battery losing its charge whilst the motorcycle is not being used.

A typical disc lock attached through one of the holes in the disc

A disc lock combined with a security cable provides additional protection

A typical alarm/immobiliser system

REF•22 Security

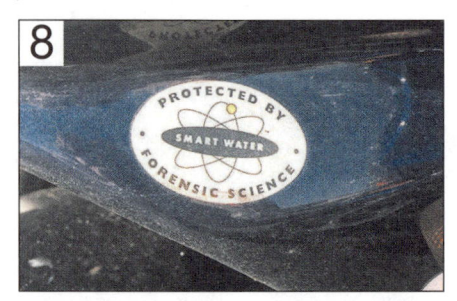

Indelible markings can be applied to most areas of the bike – always apply the manufacturer's sticker to warn off thieves

Chemically-etched code numbers can be applied to main body panels . . .

. . . again, always ensure that the kit manufacturer's sticker is applied in a prominent position

Security marking kits

Pros: *Very cheap and effective deterrent. Many insurance companies will give you a discount on your insurance premium if a recognised security marking kit is used on your motorcycle.*

Cons: *Does not prevent the motorcycle being stolen by joyriders.*

● There are many different types of security marking kits available. The idea is to mark as many parts of the motorcycle as possible with a unique security number **(see illustrations 8, 9 and 10)**. A form will be included with the kit to register your personal details and those of the motorcycle with the kit manufacturer. This register is made available to the police to help them trace the rightful owner of any motorcycle or components which they recover should all other forms of identification have been removed. Always apply the warning stickers provided with the kit to deter thieves.

Ground anchors, wheel clamps and security posts

Pros: *An excellent form of security which will deter all but the most determined of thieves.*

Cons: *Awkward to install and can be expensive.*

● Whilst the motorcycle is at home, it is a good idea to attach it securely to the floor or a solid wall, even if it is kept in a securely locked garage. Various types of ground anchors, security posts and wheel clamps are available for this purpose **(see illustration 11)**. These security devices are either bolted to a solid concrete or brick structure or can be cemented into the ground.

Permanent ground anchors provide an excellent level of security when the bike is at home

Security at home

A high percentage of motorcycle thefts are from the owner's home. Here are some things to consider whenever your motorcycle is at home:
● Where possible, always keep the motorcycle in a securely locked garage. Never rely solely on the standard lock on the garage door, these are usual hopelessly inadequate. Fit an additional locking mechanism to the door and consider having the garage alarmed. A security light, activated by a movement sensor, is also a good investment.
● Always secure the motorcycle to the ground or a wall, even if it is inside a securely locked garage.
● Do not regularly leave the motorcycle outside your home, try to keep it out of sight wherever possible. If a garage is not available, fit a motorcycle cover over the bike to disguise its true identity.
● It is not uncommon for thieves to follow a motorcyclist home to find out where the bike is kept. They will then return at a later date. Be aware of this whenever you are returning home on your motorcycle. If you suspect you are being followed, do not return home, instead ride to a garage or shop and stop as a precaution.
● When selling a motorcycle, do not provide your home address or the location where the bike is normally kept. Arrange to meet the buyer at a location away from your home. Thieves have been known to pose as potential buyers to find out where motorcycles are kept and then return later to steal them.

Security away from the home

As well as fitting security equipment to your motorcycle here are a few general rules to follow whenever you park your motorcycle.
● Park in a busy, public place.
● Use car parks which incorporate security features, such as CCTV.
● At night, park in a well-lit area, preferably directly underneath a street light.
● Engage the steering lock.
● Secure the motorcycle to a solid, immovable object such as a post or railings with an additional lock. If this is not possible, secure the bike to a friend's motorcycle. Some public parking places provide security loops for motorcycles.
● Never leave your helmet or luggage attached to the motorcycle. Take them with you at all times.

Lubricants and fluids

A wide range of lubricants, fluids and cleaning agents is available for motor-cycles. This is a guide as to what is available, its applications and properties.

Four-stroke engine oil

- Engine oil is without doubt the most important component of any four-stroke engine. Modern motorcycle engines place a lot of demands on their oil and choosing the right type is essential. Using an unsuitable oil will lead to an increased rate of engine wear and could result in serious engine damage. Before purchasing oil, always check the recommended oil specification given by the manufacturer. The manufacturer will state a recommended 'type or classification' and also a specific 'viscosity' range for engine oil.
- The oil 'type or classification' is identified by its API (American Petroleum Institute) rating. The API rating will be in the form of two letters, e.g. SG. The S identifies the oil as being suitable for use in a petrol (gasoline) engine (S stands for spark ignition) and the second letter, ranging from A to J, identifies the oil's performance rating. The later this letter, the higher the specification of the oil; for example API SG oil exceeds the requirements of API SF oil. **Note:** *On some oils there may also be a second rating consisting of another two letters, the first letter being C, e.g. API SF/CD. This rating indicates the oil is also suitable for use in a diesel engines (the C stands for compression ignition) and is thus of no relevance for motorcycle use.*
- The 'viscosity' of the oil is identified by its SAE (Society of Automotive Engineers) rating. All modern engines require multigrade oils and the SAE rating will consist of two numbers, the first followed by a W, e.g. 10W/40. The first number indicates the viscosity rating of the oil at low temperatures (W stands for winter – tested at –20°C) and the second number represents the viscosity of the oil at high temperatures (tested at 100°C). The lower the number, the thinner the oil. For example an oil with an SAE 10W/40 rating will give better cold starting and running than an SAE 15W/40 oil.
- As well as ensuring the 'type' and 'viscosity' of the oil match the recommendations, another consideration to make when buying engine oil is whether to purchase a standard mineral-based oil, a semi-synthetic oil (also known as a synthetic blend or synthetic-based oil) or a fully-synthetic oil. Although all oils will have a similar rating and viscosity, their cost will vary considerably; mineral-based oils are the cheapest, the fully-synthetic oils the most expensive with the semi-synthetic oils falling somewhere in-between. This decision is very much up to the owner, but it should be noted that modern synthetic oils have far better lubricating and cleaning qualities than traditional mineral-based oils and tend to retain these properties for far longer. Bearing in mind the operating conditions inside a modern, high-revving motorcycle engine it is highly recommended that a fully synthetic oil is used. The extra expense at each service could save you money in the long term by preventing premature engine wear.
- As a final note always ensure that the oil is specifically designed for use in motorcycle engines. Engine oils designed primarily for use in car engines sometimes contain additives or friction modifiers which could cause clutch slip on a motorcycle fitted with a wet-clutch.

Two-stroke engine oil

- Modern two-stroke engines, with their high power outputs, place high demands on their oil. If engine seizure is to be avoided it is essential that a high-quality oil is used. Two-stroke oils differ hugely from four-stroke oils. The oil lubricates only the crankshaft and piston(s) (the transmission has its own lubricating oil) and is used on a total-loss basis where it is burnt completely during the combustion process.
- The Japanese have recently introduced a classification system for two-stroke oils, the JASO rating. This rating is in the form of two letters, either FA, FB or FC – FA is the lowest classification and FC the highest. Ensure the oil being used meets or exceeds the recommended rating specified by the manufacturer.
- As well as ensuring the oil rating matches the recommendation, another consideration to make when buying engine oil is whether to purchase a standard mineral-based oil, a semi-synthetic oil (also known as a synthetic blend or synthetic-based oil) or a fully-synthetic oil. The cost of each type of oil varies considerably; mineral-based oils are the cheapest, the fully-synthetic oils the most expensive with the semi-synthetic oils falling somewhere in-between. This decision is very much up to the owner, but it should be noted that modern synthetic oils have far better lubricating properties and burn cleaner than traditional mineral-based oils. It is therefore recommended that a fully synthetic oil is used. The extra expense could save you money in the long term by preventing premature engine wear, engine performance will be improved, carbon deposits and exhaust smoke will be reduced.

Lubricants and fluids

- Always ensure that the oil is specifically designed for use in an injector system. Many high quality two-stroke oils are designed for competition use and need to be pre-mixed with fuel. These oils are of a much higher viscosity and are not designed to flow through the injector pumps used on road-going two-stroke motorcycles.

Transmission (gear) oil

- On a two-stroke engine, the transmission and clutch are lubricated by their own separate oil bath which must be changed in accordance with the Maintenance Schedule.
- Although the engine and transmission units of most four-strokes use a common lubrication supply, there are some exceptions where the engine and gearbox have separate oil reservoirs and a dry clutch is used.
- Motorcycle manufacturers will either recommend a monograde transmission oil or a four-stroke multigrade engine oil to lubricate the transmission.
- Transmission oils, or gear oils as they are often called, are designed specifically for use in transmission systems. The viscosity of these oils is represented by an SAE number, but the scale of measurement applied is different to that used to grade engine oils. As a rough guide a SAE90 gear oil will be of the same viscosity as an SAE50 engine oil.

Shaft drive oil

- On models equipped with shaft final drive, the shaft drive gears are will have their own oil supply. The manufacturer will state a recommended 'type or classification' and also a specific 'viscosity' range in the same manner as for four-stroke engine oil.
- Gear oil classification is given by the number which follows the API GL (GL standing for gear lubricant) rating, the higher the number, the higher the specification of the oil, e.g. API GL5 oil is a higher specification than API GL4 oil. Ensure the oil meets or exceeds the classification specified and is of the correct viscosity. The viscosity of gear oils is also represented by an SAE number but the scale of measurement used is different to that used to grade engine oils. As a rough guide an SAE90 gear oil will be of the same viscosity as an SAE50 engine oil.
- If the use of an EP (Extreme Pressure) gear oil is specified, ensure the oil purchased is suitable.

Fork oil and suspension fluid

- Conventional telescopic front forks are hydraulic and require fork oil to work. To ensure the forks function correctly, the fork oil must be changed in accordance with the Maintenance Schedule.
- Fork oil is available in a variety of viscosities, identified by their SAE rating; fork oil ratings vary from light (SAE 5) to heavy (SAE 30). When purchasing fork oil, ensure the viscosity rating matches that specified by the manufacturer.
- Some lubricant manufacturers also produce a range of high-quality suspension fluids which are very similar to fork oil but are designed mainly for competition use. These fluids may have a different viscosity rating system which is not to be confused with the SAE rating of normal fork oil. Refer to the manufacturer's instructions if in any doubt.

Brake and clutch fluid

- All disc brake systems and some clutch systems are hydraulically operated. To ensure correct operation, the hydraulic fluid must be changed in accordance with the Maintenance Schedule.
- Brake and clutch fluid is classified by its DOT rating with most motorcycle manufacturers specifying DOT 3 or 4 fluid. Both fluid types are glycol-based and can be mixed together without adverse effect; DOT 4 fluid exceeds the requirements of DOT 3 fluid. Although it is safe to use DOT 4 fluid in a system designed for use with DOT 3 fluid, never use DOT 3 fluid in a system which specifies the use of DOT 4 as this will adversely affect the system's performance. The type required for the system will be marked on the fluid reservoir cap.
- Some manufacturers also produce a DOT 5 hydraulic fluid. DOT 5 hydraulic fluid is silicone-based and is not compatible with the glycol-based DOT 3 and 4 fluids. Never mix DOT 5 fluid with DOT 3 or 4 fluid as this will seriously affect the performance of the hydraulic system.

Coolant/antifreeze

- When purchasing coolant/antifreeze, always ensure it is suitable for use in an aluminium engine and contains corrosion inhibitors to prevent possible blockages of the internal coolant passages of the system. As a general rule, most coolants are designed to be used neat and should not be diluted whereas antifreeze can be mixed with distilled water to provide a coolant solution of the required strength. Refer to the manufacturer's instructions on the bottle.
- Ensure the coolant is changed in accordance with the Maintenance Schedule.

Chain lube

- Chain lube is an aerosol-type spray lubricant specifically designed for use on motorcycle final drive chains. Chain lube has two functions, to minimise friction between the final drive chain and sprockets and to prevent corrosion of the chain. Regular use of a good-quality chain lube will extend the life of the drive chain and sprockets and thus maximise the power being transmitted from the transmission to the rear wheel.
- When using chain lube, always allow some time for the solvents in the lube to evaporate before riding the motorcycle. This will minimise the amount of lube which will

Lubricants and fluids REF•25

'fling' off from the chain when the motorcycle is used. If the motorcycle is equipped with an 'O-ring' chain, ensure the chain lube is labelled as being suitable for use on 'O-ring' chains.

Degreasers and solvents

● There are many different types of solvents and degreasers available to remove the grime and grease which accumulate around the motorcycle during normal use. Degreasers and solvents are usually available as an aerosol-type spray or as a liquid which you apply with a brush. Always closely follow the manufacturer's instructions and wear eye protection during use. Be aware that many solvents are flammable and may give off noxious fumes; take adequate precautions when using them (see Safety First!).

● For general cleaning, use one of the many solvents or degreasers available from most motorcycle accessory shops. These solvents are usually applied then left for a certain time before being washed off with water.

Brake cleaner is a solvent specifically designed to remove all traces of oil, grease and dust from braking system components. Brake cleaner is designed to evaporate quickly and leaves behind no residue.

Carburettor cleaner is an aerosol-type solvent specifically designed to clear carburettor blockages and break down the hard deposits and gum often found inside carburettors during overhaul.

Contact cleaner is an aerosol-type solvent designed for cleaning electrical components. The cleaner will remove all traces of oil and dirt from components such as switch contacts or fouled spark plugs and then dry, leaving behind no residue.

Gasket remover is an aerosol-type solvent designed for removing stubborn gaskets from engine components during overhaul. Gasket remover will minimise the amount of scraping required to remove the gasket and therefore reduce the risk of damage to the mating surface.

Spray lubricants

● Aerosol-based spray lubricants are widely available and are excellent for lubricating lever pivots and exposed cables and switches. Try to use a lubricant which is of the dry-film type as the fluid evaporates, leaving behind a dry-film of lubricant. Lubricants which leave behind an oily residue will attract dust and dirt which will increase the rate of wear of the cable/lever.

● Most lubricants also act as a moisture dispersant and a penetrating fluid. This means they can also be used to 'dry out' electrical components such as wiring connectors or switches as well as helping to free seized fasteners.

Greases

● Grease is used to lubricate many of the pivot-points. A good-quality multi-purpose grease is suitable for most applications but some manufacturers will specify the use of specialist greases for use on components such as swingarm and suspension linkage bushes. These specialist greases can be purchased from most motorcycle (or car) accessory shops; commonly specified types include molybdenum disulphide grease, lithium-based grease, graphite-based grease, silicone-based grease and high-temperature copper-based grease.

Gasket sealing compounds

● Gasket sealing compounds can be used in conjunction with gaskets, to improve their sealing capabilities, or on their own to seal metal-to-metal joints. Depending on their type, sealing compounds either set hard or stay relatively soft and pliable.

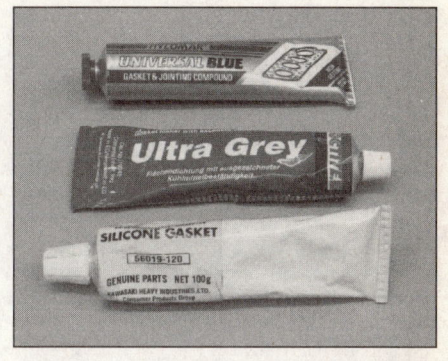

● When purchasing a gasket sealing compound, ensure that it is designed specifically for use on an internal combustion engine. General multi-purpose sealants available from DIY stores may appear visibly similar but they are not designed to withstand the extreme heat or contact with fuel and oil encountered when used on an engine (see 'Tools and Workshop Tips' for further information).

Thread locking compound

● Thread locking compounds are used to secure certain threaded fasteners in position to prevent them from loosening due to vibration. Thread locking compounds can be purchased from most motorcycle (and car) accessory shops. Ensure the threads of the both components are completely clean and dry before sparingly applying the locking compound (see 'Tools and Workshop Tips' for further information).

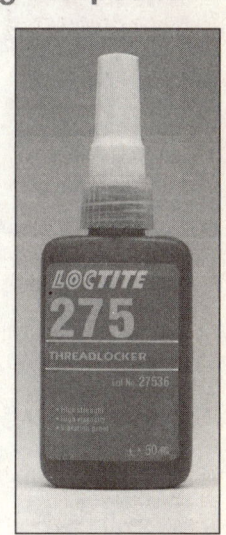

Fuel additives

● Fuel additives which protect and clean the fuel system components are widely available. These additives are designed to remove all traces of deposits that build up on the carburettors/injectors and prevent wear, helping the fuel system to operate more efficiently. If a fuel additive is being used, check that it is suitable for use with your motorcycle, especially if your motorcycle is equipped with a catalytic converter.

● Octane boosters are also available. These additives are designed to improve the performance of highly-tuned engines being run on normal pump-fuel and are of no real use on standard motorcycles.

Conversion factors

Length (distance)
Inches (in)	x 25.4	= Millimetres (mm)	x 0.0394	= Inches (in)
Feet (ft)	x 0.305	= Metres (m)	x 3.281	= Feet (ft)
Miles	x 1.609	= Kilometres (km)	x 0.621	= Miles

Volume (capacity)
Cubic inches (cu in; in^3)	x 16.387	= Cubic centimetres (cc; cm^3)	x 0.061	= Cubic inches (cu in; in^3)
Imperial pints (Imp pt)	x 0.568	= Litres (l)	x 1.76	= Imperial pints (Imp pt)
Imperial quarts (Imp qt)	x 1.137	= Litres (l)	x 0.88	= Imperial quarts (Imp qt)
Imperial quarts (Imp qt)	x 1.201	= US quarts (US qt)	x 0.833	= Imperial quarts (Imp qt)
US quarts (US qt)	x 0.946	= Litres (l)	x 1.057	= US quarts (US qt)
Imperial gallons (Imp gal)	x 4.546	= Litres (l)	x 0.22	= Imperial gallons (Imp gal)
Imperial gallons (Imp gal)	x 1.201	= US gallons (US gal)	x 0.833	= Imperial gallons (Imp gal)
US gallons (US gal)	x 3.785	= Litres (l)	x 0.264	= US gallons (US gal)

Mass (weight)
Ounces (oz)	x 28.35	= Grams (g)	x 0.035	= Ounces (oz)
Pounds (lb)	x 0.454	= Kilograms (kg)	x 2.205	= Pounds (lb)

Force
Ounces-force (ozf; oz)	x 0.278	= Newtons (N)	x 3.6	= Ounces-force (ozf; oz)
Pounds-force (lbf; lb)	x 4.448	= Newtons (N)	x 0.225	= Pounds-force (lbf; lb)
Newtons (N)	x 0.1	= Kilograms-force (kgf; kg)	x 9.81	= Newtons (N)

Pressure
Pounds-force per square inch (psi; lbf/in^2; lb/in^2)	x 0.070	= Kilograms-force per square centimetre (kgf/cm^2; kg/cm^2)	x 14.223	= Pounds-force per square inch (psi; lbf/in^2; lb/in^2)
Pounds-force per square inch (psi; lbf/in^2; lb/in^2)	x 0.068	= Atmospheres (atm)	x 14.696	= Pounds-force per square inch (psi; lbf/in^2; lb/in^2)
Pounds-force per square inch (psi; lbf/in^2; lb/in^2)	x 0.069	= Bars	x 14.5	= Pounds-force per square inch (psi; lbf/in^2; lb/in^2)
Pounds-force per square inch (psi; lbf/in^2; lb/in^2)	x 6.895	= Kilopascals (kPa)	x 0.145	= Pounds-force per square inch (psi; lbf/in^2; lb/in^2)
Kilopascals (kPa)	x 0.01	= Kilograms-force per square centimetre (kgf/cm^2; kg/cm^2)	x 98.1	= Kilopascals (kPa)
Millibar (mbar)	x 100	= Pascals (Pa)	x 0.01	= Millibar (mbar)
Millibar (mbar)	x 0.0145	= Pounds-force per square inch (psi; lbf/in^2; lb/in^2)	x 68.947	= Millibar (mbar)
Millibar (mbar)	x 0.75	= Millimetres of mercury (mmHg)	x 1.333	= Millibar (mbar)
Millibar (mbar)	x 0.401	= Inches of water (inH$_2$O)	x 2.491	= Millibar (mbar)
Millimetres of mercury (mmHg)	x 0.535	= Inches of water (inH$_2$O)	x 1.868	= Millimetres of mercury (mmHg)
Inches of water (inH$_2$O)	x 0.036	= Pounds-force per square inch (psi; lbf/in^2; lb/in^2)	x 27.68	= Inches of water (inH$_2$O)

Torque (moment of force)
Pounds-force inches (lbf in; lb in)	x 1.152	= Kilograms-force centimetre (kgf cm; kg cm)	x 0.868	= Pounds-force inches (lbf in; lb in)
Pounds-force inches (lbf in; lb in)	x 0.113	= Newton metres (Nm)	x 8.85	= Pounds-force inches (lbf in; lb in)
Pounds-force inches (lbf in; lb in)	x 0.083	= Pounds-force feet (lbf ft; lb ft)	x 12	= Pounds-force inches (lbf in; lb in)
Pounds-force feet (lbf ft; lb ft)	x 0.138	= Kilograms-force metres (kgf m; kg m)	x 7.233	= Pounds-force feet (lbf ft; lb ft)
Pounds-force feet (lbf ft; lb ft)	x 1.356	= Newton metres (Nm)	x 0.738	= Pounds-force feet (lbf ft; lb ft)
Newton metres (Nm)	x 0.102	= Kilograms-force metres (kgf m; kg m)	x 9.804	= Newton metres (Nm)

Power
Horsepower (hp)	x 745.7	= Watts (W)	x 0.0013	= Horsepower (hp)

Velocity (speed)
Miles per hour (miles/hr; mph)	x 1.609	= Kilometres per hour (km/hr; kph)	x 0.621	= Miles per hour (miles/hr; mph)

Fuel consumption*
Miles per gallon, Imperial (mpg)	x 0.354	= Kilometres per litre (km/l)	x 2.825	= Miles per gallon, Imperial (mpg)
Miles per gallon, US (mpg)	x 0.425	= Kilometres per litre (km/l)	x 2.352	= Miles per gallon, US (mpg)

Temperature
Degrees Fahrenheit = (°C x 1.8) + 32   Degrees Celsius (Degrees Centigrade; °C) = (°F - 32) x 0.56

It is common practice to convert from miles per gallon (mpg) to litres/100 kilometres (l/100km), where mpg x l/100 km = 282

MOT Test Checks

About the MOT Test

In the UK, all vehicles more than three years old are subject to an annual test to ensure that they meet minimum safety requirements. A current test certificate must be issued before a machine can be used on public roads, and is required before a road fund licence can be issued. Riding without a current test certificate will also invalidate your insurance.

For most owners, the MOT test is an annual cause for anxiety, and this is largely due to owners not being sure what needs to be checked prior to submitting the motorcycle for testing. The simple answer is that a fully roadworthy motorcycle will have no difficulty in passing the test.

This is a guide to getting your motorcycle through the MOT test. Obviously it will not be possible to examine the motorcycle to the same standard as the professional MOT tester, particularly in view of the equipment required for some of the checks. However, working through the following procedures will enable you to identify any problem areas before submitting the motorcycle for the test.

It has only been possible to summarise the test requirements here, based on the regulations in force at the time of printing. Test standards are becoming increasingly stringent, although there are some exemptions for older vehicles. More information about the MOT test can be obtained from the TSO publications, *How Safe is your Motorcycle* and *The MOT Inspection Manual for Motorcycle Testing*.

Many of the checks require that one of the wheels is raised off the ground. If the motorcycle doesn't have a centre stand, note that an auxiliary stand will be required. Additionally, the help of an assistant may prove useful.

Certain exceptions apply to machines under 50 cc, machines without a lighting system, and Classic bikes - if in doubt about any of the requirements listed below seek confirmation from an MOT tester prior to submitting the motorcycle for the test.

Check that the frame number is clearly visible.

Electrical System

Lights, turn signals, horn and reflector

- With the ignition on, check the operation of the following electrical components. **Note:** *The electrical components on certain small-capacity machines are powered by the generator, requiring that the engine is run for this check.*
  a) Headlight and tail light. Check that both illuminate in the low and high beam switch positions.
  b) Position lights. Check that the front position (or sidelight) and tail light illuminate in this switch position.
  c) Turn signals. Check that all flash at the correct rate, and that the warning light(s) function correctly. Check that the turn signal switch works correctly.
  d) Hazard warning system (where fitted). Check that all four turn signals flash in this switch position.
  e) Brake stop light. Check that the light comes on when the front and rear brakes are independently applied. Models first used on or after 1st April 1986 must have a brake light switch on each brake.
  f) Horn. Check that the sound is continuous and of reasonable volume.
- Check that there is a red reflector on the rear of the machine, either mounted separately or as part of the tail light lens.
- Check the condition of the headlight, tail light and turn signal lenses.

Headlight beam height

- The MOT tester will perform a headlight beam height check using specialised beam setting equipment **(see illustration 1)**. This equipment will not be available to the home mechanic, but if you suspect that the headlight is incorrectly set or may have been maladjusted in the past, you can perform a rough test as follows.
- Position the bike in a straight line facing a brick wall. The bike must be off its stand, upright and with a rider seated. Measure the height from the ground to the centre of the headlight and mark a horizontal line on the wall at this height. Position the motorcycle 3.8 metres from the wall and draw a vertical line up the wall central to the centreline of the motorcycle. Switch to dipped beam and check that the beam pattern falls slightly lower than the horizontal line and to the left of the vertical line **(see illustration 2)**.

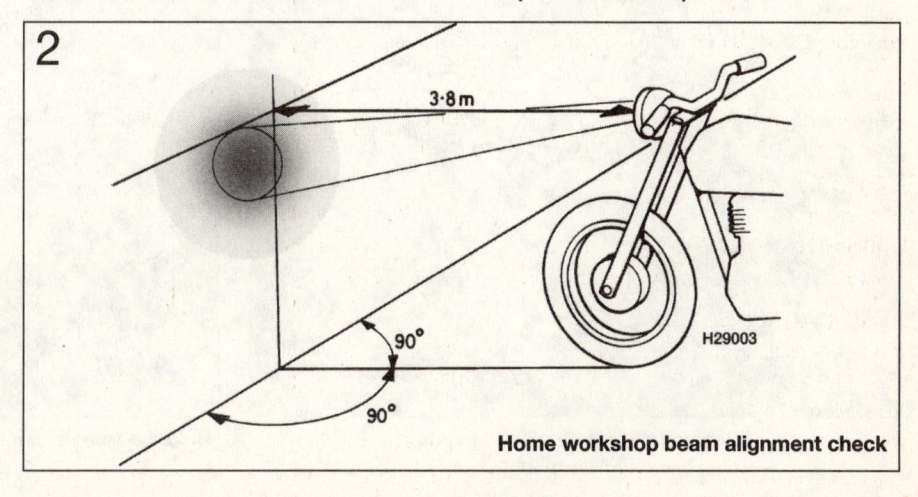

Headlight beam height checking equipment

Home workshop beam alignment check

MOT Test Checks

Exhaust System and Final Drive

Exhaust

● Check that the exhaust mountings are secure and that the system does not foul any of the rear suspension components.
● Start the motorcycle. When the revs are increased, check that the exhaust is neither holed nor leaking from any of its joints. On a linked system, check that the collector box is not leaking due to corrosion.

● Note that the exhaust decibel level ("loudness" of the exhaust) is assessed at the discretion of the tester. If the motorcycle was first used on or after 1st January 1985 the silencer must carry the BSAU 193 stamp, or a marking relating to its make and model, or be of OE (original equipment) manufacture. If the silencer is marked NOT FOR ROAD USE, RACING USE ONLY or similar, it will fail the MOT.

Final drive

● On chain or belt drive machines, check that the chain/belt is in good condition and does not have excessive slack. Also check that the sprocket is securely mounted on the rear wheel hub. Check that the chain/belt guard is in place.
● On shaft drive bikes, check for oil leaking from the drive unit and fouling the rear tyre.

Steering and Suspension

Steering

● With the front wheel raised off the ground, rotate the steering from lock to lock. The handlebar or switches must not contact the fuel tank or be close enough to trap the rider's hand. Problems can be caused by damaged lock stops on the lower yoke and frame, or by the fitting of non-standard handlebars.
● When performing the lock to lock check, also ensure that the steering moves freely without drag or notchiness. Steering movement can be impaired by poorly routed cables, or by overtight head bearings or worn bvearings. The tester will perform a check of the steering head bearing lower race by mounting the front wheel on a surface plate, then performing a lock to lock check with the weight of the machine on the lower bearing (see illustration 3).
● Grasp the fork sliders (lower legs) and attempt to push and pull on the forks

Front wheel mounted on a surface plate for steering head bearing lower race check

(see illustration 4). Any play in the steering head bearings will be felt. Note that in extreme cases, wear of the front fork bushes can be misinterpreted for head bearing play.
● Check that the handlebars are securely mounted.
● Check that the handlebar grip rubbers are secure. They should by bonded to the bar left end and to the throttle cable pulley on the right end.

Front suspension

● With the motorcycle off the stand, hold the front brake on and pump the front forks up and down (see illustration 5). Check that they are adequately damped.

Checking the steering head bearings for freeplay

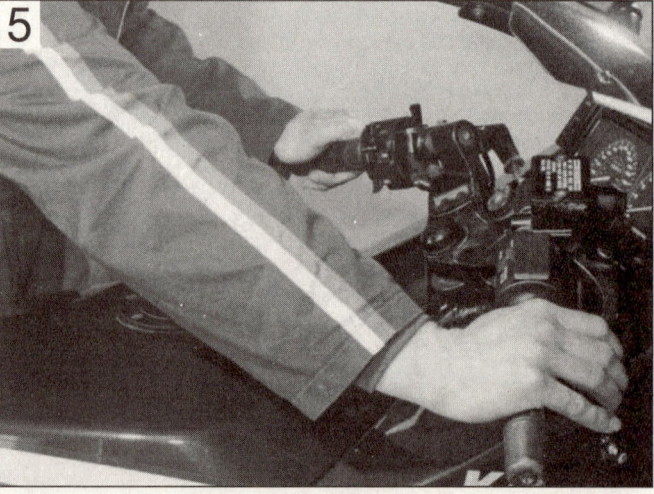

Hold the front brake on and pump the front forks up and down to check operation

MOT Test Checks REF•29

Inspect the area around the fork dust seal for oil leakage (arrow)

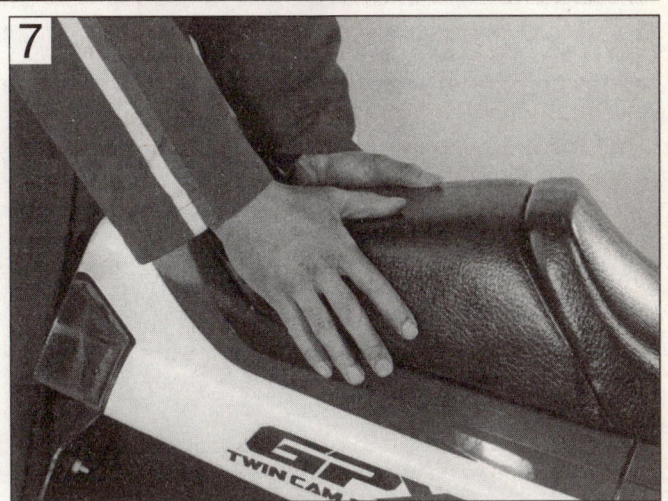

Bounce the rear of the motorcycle to check rear suspension operation

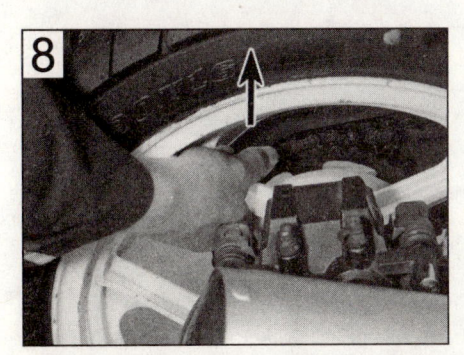

Checking for rear suspension linkage play

● Inspect the area above and around the front fork oil seals **(see illustration 6)**. There should be no sign of oil on the fork tube (stanchion) nor leaking down the slider (lower leg). On models so equipped, check that there is no oil leaking from the anti-dive units.
● On models with swingarm front suspension, check that there is no freeplay in the linkage when moved from side to side.

Rear suspension

● With the motorcycle off the stand and an assistant supporting the motorcycle by its handlebars, bounce the rear suspension **(see illustration 7)**. Check that the suspension components do not foul on any of the cycle parts and check that the shock absorber(s) provide adequate damping.
● Visually inspect the shock absorber(s) and check that there is no sign of oil leakage from its damper. This is somewhat restricted on certain single shock models due to the location of the shock absorber.
● With the rear wheel raised off the ground, grasp the wheel at the highest point and attempt to pull it up **(see illustration 8)**. Any play in the swingarm pivot or suspension linkage bearings will be felt as movement. **Note:** *Do not confuse play with actual suspension movement.* Failure to lubricate suspension linkage bearings can lead to bearing failure **(see illustration 9)**.
● With the rear wheel raised off the ground, grasp the swingarm ends and attempt to move the swingarm from side to side and forwards and backwards - any play indicates wear of the swingarm pivot bearings **(see illustration 10)**.

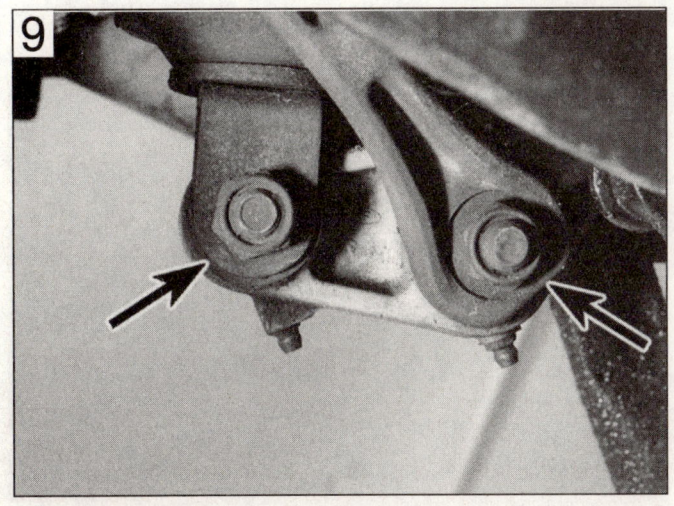

Worn suspension linkage pivots (arrows) are usually the cause of play in the rear suspension

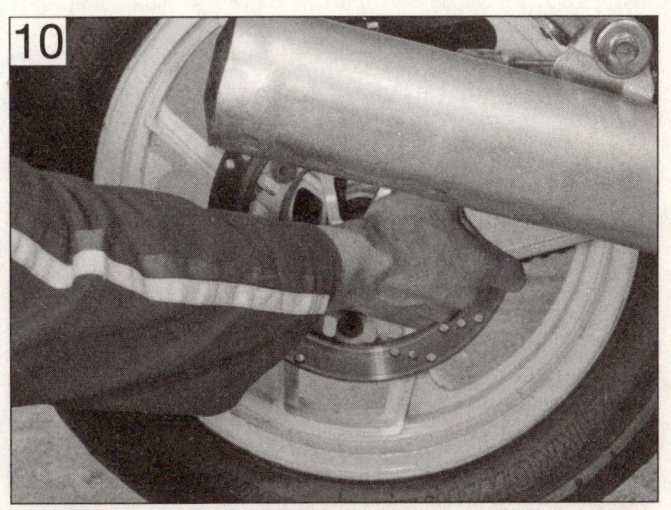

Grasp the swingarm at the ends to check for play in its pivot bearings

REF•30 MOT Test Checks

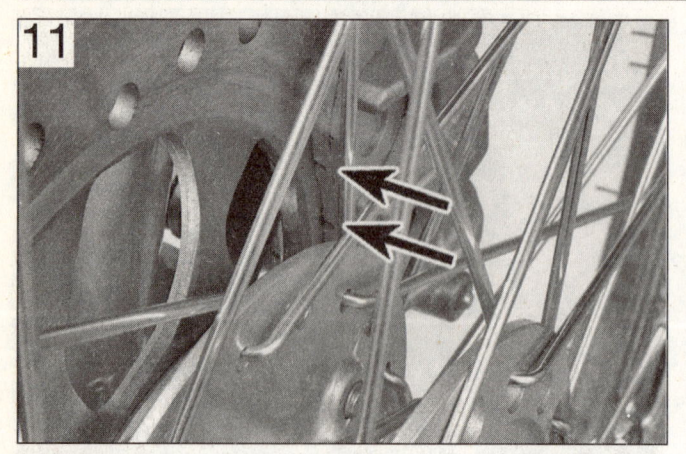

Brake pad wear can usually be viewed without removing the caliper. Most pads have wear indicator grooves (arrowed) and some also have indicator tangs or cut-outs.

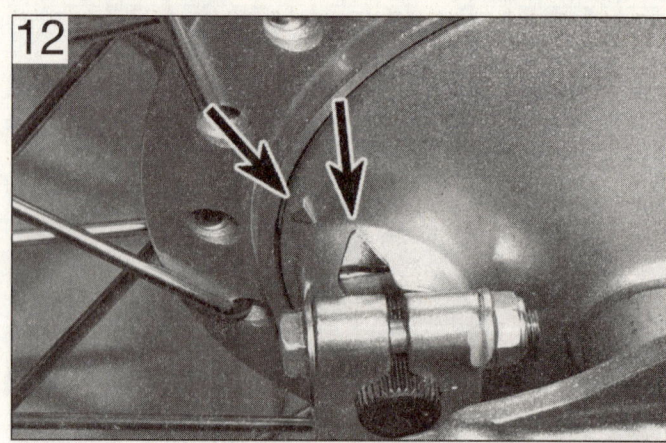

On drum brakes, check the angle of the operating lever with the brake fully applied. Most drum brakes have a wear indicator pointer or scale.

Brakes, Wheels and Tyres

Brakes

- With the wheel raised off the ground, apply the brake then free it off, and check that the wheel is about to revolve freely without brake drag.
- On disc brakes, examine the disc itself. Check that it is securely mounted and not cracked.
- On disc brakes, view the pad material through the caliper mouth and check that the pads are not worn down beyond the limit **(see illustration 11)**.
- On drum brakes, check that when the brake is applied the angle between the operating lever and cable or rod is not too great **(see illustration 12)**. Check also that the operating lever doesn't foul any other components.
- On disc brakes, examine the flexible hoses from top to bottom. Have an assistant hold the brake on so that the fluid in the hose is under pressure, and check that there is no sign of fluid leakage, bulges or cracking. If there are any metal brake pipes or unions, check that these are free from corrosion and damage. Where a brake-linked anti-dive system is fitted, check the hoses to the anti-dive in a similar manner.
- Check that the rear brake torque arm is secure and that its fasteners are secured by self-locking nuts or castellated nuts with split-pins or R-pins **(see illustration 13)**.
- On models with ABS, check that the self-check warning light in the instrument panel works.
- The MOT tester will perform a test of the motorcycle's braking efficiency based on a calculation of rider and motorcycle weight. Although this cannot be carried out at home, you can at least ensure that the braking systems are properly maintained. For hydraulic disc brakes, check the fluid level, lever/pedal feel (bleed of air if its spongy) and pad material. For drum brakes, check adjustment, cable or rod operation and shoe lining thickness.

Wheels and tyres

- Check the wheel condition. Cast wheels should be free from cracks and if of the built-up design, all fasteners should be secure. Spoked wheels should be checked for broken, corroded, loose or bent spokes.
- With the wheel raised off the ground, spin the wheel and visually check that the tyre and wheel run true. Check that the tyre does not foul the suspension or mudguards.
- With the wheel raised off the ground, grasp the wheel and attempt to move it about the axle (spindle) **(see illustration 14)**. Any play felt here indicates wheel bearing failure.

Brake torque arm must be properly secured at both ends

Check for wheel bearing play by trying to move the wheel about the axle (spindle)

MOT Test Checks REF•31

Checking the tyre tread depth

Tyre direction of rotation arrow can be found on tyre sidewall

Castellated type wheel axle (spindle) nut must be secured by a split pin or R-pin

Two straightedges are used to check wheel alignment

- Check the tyre tread depth, tread condition and sidewall condition **(see illustration 15)**.
- Check the tyre type. Front and rear tyre types must be compatible and be suitable for road use. Tyres marked NOT FOR ROAD USE, COMPETITION USE ONLY or similar, will fail the MOT.
- If the tyre sidewall carries a direction of rotation arrow, this must be pointing in the direction of normal wheel rotation **(see illustration 16)**.
- Check that the wheel axle (spindle) nuts (where applicable) are properly secured. A self-locking nut or castellated nut with a split-pin or R-pin can be used **(see illustration 17)**.
- Wheel alignment is checked with the motorcycle off the stand and a rider seated. With the front wheel pointing straight ahead, two perfectly straight lengths of metal or wood and placed against the sidewalls of both tyres **(see illustration 18)**. The gap each side of the front tyre must be equidistant on both sides. Incorrect wheel alignment may be due to a cocked rear wheel (often as the result of poor chain adjustment) or in extreme cases, a bent frame.

General checks and condition

- Check the security of all major fasteners, bodypanels, seat, fairings (where fitted) and mudguards.
- Check that the rider and pillion footrests, handlebar levers and brake pedal are securely mounted.
- Check for corrosion on the frame or any load-bearing components. If severe, this may affect the structure, particularly under stress.

Sidecars

A motorcycle fitted with a sidecar requires additional checks relating to the stability of the machine and security of attachment and swivel joints, plus specific wheel alignment (toe-in) requirements. Additionally, tyre and lighting requirements differ from conventional motorcycle use. Owners are advised to check MOT test requirements with an official test centre.

REF•32 Storage

Preparing for storage

Before you start

If repairs or an overhaul is needed, see that this is carried out now rather than left until you want to ride the bike again.

Give the bike a good wash and scrub all dirt from its underside. Make sure the bike dries completely before preparing for storage.

Engine

● Remove the spark plug(s) and lubricate the cylinder bores with approximately a teaspoon of motor oil using a spout-type oil can (**see illustration 1**). Reinstall the spark plug(s). Crank the engine over a couple of times to coat the piston rings and bores with oil. If the bike has a kickstart, use this to turn the engine over. If not, flick the kill switch to the OFF position and crank the engine over on the starter (**see illustration 2**). If the nature on the ignition system prevents the starter operating with the kill switch in the OFF position, remove the spark plugs and fit them back in their caps; ensure that the plugs are earthed (grounded) against the cylinder head when the starter is operated (**see illustration 3**).

Warning: It is important that the plugs are earthed (grounded) away from the spark plug holes otherwise there is a risk of atomised fuel from the cylinders igniting.

HAYNES HiNT *On a single cylinder four-stroke engine, you can seal the combustion chamber completely by positioning the piston at TDC on the compression stroke.*

● Drain the carburettor(s) otherwise there is a risk of jets becoming blocked by gum deposits from the fuel (**see illustration 4**).

● If the bike is going into long-term storage, consider adding a fuel stabiliser to the fuel in the tank. If the tank is drained completely, corrosion of its internal surfaces may occur if left unprotected for a long period. The tank can be treated with a rust preventative especially for this purpose. Alternatively, remove the tank and pour half a litre of motor oil into it, install the filler cap and shake the tank to coat its internals with oil before draining off the excess. The same effect can also be achieved by spraying WD40 or a similar water-dispersant around the inside of the tank via its flexible nozzle.

● Make sure the cooling system contains the correct mix of antifreeze. Antifreeze also contains important corrosion inhibitors.

● The air intakes and exhaust can be sealed off by covering or plugging the openings. Ensure that you do not seal in any condensation; run the engine until it is hot,

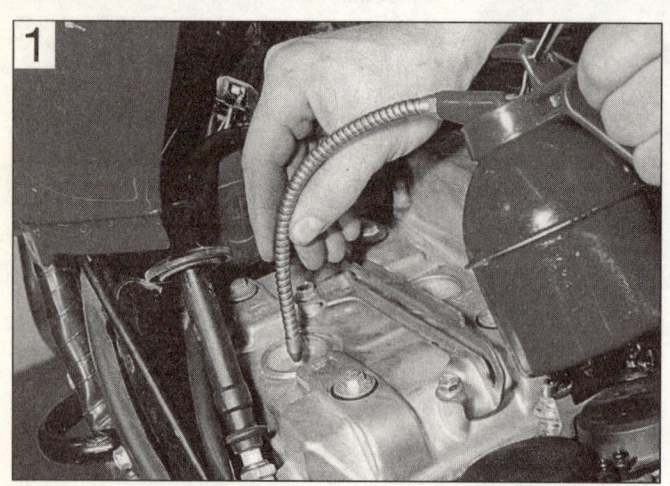

1 Squirt a drop of motor oil into each cylinder

2 Flick the kill switch to OFF . . .

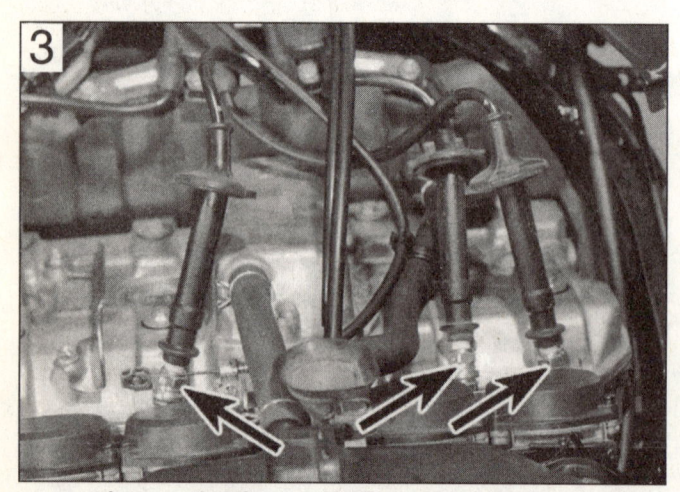

3 . . . and ensure that the metal bodies of the plugs (arrows) are earthed against the cylinder head

4 Connect a hose to the carburettor float chamber drain stub (arrow) and unscrew the drain screw

Storage REF•33

Exhausts can be sealed off with a plastic bag

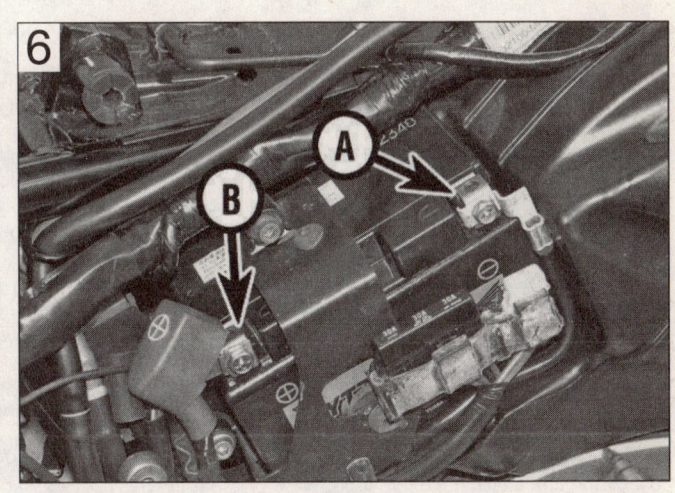

Disconnect the negative lead (A) first, followed by the positive lead (B)

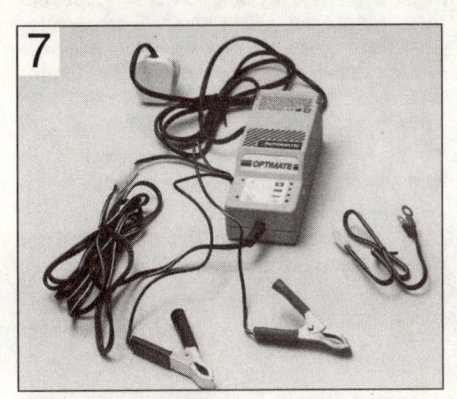

Use a suitable battery charger - this kit also assess battery condition

then switch off and allow to cool. Tape a piece of thick plastic over the silencer end(s) **(see illustration 5)**. Note that some advocate pouring a tablespoon of motor oil into the silencer(s) before sealing them off.

Battery
● Remove it from the bike - in extreme cases of cold the battery may freeze and crack its case **(see illustration 6)**.
● Check the electrolyte level and top up if necessary (conventional refillable batteries). Clean the terminals.
● Store the battery off the motorcycle and away from any sources of fire. Position a wooden block under the battery if it is to sit on the ground.
● Give the battery a trickle charge for a few hours every month **(see illustration 7)**.

Tyres
● Place the bike on its centrestand or an auxiliary stand which will support the motorcycle in an upright position. Position wood blocks under the tyres to keep them off the ground and to provide insulation from damp. If the bike is being put into long-term storage, ideally both tyres should be off the ground; not only will this protect the tyres, but will also ensure that no load is placed on the steering head or wheel bearings.
● Deflate each tyre by 5 to 10 psi, no more or the beads may unseat from the rim, making subsequent inflation difficult on tubeless tyres.

Pivots and controls
● Lubricate all lever, pedal, stand and footrest pivot points. If grease nipples are fitted to the rear suspension components, apply lubricant to the pivots.
● Lubricate all control cables.

Cycle components
● Apply a wax protectant to all painted and plastic components. Wipe off any excess, but don't polish to a shine. Where fitted, clean the screen with soap and water.
● Coat metal parts with Vaseline (petroleum jelly). When applying this to the fork tubes, do not compress the forks otherwise the seals will rot from contact with the Vaseline.
● Apply a vinyl cleaner to the seat.

Storage conditions
● Aim to store the bike in a shed or garage which does not leak and is free from damp.
● Drape an old blanket or bedspread over the bike to protect it from dust and direct contact with sunlight (which will fade paint). This also hides the bike from prying eyes. Beware of tight-fitting plastic covers which may allow condensation to form and settle on the bike.

Getting back on the road

Engine and transmission
● Change the oil and replace the oil filter. If this was done prior to storage, check that the oil hasn't emulsified - a thick whitish substance which occurs through condensation.
● Remove the spark plugs. Using a spout-type oil can, squirt a few drops of oil into the cylinder(s). This will provide initial lubrication as the piston rings and bores comes back into contact. Service the spark plugs, or fit new ones, and install them in the engine.
● Check that the clutch isn't stuck on. The plates can stick together if left standing for some time, preventing clutch operation. Engage a gear and try rocking the bike back and forth with the clutch lever held against the handlebar. If this doesn't work on cable-operated clutches, hold the clutch lever back against the handlebar with a strong elastic band or cable tie for a couple of hours **(see illustration 8)**.
● If the air intakes or silencer end(s) were blocked off, remove the bung or cover used.
● If the fuel tank was coated with a rust

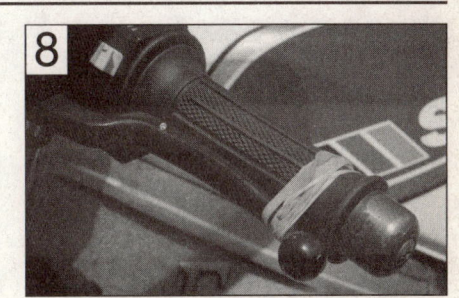

Hold clutch lever back against the handlebar with elastic bands or a cable tie

Storage

preventative, oil or a stabiliser added to the fuel, drain and flush the tank and dispose of the fuel sensibly. If no action was taken with the fuel tank prior to storage, it is advised that the old fuel is disposed of since it will go off over a period of time. Refill the fuel tank with fresh fuel.

Frame and running gear

- Oil all pivot points and cables.
- Check the tyre pressures. They will definitely need inflating if pressures were reduced for storage.
- Lubricate the final drive chain (where applicable).
- Remove any protective coating applied to the fork tubes (stanchions) since this may well destroy the fork seals. If the fork tubes weren't protected and have picked up rust spots, remove them with very fine abrasive paper and refinish with metal polish.
- Check that both brakes operate correctly. Apply each brake hard and check that it's not possible to move the motorcycle forwards, then check that the brake frees off again once released. Brake caliper pistons can stick due to corrosion around the piston head, or on the sliding caliper types, due to corrosion of the slider pins. If the brake doesn't free after repeated operation, take the caliper off for examination. Similarly drum brakes can stick due to a seized operating cam, cable or rod linkage.
- If the motorcycle has been in long-term storage, renew the brake fluid and clutch fluid (where applicable).
- Depending on where the bike has been stored, the wiring, cables and hoses may have been nibbled by rodents. Make a visual check and investigate disturbed wiring loom tape.

Battery

- If the battery has been previously removal and given top up charges it can simply be reconnected. Remember to connect the positive cable first and the negative cable last.
- On conventional refillable batteries, if the battery has not received any attention, remove it from the motorcycle and check its electrolyte level. Top up if necessary then charge the battery. If the battery fails to hold a charge and a visual checks show heavy white sulphation of the plates, the battery is probably defective and must be renewed. This is particularly likely if the battery is old. Confirm battery condition with a specific gravity check.
- On sealed (MF) batteries, if the battery has not received any attention, remove it from the motorcycle and charge it according to the information on the battery case - if the battery fails to hold a charge it must be renewed.

Starting procedure

- If a kickstart is fitted, turn the engine over a couple of times with the ignition OFF to distribute oil around the engine. If no kickstart is fitted, flick the engine kill switch OFF and the ignition ON and crank the engine over a couple of times to work oil around the upper cylinder components. If the nature of the ignition system is such that the starter won't work with the kill switch OFF, remove the spark plugs, fit them back into their caps and earth (ground) their bodies on the cylinder head. Reinstall the spark plugs afterwards.
- Switch the kill switch to RUN, operate the choke and start the engine. If the engine won't start don't continue cranking the engine - not only will this flatten the battery, but the starter motor will overheat. Switch the ignition off and try again later. If the engine refuses to start, go through the fault finding procedures in this manual. **Note:** *If the bike has been in storage for a long time, old fuel or a carburettor blockage may be the problem. Gum deposits in carburettors can block jets - if a carburettor cleaner doesn't prove successful the carburettors must be dismantled for cleaning.*
- Once the engine has started, check that the lights, turn signals and horn work properly.
- Treat the bike gently for the first ride and check all fluid levels on completion. Settle the bike back into the maintenance schedule.

Fault Finding REF•35

This Section provides an easy reference-guide to the more common faults that are likely to afflict your machine. Obviously, the opportunities are almost limitless for faults to occur as a result of obscure failures, and to try and cover all eventualities would require a book. Indeed, a number have been written on the subject.

Successful troubleshooting is not a mysterious 'black art' but the application of a bit of knowledge combined with a systematic and logical approach to the problem. Approach any troubleshooting by first accurately identifying the symptom and then checking through the list of possible causes, starting with the simplest or most obvious and progressing in stages to the most complex.

Take nothing for granted, but above all apply liberal quantities of common sense.

The main symptom of a fault is given in the text as a major heading below which are listed the various systems or areas which may contain the fault. Details of each possible cause for a fault and the remedial action to be taken are given, in brief, in the paragraphs below each heading. Further information should be sought in the relevant Chapter.

1 Engine doesn't start or is difficult to start
- [ ] Starter motor doesn't rotate
- [ ] Starter motor rotates but engine does not turn over
- [ ] Starter works but engine won't turn over (seized)
- [ ] No fuel flow
- [ ] Engine flooded
- [ ] No spark or weak spark
- [ ] Compression low
- [ ] Stalls after starting
- [ ] Rough idle

2 Poor running at low speed
- [ ] Spark weak
- [ ] Fuel/air mixture incorrect
- [ ] Compression low
- [ ] Poor acceleration

3 Poor running or no power at high speed
- [ ] Firing incorrect
- [ ] Fuel/air mixture incorrect
- [ ] Compression low
- [ ] Knocking or pinking
- [ ] Miscellaneous causes

4 Overheating
- [ ] Engine overheats
- [ ] Firing incorrect
- [ ] Fuel/air mixture incorrect
- [ ] Compression too high
- [ ] Engine load excessive
- [ ] Lubrication inadequate
- [ ] Miscellaneous causes

5 Clutch problems
- [ ] Clutch slipping
- [ ] Clutch not disengaging completely

6 Gearchanging problems
- [ ] Doesn't go into gear, or lever doesn't return
- [ ] Jumps out of gear
- [ ] Overselects

7 Abnormal engine noise
- [ ] Knocking or pinking
- [ ] Piston slap or rattling
- [ ] Valve noise
- [ ] Other noise

8 Abnormal driveline noise
- [ ] Clutch noise
- [ ] Transmission noise
- [ ] Final drive noise

9 Abnormal frame and suspension noise
- [ ] Front end noise
- [ ] Shock absorber noise
- [ ] Brake noise

10 Oil pressure warning light comes on
- [ ] Engine lubrication system
- [ ] Electrical system

11 Excessive exhaust smoke
- [ ] White smoke
- [ ] Black smoke
- [ ] Brown smoke

12 Poor handling or stability
- [ ] Handlebar hard to turn
- [ ] Handlebar shakes or vibrates excessively
- [ ] Handlebar pulls to one side
- [ ] Poor shock absorbing qualities

13 Braking problems
- [ ] Brakes are spongy, don't hold
- [ ] Brake lever or pedal pulsates
- [ ] Brakes drag

14 Electrical problems
- [ ] Battery dead or weak
- [ ] Battery overcharged

REF•36 Fault Finding

1 Engine doesn't start or is difficult to start

Starter motor doesn't rotate

- ☐ Engine kill switch OFF.
- ☐ Fuse blown. Check main fuse and FI/ignition fuse (Chapter 8).
- ☐ Battery voltage low. Check and recharge battery (Chapter 8).
- ☐ Starter motor defective. Make sure the wiring to the starter is secure. Make sure the starter relay clicks when the start button is pushed. If the relay clicks, then the fault is in the wiring or motor (Chapter 8).
- ☐ Starter switch not contacting. The contacts could be wet, corroded or dirty. Disassemble and clean the switch (Chapter 8).
- ☐ Wiring open or shorted. Check all wiring connections and harnesses to make sure that they are dry, tight and not corroded. Also check for broken or frayed wires that can cause a short to earth (ground) (see *Wiring diagrams*, Chapter 8).
- ☐ Ignition switch defective. Check the switch and replace with a new one if it is defective (Chapter 8).
- ☐ Engine kill switch defective. Check for wet, dirty or corroded contacts. Clean or replace the switch with a new one as necessary (Chapter 8).
- ☐ Faulty neutral switch, sidestand switch or clutch switch. Check the wiring to each switch and the switch itself (Chapter 8).
- ☐ Faulty diode (Chapter 8).
- ☐ Fuel injection system shutdown due to system fault (Chapter 4).

Starter motor rotates but engine does not turn over

- ☐ Starter clutch defective. Inspect and repair or replace with a new one (Chapter 2).
- ☐ Damaged idler or starter gears. Inspect and replace the damaged parts (Chapter 2).

Starter works but engine won't turn over (seized)

- ☐ Seized engine caused by one or more internally damaged components. Failure due to wear, abuse or lack of lubrication. Damage can include seized valves, followers, camshafts, pistons, crankshaft, connecting rod bearings, or transmission gears or bearings. Refer to Chapter 2 for engine disassembly.

No fuel flow

- ☐ No fuel in tank.
- ☐ Fuel tank breather hose obstructed.
- ☐ Faulty fuel cut-off relay. Check the relay (Chapter 4).
- ☐ Fuel pump faulty or blocked (Chapter 4).
- ☐ Fuel hose clogged. Remove the fuel hose and carefully blow through it.
- ☐ Fuel rail or injector clogged. For all of the injectors to be clogged, either a very bad batch of fuel with an unusual additive has been used, or some other foreign material has entered the tank. In some cases, if a machine has been unused for several months, the fuel turns to a varnish-like liquid which can cause an injector needle to stick to its seat. Drain the tank and fuel system (Chapter 4).

Engine flooded

- ☐ Injector needle valve worn or stuck open causing excess fuel to be admitted to the throttle body. In this case, the injectors should be renewed.
- ☐ Starting technique incorrect. Under normal circumstances (i.e. if all the components of the fuel injection system are good) the machine should start with the throttle closed.

No spark or weak spark

- ☐ Ignition switch OFF.
- ☐ Engine kill switch turned to the OFF position.
- ☐ Ignition or kill switch shorted. This is usually caused by water, corrosion, damage or excessive wear. The switches can be disassembled and cleaned with electrical contact cleaner. If cleaning does not help, replace the switches (Chapter 8).
- ☐ Battery voltage low. Check and recharge the battery as necessary (Chapter 8).
- ☐ Spark plug caps not making good contact. Make sure that the caps fit snugly over the plug ends.
- ☐ Spark plugs dirty, defective or worn out. Locate reason for fouled plugs using spark plug condition chart on the inside back cover and follow the plug maintenance procedures (Chapter 1).
- ☐ Incorrect spark plugs. Wrong type or heat range. Check and install correct plugs (Chapter 1).
- ☐ Ignition coil or spark plug cap defective. Test and renew if necessary (Chapter 4).
- ☐ Fuel injection system shutdown due to system fault (Chapter 4).
- ☐ Crankshaft position (CKP) sensor defective (Chapter 4).
- ☐ Faulty engine stop relay or lean angle sensor (Chapter 4).
- ☐ Engine control module (ECM) defective (Chapter 4).
- ☐ Wiring shorted or broken between:
    a) Ignition switch and engine kill switch (or blown fuse)
    b) ECM and engine kill switch
    c) ECM and ignition coils
    d) ECM and CKP sensor
- ☐ Make sure that all wiring connections are clean, dry and tight. Look for chafed and broken wires (Chapters 4 and 8).

Fault Finding

1 Engine doesn't start or is difficult to start (continued)

Compression low

- [ ] Spark plugs loose. Remove the plugs and inspect their threads. Reinstall and tighten securely (Chapter 1).
- [ ] Cylinder head not sufficiently tightened down. If the cylinder head is suspected of being loose, then there's a chance that the gasket or head is damaged if the problem has persisted for any length of time. The head bolts should be tightened to the proper torque and in the correct sequence (Chapter 2).
- [ ] Improper valve clearance. This means that the valve is not closing completely and compression pressure is leaking past the valve. Check and adjust the valve clearances (Chapter 1).
- [ ] Cylinder and/or piston worn. Excessive wear will cause compression pressure to leak past the rings. This is usually accompanied by worn rings as well. A top-end overhaul is necessary (Chapter 2).
- [ ] Piston rings worn, weak, broken, or sticking. Broken or sticking piston rings usually indicate a lubrication or fuelling problem that causes excess carbon deposits to form on the pistons and rings. Top-end overhaul is necessary (Chapter 2).
- [ ] Piston ring-to-groove clearance excessive. This is caused by excessive wear of the piston ring lands. Piston renewal is necessary (Chapter 2).
- [ ] Cylinder head gasket damaged. If a head is allowed to become loose, or if excessive carbon build-up on the piston crown and combustion chamber causes extremely high compression, the head gasket may leak. Retorquing the head is not always sufficient to restore the seal, so a new gasket is necessary (Chapter 2).
- [ ] Cylinder head warped. This is caused by overheating or improperly tightened head bolts. Machine shop resurfacing or head renewal is necessary (Chapter 2).
- [ ] Valve spring broken or weak. Caused by component failure or wear; the springs must be renewed (Chapter 2).
- [ ] Valve not seating properly. This is caused by a bent valve (from over-revving or improper valve adjustment), burned valve or seat (improper fuelling) or an accumulation of carbon deposits on the seat. The valves must be cleaned and/or renewed and the seats serviced (Chapter 2).

Stalls after starting

- [ ] Engine idle speed incorrect. Faulty idle speed control system (Chapter 4).
- [ ] Ignition malfunction (Chapter 4).
- [ ] Fuel injection system malfunction (Chapter 4).
- [ ] Fuel contaminated. The fuel can be contaminated with either dirt or water, or can change chemically if the machine has been unused for several months. Drain the tank and fuel system (Chapter 4).
- [ ] Intake air leak. Check for loose throttle body-to-intake duct connections or a loose or damaged PAIR vacuum hose (Chapter 4).

Rough idle

- [ ] Idle speed incorrect (Chapter 4).
- [ ] Ignition fault (Chapter 4).
- [ ] Fuel injection system malfunction (Chapter 4).
- [ ] Fuel contaminated. The fuel can be contaminated with either dirt or water, or can change chemically if the machine has been unused for several months. Drain the tank and the fuel system (Chapter 4).
- [ ] Intake air leak. Check for loose throttle body-to-intake duct connections or a loose or damaged PAIR vacuum hose (Chapter 4).
- [ ] Air filter clogged. Clean the air filter element or replace it with a new one (Chapter 1).

2 Poor running at low speeds

Spark weak

- [ ] Battery voltage low. Check and recharge battery (Chapter 8).
- [ ] Spark plug caps not making good contact. Make sure that the caps fit snugly over the plug ends.
- [ ] Spark plugs dirty, defective or worn out. Locate reason for fouled plugs using spark plug condition chart on the inside back cover and follow the plug maintenance procedures (Chapter 1).
- [ ] Incorrect spark plugs. Wrong type or heat range. Check and install correct plugs (Chapter 1).
- [ ] Ignition coil or spark plug cap defective. Test and renew if necessary (Chapter 4).

Fuel/air mixture incorrect

- [ ] Fuel tank breather hose obstructed.
- [ ] Fuel pump faulty or blocked (Chapter 4).
- [ ] Fuel hose clogged. Remove the fuel hose and carefully blow through it.
- [ ] Fuel rail or injector clogged. For all of the injectors to be clogged, either a very bad batch of fuel with an unusual additive has been used, or some other foreign material has entered the tank. In some cases, if a machine has been unused for several months, the fuel turns to a varnish-like liquid which can cause an injector needle to stick to its seat. Drain the tank and fuel system (Chapter 4).
- [ ] Intake air leak. Check for loose throttle body-to-intake duct connections, or loose or damaged vacuum hoses (Chapter 4).
- [ ] Air filter clogged. Clean the air filter element or replace it with a new one (Chapter 1).

Compression low

- [ ] Spark plugs loose. Remove the plugs and inspect their threads. Reinstall and tighten securely (Chapter 1).
- [ ] Cylinder head not sufficiently tightened down. If the cylinder head is suspected of being loose, then there's a chance that the gasket or head is damaged if the problem has persisted for any length of time. The head bolts should be tightened to the proper torque and in the correct sequence (Chapter 2).
- [ ] Improper valve clearance. This means that the valve is not closing completely and compression pressure is leaking past the valve. Check and adjust the valve clearances (Chapter 1).
- [ ] Cylinder and/or piston worn. Excessive wear will cause compression pressure to leak past the rings. This is usually accompanied by worn rings as well. A top-end overhaul is necessary (Chapter 2).
- [ ] Piston rings worn, weak, broken, or sticking. Broken or sticking piston rings usually indicate a lubrication or fuelling problem that causes excess carbon deposits to form on the pistons and rings. Top-end overhaul is necessary (Chapter 2).
- [ ] Piston ring-to-groove clearance excessive. This is caused by excessive wear of the piston ring lands. Piston renewal is necessary (Chapter 2).
- [ ] Cylinder head gasket damaged. If the head is allowed to become loose, or if excessive carbon build-up on the piston crown and combustion chamber causes extremely high compression, the head gasket may leak. Retorquing the head is not always sufficient to restore the seal, so a new gasket is necessary (Chapter 2).
- [ ] Cylinder head warped. This is caused by overheating or improperly tightened head bolts. Machine shop resurfacing or head renewal is necessary (Chapter 2).
- [ ] Valve spring broken or weak. Caused by component failure or wear; the springs must be renewed (Chapter 2).
- [ ] Valve not seating properly. This is caused by a bent valve (from over-revving or improper valve adjustment), burned valve or seat (improper fuelling) or an accumulation of carbon deposits on the seat (from fuelling or lubrication problems). The valves must be cleaned and/or renewed and the seats serviced (Chapter 2).

Poor acceleration

- [ ] Timing not advancing. The crankshaft position sensor (CKP) or the engine control module (ECM) may be defective (Chapter 4). If so, they must be renewed.
- [ ] Engine oil viscosity too high. Using a heavier oil than that recommended in Chapter 1 can damage the oil pump or lubrication system and cause drag on the engine.
- [ ] Brakes dragging. Usually caused by debris which has entered the brake caliper piston seals, or from a warped disc or bent axle (Chapter 6).

Fault Finding REF•39

3 Poor running or no power at high speed

Firing incorrect
- [ ] Spark plug caps not making good contact. Make sure that the caps fit snugly over the plug ends and that the wiring is secure.
- [ ] Spark plugs dirty, defective or worn out. Locate reason for fouled plugs using spark plug condition chart on the inside back cover and follow the plug maintenance procedures (Chapter 1).
- [ ] Incorrect spark plugs. Wrong type or heat range. Check and install correct plugs (Chapter 1).
- [ ] Ignition coil or spark plug cap defective. Test and renew if necessary (Chapter 4).
- [ ] Faulty ECM (engine control module) (Chapter 4).

Fuel/air mixture incorrect
- [ ] Fuel tank breather hose obstructed.
- [ ] Fuel pump faulty or blocked (Chapter 4).
- [ ] Fuel hose clogged. Remove the fuel hose and carefully blow through it.
- [ ] Fuel rail or injector clogged. For all of the injectors to be clogged, either a very bad batch of fuel with an unusual additive has been used, or some other foreign material has entered the tank. In some cases, if a machine has been unused for several months, the fuel turns to a varnish-like liquid which can cause an injector needle to stick to its seat. Drain the tank and fuel system (Chapter 4).
- [ ] Intake air leak. Check for loose throttle body-to-intake duct connections, or loose or damaged vacuum hoses (Chapter 4).
- [ ] Air filter clogged. Clean the air filter element or replace it with a new one (Chapter 1).

Compression low
- [ ] Spark plugs loose. Remove the plugs and inspect their threads. Reinstall and tighten securely (Chapter 1).
- [ ] Cylinder head not sufficiently tightened down. If the cylinder head is suspected of being loose, then there's a chance that the gasket or head is damaged if the problem has persisted for any length of time. The head bolts should be tightened to the proper torque and in the correct sequence (Chapter 2).
- [ ] Improper valve clearance. This means that the valve is not closing completely and compression pressure is leaking past the valve. Check and adjust the valve clearances (Chapter 1).
- [ ] Cylinder and/or piston worn. Excessive wear will cause compression pressure to leak past the rings. This is usually accompanied by worn rings as well. A top-end overhaul is necessary (Chapter 2).
- [ ] Piston rings worn, weak, broken, or sticking. Broken or sticking piston rings usually indicate a lubrication or fuelling problem that causes excess carbon deposits to form on the pistons and rings. Top-end overhaul is necessary (Chapter 2).
- [ ] Piston ring-to-groove clearance excessive. This is caused by excessive wear of the piston ring lands. Piston renewal is necessary (Chapter 2).
- [ ] Cylinder head gasket damaged. If a head is allowed to become loose, or if excessive carbon build-up on the piston crown and combustion chamber causes extremely high compression, the head gasket may leak. Retorquing the head is not always sufficient to restore the seal, so a new gasket is necessary (Chapter 2).
- [ ] Cylinder head warped. This is caused by overheating or improperly tightened head bolts. Machine shop resurfacing or head renewal is necessary (Chapter 2).
- [ ] Valve spring broken or weak. Caused by component failure or wear; the springs must be replaced with new ones (Chapter 2).
- [ ] Valve not seating properly. This is caused by a bent valve (from over-revving or improper valve adjustment), burned valve or seat (improper fuelling) or an accumulation of carbon deposits on the seat (from fuelling or lubrication problems). The valves must be cleaned and/or renewed and the seats serviced (Chapter 2).

Knocking or pinking
- [ ] Carbon build-up in combustion chamber. Use of a fuel additive that will dissolve the adhesive bonding the carbon particles to the piston crown and chamber is the easiest way to remove the build-up. Otherwise, the cylinder head will have to be removed and decarbonised (Chapter 2).
- [ ] Incorrect or poor quality fuel. Old or improper grades of fuel can cause detonation. This causes the piston to rattle, thus the knocking or pinking sound. Drain old fuel and always use the recommended fuel grade.
- [ ] Spark plug heat range incorrect. Uncontrolled detonation indicates the plug heat range is too hot. The plug in effect becomes a glow plug, raising cylinder temperatures. Install the proper heat range plug (Chapter 1).
- [ ] Improper air/fuel mixture. This will cause the cylinders to run hot, which leads to detonation. A blockage in the fuel system or an air leak can cause this imbalance (Chapter 4).

Miscellaneous causes
- [ ] Throttle valve doesn't open fully. Adjust the throttle twistgrip freeplay (Chapter 1).
- [ ] Clutch slipping due loose or worn clutch components (Chapter 2).
- [ ] Timing not advancing. The crankshaft position sensor (CKP) or the engine control module (ECM) may be defective (Chapter 4). If so, they must be replaced with new ones.
- [ ] Engine oil viscosity too high. Using a heavier oil than the one recommended in Chapter 1 can damage the oil pump or lubrication system and cause drag on the engine.
- [ ] Brakes dragging. Usually caused by debris which has entered the brake caliper piston seals, or from a warped disc or bent axle (Chapter 6).

REF•40 Fault Finding

4 Overheating

Engine overheats

- [ ] Coolant level low. Check the level and add coolant (see *Pre-ride checks*).
- [ ] Leak in cooling system. Check cooling system hoses and radiator for leaks and other damage. Repair or renew parts as necessary (Chapter 3).
- [ ] Faulty thermostat. Check and renew as described in Chapter 3.
- [ ] Faulty radiator cap. Remove the cap and have it pressure tested.
- [ ] Coolant passages clogged. Have the entire system drained and flushed, then refill with fresh coolant.
- [ ] Water pump defective. Remove the pump and check the components (Chapter 3).
- [ ] Clogged or damaged radiator fins (Chapter 3).
- [ ] Faulty cooling fan, relay or ECT sensor (Chapter 3).

Firing incorrect

- [ ] Wrongly connected ignition coil wiring or plug leads.
- [ ] Spark plugs dirty, defective or worn out. Locate reason for fouled plugs using spark plug condition chart on the inside back cover and follow the plug maintenance procedures (Chapter 1).
- [ ] Incorrect spark plugs. Wrong type or heat range. Check and install correct plugs (Chapter 1).
- [ ] Ignition coil or spark plug cap defective. Test and replace with a new one if necessary (Chapter 4).
- [ ] Faulty ECM (engine control module) (Chapter 4).

Fuel/air mixture incorrect

- [ ] Fuel tank breather hose obstructed.
- [ ] Fuel pump faulty or blocked (Chapter 4).
- [ ] Fuel hose clogged. Remove the fuel hose and carefully blow through it.
- [ ] Fuel rail or injector clogged. For all of the injectors to be clogged, either a very bad batch of fuel with an unusual additive has been used, or some other foreign material has entered the tank. In some cases, if a machine has been unused for several months, the fuel turns to a varnish-like liquid which can cause an injector needle to stick to its seat. Drain the tank and fuel system (Chapter 4).
- [ ] Intake air leak. Check for loose throttle body-to-intake duct connections, or loose or damaged vacuum hoses (Chapter 4).
- [ ] Air filter clogged. Clean the air filter element or replace it with a new one (Chapter 1).

Compression too high

- [ ] Carbon build-up in combustion chamber. Use of a fuel additive that will dissolve the adhesive bonding the carbon particles to the piston crown and chamber is the easiest way to remove the build-up. Otherwise, the cylinder head will have to be removed and decarbonised (Chapter 2).
- [ ] Improperly machined head surface or installation of incorrect gasket during engine assembly.

Engine load excessive

- [ ] Clutch slipping due to loose or worn clutch components (Chapter 2).
- [ ] Engine oil level too high. Too much oil will cause pressurisation of the crankcase and inefficient engine operation. Check Specifications and drain to proper level (Chapter 1 and *Pre-ride checks*).
- [ ] Engine oil viscosity too high. Using a heavier oil than the one recommended in Chapter 1 can damage the oil pump or lubrication system as well as cause drag on the engine.
- [ ] Brakes dragging. Usually caused by debris which has entered the brake caliper piston seals, or from a warped disc or bent axle (Chapter 6).

Lubrication inadequate

- [ ] Engine oil level too low. Friction caused by intermittent lack of lubrication or from oil that is overworked can cause overheating. The oil provides a definite cooling function in the engine. Check the oil level (see *Pre-ride checks*).
- [ ] Low engine oil pressure. Check the pressure (Chapter 2).
- [ ] Blocked oil filter or oil cooler (Chapters 1 and 2).
- [ ] Poor quality engine oil or incorrect viscosity or type. Oil is rated not only according to viscosity but also according to type. Some oils are not rated high enough for use in this engine. Check the Specifications section and change to the correct oil (Chapter 1).

Miscellaneous causes

- [ ] Modification to exhaust system. Most aftermarket exhaust systems cause the engine to run leaner, which make them run hotter. When installing an accessory exhaust system, always check with the manufacturer/supplier as to whether the ECM requires re-mapping.

Fault Finding REF•41

5 Clutch problems

Clutch slipping
- [ ] Insufficient clutch cable freeplay. Check and adjust (Chapter 1).
- [ ] Clutch plates worn or warped. Overhaul the clutch assembly (Chapter 2).
- [ ] Clutch springs broken or weak. Old or heat-damaged (from slipping clutch) springs should be renewed (Chapter 2).
- [ ] Faulty clutch release mechanism. Replace any defective parts with new ones (Chapter 2).
- [ ] Clutch centre or housing unevenly worn. This causes improper engagement of the plates. Replace the damaged or worn parts (Chapter 2).

Clutch not disengaging completely
- [ ] Excessive clutch cable freeplay. Check and adjust (see Chapter 1).
- [ ] Faulty clutch release mechanism. Replace any defective parts with new ones (Chapter 2).
- [ ] Clutch plates warped or damaged. This will cause clutch drag, which in turn will cause the machine to creep. Overhaul the clutch assembly (Chapter 2).
- [ ] Clutch springs fatigued or broken. Check and renew the springs (Chapter 2).
- [ ] Engine oil deteriorated. Old, thin oil will not provide proper lubrication for the plates, causing the clutch to drag. Renew the oil and filter (Chapter 1).
- [ ] Engine oil viscosity too high. Using a heavier oil than recommended in Chapter 1 can cause the plates to stick together. Change to the correct weight oil.
- [ ] Clutch housing guide seized on the transmission input shaft. Lack of lubrication, severe wear or damage can cause the bearing to seize. Overhaul of the clutch, and perhaps transmission, may be necessary to repair the damage (Chapter 2).
- [ ] Loose clutch centre nut. Causes housing and centre misalignment putting a drag on the engine. Engagement adjustment continually varies. Overhaul the clutch assembly (Chapter 2).

6 Gearchanging problems

Doesn't go into gear or lever doesn't return
- [ ] Clutch not disengaging (above).
- [ ] Gearchange mechanism stopper arm spring weak or broken, or arm roller broken or worn. Replace the spring or arm with a new one (Chapter 2).
- [ ] Selector fork(s) bent, worn or seized. Overhaul the transmission (Chapter 2).
- [ ] Gear(s) stuck on shaft. Most often caused by a lack of lubrication or excessive wear in transmission bearings and bushes. Overhaul the transmission (Chapter 2).
- [ ] Selector drum binding. Caused by lubrication failure or excessive wear. Replace the drum and/or its bearing with a new one (Chapter 2).
- [ ] Gearchange mechanism return spring weak or broken (Chapter 2).
- [ ] Gearchange linkage arm broken. Splines stripped out of arm or shaft, caused by a loose linkage arm pinch bolt or from dropping the machine (Chapter 2).

Jumps out of gear
- [ ] Selector fork(s) worn (Chapter 2).
- [ ] Selector fork groove(s) in selector drum worn (Chapter 2).
- [ ] Gear pinion dogs or dog slots worn or damaged. The gear pinions should be inspected and renewed. No attempt should be made to repair the worn parts.

Overselects
- [ ] Gearchange mechanism stopper arm spring weak or broken, or arm roller broken or worn. Renew the spring or arm (Chapter 2).
- [ ] Gearchange mechanism return spring weak or broken (Chapter 2).

Fault Finding

7 Abnormal engine noise

Knocking or pinking

- [ ] Carbon build-up in combustion chamber. Use of a fuel additive that will dissolve the adhesive bonding the carbon particles to the piston crown and chamber is the easiest way to remove the build-up. Otherwise, the cylinder head will have to be removed and decarbonised (Chapter 2).
- [ ] Incorrect or poor quality fuel. Old or improper grades of fuel can cause detonation. This causes the pistons to rattle, thus the knocking or pinking sound. Drain old fuel and always use the recommended fuel grade.
- [ ] Spark plug heat range incorrect. Uncontrolled detonation indicates the plug heat range is too hot. The plug in effect becomes a glow plug, raising cylinder temperatures. Install the proper heat range plug (Chapter 1).
- [ ] Improper air/fuel mixture. This will cause the cylinders to run hot, which leads to detonation. A blockage in the fuel system or an air leak can cause this imbalance (Chapter 4).

Piston slap or rattling

- [ ] Cylinder-to-piston clearance excessive. Cylinder and/or piston worn, usually accompanied by worn rings as well. A top-end overhaul is necessary (Chapter 2).
- [ ] Piston ring(s) worn, broken or sticking. Overhaul the top-end (Chapter 2).
- [ ] Piston pin, piston pin bore or connecting rod small-end worn from high mileage or seized due to lack of lubrication (Chapter 2).
- [ ] Piston seizure damage. Usually from lack of lubrication or overheating. Replace the pistons and upper crankcase, as necessary (Chapter 2).
- [ ] Connecting rod big-end clearance excessive. Caused by excessive wear or lack of lubrication. Replace worn parts.
- [ ] Connecting rod bent. Caused by over-revving, trying to start a badly flooded engine or from ingesting a foreign object into the combustion chamber. Replace the damaged parts (Chapter 2).

Valve noise

- [ ] Incorrect valve clearances – check and adjust (Chapter 1).
- [ ] Valve spring broken or weak. Check and replace weak valve springs with new ones (Chapter 2).
- [ ] Camshaft or camshaft journals in the cylinder head worn or damaged. Lubrication failure at high rpm is usually the cause of damage due to insufficient oil or failure to change the oil at the recommended intervals. Since there are no replaceable bearings in the head, the head itself will have to be replaced with a new one (Chapter 2).

Other noise

- [ ] Cylinder head gasket leaking. Check around the joint for blowing with the engine running.
- [ ] Exhaust pipe leaking at cylinder head connection. Caused by incorrect fit of pipe(s), loose exhaust flange or damaged gasket. All exhaust system fasteners should be tightened evenly and carefully to avoid leaks (Chapter 4).
- [ ] Crankshaft runout excessive. Caused by a bent crankshaft (from over-revving) or damage from an upper cylinder component failure. Can also be attributed to dropping the machine on either of the crankshaft ends.
- [ ] Engine mounting bolts loose – ensure all the bolts are tightened to the specified torque settings (Chapter 2).
- [ ] Crankshaft bearings worn (Chapter 2).
- [ ] Cam chain rattle, due to worn chain or defective tensioner. Also worn chain tensioner/guide blades (Chapter 2).

8 Abnormal driveline noise

Clutch noise

- [ ] Clutch housing/friction plate clearance excessive (Chapter 2).
- [ ] Wear between the clutch housing splines and input shaft splines (Chapter 2).
- [ ] Worn release bearing (Chapter 2).

Transmission noise

- [ ] Bearings worn. Also includes the possibility that the shafts are worn. Overhaul the transmission (Chapter 2).
- [ ] Gears worn or chipped (Chapter 2).
- [ ] Metal chips jammed in gear teeth. Probably pieces from a broken clutch, gear or selector mechanism that were picked up by the gears. This will cause early bearing failure (Chapter 2).
- [ ] Engine oil level too low. Causes a howl from transmission. Also affects engine power and clutch operation (see *Pre-ride checks*).

Final drive noise

- [ ] Chain not adjusted properly (Chapter 1).
- [ ] Front or rear sprocket loose. Tighten fasteners (Chapter 6).
- [ ] Sprockets and/or chain worn. Fit new sprockets and chain (Chapter 6).
- [ ] Rear sprocket warped. Fit a new sprocket (Chapter 6).
- [ ] Rubber dampers worn in sprocket coupling (Chapter 6).

Fault Finding   REF•43

9 Abnormal frame and suspension noise

Front end noise

- ☐ Low fluid level or improper viscosity oil in forks. This can sound like spurting and is usually accompanied by irregular fork action (Chapter 5).
- ☐ Spring weak or broken. Makes a clicking or scraping sound. Fork oil, when drained, will have a lot of metal particles in it (Chapter 5).
- ☐ Steering head bearings loose or damaged. Clicks when braking. Check and adjust or replace with new ones as necessary (Chapters 1 and 5).
- ☐ Fork yoke clamp bolts loose – ensure all the bolts are tightened to the specified torque (Chapter 6).
- ☐ Forks bent. Good possibility if machine has been dropped. Replace the inner and outer tubes with new ones as required (Chapter 5).
- ☐ Front axle or axle pinch bolts loose. Tighten them to the specified torque (Chapter 6).
- ☐ Loose or worn wheel bearings. Check and replace with new ones as needed (Chapters 1 and 6).

Shock absorber noise

- ☐ Fluid level incorrect. Indicates a leak caused by defective seal. Shock will be covered with oil. Replace shock with a new one or seek advice on repair from a suspension specialist (Chapter 5).
- ☐ Defective shock absorber with internal damage. This is in the body of the shock and can't be remedied. The shock must be replaced with a new one or rebuilt (Chapter 5).
- ☐ Bent or damaged shock body. Replace the shock with a new one (Chapter 5).

Brake noise

- ☐ Squeal caused by pad shim not installed or positioned correctly (where fitted) (Chapter 6).
- ☐ Squeal caused by dust on brake pads. Usually found in combination with glazed pads. Clean using brake cleaning solvent (Chapter 6).
- ☐ Pads glazed. Caused by excessive heat from prolonged hard use or from contamination. DO NOT use sandpaper, emery cloth, carborundum cloth or any other abrasive to roughen the pad surfaces as abrasives will stay in the pad material and damage the disc. A very fine flat file can be used, but new pads is the best remedy (Chapter 6).
- ☐ Contamination of brake pads. Oil or brake fluid can cause the brake pads to chatter or squeal. Fit new pads. Identify the cause of the contamination, especially check the caliper piston seals for leaking fluid. Clean disc thoroughly with brake system cleaner (Chapter 6).
- ☐ Disc warped. Can cause a chattering, clicking or intermittent squeal. Usually accompanied by a pulsating lever and uneven braking. Replace the disc with new one (Chapter 6).
- ☐ Loose or worn wheel bearings. Check and replace with new ones as needed (Chapters 1 and 6).

10 Oil pressure warning light comes on

Engine lubrication system

- ☐ Engine oil level low. Inspect for leak or other problem causing low oil level and add recommended oil (see Pre-ride checks).
- ☐ Engine oil pump defective, blocked oil strainer gauze or failed pressure relief valve. Carry out an oil pressure check (Chapter 2).
- ☐ Engine oil viscosity too low. Very old, thin oil or an improper weight of oil used in the engine. Change to correct oil (Chapter 1).
- ☐ Camshaft or crankshaft journals worn. Excessive wear causing drop in oil pressure. Abnormal wear could be caused by oil starvation at high rpm from low oil level or improper weight or type of oil (Chapter 1).

Electrical system

- ☐ Oil pressure switch defective. Check the switch according to the procedure in Chapter 8. Replace it with a new one it if is defective.
- ☐ Oil pressure warning LED defective. Check for pinched, shorted, disconnected or damaged wiring (Chapter 8).

REF•44 Fault Finding

11 Excessive exhaust smoke

White smoke

- ☐ Piston rings worn or broken, causing oil from the crankcase to be pulled past the piston into the combustion chamber. Replace the rings with new ones (Chapter 2).
- ☐ Cylinders worn or scored. Caused by overheating or oil starvation. Rebore cylinders (Chapter 2).
- ☐ Valve stem oil seal damaged or worn. Replace the oil seals with new ones (Chapter 2).
- ☐ Valve guide worn. Perform a complete valve job (Chapter 2).
- ☐ Engine oil level too high, which causes the oil to be forced past the rings. Drain oil to the proper level (see *Pre-ride checks*).
- ☐ Head gasket broken between oil return and cylinder. Causes oil to be pulled into the combustion chamber. Replace the head gasket with a new ones and check the head for warpage (Chapter 2).
- ☐ Abnormal crankcase pressurisation which forces oil past the rings, usually caused by a clogged breather.

Black smoke

- ☐ Air filter clogged. Clean the air filter element or replace it with a new one (Chapter 1).
- ☐ Fuel injection system malfunction (Chapter 4).

Brown smoke

- ☐ Air filter poorly sealed or not installed (Chapter 1).
- ☐ Fuel injection system malfunction (Chapter 4).

12 Poor handling or stability

Handlebar hard to turn

- ☐ Steering head bearing adjuster nut too tight. Check adjustment as described in Chapter 1.
- ☐ Bearings damaged. Roughness can be felt as the bars are turned from side-to-side. Replace the bearings with new ones (Chapter 5).
- ☐ Races dented or worn. Denting results from wear in only one position (e.g., straight ahead), from a collision or hitting a pothole or from dropping the machine. Replace the bearings with new ones (Chapter 5).
- ☐ Steering stem lubrication inadequate. Causes are grease getting hard from age or being washed out by high pressure car washes. Disassemble steering head and repack bearings (Chapter 5).
- ☐ Steering stem bent. Caused by a collision, hitting a pothole or by dropping the machine. Replace damaged part. Don't try to straighten the steering stem (Chapter 5).
- ☐ Front tyre air pressure too low (see *Pre-ride checks*).

Handlebar shakes or vibrates excessively

- ☐ Tyres worn or out of balance (Chapter 6).
- ☐ Swingarm bearings worn. Replace the bearings with new ones (Chapter 5).
- ☐ Wheel rim(s) warped or damaged. Inspect wheels for runout (Chapter 6).
- ☐ Wheel bearings worn. Worn front or rear wheel bearings can cause poor tracking. Worn front bearings will cause wobble (Chapters 1 and 6).
- ☐ Fork yoke clamp bolts or handlebar clamp bolts loose. Tighten them to the specified torque (Chapter 5).
- ☐ Engine mounting bolts loose. Will cause excessive vibration with increased engine rpm – ensure all the bolts are tightened to the specified torque settings (Chapter 2).

Machine pulls to one side

- ☐ Frame bent. Definitely suspect this if the machine has been dropped. May or may not be accompanied by cracking near the steering head, swingarm mountings or engine mountings. Replace the frame with a new one (Chapter 5).
- ☐ Wheels out of alignment. Caused by poor chain adjustment, improper location of axle spacers or from bent steering stem or frame (Chapters 1 and 5).
- ☐ Forks bent. Disassemble the forks and replace the damaged parts (Chapter 5).
- ☐ Swingarm bent or twisted. Replace the arm with a new one (Chapter 5).
- ☐ Fork oil level uneven. Check and add or drain as necessary (Chapter 5).

Poor shock absorbing qualities

- ☐ Too hard:
  - a) Suspension adjustment incorrect.
  - b) Fork oil level excessive (Chapter 5).
  - c) Fork oil viscosity too high. Use a lighter oil (see the Specifications in Chapter 5).
  - d) Fork tube bent. Causes a harsh, sticking feeling (Chapter 5).
  - e) Fork internal damage (Chapter 5).
  - f) Shock shaft or body bent or damaged (Chapter 5).
  - g) Shock internal damage.
  - h) Tyre pressure too high (see *Pre-ride checks*).
- ☐ Too soft:
  - a) Suspension adjustment incorrect.
  - b) Fork oil level too low (Chapter 5).
  - c) Fork oil viscosity too light (Chapter 5).
  - d) Fork springs weak or broken (Chapter 5).
  - e) Fork or shock oil leaking (Chapter 5).
  - f) Shock internal damage (Chapter 5).

Fault Finding REF•45

13 Braking problems

Brakes are spongy, don't hold
- [ ] Low brake fluid level (see *Pre-ride checks*).
- [ ] Air in hydraulic system. Caused by inattention to master cylinder fluid level or by leakage. Locate problem and bleed brakes (Chapter 6).
- [ ] Pad or disc worn (Chapters 1 and 6).
- [ ] Contaminated pads. Caused by contamination with oil, grease, brake fluid, etc. Fit new pads. Identify the cause of the contamination, especially check the caliper piston seals for leaking fluid. Clean disc thoroughly with brake system cleaner (Chapter 6).
- [ ] Brake fluid deteriorated. Fluid is old or contaminated. Drain system, replenish with new fluid and bleed the system (Chapter 6).
- [ ] Master cylinder internal seals worn or damaged causing fluid to bypass (Chapter 6).
- [ ] Master cylinder bore scratched by foreign material or broken spring. Fit a new master cylinder (Chapter 6).
- [ ] Disc warped. Replace disc and pads (Chapter 6). Replace both front discs if the fault occurs on the front brake.
- [ ] C-ABS system faulty (where fitted - Chapter 6).

Brake lever or pedal pulsates
- [ ] Disc warped. Replace disc with new one (Chapter 6). Replace both front discs if the fault occurs on the front brake.
- [ ] Axle bent. Replace axle with new one (Chapter 6).
- [ ] Brake caliper bolts loose – tighten the bolts to the specified torque (Chapter 6).
- [ ] Wheel warped or otherwise damaged (Chapter 6).
- [ ] Wheel bearings damaged or worn (Chapters 1 and 6).
- [ ] C-ABS system faulty (where fitted - Chapter 6).

Brakes drag
- [ ] Master cylinder piston seized. Caused by wear or damage to piston or cylinder bore (Chapter 6).
- [ ] Lever balky or stuck. Check pivot and lubricate (Chapter 6).
- [ ] Brake caliper piston seized in bore. Caused by corrosion or ingestion of dirt past deteriorated seal (Chapter 6).
- [ ] Brake caliper binds. Caused by inadequate lubrication of caliper slider pins (Chapter 6).
- [ ] Brake pad damaged. Pad material separated from backing plate. Usually caused by faulty manufacturing process or from contact with chemicals. Fit new pads (Chapter 6).
- [ ] Pads improperly installed (Chapter 6).
- [ ] Brake caliper incorrectly installed (Chapter 6).
- [ ] C-ABS system faulty (where fitted - Chapter 6).

14 Electrical problems

Battery dead or weak
- [ ] Battery faulty. Caused by sulphated plates which are shorted through sedimentation. Confirm with battery condition check (Chapter 8).
- [ ] Broken battery terminal making only occasional contact.
- [ ] Battery leads making poor contact (Chapter 8).
- [ ] Load excessive. Caused by addition of high wattage lights or other electrical accessories.
- [ ] Ignition switch defective. Switch either earths (grounds) internally or fails to shut off system. Renew the switch (Chapter 8).
- [ ] Regulator/rectifier defective (Chapter 8).
- [ ] Alternator stator coil open or shorted (Chapter 8).
- [ ] Charging system fault. Check for excessive current leakage (Chapter 8).
- [ ] Wiring faulty. Wiring grounded (earthed) or connections loose in ignition, charging or lighting circuits (Chapter 8).

Battery overcharged
- [ ] Regulator/rectifier defective. Overcharging is noticed when battery gets excessively warm (Chapter 8).
- [ ] Battery faulty. Confirm with battery condition check (Chapter 8).
- [ ] Battery amperage too low, wrong type or size of battery. Install manufacturer's specified amp-hour battery to handle charging load (Chapter 8).

Technical Terms Explained

A

ABS (Anti-lock braking system) A system, usually electronically controlled, that senses incipient wheel lockup during braking and relieves hydraulic pressure at wheel which is about to skid.
Aftermarket Components suitable for the motorcycle, but not produced by the motorcycle manufacturer.
Allen key A hexagonal wrench which fits into a recessed hexagonal hole.
Alternating current (ac) Current produced by an alternator. Requires converting to direct current by a rectifier for charging purposes.
Alternator Converts mechanical energy from the engine into electrical energy to charge the battery and power the electrical system.
Ampere (amp) A unit of measurement for the flow of electrical current. Current = Volts ÷ Ohms.
Ampere-hour (Ah) Measure of battery capacity.
Angle-tightening A torque expressed in degrees. Often follows a conventional tightening torque for cylinder head or main bearing fasteners **(see illustration)**.

Angle-tightening con-rod bolts

Antifreeze A substance (usually ethylene glycol) mixed with water, and added to the cooling system, to prevent freezing of the coolant in winter. Antifreeze also contains chemicals to inhibit corrosion and the formation of rust and other deposits that would tend to clog the radiator and coolant passages and reduce cooling efficiency.
Anti-dive System attached to the fork lower leg (slider) to prevent fork dive when braking hard.
Anti-seize compound A coating that reduces the risk of seizing on fasteners that are subjected to high temperatures, such as exhaust clamp bolts and nuts.
API American Petroleum Institute. A quality standard for 4-stroke motor oils.
Asbestos A natural fibrous mineral with great heat resistance, commonly used in the composition of brake friction materials. Asbestos is a health hazard and the dust created by brake systems should never be inhaled or ingested.
ATF Automatic Transmission Fluid. Often used in front forks.
ATU Automatic Timing Unit. Mechanical device for advancing the ignition timing on early engines.
ATV All Terrain Vehicle. Often called a Quad.
Axial play Side-to-side movement.
Axle A shaft on which a wheel revolves. Also known as a spindle.

B

Backlash The amount of movement between meshed components when one component is held still. Usually applies to gear teeth.
Ball bearing A bearing consisting of a hardened inner and outer race with hardened steel balls between the two races.
Bearings Used between two working surfaces to prevent wear of the components and a build-up of heat. Four types of bearing are commonly used on motorcycles: plain shell bearings, ball bearings, tapered roller bearings and needle roller bearings.
Bevel gears Used to turn the drive through 90°. Typical applications are shaft final drive and camshaft drive **(see illustration)**.

Bevel gears are used to turn the drive through 90°

BHP Brake Horsepower. The British measurement for engine power output. Power output is now usually expressed in kilowatts (kW).
Bias-belted tyre Similar construction to radial tyre, but with outer belt running at an angle to the wheel rim.
Big-end bearing The bearing in the end of the connecting rod that's attached to the crankshaft.
Bleeding The process of removing air from an hydraulic system via a bleed nipple or bleed screw.
Bottom-end A description of an engine's crankcase components and all components contained there-in.
BTDC Before Top Dead Centre in terms of piston position. Ignition timing is often expressed in terms of degrees or millimetres BTDC.
Bush A cylindrical metal or rubber component used between two moving parts.
Burr Rough edge left on a component after machining or as a result of excessive wear.

C

Cam chain The chain which takes drive from the crankshaft to the camshaft(s).
Canister The main component in an evaporative emission control system (California market only); contains activated charcoal granules to trap vapours from the fuel system rather than allowing them to vent to the atmosphere.
Castellated Resembling the parapets along the top of a castle wall. For example, a castellated wheel axle or spindle nut.
Catalytic converter A device in the exhaust system of some machines which converts certain pollutants in the exhaust gases into less harmful substances.
Charging system Description of the components which charge the battery, ie the alternator, rectifier and regulator.
Circlip A ring-shaped clip used to prevent endwise movement of cylindrical parts and shafts. An internal circlip is installed in a groove in a housing; an external circlip fits into a groove on the outside of a cylindrical piece such as a shaft. Also known as a snap-ring.
Clearance The amount of space between two parts. For example, between a piston and a cylinder, between a bearing and a journal, etc.
Coil spring A spiral of elastic steel found in various sizes throughout a vehicle, for example as a springing medium in the suspension and in the valve train.
Compression Reduction in volume, and increase in pressure and temperature, of a gas, caused by squeezing it into a smaller space.
Compression damping Controls the speed the suspension compresses when hitting a bump.
Compression ratio The relationship between cylinder volume when the piston is at top dead centre and cylinder volume when the piston is at bottom dead centre.
Continuity The uninterrupted path in the flow of electricity. Little or no measurable resistance.
Continuity tester Self-powered bleeper or test light which indicates continuity.
Cp Candlepower. Bulb rating commonly found on US motorcycles.
Crossply tyre Tyre plies arranged in a criss-cross pattern. Usually four or six plies used, hence 4PR or 6PR in tyre size codes.
Cush drive Rubber damper segments fitted between the rear wheel and final drive sprocket to absorb transmission shocks **(see illustration)**.

Cush drive rubbers dampen out transmission shocks

D

Decarbonisation The process of removing carbon deposits - typically from the combustion chamber, valves and exhaust port/system.
Degree disc Calibrated disc for measuring piston position. Expressed in degrees.
Detonation Destructive and damaging explosion of fuel/air mixture in combustion chamber instead of controlled burning.
Dial gauge Clock-type gauge with adapters for measuring runout and piston position. Expressed in mm or inches.

Technical Terms Explained

Diaphragm The rubber membrane in a master cylinder or carburettor which seals the upper chamber.
Diaphragm spring A single sprung plate often used in clutches.
Direct current (dc) Current produced by a dc generator.
Diode An electrical valve which only allows current to flow in one direction. Commonly used in rectifiers and starter interlock systems.
Disc valve (or rotary valve) A induction system used on some two-stroke engines.
Double-overhead camshaft (DOHC) An engine that uses two overhead camshafts, one for the intake valves and one for the exhaust valves.
Drivebelt A toothed belt used to transmit drive to the rear wheel on some motorcycles. A drivebelt has also been used to drive the camshafts. Drivebelts are usually made of Kevlar.
Driveshaft Any shaft used to transmit motion. Commonly used when referring to the final driveshaft on shaft drive motorcycles.

E

Earth return The return path of an electrical circuit, utilising the motorcycle's frame.
ECU (Electronic Control Unit) A computer which controls (for instance) an ignition system, or an anti-lock braking system.
EGO Exhaust Gas Oxygen sensor. Sometimes called a Lambda sensor.
Electrolyte The fluid in a lead-acid battery.
EMS (Engine Management System) A computer controlled system which manages the fuel injection and the ignition systems in an integrated fashion.
Endfloat The amount of lengthways movement between two parts. As applied to a crankshaft, the distance that the crankshaft can move side-to-side in the crankcase.
Endless chain A chain having no joining link. Common use for cam chains and final drive chains.
EP (Extreme Pressure) Oil type used in locations where high loads are applied, such as between gear teeth.
Evaporative emission control system Describes a charcoal filled canister which stores fuel vapours from the tank rather than allowing them to vent to the atmosphere. Usually only fitted to California models and referred to as an EVAP system.
Expansion chamber Section of two-stroke engine exhaust system so designed to improve engine efficiency and boost power.

F

Feeler blade or gauge A thin strip or blade of hardened steel, ground to an exact thickness, used to check or measure clearances between parts.
Final drive Description of the drive from the transmission to the rear wheel. Usually by chain or shaft, but sometimes by belt.
Firing order The order in which the engine cylinders fire, or deliver their power strokes, beginning with the number one cylinder.
Flooding Term used to describe a high fuel level in the carburettor float chambers, leading to fuel overflow. Also refers to excess fuel in the combustion chamber due to incorrect starting technique.
Free length The no-load state of a component when measured. Clutch, valve and fork spring lengths are measured at rest, without any preload.
Freeplay The amount of travel before any action takes place. The looseness in a linkage, or an assembly of parts, between the initial application of force and actual movement. For example, the distance the rear brake pedal moves before the rear brake is actuated.
Fuel injection The fuel/air mixture is metered electronically and directed into the engine intake ports (indirect injection) or into the cylinders (direct injection). Sensors supply information on engine speed and conditions.
Fuel/air mixture The charge of fuel and air going into the engine. See Stoichiometric ratio.
Fuse An electrical device which protects a circuit against accidental overload. The typical fuse contains a soft piece of metal which is calibrated to melt at a predetermined current flow (expressed as amps) and break the circuit.

G

Gap The distance the spark must travel in jumping from the centre electrode to the side electrode in a spark plug. Also refers to the distance between the ignition rotor and the pickup coil in an electronic ignition system.
Gasket Any thin, soft material - usually cork, cardboard, asbestos or soft metal - installed between two metal surfaces to ensure a good seal. For instance, the cylinder head gasket seals the joint between the block and the cylinder head.
Gauge An instrument panel display used to monitor engine conditions. A gauge with a movable pointer on a dial or a fixed scale is an analogue gauge. A gauge with a numerical readout is called a digital gauge.
Gear ratios The drive ratio of a pair of gears in a gearbox, calculated on their number of teeth.
Glaze-busting see **Honing**
Grinding Process for renovating the valve face and valve seat contact area in the cylinder head.
Gudgeon pin The shaft which connects the connecting rod small-end with the piston. Often called a piston pin or wrist pin.

H

Helical gears Gear teeth are slightly curved and produce less gear noise that straight-cut gears. Often used for primary drives.
Helicoil A thread insert repair system. Commonly used as a repair for stripped spark plug threads (**see illustration**).

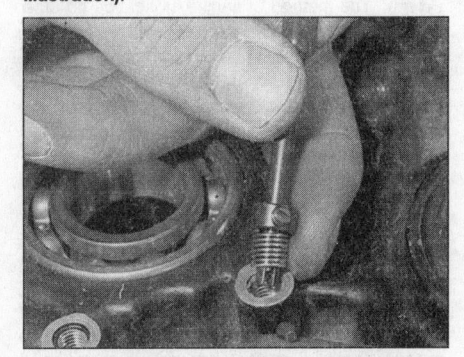

Installing a Helicoil thread insert

Honing A process used to break down the glaze on a cylinder bore (also called glaze-busting). Can also be carried out to roughen a rebored cylinder to aid ring bedding-in.
HT (High Tension) Description of the electrical circuit from the secondary winding of the ignition coil to the spark plug.
Hydraulic A liquid filled system used to transmit pressure from one component to another. Common uses on motorcycles are brakes and clutches.
Hydrometer An instrument for measuring the specific gravity of a lead-acid battery.
Hygroscopic Water absorbing. In motorcycle applications, braking efficiency will be reduced if DOT 3 or 4 hydraulic fluid absorbs water from the air - care must be taken to keep new brake fluid in tightly sealed containers.

I

lbf ft Pounds-force feet. An imperial unit of torque. Sometimes written as ft-lbs.
lbf in Pound-force inch. An imperial unit of torque, applied to components where a very low torque is required. Sometimes written as in-lbs.
IC Abbreviation for Integrated Circuit.
Ignition advance Means of increasing the timing of the spark at higher engine speeds. Done by mechanical means (ATU) on early engines or electronically by the ignition control unit on later engines.
Ignition timing The moment at which the spark plug fires, expressed in the number of crankshaft degrees before the piston reaches the top of its stroke, or in the number of millimetres before the piston reaches the top of its stroke.
Infinity (∞) Description of an open-circuit electrical state, where no continuity exists.
Inverted forks (upside down forks) The sliders or lower legs are held in the yokes and the fork tubes or stanchions are connected to the wheel axle (spindle). Less unsprung weight and stiffer construction than conventional forks.

J

JASO Quality standard for 2-stroke oils.
Joule The unit of electrical energy.
Journal The bearing surface of a shaft.

K

Kickstart Mechanical means of turning the engine over for starting purposes. Only usually fitted to mopeds, small capacity motorcycles and off-road motorcycles.
Kill switch Handebar-mounted switch for emergency ignition cut-out. Cuts the ignition circuit on all models, and additionally prevent starter motor operation on others.
km Symbol for kilometre.
kmh Abbreviation for kilometres per hour.

L

Lambda (λ) sensor A sensor fitted in the exhaust system to measure the exhaust gas oxygen content (excess air factor).

Technical Terms Explained

Lapping see Grinding.
LCD Abbreviation for Liquid Crystal Display.
LED Abbreviation for Light Emitting Diode.
Liner A steel cylinder liner inserted in a aluminium alloy cylinder block.
Locknut A nut used to lock an adjustment nut, or other threaded component, in place.
Lockstops The lugs on the lower triple clamp (yoke) which abut those on the frame, preventing handlebar-to-fuel tank contact.
Lockwasher A form of washer designed to prevent an attaching nut from working loose.
LT Low Tension Description of the electrical circuit from the power supply to the primary winding of the ignition coil.

M

Main bearings The bearings between the crankshaft and crankcase.
Maintenance-free (MF) battery A sealed battery which cannot be topped up.
Manometer Mercury-filled calibrated tubes used to measure intake tract vacuum. Used to synchronise carburettors on multi-cylinder engines.
Micrometer A precision measuring instrument that measures component outside diameters **(see illustration)**.

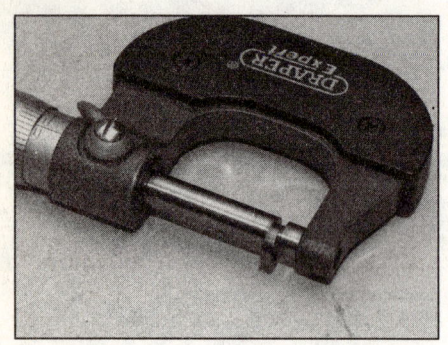

Tappet shims are measured with a micrometer

MON (Motor Octane Number) A measure of a fuel's resistance to knock.
Monograde oil An oil with a single viscosity, eg SAE80W.
Monoshock A single suspension unit linking the swingarm or suspension linkage to the frame.
mph Abbreviation for miles per hour.
Multigrade oil Having a wide viscosity range (eg 10W40). The W stands for Winter, thus the viscosity ranges from SAE10 when cold to SAE40 when hot.
Multimeter An electrical test instrument with the capability to measure voltage, current and resistance. Some meters also incorporate a continuity tester and buzzer.

N

Needle roller bearing Inner race of caged needle rollers and hardened outer race. Examples of uncaged needle rollers can be found on some engines. Commonly used in rear suspension applications and in two-stroke engines.
Nm Newton metres.
NOx Oxides of Nitrogen. A common toxic pollutant emitted by petrol engines at higher temperatures.

O

Octane The measure of a fuel's resistance to knock.
OE (Original Equipment) Relates to components fitted to a motorcycle as standard or replacement parts supplied by the motorcycle manufacturer.
Ohm The unit of electrical resistance. Ohms = Volts ÷ Current.
Ohmmeter An instrument for measuring electrical resistance.
Oil cooler System for diverting engine oil outside of the engine to a radiator for cooling purposes.
Oil injection A system of two-stroke engine lubrication where oil is pump-fed to the engine in accordance with throttle position.
Open-circuit An electrical condition where there is a break in the flow of electricity - no continuity (high resistance).
O-ring A type of sealing ring made of a special rubber-like material; in use, the O-ring is compressed into a groove to provide the sealing action.
Oversize (OS) Term used for piston and ring size options fitted to a rebored cylinder.
Overhead cam (sohc) engine An engine with single camshaft located on top of the cylinder head.
Overhead valve (ohv) engine An engine with the valves located in the cylinder head, but with the camshaft located in the engine block or crankcase.
Oxygen sensor A device installed in the exhaust system which senses the oxygen content in the exhaust and converts this information into an electric current. Also called a Lambda sensor.

P

Plastigauge A thin strip of plastic thread, available in different sizes, used for measuring clearances. For example, a strip of Plastigauge is laid across a bearing journal. The parts are assembled and dismantled; the width of the crushed strip indicates the clearance between journal and bearing.
Polarity Either negative or positive earth (ground), determined by which battery lead is connected to the frame (earth return). Modern motorcycles are usually negative earth.
Pre-ignition A situation where the fuel/air mixture ignites before the spark plug fires. Often due to a hot spot in the combustion chamber caused by carbon build-up. Engine has a tendency to 'run-on'.
Pre-load (suspension) The amount a spring is compressed when in the unloaded state. Preload can be applied by gas, spacer or mechanical adjuster.
Premix The method of engine lubrication on older two-stroke engines. Engine oil is mixed with the petrol in the fuel tank in a specific ratio. The fuel/oil mix is sometimes referred to as "petroil".
Primary drive Description of the drive from the crankshaft to the clutch. Usually by gear or chain.
PS Pfedestärke - a German interpretation of BHP.
PSI Pounds-force per square inch. Imperial measurement of tyre pressure and cylinder pressure measurement.
PTFE Polytetrafluroethylene. A low friction substance.
Pulse secondary air injection system A process of promoting the burning of excess fuel present in the exhaust gases by routing fresh air into the exhaust ports.

Q

Quartz halogen bulb Tungsten filament surrounded by a halogen gas. Typically used for the headlight **(see illustration)**.

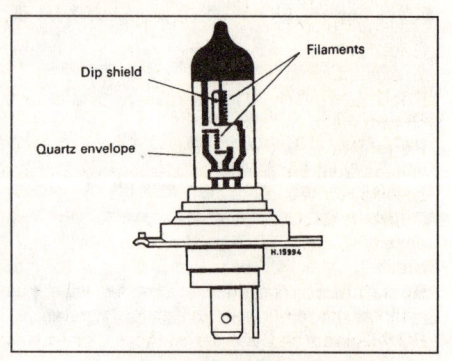

Quartz halogen headlight bulb construction

R

Rack-and-pinion A pinion gear on the end of a shaft that mates with a rack (think of a geared wheel opened up and laid flat). Sometimes used in clutch operating systems.
Radial play Up and down movement about a shaft.
Radial ply tyres Tyre plies run across the tyre (from bead to bead) and around the circumference of the tyre. Less resistant to tread distortion than other tyre types.
Radiator A liquid-to-air heat transfer device designed to reduce the temperature of the coolant in a liquid cooled engine.
Rake A feature of steering geometry - the angle of the steering head in relation to the vertical **(see illustration)**.

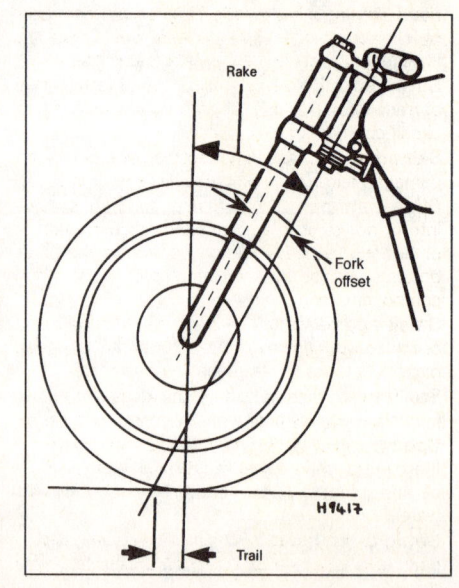

Steering geometry

Technical Terms Explained

Rebore Providing a new working surface to the cylinder bore by boring out the old surface. Necessitates the use of oversize piston and rings.
Rebound damping A means of controlling the oscillation of a suspension unit spring after it has been compressed. Resists the spring's natural tendency to bounce back after being compressed.
Rectifier Device for converting the ac output of an alternator into dc for battery charging.
Reed valve An induction system commonly used on two-stroke engines.
Regulator Device for maintaining the charging voltage from the generator or alternator within a specified range.
Relay A electrical device used to switch heavy current on and off by using a low current auxiliary circuit.
Resistance Measured in ohms. An electrical component's ability to pass electrical current.
RON (Research Octane Number) A measure of a fuel's resistance to knock.
rpm revolutions per minute.
Runout The amount of wobble (in-and-out movement) of a wheel or shaft as it's rotated. The amount a shaft rotates 'out-of-true'. The out-of-round condition of a rotating part.

S

SAE (Society of Automotive Engineers) A standard for the viscosity of a fluid.
Sealant A liquid or paste used to prevent leakage at a joint. Sometimes used in conjunction with a gasket.
Service limit Term for the point where a component is no longer useable and must be renewed.
Shaft drive A method of transmitting drive from the transmission to the rear wheel.
Shell bearings Plain bearings consisting of two shell halves. Most often used as big-end and main bearings in a four-stroke engine. Often called bearing inserts.
Shim Thin spacer, commonly used to adjust the clearance or relative positions between two parts. For example, shims inserted into or under tappets or followers to control valve clearances. Clearance is adjusted by changing the thickness of the shim.
Short-circuit An electrical condition where current shorts to earth (ground) bypassing the circuit components.
Skimming Process to correct warpage or repair a damaged surface, eg on brake discs or drums.
Slide-hammer A special puller that screws into or hooks onto a component such as a shaft or bearing; a heavy sliding handle on the shaft bottoms against the end of the shaft to knock the component free.
Small-end bearing The bearing in the upper end of the connecting rod at its joint with the gudgeon pin.
Spalling Damage to camshaft lobes or bearing journals shown as pitting of the working surface.
Specific gravity (SG) The state of charge of the electrolyte in a lead-acid battery. A measure of the electrolyte's density compared with water.
Straight-cut gears Common type gear used on gearbox shafts and for oil pump and water pump drives.
Stanchion The inner sliding part of the front forks, held by the yokes. Often called a fork tube.

Stoichiometric ratio The optimum chemical air/fuel ratio for a petrol engine, said to be 14.7 parts of air to 1 part of fuel.
Sulphuric acid The liquid (electrolyte) used in a lead-acid battery. Poisonous and extremely corrosive.
Surface grinding (lapping) Process to correct a warped gasket face, commonly used on cylinder heads.

T

Tapered-roller bearing Tapered inner race of caged needle rollers and separate tapered outer race. Examples of taper roller bearings can be found on steering heads.
Tappet A cylindrical component which transmits motion from the cam to the valve stem, either directly or via a pushrod and rocker arm. Also called a cam follower.
TCS Traction Control System. An electronically-controlled system which senses wheel spin and reduces engine speed accordingly.
TDC Top Dead Centre denotes that the piston is at its highest point in the cylinder.
Thread-locking compound Solution applied to fastener threads to prevent slackening. Select type to suit application.
Thrust washer A washer positioned between two moving components on a shaft. For example, between gear pinions on gearshaft.
Timing chain See **Cam Chain**.
Timing light Stroboscopic lamp for carrying out ignition timing checks with the engine running.
Top-end A description of an engine's cylinder block, head and valve gear components.
Torque Turning or twisting force about a shaft.
Torque setting A prescribed tightness specified by the motorcycle manufacturer to ensure that the bolt or nut is secured correctly. Undertightening can result in the bolt or nut coming loose or a surface not being sealed. Overtightening can result in stripped threads, distortion or damage to the component being retained.
Torx key A six-point wrench.
Tracer A stripe of a second colour applied to a wire insulator to distinguish that wire from another one with the same colour insulator. For example, Br/W is often used to denote a brown insulator with a white tracer.
Trail A feature of steering geometry. Distance from the steering head axis to the tyre's central contact point.
Triple clamps The cast components which extend from the steering head and support the fork stanchions or tubes. Often called fork yokes.
Turbocharger A centrifugal device, driven by exhaust gases, that pressurises the intake air. Normally used to increase the power output from a given engine displacement.
TWI Abbreviation for Tyre Wear Indicator. Indicates the location of the tread depth indicator bars on tyres.

U

Universal joint or U-joint (UJ) A double-pivoted connection for transmitting power from a driving to a driven shaft through an angle. Typically found in shaft drive assemblies.
Unsprung weight Anything not supported by the bike's suspension (ie the wheel, tyres, brakes, final drive and bottom (moving) part of the suspension).

V

Vacuum gauges Clock-type gauges for measuring intake tract vacuum. Used for carburettor synchronisation on multi-cylinder engines.
Valve A device through which the flow of liquid, gas or vacuum may be stopped, started or regulated by a moveable part that opens, shuts or partially obstructs one or more ports or passageways. The intake and exhaust valves in the cylinder head are of the poppet type.
Valve clearance The clearance between the valve tip (the end of the valve stem) and the rocker arm or tappet/follower. The valve clearance is measured when the valve is closed. The correct clearance is important - if too small the valve won't close fully and will burn out, whereas if too large noisy operation will result.
Valve lift The amount a valve is lifted off its seat by the camshaft lobe.
Valve timing The exact setting for the opening and closing of the valves in relation to piston position.
Vernier caliper A precision measuring instrument that measures inside and outside dimensions. Not quite as accurate as a micrometer, but more convenient.

Wet liner arrangement

VIN Vehicle Identification Number. Term for the bike's engine and frame numbers.
Viscosity The thickness of a liquid or its resistance to flow.
Volt A unit for expressing electrical "pressure" in a circuit. Volts = current x ohms.

W

Water pump A mechanically-driven device for moving coolant around the engine.
Watt A unit for expressing electrical power. Watts = volts x current.
Wear limit see **Service limit**
Wet liner A liquid-cooled engine design where the pistons run in liners which are directly surrounded by coolant **(see illustration)**.
Wheelbase Distance from the centre of the front wheel to the centre of the rear wheel.
Wiring harness or loom Describes the electrical wires running the length of the motorcycle and enclosed in tape or plastic sheathing. Wiring coming off the main harness is usually referred to as a sub harness.
Woodruff key A key of semi-circular or square section used to locate a gear to a shaft. Often used to locate the alternator rotor on the crankshaft.
Wrist pin Another name for gudgeon or piston pin.

Index

Note: *References throughout this index are in the form - "Chapter number" • "Page number"*

A

ABS system – 6•22, 6•23, 6•25
Air filter – 1•22
Air filter housing – 4•5
Air intake system – 4•19
Alternator – 8•33

B

Battery – 8•4
   charging – 8•5
   check – 1•24
   specifications – 8•1
Bodywork – 7•1 et seq
Brake
   ABS system – 6•22, 6•23, 6•25
   bleeding – 6•19
   calipers – 6•6, 6•13
   discs – 6•9, 6•15
   fault finding – REF•45
   fluid change – 1•10, 6•22
   fluid levels – 0•12
   hoses and fittings – 6•18
   master cylinders – 6•9, 6•15
   pads – 1•9, 6•4, 6•11
   specifications – 0•17, 6•1
   system check – 1•10
Brake lever – 5•7
   span adjuster – 1•10
Brake light
   bulb – 8•8
   circuit check – 8•8
Brake light switches – 8•17
   check – 1•10
Brake pedal – 5•3
   height adjustment – 1•10
Bulbs
   brake/tail light (CBF) – 8•13
   headlight – 8•8
   instruments (CBF600N/NA) – 8•21
   licence plate – 8•13
   sidelight – 8•8
   turn signal 8•15
   wattage – 8•2

C

C-ABS system – 6•22, 6•23, 6•25
Cables
   clutch – 1•10, 2•32
   lubrication – 1•22
   throttle – 1•11, 4•24
Calipers (brake)
   front – 6•1, 6•6
   rear – 6•2, 6•13

Cam chain and blades/guides – 2•18
Cam chain tensioner – 2•12
Camshafts – 2•2, 2•13
Catalytic converter – 4•29
Centrestand (CBF) – 5•4
   check – 1•18
Chain – 6•34, REF•18
   check and adjustment – 1•7
   cleaning and lubrication – 1•8
   specifications – 1•2, 6•3
Charging system – 8•1, 8•33
CKP sensor – 4•16
Clutch – 2•26
   cable renewal – 2•32
   check and cable adjustment – 1•10
   fault finding – REF•41
   specifications – 2•3
Clutch lever – 5•7
Clutch switch – 8•27
Cockpit surround (CBF600S/SA) – 7•14
Coils (ignition) – 4•30
Colour code – 0•9
Connecting rods – 2•4, 2•44
Coolant – 1•2
   change – 1•16
   level check – 0•14
   reservoir – 3•7
Cooling system – 3•1 et seq
   check – 1•15
   ECT sensor – 3•4
   fan and fan relay – 3•2
   hoses, pipes and unions – 3•8
   pressure cap – 3•1, 3•6
   radiator – 3•5
   temperature display – 3•3
   thermostat – 3•4
   water pump – 3•6
Conversion factors – REF•26
Crankcase – 2•38, 2•41
Crankcase breather – 1•9
Crankshaft and bearings – 2•4, 2•42
Cylinder bores – 2•4, 2•41
Cylinder compression check – 2•7
Cylinder head – 2•2, 2•19, 2•20

D

Delay valve – 6•27
Dimensions (model) – 0•16
Diode block – 8•28
Disc (brake)
   front – 6•2, 6•9
   rear – 6•2, 6•15
Drive chain – 6•34, REF•18
   check and adjustment – 1•7
   cleaning and lubrication – 1•8
   specifications – 1•2, 6•3

E

ECM – 4•17
ECT sensor – 3•4, 4•14
Electrical system – 8•1 et seq
   alternator – 8•33
   battery – 8•4, 8•5
   brake light switches – 8•17
   brake/tail light – 8•13
   clutch switch – 8•27
   diode block – 8•28
   fault finding – 8•3, REF•45
   fuses – 8•6
   handlebar switches – 8•25
   headlight and sidelight – 8•8, 8•11
   horn – 8•28
   ignition switch – 8•24
   instruments – 8•18, 8•20
   licence plate light – 8•13
   lighting system check – 8•7
   neutral switch – 8•26
   oil pressure switch – 8•23
   regulator/rectifier – 8•36
   sidestand switch – 8•27
   starter motor – 8•30
   starter relay – 8•29
   turn signals – 8•14, 8•15, 8•16
   wiring diagrams – 8•38
Engine – 2•1 et seq
   bearings – 2•42
   cam chain and blades/guides – 2•18
   cam chain tensioner – 2•12
   camshafts and followers – 2•13
   connecting rods and bearings – 2•44
   crankcase – 2•38, 2•41
   crankcase breather – 1•9
   crankshaft and main bearings – 2•42
   cylinder compression check – 2•7
   cylinder head – 2•19, 2•20
   fault finding – REF•36
   leak-down test – 2•7
   oil cooler – 2•10
   oil filter – 1•13
   oil level – 0•11
   oil pressure check – 2•7
   oil pressure relief valve – 2•35
   oil pump – 2•36
   oil sump and strainer – 2•35
   piston rings – 2•48
   pistons – 2•47
   removal and installation – 2•8
   running-in procedure – 2•58
   specifications – 0•17, 1•2, 2•1
   starter clutch and gears – 2•23
   valve clearance adjustment – 1•23
   valve cover – 2•11

Index

Engine management system – 4•1 et seq
  air filter housing and throttle bodies – 4•5
  air intake system – 4•19
  ECM – 4•17
  engine stop relay – 4•18
  fault diagnosis – 4•12
  fuel cut-off relay – 4•19
  fuel rails and injectors – 4•10
  idle speed control system – 4•20
  sensors – 4•14
  specifications – 4•1
Engine number – 0•9
Exhaust system – 4•26

F

Fairing
  CBF600S/SA – 7•15
  CBR600F/FA – 7•9
Fairing side panels
  CBF600S/SA – 7•14
  CBR600F/FA – 7•8
Fan – 3•2
Fan relay – 3•3
Fault codes – 4•13, 4•33, 6•23
Fault diagnosis
  C-ABS system – 6•23
  electrical system – 8•3
  fuel injection system – 4•12
  immobiliser system – 4•33
Fault finding – REF•35 et seq
Filter
  air – 1•22
  engine oil – 1•13
Footrests – 5•2
Frame – 5•2
Frame number – 0•9
Front brake
  calipers – 6•6
  discs – 6•9
  pads – 6•4
  master cylinder – 6•9
Front forks
  adjustment – 5•26
  check – 1•18
  oil change – 5•9
  overhaul – 5•12
  removal and installation – 5•8
  specifications – 5•1
Front mudguard
  CB and CBR – 7•4
  CBF – 7•12
Front wheel – 6•29
Fuel system
  check – 1•11
  specifications – 4•1
Fuel gauge and level sensor – 4•2, 4•23

Fuel pressure check – 4•22
Fuel pump – 4•22
Fuel rails and injectors – 4•10
Fuel tank – 4•3
  capacity – 0•17, 4•1
Fuses – 8•2, 8•6

G

Gearchange lever and linkage – 5•3
Gearshafts – 2•50, 2•51
Gearchange mechanism – 2•33
  fault finding – REF•41

H

Handlebar levers – 5•7
Handlebar switches – 8•25
Handlebar weights – 5•6
Handlebars – 5•4
Headlight – 8•11
  aim – 1•17
  bulb – 8•8
  circuit check – 8•7
Headlight covers
  CB 2007 to 2010 – 7•2
  CB 2011-on – 7•6
Horn – 8•28

I

IAT sensor – 4•15
Idle speed control system – 4•20
Ignition switch – 8•24
Ignition system
  check – 4•29
  coils – 4•30
  ECM – 4•17
  specifications – 4•2
  timing – 4•31
Immobiliser system – 4•32
Injectors (fuel) – 4•10
Instruments – 8•18, 8•20
Instrument cover (CBR) – 7•10
Instrument covers (CB 2011-on) – 7•6

L

Leak-down test – 2•7
Lean angle sensor – 4•17
Licence plate light
  bulb – 8•13
  circuit check – 8•8
Lighting system – 8•7

Lubricants
  general – REF•23
  recommended – 1•2
Lubrication
  cables – 1•22
  pivot points – 1•22

M

Maintenance schedule – 1•3
MAP sensor – 4•14
Master cylinder
  front – 6•2, 6•9
  rear – 6•2, 6•15
Mirrors
  CB and CBF600N/NA – 7•5
  CBF600S/SA – 7•16
  CBR – 7•10
Model development – 0•18
Model dimensions – 0•16
Modulator (C-ABS) – 6•26
MOT Test Checks – REF•27

N

Neutral switch – 8•26

O

Oil (engine) – 1•2
  filter and change – 1•13
  level – 0•11
Oil (front forks) – 5•1, 5•9
Oil cooler – 2•10
Oil pressure check – 2•7
Oil pressure switch – 8•23
Oil pump – 2•3, 2•36
Oil strainer – 2•35
Oil sump – 2•35
Oxygen sensor – 4•15

P

Pads (brake) – 1•9, 6•4, 6•11
PAIR (pulse secondary air supply) system – 1•17, 4•2, 4•28
Piston rings – 2•4, 2•48
Pistons – 2•4, 2•47
Pressure cap – 3•1, 3•6
Pressure relief valve – 2•35
Proportional control valve – 6•26
Pulse ring – 6•25, 6•26
Pump
  fuel – 4•22
  oil – 2•36
  water – 3•6

Index

R

Radiator – 3•5
Rear brake
  caliper – 6•13
  disc – 6•15
  master cylinder – 6•15
  pads – 6•11
Rear mudguard
  CB 2007 to 2010 – 7•5
  CB 2011-on and CBR – 7•7
  CBF – 7•12
Rear suspension
  checks – 1•19
  shock absorber – 5•22, 5•26
  swingarm – 5•24
Rear wheel – 6•30
Regulator/rectifier – 8•36
Relay
  engine stop – 4•18
  fan – 3•3
  fuel cut-off – 4•19
  headlight – 8•7
  starter – 8•29
  turn signal – 8•14
Resistor – 8•2

S

Safety – 0•10, 0•15
Seat
  CB and CBR – 7•2
  CBF – 7•10
Seat cowl
  CB 2007 to 2010 – 7•4
  CB 2011-on and CBR – 7•2
  CBF – 7•12
Security – REF•20
Selector drum and forks – 2•3, 2•57
Side covers
  CB – 7•2
  CBR – 7•7
  CBF – 7•13
Sidelight (front)
  bulb – 8•8
  circuit check – 8•8
Sidestand – 5•4
  check – 1•18
Sidestand switch – 8•27
Spark plugs – 1•2, 1•12
Speed sensor (C-ABS) – 6•25
Speed sensor (speedometer) – 8•20, 8•23
Speedometer – 8•20
Sprocket coupling – 6•36
  bearing – 6•33
Sprocket cover – 6•35
Sprockets – 6•35
  check – 1•9
  sizes – 6•3
Starter clutch – 2•3, 2•23
Starter interlock circuit – 1•18
Starter motor – 8•2, 8•30
Starter relay – 8•29
Steering
  checks – 0•13
  head bearings – 1•19, 5•1, 5•21
Steering stem – 5•19
Storage – REF•32
Suspension
  adjustment – 5•26
  checks – 0•13, 1•18
  specifications – 0•17
Swingarm – 1•19, 5•24

T

Tachometer – 8•21
Tail light – 8•13
  bulb – 8•13
  circuit check – 8•8
Temperature display – 3•3
Thermostat – 3•1, 3•4
Throttle bodies – 4•5
Throttle cables – 4•24
  freeplay check and adjustment – 1•11
Throttle position sensor – 4•15
Tools and Workshop Tips – REF•2 et seq
Torque settings – 1•2, 2•6, 3•1, 4•2, 5•2, 6•3, 7•1, 8•2
Transmission
  selector drum and forks – 2•57
  shafts – 2•50, 2•51
  specifications – 2•5
Trim clips – 7•1
Turn signal – 8•16
  bulbs – 8•15
  circuit check – 8•14
Tyres – 6•34
  checks and pressures – 0•15, 1•21
  sizes – 6•3

V

Valve clearances – 1•2, 1•23
Valve cover – 2•11
Valves – 2•2,
VIN – 0•9

W

Water pump – 3•6
Weight (model) – 0•16
Wheel – 6•29, 6•30
  alignment check – 6•28
  checks – 1•21
  inspection and repair – 6•27
  specifications – 6•3
Wheel bearings – 6•31
  checks – 1•21
Wheel speed sensor – 6•25
Windshield
  CBF600S/SA – 7•14
  CBR600F/FA – 7•10
Wiring diagrams – 8•38 et seq

Haynes Motorcycle Manuals – The Complete List

Title	Book No
APRILIA RS50 (99 - 06) & RS125 (93 - 06)	4298
Aprilia RSV1000 Mille (98 - 03)	♦ 4255
Aprilia SR50	4755
BMW 2-valve Twins (70 - 96)	♦ 0249
BMW F650	♦ 4761
BMW K100 & 75 2-valve Models (83 - 96)	♦ 1373
BMW R850, 1100 & 1150 4-valve Twins (93 - 04)	♦ 3466
BMW R1200 (04 - 06)	♦ 4598
BSA Bantam (48 - 71)	0117
BSA Unit Singles (58 - 72)	0127
BSA Pre-unit Singles (54 - 61)	0326
BSA A7 & A10 Twins (47 - 62)	0121
BSA A50 & A65 Twins (62 - 73)	0155
Chinese Scooters	4768
DUCATI 600, 620, 750 and 900 2-valve V-Twins (91 - 05)	♦ 3290
Ducati MK III & Desmo Singles (69 - 76)	◊ 0445
Ducati 748, 916 & 996 4-valve V-Twins (94 - 01)	♦ 3756
GILERA Runner, DNA, Ice & SKP/Stalker (97 - 07)	4163
HARLEY-DAVIDSON Sportsters (70 - 08)	♦ 2534
Harley-Davidson Shovelhead and Evolution Big Twins (70 - 99)	♦ 2536
Harley-Davidson Twin Cam 88 (99 - 03)	♦ 2478
HONDA NB, ND, NP & NS50 Melody (81 - 85)	◊ 0622
Honda NE/NB50 Vision & SA50 Vision Met-in (85 - 95)	◊ 1278
Honda MB, MBX, MT & MTX50 (80 - 93)	0731
Honda C50, C70 & C90 (67 - 03)	0324
Honda XR80/100R & CRF80/100F (85 - 04)	2218
Honda XL/XR 80, 100, 125, 185 & 200 2-valve Models (78 - 87)	0566
Honda H100 & H100S Singles (80 - 92)	◊ 0734
Honda CB/CD125T & CM125C Twins (77 - 88)	◊ 0571
Honda CG125 (76 - 07)	◊ 0433
Honda NS125 (86 - 93)	3056
Honda CBR125R (04 - 07)	4620
Honda MBX/MTX125 & MTX200 (83 - 93)	◊ 1132
Honda CD/CM185 200T & CM250C 2-valve Twins (77 - 85)	0572
Honda XL/XR 250 & 500 (78 - 84)	0567
Honda XR250L, XR250R & XR400R (86 - 03)	2219
Honda CB250 & CB400N Super Dreams (78 - 84)	◊ 0540
Honda CR Motocross Bikes (86 - 01)	2222
Honda CRF250 & CRF450 (02 - 06)	2630
Honda CBR400RR Fours (88 - 99)	◊ ♦ 3552
Honda VFR400 (NC30) & RVF400 (NC35) V-Fours (89 - 98)	◊ ♦ 3496
Honda CB500 (93 - 02) & CBF500 03 - 08	◊ 3753
Honda CB400 & CB550 Fours (73 - 77)	0262
Honda CX/GL500 & 650 V-Twins (78 - 86)	0442
Honda CBX550 Four (82 - 86)	◊ 0940
Honda XL600R & XR600R (83 - 08)	♦ 2183
Honda XL600/650V Transalp & XRV750 Africa Twin (87 to 07)	♦ 3919
Honda CBR600F1 & 1000F Fours (87 - 96)	♦ 1730
Honda CBR600F2 & F3 Fours (91 - 98)	♦ 2070
Honda CBR600F4 (99 - 06)	♦ 3911
Honda CB600F Hornet & CBF600 (98 - 06)	◊ ♦ 3915
Honda CBR600RR (03 - 06)	♦ 4590
Honda CB650 sohc Fours (78 - 84)	0665
Honda NTV600 Revere, NTV650 and NT650V Deauville (88 - 05)	◊ ♦ 3243
Honda Shadow VT600 & 750 (USA) (88 - 03)	2312
Honda CB750 sohc Four (69 - 79)	0131
Honda V45/65 Sabre & Magna (82 - 88)	0820
Honda VFR750 & 700 V-Fours (86 - 97)	♦ 2101
Honda VFR800 V-Fours (97 - 01)	♦ 3703
Honda VFR800 V-Tec V-Fours (02 - 05)	♦ 4196
Honda CB750 & CB900 dohc Fours (78 - 84)	0535
Honda VTR1000 (FireStorm, Super Hawk) & XL1000V (Varadero) (97 - 08)	♦ 3744
Honda CBR900RR FireBlade (92 - 99)	♦ 2161
Honda CBR900RR FireBlade (00 - 03)	♦ 4060
Honda CBR1000RR Fireblade (04 - 07)	♦ 4604
Honda CBR1100XX Super Blackbird (97 - 07)	♦ 3901
Honda ST1100 Pan European V-Fours (90 - 02)	♦ 3384
Honda Shadow VT1100 (85 - 98)	2313
Honda GL1000 Gold Wing (75 - 79)	0309

Title	Book No
Honda GL1100 Gold Wing (79 - 81)	0669
Honda Gold Wing 1200 (USA) (84 - 87)	2199
Honda Gold Wing 1500 (USA) (88 - 00)	2225
KAWASAKI AE/AR 50 & 80 (81 - 95)	1007
Kawasaki KC, KE & KH100 (75 - 99)	1371
Kawasaki KMX125 & 200 (86 - 02)	◊ 3046
Kawasaki 250, 350 & 400 Triples (72 - 79)	0134
Kawasaki 400 & 440 Twins (74 - 81)	0281
Kawasaki 400, 500 & 550 Fours (79 - 91)	0910
Kawasaki EN450 & 500 Twins (Ltd/Vulcan) (85 - 07)	2053
Kawasaki EX500 (GPZ500S) & ER500 (ER-5) (87 - 08)	♦ 2052
Kawasaki ZX600 (ZZ-R600 & Ninja ZX-6) (90 - 06)	♦ 2146
Kawasaki ZX-6R Ninja Fours (95 - 02)	♦ 3541
Kawasaki ZX-6R (03 - 06)	♦ 4742
Kawasaki ZX600 (GPZ600R, GPX600R, Ninja 600R & RX) & ZX750 (GPX750R, Ninja 750R)	♦ 1780
Kawasaki 650 Four (76 - 78)	0373
Kawasaki Vulcan 700/750 & 800 (85 - 04)	♦ 2457
Kawasaki 750 Air-cooled Fours (80 - 91)	0574
Kawasaki ZR550 & 750 Zephyr Fours (90 - 97)	♦ 3382
Kawasaki Z750 & Z1000 (03 - 08)	♦ 4762
Kawasaki ZX750 (Ninja ZX-7 & ZXR750) Fours (89 - 96)	♦ 2054
Kawasaki Ninja ZX-7R & ZX-9R (94 - 04)	♦ 3721
Kawasaki 900 & 1000 Fours (73 - 77)	0222
Kawasaki ZX900, 1000 & 1100 Liquid-cooled Fours (83 - 97)	♦ 1681
KTM EXC Enduro & SX Motocross (00 - 07)	4629
MOTO GUZZI 750, 850 & 1000 V-Twins (74 - 78)	0339
MZ ETZ Models (81 - 95)	◊ 1680
NORTON 500, 600, 650 & 750 Twins (57 - 70)	0187
Norton Commando (68 - 77)	0125
PEUGEOT Speedfight, Trekker & Vivacity Scooters (96 - 08)	◊ 3920
PIAGGIO (Vespa) Scooters (91 - 06)	3492
SUZUKI GT, ZR & TS50 (77 - 90)	0799
Suzuki TS50X (84 - 00)	◊ 1599
Suzuki 100, 125, 185 & 250 Air-cooled Trail bikes (79 - 89)	0797
Suzuki GP100 & 125 Singles (78 - 93)	◊ 0576
Suzuki GS, GN, GZ & DR125 Singles (82 - 05)	◊ 0888
Suzuki GSX-R600/750 (06 - 09)	♦ 4790
Suzuki 250 & 350 Twins (68 - 78)	0120
Suzuki GT250X7, GT200X5 & SB200 Twins (78 - 83)	◊ 0469
Suzuki GS/GSX250, 400 & 450 Twins (79 - 85)	0736
Suzuki GS500 Twin (89 - 06)	♦ 3238
Suzuki GS550 (77 - 82) & GS750 Fours (76 - 79)	0363
Suzuki GS/GSX550 4-valve Fours (83 - 88)	1133
Suzuki SV650 & SV650S (99 - 08)	♦ 3912
Suzuki GSX-R600 & 750 (96 - 00)	♦ 3553
Suzuki GSX-R600 (01 - 03), GSX-R750 (00 - 03) & GSX-R1000 (01 - 02)	♦ 3986
Suzuki GSX-R600/750 (04 - 05) & GSX-R1000 (03 - 06)	♦ 4382
Suzuki GSF600, 650 & 1200 Bandit Fours (95 - 06)	♦ 3367
Suzuki Intruder, Marauder, Volusia & Boulevard (85 - 06)	♦ 2618
Suzuki GS850 Fours (78 - 88)	0536
Suzuki GS1000 Four (77 - 79)	0484
Suzuki GSX-R750, GSX-R1100 (85 - 92), GSX600F, GSX750F & GSX1100F (Katana) Fours	♦ 2055
Suzuki GSX600/750F & GSX750 (98 - 02)	♦ 3987
Suzuki GS/GSX1000, 1100 & 1150 4-valve Fours (79 - 88)	0737
Suzuki TL1000S/R & DL1000 V-Strom (97 - 04)	♦ 4083
Suzuki GSF650/1250 (05 - 09)	♦ 4798
Suzuki GSX1300R Hayabusa (99 - 04)	♦ 4184
Suzuki GSX1400 (02 - 07)	♦ 4758
TRIUMPH Tiger Cub & Terrier (52 - 68)	0414
Triumph 350 & 500 Unit Twins (58 - 73)	0137
Triumph Pre-Unit Twins (47 - 62)	0251
Triumph 650 & 750 2-valve Unit Twins (63 - 83)	0122
Triumph Trident & BSA Rocket 3 (69 - 75)	0136
Triumph Bonneville (01 - 07)	♦ 4364
Triumph Daytona, Speed Triple, Sprint & Tiger (97 - 05)	♦ 3755
Triumph Triples and Fours (carburettor engines) (91 - 04)	♦ 2162
VESPA P/PX125, 150 & 200 Scooters (78 - 06)	0707
Vespa Scooters (59 - 78)	0126
YAMAHA DT50 & 80 Trail Bikes (78 - 95)	◊ 0800
Yamaha T50 & 80 Townmate (83 - 95)	◊ 1247

Title	Book No
Yamaha YB100 Singles (73 - 91)	◊ 0474
Yamaha RS/RXS100 & 125 Singles (74 - 95)	0331
Yamaha RD & DT125LC (82 - 95)	◊ 0887
Yamaha TZR125 (87 - 93) & DT125R (88 - 07)	◊ 1655
Yamaha TY50, 80, 125 & 175 (74 - 84)	◊ 0464
Yamaha XT & SR125 (82 - 03)	◊ 1021
Yamaha YBR125	4797
Yamaha Trail Bikes (81 - 00)	2350
Yamaha 2-stroke Motocross Bikes 1986 - 2006	2662
Yamaha YZ & WR 4-stroke Motocross Bikes (98 - 08)	2689
Yamaha 250 & 350 Twins (70 - 79)	0040
Yamaha XS250, 360 & 400 sohc Twins (75 - 84)	0378
Yamaha RD250 & 350LC Twins (80 - 82)	0803
Yamaha RD350 YPVS Twins (83 - 95)	1158
Yamaha RD400 Twin (75 - 79)	0333
Yamaha XT, TT & SR500 Singles (75 - 83)	0342
Yamaha XZ550 Vision V-Twins (82 - 85)	0821
Yamaha FJ, FZ, XJ & YX600 Radian (84 - 92)	2100
Yamaha XJ600S (Diversion, Seca II) & XJ600N Fours (92 - 03)	♦ 2145
Yamaha YZF600R Thundercat & FZS600 Fazer (96 - 03)	♦ 3702
Yamaha FZ-6 Fazer (04 - 07)	♦ 4751
Yamaha YZF-R6 (99 - 02)	♦ 3900
Yamaha YZF-R6 (03 - 05)	♦ 4601
Yamaha 650 Twins (70 - 83)	0341
Yamaha XJ650 & 750 Fours (80 - 84)	0738
Yamaha XS750 & 850 Triples (76 - 85)	0340
Yamaha TDM850, TRX850 & XTZ750 (89 - 99)	◊ ♦ 3540
Yamaha YZF750R & YZF1000R Thunderace (93 - 00)	♦ 3720
Yamaha FZR600, 750 & 1000 Fours (87 - 96)	♦ 2056
Yamaha XV (Virago) V-Twins (81 - 03)	♦ 0802
Yamaha XVS650 & 1100 Drag Star/V-Star (97 - 05)	♦ 4195
Yamaha XJ900F Fours (83 - 94)	♦ 3239
Yamaha XJ900S Diversion (94 - 01)	♦ 3739
Yamaha YZF-R1 (98 - 03)	♦ 3754
Yamaha YZF-R1 (04 - 06)	♦ 4605
Yamaha FZS1000 Fazer (01 - 05)	♦ 4287
Yamaha FJ1100 & 1200 Fours (84 - 96)	♦ 2057
Yamaha XJR1200 & 1300 (95 - 06)	♦ 3981
Yamaha V-Max (85 - 03)	♦ 4072
ATVs	
Honda ATC70, 90, 110, 185 & 200 (71 - 85)	0565
Honda Rancher, Recon & TRX250EX ATVs	2553
Honda TRX300 Shaft Drive ATVs (88 - 00)	2125
Honda Foreman (95 - 07)	2465
Honda TRX300EX, TRX400EX & TRX450R/ER ATVs (93 - 06)	2318
Kawasaki Bayou 220/250/300 & Prairie 300 ATVs (86 - 03)	2351
Polaris ATVs (85 - 97)	2302
Polaris ATVs (98 - 06)	2508
Yamaha YFS200 Blaster ATV (88 - 06)	2317
Yamaha YFB250 Timberwolf ATVs (92 - 00)	2217
Yamaha YFM350 & YFM400 (ER and Big Bear) ATVs (87 - 03)	2126
Yamaha Banshee and Warrior ATVs (87 - 03)	2314
Yamaha Kodiak and Grizzly ATVs (93 - 05)	2567
ATV Basics	10450
TECHBOOK SERIES	
Twist and Go (automatic transmission) Scooters Service and Repair Manual	4082
Motorcycle Basics TechBook (2nd Edition)	3515
Motorcycle Electrical TechBook (3rd Edition)	3471
Motorcycle Fuel Systems TechBook	3514
Motorcycle Maintenance TechBook	4071
Motorcycle Modifying	4272
Motorcycle Workshop Practice TechBook (2nd Edition)	3470

◊ = not available in the USA   ♦ = Superbike

The manuals on this page are available through good motorcycle dealers and accessory shops.
In case of difficulty, contact: **Haynes Publishing**
(UK) +44 1963 442030   (USA) +1 805 498 6703
(SV) +46 18 124016
(Australia/New Zealand) +61 3 9763 8100

Preserving Our Motoring Heritage

The Model J Duesenberg Derham Tourster. Only eight of these magnificent cars were ever built – this is the only example to be found outside the United States of America

Almost every car you've ever loved, loathed or desired is gathered under one roof at the Haynes Motor Museum. Over 300 immaculately presented cars and motorbikes represent every aspect of our motoring heritage, from elegant reminders of bygone days, such as the superb Model J Duesenberg to curiosities like the bug-eyed BMW Isetta. There are also many old friends and flames. Perhaps you remember the 1959 Ford Popular that you did your courting in? The magnificent 'Red Collection' is a spectacle of classic sports cars including AC, Alfa Romeo, Austin Healey, Ferrari, Lamborghini, Maserati, MG, Riley, Porsche and Triumph.

A Perfect Day Out

Each and every vehicle at the Haynes Motor Museum has played its part in the history and culture of Motoring. Today, they make a wonderful spectacle and a great day out for all the family. Bring the kids, bring Mum and Dad, but above all bring your camera to capture those golden memories for ever. You will also find an impressive array of motoring memorabilia, a comfortable 70 seat video cinema and one of the most extensive transport book shops in Britain. The Pit Stop Cafe serves everything from a cup of tea to wholesome, home-made meals or, if you prefer, you can enjoy the large picnic area nestled in the beautiful rural surroundings of Somerset.

John Haynes O.B.E., Founder and Chairman of the museum at the wheel of a Haynes Light 12.

The 1936 490cc sohc-engined International Norton – well known for its racing success

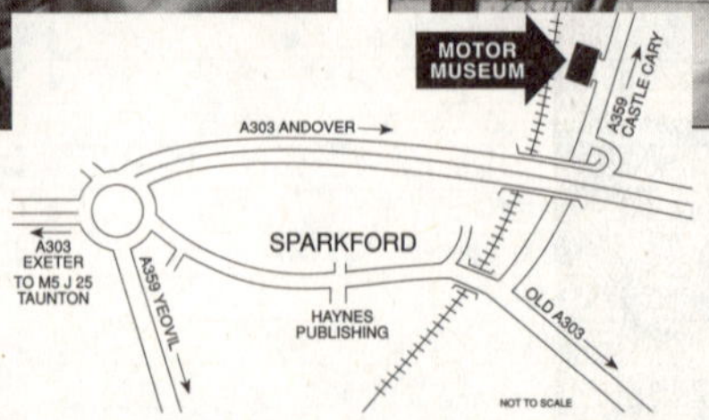

The Museum is situated on the A359 Yeovil to Frome road at Sparkford, just off the A303 in Somerset. It is about 40 miles south of Bristol, and 25 minutes drive from the M5 intersection at Taunton.
Open 9.30am - 5.30pm (10.00am - 4.00pm Winter) 7 days a week, *except Christmas Day, Boxing Day and New Years Day*
Special rates available for schools, coach parties and outings   Charitable Trust No. 292048